Sport in the Global Society

General Editor: J.A. Mangan

WOMEN, SPORT AND SOCIETY IN MODERN CHINA

SPORT IN THE GLOBAL SOCIETY

General Editor: J.A. Mangan

The interest in sports studies around the world is growing and will continue to do so. This unique series combines aspects of the expanding study of *sport in the global society*, providing comprehensiveness and comparison under one editorial umbrella. It is particularly timely, with studies in the political, cultural, anthropological, ethnographic, social, economic, geographical and aesthetic elements of sport proliferating in institutions of higher education.

Eric Hobsbawm once called sport one of the most significant practices of the late nineteenth century. Its significance was even more marked in the late twentieth century and will continue to grow in importance into the new millennium as the world develops into a 'global village' sharing the English language, technology and sport.

Other Titles in the Series

WOMEN, SPORT AND SOCIETY IN MODERN CHINA

Holding Up *More* than Half the Sky

DONG JINXIA

Peking University

FRANK CASS
LONDON • PORTLAND, OR

First published in 2003 in Great Britain by
FRANK CASS PUBLISHERS
Crown House, 47 Chase Side, Southgate
London, N14 5BP

and in the United States of America by
FRANK CASS PUBLISHERS
c/o ISBS, 5824 N.E. Hassalo Street
Portland, Oregon 97213-3644

Website: www.frankcass.com

British Library Cataloguing in Publication Data

Jinxia, Dong
    Women, sport and society in modern China: holding up
    more than half the sky – (Sport in the global society; 35)
    1. Women athletes – China 2. Sports – Social aspects –
    China
    I. Title
    306.4′83′0951

ISBN 0-7146-5235-0 (cloth)
ISBN 0-7146-8214-4 (paper)
ISSN 1368-9789

Library of Congress Cataloging-in-Publication Data

Dong, Jinxia, 1962–
    Women, sport, and society in modern China: holding up more
    than half the sky / Dong Jinxia.
      p. cm. – (Sport in the global society, ISSN 1368-9789)
    Includes bibliographical references and index.
    ISBN 0-7146-5235-0 (cloth: alk. paper) – ISBN 0-7146-8214-4
    (pbk.: alk. paper)
    1. Sport for women–China 2. Sports and state–China. I. Title.
    II. Series.

GV709.18.C6 D66 2002
796′.082′0973–dc21   2002031421

Printed in Great Britain by
MPG Books Ltd, Bodmin, Cornwall

Contents

Acknowledgements

This book began as a doctoral thesis under the supervision of Professor J.A. Mangan at the International Research Centre for Sport, Socialization and Society. I am grateful to all those who have helped see this book through to publication but three people deserve special mention and very special thanks. My husband Zhong Bingshu has been a tower of strength in the years that I have been in the West. To use an appropriate English expression, he has held the domestic fort against all challenges. In China in my absence, to adapt a famous Chinese expression, he has held up all the sky! I owe him the most profound thanks. Then my daughter Zhong Yijing has endured long years of separation from her mother without complaint (except about missing her cooking) and with understanding. She is truly exceptional in her maturity, in her resilience and in her patience. These qualities displayed during my absence can never be forgotten. Finally, with regard to my supportive trio of helpers, Professor J.A. Mangan has proved to be a most exceptional supervisor. His intelligence, his attention to detail, his sympathy for my subject, his long hours of patient assistance, have ensured the completion of this book. When I chose to study at his international research centre, without fully appreciating the fact I made the wisest of decisions. His sound advice, his meticulousness and his constant support too can never be forgotten.

Others have made their contributions to this book. I acknowledge with gratitude the support of the University of Strathclyde Research Student Committee for the financial support that was extended to me at a crucial moment in my studies, when the cost of completion seemed simply too much. The authorities of Beijing University of Physical Education, in particular Principal Jin Jichun, Vice-Principals Zhang Wangzhen, Tian Maijiu and Xing Wenhua, and the Head of the Gymnastics Department Xiao Guanglai have shown sympathetic understanding and provided practical assistance throughout my period of study. I should like to place on record my gratitude to them.

Fellow academics in China and the West provided information, advice and comment that allowed me to see my way more clearly. I mention with thanks in this context Professor Jennifer Hargreaves, Dr Ren Hai, Liu Yueye, Pat Elsmie, Ian and Lesley Whyte, and Denise and Graham Jackson. I shall remember with affection my fellow research students in IRCSSS, Hamad Ndee and Gwang Ok, for their friendship, company and encouragement.

In a very real sense, this book has been my intellectual 'Long March' – arduous, difficult and demanding. I shall always remember all those who urged me on and offered help to me on my way, but understandably I shall remember most often and most warmly the trio who marched with me step by step – in spirit in China and in life in Britain. Thankyou.

DJ
Beijing
February 2003

List of Abbreviations

ACSF:	All China Sports Federation
BIPE:	Beijing Institute of Physical Education
BMSC:	Beijing Municipal Sports Commission
BUPE:	Beijing University of Physical Education
CCCL:	Central Committee of the Communist League
CCP:	Chinese Communist Party
CWVT:	Chinese women's volleyball team
CR:	Cultural Revolution
GLF:	Great Leap Forward
IAAF:	International Amateur Athletic Federation
IOC:	International Olympic Committee
NSA:	National Swimming Association
NSC:	National Sports Commission
PLA:	People's Liberation Army
PRC:	People's Republic of China
SEZ:	Special Economic Zone
SSC:	Sichuan Sports Commission
WPS:	'workers, peasants and soldiers'

Foreword

With great pride I have presented medals to Li Lingwei, Fu Mingxia, Wang Liping and Ge Fei, as well as many other Chinese women athletes at the Olympic Games and other major international competitions. The success of these Chinese women have not only helped China to win world recognition, but have also aroused worldwide interest. Why are Chinese women athletes so impressive? How could they become so impressive? Are the Chinese people as impressed by them as the rest of the world? These are some of the questions asked by the world's media. My international and Chinese colleagues, acquaintances and academic friends have also frequently asked me the same questions. In order to provide convincing answers, it is necessary to explore the relationship between women and sport in modern Chinese society in terms of cultural traditions, recent history, economic developments, modernisation and international politics. The subject calls for a careful and comprehensive study.

In her book, Dr Dong Jinxia has offered fascinating and thoughtful answers to these questions and she has responded to the call for a serious consideration of women and sport in modern China. In a sentence – she fills a gap. China and the world beyond China will be intrigued by her study. *Women, Sport and Society in Modern China* is the first survey of the subject in the English language, and thus the first available to the world beyond China. In this book Dr Dong Jinxia deals thoroughly with the evolution of women's sport in new China and its complex relationship with culture, society, economics and politics.

Based on her experience as a woman athlete, a coach and a sports university academic, she is able to discuss with authority and insight political sports ideologies, centralised planning arrangements, winning-orientated sports policies, the issues of the politicisation of sport, the commercialisation of sport and attitudes to performance-enhancing drugs.

First and foremost her book is a study of Chinese women in a time of change. It is a commentary on the reformation of gender attitudes, expectations, responses and demands in contemporary China. In this reformation women athletes have acted as Pioneers; as Dong Jinxia rightfully states, they have held up *more* than half the sky. Dong Jinxia is an remarkable and faithful witness of their achievements.

LU SHENGRONG
President of the International Badminton Federation (1993–2001)
Member of the IOC (1996–2000)
Member of the Women and Sports Working Group of the IOC (1995–)
January 2003

Series Editor's Foreword

Dong Jinxia's *Women, Sport and Society in Modern China* deals with a present belief in equality increasingly instilled in women's minds: 'Women have the courage and the capacity – the product of history – to confront modern dilemmas and overcome them. Sportswomen for their part today are aware of their possibilities and confident in their aspirations as never before. Women in general are conscious of their rights and ready to fight against social bias and injustice ... If and when women's equality with men is fully achieved, women could well hold up more than half the sky – in Chinese sport *and* society.'[1]

In short, *Women, Sport and Society in Modern China* is about far more than just sport. 'The wise man points to the moon', so the Chinese saying goes, 'but the fool looks at the finger'. Dong Jinxia is purposefully moon-gazing (or perhaps more aptly sky-gazing) and she is certainly not mesmerised by any finger. Nor, however, is she starry eyed: she notes the challenges; she is aware of the difficulties. There is a long march ahead – but women are on the move – and sportswomen are among 'the spear-carriers' in the vanguard. Her concluding remarks are cautious and sober. Nevertheless what she makes clear in page after page of evidence and argument, is that in the world of international sport – so significant in terms of national status – Chinese women have more than an edge over Chinese men: they hold up *more* than half the sky – and this has resonances for the women of China. As she remarks in her opening sentence to the Prologue: ' "Women hold up half the sky" and "Women can do what men can do" are not just popular slogans peddled by Chairman Mao, but recent actualities in China's elite sport'.[2]

This is their story. It is a tale for modern times: of gender challenge and change; of the release of women's potential; of their demonstrated capacities; of their determination to free their talents. The story is not yet fully told. It is to be hoped that Dong Jinxia, who herself personifies so well the qualities outlined above in the first paragraph, will add to it with the acumen that characterises *Women, Sport and Society in Modern China* – perhaps after the Beijing Olympics!

J. A. MANGAN
International Research Centre
for Sport, Socialization and Society
De Montfort University (Bedford)
February 2003

PROLOGUE

From Dominated Domestic to Olympic Champion: Ideology, Gender and Elite Sport in China

Introduction

'Women hold up half the sky' and 'Women can do what men do' are not just popular slogans peddled by Chairman Mao, but recent actualities of China's elite sport.[1] Indeed, in this setting women can be said to hold up more than 'half the sky' and do more than men do. At the 1992, 1996 and 2000 Olympic Games, Chinese female participants outnumbered their male counterparts and played a major part in progressively raising China's position[2] in the medal table (see Table 1). In every Olympics since 1988 women have increased their representation over men.

These extraordinary performances have thrust Chinese sportswomen into the global limelight and sparked considerable interest around the world. Many associated with sport in a variety of roles have pondered on the reasons for the sudden rise to prominence of Chinese women. An increasing number of research papers, articles and books have been published on the subject. An outstanding example is Fan Hong's *Footbinding, Feminism and Freedom: The Liberation of Women's Bodies in Modern China*, which provides a valuable historical background to women's physical emancipation, a prerequisite of their later performance in modern sport in China. Her account of the evolution of Chinese women's sport not only fills in the gaps

TABLE 1

WOMEN'S CONTRIBUTION TO CHINESE SUCCESS AT THE OLYMPIC GAMES

Olympic Games	1988		1992		1996		2000	
	P	G	P	G	P	G	P	G
men	161	2	118	4	110	7	93	11.5
women	137	3	132	12	200	9	188	16.5
percentage	46%	60%	52.8%	75%	64.5%	56%	66.9%	58.9%

Note: P=participants; G=gold medals; percentage=proportion of women in the total

Sources: http://www.Olympics.com/eng/countries/chin/medal.htm and http://202.84.17.73/aoyun/ayhg/25/gaikuang_25.htm.

of previously male-centred historiography, but also serves the purpose of revealing the historical struggle for women's access to, and success in, sport before the creation of Communist China in 1949. A complementary study, Susan Brownell's *Training the Body for China: Sports in the Moral Order of the People's Republic*, sheds light on contemporary Chinese society and sport. In addition, her comparative consideration of China and the West provides further valuable insights into Chinese women and sport in a global as well as a national context. However, elite sport is not the central focus of Brownell's study. Consequently, her information on elite sport is limited – mostly obtained from amateur college athletes. Furthermore, her inquiry covers the period before elite provincial athletes were allowed privileged access to universities in the 1990s. Given the substantial existing differences between college athletes and provincial and national elite athletes in China at the time, her inquiries only present part of the picture of modern Chinese women and their sport – and the less significant part. In other words, the complex interrelationship between elite sport, women and society has yet to be analysed adequately. There are journalistic articles[3] about Chinese elite women athletes, such as Ming Li and Bing Wei's 'Chinese Women in Elite Sport: A Cultural Inquiry'.[4] Most of these articles, however, are mainly descriptive, and lack a systematic and convincing analysis of the nature of elite women's sport and its complicated relationship with society, culture, and indeed politics. The causes of Chinese women's success in world sport – the focus of so much international curiosity – remain to be satisfactorily explored.

Despite a growing interest, therefore, there remains a paucity of analytical literature on Chinese elite women's sport, not only in China but throughout the world. This is due to a variety of factors. First, in China feminist studies have shown little or no interest in sport because of its perceived insignificance compared to other subjects of inquiry. Consequently, although some feminists have endeavoured to restore Chinese women to history,[5] it is difficult to find any consideration of sport in the mainstream feminist (or other) works of the reform era after 1978. Second, gender has not until recently been considered an important part of sports research (or statistics) in China. Sportswomen are not actively involved in the feminist movement and studies of them in sports research have mostly concentrated on general technical issues relevant to sports performance. Thus, most figures and data, in both scientific studies and official statistics, do not have separate indexes for men and women. Finally, North American and European feminist studies of sport, based mostly on the experiences of white, middle-class women, too often ignore issues of ethnic diversity. They lack local insight on the diversity of sportswomen's lives in various parts of the globe as a product of disparate cultures, and their part in constructing specific gender relations and meanings through and in sport.[6] The result is that Chinese women in sport have rarely been examined satisfactorily by western sports academics.[7] What is clearly required to satisfy the considerable international curiosity about the rise to pre-eminence of modern Chinese women in sport is at least one study from the 'inside' (China), but in the linguistic medium of the 'outside' (English). This is the ambition of this study.

To this day, many questions pertaining to Chinese women and elite sport remain unanswered. For example, is China's success in sport merely chance – the result of an unplanned and unpremeditated combination of fortunate but unforeseen circumstances; or a product of regularities of circumstance and intention that can be located by careful inquiry? If so, what factors have contributed to the success of Chinese women, once captive in the home and crippled with 'bound feet', in international sports competitions? Have performance-enhancing drugs played an important part? What dramatic changes have taken place in society, and women's lives in particular, in the 'New China' – the common expression for China, in China and elsewhere, for the period from the Communist Revolution of 1949 to the present – that may have had an impact on elite sport? Some have certainly taken place. Furthermore, what impact will these changes have on the future of Chinese women's elite sport? To answer these difficult, interlocked and complicated questions, it is necessary to scrutinise the recent evolution of women's sport in the 'New China' since 1949, and the intertwined relationships between politics, economics, culture, society, women, and women's sport.

Crucial Concepts

1. Elite sport

Elite sport is used in this study to refer to high-level (provincial, national and international) competitive sport, one of the three elements of China's sport: high-level competitive sport, mass sport and school sport.

2. Elite athlete

Any athlete who is admitted to a provincial, municipal or army (and above) elite sports team is defined as an elite athlete in this study. An elite athlete devotes most of her/his time to athletic training and receives free coaching, board, subsistence and medical care as well as a wage equivalent to that of a state worker. The Chinese elite athlete is a product of Chinese socialism.[8]

3. Culture

Edward B. Tylor wrote in 1871: 'Culture or civilisation, taken in its wide ethnographic sense, is that complex whole which includes knowledge, belief, art, morals, law, custom, and any other capabilities and habits acquired by man as a member of society.'[9] The concept of culture has been refined and advanced in several different directions since Tylor laid down the basis for modern anthropological theories of culture.[10] The concept of culture employed here, as well as drawing on Tylor, draws on Clyde Kluckhohn:[11]

> A culture is learned by individuals as the result of belonging to some particular group, and it constitutes that part of learned behaviour which is shared with others … Culture regulates our lives at every turn. It is true that any culture is a set of techniques for adjusting both to the external environment and to other men. However, cultures create problems as well as solve them.

This definition nicely captures the relationship between culture and control. Furthermore, it points up advantages and disadvantages inherent in cultures. It also emphasises the dynamic nature of the cultural process in which individuals both learn and adjust their behaviour and technique. It is highly relevant, as will be demonstrated, to modern China and its elite sportswomen.

4. Gender

Gender is a cultural construct, a collective representation that pressures people into acting in certain ways.[12] It is different from the biological sex characteristics that encompass the morphological and physiological distinctions by which humans (and other life forms) are categorised as male and female.[13] Gender refers to the distinctive roles, behaviours, mental and emotional characteristics required of females and males by a society.[14]

5. Confucianism

Confucianism, as an intellectual and ethical tradition, is many centuries old. In the second century BCE, Confucianism was adopted as the state ideology.[15] Based on the ideas of the Chinese scholar Confucius (*Kong Zhi*),[16] Confucianism regards morality, obedience and hierarchy[17] as sources of order and harmony: domestic, regional and national. The 'Four Books' (*si shu*)[18] and the 'Five Classics' (*wu jing*)[19] constitute the Confucian canon, in which ritual or morality (*li*) are at the centre. Thus, in the traditional family, the 'father' had absolute authority. He was the head of a hierarchy arranged by generation, age and sex. Individualism was suppressed and dependence was encouraged, and in this way peaceful cooperation was pursued – and hopefully achieved. Within this ideal and in reality, according to the 'Five Relationships' (*wu chang*)[20] of Confucian teaching, the female was submissive to the male. A woman had to adhere to 'Three Obediences' (*sang cong*): obedience to her father when unmarried, to her husband upon marriage, and to her son when widowed. Hence, a woman's low status in society was determined by her required submissive and subordinate role in the family. Her place was in the home where she should practise filial piety, order the ceremonials of family life and supervise daily affairs. She was expected to be compliant, humble, yielding and respectful in order to maximise family harmony and minimise family conflict. In the twentieth century, many of the core values of Confucian social thought have been subject to extensive criticism and outright rejection. However, the Confucian legacy is still visible in Chinese society. Indeed, Confucianism reinterpreted to succour capitalism is being reincarnated. As will be demonstrated later, Confucianism has played, and still plays, an important part in elite women's sport in China.

Methodology

The relationship between women, sport and society is continuously constructed, deconstructed and reconstructed over time and in space. To analyse this relationship in the context of China, historical, sociological and comparative approaches are employed in this study. It relies for the most part on archival records, published documents, ethnographic data, interviews with and surveys of elite sportswomen, and regional case studies. No previous inquiries in either China or the West have combined so many methods of collecting data to study elite women's sport in China. The time-span of this inquiry is 1949–98.

As mentioned already, there are few sources dealing directly with women's sport in the mainstream academic literature on women in Chinese history, culture and society. However, there is a wide range of sources in the mainstream literature of relevance to women and sport, such as Julia Kristeva's *About Chinese Women* (1977), Elisabeth J. Croll's *Chinese Women Since Mao* (1983), and Li Xiaojian's *Huaxia nuxing zhimi* [The Mystery of Chinese Women] (1990). Full details will be found in the bibliography. There is also a substantial amount of journalistic material, particularly in recent years, on women (elite women especially) and sport, in magazines and newspapers such as *Zhongguo tiyu* [China's Sport], *Zhongguo funu* [Chinese Women], *Xing titu* [New Sport] and *Tiyu bao* [Sports Daily]. They are fully explored in this study. In addition, the extensive official statistics on sports developments are drawn upon to provide evidence of trends over time in sports involvement, provision and achievement.

For the purposes of this inquiry 48 semi-structured interviews with sports administrators, coaches and elite athletes were conducted between 1993 and 1998. Each interview lasted between 30 minutes and two hours. The purpose of the interviews was to establish profiles of contemporary Chinese sportswomen – their personalities, ambitions, motivation and problems in elite sport. For interview contents and interviewees' backgrounds, see Appendix 2.

To explore the connection between sports achievement and the socioeconomic origins and social status of women athletes, a questionnaire was co-designed and co-conducted with Bingshu Zhong, who undertook his

Ph.D. study between 1994 and 1997 on the issue of social mobility and sport in general. Sportswomen and their social mobility were the specific concern of this questionnaire. The 274 respondents, selected according to a systematic stratified method,[21] were all elite athletes of first-grade level[22] or above across the country.[23] The contents of the questionnaire and the survey results are presented in Appendices 3 and 4 respectively.

The cultural, social and economic characteristics of China vary tremendously from place to place. Under the direct jurisdiction of the central government are four municipalities, 23 provinces and five autonomous regions,[24] which constitute the highest level of local administration in the country. It is at this level that elite sports teams function. Thus, provinces, municipalities and autonomous regions are the geographic units considered in this study.

Generally speaking, China comprises three large and diverse regions: the East (coastal), Central and the West. In order to present a representative picture of women and sport across China, Guangdong (coastal), Beijing (central) and Sichuan (south-west) have been selected as case studies.

Beijing, the capital of the People's Republic of China (PRC), is the political, commercial and cultural centre of the most highly populated country in the world. Situated in the north of China, Beijing is an independently administered municipality with about 12 million people living in an area of 16,808 square kilometres (about 6,500 square miles). It has 18 districts and counties.[25] Beijing is the location of national sports bodies, and has held most of the major national and international competitions. Beijing has produced a number of female sports celebrities over the years, including the gymnast Liu Yajun in the 1970s, the volleyball player Lang Ping in the 1980s, and the swimmer Sang Ying, as well as the football players Liu Ailin, Liu Ying and Li Xiuli in the 1990s, to name but a few.

Guangdong is located in the south of China. It covers 178,000 square kilometres with over 68 million permanent residents. Its coastline extends for 3,368 km, the longest coastline of all the provinces, and over 10 per cent of the country's total coastline. Thus, it has been a gateway to the outside world and the main entry point for various western values, ideas and customs. Modern sport was imported from the West into this province in the late nineteenth and the early twentieth centuries.[26] This early contact with modern sport left a legacy of sporting enthusiasm and paved the way in due course for the rapid expansion of elite sport among women. Since the advent of economic reform in 1979 Guangdong has been the engine for the nation's phenomenal economic thrust forward. Three of the four Special Economic Zones, initially established in 1979, are situated in the province.[27] Guangdong has produced a number of female world champions, including the diver Cheng Xiaoxia in the late 1970s and early 1980s, the weightlifter Xin Fen and four Olympic footballers in the 1990s. The pole-vaulter Sun Caiyun impressively broke the women's record four times, and the weightlifters Zhang Yuxiang and Chen Shaomin also smashed world records in 1996.[28] Clearly, Guangdong women have made indisputable contributions to elite women's sport in China.

Sichuan, an inland province in the south-west of China, is located on the upper reaches of the Yangtze River. It covers 570,000 square kilometres, some 6 per cent of China's total landmass.[29] It can be roughly divided into four parts: the western highlands, the central basin, the eastern hills, and the south-west mountain and basin areas. Chengdu, the capital of the province, is situated in the basin. As the biggest Chinese province, Sichuan has a population of 110.84 million (nearly 10 per cent of the Chinese population) and has 23 cities, counties and autonomous prefectures.[30] Interestingly, virtually all international Sichuanese sports celebrities between the late 1980s and early 1990s were women, including the 'diving queen' Gao Min, the world champion volleyball players Zhang Rongfang, Liang Xan and Wu Dan, and the 1992 Olympic shooting champion Zhang Shang.

This book is in two parts. In Part 1 (Chapters 1 to 5), case studies will be drawn upon to illustrate the historical evolution of women's sport since 1949 – both general and elite, but with a particular emphasis, as the thesis logically requires, on elite women athletes. This requires exploration of regional archives. Part 2 (Chapters 6 to 9) focuses directly on recent and contemporary issues, and is more sociological in approach. The earlier case studies are therefore considered to have served their historical purpose and will not be pursued. Attention will be concentrated on major issues of global interest, and sometimes causes for concern, such as drugs, or 'super-coaches and super-athletes'. The emphasis will be on the contemporary national and international dimension, and not on archival sources for regional histories as in Part 1, since such archives do not yet exist.

Literature Review of Women, Gender and Sport

Gender issues have been the focus of many studies in the three decades since the women's liberation movement, initiated in the mid-1960s, gained momentum in the United States and Europe.[31] The issues of equal access to education and careers have been raised, and legislative and institutional changes have resulted. Title IX in 1972 in the USA and the Sex Discrimination Act of 1975 in Britain helped to extend opportunities for girls and women to achieve their potential in every sphere, including sport.[32] On the back of these developments, sports feminism emanated mainly from North America during the 1970s.[33] Sports feminists confronted the reality of male dominance in sport and the marginalisation of female sport – the dominant gender relationship in sport. From the late 1970s onwards, Ann Hall,[34] Susan Greendorfer,[35] Susan Birrell[36] and others conducted a multifaceted analysis of women, gender and sex inequality in sport. It uncovered a hidden history of female sport, examined gender differences in the patterns of athletes' socialisation, and demonstrated how the dominant institutional forms of sport had consolidated men's privileges and power over women.[37]

Unsurprisingly, therefore, gender relations have been central to subsequent feminist studies since the 1980s. Feminist sports studies, such as Nancy Theberge's *Sport and Women's Empowerment*[38] and Susan J. Birrell's *Discourse on the Gender/Sport Relationship: From Women in Sport to Gender Relations*,[39] had shifted the focus from gender differences to gender relations within sport by the late 1980s. It was widely acknowledged that men had more dominant positions and more control of their personal lives and social activities in most societies, although the degree and nature of male superiority and dominance varied considerably.[40] This process of male dominance that ranks and rewards males over females is known as patriarchy.[41] As a 'web of structured social practice, it systematically fosters the development of men while constraining the development of women'.[42] All societies that have been studied by social scientists have some elements of patriarchy in their private and public forms of social organisation, although the extent of male dominance is uneven.[43] Thus, the theory of patriarchy has been prevalent in feminist studies. However, gender relations are not static, ahistorical configurations, but contingent social arrangements that are always being contested and, consequently, a great deal of cultural and political energy is consumed keeing them in place.[44] Some feminist scholars – R.W. Connell, for one – argued that the theory of patriarchy was thus too glibly universalistic, ahistorical, essentialist and unsophisticated, and suggested replacing the concept of patriarchy with 'masculinity' when considering gender relations.[45] Since gender relations are essentially power relations, Jennifer Hargreaves and others have advocated the use of 'hegemony theory'[46] in feminist sports studies.

> The concept of male hegemony recognises the advantages experienced by men, in general, in relation to women, but recognises, also, the inability of men to gain total control. In sport, women are not totally manipulated, and it is misleading to treat either men or women as homogeneous groups.[47]

It goes without saying that power relations are complex and require sophisticated analysis. Above all, it should be recognised that, while often denied formal power, women are seldom without informal power.[48] As inquiries became subtler by the 1990s the investigation and analysis of gender and sport both broadened and deepened. Academic work had come to focus on the attitudes of society to women in sport, and the constraints imposed on – and consequences of – women's participation in both competitive and recreational activities, as well as the limitations of these attitudes.[49] Ann Hall summarised the relevant issues associated with a feminist study of women's sport in *Gender and Sport in the 1990s: Feminism, Culture, and*

Politics and *Feminism and Sporting Bodies.*[50] She emphasised the necessity of paying attention to the relationship between gender and other social divisions, such as class and race, while recognising the pervasive influence of gender divisions on social life. In short, the field of feminist sports studies has been steadily transformed from non-theoretical investigation of the patterns of women's involvement and the psychological factors that kept women from full participation to a more theoretical, informed and balanced critical analysis of the cultural forces that work to produce the ideological practices that influence the relations between sport and gender.[51]

Feminist studies in the West, such as those by Hall and Hargreaves, provide, up to a point, a useful analytical framework for the analysis of sportswomen in China. However, as some critics have remarked, feminism in modern technological societies has been essentially a gender liberation movement by and for white, middle-class women, and consequently, the literature on gender produced by both feminists and non-feminists has been gender-confrontational, partial, limited and too narrowly focused.[52] Thus, feminist activists and scholars have often felt confused by third world and minority women's insistence that 'their interests might best be served through alliances with men, waged against race and class oppression'.[53] For their part, 'poor and minority women have often felt uneasy being lumped together with white, privileged women as mutual victims of "patriarchy".'[54] Alison Dewar has castigated the use of the experiences of western sportswomen falsely universalised as representative of all women's experiences within the sports world.[55] As far as China is concerned, the assertion that 'sport is a predominantly male preserve'[56] is inaccurate and misleading. This will be discussed in detail later. It should be stressed that western ethnocentric assertions, assumptions and interpretations are not necessarily transferable to other parts of the world with different histories, ideologies and their consequences. It is surely time for indigenous analysts to offer their insights – born of indigenous experience – rather than have others extrapolate with certainly brave confidence and sometimes bold ignorance from West to East.

Having issued this sensible caveat, it must be recognised, of course, that the subject of Chinese women and society has been the research interest of a number of western or western-trained feminist studies, such as Marilyn Young's *Women in China: Studies in Social Change and Feminism* (1973); Elisabeth J. Croll's *Feminism and Socialism in China* (1978), *Chinese Women Since Mao* (1983), and *Changing Identities of Chinese Women* (1995); Phyllis Andors's *The Unfinished Liberation of Chinese Women 1949–1980* (1983); and Rey Chow's *Woman and Chinese Modernity* (1991). Their works, which have some worthwhile things to say about women in modern China, have suggested that socialist revolution in China has greatly improved women's lives but has not yet addressed the full range of gender inequalities. All this is certainly true. With regard to women's elite sport, however, which their studies do not address, there remains considerable scope for a detailed and specific indigenous analysis that will underline the dangers of imposing western interpretations on eastern circumstances, as well as provide an eastern perspective on eastern phenomena.

Feminist studies emerged in China only after the 'open door' policy was adopted in the late 1970s. With the publication of feminist inquiries and the development of women's studies programmes at a number of universities came a new body of knowledge on women's status in general and education, employment, social mobility, political participation, family, marriage and gender relations in particular.[57] These feminist studies culminated in the fourth World Women's Conference of the United Nations in Beijing in 1995.[58] However, as mentioned earlier, these mainstream feminist studies have excluded sport and sportswomen. In sport itself there are some studies – although an insufficient number – that have explored the reasons for Chinese women's achievement in sport; but these have scarcely analysed them from a feminist perspective – or indeed an adequately comprehensive perspective. Such studies fall into three categories. One, as represented, for example, by the influential Chinese sports officials He Zhenliang and Zhang Canzhen,[59] argues that women's success in sport is attributable to recent equality of access and opportunity within sport, women's propensity for hard work and obedience, and more recently the support of men.[60] This argument is partially correct, but not wholly convincing given that many other Asian sportswomen are as obedient and hard-working as Chinese women, but have not achieved so much in sport. In addition, the terms 'obedience and hard work' convey an ambivalent message about sport and women's liberation, and are likely to lock people into a belief in the fixed innate predisposition of the female – a belief that is blind to historical and cultural changes involving women in the New China.

Another viewpoint – held, for example, by the Chinese academic Lu Yuanzhen[61] and the American scholar Susan Brownell[62] – is that Chinese sportswomen's rise to international supremacy is a manifestation of their low, rather than high, social status in society, because female athletes are assumed to come mainly from the rural and urban lower classes, with the result that they are driven to better themselves. However, this remains pure supposition. No convincing statistical data on the family origins of female athletes have been provided to support this argument, which will be considered further in Chapter 8. There is a clear danger that with such unproven assertions academics can give birth to facile mythology.

The Chinese scholars Lu Shuting and Wang Yuan offer a third point of view: women's stunning accomplishment in sport is an outcome of the combination of male dominance in the wider society with a much more equal environment in the sports community, in which gender bias against women scarcely exists, while competition and success are encouraged:[63] in short, sport is meritocratic. However, why such polarised conditions – assuming they exist – should contribute to women's success in sport, and how women athletes are stimulated by the polarised cultural arrangements of society and sport respectively, are questions left largely unexplored by these Chinese scholars. Once more, assertion is preferred to evidence.

All these opinions lack the authority of conclusive evidence. What can be said authoritatively of all three points of view is that they fail to consider adequately the effects on today's women's sport of recent historical events such as the Great Leap Forward in the late 1950s, the Cultural Revolution between 1966 and 1976, and the economic reform after 1979. Consequently confusion, contradictions and a lack of historically relevant analysis characterise inquiry into elite women's sport in contemporary China. This study will attempt to fill in gaps, resolve contradictions and reduce confusion. Sport in the modern world is a multi-faceted social phenomenon with political, cultural, economic, spiritual and aesthetic dimensions.[64] As a consequence this study argues that Chinese women's success in international competitions is an outcome of the subtle interaction of historical and cultural events, political priorities, rapid economic development, changing gender relations, international political ambitions, and an efficient sports system. This matrix of factors will now be briefly reviewed as a preliminary to the presentation of short outlines of the chapters.

Overview: Elite Women's Sport in the New China

Historical background

The Opium War (1840–42)[65] formed a watershed in the modern history of China. Following the gunboats and troops, western missionaries came to China to preach Christianity. To this end, they established various schools throughout the country. An English woman, Marry Ann Aldersey, opened the first girls' school in Ningpo in 1844. By 1876 the missionary girls' schools numbered 121 with about 2,000 female students.[66] These schools played an important part not only in eliminating illiteracy and arousing women's awareness of their individuality and oppression, but also in promoting the anti-foot-binding campaign[67] and introducing modern sport to Chinese women. These sports – including gymnastics, athletics, swimming, basketball, volleyball and table tennis – were an important and integral part of the school curriculum.[68] In the missionaries' view healthy girls made healthy mothers. However, due to the limited access to education and the influence of the deep-rooted Confucian ideas about women and the continuing practice of footbinding in many families, most women were still barred from modern education, freedom of physical movement and opportunities for sport. Progress towards modern physical emancipation would be very gradual.

By the end of the nineteenth century, China was in the throes of western invasion and partial colonisation. To revive their ancient and humiliated nation, in 1896 radical Chinese intellectuals and officials, represented by Kang Youwei[69] and Liang Qichao,[70] advocated a national Reform Movement.[71] Believing that the cause of national regeneration demanded the better health and welfare of women – strong mothers to produce strong soldiers – they launched their own anti-footbinding campaign.[72] The result was that more and more women ceased to be constrained by the cruel practice of footbinding, walked out of their homes, and made 'big strides forward' with increased vigour and vitality. Gaining a sense of control over their bodies was fundamental to the acquisition of control over themselves and their immediate environment.[73] A new sense of self-worth was gradually born in women, which at least reduced their psychological – as well as physical – dependence on men.

During the Reform Movement women's education was encouraged and extended. Female student numbers reached 177,273 by 1917 in the country as a whole. After the May 4th Movement,[74] girls' schools and colleges flourished. In 1920 women were for the first time admitted to universities and by 1924 the number of female university students had reached 665.[75] Now physical education became a subject in most schools and universities, while specialised sports schools and colleges came into being. For example, as early as 1912 a private woman's sports school was established in Guangzhou, the capital of Guangdong province.[76] In Sichuan in the mid-1920s the First Girls' Normal School[77] and Hanyuan Girls' Primary School were established,[78] followed by Sichuan Women's Musical and Physical Education School in 1928, Sichuan Women's Physical Education School in 1930 and the Physical Education Department of the National Women's Normal College in 1940.[79] Modern sport now became popular among female students, who began to appear in various domestic and international sports competitions.[80] Guangdong women played volleyball at the Eighth Provincial Games of the 'Old China' in 1921, only four years after their male counterparts first took part. Women debuted at the National Games in 1922.[81] The female swimmer Yang Xiuqiong, from Guangdong, won five medals at the Tenth Far-East Games in 1934.[82] Arguably, there was from the outset no gap between China and the West in terms of access to organised elite sport for women. In 1924, while western women competed in fencing and swimming at the Olympic Games, Chinese women played basketball, softball and volleyball at the National Games.

While liberation played its part, to some extent Chinese women's rapid access to modern sport was associated with the fact that sport was considered an activity that posed no threat to the Confucian hierarchical structure. Due to a widespread belief that women's participation in sport could hardly mount a fundamental challenge to the established order of the male-dominated society, women were able to take up modern sport without provoking strong resistance.[83] Consequently, Chinese women and men took up modern sport virtually simultaneously. This is in contrast to the West, where modern sport was a male preserve well before it became widely available to women.

Nevertheless, the chaos of civil wars (1927–37 and 1945–49) and the Anti-Japanese War (1937–45) made it hard, if not impossible, for Chinese women to engage seriously in sport and participate in the Olympic Games.[84] Neither, of course, did international women's sport itself progress significantly, due to the eruption of the Second World War. Thus, a number of women's sports were not incorporated into the Olympic Games until 1948.[85] The result was that Chinese women did not lag far behind western women in elite sport by the mid-twentieth century.[86] This should not be overlooked. In the process of inhabiting the world sports stage, Chinese women did not have as far to travel as Chinese men.

The year 1949 witnessed the establishment of the New China, in which, as noted earlier, the Communist belief in equality between men and women was stressed. Immediately, Chinese women took up organised elite sport on a large scale. Chinese women actually outstripped western women in terms of equal opportunities in organised sport. Inequality between men and women was a widespread phenomenon all over the world, including in western sport, prior to the early 1970s. Western women took part in sport in far fewer numbers than men.[87] At the 1952 Helsinki Games, there were 4,407 male but only 518 female athletes (10.5 per cent).[88] Although women's representation at the Olympic Games slowly increased over time, from 13.3 per cent in 1964 to 20.6 per cent in 1976, they were, and still are, under-represented. Even in the case of America, the world's leading sports power, female athletes made up only 26 per cent of its 1988 Olympic delegation.[89] American women had, and have, difficulties finding sponsorship, network television coverage, and support for professional projects.[90] To a certain extent, this global gender inequality favoured Chinese sportswomen, who enjoyed, on occasion, more than equal treatment in the New China. This is clearly reflected in their overrepresentation in Olympic delegations.

Modern sport had been an exclusively male preserve internationally for some time before the late nineteenth century, when it was first introduced to Chinese men.[91] Thus, there was a gap between Chinese men and their western counterparts in obtaining access to it. Moreover, Chinese traditional culture granted the highest status to men who achieved success in imperial academic examinations.[92] According to Susan Ogden, 'The very existence of an institutionalised system of recruitment based on educational achievement sets China apart from most other civilisations and countries.'[93] Initially, therefore, men's incentive to participate in modern sport was not high. In China, academic knowledge was stressed and gentleness was regarded as an important quality of masculinity. In consequence, modern sport was despised as an uncouth, lower-class activity. Mao Zedong vividly described this state of affairs early in 1917: 'Students feel that exercise is shameful. ... Flowing garments, a slow gait, a grave, calm gaze – these constitute a fine deportment, respected by society.'[94] Exercise, as a result, was considered savage and vulgar. An 'effeminate' culture[95] resulted and modern sport, emphasising aggression, strength, speed and power, was discouraged. The negative impact on men's sport of the conventional importance attached to examinations and its consequences for the definition of ideal masculinity, it is argued here, has not been given sufficient attention. One eventual consequence was men achieving relatively poorly in world sport and women being given their chance to do better, in the interest of projecting the virtues of Chinese Communism.

Contemporary Situation

Of course, sport does not occur in a social vacuum: it is an integral part of social life.[96] It reflects, and is affected by, the dominant social structures and values of the society in which it exists.[97] After the People's Republic of China (PRC) came into being in 1949, fundamental changes took place in society. The Marriage Law decreed in 1950 constituted a milestone in protecting women's rights within the household. The Land Law of the same year established, for the first time, women's right to own and inherit property.[98] Education was now widely available to them. Chinese women 'suddenly' obtained equal rights with men in the spheres of law, family and education – a more sudden, if tardy, progress than that of western women in the history of women's liberation.[99]

In China, education was essential to women's liberation – the stepping stone to their involvement in sport. Education was put at the top of the national agenda in the early 1950s. A campaign to wipe out illiteracy was initiated across the country, which witnessed the creation of numerous schools in both rural and urban areas. Within the first ten years of the new regime, women students in higher education snowballed in number from 27,000 to 150,000.[100] Education effectively awakened women's consciousness to their potential as human beings: mentally, emotionally, and physically. Among other things they began to break down traditional barriers to involvement in sport, and their attitude to sport became progressively more positive. Sport was now believed to make women healthier and happier. Many parents now encouraged their daughters and daughters-in-law to take part in physical exercise, while young men sought girlfriends from sports teams.[101] All this vigorously challenged the traditional stereotype of femininity and helped clear away, at least in part, the cultural obstacles to women's participation in sport.

In Communist China, elite sport has always been a state-sponsored activity. As part of a centralised planning system, by the mid-1950s a sports administration system had been established and China's sport became institutionalised, specialised and bureaucratised. However, elite sport has been heavily influenced by both political *and* economic policies (see Figure 1).[102] Sports investment has paralleled the state of the national economy. While gross national product increased from 362.4 billion yuan in 1978 to 1,859.84 billion yuan in 1990, for example, the sports budget rose correspondingly from 253.86 million yuan to 1,462.762 million yuan. Similarly, the sports budget dropped markedly when China was economically and politically unstable – for example, in the three-year period in the early 1960s resulting from the ill-advised Great Leap Forward (1958–60) and a series of natural disasters. The same was true of the chaotic early years of the Cultural

FIGURE 1

SPORTS BUDGET AND GROSS NATIONAL PRODUCT OVER TIME

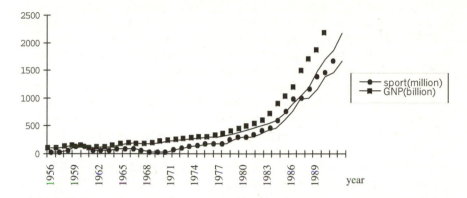

Revolution (1966–76). In contrast, both GNP and the sports budget soared dramatically after 1980, when economic reform was introduced in China. Clearly, sport has been, and still is, entwined intimately with both national politics and economics.

Furthermore, elite sport in China has been enmeshed in international politics. In the early 1950s, when China and America were dragged into the Korean War, their relationship deteriorated. As a result, the United States and its allies blocked Chinese admission to the United Nations for two decades. This had a knock-on effect on China's attempt to regain its membership of the International Olympic Committee, from which China had withdrawn in 1958 over the issue of Taiwan.[103] This international isolation prompted China to rely on itself to accelerate its economic progress and to win a place in the modern world. The Great Leap Forward (GLF) was thus launched in the late 1950s. One product of the GLF was the emergence of the 'commune' (*gongshe*), in which the Communist practices of 'eating out of the same pot' (*zhi daguo fan*) and distributing goods according to 'need' were experimented with, and household chores 'collectivised'. These innovations relieved individual women, though temporarily, from personal domestic responsibilities and made it possible *and* desirable for women to be involved in 'social production' (*shehui shengchan*), including sport, with the result that women's sport – both mass and elite – reached an unparalleled high-water mark, culminating in their participation in the First National Games in 1959. The Games were viewed as an instrument for eventual international confrontation, and a stimulus to motivate athletes and coaches. The National Games now became, and have remained, the yardstick of China's elite sport. To take part was, and is, to have arrived. The ill-advised GLF turned out to be short-lived. The impractical utopian communist practices were followed by three years of natural disasters (1959–61). The GLF and the disasters jointly brought China to the brink of economic collapse. This rebounded on sport, and elite sports teams were decimated in the early 1960s.

Before too long, another nationwide, but longer-lived political movement – the Cultural Revolution – was unleashed across the country, between 1966 and 1976. During the turbulent years between 1966 and 1969, elite sport virtually collapsed. After the early ferocious fighting between various sectors of the Red Guards and other mass organisations came to an end in 1969, provincial sports teams gradually resumed their normal activities. Sports teams provided an asylum for some young people, allowing them to evade the fighting and avoid being sent to the countryside, with the result that many parents now encouraged their children to engage in elite sport. Consequently, the number of students in sports schools reached a record high.[104] By the mid-1970s, in spite of the continued attack on 'medalism and trophyism,' at least in rhetoric, Chinese athletes had re-emerged in international competitions – for example, at the Seventh Asian Games in 1974. Female athletes began to reveal their potential and their competence in international sport.

Mao's death in 1976 marked the end of an era characterised by disruptive and damaging ideological revolution. The national entrance exams for universities, which had been abandoned during the Cultural Revolution, were reintroduced in 1978. Academic study was now a priority for the young, and parents were now reluctant to allow their children to engage in sport, with the outcome that student numbers in sports schools dropped considerably by the early 1980s. In 1978 the introduction of economic reform also brought about dramatic changes in society. The 'responsibility system of production' (*shengchan zeren zhi*) and concomitant material incentives and bonuses were re-introduced. Sport was in the vanguard of the movement to overturn the egalitarian 'big pot' (*da guo fan*) practice, in which individuality had been discouraged. The massive political and financial rewards under the new system made elite sport a magnet to many young people. The decline in participation in elite sport of the late 1970s was reversed by the mid-1980s.

In 1980 the Chinese participated in the Winter Olympic Games, but joined America and other western nations in the boycott of the Summer Olympic Games in Moscow in protest against the Soviet invasion of Afghanistan. Four years later, the Chinese won 15 gold medals at the Los Angeles Games, burying their humiliating 'nil' record in the Olympic gold medal table once and for all. This performance stirred up an intense nationalism among the Chinese and fuelled Chinese ambition to become a world sporting power. Subsequently – in 1985 – an 'Olympic Strategy' was put in place. This strategy greatly favoured women, who were considered more likely than the men to excel in international competitions.[105] Specific support at all levels and in all areas was given to promising women athletes, including the adoption of 'male sparring partners' (*nan pei nu liang*) in a number of women's sports teams. Athletic performance was the sole criterion determining the allocation of resources and the consequent strata of athletes in the sports community and in society at large. The success of women athletes proved the value of the Olympic Strategy,[106] and for women led to huge political, social and financial rewards. For example, there were 44 women among the 93 sports deputies to the fourth, sixth and seventh National People's Congresses.[107] Achievement in sport now provided the opportunity for upward social mobility.

Since the late 1970s China has gradually opened its door to the West, and technological and cultural exchanges have multiplied. Due to the obvious gap in living standards between China and the West, in the 1980s emigration became a goal of not a few, including athletes. Unexpectedly, the athlete and coach diaspora eventually resulted in 'overseas Chinese shock troops' (*haiwai juntuan*) who too frequently challenged Chinese dominance in a number of sports. In the face of this threat, China tightened its control over the international emigration of elite athletes and coaches. The central and local provincial sports governing bodies introduced a number of policies and regulations to restrain athletes from emigrating. However, after over two decades of 'opening up', this proved only partially successful. The global sports market had increasingly ensured the international mobility of athletes and made it an irreversible trend that Chinese action could no longer completely curtail.

International mobility led to the exchange of specialised sports knowledge. Accompanying the exchange of sports information and training methods, however, was the introduction of performance-enhancing drugs to China in the early 1980s. To a large extent drug-taking in sport is associated with the westernisation of Chinese society, the winning-oriented sports policy, and the personal desire for fame, wealth and success: the mentality of winning at all costs is the main cause. Following mounting incidences of drug abuse, the Chinese were internationally condemned. In response to huge international pressure and the growing tightening of international sports organisations' drug checks, in the late 1990s the Chinese started to seriously review, and then adjust, internal control over sports policy and management, and took firm action to crack down on drug abuse.

In line with general social and economic reforms, over the last decade sports administration, training and competition systems have gradually been transformed – from systems of exclusively central control and finance to systems of shared management and investment by the state, private enterprises and interested individuals. Social groups were encouraged to sponsor or manage elite sport in the early 1980s.[108] The decentralisation of sports management accelerated after the late 1980s. In addition to central and local government investment, increased levels of commercial and private sponsorship flooded into sport. The sports infrastructure of the country was considerably improved. By the mid-1990s China had 19 national sports training bases, located in 12 provinces or autonomous regions.[109] Private enterprise sports teams now emerged and mushroomed, and commercial sports clubs, a sports labour market, and western-type professional teams came into being one after another. By 1997 all individual sports associations had acquired autonomy from the National Sports Commission in financial, personnel and training management. In the meantime, local sports governing bodies and coaches acquired increasing control over their training affairs. Clearly, changes were underway, but they were not without their challenges. How were national and local interests to be reconciled? How were the coach's authority and the athlete's individuality to be squared? And how were market forces to be best used to the benefit of elite sport?

Despite continuous and often dramatic political, cultural and economic changes in the course of more than a millennium – especially in the last century[110] – the legacy of Confucianism is still strong in Chinese society, in the sports community as elsewhere, with the result that the family is still central to women's existence and family responsibilities are still their primary tasks. This tradition to a certain extent conflicts with women's pursuit of careers. In pursuit of sports careers, marriage and family often distract women from, and reduce their commitment to sport. Consequently, until recently female athletes were required to forgo their relationships with boys and delay marriage. It is not surprising that virtually all the successful female athletes achieved their best results before marriage. Thus, not infrequently, elite female athletes had to make a choice between a family and an athletic career. In consequence, many top-class sportswomen married later than other women.

As a product of the Confucian heritage, women's obedience is still stressed and favoured in Chinese society. Perhaps because of this, female athletes are often considered more obedient than their male counterparts – arguably a reason for women's more remarkable achievements. The obedient female athletes are, so the argument goes, more eager than men to win prestige for their nation, their families and themselves. They often work excessively hard. They have successfully assimilated and projected, it is often argued, the Confucian image of woman – modest and submissive, but also strong and responsible.[111]

While there is continuity, changes are inevitable. The most notable changes took place during the Cultural Revolution, when women, like men, threw themselves enthusiastically into the Red Guard movement, the Rustication Campaign and much else of a revolutionary nature. Under the slogan 'Women hold up half the sky', they demonstrated astonishing ambition, capability and courage. However, in pursuit of equality a 'sameness' was established between men and women. The denial of women's sexuality caused perplexing contradictions regarding the concept of femininity. Moreover, in the era of economic reform inaugurated in the late 1970s, values, norms and ideas changed again. Success, competitiveness and profit replaced class struggle, egalitarianism and austerity. Women, especially female athletes, as a consequence became more assertive and individualistic. In the last decade not a few female sports stars have overtly challenged conventional authoritarian management. Furthermore, in pursuit of their athletic careers an increasing number of women choose to delay marriage, and even to resume training after having children. All these developments in the periods of the Cultural Revolution and the Economic Reform are at odds with Confucian prescriptions for women's obedience and submissiveness. They have contributed to a change in gender expectations and gender relations.

Nevertheless, in the 1980s, in the context of a market economy, it was a case of two steps forward and one step back. Women in general encountered unanticipated difficulties. With demanding production quotas in a capitalist profit-directed economy, specific 'socialist' favours granted to women gradually ceased. They were made redundant first, or were not hired, on the pretext that their maternal role interfered with their job performance.[112] Acknowledging the existence of women's problems, China passed a new 'women's law' in 1992 in an attempt to prevent commercial discrimination. Women's issues attracted attention both from the state and from women themselves. This culminated in the convening of the Fourth Women's Conference of the United Nations in Beijing in 1995. Apart from recognising new capitalistic discrimination, some feminist scholars identified the still incomplete awakening of women's consciousness of their rights as the root cause of the lingering inequality of women in China.[113] Over and above the reasons discussed above, this might well be a further reason for the under-representation of women in sports coaching and administration, if not in sporting activities themselves.

What this summary amounts to is a brief consideration of the web of issues – political, economic, social, cultural and aesthetic – that will be considered more fully in the chapters summarised below, in an attempt to illustrate the complexity of the phenomena under review and the need to embrace this complexity.

Chapter Outlines

This book consists of nine chapters. Chapters 1 to 5 examine chronologically elite women's sport in the New China in terms of the interrelationship between society, women and sport. Chapter 1 centres attention on fundamental socio-economic, political and intellectual changes in society, their impact on women's lives in the early period of the New China, and their further influence on sports policies, practices and women's involvement in elite sport. By way of an exploration of the interactions between post-war economic rehabilitation, reliance on the Soviet Union and antagonism towards America, women's participation in 'social production' (*shehui shengchan*), the reasons for the early establishment of a centralised sports administration, the growth of semi-professional practice of elite sports teams, and the growth of women's involvement in elite sport are explained.

Chapter 2 covers the years between 1957 and 1965, with the focus on the period of the Great Leap Forward, which witnessed an unprecedented expansion of women's elite and mass sport. How were sports communities, like other groups in the country, motivated by the ambition to overtake western nations within a short time? What influences did the communist practice of 'commune' (*gongshe*) have on women's participation in elite sport? How did the emphasis on will power lead to excessively intensive training and a high incidence of sports injuries? And what legacy did the GLF have on the advances of women's sport in the following decades?

The Cultural Revolution between 1966 and 1976 constitutes a unique, and regrettable, episode in the political history of Communist China. However, the astonishing energy demonstrated by women during this period holds a particular fascination for feminists. Chapter 3 traces the progress of women in sport during this chaotic decade. To what extent were sports communities and athletes – and sportswomen in particular – involved in the political movement? What dialectic relationships existed between the Rustication Campaign, educational 'revolution' and sports participation, and between 'model opera' (see Chapter 3) and women's emancipation? How did sport serve political and diplomatic ends? And what was the impact on elite sportswomen? What influence in general did the Cultural Revolution have on society, women and elite sport?

The momentous year of 1979 signalled the onset of the Deng era and the restoration of China to the IOC. The inauguration of economic reform led to radical changes in society in general, and the sports community in particular. Chapter 4 reviews the first decade of economic reform (1979–89) and addresses the following issues: how elite sport evolved in the era of reform; what changes economic reform brought about in both the wider society and the sports community in the 1980s; what impact these changes had on women's social status and women in elite sport; and why Chinese sportswomen excelled in international competitions and then were regarded as national heroines.

Reforms continued into the 1990s in China, which influenced, and still influence, women's sport and sportswomen. Chapter 5 discusses the ongoing process of market-oriented economic reform in the 1990s and analyses the radical social, political and cultural changes during the transition to a market economy, their reverberations on the sports community, their role in the emergence of professional sports teams, sports clubs, league competitions and athlete transfer, and their actual and potential effects – both positive and negative – on women's elite sport.

Drugs cast a long shadow over Chinese sport in the 1990s. When and how drugs were introduced to China, why some women athletes risked the use of drugs, why drug abuse became prevalent and what attitude Chinese officials held towards drug offences are perplexing puzzles. Chapter 6 attempts to uncover the 'drug scene' in Chinese sport, evaluate the influence of drug misuse on sports achievement and speculate on the possible impact of drug control on sports policy and women's sport in the future.

Chapter 7 deals with the social and psychological characteristics of elite female athletes in China through the life stories of some famous female athletes: the Ma Family Army, the Chinese women's volleyball team and the speed skater Ye Qiaobo. The complex characteristics of modern sportswomen – among them obedience and defiance, assertion and compliance, self-interest and self-sacrifice – as well as the influence of sporting success on their later lives, social status and family, and their coaches are explored in this chapter.

Successful sportswomen in China offer fascinating examples of upward social mobility through sports achievement. Of course, not every athlete is fortunate. What factors determine upward social mobility and how athletes in China actually realise mobility through sports participation are issues considered in Chapter 8. It investigates the relationship between sport, family background and gender difference, and reflects on the associated mobility of women athletes, success and gender stratification in the sports community, and the impact of changing sports policies on athletes' mobility.

The question of why Chinese women, not men, have excelled internationally in sport calls for examination of gender relations in sport in modern China. The last chapter, therefore, probes gender relations in Chinese sport through the analysis of the recent evolution of elite sport in China, the international performance of men and women, and the rise in the confidence, assertiveness, esteem and status of women in society – and more particularly in sport. The changing and challenging relationships between sportswomen and coaches, and the crucial relationship between family and athlete, will receive particular attention.

Finally, the Epilogue brings this book to a conclusion and offers predictions for the future prospects of elite women's sport in China.

Women, Society and Sport in the Early Years of the New China

Sport in modernising communities is a serious business with key functions to perform. It is accordingly state-controlled, encouraged and shaped by utilitarian and ideological designs (it is by no means a matter merely of fun and games). In its development it is associated with health, hygiene, defence, patriotism, integration, productivity, international recognition, even cultural identity and nation-building.[1]

Self-evidently, 1 October 1949 was a watershed in Chinese history. The Chinese Communist Party (CCP) acceded to power and the People's Republic of China (PRC) came into being. China changed from a semi-feudal and semi-colonial country to a socialist independent state. However, this new regime inherited a legacy of poverty and ineffective control over provinces impoverished for over half a century – a consequence of both natural and man-made disasters. At the same time, it had to deal with threats from the United States, whose army actually intruded into Korea and came close to the border of China in the early 1950s.[2] Thus, the immediate and obvious needs for the CCP were to build newly centralised ideological, political and economic systems, develop its economy and strengthen its national defence. Sport was utilised and emphasised to serve all these ends.[3] With a stable political climate, an improved economic situation and a favourable ideology, mass sport developed quickly.[4] It generated the first wave of the sports 'craze' of the New China,[5] which provided a solid base for the development of elite sport. Following the establishment of national sports administration and training systems, systematic elite sport was born.

In tune with communist principles and political imperatives, women were encouraged to involve themselves in 'social production'[6] (*shehui shengchang*) and political activity – and in sport, for which they demonstrated considerable enthusiasm and in which they demonstrated considerable potential. Thus, the period from 1949 to 1957 witnessed the first stage of the evolution of elite women's sport in the New China.

Fundamental changes occurred in sport, especially women's sport, during the earliest years of the PRC,[7] yet even today, as mentioned in the Prologue, there is a paucity of literature on women and elite sport in these years. Why and how did Chinese women, once captive in the home with 'bound feet', so successfully and enthusiastically take part in competitive sport, which was regarded as the sphere of men? What were their motives? What was the relationship between state policy, women's involvement in sport and women's social status? And what impact did developments in the early 1950s have on Chinese women's astounding later international success? For the most part, these questions remain unanswered. This chapter will explore the issues relevant to these questions.

Analysis: Overview

Communist Sports Administration

After a few years of recovery from war-torn chaos, China began its full socialist transformation and planned reconstruction in 1953, the first year of its first Five-year Plan. Sports developments were part of this reconstruction. Organised and centralised sport replaced voluntary and decentralised sport. As befitted a socialist state, sport was exclusively financed by the state: in Brohm's words, 'Sport is mediated through the state which locks in all the structures of society as a whole.'[8] In every aspect of transformation, the Communist Party played a leading role. The Party's policies, strategies and plans determined, to a considerable extent, the direction of Chinese society, including women's sport, in post-1949 China.

The model of Chinese sports administration mirrored the wider system. Both the Party and state administrations were organised in a vast hierarchy with power flowing down from the top.[9] Sports administration was no different. A highly unified and concentrated system of sports administration was put in place following the creation of the National Sports Commission (NSC) at the end of 1952.[10] This commission was in charge of the formulation and implementation of sports policy in all its forms and the administration of the national sports programme. It liaised closely with other government ministries such as Education and National Defence. Subsequently, a lot of local sports establishments at the level of province, city or county came into being between 1953 and 1954, as illustrated by the three case studies below. A centralised system of sports administration had taken shape by the mid-1950s (see Figure 2).

Despite some variation over time, the administrative structure of Chinese sport has not changed fundamentally over the four subsequent decades. Indeed, many of the pillars of China's sports system are still in place. Once the system of sports administration was in place, training, competition and coaching systems followed. Of course, there have been changes, which will be discussed later.

FIGURE 2

ADMINISTRATIVE STRUCTURE OF CHINESE SPORT
(Note: PLA= People's Liberation Army; SC= sports commission)

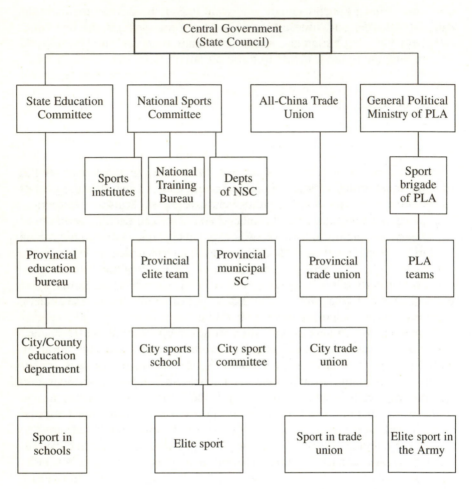

Specialisation of Sport and Women's Emancipation

As will be seen in the later case studies, some national and army sports teams were created in 1951. Following in their footsteps, between 1953 and 1958 provinces across the country organised their own specialised (now called elite) sports teams. Elite athletes lived a militarised life in a semi-sealed sporting community, and enjoyed enviable welfare benefits.[11] By taking up elite sport, men and women could obtain incomes, support them-selves, safeguard their futures, achieve self-satisfaction and lead worthwhile lives. This process, however, was not always straightforward and was seldom without struggle. The experience of 1961 women's world table-tennis champion Qou Zhonghui clearly illustrates both points:

> In 1953 when the provincial volleyball team recruited me, my community including my parents and teachers were opposed. At that time, people regarded sports men and women as having low social status and reputation. In the history of my family no one had specialised in sport. Even my brother, who had encouraged my enthusiasm, disagreed with my decision to become an elite sportswoman. He considered sport a 'youth career' and was worried about my post-athletic future. To stop me from joining the sports team, my parents even declared that if I joined the sports team I should never come back home. Nevertheless, I did join the team and did not go back home for several months. At last my family gave in. My brother, on behalf of my parents, begged me to return home on my day off. To be honest, I had never dreamed of specialising in sport. I just followed the assignment from the 'organisation' (Party). There was a popular slogan at that time: 'The need of the motherland is my wish.' This concept was deeply rooted in the minds of the 50s generation. The interest of the nation came first.[12]

This anecdote is revealing for several reasons. First, as noted earlier, sport was regarded as a career in Communist-controlled China, but not necessarily an admirable one, due to its historically low standing in society, and a general traditional bias against sport. Second, communist education in the 1950s had a deep influence on the 1950s generation (women in particular) that grew up in the New China. Following rural land reform and urban economic re-organisation in the 1950s, the centuries-old extended-kinship structure was disbanded. It effectively removed a deep-rooted source of authority in the Chinese extended family.[13] In consequence, in both cities and villages, parents and children were virtually equal in the eyes of the state. More importantly, the state deliberately launched a process of liberating women from the patriarchal family, and transforming them from 'family females' (*jiating funu*) into 'societal females' (*shehui funu*) – members of the state first and foremost.[14] Motivated by communist belief and reinforced by ideological propaganda,[15] people were expected to sacrifice themselves to the cause (*shiye*), and to the Party that had led them to communism. The 1950s generation broadly accepted that national interest took precedence over individual interest. Finally, as a consequence of these changes, Chinese women began to project a new image of growing self-confidence, assertiveness and independence that allowed them to mount a successful challenge to traditional patriarchal ideas and institutions. This new image was in sharp contrast to 'foot-bound' small women in the 'Old China'. This revolutionary change in women was to a considerable extent an outcome of communist policies and practices.

As already discussed, the CCP de facto attached great importance to women's liberation and granted women equal rights in the family and in society. Women's equal status was clearly stated in the first Constitution of the New China: 'The state protects the rights and interests of women, applies the principle of equal pay for equal work for men and women alike, and trains and selects cadres from among women.'[16] Women were also allowed access to political posts. Song Chingling,[17] for example, was elected as vice-chairwoman of the People's Central Government Committee. Shi Liang[18] and others[19] were also given leading posts in the new government. These prominent women were role models for other Chinese women. Fundamental changes took place in women's lives, as illustrated by the following quotation from Wang Yingrun, a female professor of sports physiology at Beijing University of Physical Education.

> I lived more than 30 years in the Old China, spent three years abroad, and lived 44 years in the New China. In the Old China, it was difficult to obtain a job after graduation, even for men. Although I received higher education, and had been always among the best academic performers in the university, I had to rely on my husband. As he was very brilliant, he was offered a teaching post in his college even before he graduated. He made it a condition of his employment that the college employed me. Employers did not like to recruit women at that time. More than this, even if women obtained posts, they also faced discrimination in promotion. My husband began working as a lecturer without the normal probationary period as an assistant teacher, and was promoted to associate professor within eight years. Some other universities even wanted to employ him as a professor. In contrast, I was an assistant teacher for nine years. This inequality made me determined to go abroad no matter what difficulties lay ahead. In short, women were greatly discriminated against in the Old China. Things changed dramatically in the New China. I was given a key position [director of a sports physiology department] and many honours and privileges by the Party, the government and our university.[20]

In 1950 the significant and far-reaching Marriage Law[21] was passed in order to eradicate the traditional system of marriage, which was identified as a source of female inequality, and more significantly as a barrier to wider participation in the socialist revolution. The Party declared the abolition of the 'feudal marriage system characterised by arranged and forced marriage, male superiority and female inferiority, and disregard for the interests of children'.[22]

With the acquisition of equal status in the family, women began to reassess their role and status both in the family and in society. Reassessment inevitably led to the further pursuit of wider equality in society, embracing equal employment opportunities, higher education, equal pay for equal work, and an equal voice in decision-making. Therefore, the Marriage Law brought challenge and change not only to family lives, but also to the social system. Challenge and change in turn indirectly provided the opportunity for women to participate in sport.

The CCP stressed, and believed, that women's emancipation could only be realised after women had economic independence. Thus, women were encouraged to step out of their homes to take part in economic production and even to enter the world previously inhabited largely by men. Women took on various jobs in factories, schools and hospitals. They even became successfully involved in 'male dominated' occupations such as train and tractor drivers and pilots, albeit not without resistance. In 1957, around 70 per cent of rural women were engaged in agricultural work, and the number of urban women workers and staff had reached over 3 million: a 5.5-fold increase over 1949.[23] Women now developed and tested their abilities and potential outside the home. Their actions led to a slow redefinition of women's social position and ensured their increasing independence. These developments provided the conditions for women to take up elite sport, now regarded as an occupation.

With the class system turned on its head, a number of elite female athletes in this period now came from the working class. This would have been impossible before 1949. The alpinist Pan Duo (born 1938) was one of them: a daughter of peasant slaves from Tibet, she was once a beggar in China after her parents died. When the Chinese Communist Party took control in Tibet in 1951, she became a factory worker, and in 1955 she joined the national mountaineering team. Her story will be further described in the following chapters.[24] Athletes with working-class backgrounds were, incidentally, prominent elite performers. Of the 92 athletes who qualified, for example, for the 16th Olympic Games in 1956 (which will be discussed more fully later), 27 came from the All China Trade Union that was established in 1949 and was responsible for organising sports activities for factories and enterprises throughout the country. The first Workers' Games took place in October 1955 and athletes from 17 enterprises participated in competitions covering six sports. By the end of 1956, there were 19 national enterprise sports associations, and 25,100 local sports associations affiliated to the All China Trade Union in the country. Their members numbered over a million (about ten per cent of all workers).[25]

Women's education was also an important stepping stone to involvement in both recreational and elite sport. Due to the separation between public and domestic spheres, women's education had been severely restricted in pre-1949 China (almost 90 per cent of women were illiterate). The vast majority of Chinese never stepped into a classroom, let alone participated in sport. Indeed, many women had no ambition to take part in sport, as the feudal concept of woman was still embedded deeply in their psyches. Faced with this legacy, the CCP paid considerable attention to improving women's education.[26] Between 1949 and 1951, some 3.4 million were taught to read and write.[27] The expansion of education spurred the growth of sport in schools. The two went hand in hand. Benefiting from the new Marriage Law, which stipulated a minimum age for marriage of 18 for women and 20 for men, adolescent girls could freely pursue their education. By 1958, '16 million women had learned to read, and this represented an initial step in eradicating the ignorance and backwardness of Chinese women'.[28] About 38.5 per cent of students in primary schools were girls, and female students in higher education increased gradually from 22.53 per cent in 1951 to 26.27 per cent in 1954.[29] As women's education improved, their awareness of their potentialities and the possibilities in society was awakened. They began to question the traditional norms of femininity, encapsulated in such aphorisms as 'women's lack of ability is her virtue' and 'man is superior to woman'. Thus cultural transformation laid down a further stepping stone enabling women to make their way to involvement in sport, including elite sport.

Girls' access to schooling was self-evidently helpful in this progress because physical education became an integral feature of the general curriculum. Humiliated by the image of the small and weak Asian, the Chinese were anxious to strengthen their physiques. The Korean War further reinforced a national concern with fitness. As a result, physical education was made mandatory from elementary school to university (twice a week).[30] Due to students' generally poor physiques,[31] the State Council further demanded that they should all spend one to one-and-a-half hours each day in physical exercise and physical labour in addition to mandatory twice-a-week physical education classes. Schoolgirls thus did not just learn sporting skills; more importantly, they also developed an interest in sport. By 1955, some 127,000 students in 187 schools were involved in the 'labour and defence programme' (*lao wei zhi*),[32] which provided both the incentive and amenities to realise students' sport potential and enhance the general athletic level of the whole nation. Once teachers of physical education identified a sporting talent, they often organised extracurricular sports training. An unprecedented growth of extracurricular athletics occurred. Most elite athletes in the 1950s came from schools and universities, which were the first institutional settings for women's sport.

'Specialised' sports teams now became a hallmark of – and represented the first significant development in – Chinese elite sport. Given the tension between the poor economic performance of China in the 1950s and the demand for huge investment in sports teams, the motive for introducing 'specialised' sports teams needs to be explored. The point to stress is that sport did not stand outside society: China's interest in elite sport was derived from its new identity. Hungry to obtain redress for over a century of humiliation by foreign powers, the Chinese were anxious to create a new identity in the world after the communist regime came into being, and sporting success was a useful instrument for this purpose. How to overtake the advanced sporting countries was an issue that obsessed the Chinese. However, in the early 1950s China was still characterised by widespread poverty; scarce resources of capital and expertise limited the possibility of laying down foundations for elite sport at the grass-roots level. Concentrating on selected sports talents – a logical strategy in the circumstances outlined above – was both a manifestation of Chinese political pragmatism and political elitism. As a result, national teams emerged quickly in 1951. A 'Central Sports Training Class', the predecessor of the National Training Bureau as the centre for the creation of national teams, was installed in Beijing the next year. The National Training Bureau, adopted a centralised system.[33] In Beijing, athletes of national teams enjoyed better training conditions, higher food and clothing subsidies, and more opportunities for international competition than provincial team members. By 1956 national teams for volleyball, basketball, football, table tennis, badminton, gymnastics, athletics and swimming had been established. In spite of some disputes about its management (see Chapter 5), the institution of the national team played an important part in assuring Chinese international victories.

In 1951, simultaneously with the emergence of national teams in China, the People's Liberation Army began to run 'specialised' elite sports teams. The six major military areas[34] across the country were given a quota of 3,000 places in order to establish their 'sports brigades'.[35] Why did the army race ahead of the local provinces in this regard and what influence did the army have on the development of Chinese elite sport? In attempting to answer these questions, three points should be borne in mind. First, modern sport was introduced into the army at the end of the nineteenth century and was integrated into the military training programme. As a result, the PLA had more experience of developing modern sport than most other institutions in China. Second, the qualities of sacrifice, discipline and hard work that were emphasised in the army are important attributes of modern sport. As Nan Yalan, a woman career-soldier and gymnastic coach, has stated:

> The strictness of life in the army cultivated my sense of responsibility. I spent 41 years in the national team (ten years as a gymnast, 31 years as a coach). I dedicated all my life to the cause, and sacrificed a lot. I had my first child when I was 33 and my second when I was 43. I kept coaching until the day before giving birth.[36]

Finally, a number of high-level military and party leaders such as Mao Zedong and Zhu De loved sport, and many former military officers acquired positions in sports administration[37] after the New China was set up. Marshal Helong, the vice-premier of the state, for example, was in charge of the National Sports Commission. They were undoubtedly bridges between the army and sports commissions. The PLA not only produced numerous elite athletes[38] but also greatly influenced the course of Chinese elite sport. Practices such as the public canteen, the collective dormitory, an isolated training environment and morning exercises owed much to military tradition. Among the far-reaching consequences of military influence is the training principle of 'strict, difficult and practical demands with a heavy load' (*congyan, congnan, cong shizhang chufa ji da yundongliang*), which had been widely used in the army and was borrowed by the sports community in the Great Leap Forward in the late 1950s. It is still a guiding principle of sports training. In a nutshell, sports careers resembled military careers in China in many ways. Military influences were manifested in the organisation, training and administration of athletes.

Apart from the 'specialised' sports team, another important dimension of elite sport was the sports school, which provided a talent pool of elite athletes. It acted as a bridge between amateur and 'specialised' athletes. After the NSC drafted 'Rules for Both Youth and Junior Spare-time Sports Schools' in 1955, sports schools for young students boomed. By the end of 1957, there were altogether 159 spare-time schools in 92 cities and 20 counties of the 23 provinces, autonomous regions and municipalities, and student numbers reached 17,000.[39] Some schools subsidised the students' clothes and food. Some provided students with accommodation.[40] Over 90 per cent of elite athletes experienced the training stage of spare-time sports schools. Indeed, all the Chinese Olympic champions at the Atlanta Olympic Games in 1996 had training experience in spare-time sports schools. By 1996 there were about 3,000 spare-time sports schools at county level and above across China. Students numbered over 200,000.[41] Due to its unique role in identifying future world champions, the sports school continues to flourish.

Other factors played their part in the consolidation of elite sport. In conjunction with the establishment of sports teams and sports schools, coaching and sports administration became full-time careers.[42] China had 982 full-time sports staff, including coaches, in 1953, and by 1956 the figure had soared to 6,551.[43] Increasingly people took up coaching as a career. Thus, in time a highly organised national sports programme under the control of paid administrators and professional coaches was created. Nevertheless, there were only a few female coaches in the early 1950s because coaching was a new career for women; the same was true for sports administration. The assimilation of women into competitive sport, of course, did not, and could not, remove inequality between men and women immediately, nor eradicate all at once the values shaped by a history of institutionalised feudal inequality. Economic independence through sport was an important but not all-at-once factor in women's emancipation. Women's liberation in sport and in society was a gradual process. It needed an appropriate political, social and cultural climate and, more importantly, women's own efforts and men's understanding and support in addition to the freedom brought by economic independence.

Partly because of full-time coaching opportunities, partly because of the shortage of sport experts in China (as the Guangdong case later clearly illustrates), a number of overseas Chinese returned to China to take up coaching positions in the early 1950s. Huang Jian, the coach of high-jumper Zheng Furong, who broke a world record in 1957, came from the now former Soviet Union, for example; Ma Qiwei, the coach of the women's volleyball team, came from the United States. A number of badminton coaches arrived from Indonesia. The contribution of these coaches was highly valued by the Chinese government.

With coaching as an occupation, and with a marked increase in newly organised sports activities and competitions, more sports specialists were obviously required. In 1952, there were only two institutes of physical education in the whole country, with 246 students on two-year programmes and only 79 on four-year programmes.[44] The total number of graduates of all sports colleges and sports departments of universities in 1955 was 817 at most.[45] This output could not meet the increasing demand for qualified coaches and physical educationists. In order to provide more sports specialists, 11 schools of physical education and six institutes of physical education[46] were established between 1952 and 1954. The number of students climbed to 2,699[47] (the ratio of girl students to boy students remained about one to five). Students in four-year programmes began to predominate after 1956.[48] The specialist colleges and departments played a large part in furthering growth of specialised sport for both men and women.

Competition is the essence of elite sport. Sports competition was provided for by means of a pyramid of meetings, contests and tournaments held under local, regional and national authority. Of the six thousand sports meetings held above the level of district and city between 1953 and 1956, 75 were nationwide. The number of athletes in various competitions also greatly increased over time. Table tennis provides a good example. In 1952 only 62 players took part in the first national table-tennis competition By the fourth national championships in 1957, the figure had increased to 252.[49] Meanwhile, regulations for a national sports competition system and criteria for the ranking of referees[50] and athletes[51] as well as the standards for sports including swimming and gymnastics – 16 events altogether – were published in 1956.

With the installation of various sports institutions, a coordinated network of talent identification, testing and nurturing was gradually built up. After 1952 China's sport gradually became specialised and bureaucratised. An elaborate system of regional and national organisations emerged to control and regulate sport. In spite of the varied tasks of its branches at different levels, they were inter-linked. The higher levels of the system had a right to monitor and control the lower ones. This network was labelled the 'dragon system': the national teams acted as the head of a dragon, the provincial elite sports teams and the spare-time sports schools were the body and the tail, with the head leading and controlling the others. This system played an essential part in accelerating the advance of Chinese elite sport so that by 1956 Chinese elite sport had become systematised and institutionalised.

International Recognition and Soviet Influences

As already noted, from the outset of the communist regime in 1949 Chinese sport was inextricably entwined with international political struggle. The

1952 Helsinki Olympic Games were considered a chance for the New China to enter the world competitive arena. Although Taiwan, considered by the PRC as merely the one province of China that was ruled by the Nationalist Party, was invited to the games, the New China also sent a 41-strong delegation, including 24 male basketball and football players and two female swimmers. However, only one swimmer took part in the competition due to the late arrival of most participants in Finland – a result of the delayed invitation from the IOC, which was thrown into confusion by the political reality of 'two Chinas', Taiwan and China.[52] Nevertheless, the Helsinki Olympics clearly indicated that the New China was eager to win international recognition through sport. Thereafter, to further this recognition Chinese political strategy began to shift from mass sport to elite sport.

Furthermore, after 1953, in pursuit of recognition Chinese women were encouraged to participate in increasing numbers in both national and international competitions. By 1953 there were domestic competitions for basketball, volleyball, athletics, swimming, gymnastics, cycling and various other events. Women emerged in all these sports – see Table 2. The starting point for female elite sport was virtually the same as for males. There was no obvious gap in the number of sports available to men and women. This was in striking contrast to America and other western nations, where men were involved in elite sport much earlier and had access to many more activities than women.[53] From 1954 to 1957 female Chinese athletes created new national records in an average of 25 events each year. (In the same period male athletes achieved records in 77 events.)[54] However, in the first eight years of the New China, Chinese women made faster progress in athletics than men. The best time in the 100m sprint improved from 13:2 to 11:9 seconds, and in the 80m hurdles from 13:6 to 11:2; the best height in the high-jump from 1.40m to 1.77m; in the shot put from 20.33m to 33.55–50.93m; and in the javelin from 15.22m to 32.29–47.51m.[55] Such women were in sharp contrast to the 'feet-bound' women, invisible a few years earlier. They symbolised broad social, economic and cultural changes. They were also a portent of the future: Chinese women would in time come from behind to outperform Chinese men internationally by the millennium. The signs, for those with sharp vision, were there to see from the 1950s.

Increasingly adopting an aggressive 'one China' stance[56] in the world political arena, China boycotted the Singapore international table tennis competition in 1952 because of the participation of Taiwan. This aggression was to have later consequences. The following year Chinese athletes including women, for the first time, went abroad to take part in the 20th World Table Tennis Championships and the first International Youth Friendship Games (volleyball and athletics). Subsequently, Chinese women participated in the Summer World Collegiate Games in 1954 and other world individual sporting competitions and tournaments between communist countries. By the end of 1956 the Chinese had participated in a total of 185 international competitions and tournaments, and had joined 14 interna-

TABLE 2

NUMBERS OF EVENTS AND ATHLETES OF NATIONAL COMPETITIONS, 1953

	athletics	gymnastics	cycling	swimming	table tennis
men	343	112	24	109	38
women	202	91	20	59	24

Source: *zhongguo tiyu shiye tongji nianjian, 1953* [Sports Yearbook In China, 1953], Beijing remin tiyu chuban she, 1954).

tional sports organisations, such as the International Volleyball Federation.[57] This early entrance into the world competitive arena provided a springboard for their later international victories in table tennis and volleyball. As China's first female table-tennis world champion Qiu Zhonghui recalled:

> When the national table-tennis team was established in September 1953, I came to Beijing. In 1954, I was for the first time sent abroad to compete, but failed. This failure greatly stimulated me. The next year the Chinese women's team won promotion from the second to the first division in Japan, yet we lost the crucial match against the Americans, which was regarded as a 'political' match against our enemy. After the competition I went to ask the world champion for her signature. Her arrogance badly hurt my esteem. I was determined to improve my skill. In the 1957 and 1959 world championships, the Chinese women's team advanced to third place in the world.[58]

It is clear from the above remarks that politics and sport were closely intertwined in the early experiences of Communist China and participation in international competitions stirred up an intense nationalism among Chinese athletes. One outcome was that conservative thought and practice in coaching were criticised at the national coaching seminar in Tianjin in 1955. This clearly reflected Chinese ambition to 'leap forward' in elite sport.

Through five years of strenuous and systematic endeavour, a solid foundation for Chinese elite sport had been constructed by 1956. As shown in Figure 3, sports investment had increased over the previous years, but the greatest rise was in 1956, with a 156 per cent increase.[59] Consequently, sports teams expanded and sports facilities and equipment improved remarkably. By 1956, there were 1,939 elite athletes in total, compared to 833 in 1953. As mentioned earlier, there were no precise statistical data on gender before 1962.[60] However, one thing is clear and revealing. About 43 women's basketball teams employed full-time coaches by 1957.[61] Prior to 1949, there were only 14 sports fields and nine gymnasiums in the whole country. During the three years of rehabilitation between 1949 and 1951, only seven sports fields were built. From 1952 to 1956, some 45 sports fields

FIGURE 3
EXPENDITURE ON SPORT, 1953–58

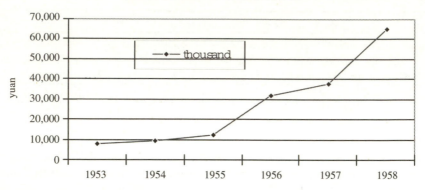

and seven gymnasiums were erected. This infrastructure, mirrored in developments in Beijing, Guangdong and Sichuan to be discussed more fully
later, provided a platform for the take-off of Chinese elite sport. To the
impetus of physical resources should be added an impetus to psychological
confidence. In 1956 the Chinese weightlifter Cheng Jinkai broke a world
record – the first in Chinese history to do so. The victory convinced China
of the possibility of catching up with the world's sporting powers.
'Advancing the level of sport' was embodied in a government work report.[62]
Elite sport became the heart of sports policy and investment.

To prepare for the 16th Olympic Games, in which the Chinese were
keen to demonstrate socialism's superiority over capitalism, China held
preliminary competitions for seven sports in October 1956, in which about
1,400 athletes from 27 provinces, municipalities and autonomous regions
took part. Ninety-two athletes were chosen to prepare for the Olympics and
49 athletes for the first time were awarded the title of 'Master of Sport'.
One of them was the female shot-putter Shi Baoshu, whose performance
(50.93m) ranked seventh in the world that year. Unfortunately, China boycotted the games in protest against the IOC's decision that Taiwan and the
PRC could both represent China in the games.[63] Chinese athletes missed the
opportunity to show the world the extent of their progress, and had to wait
until the Los Angeles Olympics of 1984 to exhibit their skills. This turn of
events involving China and the IOC demonstrates the extent to which
Chinese competitive sport, including women's sport, has been strongly
dependent on state policies and has served the purposes of politics. Chinese
elite sport for both men and women was established well before the 1980s,
when China re-entered international competitions. A vast gold mine of athletic talent was now being explored. The nuggets polished in the 1990s
became world news.

There have been occasional references earlier to the influence of the former Soviet Union on Chinese sport. Indeed, Soviet influence merits special attention in any consideration of the evolution of Chinese women's elite sport. When the PRC was founded in 1949, the former Soviet Union was a model in virtually every field because it was the first powerful communist state in the world. After the Treaty of Friendship, Alliance and Mutual Assistance and other specific treaties on diplomacy and railways were signed by China and the former USSR in February 1950, Soviet experts from all walks of life were sent to China to assist Chinese reconstruction. This policy was reinforced by the Korean War (1950–53), in which China fought against American-led United Nations forces, and a military and economic alliance with the Soviet Union produced the so-called 'lean to one side' policy of close friendship with Moscow. Soviet influence dominated the first phase of the New China.

Soviet women, who appeared to enjoy an equal relationship with men, were regarded as models for Chinese women. Media propaganda played a persistent and powerful part in this emulation process: in the magazine *New Chinese Women*, a special column was used to introduce Soviet women in all walks of life. Moreover, Soviet films and novels provided a window through which the new image of Soviet women appeared. In consequence, Chinese women were inspired by Soviet womanhood to take on new roles in both society and family.

In order to learn from the Soviet Union, China sent its sports officials, coaches and students there after 1950.[64] They inspected Soviet sports administrations, training systems and school sports. These visits undoubtedly helped the Chinese to construct their own sports system. Simultaneously, in the early 1950s the Soviet government sent teams and experts to help China develop its sport. The first Soviet delegation mainly consisted of men's and women's basketball teams. They played 33 games with different local teams throughout China between 24 December 1950 and 1 February 1951. Gymnasts, athletes, swimmers and others followed them. The Soviet colleagues' advanced skills and scientific training methods broadened Chinese perspectives and set examples. In the mid-1950s Soviet coaches were invited to China to run coaching courses on volleyball and athletics, and supervise Chinese gymnasts, swimmers and basketball players. To help regularise the teaching programmes and to improve teaching standards in sports institutes, Soviet experts were invited to sports colleges to teach, as discussed later in the Beijing case study. With the assistance of Soviet experts, teaching material including teaching plans, programmes, textbooks, rules and methods of management were all produced in China during this period. A 'Ten-Year Teaching Programme of Physical Education in Soviet Schools' and nine different sports teaching programmes for spare-time sports schools in the USSR (basketball, volleyball, athletics, swimming, gymnastics, cycling, diving, skating and skiing) as well as four teaching reference books were all translated into Chinese.[65] Many similarities between China and the former Soviet Union could be found: the centrally controlled administration, the 'specialised' sports training and specialisation at an early age. Undoubtedly, Chinese sport benefited greatly from the former Soviet Union's assistance in the early 1950s.

Nevertheless, indiscriminate copying of Soviet practices at this stage had a detrimental effect on the development of Chinese sport. For example, witnessing a Soviet gymnast retain his world title for four years with the same routine on one piece of apparatus, the Chinese tried to learn the same elements and hoped to defeat their Soviet 'brothers' by virtue of quality. Thus quality of movement was overemphasised, and innovation was ignored and even discouraged. As a result, these Chinese gymnasts failed. From this failure, and others in other sports, the Chinese learned that imitating others blindly, irrespective of their own history, practical conditions and demographic characteristics, meant that success was denied them. Innovation based both on learning from others and on one's own initiative was the gateway to victory. Nevertheless, obsequious copying was not abandoned until 1958, when relationships between the USSR and China began to deteriorate, especially after Soviet experts withdrew from China in 1960 (see Chapter 2).

Relations between China and the USSR were by no means completely harmonious. First, Stalin firmly believed in the Marxist-Leninist concept of a revolution based on the urban proletariat, while Mao believed that in a country like China the revolution should be based on the peasantry. After Stalin died in 1953, Khrushchev took over as the leader of the USSR. 'De-Stalinisation' took place, which the Chinese leadership resented. Differences intensified by the late 1950s and led to the split between the two states in the early 1960s.

In spite of the strong Soviet influence in the 1950s, western influence on the development of modern sport in China also existed. This influence was realised through those Chinese who had specialised in sport or related subjects in America, Japan or European countries prior to 1949. A number of them became influential sports authorities in the New China.[66] One of them was Chang Huilan. After graduating from a physical education normal school run by the YWCA in Shanghai in 1920, she went to America to study sport. Three years later she returned to China and lectured in the school where she had studied. She went to America again between 1925 and 1926, and between 1938 and 1946, and got her bachelor's, master's and doctor's degrees successively. Physical education, biology and public hygiene were her major subjects. She returned to China in 1946 and was employed as a professor and director of the physical education departments of several different universities. After 1952 she was a director of the Sports Anatomy Office and Dean of Shanghai Institute of Physical Education. Due to her influence and that of others (Soviet and Chinese), Chinese elite sport was influenced by both the Soviet Union and the West.

Analysis: Illustrative Case Studies

In an attempt to provide more detailed evidence of the national nature of fundamental change in the early 1950s, three case studies will cover the following aspects:

- Post-1949 organisational beginnings – a structure for sport, mass and elite;
- The formation of elite teams, the creation and recruitment of coaches and administrators;
- The provision of facilities;
- The promotion of mass sport;
- The promotion of elite sport;
- Women in the New China: masses and elitists.

Below then follows a discussion of the evolution of sport and women's sport in three representative areas of the New China – Beijing, Guangdong and Sichuan – in order to add some flesh to the skeleton presented earlier.

Beijing

At the First Plenary Session of the Chinese People's Political Consultative Conference, which was convened in Beijing a few months before the founding of the PRC in October 1949, 'advocating national sport' was incorporated into the General Plan for the New China. In response, to popularise sport and cultivate collectivism among the masses, the Beijing Municipal People's Games took place three weeks after the birth of the PRC. The games included athletics competitions, a mass callisthenics demonstration and ball-game exhibitions. The male and female participants were either students from primary and middle schools and universities or workers from factories and other enterprises. Because this was the first sports event of the communist regime many other cities and provinces sent delegations to observe it.[67] On the eve of the Korean War (1950–53), in which China fought against American-led United Nations forces, the games were repeated. About 38,000 participants took part in 175 general events and 79 basketball, football and baseball matches. The number of athletes was twice that of the previous games. Athletes were categorised into five groups according to occupation: workers, peasants, army, students (primary, middle schools and universities) and others.[68] The unprecedented scale of this event reflected the speedy mobilisation of the masses into sport in the New China.

To further promote sport, Beijing in 1950 organised municipal summer courses for physical education teachers of primary and secondary schools. Gymnastics, baseball, football, group games and dance were taught. Over 400 teachers from all parts of the city attended the courses.[69] As befitted the capital city, Beijing hosted most of the international, national and regional competitions in this period, including national competitions for table tennis, swimming, athletics, basketball and football as well as the Army Games. These competitions helped promote sport among the masses and ensured the creation of a sports infrastructure in Beijing.

Based on performances in the city's competitions in March 1951, Beijing established male and female basketball and volleyball representative teams. They took part in the qualifying competitions of the North Administrative Area[70] for the first national basketball and volleyball competitions in Beijing in the same year.[71] Subsequently, national teams for basketball and volleyball were launched in Beijing in 1951. The women's volleyball squad consisted of 11 players (including one reserve), only four fewer than the men's squad.[72] National teams for both men and women in athletics, gymnastics, swimming, weightlifting, table tennis and badminton were set up between 1953 and 1955.[73] National teams were the apex of Chinese elite sport. They prompted systematic and organised high-level athletic training. Beijing led the nation in sports initiatives and obtained remarkable results in the national competitions – in 1956, for example, producing national women's basketball and volleyball champions and winning the women's table tennis, gymnastics and swimming titles.[74] These achievements were to a considerable extent attributed to the fact that national teams and the Beijing Institute of Physical Education were located there.[75]

The Beijing Municipal Sports Commission (*Beijing shi tiyu yundong eiyuan hui*) (BMSC) was created in 1953 with 99 sports staff including coaches. Three years later, the staff numbered 436 due to the emergence of various elite sports teams.[76] This commission was responsible for policy formulation, financial planning and the overall management of sports development in the capital city. Its emergence stood as a symbol of the institutionalisation of sport in Beijing. Thereafter sport became a more centrally controlled and organised activity. One year later, following the Soviet model, BMSC established its first spare-time sports school for young students – Shi Cha Hai Sports School. This school was one of the three spare-time sports schools that were experimentally established in Beijing, Shanghai and Tianjin (the three municipal cities) respectively. To develop sport among young people was the priority of the school, which recruited 486 students for three sports: athletics, gymnastics and football.[77] However, students were required to be good at both sports activities and academic studies. Most won access to university – for example, of the 16 members of the women's basketball team, 14 entered higher education[78] – and as a result, parents encouraged their children to join the sports schools. Spare-time sports schools were expanded to two by 1956, with 747 students.[79] In order to provide sports specialists, the Beijing Institute of Physical Education was founded in 1953. In the first two years 560 and 541 students respectively were admitted to study in a two-year junior college programme. Most students with sporting talent were sent to the institute. However, 'of the over 500 enrolled students from the whole country, only two *voluntarily* applied to the institute'[80] – the result of the still powerful historical legacy of regarding sport as an entertainment, not an occupation. The stereotype of sportsmen/women as people with 'simple minds and strong muscles' remained deeply rooted. As Chen Dexin, a female student at the time, now a teacher at the university, has recalled: 'I did not feel it an honour to be enrolled in the BIPE, and even intended to change my subject after enrolment.' She added that 'There were five groups of female students in our grade, and each group consisted of about 20 individuals.'[81] This state of affairs – her attitude and the size of the groups – reflected both the determination of the Party to develop sport and a deep-seated bias against sport. It was a difficult task to turn these students into sports specialists. To motivate them, ideological propaganda was attempted and various political meetings, historical reviews, discussions, talks, films and activities were carefully organised. Thus, sports involvement, academic study and ideological education were closely integrated; the Party was not to be resisted. From 1955, the institute adopted four-year undergraduate programmes.[82]

Hand in hand with administrative and educational developments went financial assistance. With an annual sports budget of over a million yuan, sports equipment and facilities throughout Beijing improved remarkably in this period. Beijing Shooting Field and Beijing Stadium, which consisted of competition and practice halls and an indoor swimming pool, were built in 1955. These facilities laid down a strong and firm material foundation for the growth of elite sport.

In the 1950s, as mentioned earlier, a 'brother' relationship was nurtured between China and the Soviet Union, the first communist country in the world and a model for the PRC. A number of Soviet sports teams went to Beijing and other cities to display their skills. The Soviet coaching expert Gelomazhuv was invited to lecture at coaching courses in Beijing and Tianjin in 1956. About two hundred coaches attended. Between 1953 and 1957 ten Soviet experts worked at the BIPE. They supervised 215 postgraduate students, who were recruited between 1954 and 1957 and specialised in mostly sports theory, athletics, anatomy and gymnastics. These students later became the backbone of China's sports teaching and coaching. In 1956 the first national scientific sport symposium was held at the institute, and more than 300 people attended. This symposium signalled the inauguration of sports research.

Now that women were encouraged to enter male-dominated fields in pursuit of the principle of gender equality, on 'March Eighth Day' in 1952, China's first female pilots – who had begun flying training in 1950 – presented a flying exhibition in Beijing.[83] After their demonstration, they played basketball with the men's team of the Air Force Headquarters and won the match – all the female pilots had been athletes or sports enthusiasts at school. On 'May Fourth Day'[84] of the same year, 30 female motorcyclists put on another impressive show. These pilots and motorcyclists helped spell out to others, and especially to other women, the significance of sport for keeping fit and achieving social and professional success. Their skill and courage impressed both men and women; their ability contradicted conventional wisdom concerning the weak and fragile female. They were positive role models for women and encouraged some to take up physical activities.[85] Also in 1952 the first Workers' Sports Games took place in Beijing. More than 1,700 worker athletes, men and women, participated. Women workers broke national records in the javelin and the 1,500-metre and 3,000-metre cycling events. Their records not only further challenged the traditional image of weak and fragile women, but also promoted the development of elite women's sport. In the 1950s many elite athletes came from the ranks of these workers. Of course, in marked contrast to the 1990s, incentive rewards were unavailable in the 1950s because of an emphasis on communist principles. As a former female national champion Yang Yifang said:

> After I broke the national record (javelin) and became a national champion in 1953, I was awarded a medal and citation, nothing else. Oral compliments and coverage in newspapers, instead of material rewards, were the awards for me. I was not promoted to an administrative position either. It was very different from the 1980s and from today.[86]

It is evident that sport in Beijing was a centrally controlled political activity from the time of the creation of the PRC. The establishment of a sports commission, spare-time sports schools and a sports institute and major games provided an organisational structure for elite sport. Due to its unique status as the political and cultural centre of the nation, Beijing had unparalleled advantages, such as being the host city of various sports events and aid from the national teams and the BIPE in this period. All this advanced elite sport. As part of the political process, in addition, women in Beijing were strongly encouraged to be actively involved in male-dominated occupational spheres including elite sport, with the result that the popularity of sport among female school students, factory workers and military officers paved the way for the advance of this type of women's sport in the early years of the PRC.

Guangdong

Guangdong was not brought under CCP control until two weeks after the PRC was founded. When the country was divided into six greater administrative regions, each with considerable autonomy, between October 1949 and early 1953, Guangdong became part of the Central-South administrative region. Thus, sport in this province was under the joint leadership of the Central-South Sports Brigade, the provincial trade union, the provincial Cultural and Educational Bureau, and the Guangdong branch of the ACSF, which was established in 1951.[87] Sport was now promoted at every level.

After the Guangdong Provincial Sports Commission was created in July 1953, corresponding sports commissions were established in most cities and counties within the next two years.[88] Sport became a highly organised and hierarchical institution. Sports commissions administered sport at county level and above. 'Specialised' provincial sports teams and spare-time sports schools emerged in the same year. Owing to the popularity of swimming in the province, the Guangdong swimming team, formed in 1952, was one of the first elite provincial teams in the country. In 1953 'specialised' sports teams in football, basketball, men's volleyball and diving were established, and an elite table tennis team came into being the following year. By 1956 Guangdong had 130 elite athletes; before 1949 it had none. In 1953 five spare-time sports schools were created, which became a talent pool for the provincial sports teams. One year later these schools numbered 11, and by 1956 there were 306 students in these schools.[89] Due to the inauguration and expansion of these sports teams and schools, sports coaching and administration became essential. Full-time coaches and administrators soared in number from 164 in 1953 to 533 in 1956.[90] Yet sports specialists were still in short supply in these years. Consequently, a number of overseas Chinese returned to Guangdong to promote sport: between 1951 and 1957 some 34 overseas athletes, coaches and physical educationalists went from Hong Kong and Macao to Guangdong, among them Rong Guotuan, world table-tennis champion in 1956.[91] These people played their part in advancing Guangdong's elite sport – including elite women's sport. They were collectively a symbol of the ambition and idealism of the New China.

Hosting sports competitions is an effective means of promoting sport. In 1952 Guangzhou hosted the first National Swimming and Diving Competition, in which 17 men and 17 women represented Guangdong and the province came fourth.[92] This event proved to be the tip of an eventual iceberg: in 1956 alone, apart from provincial swimming, football, basketball and volleyball competitions, the Provincial Workers' Games, Provincial Youth Games[93] and the Guangdong Provincial Games were held.[94] The Provincial Games included athletics, gymnastics and cycling competitions, with football and volleyball as demonstration sports. Over 400 athletes, including 106 women, took part in the 20 events (14 for women).[95] These multi-layer and multi-level competitions stirred up provincial enthusiasm and generated momentum in elite sport. Sport, of course, was sponsored exclusively by the state. Guangdong's sports budget, in fact, for reasons outlined below, was slightly more than Beijing's (1.94 million yuan). Between 1952 and 1954 Yuexiu People's Sports Field, Guangzhou Sports Stadium and Yuexiu Swimming Pool were built. To prepare for the 1956 Olympic Games, the National Sports Commission decided to build a sports training base in Guangzhou, the capital of Guangdong province, which was climatically similar to Melbourne, the host city for that year's Olympics. This base was built in the mid-1950s and occupied an area of 121,651 square metres, consisting of a building of 9,849 square metres, a 2,017-square-metre ball-game hall and 16 other outdoor fields and courts, including an athletics field, a swimming pool, a football field, and courts for basketball, volleyball and tennis.[96] These facilities greatly improved the Guangzhou sports infrastructure. It became one of the few cities in China with the capacity to host comprehensive sports events. Furthermore, due to its unique geographic location, Guangdong gained access to modern sport and western training methods earlier than the inland provinces.[97] This early committed entrance into sport made elite women's sport more acceptable in the province than other parts of the country, including Beijing. Wen Guoxuan, an associate professor at the BIPE, recalled in 1996 that:

> Sport was very popular when I attended a prestigious middle school in Guangdong from 1949 to 1953. As I was very good at it, I applied to the BIPE in 1953 when I graduated. People did not despise me. Instead some envied me because I would have the chance to take part in competitions and travel across the country, and enjoy cadre[98] status after graduation from the institute. However, at that time, a lot of people in other places in China considered sport a non-subject.[99]

In the same year, Huang Xinhe, who also originated from Guangdong, recounted:

> Although my family placed priority on academic study, I was good at the 100m sprint in secondary school. Then I broke the 100m junior record at the South China Sports Games in 1953. I was then selected for the national athletic team as a sprinter when I was 15 years old. My parents were very proud of me. Not long after I was injured. Thus, I transferred to a junior school affiliated to the BIPE in 1955, and began to practise gymnastics.[100]

This acceptability, illustrated clearly by Wen Guoxuan and Huang Xinhe, ensured that Guangdong women dominated Chinese swimming, diving and other sporting activities during the first stage of the New China.[101] Interestingly, football too was popular among women in the province's Mei County as early as 1956 – a fact that would suggest that women had made a considerable advance in overturning traditional stereotyping.

In summary, elite sport in Guangdong advanced and became institutionalised and centrally organised after the provincial sports commission and elite sports teams and sports schools were put in place by the mid-1950s. With its geographic advantages, Guangdong not only attracted overseas experts, but also became an important national training base. As a result of the province's especially strong commitment to sport, Guangdong women were ahead of other women in the New China in taking up sport. It was for this reason that they entered 'male dominated' sports such as football as early as the mid-1950s.

Sichuan

Between 1949 and 1954 China comprised six administrative regions. Sichuan was the location of the headquarters of the South-West administrative region. In 1951 South-West teams (swimming, diving, volleyball and basketball) were created to prepare for the first national competitions of 1952. In the same year the 'Fighting Teams of the South-West Military Area' (*Xinan Junqu Zhangdou Dui*) for these activities, plus gymnastics and athletics, were established to participate in the 1952 National Army Games. Athletes of the South-West teams and fighting teams were mainly recruited from schools and colleges of the three provinces of Yunnan, Sichuan and Guizhou. A female volleyball player of the early 1950s, Wang Defen, was one of them. She joined the South-West women's volleyball team in 1951, one year prior to her graduation from Sichuan University.[102] Some members of both South-West teams and 'fighting teams' transferred to local teams and merged with athletes of the Sichuan provincial sports training classes (later called Sichuan provincial teams) in 1954, when the six administrative regions were reorganised.[103] Thus, these athletes of the South-West Brigade and the 'fighting teams' became the backbone of Sichuan elite sport in the 1950s.

The Sichuan Sports Commission (SSC) was set up in 1953. As in the case of Guangdong, this commission was a governmental body that controlled the sporting development of the province. Its establishment was a milestone in Sichuan sport. It led to the creation of elite sports teams and spare-time sports schools, which were all affiliated to the commission. To prepare for the 1953 national athletics meeting, selected athletes were assembled to undergo organised and planned training. They included women. One outstanding woman athlete was Liu Xinyu, who joined the provincial athletic team in 1953 from a high school at the age of 19, and won two third places in the year's national competition. The next year, she captured the 100m and 200m sprint and long-jumping titles. Rapid expansion of elite sports teams occurred during the years 1953–56. In 1953 Sichuan had only 58 elite athletes and 24 sports staff including coaches. By 1956 elite athletes had soared in number to 307, and sports staff to 340.[104] There were three spare-time sports schools in 1953; one year later there were another three, and by 1956, the students of these schools numbered 556.[105] From these figures, it is clear that Sichuan's elite sport was up and running by the mid-1950s. The South-West Institute of Physical Education (later named Chengdu Institute of Physical Education) was set up in 1954 to prepare sports personnel for the South-West provinces. Students of the institute often represented Sichuan in national competitions. The boom in sports teams and sports schools, of course, required well-trained sports specialists. At first, as in the case of Beijing, they came from other communist countries. It is well-known that the 1950s were characterised by the close relationship between the China and the then Soviet Union. As a result, coaches and experts from USSR and satellite communist countries such as Hungary were invited to give lectures at training courses sponsored by the National Sports Commission. Four swimming coaches from Sichuan attended these courses in the mid-1950s.[106] In addition, the tour of China by Soviet gymnasts in 1953 helped to popularise gymnastics in Sichuan in the early 1950s.[107] In other words, Soviet and eastern European influence was an important factor in shaping the direction of Chinese elite sport at both national and provincial level.

In Sichuan, the year 1953 was notable for elite sport with the emergence of the provincial sports commission, elite sports teams and sports schools. Lan Yanan, a female gymnast, went to the South-West Military Area from Zigong City in south-west Sichuan when she was in the second year of senior high school in 1951. She was selected for the national team two years later. Lan's experience represented a seismic shift from sport enthusiast to elite athlete in the first phase of the New China. She was not alone. By the mid-1950s women's elite sport was firmly consolidated. Sichuan women performed extremely well: the women's basketball team won the national title in 1955. When the National Sports Commission experimented with an A and B league system in 1956,[108] Sichuan women's volleyball and basketball teams were in group A. By 1958 they had remained ranked third to fifth in the two years of the league's existence. Even more impressive was the women's athletics team, which ranked top with five individual titles in the national competition of 1956. They excelled in nine events, far outdoing their male counterparts (two events). Due to their remarkable achievements and potential in athletics, women outnumbered men by 13 to eight in terms of the number of events with provincial elite athletes.[109] This phenomenon was rarely seen in other Chinese provinces, or indeed in the rest of the world. It highlighted the importance of performance, not gender, in the allocation of sports resources in Sichuan in the 1950s – the general situation in China some three decades later. It was a straw in the wind.

As the political and cultural centre of the South-West region, Sichuan became the main beneficiary of the South-West administrative region and military areas. However, its isolated geographical location restrained its opportunities for hosting major competitions. Before 1949 Sichuan had been physically isolated from the rest of China by its mountainous periphery, and there was no trans-provincial railway in the early 1950s. This lack of infrastructure undoubtedly limited its opportunities to hold national competitions in this period. However, this backwardness ended with the rapid economic development of the period of the first Five-Year Plan. The annual national income growth rate in Sichuan from 1952 to 1957 was 11.07 per cent, higher than the national average (8.7 per cent) and Guangdong (9.2 per cent).[110] As part and parcel of its economic development, by the mid-1950s the city of Chengdu was linked to the city of Chongqing, and the province was connected with other provincial capital cities – Kunming, Guiyang and Xi'an – by rail. Sichuan was now accessible. At the same time, sports facilities and equipment improved over time. Until the PRC was established in 1949, Sichuan had no adequate sports field or stadium. There were only 469 ill-equipped sports fields in the province.[111] This legacy more or less restrained the pace of sports development. Efforts were made to change the situation in the 1950s. First, the People's Sports Field was built in 1952 in Chengdu, the capital city of the province. It could accommodate 20,000 people. In 1955 a stadium with over 4,000 seats was erected in Chongqing, the second city of Sichuan until it became an independent municipality in 1997. The city had a new sports field the next year, and was now equipped to host national competitions. In 1957 Chongqing held its first national athletics competition.[112] Although sport prospered more than ever, the infrastructure in the province still lagged behind the growing needs of elite sport. For example, the provincial swimming team, formed in 1955, had no fixed training venue until 1981, when a swimming centre was established in Chengdu.

It is obvious that developments in elite sport in Sichuan were broadly similar in pattern and pace to Guangdong and Beijing despite early geographic isolation and a slower growth in the construction and provision of sports organisations, facilities and performances. Unsurprisingly, therefore, elite women's sport leapt forward there. As elsewhere, their astounding performances won them more than equal treatment in the allocation of resources.

Incidentally, it should not be overlooked that these three case studies also demonstrate that in the period of economic rehabilitation between 1949 and 1952,[113] sport was emphasised in China as a means of promoting national fitness. 'Broadcast Gymnastics',[114] ball games and other physical activities were popular among the masses. Most people did not know what sport was when the New China was created. In a remarkably short time Chinese sport became a centrally organised and planned social practice. Almost from the start of the PRC, under the joint administration and direction of the All China Sports Federation (ACSF)[115] mostly hand in hand with other organisations such as the trade unions and the Educational Bureau, mass sport was widely available. Peasants and workers, not just students and soldiers, participated and achieved good results all over China.[116] After specialised sports teams at national level and in the army emerged in 1951, and especially after the creation of provincial sports teams across the country, elite sport was gradually regarded more as an occupation than as a pastime. In this social change the national and army teams led the way. Increasingly, involvement in sport by the masses provided performers for the ranks of the athletic elite.

Beijing, Guangdong and Sichuan are illustrative of a more general progress in sport in the 1950s across China as a whole. In spite of inevitable variations, by the mid-1950s the regions of China presented recognisably similar characteristics of organisation and effect. Across the nation major sports institutions were widely installed in 1953; sports competitions were then institutionalised and sports facilities were greatly expanded. At the same time the establishment of sports colleges, aided by Soviet advisers, eased the shortage of sporting experts of various kinds and at various levels. By the mid-1950s, elite sport was on the fast track.[117] Simultaneously, taking advantage of the communist emphasis on equality, women in these places and elsewhere, at an unprecedented pace, stepped out of the home into society, and even into archetypal male-dominated occupations such as pilot or motorcyclist. They exhibited ability, determination and courage, and challenged the feudal concept of women's inferiority. Their actions demonstrated that women were physically and mentally strong, and encouraged more women to break through traditional social barriers to do what they had never done before. Women athletes, for example, underwent systematic and organised training, achieved ambitions and registered outstanding performances – regionally, nationally and internationally. Women's involvement in a wide range of careers helped pave the way for the acceptance of elite women's sport in the New China, and vice versa.

Conclusion

Despite the centuries-old biases against sport and against women, elite women's sport in China developed rapidly following the founding of the New China in 1949. This progress was shaped by both communist principles of equality and the Party's sports policies. First, women's emancipation was a main concern of the CCP. Fundamental changes took place in women's social status and actual lives after 1949. With freedom in marriage, improved educational opportunities and increased mobilisation in 'social production' (*shehui shengchang*), women began to participate in sport. Women now had careers and elite sport now became a career. In consequence, female elite athletes, and to a lesser extent full-time coaches of 'specialised' sports teams, emerged across the country. There were other things in their favour. Chinese women and their elite sports were greatly influenced by Soviet experiences and models in the early 1950s. Furthermore, in conjunction with the economic recovery from the wreckage of decades of war, mass sport was strongly emphasised to promote fitness. Thus sport in schools, universities, factories and the army flourished. These formed one set of foundations for elite sport, but it needed others. They were provided: between 1952 and 1956 sports institutions were established at provincial and national levels and an administrative sports system took shape. Provincial and national elite sports teams, sports schools and sports institutes were not only the foundations but the later pillars of Chinese elite sport.

Finally, this period witnessed a change of political policy from mass sport to elite sport – mainly for reasons of international politics. Chinese elite sport took off after 1956.[118] Women were well to the fore in this radical situation. As a consequence, as the three case studies of Beijing, Guangdong and Sichuan clearly illustrate, women in increasing numbers took part in various international and national competitions and made remarkable achievements. Their sports potential and ambitions would reach a fuller realisation in the records to come.

Women, Society and Elite Sport in the New China between 1957 and 1965

After the New China had made great strides in industrial development during the period of the First Five-Year Plan (1952–56),[1] the Chinese people were inspired to speed up their socialist reconstruction to catch up with the West. Influenced by Chairman Mao's ambition early in 1956[2] and stimulated by the 'anti-right' campaign in 1957,[3] the Great Leap Forward (GLF) – a massive nationwide political and economic campaign – was launched throughout China between 1958 and 1960. New and strange phenomena arose – the people's commune,[4] the campaign of smelting iron and steel,[5] and the 'communist wind'.[6] They brought about profound changes in society with unanticipated and often haphazard consequences, and greatly affected the lives of both men *and* women in China.

Chinese evaluations of the GLF have varied with the political climate over time.[7] Not until 1980, when Mao's radicalism was followed by Deng's pragmatism, were the process, causes and effects of the GLF subjected to academic inquiry. For example, Xie Chuntao's *Dayuejin kuanlang* [The Raging Waves of the Great Leap Forward] (1994) and Lu Tingyu's *Zhonghua renming gongheguo lishi jishi: quzhe fazhang (1958–1965)* [A Realistic Report of the History of the People's Republic Of China: Twisting Development (1958–65)] (1994) have described the evolution and legacy of this movement in terms of its political, social and economic impacts. In addition, both general sports historians and experts on individual sports in China have discussed sporting developments during and after the GLF.[8] However, none of them has paid much attention to women in sport in this period.

In the West a number of feminists, including Marilyn Young (*Women in China: Studies in Social Change and Feminism*, 1973), Elisabeth J. Croll (*Feminism and Socialism in China*, 1978) and Rey Chow (*Woman and Chinese Modernity*, 1991), have examined the influence of the GLF on women's emancipation, with particular regard to education, employment and family. They have ignored sport. In general, there has been little western discussion about Chinese sport during the GLF. One of the few analysts was Jonathan Kolatch, who in his book *Sports, Politics and Ideology in China* (1972) analysed the complex interaction between Chinese sport, politics and ideology during these years. However, gender was not considered in his analysis. Thus a number of issues pertaining to women and sport during the GLF remain unclear. What was the impact of the GLF both on women and, in the specific context of this study, on their access to and involvement in sport as a manifestation of a fuller, freer life in a promised political utopia of the East? Did sport suffer as much as society during the GLF? In general, what effect did the GLF have on the subsequent decades of Chinese elite sport, women's elite sport in particular? This chapter will seek answers to these questions.

Analysis: Overview

Political Goals and Elite Women's Sport

'To achieve greater, faster, better and more economic results in building socialism'[9] became the purpose of the Great Leap Forward initiated in 1958. Immediately, rapid and ambitious targets were pursued in every project throughout the country.[10] To shorten the process of Chinese modernisation, women, an untrained labour reservoir, were massively mobilised for 'social production' as an essential substitute for absent mechanical and technical resources. This mobilisation was backed by the belief that women's participation in 'social production' was an important means of liberating women. A campaign of ideological indoctrination was launched to urge women to be economically independent in order to achieve full emancipation. Wives' dependence on their husbands was criticised. In consequence, the class of 'household women' virtually disappeared overnight.[11]

When women left the home, some took up sport as an occupation. Consequently, the number of both female athletes and coaches increased considerably. As there were no gendered statistics before 1962, unfortunately it is impossible to detail precisely the changes in the number of female coaches and athletes in the years of the GLF. Nevertheless, female elite athletes numbered 3,552 by 1962, about a third of the total athletes (see Figure 4). Some sports had a higher proportion of women than others. In athletics, for example, 615 out of the 1,350 athletes in total were women (45.6 per cent). In spite of being fewer than men in absolute numbers, female athletes actually outnumbered their male counterparts in the events in which both competed – see Table 3.

The progress of women in sport was, however, by no means uncomplicated, nor was it without resistance. The story of Dong Tianshu, a player in the Chinese women's volleyball team in the 1960s, exemplifies this:

> I entered an ordinary senior high school in 1957 in Henan. Later on a coach from Beijing came to our province to select volleyball players. I was chosen. At the time I was 14 years of age and eager to escape from the tight discipline of the family. Fortunately, my mother, an emanci-

pated new woman, held that 'each career can produce a celebrity' and 'a girl should cherish her opportunity'. She encouraged me to go to Beijing. In addition, the practical benefits that a Beijing resident could bring added extra weight to her support. However, my father, a senior engineer specialising in a project on the Yellow River, did not like me to engage in sport. With my modest request for a three-month trial, and more importantly, conditioned by the socio-political climate (equality between children and parents in the eyes of the Party) at the time, he could not overtly intervene. Thus, I left home for Beijing.[12]

It is clear from this account that attitudes to women in sport varied, even within families, and in spite of society's pervasive official encouragement, the reluctance of parents, especially fathers of some social standing, could still be strong. It was women themselves who played a crucial part in changing attitudes by their insistence on devoting themselves to sport. They vigorously challenged conservative ideas about women's participation in sport and set new norms of social expectation.

As mentioned earlier, sport was an essential part of national development for the Great Leap Forward. 'Fitness for forward advance' was the mantra.

FIGURE 4

FEMALE ATHLETES IN THE EARLY 1960s

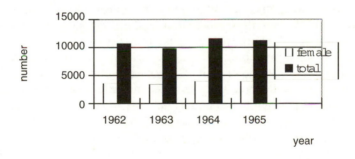

TABLE 3

NUMBER OF FEMALE AND MALE ATHLETES IN MAJOR ATHLETICS EVENTS

	sprints	400m	800m	hurdle	high-jump	long-jump	shot-put	discus	Javelin	others	total
F	120	46	40	52	63	51	29	41	45	128	615
M	105	36	48	52	38	34	22	40	52	87	735

Source: Woguo 18 ge yundong xiangmu jishu fazhan Ziliao [Material on the Technical Development of 18 sports in China], Beijing tiyu xueyuan [BIPE] (ed.), 61 nian tiyu gongzuo huiyi cankao wenxian [Reference Document of the 1961 Sports Conference].

In accordance with the Communist Party's 'mass line' (*qunzhong luxian*),[13] the whole nation was mobilised for sport.[14] 'Sports weeks' and 'sports months' were organised, and a campaign of Ten Minutes' Broadcast Exercises was launched across the country in 1958. Female workers on a scale not previously experienced now took part in all kinds of physical activity programmes organised for the workers by the trade unions – to ensure fitness for maximum productivity. Statistics on the significance of sport in raising production attendance rates were used to encourage people to engage in it, although the reliability of the statistics was doubtful due to 'boastfulness'.[15] Even those housewives still at home exercised to radio music.[16] Women's image continued to change and there was a new impetus behind this change, as a verse written in 1959 illustrated: 'Exercise has brought changes to women, a weak girl has turned into an iron one.'[17] In a sentence, mass sport leaped forward in conjunction with the Great Leap Forward in the interest of China's productivity.[18] Women were now workers, and consequently were pressurised into playing sport.

Ironically, due to the militaristic discipline adopted in the workplace during the GLF, after work many women had little time and energy for exercise, or even for their children. These factors limited both the kinds of women's participation in sport and their achievements. Sport was a regimented collective activity, and many women were forced to become involved by pressure of the political climate rather than by an awakened consciousness of increased opportunity for self-expression. As a result, sport was more like a politically enforced mass movement than a popular mass revolution.

However, it was not all regimentation and enforcement. Schools played a great part in popularising sport because they provided females with their first access to organised sport. During the GLF public education developed quickly. In 1958 about 85 per cent of school-age children were admitted to school. Compared to the preceding year, the increase was 34 per cent for primary schools, 41 per cent for secondary schools and over 50 per cent for universities.[19] On a longer time scale, the number of female students in higher education rose from 27,000 in 1949 to 150,000 in 1958.[20] Now students were required to be 'four reds': to pass the first and second grade of the Labour and Defence Programme, to become ranked athletes and to be relatively good shooters. Female students, without the double burden of productive work and household affairs that restricted the married women, participated widely in sport and improved their performances quickly. Subsequently, a number of elite female athletes emerged from higher education institutions. Simultaneously, attitudes to girls' participation in sport became more supportive. Exempt from home-centred activities, with access to education, institutions and organisations, and with increasing public acceptance, women in education found both participation and achievement in sport far easier than in the past.

Both the climate of the GLF and the general popularity of sport undoubtedly favoured the advance of elite sport. With the strong encouragement of the NSC,[21] counties, schools, enterprises, factories, communes and even neighbourhoods ran sports schools themselves. As a result, spare-time sports schools mushroomed, numbering 70,000 by 1958, compared to 159 in 1957. At the same time, the number of students in these schools soared from 17,000 in 1957 to over two million in 1958.[22] These schools provided a huge talent pool for elite sports teams. A corresponding expansion happened in national and provincial teams throughout the country. In 1957 there were only 1,939 athletes. Three years later elite athletes numbered 17,783 – over a ninefold increase. By now, virtually all elite athletes were exclusively affiliated to provincial or municipal 'specialised' sports teams.

Due to the enlargement of sports teams and schools, the need for well-trained coaches intensified. Institutes of physical education greatly expanded to meet the need. Within the brief period of the GLF the number of these institutes climbed from six to 30 – a record in Chinese history both before and after the GLF.[23] Consequently, the number of professional coaches increased at an unprecedented rate. By 1962 there were 1,734 full-time coaches, of which 16 per cent (282) were women. Three years later, the total number of coaches further increased to 2,062, of which 338 were women, about the same percentage as in 1962.[24] Despite an obvious under-representation, women were increasingly involved in coaching. Theirs was a slow but steady progress.

Following the enlargement of sports teams and the improvement of coaching quality, athletic performances improved markedly. There were only 1,218 first-grade athletes in 1957. A year later the number jumped to 9,871.[25] The number of sports masters – the highest grade for athletes – increased dramatically in 1958 and 1959 (see Figure 5). More strikingly, in the first year of the GLF, nine athletes broke six world records and 161 women broke national records in 35 events. In the next two years, over 40 world records were set annually. These performances clearly demonstrate the rapid growth of sports participation and significant progress in standards in the late 1950s. Chinese women broke through in individual and team sports such as speed skating, table tennis, shooting, gymnastics and even basketball; in gymnastics they became one of the world's top six nations. Female table tennis players won two third places (team and single competitions) at the 1959 world championships and two years later Qiu Zhonghui captured the women's world singles crown. Thereafter, Chinese players – both men and women – dominated table tennis for many years despite not participating between 1966 and 1971.

It was noticeable that by the early 1960s Chinese women had gone ahead of their male counterparts in terms of world-ranking performances in athletics, basketball, volleyball, speed skating and shooting.[26] For example, women's basketball teams defeated a number of well-known European teams including the world's third-ranked team, Czechoslovakia. In athletics, Chinese women set Asian records in virtually every event. In a nutshell, women athletes moved to the centre stage, at least in Asia, in many sports,

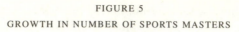

FIGURE 5

GROWTH IN NUMBER OF SPORTS MASTERS

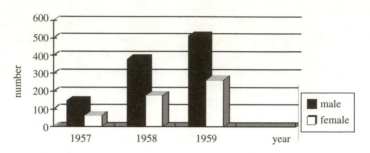

and carried Chinese hopes of stepping onto the world sporting stage. Volleyball provides a glimpse of this progress. As Dong Tianshu, a volleyball player in the early 1960s, put it:

> By the mid-1960s we [the women's volleyball team] had already reached the top three in the world in terms of our performances. Except for Japan – the world champion team at the time – we defeated most of the top world teams such as Czechoslovakia, Hungary, Bulgaria, Romania and even the Soviet Union. The Japanese head coach Daimachu Hirofumi believed that a Chinese team could become world champions in just two years if he coached it. This optimistic vision impressed the top officials of the Party and government such as Premier Zhou Enlai and Marshal He Long. They were present whenever the team competed against foreign teams. The responsibility of beating the world – the ambition of Marshal He Long – was put on the shoulders of the women's volleyball team.[27]

Thus, well before Chinese women became international celebrities in the 1980s, they had approached world level in a number of sports. Regrettably, they did not have the opportunities to demonstrate their capabilities in major international competitions until China resumed its place in the IOC in 1979. Had China not been barred from the IOC for 20 years, and had the decade-long Cultural Revolution not occurred, the Chinese would have astonished the world at least ten years earlier. Elite sport was certainly the handmaiden of political change and purpose in the period of the GLF.

As mentioned above, Chinese athletes created a number of world records in shooting and mountain climbing. These sports were categorised as national defence sports – an integral dimension of elite sport in the 1950s. Following Chairman Mao's instruction that 'every one is in a militia', national defence sport clubs boomed. For example, aviation clubs increased from ten in 1957 to 85 in 1960.[28] The number of shooters ranked first, second or third grade rose from 643 in 1957 to 33,422 in 1959, and those with the title of sports master from nine in 1957 to 162 in 1960. Mountain-climbing – another defence sport – cost China 3.6 million yuan[29] in preparing its climbers to conquer the Himalayas in 1960, when famine was spreading through the country. Priorities were brutally clear: security took precedence over the alleviation of starvation.

The momentum of elite sport, particularly in the case of women's sport, was backed by ever-increasing government investment. As illustrated in Figure 6, the heaviest investment occurred in 1959 and 1960.[30] In consequence, sports facilities greatly improved. Some 26 stadiums, 20 large sports fields and 102 standard swimming pools were built between 1958 and 1960 at various levels by sports commissions.[31] This provided a solid base for later elite sport in the New China. In effect, the GLF constituted a uniquely beneficial, if short, chapter in the story of history of Chinese modern sport. This is not always understood

Gender Culture and Training Loads

The thrust forward of Chinese women in sport in the early 1960s, to a large extent, is inseparable from the introduction of intensive training during the GLF. In response to the Party's call to 'break through superstition and liberate thought'(*puochu mixin, jiefang shixiang*), intensive training – an innovation in training philosophy – was introduced, stressed and then widely adopted after 1958. The female high-jumper Zheng Fengrong, for example, had nine training sessions each week and 309 sessions in the year before she created a world record in 1957 – a training load double that of her foreign rivals.[32] Her success was testimony to the value of intensive training in producing outstanding athletes rapidly. In 1958 the 12-year-old female gymnast Ding Xiaoming spent just five weeks learning the compulsory and optional routines required for sports master, which usually took several years. She became the youngest female gymnast with the title at the time – the average age was 19 to 20.[33]

FIGURE 6

SPORTS INVESTMENT DURING THE GREAT LEAP FORWARD

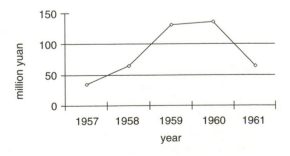

However, driven by inordinate ambition and unrealistic quotas, intensive training was often emphasised over scientific training principles and even common-sense knowledge. For example, some shooters stood still for seven hours holding a heavy 10 kg gun each day without a break or any other exercise. Long training sessions with heavy loads took place without adequate recovery time or appropriate medical supervision. As a result, athletes were exhausted and massive injuries resulted. The female athlete Yang Meiru was a typical victim of this training regime. She practised squatting with weights (bar with disk) repeatedly in order to improve her leg strength. The total weight reached over 13,000 kg in one session. Unfortunately, overwork damaged her knees and brought an end to her athletic career. According to a national survey in 1961, 50.3 per cent (348) of the 691 athletes questioned had injuries and 8.7 per cent (60) caught illnesses. Over 90 per cent of these incidents (628) happened after 1958. As a consequence of injury and illness, over 22.3 per cent (91) of these athletes had stopped training.[34] Injuries were particularly high in gymnastics: in the 1958 national gymnastic competition alone, 69 injury incidents were witnessed.[35] These injuries not only affected normal training but also endangered the careers of many athletes. Thus, intensive training resulted in mixed and contradictory results in China. On the one hand it advanced athletic performance formidably and produced young sporting stars rapidly; on the other, it led to massive sports injuries and consequently shortened a number of athletics careers.

With regard to excessive training, one could ask: what motivated the Chinese to take up often risky and unimaginably intensive training programmes, and how could Chinese women bear the 'unbearable' training loads? There are several explanations. First, situated in the 'higher and faster' climate of the GLF, the role of will-power was particularly stressed. Its value in sports improvement was frequently and irrationally exaggerated. There arose some absurd slogans, such as 'the higher the skill targets, the more revolutionary the athletes and coaches'. The result was that intensive training was regarded as a means towards creating miracles. Second, excessive intensive training was a direct result of a drive for national status in world sport. Driven by the humiliating past of western invasion and present underdevelopment, the Chinese longed for esteem, prosperity, stability and 'modernity'. Coaches and athletes in the New China were eager for immediate victories to win glory for the nation. To fulfil their mission as early as possible, intensive training was embraced enthusiastically. Third, China was, and is, a nation that pays a lot of attention to saving face (*ai mian zi*). External appearance and behaviour were, and are, important to many Chinese. It was highly likely to result in 'formalism' (*xingshi zhuyi*) – in a phrase, impression management – discernible everywhere in China, in sport as elsewhere. Intensive training was used by some to publicly demonstrate their determination and hard work rather than to actually serve training ends effectively. Quantity was extravagantly pursued. 'Formalism', in short, created the environment in which unrealistic intensive training thrived.

Finally, the historical legacy of 'eating bitterness and enduring hard labour' (*chiku lainao*) and obedience (*tihua*) – the desired qualities of Chinese women for centuries – did not disappear with the arrival of the New China. On the contrary, Chinese women were required to be obedient to the Party, state, teachers and coaches as well as parents. As a consequence of sociali-sation, athletes, particularly females, rarely defied coaches' instructions and demands, even though they were inappropriate or incorrect. The volleyball player Dong Tianshu has made this clear:

> We players were 100 per cent obedient to our coaches and leaders at the time. I never thought of asking coaches to adjust my training load even when I was sick. Exhausted and upset by my coach's demands and my poor physical condition, I cried, and even screamed, in exas-peration almost every day.[36]

To a large extent the effective adoption of excessive intensive training was inseparable from the obedience of female athletes.

Despite the negative consequences of injuries and illness, intensive training played an essential part in the breakthrough to parity or better with the leading nations. In time the Chinese gradually learned both the strengths and the weaknesses of intensive training, and the dialectic relationship between training and injury. Subsequently, modified and sensible intensive training became one of the essential training principles leading to success. It occupied, and continues to occupy, a place in modern coaching theory – but it is better understood, monitored and employed. Therefore, the philosophy of intensive training during the GLF to some extent laid down stepping stones for future strides in Chinese elite sport.

The GLF, International Conflicts and the National Games

When China launched its GLF, coincidentally, its international relations were at a low point. The establishment of the new institution of people's communes broke with the Soviet model that emphasised planned and cen-tralised industry-oriented development. The USSR strongly disapproved of this audacity. The hidden differences and disputes between these two great countries now surfaced.[37] This weakened the fraternal relationship. At the same time, tension with the United States increased over the issue of Taiwan.[38] International political confrontation, first indirectly, then directly, threatened China's standing in world sport. Taiwan, with the backing of America, gradually influenced voters in the International Olympic Committee and other sports organisations. Recognition of 'two' Chinas was the result. In protest against the IOC's acceptance of 'two Chinas',[39] the PRC withdrew from the IOC and eight other individual international sporting federations in 1958. The split from the IOC, in par-ticular, certainly reduced Chinese opportunities for international success and delayed its visibility in the international sports community for over two decades.

Nevertheless, China did not simply abandon elite sport following its departure from a large part of the world scene. It continued to be involved in some world championships, in the New Emerging Force Games, and in other international tournaments between communist countries until the eve of the Cultural Revolution. For example, in September 1958, the Chinese Army sent a team of 123 athletes to the First Army Spartakiade held in Leipzig. In 1958 and 1962 Chinese gymnasts took part in the 14th and 15th world championships.[40] In these international competitions the Chinese displayed their sporting progress, learned the latest skills and exchanged training ideas.

Despite temporary isolation, the intention of becoming a world power in sport produced a concerted effort to achieve excellence throughout the country, an effort that had the highest backing. The government and Party leaders greatly favoured elite sport and elite athletes. As Qiu Zhonghui, a famous athlete in the early 1960s, recalled:

> Whenever we were going abroad to compete, Premier Chou would meet us before departure. I met him altogether 23 times. He invited us to have dinner at his house, even corrected our training diaries. After the male player Rong Guotuan won the single title in 1959, Chairman Mao received all the players of the table tennis team. I wrote in my notebook: 'I must win glory for the motherland with the hand that Chairman Mao has held…' Apart from going out at weekends, we had no contact with outsiders. We knew nothing about the great famine. While the ordinary people ate a mixture of rice and leaves, and one cabbage lasted for two days, we were served fish, chicken and pork every day without restriction. After I knew the truth about the food shortages, I felt that we would be in debt to people if we did not achieve good results in the coming world championships.[41]

The considerable effort made to ensure success in elite sport is vividly demonstrated in the preparations for the 26th world table tennis championships in Tianjin in 1961. To guarantee victories in the first big world competition in China, the best 108 players from the whole country were assembled to practise together for a year. They were given priority in personnel and material resources. At the same time, a group of officials, including vice-minister Rong Gaotang, the chief directors of the relevant departments under the NSC, Li Menghua, Zhang Canzhen and others, were involved in the preparations. They lived in the same building and ate in the same canteen with the players, and watched their training and sometimes picked up balls for them during the daytime. Meetings were arranged in the evenings. This style of leadership became a tradition for the table tennis team and continues even today.[42] As part of this effort, by the early 1960s China had adopted a centrally planned, coordinated and target-oriented training system. This system produced abundant fruit when the Chinese re-entered the international sports arena after an interval of two decades.

The whole nation was mobilised in the effort to achieve world status. Before the world table tennis championships, the Central Committee of the Communist League (CCCL) encouraged various sectors throughout the country to organise table tennis competitions for the young from the winter of 1959 to the autumn of 1960. Some competitions attracted 5,000 to 10,000 participants. With too few female players, both the CCCL and the NSC appealed to girls to play table tennis.[43] Not long after, a girl's 'table tennis craze' resulted. Table tennis became very popular, with 90 million people now playing table tennis across the nation.[44] Elite sport in effect promoted popular sport, which in turn provided a talent base for future champions.

Nor was this all. Strategic policies were formulated in order to speed up entry into, and achievement in, world sport. Ten sports – athletics, gymnastics, swimming, football, basketball, volleyball, table tennis, shooting, weightlifting and speed skating – were given priority.[45] In the years 1959–60 the National Sports Commission appointed experts to draft teaching programmes for these sports. In 1962 instructional books for football, basketball, volleyball, swimming, gymnastics, athletics and table tennis were circulated.[46] This documentation made sports training more systematised and rationalised. As a result, in athletics, for example, the gap between Chinese and world records narrowed remarkably. A comparison of Chinese performances in domestic athletics competitions in 1960 with the world athletics records in the same year's Olympic Games revealed that five Chinese women athletes could rank among the world top eight in three events.[47] This was unquestionably significant progress compared to 1952, when China could hardly achieve world standards in athletics.

To produce experienced and nerveless 'battle-hardened' performers, China organised various international tournaments as well as national competitions. In 1958 China hosted an international volleyball tournament; the Basketball Championships of Friendly Countries (mostly communist states in Asia and Eastern Europe) were held in Beijing in 1963; and an invitation table tennis tournament followed two years later. To motivate the enthusiasm of coaches and athletes, and, more importantly, to demonstrate the progress of Chinese sport again to the world, the National Games were inaugurated in 1959. This event led to the first peak in sports development in the New China. The National Games proved a seedbed of remarkable fertility.

The games consisted of *preliminary* and *final* phases, and involved unprecedented numbers of people. Over 50 million people from 30 provinces, municipalities and autonomous regions, and the Army joined the preliminary competitions that were held in different provinces. Some 10,658 competitors participated in the final phase of the games. Women comprised a third (3,670) of them, taking part in 24 sports while men contested 36. As a result, 664 athletes broke 106 national records, and seven athletes set four world records in the games. Women performed impressively. Three women parachute jumpers broke the world record for group precision landing from an altitude of 1,000 metres, and a female shooter broke the 50m and 100m prone position records.[48] Also at the time of the National Games, Pan Duo (introduced in Chapter 1) climbed the 7,282-metre-high Muztag Mountain[49] – the highest height reached by women at the time. Two years later, she, with two other women, once more established a new record by reaching the peak of the 7,719-metre Kongur Shan.

Interestingly, Jiangsu women's volleyball team was called a 'mothers' team' at the games because five leading players of the team had children. These mothers had played volleyball for seven or eight years and, coincidentally, their husbands were all members of the provincial men's volleyball team. Who would take care of their children and household affairs when wives and husbands were both committed to sport? The answer to this question lay in the radical changes in society at large. First, during the GLF many of the tasks that had kept women in the home were collectivised, and became an integral part of 'social production' following the establishment of public canteens,[50] schools, nurseries[51] and other services[52] in the working units and neighbourhoods.[53] Thus the social role of the family and patriarchal authority over women were greatly weakened. 'For the first time, women could forgo household chores and throw themselves totally into "social production". For the generations of women who had been tied to the kitchen, this was an extraordinary transformation.'[54] The rapid formation of people's communes and the development of a communal spirit laid the ideological and organisational foundations for the nationwide promotion of sport.

Second, women were encouraged to mobilise into diverse occupational fields during the GLF, which brought about concomitant changes in roles in the family. The wife, like the husband, now supported the family. In response, the husband had to take on some household chores. In the context of leaping forward to pure communism, the relationship between wife and husband was now called comradeship. This undoubtedly challenged, if it did not fundamentally change, the traditional domestic division of labour. This state of affairs ensured that the GLF took women's liberation a step forward. Women gradually enjoyed a more independent role and status in society, workplace and home. In turn, they broadened their experience, knowledge and views, and fulfilled their potential outside the home. All these advantages greatly enriched their lives. The keys to advantages were opportunity and time. With regard to the impact of the GLF on women's emancipation, Phyllis Andors has rightly pointed out:

> The mass mobilisation of women during the GLF put sharp and intensified pressure on the traditional view which defined women uniquely within the nexus of familial-oriented activities … the GLF never challenged the priority of increased production.[55]

In these changed circumstances, attitudes to women's participation in sport underwent fundamental changes. Married women were allowed opportunities to continue their athletic careers. Not only this, they were given legitimate and sanctioned time to do this.

While mother athletes were active on playing fields and elsewhere, a number of young faces emerged at the National Games. A 14-year-old diver, Zhou Xiyang from Beijing, won a gold medal at the games: a year earlier she could not even swim. A 12-year-old gymnast, Ding Zhaofang from Jiangsu, became the champion of sports acrobatics. In China their successes set new standards of training and raised the possibility of the early specialisation that became popular in the 1970s in eastern Europe and was later accepted gradually by western nations. Early specialisation in sport was a milestone in Chinese competitive sport. Young talents blossomed. By way of example, the 17-year-old female high-jumper Fu Shueyuan cleared 1.58 metres, higher than the 1958 world record of 1.55 metres. This early specialisation – one of the main reasons for Chinese success – now became a widely accepted training principle.

The National Games were, of course, nationwide, but to prepare for them each province held its provincial games or similar competitions to select candidates, and assembled athletes to undertake intensive training. As a parachute jumper, Guo Zhi, reiterates:

> I took part in the Shanxi Provincial Games in 1958 as a basketball player. Coaches of some provincial teams, including parachuting, went to the local delegations to select athletes for the coming National Games. I was selected. At the time I was in the final year of high school and reluctant to enrol in the provincial team. I would have preferred to go to university. However, under pressure from my physical education teacher, I went to the provincial sports commission. Thus I began my career as a parachutist. At first we trained with the Army soldiers. Later on, a training camp was organised in Xinxiang, a county in Henan province. Athletes from Beijing, Henan, Anhui, and Shanxi [provinces], coached by army instructors, practised together. After the National Games most of these teams were dismantled, but our team survived because of our remarkable achievements in the games [breaking three world records]. Since then, I have never been left out of the sports community.[56]

Guo Zhi's experience demonstrates that local sports commissions were preoccupied with the National Games, which were, and still are, yardsticks for sports planners to evaluate training techniques, performance and administration – see Table 4.

Apart from the National Games and provincial games or their equivalents, there were various kinds of national and regional sporting meetings and tournaments during the GLF. For example, ten national gymnastics competitions took place in 1958. In the same year the National Middle

TABLE 4

NEW WORLD AND NATIONAL RECORDS AT THE NATIONAL GAMES

	1st Games	2nd Games	3rd Games	4ths Games	5th Games	6th Games	7th Games	8th Games
World Records	4	9	3	5	3	15	21	41
National Records	106	130	63	102	61		117	66

Source: http://www.sports.gov.cn/xinxi/dbindex.html.

School Athletics Meeting attracted 830 competitors aged below 17. In total, there were 64 national and 1,174 provincial or municipal sporting competitions in 1958, more than double those of 1956 (30 and 437 respectively).[57] These activities, it could be argued, more than made up for the limited opportunities for international competition and paved the way for future inroads in global contests.

In the meantime, there were innovations in the competition system. The national volleyball championships may serve as an example. They now comprised two rounds and four phases of competition, not just one. Players had to participate in two phases of competition within a month. Thus, competitive intensity increased. This unquestionably promoted the development of volleyball[58] and, by extension, other sports.

In short, the National Games in the New China effectively stimulated Chinese enthusiasm for elite sport and made up for the loss of major international competition as a result of the departure from the IOC and other organisations. Consequently, the ambition for world supremacy never faded.

Post-GLF Adjustment and Reform

Due to 'adventurousness' in economic development, and the consequent imbalance between heavy and light industries and between agriculture and industry, the Chinese economy came under serious threat by 1959. This economic situation was worsened by severe natural disasters between 1959 and 1961.[59] At this crucial point, the already strained Sino-Soviet relationship further deteriorated and resulted in the complete withdrawal of Soviet experts and technical blueprints.[60] This split from the USSR exacerbated the emergent economic crisis and triggered China into famine. The people's living standards declined sharply in 1960,[61] and remained below the pre-GLF level until around 1965.[62] Due to widespread malnutrition and related illnesses, the Chinese population dropped by about 20 million from 1959 to 1961. The GLF was finally suspended at the end of 1960. A difficult three-year period (1960–62) followed. Suffice it to say the GLF did not facilitate economic development, but on the contrary imposed man-made obstacles to economic modernisation.

During the difficult three-year period, the radical policies introduced during the GLF were abandoned. Public canteens and nurseries in the communes were dismantled, and concomitantly a number of women returned to their previous domestic roles, once again assuming the full burden of household affairs. In line with the Party's policy of 'adjustment, consolidation, strength and promotion' advocated in the Ninth Plenary of the Eighth Congress of the CCP in January 1961, a short-term resuscitation of the economy was attempted between 1961 and 1963.

Affected by the depressed economy, the 'Great Leap Forward' in sport came to an end after 1961 – sport followed economic fluctuations closely with about a one-year time lag. Government sports investment slumped steeply in the same year (see Figure 6). No grade tests were organised and national competitions declined in number from 52 in 1960 to 21 in 1962. Simultaneously, spare-time sports schools virtually stopped normal training and many vanished; the institutes of physical education were reorganised and their number dropped from 30 to ten.[63] China's sport shrank. The ups and downs of Chinese sport around the period of the GLF highlight the close and complex relationship between sport, economics and politics.

During the three difficult years provincial and municipal elite sports teams were also scaled down and reorganised. Most military sports were abandoned. Consequently, the number of elite athletes decreased from 17,783 in 1960 to 10,659 in 1962. Now limited resources were concentrated on such key sports as athletics, gymnastics, swimming, football, basketball, volleyball, table tennis, shooting, weightlifting and speed skating. Marshal He Long, the director of the National Sports Commission (NSC), bluntly declared in 1962 that in the future the NSC would direct its attention exclusively to elite sport, and that provincial and municipal-level sports commissions would be responsible for mass and national defence sports.[64] Elite sport now became the focus of the NSC, the central governing body of sport.

Clearly, the failure of the 'utopian' practices of 1958–60 did not eliminate the desire for a rapid and dramatic breakthrough to world sport, but it put an end to the hope of achieving this breakthrough overnight. The GLF did not end Chinese efforts to change their backwardness by mass mobilisation, but it shifted the balance of forces toward sobriety, caution and scepticism, and forced everyone to undergo the painful process of lowering levels of aspiration for themselves and for China.[65]

The economic setbacks and associated power struggle[66] after the GLF gravely obstructed sports development. Fortunately, this downturn did not last long. After 1962 the Chinese economy recovered substantially,[67] and living standards improved. Like science, technology and education,[68] sport resumed its momentum. Sports schools gradually reverted to normal training. Their number picked up by 1,800, with 140,000 students in 1965. It should be noted that the sports boarding school[69] was created in 1963 and gradually expanded. This type of school formed a bridge between the spare-time sports school and the sports team, and became an immediate source of elite athletes. By 1965 there were 13 across the country.[70]

By 1962 international competitions were back on the agenda. In 1963 China sent 229 athletes to the first New Emerging Force Games,[71] which took place in Jakarta, Indonesia, and in which over 2,000 athletes from 48 countries, including the Soviet Union, Japan, Brazil, France, East Germany and others, participated. China came first with 65 gold, 56 silver and 47 bronze medals (the Soviet Union and its satellite countries sent only small teams). This performance demonstrated Chinese potential and fed its ambition for sporting supremacy in the future.

Sport's renewed impetus was assisted by strategic publications. Based on the teaching programmes for 11 sports – athletics, swimming, gymnastics, football, basketball, volleyball, table tennis, weightlifting, skating, diving and shooting – issued in 1959 and 1960, seven textbooks for football, basketball, volleyball, swimming, gymnastics, athletics and table tennis were published in 1962.[72] The following year coaches' ranking system regulations were published. There were five categories from high to low level: National, first, second, third and assistant coaches.[73] Simultaneously, new ranking systems for athletes and referees were issued by the NSC. These innovations marked the beginning of an even more systematic management of elite sport in China. Based on the experiences of the previous years, a sporting policy of 'combining popularity with advancement, greatly developing mass sport, promoting technical levels and continually creating new records based on mass sport' (*puji yu tigao xiang jiehe, dali fazhang qunzhong tiyu, tigao yundong jishu shuiping, zai qunzhong tiyu de jichu shang budui chuzhao xing jilu*) was advocated in 1964. This policy underpinned Chinese sport for the following two decades.

Due to the closeness of the deadline of the Ten-Year Sports Development Plan,[74] drawn up in 1958, sports progress accelerated by the mid-1960s. In 1965 Chinese athletes smashed 29 world records and 202 national records.[75] More importantly, the Chinese were now on a par with the world's leading countries in some sports. Of the top ten female high jumpers in the world, five were Chinese. The remarkable performances of Chinese sportswomen thrilled and inspired much of the nation. After watching competitions against the visiting Japanese volleyball team – world champions in 1962 and Olympic champions in 1964 – Chinese government officials, including Premier Zhou Enlai, valued the Chinese girls' prospects and gave them official support. The Japanese coach Daimachu Hirofumi was brought to China to coach the Chinese players for a month in April 1965, to the advantage of Chinese volleyball. The future lay with China.

The year 1965 witnessed a second wave of developments in sport, which came to its crest in the Second National Games. At the games 24 athletes broke nine world records and 331 athletes smashed over a hundred national records. These performances spurred on sports people, elite athletes in particular, to drive for world supremacy.

Analysis: Illustrative Case Studies

Again, to provide regional evidence of the intricate evolution of elite women's sport during the GLF, three regional case studies are presented below, covering:

- Sporting developments at the time of the GLF;
- The interdependence of politics, economy and sport;
- Political and economic policies and their impact on sport and gender relations during and after the GLF.

Beijing

As mentioned in the previous chapter, Beijing led China in sport in the early 1950s. This advantage continued into the late 1950s – see Table 5. By July 1958, Beijing ranked first in the national evaluation system in terms of four crucial indicators: sports masters, ranked athletes, qualifiers for the Labour Defence Programme,[76] and spare-time sports schools.[77] At this time, standards in some women's sports in the city were approaching world level.[78] With the launch of the Great Leap Forward there was a special enthusiasm for sport. Indeed, in conjunction with the GLF, a 'Month of Sports Leaping Forward' event was organised in Beijing from May to July 1958.

Mass sport, including sport in school and university, reached an unprecedented peak in Chinese history during the GLF. Women benefited in Beijing as elsewhere. For example, Han Juyuan, a female student at the Beijing Institute of Iron and Steel, broke the national record for hand grenade throwing in 1958. Wei Yu, the first female doctor of electronics and now vice-minister of the National Education Committee, passed the first grade of gymnastics in 1959 while at university.

The Beijing Institute of Physical Education played a crucial part in the 'Great Leap Forward of Sport', producing valuable specialist sports 'workers'. It sent 600 teachers and students to factories and schools to promote mass sport, and its fourth-year students were dispatched to provincial and municipal sports commissions to assist in the establishment of sports teams during these years.[79] To provide provincial sports teams and sports schools with well-trained coaches, a new department, the sports coaching

TABLE 5

BEIJING'S RANKING IN MAJOR NATIONAL SPORTS COMPETITIONS IN 1958

	athletics	gymnastics	cycling	basketball	volleyball	table tennis
men	2	6	7-8	1	1	1
women	1	5	2	1	2	1

Source: Guijia tiwei xuanchuang bu [Propaganda Department of the NSC], 3 (1958), pp.62–109.

department, was established in the BIPE at the end of 1957. It continues to this day.[80] It set a precedent: henceforward, the formal educational preparation of coaches was mainly organised by colleges of physical education.[81] These actions reflected the fact that physical education institutions were in the vanguard of both elite and mass sport development in the 1950s.

To realise the goal set by the NSC's Ten-year Plan, a campaign of 'greatly passing sports grades' began in 1958 and lasted for more than one year. Its purpose was to upgrade sports standards within a short time. This was dramatically revealed in the ambitious targets announced by the president of the BIPE: 30 world-level athletes within a year. In consequence, diversified tests and competitions took place day and night. Targets, however, became symbols of political enthusiasm, and lost touch with reality. Some students got up to practise at two o'clock in the morning. Some took part in more than ten tests in one day. In the wake of zealous commitment, falsification and flexibility accompanied the tests. As Cheng Dexin, a female gymnast at the BIPE at the time, has recounted, 'some students failed in the morning and tried again in the afternoon and/or evening until they reached the standards for the rank. Judging was not very strict.'[82] As a result, each student at the BIPE obtained on average 8.81 different athletic rankings within a month.

Sport appeared to develop on a spectacular scale, yet the reality was somewhat different due to the widespread exaggeration of performance quotas: a phenomenon that came to be called 'boastfulness'. Huang Xinhe has stated:

> My husband was criticised for three months just because he had critical views of the unreal, unscientific training programme. Those who advocated caution were accused of conservatism. I was a little conservative in training goals at the time, but others put forward unrealistic goals such as two full scores out of the four pieces of apparatus for women, and performing the five or six most difficult elements in a floor routine. Unquestionably, this approach had its drawbacks. Among other things, it caused a high incidence of sports injuries. I myself had an operation on my knee as a result of excessive training.[83]

The emphasis on targets resulted in a highly competitive atmosphere, which on occasion stimulated dangerous, if on occasion successful, commitment. Professor Huang Xinhe continued:

> One week prior to the first National Games I had a serious head injury in training. Three days before the games I was released from hospital. Encouraged by the momentum of the GLF, I forgot both the pain and the danger and concentrated on competition. As a result, I won the floor exercise title and fourth place overall in the competition. In spite of the obvious absurdities, the GLF played a positive part in the development of elite women's sport.[84]

Due to the mounting incidence of injuries and illness, the medical care of athletes became an urgent issue that could not be ignored. The Beijing Sports Medical Research Institute was thus set up at the Beijing Medical College in 1958. It was responsible for providing medical consultations for athletes, curing sports injuries and monitoring athletes' health. Thereafter, sports medicine became an important subject and attracted growing attention. Similarly, sports research came onto the agenda. In 1958 the National Sports Scientific Research Institute was established in the Beijing in order to help coaches and athletes improve sports performances. Thus most projects carried out by the institute focused on sports training and competitions.

Throughout Beijing, sport was leaping forward. To create good results in the first National Games mentioned earlier, the Beijing Municipal Sports Commission established elite teams for diving, gymnastics, cycling and swimming in 1958.[85] This year witnessed a huge rise in the number of athletes – from 89 to a record level of 1,070 within the year. Simultaneously, sports schools expanded. In 1958 there were six spare-time sports schools with 3,000 students in nine sports in Beijing. By 1960 there were ten schools with 7,990 students (including 1,282 from the national defence sports).[86] This expansion of elite sports teams and sports schools resulted in abundant opportunities for full-time coaching. By the eve of the Cultural Revolution in 1966, professional coaches totalled 534 in Beijing. However, from the point of view of equality, there was a fly in the ointment. Only 38 were women.[87] It is evident that men still heavily dominated coaching positions in the mid-1960s. To be on a par with men in coaching women had – and still have – a long way to go. This will be discussed later.

While elite athletes were mainly selected from schools in Beijing, neighbouring cities such as Kaifeng, Zhengzhou, Qingtao, Jinan, Dalian and Taiyuan provided reserve resources for Beijing sports teams. In 1957 Beijing coaches went to these places deliberately to select athletes. There were other efforts to promote elite sport. Beijing men and women volleyball teams went to Shandong province to help accelerate elite sport. They stayed there for over a year. As a result, Shandong women's team won a silver medal at the second National Games. In turn, Shandong provided Beijing with a number of potentially good players.[88] It is clear that Beijing had bilateral ties with neighbouring provinces as well as cities in the 1950s and some mobility of athletes from provinces and cities to Beijing existed in this period – for the greater glory of Beijing. Moreover, experts in and outside the sports community gave full support and assistance to sports teams. Actors and actresses from the Beijing Opera Troupe and Ballet Troupe were often invited to teach acrobatics and choreography to the gymnastic and diving teams. The apparent cooperation and support between different sectors and places to some extent mirrored the social climate, which demanded communist collectivism at the time.

It was not only athletes but also facilities that were improved or created. To host the first National Games in 1959 Beijing Worker's Sports Field was specially built. It occupied a 35-hectare area and comprised a central sports field with a capacity of 80,000 seats, a four-storey building for training, accommodation and board, 17 ball courts and a swimming pool. It has been the main venue for domestic and international competitions ever since. In the same year a cycling racetrack and a motorcycle ring road were constructed. These facilities greatly improved Beijing's sporting infrastructure, the culmination of years of gradual improvement – of performers and facilities. It paid off: after these years of special preparation, Beijing succeeded in organising the National Games, to which it sent 467 participants and at which it won second place. In short, energised by the GLF, in a few short years Beijing had provided an outstanding venue and achieved outstanding results.

Yet all was far from perfect. To launch a 'satellite' (*Weixing*) – to achieve outstanding accomplishments – at the first National Games, the classroom work of the student athletes at the BIPE was cancelled and most of the time was devoted to training. Due to the leftist political climate, will-power was greatly emphasised. The violation of scientific principles in athletic training became pervasive. Cheng Dexin has revealed that 'we had four training sessions each day: from early morning to late at night. We were so tired that we often fell asleep when we sat down at the edge of the floor.'[89] In spite of the apparent inappropriateness of these activities, the National Games were an important impetus to the development of elite sport. Some 293 BIPE students took part in the first National Games; 23 of them broke 25 national records and 83 won gold medals.

The rapid development of sport, unfortunately, was disrupted by the end of the decade. As a combination of the legacy of the GLF's adventurism, unusual natural disasters between 1959 and 1961, and the collapse of Sino-Soviet relations, the early 1960s witnessed a difficult three-year period (1960–62). Lan Yiansheng, an official of the Chinese Sports Science Association, has vividly reflected upon the consequences of the deterioration of the economic situation: 'When we got up in the morning, our eyes were too swollen to open. So were our bodies. At first, we thought of it as weight increase instead of malnutrition. After 1961 we hardly had training sessions.'[90] Due to malnutrition, 13 per cent of students could not follow physical education classes or engage in intense physical activities at the Beijing Second Female Middle School.[91] Others were weakened, if not seriously, by the conditions. As a result, extracurricular sports activities became almost non-existent. Influenced by the economic crisis, sporting investment fell markedly, which led to the reduction or elimination of elite sports teams. The number of elite athletes in Beijing sharply decreased from 1070 in 1958 to 374 in 1960. Similarly, students in sports schools declined from 7,990 in 1960 to 200 by 1961.[92] Fluctuation in sporting performance closely paralleled socio-economic change. However, after a few years, the economy improved and sports activities picked up. Elite athletes numbered 453 (female, 158) in 1962 and 583 (female, 201) in 1965. The pay-off came quickly: the Second National Games were held in Beijing in 1965, and Beijing came third.

It is clear from the above that Beijing's elite sport, for men and women, experienced a wavelike process of rise, fall and revival between the late 1950s and the first half of the 1960s. During the years of the GLF, sport developed on an unparalleled scale. This was both symbolised and rein-forced by the first National Games. Mutual support and cooperation were apparent between different sectors of the community, between various areas and between different provinces. However, all was far from ideal. Due to a naive subscription to leftist dogma, unrealistic training quotas and blind intensive training, excessive sports-related injuries and diseases occurred. Nevertheless, after a few years of adjustment following the GLF, Beijing felt ready to attempt to produce a world elite. This will be discussed later.

Guangdong

By the late 1950s sport was very popular in Guangdong. Twenty-one coun-ties were awarded the title of 'Sports Popular Unit'. Specialist sports coun-ties emerged – for example, Tai Shan Volleyball County, Dong Guan Swimming County and Mei County Football County. Guangdong was posi-tioned at fifth, eighth, 13th, and seventh respectively in the four areas of sports master, ranked athletes, qualifiers for the Labour Defence Programme and spare-time sports schools in the country.[93] The popularity of sport pro-vided a congenial climate for elite sport. Twenty-five cities and counties in the province were honoured as training bases for elite sport.

During the GLF, sports schools boomed after the Guangdong Provincial Sports Commission decentralised responsibility for them. As a result, the number of sports schools in Guangdong reached an unprecedented level – 1,956 in July 1958. Over a hundred sports schools came into being within five days.[94] Between April and October 1958, Guangdong established 40,000 sports schools in 84 cities and counties. The number of students reached 1.4 million.[95] There were 28 provincial-level key spare-time sports schools employing 128 coaches for 4,770 students by the early 1960s.[96] Most elite athletes were produced from these key schools,[97] which established a talent base for elite sports teams. In addition, in 1957 Guangdong had 17 provincial 'specialised' teams for 12 sports, including women's volleyball, gymnastics and athletics.[98] They employed 1,048 elite athletes in 1958, about an eightfold increase over 1956 (130). Interestingly, women outnum-bered men in athletics with 28 against 26 in 1960.[99]

In conjunction with the expansion of sports teams, performances improved remarkably. Guangdong was now in the top flight in many sports including gymnastics, swimming, diving, table tennis and weightlifting. To prepare for the first National Games, many sports organised concentrated training. For example, 40 male and 40 female divers were assembled to undertake systematic training together. With 319 participants, Guangdong won fourth place at the National Games in 1959. The women won the gym-nastics team championship and the platform diving title, came second in the

200m sprint and won three third places in other athletics events.[100] There was no sizeable gap between men and women in terms of their performances in the national competitions – see Table 6. In consequence, women were justifiably treated on a par with men in the pursuit of success.

The rapid growth of elite sports teams and sports schools was accompanied by an increase in full-time qualified coaches. By the eve of the Cultural Revolution in 1966, Guangdong had 580 full-time coaches, of whom only four were women.[101] This obvious under-representation of women demonstrated an inescapable reality that however well they performed, it was not easy for women to enter coaching. Later this will be discussed further. To provide formally trained sports coaches and cadres for the province, two new institutes of physical education and 12 sports schools were founded in 1958. In addition, in 1960 a national coaching course for spare-time sports schools in athletics, swimming and gymnastics was held in Guangdong (and Beijing), and 220 coaches attended. Coaching education was certainly now on track.

These developments were only one part of the rapid social changes in sport during the GLF that were characterised by the extreme emphasis on speed, quotas and will-power. Unfortunately, there were bad summer floods in Guangdong in 1959, leading to food shortages, disease, malnutrition and increased mortality. The collapse of the economy brought the GLF to an end in the autumn of 1960, and there was now a period of retrenchment and reorganisation. The number of elite athletes declined sharply from 1,799 in 1960 to 559 (women, 206) in 1962. The number of students in sports schools slumped from 45,766 in 1960 to 2,857 in 1963. After 1963 the decline of elite sport was reversed. It was in this year that the Scientific Research Office of the Guangdong Sports Commission – the third scientific research organisation to be established in China – was set up and sporting research began to take off in Guangdong. In 1965 elite athletes increased to 651 (female, 220)[102] and spare-time sports schools students to 5,094, figures albeit still below the level of 1958.[103] Guangdong was allocated 300 places for the second National Games, the same number as Beijing. At the games Guangdong retained its fourth place.

It is clear from the above facts and figures that Guangdong resembled Beijing in sporting development. The year 1958 witnessed the rapid expan-

TABLE 6

GUANGDONG'S RANKINGS IN MAJOR NATIONAL SPORTS COMPETITIONS, 1958

	athletics	gymnastics	cycling	basketball	volleyball	table tennis
men	22	3	11	9	3	2
women	21	5	11	5	11	3

Source: Guijia tiwei xuanchuang bu [Propaganda Department of the NSC], 3 (1958), pp.62–109.

sion of sports teams and schools, with the greatest number of elite athletes occurring in 1960. As in Beijing, there was little difference in opportunity and performance (in terms of success) between men and women. In contrast, coaching positions were predominantly occupied by men. The establishment of sports institutes and schools made coaching education in the province more institutionalised and professional. After two years' retrenchment, by 1963 elite sport had started to recover.

Sichuan

Sichuan was a highly active province during the GLF. Communes were introduced not just in the countryside, but also in the cities. Urban communes emerged in Chengdu, the capital city of the biggest province in China, in 1958, two years ahead of most other cities. Most housewives were organised into small workshop groups while a number of them looked after the children, the sick and the aged and did the cooking. The spirit of the commune infiltrated the personal lives of both men and women. In the case of women, it laid the foundations for them to be actively involved in elite sport. It allowed them the freedom to be involved.

Regarding the popularity of sport, Sichuan was an average province. Only five counties in Sichuan were regarded as 'Sports Popular Units' (*tiyu xianjin danwei*) in 1958.[104] Sichuan ranked eighth, 19th, 16th and tenth respectively in the four areas of sports master, ranked athletes, qualifiers for the Labour Defence system, and spare-time sports schools.[105] Nevertheless, sport was greatly emphasised and gradually became popular with many boys and girls during the GLF. As Jung Chang has recounted in *Wild Swans*:

> There was no political education, but we did have to do a lot of sports: running, high jump and long jump, as well as compulsory gym and swimming. We each had one after-school sport: I was selected for tennis. At first my father was against the prospect of my becoming a sportswoman, which was the purpose of the training.[106]

In 1958 Sichuan had 772 spare-time sports schools (far fewer than Guangdong), one institute of physical education and two sports schools. About 10,645 students enrolled in spare-time sports schools in 1960, well behind Guangdong. In imitation of Beijing, a sports clinic was opened in the Institute of Physical Education at Chengdu in October 1958. It produced numerous physiotherapists and high-quality applied research, and in time became well-known in China.

As in other places, representation at the National Games became the target for Sichuan sport. To prepare for the first National Games, a number of 'temporarily assembled' teams for gymnastics, table tennis, cycling, shooting, ski flying and other sports were set up in 1958. Athletes doubled in number from 307 in 1956 to 778 in 1958. Sichuan sent 467 athletes (the same number as Beijing and Guangdong) to the first National Games. It came 19th at the games, somewhere near the lower middle level in China. In the immediate aftermath of the National Games, most elite teams for sports including gymnastics, cycling, shooting and ski flying were formally established. The games had stimulated 'specialised' training in the province.

Interestingly, in the 1950s a number of provincial sports teams were controlled by local city sports commissions, as in Chongqing (swimming, diving and table tennis) and Chengdu (cycling), and the Chengdu Institute of Physical Education (gymnastics). This decentralisation of sports management had two effects. First, it promoted elite sport widely by taking advantage of local resources and expertise. Second, as a consequence it alleviated the financial and administrative burdens of the Provincial Sports Commission. This cooperation between sports bodies at different levels typified the general collectivist atmosphere during the GLF.

However, due to extreme adventurism during the GLF, Sichuan was more vulnerable to post-GLF natural disasters. A severe famine led to the deaths of over eight million in the province.[107] This disastrous economic situation adversely affected the development of elite sport – at least temporarily. The number of elite athletes began to decline: from 778 in 1958 to 614 in 1960. Following the disintegration of some sports teams such as the cycling team in 1962, the number of athletes further slumped to 451 in 1963. Things then got better in the province. After a period of adjustment and reorganisation, Sichuan spare-time sports schools picked up, and numbered 193, with 10,143 students in 1965.[108] In the same year Sichuan was allocated the same number of representatives as Beijing and Guangdong (300) at the second National Games, at which it won nine gold medals, one less than at the first National Games.

However, Sichuan's elite sportswomen put the province among the top six in many sports in the country. Its women's basketball team won the national title twice, in 1955 and 1960. The women's volleyball team won the second National Games and started their domination in this sport for almost 20 years. In general women's performances were superior to men's in most national competitions – see Table 7. As a result, increasing numbers of women were given places in sports teams. In 1962 women athletes were almost 40 per cent of the total, and this proportion was higher than in Beijing or Guangdong. Women even outnumbered men in some sports. For example, of the 65 athletes specialising in athletics in 1960, 39 were women.[109] They became the backbone of the province in sport.

In contrast to female athletes, however, female coaches were only about 10 per cent (20) of the total at the time.[110] This 10 per cent certainly pulled their weight. Wang Defen, a volleyball player in the early 1950s, mentioned already in Chapter 1, set a good example. After she became an assistant coach of the provincial women's team in 1957 she continued playing. The next year she was pregnant, but she kept coaching until the day she gave

TABLE 7

SICHUAN'S RANKINGS IN MAJOR NATIONAL SPORTS COMPETITIONS IN 1958

	athletics	gymnastics	cycling	basketball	volleyball	table tennis
men	11	9	24	7	6	5
women	3	2	23	4	4	6

Source: Guijia tiwei xuanchuang bu [Propaganda Department of the NSC], 3 (1958), pp.62–109.

birth. Unfortunately, she lost her daughter due to prenatal overwork and inadequate puerperal treatment. Nevertheless she did not lose her commitment. As a reward, she was promoted to head coach, and while she coached, she continued playing. Her team won fifth place at the first National Games.[111] Wang's story is typical of many. She symbolised the qualities of many Chinese sportswomen in the 1950s – fortitude and determination. Her story demonstrated that women had to be extremely capable and extremely committed and often ready to sacrifice family responsibilities in pursuit of their coaching careers.

In many ways, the development of sport in Sichuan was similar to Beijing and Guangdong, but there were differences. Unlike in Beijing and Guangdong, local sports commissions below the provincial level were directly involved in managing elite sport. In addition, Sichuan women had more remarkable achievements than the women of the other two provinces. This promoted their standing in provincial sports teams despite Sichuan suffering badly from the legacy of the GLF.

In summary, inspired by the enthusiasm for the rapid construction of socialism, a 'great leap forward' occurred in elite sport in Beijing, Guangdong and Sichuan. The brief period of 1958–59 formed the heyday of elite sport in terms of the scale of sports teams and schools, sports investment and infrastructure construction. The ambitious plan to catch up with the advanced countries of the world in sport mirrored the nation's economic ambitions. It stimulated mutual support between different sectors and different places, intensive training, defensive 'boastfulness' and arbitrary goals.[112] In spite of the obvious weaknesses and drawbacks of the GLF, sport de facto flourished in the late 1950s. This is not widely appreciated. However, restrained by the condition of the post-GLF Chinese economy, elite sport had to shrink. Thus, the year 1960 witnessed a sharp fall in sports investment. After a few years of economic improvement, adjustment and reorganisation, and the abandoning of the radical policies of the GLF, elite sport returned to the pre-GLF level by 1963 and developed steadily in the following two years. The ambition to catch up with the world's athletic powers did not fade. The second National Games were a symbol of this aspiration.

Conclusion

The Great Leap Forward is of considerable significance in the history of the New China, in spite of its short time span. The establishment of the communes greatly affected Chinese lives, both men and women, and provided opportunities for women to reach their full potential in a number of careers, including elite sport. As far as women are concerned, the GLF provided a congenial social environment for women to take up elite sport. During the GLF both mass and elite sport developed at an unprecedented speed. This was manifested in fiscal budgets, the number of elite athletes, organised competitions, athletic performances and the construction of sports facilities, as well as the expansion of sports schools and colleges of physical education. The result was that sportswomen became increasingly visible in national and international competitions. However, it was not all progress. The unrealistic emphasis on intensive training and on will-power led to unrealistic targets, neglect of scientific training and numerous incidents of athletic injury and illness. In truth, in its short life, the GLF left its mark on women's elite sport in both positive and negative ways.

On the wider political front, it is now widely accepted that the GLF, viewed in retrospect, was a disastrous event that caused calamitous economic setbacks, damaged foreign relations and opened serious political wounds that did not heal for years. The utopian ambition of the GLF to realise communist principles and ideals within 'today and not forward' had disastrous consequences: the most tragic was a widespread famine that claimed millions of lives. The 'Leap' also directly undermined social and economic development. There was a knock-on consequence for sport. However, after a phase of post-GLF reorganisation and adjustment, Chinese sport bounced back to an impressive level. Revival, however, was soon to be disrupted by yet another political movement – the Cultural Revolution. It will be the focus of the next chapter.

Women, Society and Elite Sport during the Cultural Revolution (1966–76)

By the mid-1960s a struggle for power within the Chinese Communist Party had escalated.[1] The 'Socialist Education Movement' (*shehui zhuyi jiaoyu yundong*)[2] now shifted its emphasis from correcting the 'incorrect' behaviour of grass-roots cadres to discrediting the Party leaders who were accused of 'taking the bourgeois road' (*zhou ziben zhuyi daolu*). Political criticism of an ideological nature touched the fields of history, philosophy, economy and literature,[3] culminating in the debate over the historical play *Hai Rui's Dismissal from Office* (*Hai Rui ba guan*).[4] All this served as the prelude to the now notorious and at the time horrific phenomenon of the decade-long Cultural Revolution. As a product of the misguided ideas of a misguided leader, this movement tore the Chinese Communist Party and society apart, propelled China into international isolation, drastically undermined its economy[5] and wasted a generation of its youth. Although the Cultural Revolution came to an end a quarter of a century ago, it has left its mark on virtually every aspect of Chinese society – political, economical, cultural and, in this setting, elite women's sport.

Following the official rejection of the Cultural Revolution in China in 1981,[6] descriptive chronologies[7] and critical investigations of Chinese politics, economy and culture during this turbulent period, have been published. Xiao Di's *Wenge zhi mi* [The Mystery of the Cultural Revolution], for example, has analysed its social and historical causes through a description of its complicated evolution and the rise and fall of key statesmen at the time.[8] Xiao Jie's *Zhongguo zhiqing miweng lu* [The Secret Records of Chinese Educated Youths] has recounted the factual, if seemingly implausible, stories of 'educated youths' during the chaotic decade.[9] These studies have confronted, honestly and directly, the psychological and sociological roots of the abnormal behaviour inspired by the 'revolutionary ideal'. However, they omit any consideration of sport. Since the mid-1980s some journalistic articles about sport during the Cultural Revolution have appeared, for example Tan Hua's 'Wenge zhong nongcun tiyu "xingsheng" xianxiang de sikao' [Reflections on the Prosperous Sports in the Countryside during the Cultural Revolution][10] and Hao Jie's 'Wenge qijian shanxi qunzhong tiyu chutan' [Studies of Mass Sport in Shan Xi during the Cultural Revolution];[11] however, they are mostly about mass sport. The result is that a number of issues associated with elite women's sport during the Cultural Revolution have remained unexplored.

For their part, Sinologists in the West have produced numerous studies on the Cultural Revolution spanning ideology, politics, economics, culture and education,[12] but have mostly ignored sport. Since the mid-1980s, some western sports sociologists and historians have developed, belatedly, an increasing interest in Chinese sport. Donald W. Calhoun, for example, devotes one chapter in his book *Sport, Culture, and Personality* to it. He makes passing reference to the Cultural Revolution. Regrettably, confused by the rhetoric of 'friendship first and competition second', he makes a bold but ill-informed claim: that the Chinese at that time lacked the keenness to win.[13] This misconception will be put right in due course in this chapter. Zhong Qingyi's 'The Effects of the "Great Cultural Revolution" on Sport in China, 1966–1976', for the first time, focused in depth on the Cultural Revolution and its impact on sport.[14] However, in his limited analysis, the interaction between state policy, women's status and their sport, particularly elite sport, is virtually overlooked. It is not surprising, therefore, given the neglect of these commentators, that some issues regarding elite women's sport during and after the Cultural Revolution are still unclear. How did society, politics and sport interact during the decade from the mid-1960s to the mid-1970s? How did the Cultural Revolution affect both women in society and sportswomen and their elite sport? What was the long-term impact of the Cultural Revolution on elite women's sport? Answers to these questions will provide the substance of this chapter.

Analysis: Overview

The Red Guard Movement, Women and Sport

It is now well known that the endorsement of the Circular of the Central Committee of the Communist Party of China[15] on 16 May 1966 marked the official start of the decade-long Cultural Revolution. Masterminded by Mao, the Revolution initially was used in his fight against high-level Party bureaucrats. To win the battle, Mao turned for assistance to the masses, especially the young. In this battle, the wall-poster (*da zhibao*) was employed as a useful tool of confrontation and accusation. After a female philosophy teacher at Beijing University, Nie Yuanzi,[16] wrote the first ever wall-poster on 25 May 1966, a nationwide campaign of writing and reading wall-posters was unleashed.[17] Most athletes and coaches, like people in other fields, were absorbed into the campaign. Wall-posters were everywhere. Seminar rooms, dormitories, dining rooms and gymnasiums, and even corridors and passages in sports buildings were covered with a variety of these posters. Some of them criticised the leading officials of the National Sports Commission for implementing allegedly 'capitalist' and anti-Mao policies. Then, reinforced by Mao's own poster[18] in August, the movement exploded. Old and young, men and women wrote and read posters. Huang Kuangrou, a little girl in the 1960s and now a sports administrator, has joked: 'My good brush calligraphy may be attributed to the practice of writing wall-posters.'[19] The wall-poster was one of the 'four big' (*si da*) propaganda strategies of the radicals – the other three being 'speaking out and airing views in a big way' (*da yanlun*), 'serious debate' (*da bianlun*) and 'let the masses educate themselves' (*gaungda qunzhong ziji jiaoyu ziji*). Advocacy was even written into the Party document 'Resolution on the Cultural Revolution' (*Guanyu wenhua da geming de jueding*).[20] This resolution, incidentally, formally stated that the aim of the Cultural Revolution was to denounce the powers 'taking the capitalist road' and to attack 'bourgeois academic privileges'. It was a green light. Thereafter, the Cultural Revolution became a frenzied movement, culminating in the excesses of the Red Guards.[21]

The Red Guards were launched in August 1966, when Mao appeared wearing a Red Guard arm band at the 'mass rally of a million people' (*baiwang qunzhong jihui*) in Tiananmen Square.[22] The guards immediately spread across the whole country, and most students in schools and colleges joined. Thousands of the Red Guards came from all over China to Beijing to see Chairman Mao.[23] Free accommodation, board and transport encouraged this nationwide pilgrimage. In Beijing every effort was made to look after the pilgrims. Even the playing fields and seats in the Workers' Athletic Stadium in Beijing were used to accommodate them.[24] After being received by Mao, the Red Guards embarked on a 'revolutionary big march' (*gemin da chuanlian*). To these youths, the march was a chance to recreate something of the experience of the famous 'Long March' of 1935.[25] A female Red Guard of the 1960s, Huang Kuanrou, has recalled:

> I was a girl of 16 years of age at the time. I came to Beijing from Changchun, Jilin province, in the north-east part of China, to see Chairman Mao and listen to his instructions. Then I joined others marching to Yanan [the base of the CCP during the Civil Wars] and other revolutionary bases, including Jiangxi and Hunan, in the footsteps of Chairman Mao.[26]

Hand in hand with the mobilisation of the Red Guards went the countrywide campaign[27] of attacking the 'Four Old Things' (*si jiu*)[28] and 'Five Types of Black Elements' (*hei wu lai*).[29] The unprecedented humiliation, torture and even murder of many 'elitists' in all walks of life resulted. 'Class struggle was constructed in a free-hand way that legitimated factional warfare, economic disruption, even assault upon the party-state apparatus, all of which was extremely damaging to the interests, even the lives, of both masses and cadres.'[30]

Those in sport were not spared. The table tennis coach Fu Qifang[31] and the first Chinese world champion Rong Guotuan,[32] who had once lived in

Hong Kong, were accused of spying and forced to commit suicide. The director of the National Sports Commission, Vice-Premier Marshal He Long[33] was arrested, beaten and denied any treatment for his ailments. He died within a few years. In volleyball circles alone, about 300 people were assaulted, imprisoned and sentenced to re-education through hard labour.[34] The Cultural Revolution, a heartless and cruel mass movement, brought China to the brink of anarchy. Now children were incited to denounce their parents and athletes were encouraged to condemn coaches. The masses were enticed to rebel against authority. Husbands were forced to accuse wives, and wives their husbands. Divorce and marriage for political insurance became commonplace. Such ruthless political actions resulted in the distortion of people's minds and undermined family relations that had been valued for thousands of years.[35] Those who did not divorce their 'black element' spouses had to suffer harsh treatment with them. The experience of the first-ever Chinese female world table tennis champion, Qiu Zhonghui, provides a glimpse of this traumatic state of affairs:

> My husband was labelled a 'suspected spy' because he grew up in the former USSR [any connection with foreign countries was suspect at the time]. I was pressurised to divorce him in order to demonstrate a politically correct attitude. But I did not because I trusted him. Due to the political position of my husband, I could not go abroad or be received by the central government leaders. Under the huge pressure my hair turned grey within two years. The Cultural Revolution made me politically mature. I started to study political issues, and indeed read Marxist and Leninist works.[36]

After the outset of the Cultural Revolution, athletic training was replaced by denunciation meetings, street marches and other revolutionary activities. International activities were virtually abandoned following the first Asian Games of the New Emerging Forces (GANEFO) in July 1966. Sports organisations were immobilised, competitions no longer existed and facilities were wrecked. The once esteemed world champions were now criticised as 'bourgeois favourites' (*zhichan jieji de hongren*) and competitiveness in sport was termed a 'bourgeois cups-and-medals mania' (*zhichan jieji de jinbiao zhuyi*). A former member of the national women's volleyball team, Dong Tianshu, has recalled the times:

> Due to an international competition in Laos in November 1966, we continued training while taking part in the Revolution [mainly writing wall-posters]. When we returned to Guangzhou after the competition, the 'rebel sector' (*zhao fan pai*) from Beijing was waiting there to criticise us. We were regarded as the 'conservative sector'(*baohuang pai*) because we had won honours for the country. Consequently, we had to give up the forthcoming world championships in 1967. Later we went

to grass-roots factories and into the countryside to demonstrate our volleyball skills. After the National Sports Commission was denounced as an 'independent kingdom' (*duli wangguo*)[37] in 1968, training activities came to a halt.[38]

One outcome of such extremism was that the best years of talented athletes were squandered. For example, among the volleyball teams at the 1972 Five Ball Events Games, there were five female teams whose players were over 25 years of age.[39] The best six men and women gymnasts in the national gymnastic competition in 1972 all belonged to the pre-CR generation.[40]

After mid-1967 the Cultural Revolution developed beyond wall-posters and demonstrations into a full-scale physical struggle for state power, which resulted in violent fighting between different factions.[41] By 1968, everything was in chaos. The furious fighting brought China to the brink of economic collapse. The gross national product reportedly dropped from 306.2 billion yuan in 1966 to 264.8 billion yuan in 1968.[42] This directly rebounded on sport. Sporting investment fell annually from 89.964 million yuan in 1966 to 27.39 million yuan in 1968. The steepest slumps happened in 1967 and 1968 respectively: in 1967 there was a drop of 33 per cent on 1966 and then in 1968 there was a drop of 54.6 per cent on the previous year.[43] The diminished sports funding led to a shrinking of elite sports teams. Some 13 national defence sports were abandoned. The number of elite athletes and coaches dropped from 11,292 and 2,062 in 1965 to 6,288 and 1,530 in 1970 respectively.[44]

Women, especially female students,[45] demonstrated unusual vitriolic energy in the struggles of the Cultural Revolution. They appeared to overcompensate for a past lack of esteem. They joined men in invading private houses, public temples and churches to confiscate property, remove statues and tear up hymnbooks.[46] They set up portraits of Mao and quotations from his writings. A young woman at the time, Pan Yongzhi, now a deputy director of the Physical Education Department of the Beijing University of Physical Education (BUPE), commented later:

> There was little difference between girl and boy rebels. In fact, girls were occasionally fiercer than boys. Whatever they did, they always felt that justice was on their side. Those who had not been very good at academic study or sport were more radical than others.[47]

Jung Chang's vivid description of a female Red Guard in her book *Wild Swans* provided further evidence of female rebellion in the 1960s:

> Now she pulled it [a belt] off and pointed it at his nose – a stylised Red Guard posture – while she screamed at him. ... All of a sudden she was far from gentle, shy or lovely. She was all hysterical ugliness.[48]

The role of the destroyers of the 'Four Old Things' brought young women into sharp conflict with authority and the older generations.[49] Why did these once obedient women suddenly become radical rebels? This is a complex issue that involved family, school and society. First, this generation of students had grown up in the New China. They had been bombarded by propaganda about female equality all their lives, and fully subscribed to the stated belief that 'women can do what men do'. However, while women's equality had been stressed, simultaneously obedience, self-sacrifice, discipline and a rigid hierarchy had been reinforced in school and family. Thus, female students 'experienced enough of the repressive inhibitions of conformity in their socialisation to have built up explosive frustrations and raging anger at anyone they thought might be getting away with not being equally disciplined and in control of themselves'.[50] Thus, rebellious impulses were buried deeply beneath historic obedience. These impulses were both strengthened and sanctioned when Mao called on the young to denounce their seniors during the Cultural Revolution. Consequently, on numerous occasions, 'it is not a son, but a daughter who leads an assault on the real father, by getting a "symbolic father" [Mao] to support her'.[51] It can be inferred that obedience to authority was transferred from the home or school to the paramount leader Mao. Once he had publicly endorsed revolution, it became legitimate for everyone with a grievance to join in, and the movement proliferated rapidly. The contrary characteristics of obedience and rebelliousness were displayed in women's gratitude to the saviour Mao and hatred towards the 'bourgeois roaders'.[52]

The Mao cult reached its climax during the Cultural Revolution. Mao's works were regarded as the gospel and a magic instrument of revolution. Everyone, men and women, the old and the young, memorised and recited passages from the 'little red book' of Mao's works and achieved exceptional fluency. People carried the little red book with them everywhere as a symbol of Mao worship. Bizarrely, in 1967 a set of physical exercises, which comprised 18 parts, each part representing one item from Mao's works, was created and seen on screen; its music was heard on the radio. Thousands of people learned the exercises. Political and athletic activities were thus melded into one, and this fusion was clearly reflected in the articles published in the journal *China's Sports* (*zhongguo tiyu*) in the period leading up to the Cultural Revolution.[53] They were packed with Mao's political thought and there was very little information on technical training. The following quotation from the journal demonstrates the new political tone:[54]

> In the case of our sportsmen, we insist that politics must be in command of their day-to-day work to ensure success so that ideological revolution is used to bring about a revolution in the techniques and skills employed, so that the results of the ideological and political work find expression in day-to-day work, and athletes who are both 'red and expert' are produced.

Swimming, Mao's favoured sport, presents another illustration of the merging of politics and sport. The picture of Mao swimming across the Yangtze on 16 July 1966 appeared everywhere – a blatant symbol of his fitness, both physically and politically, to remain at the helm of the country.[55] Swimming was used to serve the power struggle.[56] However, the outcome had one unsuspected virtue. Mao's action inspired hundreds and thousands of people to learn to swim. Each year there were provincial or city swimming contests across rivers or lakes throughout the country. Swimming was in vogue. This popularity made its contribution to the creation of elite swimmers in the early 1980s.

The unparalleled worship of god-like Mao was underpinned by a 'highly controlled culture and art to ensure people lost their reflective and linguistic abilities, even their personalities and reason'.[57] Towards the end of the 1960s the practice of 'asking for [political] instruction in the morning and submitting reports in the evening'[58] became commonplace throughout the whole of the country. Sportsmen and women were no exception. Prior to and after training and competitions, athletes recited Mao's works in order to both sharpen and illustrate their ideological commitment and determination. 'Redness', judged by inner conviction, was stressed above all else. Now political study was not simply confined to specific periods on the timetable. Political slogans such as 'continuous revolution in thought leads to revolution in sport skills', and 'treat training and competition in a revolutionary manner' were included in meetings, in training summaries and even in the diaries of both coaches and athletes. Regarding the politicised life of China during the Cultural Revolution, Guang Hong has commented:

> In recorded history, no other nation at any other time has been enthusiastic about politics on such a wide scale as the Chinese people in the Cultural Revolution. Those who normally did not pay any attention to politics now studied the words of newspapers carefully in case of changes in policy.[59]

In short, politics permeated every part of Chinese society, including the sporting community. Elite sport suffered heavily from the violent fighting, anarchy and political indoctrination. And yet politics even in these horrendous circumstances had its uses. The Mao cult resulted in the increasing popularity of swimming and, indeed, other forms of physical exercise.

Women's Liberation, Model Operas and Sportswomen

From the mid-1960s onwards, popular pre-Cultural-Revolution films, operas and other works were criticised and prohibited. Replacing them were eight 'model operas',[60] which were exclusively shown day and night in theatres and cinemas, and broadcast on the radio. The message of the operas spilled over into the worlds of sport, art and drama. Some athletes became actors and actresses in the operas, and went to factories and communes to popularise them. Some sports such as gymnastics and figure skating choreographed their routines utilising the music of the model operas. In the winter of 1967 figure skaters from Beijing Municipal Spare-time Sports School put on an ice show choreographed according to the story of the White-haired Girl, one of the model operas. The female skater, who played the role of the positive but exploited heroine, fell on the ice several times doing difficult jumps. Spectators laughed. In contrast, the male skater, who played the role of an exploitative landlord, won enthusiastic applause from the spectators for his excellent performance.[61] To link 'revolutionary opera' with sport continually did not win the gratitude of the public. This ridiculous practice in the China of the Cultural Revolution made Chinese sports 'lose their intrinsic value. There were no sports for sport's sake.'[62]

It should be noted that these model operas presented a wholesome image of revolutionary heroines and portrayed women as militant fighters for the revolution, ready to sacrifice family for the cause.[63] Undoubtedly, these operas further challenged the concept of the traditional family and historical femininity. A generation of girls sang the songs of the operas and emulated the behaviour of the heroines in the operas. They absorbed, uncritically, what they heard on the radio or watched on the screen and saw in the theatre. Their view of the world was shaped to a considerable degree by the unrelenting operatic message. Since these girls were socialised to act like the female characters of the operas, there was an undeniable emancipatory element to this aspect of the Cultural Revolution.

Intoxicated by the operas, women deliberately wore grey-blue uniforms and cut their hair short to resemble men. Cosmetics, colourful clothes, skirts and tight trousers were considered degenerate 'bourgeois goods' and destroyed. Consequently, to show women's equality, natural differences between men and women were often denied: 'Sex equality is equated with almost total blindness to sexuality.'[64] Mao's poem 'Doff Femininity and Don Military Attire'[65] further encouraged this 'new' image of women. Thus, the state had a penetrating and profound influence on gender values and behaviour.

Socialist policies during the Cultural Revolution not only constructed a 'sameness' between men and women, but also desexualised the Chinese – at least publicly. Any reference to love was deleted from the hearing and vision of the population. In sports teams love affairs were frowned on and considered a distraction from commitment to sports training. When an athlete had a lover, she was often humiliated in public and even expelled from sports teams. In some respects, Chinese people were de-gendered and de-sexed. They suffered extreme sexual repression. This de-gendered practice of inviting women to enter the male world made 'men of women',[66] and reflected only too clearly the legacy of a deeply rooted female inferiority. Of course, it also demonstrated political manipulation.

This new image of women was further fortified by the campaign of 'Learning From Dazhai and Daqing'.[67] Early in 1963 the 'Iron Girls' Team'[68] in Dazhai was established to control severe flooding. The leader of the team, Guo Fengnian, later became a national role model and was promoted to an important leadership position during the Cultural Revolution.[69] Then an all-woman well-drilling team was set up in Daqing in 1974. Rebutting the idea that men are superior to women, in 1976 this team set a record of 10,303 metres drilled within one month.[70] Such developments demonstrated that the 'women's issue' was particularly important in what was now becoming a heated political and ideological climate. Mao once again wanted women on his side of the political divide. The state was given considerable power to change women's ideas, behaviour and status. Women, especially young female students, admired and emulated the model heroines. This had its resonance for sport. In 1975, the female alpinist Panduo became the first woman in the world to climb the highest summit of the Himalayas, Mount Everest, from the northern slope. Through her timely action she demonstrated now valued female qualities of fortitude, ambition and obedience:

> In 1975 I was already a mother of three children. Five months after I gave birth to my third child, I stopped breastfeeding and came to Beijing to join the training camp. At the government's request, and motivated by my own strong desire, I overcame various difficulties and conquered the Himalayas.

Her self-evaluation was food and drink to the propagandists of the Cultural Revolution: 'I have a very strong personality, and always want to be the best at whatever I do. I believe I would also have succeeded in any other occupation if I had not engaged in mountain-climbing.'[71]

Another event, the 'Criticising Lin Biao and Confucius Campaign' (1973–6),[72] while essentially an instrument in the power struggle, to some extent brought a fresh impetus to women's pursuit of equality.[73] As Confucian doctrine had long been seen as responsible for attitudes, values and behaviour inimical to socialist development, this fresh critique of Confucianism naturally led to criticism, once again, of one of its main principles: male supremacy. It gave new life to communist idealism – or perhaps expediency. Women, after violently criticising Confucianism, among other things, more assertively than ever refused to subscribe to the long-standing and not yet extinct belief in women's inferiority. They quoted Mao's saying 'Times have changed, and women and men are equal. Whatever men can accomplish, women can as well.' Indeed, many jobs once reserved for men, including driving locomotives and flying aeroplanes, were made more available to women. Little gender difference existed in job assignment, subject choice and sports participation. Women's political representation reached a peak in the late 1960s.[74] All this certainly had some positive impact on elite women's sport. The overall percentage of female athletes increased from 34.9 per cent in 1965 to 37.5 per cent in 1970, and then to 39.8 per cent in 1975. Their representation in coaching positions also rose from 16.4 per cent to 17.1 per cent and then 18.7 per cent in the same period.[75] Discrimination against women at this time was less in China than in many other countries.[76]

In spite of the assertive advance of women's liberation in the Cultural Revolution, gender inequalities remained in Chinese society. Some feminists argued that the slogan 'women can do what men do' simply perpetuated deeply rooted inequality because women were measured against men and judged by how well they fulfilled male roles.[77] Thus, they argued, the new opportunities that opened up for women during the Cultural Revolution did not substantially change the reality of male dominance despite some positive outcomes for women's emancipation.

The Rustication Campaign, Education and Sports Teams

In the summer of 1968, Mao authorised the armed forces to move into schools, universities, factories and many other institutions such as the National Sports Commission to stop the disruptive and often violent strife between rival mass organisations. Not only this, but the large-scale 'rustication campaign' (*shanshang xiaxian*) was launched to reduce the violence and at the same time to alleviate unemployment in the cities.[78] This campaign lasted more than ten years. Most of the middle-school and college graduates between 1966 and 1968 were sent to the countryside to reform themselves through manual labour. Thus, a unique generation of uneducated 'educated youths' resulted.

Young educated women worked with men in the fields and on construction sites. As mentioned earlier, there was virtually no gender difference in job assignment. As Shou Xiaoyu, a female educated youth in Beidafang (a military construction camp in Helongjian province) and now a sports official in the National Swimming Association, has recalled:

> We girls had to do as harsh labour as boys and sometimes even harsher labour than them in order to demonstrate the competence of 'half the sky'. We sometimes got up at three o'clock in the morning to begin our work. Without a strong body, this was simply unbearable. But without impressive work records, it would be impossible for a girl to become a 'good youth' and be recommended for a factory, the army or a college.[79]

This story illustrates clearly that women were, and had to be, capable of occupations far beyond childbearing and household management. In a so-called 'equal' environment, these educated girls indeed 'realised their potential' in the most demanding manual activities. Another young girl at the time, Xiong Li, provides the clearest evidence of this: 'I left Beijing for Beidafang in 1968 after I graduated from middle school. I did all kinds of work, including farming, lumbering, making charcoal, digging a well, [and] building houses.'[80]

While educated city girls 'developed their capacities' in the countryside, they brought to the countryside modern ideas from the city. As a result, they were often regarded as role models for rural women in demeanour and in dress. These educated young women thus played a positive role in changing, modernising and radicalising rural women's attitudes and behaviour.

Nevertheless, the filth, poverty, hardship and backwardness of the countryside made it difficult, if not impossible, for the city-educated young to be assimilated fully into the peasants' community.[81] Furthermore, the hard, boring and colourless rural life was even more strictly controlled than urban life by the state.[82] In these circumstances, the majority of the educated young wanted to return to the cities as early as possible. However, there were very few roads open to the cities. In 1970 a new route was opened – higher educational institutions resumed enrolment. Only a handful of the educated young could obtain access to universities, and those with sporting talent had a second chance: they could be recommended for the colleges of physical education.

Also in 1970, elite sports teams began to be reinstated and reconstructed, and the recruitment of elite athletes recommenced, creating another route to the cities. Those educated young with exceptional sporting ability were now admitted to provincial sports teams. As one girl at the time stated in later life:

> After I graduated from primary school in 1966 I stayed at home for three years. Then I went into the countryside in 1969. One year later I was recruited into a provincial table tennis team because I had been a student in a sports spare-time school prior to the Cultural Revolution. However, only a few like me could enter sports teams from the countryside.[83]

While the sports team was used as a springboard for the educated young to 'leap' back to the cities, it also provided a safe haven in the cities for many young people who otherwise would have been sent to the countryside. The Asian women's javelin record holder in 1980, Tang Guoli, has recently remarked of the time:

> At the time we had nothing to do. I considered the training in spare-time sports school play, and I did not expect success in sport. My parents encouraged me to engage in sport to avoid being an 'educated youth' in the countryside, which was the destination of my elder brother and some of my classmates.[84]

This magnetic attraction of sports teams was further reinforced by the limited job opportunities available in society in the 1970s and the real benefits of sports team membership, which included a secure salary, a full stomach and free clothing, and, even more importantly, a post-sport job in the city. All this did not, and could not, escape the notice of parents from various backgrounds. They encouraged their children to take up sport. The first players of the world-famous Chinese women's volleyball team and the skater Ye Qiaobo, who will be discussed in Chapter 7, belonged to this generation. Jin Dongxian, a female shooting world record holder in the late 1970s, has claimed: 'The first group of shooters in the 1970s was different from today's. They had outstanding psychological and intellectual qualities.'[85] In some respects, then, despite general negative repercussions, the 'Rustication Campaign' was in fact good for elite women's sport.

The Rustication Campaign had another indirect but profound influence on elite sport. Heavy labour, as mentioned already, made the 'educated youths' strong and poor facilities made them self-reliant. They often demonstrated unbelievable endurance and single-minded determination. They took these qualities into sport. Not only this, but those coaches who had been 'educated youths' later worked extraordinarily hard. They often tried hard to compensate for their lost time and to fulfil their unrealised dreams through their athletes.

Many of the rusticated young, who had lost their youth pointlessly, deprived of educational opportunities and professional training, became sceptical about the future and their leaders. As Franz Michael commented in 1990: 'For many of this generation, neither the ethical concepts of the past nor the new attempts by the party to teach "scientific socialism" could fill the void of the loss of their faith.'[86] They came to believe only in their children and their children's futures. Thus, in compensation for their loss of educational opportunities, the generation of the Cultural Revolution paid special attention to their children's education. Pan Yongzhi, mentioned earlier, who in reality spoke for many, once declared: 'As my academic study was affected severely by the Cultural Revolution, now I pay great attention to my son's study. It is a top priority. Nothing will interfere with it.'[87]

In spite of the reopening of higher education institutions in the early 1970s, the majority of teachers continued to be maligned as 'bourgeois' intellectuals and subjected to ruthless persecution and onslaught. In July, 1973 *Liaoning Ribao* [Liaoning Daily] published the 'educated youth' Zhang Diesheng's now famous letter, which was written on the back of a test paper for the college entrance examination. In the letter Chang wrote:

> I have loved my work in agricultural production, and have been devoted to it ever since I came to countryside in 1968. The 18 hours' heavy work each day make it impossible for me to study. … Although I do not write anything on the paper as required here, I do not feel disgraced. I could have got some marks if I opened books, but that would make me unhappy. I feel fortunate that I have had the experience of the new educational system, recommended by peasants and cadres.

Although he obtained nil in physics and chemistry, he was praised. He defined the acceptable orthodoxy in the important struggle between two 'lines' and two 'thoughts' – one radical and one moderate.[88] Education thus became a battleground in the struggle for power. Zhang was regarded as a hero with a 'nil' score. Pointedly, he was admitted to college and even became one of the college leaders. Zhang's action conveyed the message that 'knowledge is useless'. Zhang's elevation to hero status did not encourage teachers and students to pursue academic success. Consequently, teaching became mediocre, standards deteriorated and confrontation between teachers and students surfaced occasionally. Another student, this time a 12-year-old girl Huang Shuang, a primary school pupil in Beijing, also acquired heroic status and became 'a little model heroine of rebellion' for criticising her teachers in a diary that was published and circulated throughout China.[89]

While academic study was discouraged, students had plenty of time and energy to play. Parents of various backgrounds, including intellectuals who were traditionally against sport, encouraged their children to take part in organised sporting activities either to keep fit or use up their energy to avoid becoming troublemakers. This favourable attitude to sport was to some extent bolstered by the continuing emphasis on class struggle in society. Huang Yalin, a young female teacher at the BUPE, vividly described this link through her own experience:

> During the Cultural Revolution we were always in a state of upset and fear. My parents were labelled 'black five elements' because my grandfather was a big landlord in the Old China. I remember that my doctor parents swept floors all day at the hospital instead of seeing patients. They were frequently attacked in denunciation meetings. Due to my family origin, I was also accused and humiliated by other children. This experience had a long-term impact on my mentality. Even today I still shiver whenever I recall it. As a child of 'black five elements', I had no control over my future. I had to learn a speciality. When Huang Shuang was set up as a 'little model heroine of rebellion', academic study was discouraged, but sport was popular. Thus, I chose to engage in sport although I was not an athlete by nature.[90]

Clearly, the discouragement of academic performance and the discrediting of 'black five elements' during the Cultural Revolution made sport more than acceptable to young people and their parents, including intellectuals – an unusual phenomenon in Chinese history. The result was that sports schools prospered. There were 121,732 students in 1972, and by 1976 the figure soared to 305,516.[91]

In short, while the Rustication Campaign and the antagonism towards academic studies caused undeniable negative consequences in social, economic and cultural matters, they had unanticipated constructive impacts on sporting involvement and commitment. This should not be overlooked.

Revival of Elite Sport and a 'Sports Revolution'

The convening of the Ninth Party Congress[92] in April 1969 marked the end of the most destructive phase of the Cultural Revolution. The Party and government administration began to slowly rebuild the foundations of society. After the Party deputy chairman and defence minister Lin Biao allegedly died in a plane crash in Mongolia in 1971, many officials criticised and dismissed between 1966 and 1969 were reinstated.[93] Consequently, in the early 1970s the economic situation improved remarkably and sporting investment increased steadily (see Figure 7).[94] The increased investment resulted in the expansion of sports teams: by 1972 there were 9,046 elite athletes.[95]

With the recovery of domestic stability, attention turned to re-entry into the international arena. Between 1969 and 1971 China adjusted its foreign policies.[96] Diplomats who had been recalled to China during the Cultural Revolution returned to their posts.[97] To find a way out of its diplomatic isolation, China chose to reach a rapprochement with the United States. After four years of absence from international sports circles, the Chinese table tennis team reappeared in the 30th world championships in Tokyo in 1970. Although the Chinese did not win any title – a direct consequence of the destructive Cultural Revolution – they played a crucial part in restoring Chinese diplomatic relations with the United States and other western nations.[98] After the championships, the American table tennis team visited Beijing on their way home. This visit proved to be a catalyst for the announcement by the US President, Richard Nixon, of 'five new measures to relax the tension between America and China'. After Dr Kissinger's clandestine visit to China in 1971, President Nixon made his first visit to China the following year. The improved bilateral relationship between the two superpowers precipitated the expulsion of Taiwan from the United Nations and the admission of the PRC in October 1971. This episode was internationally known as 'ping-pong diplomacy', and to some extent it created a new con-

FIGURE 7

SPORTS INVESTMENT DURING THE CULTURAL REVOLUTION

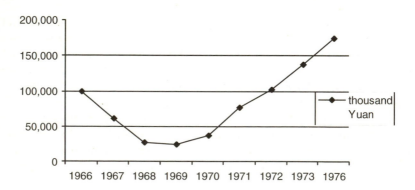

stellation in world politics. Undeniably, sport had functioned as a vehicle for improving international relations. To serve national diplomacy, international sports contacts were extended beyond communist and third-world nations.[99] In one year alone, 1970, Chinese athletes visited Switzerland, Denmark and Yugoslavia as well as communist nations. Then, following in America's footsteps, a number of sports teams from democratic nations such as Canada, Britain, Australia and Japan came to China to play table tennis in 1971.[100]

After 1972, China dominated world table tennis. International success inspired the nation's enthusiasm for the sport. The game of the 'small white ball' was played by all, from girls and boys in school to high-level officials including Chairman Mao and Premier Chou. The three-time world champion Zhuang Zedong became a national hero and was given enormous political honours: head of the National Sports Commission and member of the Central Committee of Communist Party of China. Unfortunately, in this period of Chinese history, 'sport … often suffered when brought into the political arena, was abused and then left to lick its wounds'.[101] Zhuang was later denounced and reduced to an ordinary sports worker in Shanxi province following the overthrow of the 'Gang of the Four' (*siren bang*)[102] in 1976.

When China gradually renewed its contacts with foreign nations in the early 1970s, the slogan 'friendship first, competition second'[103] was loudly voiced in China. This has led some foreign observers such as John Hoberman to claim that Chinese sport in Mao's era specialised in an inflexible etiquette based on the eradication of hostile or aggressive feelings toward an opponent, and that it placed much less value on competitive struggle than its western or Soviet bloc counterparts.[104] It certainly looked as if this was the case. Yet at the time in China there was occasionally a huge gap between official rhetoric and practical behaviour. For political reasons the Chinese sometimes deliberately lost to friendly 'socialist countries'. Yet in practice, the Chinese attached great significance to winning selective international competitions. The slogan 'winning glories for the motherland' was seen in every training hall and stimulated athletes to achieve good results in designated competitions. To raise standards, a national training and competition camp was organised for athletes, divers, water polo players and gymnasts in 1971, and at the same time various competitions were launched throughout the country. In 1972 alone there were 17 national and 256 provincial or municipal competitions for all sports. Consequently, sports performances, women's in particular, improved quickly. In 1971 the Chinese won the men's single and team titles and women's single and mixed pair gold medals in the world table tennis championships. In the same year women established ten out of 14 new national records. Women continued to make impressive progress in the following years.[105] In short, the Chinese made a desperate effort to improve their sporting performance. To win international competitions was their ambition. The slogan 'friendship first' was, on occasion, a misleading assertion – a naked political tool and the rhetorical product of a short-lived political era.

How could the Chinese sometimes advocate 'friendship first' while on other occasions seek strenuously to defeat their opponents? To understand this paradox, one must understand the complications of the period. In the era of 'politics in command', athletes had to act according to the instructions of the 'organisation' (the Party). To serve political ends, Chinese athletes were sometimes required to conceal any open competitive intent. However, the competitive compulsion was hard to eliminate. On these occasions, when it was demanded, the Chinese temporarily conceded their individual ambition to the collective or the national interest. This quality of self-sacrifice was arguably rooted in Chinese cultural tradition:

> The Chinese sense of identity comes from the notion of a great self, or *da-wuo* (nation), and from the necessity of sacrificing the smaller self to fulfil the greater self. … The glorification of sacrifice became an acknowledgement that individuals deserved to be rewarded for the sacrifices they have to make for their group.[106]

This concession was facilitated by authority. Sacrifice and reward were the siblings of Chinese sports management. The table tennis players who, when required, conceded and lost the chance of becoming world champions, were highly praised and promoted to important positions. For example, one of them, Li Furong,[107] later became the deputy director of the National Sports Commission.

There is another point to make here. Sporting competitions were closely tied to the desire for compensatory prestige. Friendship could bring goodwill for the nation, but failure would cause the individual Chinese to lose face.[108] Thus, in case of defeat not a few athletes often acted in the spirit of 'friendship'. They kept smiling whatever the result. In this way, they could claim a superiority of sorts. This trait of separating emotion from action on occasion confused some foreigners. Some even thought they were despised by the Chinese and, although victorious, felt humiliated.[109] In fact, individual Chinese, up to a point, saved face in defeat.

As mentioned earlier, sports teams were greatly reduced during the chaotic years of the Cultural Revolution. This resulted in a shortage of young talented athletes. In response, a sport-specific middle school 'training brigade for young athletes' (*Qing xun dui*) was founded in 1971 in the BIPE. Some 398 student athletes, including 173 females, were recruited from 28 Chinese provinces and municipalities.[110] After graduation, these students were sent to provincial and army sports teams throughout the country. Some later became popular sports stars, such as Cao Huiying, Yang Xi and Chen Zhaodi, members of the world champion Chinese women's volleyball team in the early 1980s. In addition, the BIPE established an archery team in 1972, and produced several female world record archers in the late 1970s, including Song Shuxian, Huang Shuyan and Meng Fanai. Apart from cultivating elite athletes, the BIPE returned to the task of training coaches, administrators and physical educationists for the whole of the country. It re-enrolled students in 1972. In the following years some 2,272 'workers, peasants and soldiers' (WPS) students[111] were admitted to the institute. To fill the talent vacuum caused by the traumatic political movement in the late 1960s, young and promising athletes had to be nurtured rapidly. To this end, many provinces began to establish junior sports teams. These young athletes shouldered a historic mission – to project the Chinese image in the world. To narrow the now enlarged gap between China and the advanced sporting powers, intensive training of the type that was once popular during the Great Leap Forward in the late 1950s was again favoured. The Hunan provincial women's gymnastic team set an example. Between 1971 and 1973 the team underwent training for 335 days each year (2,680 training hours). The maximum training hours for a week reached 62.[112] Hard work produced mixed results. The team won the national championships in 1972 and then dominated the country for decades. The gymnasts, however, suffered massive sports injuries – an inevitable result of overemphasis on intensive training. The Hunan women's gymnastics team was merely the prominent tip of the iceberg: the echoes of the GLF, analysed in the last chapter, reverberated through the 1960s and 1970s. Indeed, vestiges of the GLF mentality persisted even after the 1970s in China's sporting communities.

Elite sport was now back on the agenda. China's place in the Asian Sports Federation was restored in September 1973. The next year the New China, for the first time, sent 269 athletes to the seventh Asian Games in India and came second in the total points table.[113] The games provided a stage for the Chinese to show both their potential and their progress in sport.

In spite of obvious progress in the early 1970s, China still lagged far behind the advanced powers in most sports, and had not returned to pre-1966 performances in a number of events. For example, 45 Chinese athletes took part in 35 track and field events at the 1974 Asian Games, but won only five gold medals. At the 1975 National Games, the performances in 23 of the 35 events were poorer than a decade earlier.[114] Chinese women's and men's volleyball teams ranked just 14th and 15th respectively at the 1974 world championships. In 1962 both men and women were ninth.[115] Needless to say, the deterioration in performance was a direct consequence of the Cultural Revolution. It had interrupted the systematic training of sports teams for half a decade. This was the downside of sport during the Cultural Revolution.

Nevertheless, the third National Games in 1975 – ten years after the previous games – generated momentum for elite sport. Despite the introduction of an age limit and limitations placed on the numbers in each delegation, the total number of participants reached over 10,000. Numerous new sports stars emerged in the games, including the 13-year-old female gymnast Liu Yaojun, who won the all-around title, the 15-year-old athlete Lin Zhenglan, who won the 1500m track event, and a number of young volleyball players, who had excellent physiques and the physical ability to match any contemporary international stars. In addition, female shooters smashed three and equalled two world records, and 16 junior male and female swimmers broke national swimming records. These young talents became internationally prominent by the end of the 1970s and throughout the early 1980s. Chinese sporting victories in the early years of the reform era were in part attributed, with good reason, to the stimulus given to sport in the second half of the Cultural Revolution. Chinese elite sport, women's sport in particular, did not, as is widely believed, wholly regress or stand still throughout the whole decade of the Cultural Revolution.[116] It went both backwards and forwards. It pushed back some mature athletes but it gave a push forward to some immature athletes.

However, influenced by leftist ideology, an uncongenial political atmosphere was still pervasive in elite sports circles in the mid-1970s.[117] Sport was required to serve workers, peasants and soldiers (WPS).[118] At the 1975 National Games a review group of WPS was set up to evaluate athletes, coaches and referees in terms of their behaviour, skills and political consciousness. This practice was regarded as a new-born 'baby' of the Cultural Revolution. Thus, the third National Games were imbued with unhelpful political implications. It was no wonder that performances failed to match those of the pre-Cultural Revolution years.

Nor did it end there. In 1976, following the re-emergence of the ideological struggle between the more pragmatic veteran party officials and the ultra-left radicals represented by the 'Gang of the Four' (*siren bang*), another political campaign 'counterattacking the rightist reversing of a verdict' was launched.[119] In tune with this general political climate, Zhuang Zedong, the former world table tennis champion and now director of the National Sports Commission, introduced a 'sports revolution' (*tiyu geming*) aimed at the rejection of 'medals and trophyism' and individualism in sport. The sports revolution was first introduced in the National Gymnastic Competition for 12 Provinces in 1976. First, the term 'competition' was completely forbidden, replaced by 'review and show for workers, peasants and soldiers'.[120] Second, in the 'show' a reviewing group of WPS and a discussion group (the actual judges) were installed to evaluate gymnasts collectively. Once all gymnasts ended their performances, the WPS group and the discussion group met all the teams, discussing athletic styles and techniques, but also political attitudes. Model athletes and teams, who scored highly in all three categories, were praised. This innovation – unseen hitherto in the history of China and other parts of the world – was obviously detrimental to high performance. Sport was utilised forcefully to serve political ends. Fortunately, this leftist stupidity was prematurely aborted following the death of Mao and the overthrow of the Gang of Four in September 1976. Happily the month-long 'sports revolution' had little, if any, influence on Chinese sport.

The Cultural Revolution came to an end in 1976, but its legacy remains. As Liang Heng has stated:

> In China the clouds of the past would not dissipate, not for the next 50 years at least, for too many of us had been shaped during the terrible era, and our relationships with each other and our attitudes to the world around us had been affected too deeply.[121]

Having lived through the nightmare of the Cultural Revolution, 'people had become wiser and more cynical than before. They had witnessed the utter futility and irrationality of political struggle and the unpredictability of one's fortune as political winds shifted direction.'[122] The experience of the Cultural Revolution instilled in many Chinese men and women a greater readiness to challenge authority and scepticism about the promises and motives of political leaders. Many regretted the murders they had committed as they blindly carried out Mao's political witch-hunts. They were weary of his promises of a worker's utopia, exhausted by vicious political campaigns and disillusioned by years of sacrifice for the collective.[123] Free of the chaos and disasters of the decade-long political movement, the Chinese moved quickly to achieve modernisation. Thus, ironically, 'without the Cultural Revolution, Chinese economic reform would not have come so early'.[124]

Analysis: Illustrative Case Studies

To further chart the ebb and flow of the politics of the Cultural Revolution and their influence on Chinese women and their sport, it is helpful to present once again three case studies (Beijing, Guangdong and Sichuan) in terms of

- The Red Guard movement in the first half of the Cultural Revolution;
- The influences of the Cultural Revolution on sports development;
- The reorganisation of the sports system in the second half of the Cultural Revolution;
- Women's elite sport in the Cultural Revolution.

Beijing

From 1 April to 20 May 1966, less than a month before the inauguration of the Cultural Revolution, a comprehensive coaching course for coaches of spare-time sports schools was organised in Beijing. Over 800 coaches covering eight sports, including athletics, swimming, gymnastics, basketball, volleyball, football, table tennis and weightlifting, attended it.[125] This fact suggests that the sports community in Beijing was not in the forefront of the Cultural Revolution. However, the Beijing Municipal Sports Commission was soon put under the supervision of the Cultural Revolution military representatives. By August, the 'rebellion sector'(*zhao fan pai*)[126] started to attack Party organisations, authoritarian and professional elitists in every unit. In the words of an activist,

Although only a few were rebels in our Party branch (the majority were conservatives or loyalists, with a very few in between), public accusations and humiliations were prevalent. The denounced were disgraced by 'sitting in a jet' (being forced to adopt a position with their arms held behind them and their bodies tilted forward, like a jet). Endless street marches and denunciation meetings took place day and night between 1965 and 1970.[127]

In spite of the escalating political climate, the Asian table tennis tournament took place on schedule in Beijing between the end of August and early September 1966. However, this was the last international activity before chaos raged across the country. Sporting organisations were immobilised for several years. A number of sports officials, coaches and athletes were discredited, tortured and purged for various alleged reasons, including being 'capitalist roaders' (*zhou zhi pai*), spies and much else. At the end of 1967 two deputy directors and three other branch directors of the Beijing Municipal Sports Commission were arrested and put in jail for eight years.[128] A number of players were dispatched to factories or sent back to their home towns. Most athletes quickly married. In consequence, between 1965 and 1970 the number of athletes decreased from 586 to 109 and the number of coaches from 331 to 52.[129] Clearly, the Cultural Revolution had a detrimental effect on elite sport in the capital city.

After Mao instructed in 1966 that 'education must serve proletarian politics and be combined with productive labour', physical labour was emphasised not just for students but also for cadres. 'May Seventh cadre schools' (*wu qi gangxiao*)[130] were thus initiated in rural areas across the country in 1968. By 1970 about 400 Beijing coaches and athletes had been sent there and to factories. There they partly engaged in physical labour and partly studied the new ideology of the Cultural Revolution to re-educate themselves.

It was not until 1971 that most sports teams returned to normal training.[131] The number of elite athletes in Beijing increased from 370 in 1972 to 474 in 1973 and then to 505 in 1975. This approached the pre-CR level. These athletes, trained by 118 full-time coaches, specialised in football, basketball, volleyball, table tennis, tennis, athletics, gymnastics, swimming, diving, cycling and weightlifting. Following the resumption of sports teams, spare-time sports schools were gradually restored and expanded. In 1973 there were five sports schools with 4,000 students in the city.[132] A year later the schools leapt in number to 21 with 5,900 students. These schools, which employed some 302 full-time and 78 part-time coaches,[133] became a major source of elite athletes in Beijing. In addition to the sports schools, specialised sports classes in normal primary and middle schools were another source of future champions. There were 21 specialised sports classes in 16 schools across Beijing. These normal schools, sport schools and 'specialised' sports teams formed a matrix of talent cultivation.

In the first half of the 1970s, Beijing hosted a number of international and national competitions, including the Asia-Africa-Latin-America table tennis tournament in 1971, the first Asian table tennis championships in 1972 and the third National Games in 1975. For the National Games the capital provided over 630 athletes, including some student athletes, and came second in the medal count.

In summary, in Beijing during the Cultural Revolution numerous people were victimised and sports talents were aborted. However, with the end of the most vicious power struggles in 1969, in the early 1970s elite athletes began to return to regular training and competitions. By the mid-1970s Beijing elite sport had made a quite spectacular recovery, culminating in the third National Games.

Guangdong

Following Beijing's example, Red Guard attacks on the 'Four Old Things' (*si jiu*) and 'revolutionary marches' (*Gemin da chuanlian*) all typified Guangdong in the early months of the Cultural Revolution.[134] However, an international trade fair continued to take place in Guangzhou. This acted to some degree as a brake on chaos.[135] Nevertheless, the Provincial Sports Commission suffered immediate setbacks, and administrative organisation broke down and ceased to function normally. In May 1968 the Guangdong Sports Commission was taken over by an army group from the provincial military area and renamed the Guangdong Sports Bureau. Three months later this was replaced by the Revolutionary Committee of the Guangdong Provincial Sports Commission. It remained in existence until June 1978, when the Guangdong Provincial Sports Commission was reinstated.[136]

As in Beijing, many elite athletes, coaches and officials were under political surveillance during the Cultural Revolution, and a good number of them were sent to May Seventh cadre schools (*wu qi gang xiao*) or assigned to factories. Meanwhile, some 70 per cent of sports teams stopped normal training. The provincial Wushu (martial arts), weightlifting and tennis teams were disbanded[137] because they were considered either despicable feudal remnants or harmful bourgeois sports. Consequently, by the end of the 1960s, the number of athletes and coaches had sharply declined. In 1965 there were 651 elite athletes. Five years later, there were only 158. Similarly, the number of coaches decreased from 90 in 1965 to 30 in 1970.[138] During the furious years of the Cultural Revolution sports schools were also closed and sports fields and equipment were ruined.[139] As a consequence, by 1972 the number of sports fields and stadiums in Guangdong province had fallen below that of the national average and Guangdong now ranked eighth and 15th respectively among the 30 provinces and municipalities of the nation (except Taiwan).[140] It goes without saying that the destructive Cultural Revolution had baleful reverberations for Guangdong's sport.

In 1971, after the death of Lin Biao, Mao's designated successor, economic and political reconstruction accelerated. The next year 16 provincial sports teams resumed normal daily training in Guangdong. By 1975 Guangdong, with its 552 elite athletes supervised by 115 coaches, again exerted its strong influence in sport. It provided 32 athletes to the 1974 Asian Games. The next year it sent 447 athletes (fewer than Beijing) to the third National Games, in which it ranked first in the medal count.[141] Guangdong was once again one of the top provinces in elite sport.

In summary, Guangdong's elite sport was damaged by the Cultural Revolution, as revealed in the disintegration of its sports governing body, its ruined sports facilities, and the greatly reduced numbers of its coaches and athletes. Nevertheless, after sports training was normalised in 1972, Guangdong once again became the backbone of China's elite sport. Once again, it is clear from the regional case study that sport was not hindered for the whole of the Cultural Revolution.

Sichuan

As in Beijing and Guangdong, virtually all sports teams in Sichuan abandoned normal training following the eruption of the Cultural Revolution. Athletes joined the Red Guard movement, about which Zhang Manlei, a gymnastic coach at the time, has stated: 'We marched on foot to Guizhou and Yunan provinces. It was hard, but full of fun.'[142] During the first years, wall-posters criticising the 'bourgeois roaders' (*zou zi pai*) were everywhere. Large-scale violence was rampant,[143] and consequently a number of sports officials, coaches and athletes suffered inhuman treatment. One of them was the female coach of the Sichuan women's volleyball team, Wang Defen (quoted above). She was jailed for six years both because of her family origins[144] and because of her celebrity status before the Cultural Revolution.

Sichuan's economy was badly affected by the political turbulence in 1967 and 1968.[145] This directly impinged on sporting development. For example, Sichuan's sports expenditure decreased from 4.4 million yuan in 1965 to 2.17 million yuan in 1970. During this time, the total number of athletes in the province rose by only 11, from 424 in 1965 to 435 in 1970.[146] However, due to the 'third front' (*sanxian*)[147] defence project initiated in the mid-1960s, Sichuan received huge sums from central government. This might be one of reasons that Sichuan sports teams recommenced their normal training in 1970, earlier than in Beijing and Guangdong. The numbers of both coaches and athletes in the province quickly climbed close to the 1965 level.[148] Coaches were gradually summoned back from the May Seventh cadre schools and factories. New athletes were recruited. The volleyball player Zhang Rongfang, the key member of the Chinese women's volleyball team between 1976 and 1986, for example, was admitted to the provincial youth team in 1970 and two years later to the adult provincial team. Swimming, diving and table tennis teams, which had been the responsibility of Chongqing City's Sports Commission, returned to the care of the Provincial Sports Commission in Chengdu. Thus, elite sports management became more centralised. In 1975 Sichuan sent 383 athletes to the third National Games, in which it ranked 17th out of the 31 provincial, municipal and military delegations in the medal count. Although Sichuan never became a leading province in sport, its women's volleyball team won the National Games in 1975 and subsequently dominated the country for over a decade.

Beijing, Guangdong and Sichuan show quite clearly that numerous coaches and athletes were entangled in the political movement raised in support of Mao and his fresh revolutionary ambitions. In consequence, elite sport suffered badly. Normal sporting competition and training were disrupted for several years. Sports experts were purged, persecuted and even tortured and killed. Sports talents were pitifully wasted. Nevertheless, early in 1970 normality was restored up to a point. Pre-CR policies and practices were partially revived. Sports teams and schools were reconstructed and athletes re-emerged in national and international competitions.

It should be noted, however, that between 1965 and 1970 in all three places – Beijing, Guangdong and Sichuan – the absolute number of athletes in total declined, but the percentages of women athletes all increased (see Figure 8). Possible explanations are that more men left sports teams for the Red Guard movement in the late 1960s or/and more women were recruited into sports teams in 1970. Whatever the reasons, women's sport seemed to be in a better situation than men's in the early 1970s, which arguably laid down a basis for their international success in the 1980s.

Conclusion

The Cultural Revolution brought China to the brink of political, economic and social eclipse. The sky was truly dark. Elite sport suffered harshly

FIGURE 8

CHANGES IN THE PERCENTAGE OF FEMALE ATHLETES, 1965–70

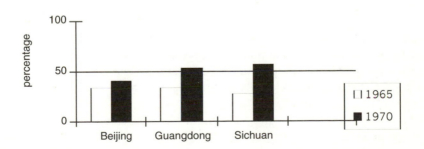

between 1966 and 1969. Numerous elite athletes, coaches and administrators were purged, persecuted and tortured. Sports training was disrupted and sports schools were shut down. International sporting contacts virtually ended and sports facilities were widely ruined. However, elite sport did not remain in this state for the whole decade of the Cultural Revolution. Sports teams at provincial level began to recruit once again in the early 1970s, when the Rustication Campaign was under way and academic study was discouraged in society. They provided a haven for many young people who otherwise would have been sent to the countryside. In this, for them, relatively advantageous setting, the steady progress of young female athletes in the 1970s laid down a foundation for their later rapid breakthrough in international contests.

Sport is frequently used as a political instrument. The China of the 1970s illustrates this fact well. The 'ping-pong diplomacy' of 1970 helped restore Chinese diplomatic relations and sporting exchanges with United States, Japan and other nations. The policy of 'friendship first, competition second' became politically desirable. Nevertheless, there was a discrepancy between the rhetoric and practice in China during the Cultural Revolution. The impulse to win sporting victories never wholly vanished from Chinese minds. It was just hidden under the loud rhetoric of 'friendship first'. For a brief moment, in addition, sport was regarded as a crucial means of reinforcing a particular nonsensical ambition, political 'people power', as manifested in the short-lived 'sports revolution' of 1976. In short, sport was tightly enmeshed with politics during the Cultural Revolution, which in general had an adverse influence on the development of competitive sport.

The Cultural Revolution greatly influenced the lives of the Chinese people, especially young women. They were part and parcel of the Red Guard movement, the Rustication Campaign, and the anti-Lin and anti-Confucius Campaign. Rebellious impulses that had been deeply buried beneath historic obedience surfaced during the turbulent decade. Their rebellion was aroused directly and calculatedly by Mao, whose personality cult reached a pinnacle during the Cultural Revolution. Following Mao's assertion that 'women and men are equal', women were required to behave like men in manner and even in dress. The 'model operas', though primarily used to serve political purposes, had a considerable impact on the women of the Cultural Revolution generation. They began to question the concepts of the traditional family and historic femininity. This, in turn, affected the attitudes to, and involvement of, women in sport – in athletic participation, coaching commitment and administrative management – with the striking result of an increased proportion of successful female athletes and coaches. This striking result in the 1980s will be analysed next.

Women, Society and Elite Sport in the First Decade of Economic Reform (1977–89)

Mao's death in September 1976 marked the end of an era. China began to bring order out of chaos.[1] Fundamental changes, however, did not occur until the pivotal third plenum of the eleventh Central Committee of the Chinese Communist Party on 22 December 1978.[2] Thereafter, the Party broke away from the long and crushing bondage of 'leftist' practice and embraced pragmatic economic and social reforms.[3] At this momentous turning point in modern Chinese history, Chinese athletes took part in the eighth Asian Games in Bangkok and won 12 gold, 12 silver and 13 bronze medals. Sport became an immediate window to the world, through which China's changing image was reflected.

The year 1979 was another turning point both in economic reform and elite sport in China. The inauguration of 'economic reform and opening up to the outside' (*jingji gaige yu duiwai kaifang*) led to impressive economic progress. Increasingly, from this moment, China grew much wealthier, while the Chinese seat on the International Olympic Committee was reoccupied.[4] Chinese athletes, women in particular, became involved continually and comprehensively in international competitions, achieving astonishing results.[5] In all these things the decade 1979–89 contrasted sharply with the previous years dominated by Mao Zedong. Hand in hand with Chinese economic and social changes, elite sport underwent dramatic changes in ideology, administration and training as well as performance. These changes led to, and interacted with, shifts in cultural attitudes, including attitudes to women and to elite women's sport. These cultural transformations were both influenced by, and contributed to, economic and social advances.

With the increasing visibility of Chinese women in world sport, some have pondered on the reasons for their success.[6] Nevertheless, no comprehensive study has examined women and elite sport within the changed and changing socio-political, cultural and economic contexts of the reform era. To understand why Chinese women suddenly gained celebrity status in world sport in the 1980s and what impact socio-economic reform had on both elite women's sport and sportswomen, it is necessary to analyse the relationship between economic and political transformations, cultural changes and sports developments in the surge of system-wide structural reform.

Analysis: Overview

Reform, Pluralism and Elite Sport

Economic reform was unleashed in China in the late 1970s. Based on the concept of 'household responsibility' *(jiating chenbao zhi)*[7] initiated in the countryside, private and corporate businesses were introduced in the early 1980s. The rapid growth of non-state enterprises resulted.[8] These reforms brought about a remarkable improvement in the Chinese economy. According to official figures, its gross national income rose from 358.8 billion yuan in 1978 to 696.2 billion yuan in 1984, a 94 per cent increase.[9] As a result, people's living standards improved markedly.[10]

A prosperous economy paved the way for the rapid development of elite sport. Government sports funding soared from 253.86 million in 1978 to 598.671 million yuan in 1984, a rise of 135.8 per cent. By 1990, it reached 1,462.762 million yuan, a 149.35 per cent increase.[11] The augmented investment resulted in the expansion of sports facilities. By 1988 China had 528,112 sports fields and gymnasiums, of which 40.9 per cent (215,997.8) were built within the decade 1979–88.[12] These improved sports facilities provided the basis for the steady Chinese advance on the world sporting scene.

With economic progress went changes in the political climate. In 1981 the Cultural Revolution was officially rejected. Innovatory socialist principles were no longer regarded as dogmas that would provide specific and infallible solutions to immediate political problems. Now political stability and economic development were stressed: 'Pragmatic adoption of a policy to solve pressing concrete problems replaced utopian efforts to transform society in the name of egalitarian goals.'[13] Consequently, the space available for private life was expanded, and at the same time, intellectuals and professionals were allowed greater autonomy. Harry Harding succinctly and astutely describes these changes as follows:

> The Party no longer interferes in the details of the daily lives of most citizens. A system of law, which guarantees the Chinese people certain substantive and procedural rights, increasingly constrains the exercise of political power. Greater opportunities have been opened for Chinese outside government, particularly intellectuals, to express their views on national policy. Discussion of political issues, both in private and in public, is more lively, frank, and detailed. And the tone of political discourse is less charismatic, more secular, less ideological, and more rational. On balance, the political system is more open and relaxed than at any time since 1949.[14]

Competitive sport was an integral part of this changing society. From early 1979 there was a shift from the use of sport to illustrate ideological principles to the presentation of sport as political performance. Mao's policy of 'friendship first, competition second' was abandoned. Competitive sport was now high on the national agenda. In 1979 the National Sports Committee sponsored 96 national competitions, in which 41,367 athletes participated.[15] At the same time the system of ranking athletes, coaches and referees, which had been disrupted during the Cultural Revolution, was reintroduced. This helped regularise training activities and motivate athletes and coaches to improve their skills. From 1980 the National Sports Commission organised experts from 22 different sports research institutes and departments across the country to carry out 27 research projects on talent identification for over ten sports. In addition, 162 experts spent almost six years in formulating junior training programmes for nine sports, including athletics, swimming, gymnastics, weightlifting and some ball games.[16] All these projects were manifestations of the Chinese endeavour to achieve global sports supremacy.

In tune with economic reform, with its profit motive, rewards, victory and success became major aims in elite sports circles. From the early 1980s onwards material incentives, together with social prizes, were steadily used as important means to motivate athletes. The winner of one gold medal at the 1984 Olympic Games was given a 8,000-yuan winning bonus (average per-capita income that year was 372.7 yuan). By 1988 this bonus had risen to 18,000 yuan (with silver and bronze medallists receiving 5,000 and 3,000 respectively). Compared to the per-capita income of 881.8 yuan at the time, this was a huge sum of money.

Material rewards in sport sparked off controversy. Economic reform, of course, was carried out over a transitional period when many elements of the old system coexisted with the new. Thus, old ideas still prevailed in society in the early 1980s. The egalitarian system of 'eating from the same big pot' (*ci da guo fan*) continued to dominate Chinese thinking and behaviour. In the face of the prolonged curtailment of material incentives under past communism, the emphasis on elitism in sport through the use of financial rewards seriously challenged Maoist egalitarianism. Consequently, an intensive debate about the contrasting values of socialist (egalitarian) and bourgeois (competitive) sport arose. It was short-lived. Not long after, material rewards were widely accepted and regarded as an effective means to motivate athletes. The sports community now stood at the forefront of China's transformation to a more commercially competitive economy. Athletes played a leading part in promoting a change from a command economy to a market economy in the early stages of economic reform.

Despite scattered experiments, urban reform did not proceed energetically until October 1984, when the third plenum of the twelfth Central Committee was held.[17] Now price reform was introduced,[18] decentralisation was accelerated and guaranteed lifetime employment was abandoned, and the Party encouraged 'some areas and some people to get rich first'. Chinese society started to turn towards a more materialistic and pragmatic disposition. The tide of 'doing business' swept throughout the country. In 1986 there were 170,000 different kinds of business corporations and 'centres'. Two years later the figure had increased to over 400,000.[19] Regarding this situation, Connie Squires Meaney commented in 1991:

> Money – and the ability to manipulate it for profit – played a role not seen in four previous decades of communist rule. Money could now help an individual create a network of accomplices, instead of being merely a reflection of one's connections. Since one could now legitimately acquire wealth (and spend it as well), economic competition partially replaced political competition as a focus of upward mobility, and the stakes rose precipitously.[20]

In conjunction with these vigorous economic and general reforms, sport underwent extensive institutional change, namely a transformation from being an exclusively centrally sponsored and centrally controlled system to a multi-level, multi-channel system. In 1984, a western-modelled sports lottery was first piloted in the special economic zones (*jinji tequ*) (this will be discussed later) and the 14 coastal 'opening' cities. Given the fact that gambling had previously been illegal under 'old' communism, this was undoubtedly a bold action. This innovation, however, intensified the now pervasive mentality of 'getting rich quickly' (*jinkuai zhifu*) and threatened to seriously corrode the former social values and priorities of the Chinese people, especially the young.

Also in 1984 corporations and private individuals were invited to sponsor sports. By 1985 high-level sports teams run by enterprises were proclaimed in 26 provinces, autonomous regions and municipalities.[21] These teams were run either by the enterprises themselves or jointly by enterprises and sports commissions. In addition, in the late 1980s corporate and private sponsorship of sports clubs emerged and then expanded. This was considered a radical move away from the conventional centralised sports system. However, these reforms gave rise to some problems, including the absence of a legal basis for the new kind of relationship between enterprises and sports commissions, a reluctance on the part of sports teams to take responsibility for running their own enterprises, an increasing income gap between various sports teams and a low level of enterprise skill in running sports teams.[22]

In addition to corporations and private individuals, in 1986 universities were also encouraged to run elite sports teams. This innovation was pioneered by 55 universities and colleges. In spite of the laudable intention to sponsor super-athletes of super intelligence, the result was not fully satisfactory. Given that most sports students were retired athletes from local or national elite sports teams or those without potential for world performance, it was unlikely that they could reach world standards. Their intelligence too was frequently not in the first rank. This practice, however, helped promote sport in higher education institutions. With the involvement of various social sectors in elite sport, the state and provincial sports commissions now focused mostly on Olympic sports with multiple medal potential, such as athletics and swimming, and on sports at which the Chinese were already superior, for example, gymnastics, table tennis and diving. This emphasis will be further analysed in the course of this chapter.

After 1988 even more radical reforms were on the agenda. Twelve sports (20 per cent of the total) were chosen to experiment with the 'enterprisation' (*shiti hua*) of sporting associations – the transformation from government agencies to public organisations. It was intended that through 'enterprisation', the associations would become more self-reliant and help lift much of the financial and administrative burden from the central government, which could then focus its resources mostly on medal-oriented sports. Three different approaches were adopted in the process of 'exterprisation'. Football, tennis, chess, martial arts and boxing continued to receive the basic state budget, but now financed non-budget expenses themselves. Associations such as those for mountain climbing and motorcycling were to completely finance themselves without state investment, but to remain under the aegis of the National Sports Commission. Others, such as the triathlon, bridge and sports dance, became mass organisations and financially managed themselves.[23] This experimentation continued into the 1990s when institutional sporting reform took place on a wider scale: this will be described in the following chapter.

In the mid-1980s, employment policy regarding coaches and administrators was also transforming the sporting scene. Early in 1985, the National Sports Commission demanded that the authority for sports teams should gradually shift from team leaders to head coaches. The system of head coach responsibility, equivalent to 'managerial responsibility' in industry, was progressively embraced by sports teams.[24] By 1992, about 38 per cent of sports teams throughout the country had already adopted the system.[25]

As part and parcel of the sporting reforms, the system of competition underwent radical change. Corporations, local government and even private businessmen played an increasingly important part in sponsoring various kinds of competition. By the mid-1980s comprehensive national sporting events had became regularised: the National Games, the National Youth Games, the National City Games and the National Minority Games were now to take place every four years. Every sport also had at least a formal government-financed national competition annually, supplemented by other tournaments and enterprise-sponsored competitions.[26]

Nevertheless, there were zigzags, advances and retreats in the socioeconomic reforms. The urban reforms introduced in 1984 resulted in unprecedented inflation,[27] which was intensified by the problem of profiteering and the two-track price system.[28] Corruption, bribery and other economic crimes increased significantly.[29] Widespread urban opposition to the negative impacts of economic reform grew in the second half of the 1980s, and there was a resurgence of the demand for more democracy. These developments, to some extent, led to the Tiananmen Student Movement in

1989.[30] A temporary setback in the Chinese economy and other aspects including sport[31] followed. After the student movement, some western governments and international aid agencies imposed a series of economic sanctions. High-level official exchanges were suspended. Foreign companies and capital were largely withdrawn from China. Foreign investment stalled in late 1989. The loss of foreign investment in 1989 was estimated as worth between one and two billion US dollars while tourism revenue fell by one billion dollars.[32] The growth rate of the gross domestic product (GDP) declined from more than 10 per cent in the 1980s to 4 per cent in 1989–90.[33] Chinese economic reform slowed down. This sudden change in both international and domestic politics and the economy cast a dark shadow over Chinese sport, especially on the forthcoming Asia Games in 1990. This will be discussed in the next chapter.

'Opening up', Nationalism and Olympic Strategy

With the introduction of the open-door policy, China made a concerted effort to become integrated into the world economy. In 1980 four 'special economic zones' (*jinji tequ*)[34] were established in an attempt to attract foreign capital, investment, enterprise and technology. In 1984 another 14 coastal cities[35] were empowered to practise the same policies as the SEZs to attract overseas investment. The result was that China's trade and investment links with other countries rapidly expanded.[36] More than 10,000 foreign joint ventures were established between 1978 and 1987, involving contracts of about $30 billion. Foreign loan contracts amounted to around $40 billion.[37] Now western influence was visible everywhere – in international hotels, joint ventures and foreign-owned enterprises, and foreign products in television advertisements and on advertising billboards.

Benefiting from the open-door policy and renewal of Chinese membership of the IOC in late 1979, Chinese athletes set out to conquer the world – see Table 8. The 15-year-old female gymnast Ma Yanhong took the lead. She won a world title in the world gymnastic championships in December, 1979. Following her were numerous female world champions in fencing,

TABLE 8

NUMBER OF INTERNATIONAL COMPETITIONS IN WHICH CHINESE
ATHLETES PARTICIPATED, 1976–79

	countries	occasions	number
1976	86	231	3,715
1977	87	231	3,872
1978	92	342	5,644
1979	92	450	5,243

Source: *1979 nian zhongguo tiyu nianjie* [Sports Yearbooks in China in 1979], p.889.

judo, shooting, diving, table tennis and badminton.[38] These early victories greatly inspired the Chinese people. The slogan 'Go beyond Asia and join the advanced world ranks' (*zhouchu yazhou, chongxiang shijie*), put forward by the Chinese diving team in 1980, became their overt ambition. This year saw the Chinese re-enter the Olympic Games after an absence of over two decades. China planned, and indeed prepared, to take part in both winter and summer games. As the former athlete Li Xiaohui has stated:

> To prepare for the 1980 Olympic Games, the state for the first time sent our athletes and coaches abroad to train for three months. We were divided into three groups by sport. Our group, comprising coaches and athletes in discus, javelin, distance running and high-jump, plus two doctors, went to West Germany. The two other groups went to America and the Soviet Union respectively.[39]

In 1980, 26 Chinese men and women made their debut at the 13th Winter Olympics at Lake Placid. However, politics and sport remained closely intertwined. China joined the United States and other western nations in boycotting the Moscow Summer Games in response to the Soviet invasion of Afghanistan. Regrettably, this boycott brutally deprived a number of Chinese athletes of the lifetime chance to participate in the Olympics, and also delayed Chinese visibility in this biggest of international sports events for another four years.

Fortunately, other international competitions were open to the Chinese. In 1981 the Chinese women's volleyball team (CWVT) for the first time defeated Japan and won the World Cup. This was the start of its world dominance. Between 1981 and 1986, the team won five world titles in succession.[40] These victories gave the Chinese a chance to enjoy the experience of international success. A huge wave of patriotism resulted across the whole country. Wild celebrations took place. Thousands of articles, photographs and paintings as well as a television series were devoted to these young women. They became hugely popular and greatly admired and were regarded as heroines – models for all. The spirit of the CWVT (*nupai jinsheng*) became a political slogan spurring on millions of Chinese to strive for the 'four modernisations' – modern industry, modern agriculture, modern national defence, and modern science and technology. Chinese political and sports officials openly acknowledged that they viewed sport as an instrument for the promotion of national pride and identity. The projection of successful Chinese athletes, in particular women athletes, shows this statement to be wholly correct. Thus, the CWVT was a political tool.[41] Such sporting performances strengthened the cohesion of the Chinese nation, provided it with a new pride and demonstrated a new, confident face of China to the world.

In this heady climate, sport was often the handmaiden of crude chauvinism. This is vividly revealed by the words of the head coach Yuan

Weimin to his players on the crucial occasion of the last set of the 1981 volleyball world cup final against Japan.[42]

> Think of where you are playing – Japan, the home of Japanese invaders
> who killed hundreds of thousands of Chinese in the Second World War.
> You are representing the Chinese nation. People in the motherland need
> you to risk your life to fight and to win all the rounds. If you don't win
> this game, you will regret it all your life.[43]

These patriotic words aroused the female players to an all-out effort and ultimate victory. Obviously, this intense approach to the game against Japan had the deepest social and historic roots. The bitter history of invasion by Japan (and the western nations) in the century before 1949 bred anti-Japanese (and anti-western) sentiments. They were reinforced by films, television programmes, textbooks and much else. Although attitudes and government policy had gradually changed and the tilt towards these powers increased by the early 1980s, a basic attitude of distrust remained in most Chinese minds. When the commercial goods of the 'enemy' Japan filled every corner of the land in the early 1980s, many Chinese felt humiliated – it was 'losing face' (*diulian*). In addition, in the Maoist era the Chinese people were told, many believed it at the time, that they were living in a 'socialist heaven'. After the door was opened up to the outside at the end of the 1970s, most Chinese were astonished by the backwardness of their country and the severity of its problems. A crisis of belief in the Party and the nation resulted. As they struggled to regain their lost dignity, the Chinese people found little scope for hope. As a weapon to counteract public discontent, the government called upon the forces of nationalism, including those xenophobic tendencies that remained deeply embedded in the psyches of a considerable proportion of Chinese people. Sport gave them at least some measure of pride, dignity and confidence at a time of low national morale.

The 1984 Olympic Games formed a great divide in China's Olympic history. China, for the first time, sent a large delegation of 225 athletes to the games. The Chinese did not just break their 'nil' record in the Olympic medal chart; they won 15 gold medals. This astonishing achievement greatly changed China's image in the world, and stimulated people from all walks of life to work hard to help strengthen and modernise the Chinese nation. Competitiveness and success in sport were thus transferred to the whole of society. Consequently, a strong nationalism was once again aroused in many Chinese at home and abroad.[44] Certainly in the case of China at this time, the following assertion rings true: 'Apart from war, no other form of bonding serves to unite a nation better than representational sports and nowhere is the sport-place bond more graphically illustrated than in the Olympic Games.'[45]

The 1984 Olympic Games marvellously demonstrate the significance of international sporting success for a positive national image, self-esteem and self-confidence. Olympic victory now occupied China's attention. In 1985

FIGURE 9

BUDGETS FOR ELITE SPORTS TEAMS, 1980–90

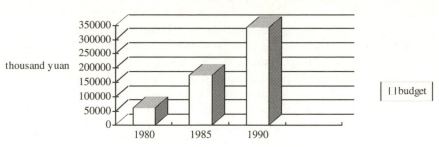

the Olympic Strategy was put forward by the Society of Strategic Research for the Development of Physical Education and Sport (*tiyu fazhan zhanlue yantiu hui*). This society, composed of 64 sports specialists and sports workers,[46] was set up in late 1984. The Olympic Strategy became the blueprint for elite sports programmes in China. In the 1980s the National Sports Commission (NSC) allocated six 'departments' (*shi*) to elite sport,[47] but only one to mass sport (*qunti shi*). Elite sport now consumed two-thirds of the state's sporting budget.[48] Elite sports teams were major beneficiaries. Figure 9 shows the increased investment in elite sports teams between 1980 and 1990.[49] Given the crucial part played by coaches in raising the standards of Chinese sport, more coaches – an increase from 2,829 in 1979 to 4,926 in 1985 – were now employed for elite sports teams.[50]

In line with the Olympic Strategy, emphasis was shifted to Olympic sports and all available resources in China were concentrated on a few key sports in which athletes had the best opportunities of winning medals in the Olympic Games. Athletics and swimming were two of the key sports. As a result, the number of athletes in these sports increased substantially: for example, between 1982 and 1987 there was an increase of 3,000 elite swimmers.[51] Standards in these sports also improved dramatically. Chinese women walkers won two world championships in individual and team events in 1983, and created world records on 14 occasions between 1983 and 1987. To advance performances in athletics and swimming, from 1986 onwards special annual gold and silver awards were established for swimmers and athletes. This helped drive improvement in these sports. At the 1986 Asian Games athletes and swimmers won 32 gold medals, a third of the Chinese total.[52] Although China suffered a disastrous overall defeat at the 1988 Olympic Games, which will be discussed below, Chinese female swimmers made a substantial breakthrough, winning three silver medals and a third place in the world rankings. In 1989, the shot putter Huang Zhihong became the first woman world champion in the event from China, and indeed Asia.

However, the road to world supremacy was full of twists and turns. In 1988 the Chinese suffered an unanticipated blow at the 24th Olympic Games. Inspired by the achievements in the 1984 Olympics, the Chinese were very optimistic about the Seoul games. The conservative goals set by the National Sports Commission were to win eight to ten gold medals and become one of the top six nations at the games.[53] But popular expectation was that China would come fourth and win 15 to 20 gold medals.[54] In these circumstances, a large delegation of 445 members, including 298 athletes (46 per cent were women), was sent to Korea. Unfortunately, the results were disappointing: Chinese athletes won only five gold medals and China was placed 11th, lagging behind even South Korea.[55] For most Chinese this was a total fiasco – a 'defeat of the troops in Seoul' (*bingbai hancheng*).[56]

The Seoul 'defeat' sparked various controversies, debates and bitter criticism across the country. Some questioned whether the result of five gold medals was worth the 1988 one-billion-yuan sports budget, of which 0.22 billion yuan went to the 17,000 elite athletes.[57] Although Zhao Yu had sharply criticised the medal-oriented sports policy in his book *Qiangguo meng* [Superpower Dream], published before the Seoul Games, saying that 'Olympic gold medals deprived most Chinese people of the opportunity of exercise for good health',[58] the criticism then had not been treated seriously. Indeed it had been suppressed by governing bodies in sport.[59] Consequently, the problems in the sports system and the need for radical reform were masked by indifference to criticism and hidden under the phenomenal success of Chinese athletes in international competitions between 1979 and 1988.

Another problem arising from the winning-oriented policy should not be overlooked. Most provincial sports commissions invested large amounts in adult teams rather than juvenile teams because the competition results of adult teams received publicity. According to a survey by the Tianjin Municipal Sports Commission in 1990, most training expenses (50.8 per cent) and coaches (the ratio of coaches to athletes was 1:3 or below) were concentrated on adult elite sports teams. Consequently, a serious shortage of investment in junior elite sports teams and sports schools resulted: they received only 17.7 per cent and 24.13 per cent respectively of total investment. The ratio of coaches to junior athletes was 1:5–7 (or above).[60] In the long run, this practice unquestionably affected the future of Chinese elite sport.

In the aftermath of the 1988 Olympic Games, Chinese sports officials and academics debated furiously the goals of China's sports development programme and the relationship between elite and mass sport.[61] It was advocated that the two strategies – Olympics and national fitness – should go ahead hand in hand. In spite of a request, voiced increasingly loudly in all sections of society, to weaken the gold-medal emphasis, the National Sports Commission was determined to promote this emphasis.[62] As a result, the Olympics-directed policy continued after the 1988 Olympics.

To ensure good results at the 11th Asian Games in Beijing, the State National Committee allocated a special fund (about one million yuan) to 48 research projects associated with the games, involving over 300 researchers.[63] A winning-oriented sports policy dominated the sports community, from athletes to coaches, from researchers to administrators. Winning in competitions was the exclusive goal. The consequence of this unswerving pursuit of success was the astonishing achievements of Chinese athletes, women in particular, in the Olympics in the last decade of the millennium.

Sport, Success, Status and Challenge

As mentioned already, Chinese women have made crucial contributions to China's advances in world sport.[64] Their prominent performances convinced the Chinese government of their part in building an applauded national identity. As a result, many women's sports obtained special treatment. For example, the number of women athletes stayed relatively stable while the total number of athletes decreased from 17,974 in 1979 to 16,892 in 1992 – a result of the restructuring of sports teams following the implementation of the Olympic Strategy. The percentage of women athletes was 38.3 in 1979 and 39.6 in 1992.[65] This demonstrates clearly that elite women's sport was ensured priority in the investment crucial to Olympic success. In addition, to facilitate women's dominance in world sport, the practice of 'training with a male sparring partner' (*nan pei nu laing*) was widely adopted throughout the country. Male athletes were summoned to train with women in order to improve their techniques and strength. The practice eventually proved to be a major contribution to women's success in international competitions. This will be further discussed in Chapter 9.

Women's success in international sport, together with the consequent financial and social benefits, helped raise sportswomen in public esteem and promoted women's status, both in the sports community and society at large. In the words of one academic, commenting at the time:

Now it is very different from the 1960s. Excellent performances can bring athletes a lot of money and their social and financial standing is much higher than before. The state and government give close attention and full support to women's sport. Without a doubt, the present performances of Chinese women in international sports arenas have contributed to the general promotion of Chinese women's status in society. I always say provocatively in my lectures: 'Who dares to look down on Chinese women? Do it if you do not want gold medals!'[66]

Successful women athletes also inspired young girls to get involved in sport. One volleyball player from the People's Liberation Army team recalled of the time: 'When I began to practise volleyball, the Chinese women's volleyball team was at the peak of its performance. That is the main reason that my parents encouraged me to take it up.'[67]

Undeniably, where women were concerned, as elsewhere, significant cultural changes were taking place in the China of the 1980s. The conventional practices and norms in Chinese sport were increasingly at odds with the changed society. The story of the women's table tennis world champion He Zhili in 1987 reflected the dynamic and complex process of cultural change and the resistance to this change. 'Conceding' (*ranqiu*) to team-mates had been considered a strategy to guarantee Chinese dominance in world table tennis by the 1980s.[68] In the semi-finals of the 1987 world championships He Zhili, who had been defeated by the Korean player Liang Yingzi a year earlier, was instructed to lose to her team-mate Guan Jianhua so that she would play against Liang in the final. Unexpectedly, He Zhili boldly and stubbornly defied her coaches' instructions. Instead, she defeated Guan and won her place in the final. In the face of severe punishment for her defiance, He refused to accept humiliation, resisted pressure, and then defeated her Korean rival, winning the world title. By her action He demonstrated considerable courage in defying the 'common' norms in sport, which demanded the unconditional obedience of athletes to their coaches, and personal sacrifice in the interests of the group and the state. She demonstrated that sportswomen in the era of reform had become more independent, more individualistic and more self-assertive. He Zhili proved that women were involved 'in the dialectic of cultural struggle and active agents in the transformation of culture'.[69] They both initiated change and were part of change. Sport reflected society. The result was that, as Barnett A. Doak has pointed out, 'the Chinese now enjoy more freedom of inquiry, expression, lifestyle, [and] while not unlimited, these freedoms far exceed those during the final years of Mao's life and are arguably greater than at any time since 1949'.[70]

The forces of conservatism, however, were far from spent. Despite winning a gold medal for China, He Zhili was later bitterly criticised for putting individual interest before the national and collective interest. She was punished for this: she lost her chance to take part in the 1988 Olympic Games and various other major competitions. Frustrated by this treatment, she put an end to her playing career in China and migrated to Japan in 1989. He Zhili won much sympathy.[71] Her story illustrates that while change was in the air, traditional forces were resilient and cultural change was neither a straightforward nor a smooth process. Change and continuity are a recurrent theme of Chinese sport in the 1990s, as they are in history itself, and will be analysed in the next chapter.

In the 1980s Chinese women were seriously involved in previously 'men only' sports such as football, weightlifting and even body-building. Their presence in these 'male' sports was unquestionably a challenge to traditional gender stereotypes that still existed in many minds. Not only this, but in these activities the adoption of modern fashion caused great concern. When women, for the first time, stepped on stage in bikinis instead of one-piece swimming suits in 1986, it caused controversy over their 'decency'.

How did these women stand up against such conservatism? One female body-building champion declared later:

> There had to be someone brave enough to be the first to wear a bikini. I was determined to be this 'someone' so that others would follow suit. Otherwise there would be no progress in the sport of body-building among women. They would avoid it.[72]

Contrary to expectations, the response was favourable. The same athlete remarked: 'Spectators were very polite and well-behaved at the Shenyang contest. They applauded us in appreciation not only of our figures, but also of our boldness in rejecting outmoded ideas.'[73] Women's participation in these 'male sports' sturdily defied the stereotypical expectation about their appropriateness for women, while women's own assertion within their sports began the progress of newly defining the female image.

Body-building in bikinis may have been surprisingly well received, but taking up soccer was another story. The Chinese men's soccer team failed to realise its ambition of going beyond Asia. In contrast, the women's soccer team succeeded in their similar ambition. In 1986 their outstanding performance at the Asian Football Championships resulted in the creation of a national women's football team. However, the training and living conditions for the team were far from luxurious. Initially they trained at a base in Guangdong province. They were housed in a former warehouse. There were no electric fans in the summer and no hot water for showers. Due to the shortage of dinner tables, those who arrived late for meals had to stand. In addition, there were so many mosquitoes that at one meal, one player was bitten 27 times.[74] The situation gave rise to a belief that women were being penalised for taking up a predominantly male sport. The unequal treatment of men and women had a two-edged impact on women's football. On the one hand, it stimulated some female players to work extremely hard to win good results in international competitions in order to obtain improvements in training and living conditions. On the other hand, it discouraged some from involvement in the new sport. This was reflected in the declining number of women's soccer teams throughout the country by the end of the 1980s.[75]

Higher Education, Occupational Choices and Elite Sport

In the context of economic reform, the most notable change for young Chinese people came in the education system. After 1977 the old system of elite education was restored, and in 1980 leading schools were reopened. In 1977 physical education colleges, like other higher education institutions, began to admit students by national examinations for both academic and sports subjects. At the end of the 1970s, due to high unemployment and underemployment, the chance of receiving higher education and, more importantly, leaving, or avoiding going to, the countryside was a powerful incentive for most young people. In the late 1970s about 2,000 students were recruited each year by sports institutes across the country. Some eminent athletes and coaches, such as Tang Guoli, the Asian javelin record-holder in 1980, emerged from this generation of students. From 1979 postgraduate sports students were also recruited. In and after the 1980s, these sports postgraduates played a crucial part in research and administration. Some even became famous coaches, such as Chou Ming,[76] the coach of several world champion swimmers.

The quality of coaches is the most important factor in ensuring sporting success. During the Cultural Revolution, coaching education was badly affected. To put things right, in 1983 sports colleges began to run two-year courses for coaches and administrators, starting in Beijing and Shanghai. Enrolment increased from 604 in 1983 to 1,300 in 1985, and thereafter the figure remained around 1,000.[77] From 1986 coaches of elite sports teams were required to possess certificates from higher education institutions.[78]

By the mid-1980s, the quasi-traditional pressure for educational success, and for the status it was presumed to bring, was so strong in society at large that education became viewed as a source of significant opportunity for the successful individual. The school system again became highly competitive. Academic performance was stressed and good exam results ensured a promising career start. Once students were admitted to university, they were firmly on the escalator to cadredom. Cadre and technical jobs in state enterprises came with higher education. It also led to top Party and government positions that were strenuously pursued by the young before the mid-1980s. Thus higher education was exceptionally attractive. According to one survey, more than 80 per cent of parents were willing to support their sons or daughters through either university or graduate school, although the expenses involved represented a large slice of an average family's income.[79] This emphasis on academic study, with its deep roots in Chinese history,[80] to some extent discouraged the involvement of young people in sport. With a return to an emphasis on education, the associated reinstitution of university entrance examinations marked the beginning of a downward spiral in grass-roots support for sports schools.[81]

Along with increased educational opportunities went increased job opportunities in society. After the Cultural Revolution, class struggle was subordinated to economic progress, job opportunities multiplied, and the sports team was no longer overwhelmingly the first choice that it had been in the 1960s and 1970s. Not long after, the increasing opposition of urbanites, especially intellectuals, to sport as a career surfaced. This opposition was also largely associated with a crude athletic stereotype: athletes have 'four developed limbs and an undeveloped brain' (*sizhi fada, tounao jiandan*). Then again, the 'one child' policy, which was adopted in 1979, adversely affected the involvement of young people in sport. Parents, especially in the cities, focused all their energies, hopes and aspirations on their single child. In the minds of most Chinese, there was the dream that their children might be able to achieve what they had failed to accomplish. They hoped against hope that their child would have everything that had been unavailable to them during the Cultural Revolution. Ironically, this compensatory urge occasionally resulted in the 'little emperor syndrome' – spoiled children who were overindulged and could not stomach hard work. Parents worried about the next generation, and at the same time tried to create a comfortable life for it. As a result, few parents encouraged their child to engage in sport. It was too much like hard work. According to an inquiry in Shenzhen, only two per cent of parents wished their children to become sports stars. All this led to the scaling down of the numbers of students in spare-time sports schools from 307,550 in 1977 to 226,472 in 1984. Overfeeding and the lack of physical activities collectively resulted in the emergence of obese children in the 1990s.[82] This phenomenon threatened to reduce further the talent pool for future elite athletes.

While the total number of students in sports schools fell in the early 1980s, the number of athletes from the countryside increased. The best of them included most of the well-known runners of the 'Ma Family Army' (see Chapter 5). Why did the situation occur? How could peasants ignorant of modern sport be involved in sport? What was their motivation? To explore this phenomenon, it is necessary to look at the influence of economic reform on peasants' lives.

After the rural productivity reforms in 1978, agricultural output increased remarkably and the living standards of peasants improved considerably.[83] Their average annual income reportedly increased from 133.6 yuan in 1978 to 309.8 yuan in 1983, a 131 per cent rise.[84] They now owned televisions and other electric appliances, and watching television became the most popular family activity. Television changed the life of the Chinese peasant. It became possible for more and more girls in the countryside to gain access to information about a variety of opportunities, including opportunities in sport. Furthermore, in spite of improved living standards in the countryside, the income gap between the average city dweller and the average rural person steadily increased after the mid-1980s. Peasant families, therefore, were less opposed to urban sports opportunities. Economic reform was thus accompanied by mobility: an increasing number of rural people left the land to get jobs in county towns or cities. Nevertheless, most athletes were still from the cities.

To recruit more sporting talent, it was necessary to reduce the tension between academic study and sports training. In 1979 the sports boarding school, which had been experimented with in 1963, re-emerged. It was run either by institutes of physical education or by provincial or city sports commissions. Students usually studied in the morning and trained in the afternoon. By 1981 there were 484 students in sports boarding schools attached to institutes of physical education; by 1991 the figure had increased to 1,135. Students affiliated to local sports commissions increased from 5,070 in 1981 to 27,057 in 1991.[85] To some extent this kind of school helped reduce the confrontation between academic study and athletic training. It was welcomed by some parents.

To further eliminate problems associated with athletic involvement and academic commitment, athletes on some provincial or national teams also became university or college students, as will be described in the Beijing case study below. After some years of study – usually longer than normal students because of their intensive involvement in sport – these athletes could obtain university degrees. This approach was gradually adopted by more and more sports teams. The dual role of athlete and student broadened the range of job choices for retired athletes and, to an extent, eased the fear of dead-end post-athletic careers. The result was that more talented people were attracted to sport. However, matters remained far from ideal, and in practice university and sports teams faced severe challenges. For a university to ensure academic quality, it had to insist on adequate standards from students. This meant that athletes had to spend long hours in study in order to succeed academically. Athletic teams too had their own standards for training and competition. Could students concentrate on studying after equally long hours of athletic training? It was undoubtedly a hard road for ambitious athletes. Only the exceptional trained and studied successfully.

In accordance with these education-related reforms, competition regulations underwent some changes. In the national competitions, for example, the former divisions between 'amateur' (*yeyu*) and 'specialised' (*zhuangye*) athletes no longer applied. Competitions were now based on age and technical level. However, this change had an unfortunate consequence for spare-time sports schools. Athletes in these schools were hardly of the same standard as those in elite provincial sports teams. Consequently, those who were not admitted into provincial teams would stop training at a very early age. In gymnastics, for example, there were very few gymnasts aged over ten in sports schools, and as a result there was a crisis in the popularity of gymnastics in society. Reduced spectator numbers for the sport later became an issue that threatened the existence of gymnastics under the market-oriented reforms of the 1990s.

In 1985 the number of students in sports schools started to pick up and reached 301,558 by 1991.[86] This rise in sports participation was inseparable from changing social values and norms. As stated above, in the post-Mao period, intellectuals gained both more prestige and respect than before. However, this increased social esteem did not lead to significant economic benefits. For example, the salary of a university professor was between 300 to 400 yuan (US$40–50), less than that of an ordinary waitress in a joint-venture hotel. Intellectuals were often embarrassed at being too poor to eat out. As a result, the post of college/high school teacher, which used to be highly respected and much envied by most Chinese, lost its former popularity. Undoubtedly, the sharp contrast between intellectuals' incomes and those of businessmen, sports stars or film stars affected people's attitudes to education and to career choice. Social status, of course, is attached to particular occupations.[87] In the transition to a market economy, financial rewards symbolised occupational prestige. Within this setting, not a few believed that success in elite sport could increase their wealth and bring them fame. This belief was reinforced by the commercialisation of sport. For its potential in securing both social prestige and economic rewards, sport was once again viewed as an attractive career for many young girls and boys.[88]

Despite the various reforms mentioned above, no fundamental changes came about in administrative and training systems in sport before the early 1990s. Centralised administration and the 'one dragon' training system were still widespread. The shift in emphasis in sports policy, from institutions to investment performance, was exclusively associated with elite sport. The case studies below make this very clear.

Analysis: Illustrative Case Studies

Once again, three regional case studies (Beijing, Guangdong and Sichuan) aim to put flesh on the skeleton by way of evidence of changing local socio-economic conditions and their impact on sportswomen and elite sport. In specific, three regional phenomena will receive attention:

- Economic and social reform and associated changes in sports ideology and management;
- Higher education reform, increased occupational choice and enhanced sports involvement;
- Opening-up and related international success in sport.

Beijing

When the fourth National Games were convened in Beijing in September 1979,[89] officials of the International Olympic Committee (IOC) were invited to observe the event for the first time. This invitation signalled both the renewed emphasis by the state on elite sport and the Chinese desire to rejoin the IOC. As host city, Beijing sent 509 athletes to the games and retained its influential position in elite sport with second place in the medal count.

Unexpectedly, Beijing fell to fourth place at the fifth National Games, which took place in Shanghai in 1983. This was partly due to its sending fewer participants than to the previous games – some 390. Even more surprisingly, Beijing came 20th in the gold medal count at the 1985 National Youth Games.[90] The capital's disappointing performance at these major domestic games caused widespread concern. Both internal difficulties and external challenges were considered responsible for this decline.

As mentioned above with reference to China generally, the conflict between sports training and academic endeavour became intensified following the resumption of national college entrance exams in 1978. In Beijing, as elsewhere, going to university and then obtaining a good job was now the aim of parents, pupils and schools. Consequently, the attraction of sport as a window of opportunity diminished. It became increasingly difficult to recruit, coach and retain athletes. According to a survey in the Haidian district of Beijing, only 1.3 per cent of parents encouraged their children to take up competitive sport. By contrast, 95 per cent objected to their involvement.[91] This attitude certainly undermined the recruitment of talented athletes and their commitment to elite sport. In addition to this 'domestic' setback, in sport Beijing also faced a vigorous challenge from Guangdong, Laioning and Shanghai. These regions were economically strong and possessed considerable sports potential throughout the 1980s. Beijing failed to withstand their intense challenge.

To reverse this decline, after 1986 Beijing introduced structural changes in elite sport. First, in order to combine specialised sports training with academic study, five city-level sports schools and 18 district branches were built. Two layers were thus added between elite sports team and spare-time sports school or sports classes in normal schools. This four-layered training network absorbed 7,000 athletes. Second, elite sports teams were incorporated into the normal educational system.[92] Accordingly, athletes became students and their wages were replaced by studentships.[93] This was a clear attempt to harmonise the two pursuits of academic studies and sports training. Although priority was still given to training, and academically the athlete-students could hardly match normal students,[94] athletes' educational level improved by the 1990s – see Table 9. To an extent, this made their post-athletic lives more secure.

In spite of the above measures, Beijing only managed to retain fourth place at the sixth National Games in Guangzhou in 1987. The following year, therefore, Beijing directed its attention to the management of sports teams. A full-time post of 'class director' was established. This director was to be financially and administratively responsible for a sports 'class' that embraced several teams; to monitor the teams; and to assess coaches' behaviour to maximise their effectiveness.[95] As a result, a three-level management system for elite sport was created in Beijing, namely institute, class and team.

In addition, the employment of coaches was overhauled. Coaches were no longer permanently employed. Contracts were introduced, with a normal

TABLE 9

EDUCATIONAL LEVEL OF ATHLETES IN BEIJING, 1994

	college	vocational school	High school	Junior school	Primary school	total
athletes	63	365	59	172	75	734

Source: *Tiyu shiye tongji nianjian (neibu ziliao)* [Statistical Yearbook of Sport (internal materials)], 1994.

coaching period of six years, to be reviewed every two years. Once contracted performance quotas were achieved, the coach could receive a winning bonus. Furthermore, on signing a contract the coach put down a deposit of 1,200 yuan. If the performance quota was not reached, the deposit was forfeited. However, those coaches who excelled would then be directly employed on contract without a deposit being put down.[96] It was obvious that economic reform had profoundly affected every corner of Chinese society. By the mid-1980s incentive rewards had become effective stimulants for both athletes and coaches, including those of the spare-time sports schools.[97] Also between 1980 and 1990, Beijing's budget for elite sports teams was increased from 3,447,000 yuan to 14,617,000 yuan.[98] This aided the rapid expansion of elite sports teams in the early part of the decade. Beijing had 309 female athletes in 1979, a figure that had increased to 368 by 1985, although it went down to 330 by 1990.[99] The reasons will be discussed below.

One sporting initiative in the mid-1980s was to encourage social groups to sponsor sports. Exclusive management by the Sports Commission gave way to cooperation between various social agencies and the Sports Commission. This change was implemented in the run-up to the Beijing Asian Games.[100] The organising committee of the games followed the example of the sixth National Games held in 1987 in Guangzhou, the capital of Guangdong province. Apart from central and municipal government investment,[101] about a quarter of the 2.5 billion yuan needed to host the games came from other sources. To achieve this, the Foundation of the Asian Games was set up. Individuals, in particular, donated money on an unprecedented scale: from the young to the old, overseas Chinese to indigenous schoolchildren, and ordinary workers to celebrities. The total amount donated reached an equivalent of 600 million yuan by early January 1990.[102] All this marked a shift in the financial management of sport from exclusive state investment to joint sponsorship by government and society, and from a non-profit system to a profit system.

To improve on the central government's insufficient funding and ostensibly ineffective management, decentralisation began. From the mid-1980s district/county sports commissions in Beijing were inspired to finance themselves by any and all means. Both sports or non-sports activities were encouraged, such as running a restaurant, starting a night market or opening sports centres to the public. The scheme was a success. For example, the Shichahai Sports School's net profits of 200,000 yuan in 1987 increased to 400,000 yuan in 1990.[103] Growing financial strength allowed local sports organisations greater independence in determining the priorities for sports investment. However, not everyone could be successful. In fact, these commercial activities also had a negative influence on the general development of sport: some public sports fields and stadiums actually deteriorated and decreased in number. Nationally Beijing fell to below 20th place in general sports provision and facilities by the mid-1980s.[104]

It is obvious from the above that Beijing no longer led the nation in elite sport after economic reform was initiated in the late 1970s. Both internal and external factors accounted for this. Nevertheless, formidable changes did occur in the sports community. Incentive rewards, winning bonuses and coaching contracts were all introduced within a decade. To maintain Beijing's national sporting supremacy was the purpose of all these changes. They failed. Commercialisation, entrepreneurship and financial incentives, at least those that were achieved, were surely not enough. This is clear from achievements in Guangdong.

Guangdong

After the Cultural Revolution was officially abandoned in 1978, the Revolutionary Committee of the Guangdong Provincial Sports Commission was abolished and replaced by the now reconstituted Guangdong Provincial Sports Commission.[105] Guangdong sent 392 athletes to the fourth National Games in 1979 and ranked third in the medal count. In the same year, out of four special economic zones, three (Zhuhai, Shantou and Shenzhen) were established in Guangdong Province. In 1980 the whole of Hainan Island, an underdeveloped area in Guangdong, was granted SEZ status (it was elevated to an independent province in 1992). As a result, Guangdong, especially these SEZ cities and other secondary cities in the Pearl River delta,[106] had greater economic opportunities than other places. Shenzhen was a typical example. This new city enjoyed the highest standard of living and wages in the country, with a 500 per cent increase in average income during the 1980s. In consequence, per-capita income in Guangdong rose from below the national average in 1980 to 64 per cent above it in 1991.[107] While national GNP and industrial output growth between 1979 and 1991 averaged 8.7 per cent and 10.1 per cent respectively, Guangdong's averages stood at 11.5 per cent and 20 per cent respectively.[108] This favourable economic situation provided an amenable climate for the promotion of elite sport. Guangdong's sports budget for elite teams surged from 2,091,000 yuan in 1980 to 23,996,000 yuan in 1990.[109]

The increased investment produced results. In 1983 Guangdong topped the National Games medal chart for the first time. At the 1986 Asian Games, athletes from the province won 24 gold medals, third in the country in this regard. At the 1988 Olympic Games, Guangdong athletes won two silver medals and five bronze medals, with 13 athletes entering the world top six. The province's leading position continued into the 1990s. At the 1990 Asian Games, Guangdong athletes won 42 gold medals, far ahead of other provinces. In total, they won 154 world titles between 1978 and 1992.[110]

Riding the wave of the economic boom, elite sport flourished. As elsewhere, exclusive state investment in, and management of, sport ceased after economic reform was introduced in the late 1970s. The first enterprise-run sports team – the Guangzhou Soccer Team, run by the Baiyunshan

Pharmaceutical Factory – emerged in October 1984. By the mid-1980s joint contracts with public and private organisations had become a trend. By 1992, enterprise-run sports teams numbered 24,921. With increased economic power and the decentralisation of sports management, cities, counties, enterprises and universities were encouraged to run elite sports teams and to employ athletes from outside their own city or county.[111] Guangzhou, Shenzhen and other cities followed suit, leading to the recruitment of a considerable number of athletes and coaches. Numbers of female athletes in Guangdong increased from 271 in 1979 to 414 in 1990.[112]

Guangdong not only kept its dominant position in elite sport but also pioneered the incorporation of commercialism into sport, notably at the 1987 National Games, which it hosted. The organising committee of the games sold advertising rights for the games mascot, emblem and song to corporations, and borrowed practices such as lottery tickets and tour groups from the West. In turn, the commercialisation of sport at the Guangzhou Games set the example for the Beijing Asian Games in 1990.

Guangdong women performed outstandingly in many sports. Among the prominent performers were the world diving champions Chen Xiaoxia and Li Qiaoxie, the 1990 Asian Games weightlifting champion Xin Fen and a number of female football players. Guangdong women took up some 'men's sports', including weightlifting, judo, body-building and football. Guangdong sponsored the first women's football tournament in 1981, which resulted in the establishment of two women's football teams (Guangdong and Guangzhou). Since 1982, Guangdong women's football team has been one of the most powerful teams in China.[113] In addition, women from the province took part for the first time in the national judo competition in 1986.[114] These new sports sprouted, spread and flourished in the province. Guangdong hosted an international women's football tournament in 1988, in which Chinese women demonstrated their competitive spirit and great potential. A television documentary was made to record the history of women's soccer. These events undoubtedly promoted the popularity of football among girls. In 1990, Banqiu [Half Ball] Women's Football Club was set up, marking the birth of the first women's professional football team in China.[115]

Furthermore, as a well-sited gateway to the outside world, Guangdong undertook sports exchanges with foreign countries more easily and more swiftly than other parts of China. About a fifth of the whole country's international activities (travelling to foreign countries or receiving foreign teams) took place in Guangdong. The Provincial International Sport and Touring Corporation, established in 1979, took care of these sports exchanges.

Other factors played their part in Guangdong sporting success. As about 90 per cent of Hong Kong and Macao Chinese had a Guangdong background, the province received many donations from overseas Chinese for sport.[116] In Guangzhou, the capital city of the province, the amount of sponsorship jumped from 1.2 million yuan in 1985 to 2.5 million yuan in 1988.[117] Shenzhen's ability to attract sponsorship was even more phenomenal. In 1988, it obtained over 3 million yuan in sponsorship, three times the government's annual sports budget.[118] Subsequently and consequently, sports facilities improved remarkably in the province. Some 44 sports fields, 41 stadiums, three indoor swimming pools and 394 outdoor pools, 152 tennis courts and three golf courses were built between 1979 and 1991.[119] In 1988 Guangdong province ranked first in the country in terms of sports facilities and equipment.

In spite of the impressive improvement in sports infrastructure, however, the general situation in Guangdong was far from ideal. Only ten out of the 76 counties in the province met the standard of 'two fields [one athletics field and one ball-game court with lights and seats for spectators], one pool and one gymnasium' that was demanded by the National Sports Commission. The per-capita sports budget was still quite low: only ten fen (less than one penny) for 62 counties and even less than two or three fen in some counties in the mid-1980s.[120] It was hard, if not impossible, for the government, despite its new affluence, to invest extensively in mass sport.

It is evident that Guangdong was in the forefront of virtually every major sporting reform. It pioneered commercial clubs, individual sponsorship and the transfer of athletes – all very different from the conventional practices of the past. Sportswomen benefited from this torrent of changes. These changes were dependent on the successful espousal of capitalism – its principles and its practices – but particularly from the geographical location of the province, which allowed their especially successful introduction.

Sichuan

Sichuan was the first province to abolish the egalitarian reward system by reintroducing a contract system in agriculture and in industry as early as in 1978. This breakthrough from 'egalitarianism' also occurred in sport.[121] When the Sichuan women's volleyball team won the national title again in 1978, they gained the title of 'hard-working and vigorously fighting sports team', and each player was awarded a 280-yuan bonus. In view of the fact that the average per-capita income in the province was 238 yuan per year, and material rewards had not existed previously in the New China, this bonus was an alluring stimulus. This bold innovation shocked sports communities across the country.

When economic reform occurred on a large scale in Sichuan in the early 1980s, elite sport took off. Sichuan's ranking in the medal count at the National Games rose from 19th in 1979 to 11th in 1983. It moved to sixth place in the medal count at the 1987 National Games. This rapid progress was largely attributed to women's efforts. The number of elite female athletes increased from 303 in 1979 to 378 in 1990.[122] The women's volleyball team, mentioned earlier, won the National Games four successive times between 1965 and 1987 – the only ball-game team with these accomplishments in the whole of the country. The players represented the traditional special qualities of Sichuan women: vivacity, intelligence and persistence. Zhang Rongfang, Zhu Lin, Liang Yan and Wu Dan later became the back-bone of the Chinese women's volleyball team that dominated world volleyball for the most of the 1980s. Gao Min was another sports star from the province. She captured more than 70 medals and 11 world and Olympic titles in her six years of international competition between 1986 and 1992. She was regarded as a 'diving queen'.

Sports investment increased markedly following the introduction of economic reform in 1979. The per-capita sports budget in Sichuan rose from 0.15 yuan in 1979 to 0.51 yuan in 1986, although it was still below the national average (0.87 yuan).[123] The government budget for Sichuan elite sports teams increased sevenfold, from 3,040,000 yuan in 1980 to 21,639,000 yuan in 1990.[124] The enlarged budget made it possible for elite teams to expand. New sports such as boat-racing and waterskiing for men and women, women's weightlifting and football obtained elite teams in the mid-1980s. By the end of the 1980s there were 58 elite sports teams with 1,219 athletes specialising in 39 sports in Sichuan.[125]

Thise substantial sports investment bore other fruit: the improvement of sporting facilities. An international-standard swimming hall was erected in 1981, which provided elite swimmers with a permanent training location. Moreover, between 1982 and 1986, eight sports fields, ten stadiums and 107 swimming pools were built in the province.[126] New equipment and facilities greatly improved the training condition of elite athletes in the province.

In conjunction with economic reform, from 1985 onwards the Sichuan Sports Commission cooperated with large business enterprises to organise sporting activities and to run elite sports teams, spare-time sports schools and sports classes. The provincial basketball teams for men and women and the women's football team, for example, were now co-managed by the sports commission and two steel plants.[127]

Nevertheless, while Sichuan continued to push forward its post-Mao rural and urban reforms in the early 1980s, the rapid development of China's south-east coast gradually overshadowed Sichuan's progress. From 1981 to 1989, the growth of income in Sichuan was 8.3 per cent, lower than the national average (8.7 per cent) and Guangdong (11.6 per cent).[128] This fact undoubtedly held back the development of both elite and mass sports. For example, the newly established Provincial Sports Research Institute (1980) was handicapped by a limited budget and poor equipment. By the mid-1980s, this institute employed only 13 people. Of the 214 counties in the province, only five reached the NSC's requirement of 'two fields, one pool and one gymnasium'. Some 45 counties had none of these facilities. As in Beijing, the limited sports facilities were often used for business purposes, such as furniture exhibitions.[129] In short, while there were improvements in sports facilities and equipment, much was still to be done. In addition elite sport was favoured at the expense of mass sport – a situation typical of Beijing and Guangdong, and indeed China as a whole.

In summary, Beijing, Guangdong and Sichuan provide local evidence that the first decade of economic reform (1979–89) witnessed radical changes in elite sport. Sports budgets rose markedly in Guangdong, to a lesser extent in Sichuan and gradually in Beijing. Nevertheless, despite variations in the pace and emphasis of reforms, all three regions underwent fundamental changes during this process. The introduction of incentive rewards, the contracted employment of coaches and the integration of business enterprises into sports management were the most influential steps in sports reform. What factors motivated the sports community to embark on these reforms and, more to the point, what impact these reforms had on elite women's sport and on elite sportswomen will be examined in detail in the next chapter.

Conclusion

In the late 1970s China began its policy of economic reform and 'opening up' to the outside. At the same time, its seat at the IOC was restored. Economic reform provided a congenial climate for elite sport. Sporting investment increased annually after 1979. Chinese athletes achieved astounding victories in international competitions, culminating in the successful 1984 Olympic Games. These athletes generated wave after wave of nationalism throughout the country. Sport was utilised as an effective means to promote China's image in the world and to spur on the nation to modernise itself. To ensure future success in the Olympic Games, an 'Olympic Strategy' was designed in the mid-1980s. Due to their remarkable performances in world contests, Chinese women were beneficiaries of this strategy, which furthered their sports successes in the 1980s and then in the 1990s. In turn, women athletes increasingly enjoyed high social status, respect and esteem.

Rapid economic and social transformation resulted in widely pervasive competition, commercialism and consumerism. The sporting community was at the forefront of China's shift toward a more commercial, competitive consumer culture. In the mid-1980s radical changes took place in sport. The system of increased responsibility for head coaches and corporation and private sponsorship of sports clubs were widely introduced. Exclusive state sponsorship and control of sport was replaced by the joint sponsorship by the state, public organisations and private individuals.

The emphasis on higher education after 1977 and the national one-child policy challenged, and reduced, the involvement of the young in sport in the early 1980s. To resolve the conflict between education and sports training, sports boarding schools and high-level sports teams run by universities, or jointly run by sports commissions and universities, were created. All this improved educational opportunities and practices. Consequently, coupled with the rising social and economic status of elite athletes, sport resurfaced as an attractive career after the mid-1980s.

Women, Society and Elite Sport in the Transition to a Market Economy (1990–98)

In the immediate aftermath of the repression of the student movement on 4 June 1989, economic reform slowed down. However, three years later, in early 1992, Deng Xiaoping's dramatic statement in southern China abruptly changed matters.[1] Establishing a market system to replace the planned socialist commodity economy previously endorsed in the Constitution now became the aim. Capitalism was given a bright green light. As a result, the process of internal economic and general reform accelerated, alongside contact with the external world.[2]

Economic, social, political, and cultural changes now under way in the fast transition to a market economy affected sports policies, strategies and plans. In the 1990s, as a consequence, changes in Chinese sport have attracted close attention from officials and scholars. A national symposium on a strategy for sports development until 2010, for example, was held in November 1996, at which national and provincial sports officials presented papers on various issues including sports policy, institutional reform, sports industrialisation, sports law and the future development of elite sport in the context of market-oriented reform. However, these papers merely covered standard interests. They certainly cannot be considered a comprehensive sociological survey of Chinese sport.[3] In particular, the effect of the changing national environment on sportswomen and their elite sport remains unexplored to this day in official documents, academic studies and professional symposia. This chapter will address this shortcoming by looking at the economic, social and cultural changes brought about by the market-oriented reforms, their influence on Chinese sport, women's elite sport in particular, and the consequent challenges and dilemmas that have faced, are facing and will face sportswomen in China.

Analysis: Overview

Integration of the Olympic and National Games

Sport is often used as an effective political instrument. Instances of this have already been given in the specific case of China.[4] The ability to host a big international sports competition, for example, has been a symbol of Chinese political stabilisation and economic prosperity.[5] Although the harsh crackdown on the student movement in 1989 brought uncertainty about the 1990 Asian Games, Beijing successfully hosted the games and China harvested a crop of medals.[6] These performances consolidated China's image as a major sports power in Asia and swept away the memory of the poor showing in the 1988 Olympics. Through sport China made a political statement.

Success provided the stimulus for Beijing to bid to host the Olympic Games in 2000, in an attempt once again to serve political needs. As President Jiang Zemin stated: 'The bid was made to further China's domestic stability and economic prosperity. The quest for the Olympics was to raise national morale and strengthen the cohesion of the Chinese people both in the mainland and overseas.'[7] Irrespective of political considerations, this bid greatly promoted the development of elite sport in China, especially in Beijing. This will be described later in the Beijing case study.

As mentioned earlier, China's ambition is to become a sporting world power in the foreseeable future. Olympic victory is the embodiment of this ambition. Thus, after the 1990 Asian Games, China immediately directed its attention to the coming Olympic Games. In 1991 the National Sports Commission (NSC) gave the status of 'key Olympic sport' to 16 sports including athletics, swimming and gymnastics. These sports enjoyed favourable treatment in virtually every aspect from budget to training arrangements.[8] Olympic performance was the unblinking focus of state sports officials.

Nonetheless, for provincial sports officials the first priority was high ranking at the National Games. To obtain the best results, each province or municipality made its four-year sports plan in conjunction with the National Games cycle. The games were thus central to all athletes' recruitment and retirement, competition arrangements and financial allocations. But the differences between the Olympic Games and the National Games in the timing of the competitions and types of events led to problems: in the late 1980s best performances had not infrequently occurred at the National Games rather than the Olympics. At the 1987 National Games, for example, 15 world records were established, but at the 1988 Olympic Games the Chinese won just five gold medals. This discrepancy alarmed sports governing bodies.

To secure Olympic success, therefore, early in the 1990s the NSC adjusted its policies on the National Games. First of all, the timing of the National Games was changed from the year before the Olympics to the year after. Thus, the seventh National Games were postponed from 1991 to 1993. To further stimulate local enthusiasm for the Olympics, the NSC announced in 1991 that the results of the Olympic Games in 1992 would be incorporated into the scoring system of the National Games in 1993.[9] These changes saw immediate results at the Barcelona Games in 1992. China won 16 gold medals and came fourth in the medal count. It goes without saying that state sports policy played an essential part in achieving these results.

In spite of the growing emphasis on Olympic performance, as late as the early 1990s local sports commissions had not adequately adapted their domestic-oriented strategies and practices. To reduce conflict between national and local practice, the NSC issued a directive in 1993 to the effect that only Olympic sports and the traditional Chinese sport of martial arts would be incorporated into the 1997 National Games. This simple action demonstrated quite explicitly the national determination to achieve major Olympic success.

This policy shift stimulated unprecedented enthusiasm for Olympic victory from local sports officials. In gymnastics prior to the 1996 Atlanta Games, for example. nine internal trials were organised to select seven gymnasts. Fierce competition emerged not only among promising candidates but also among the officials of the relevant provinces. These officials not only travelled hundreds or even thousands of miles to be with their gymnasts at trials but also endeavoured to provide the best support. To guarantee that the male gymnast Li Jin made the team, Hunan province sent two male staff, including a physiotherapist, to Beijing to look after his daily routine and nutrition for four months. Other provinces provided their key athletes with expensive medical equipment to aid their recovery from injuries and intensive training. Such practices were all aimed at winning places on the Olympic team. For the first time Olympic victory attracted intense attention from grass-roots sports officials.

The national Olympics-oriented policy also led to the reorganisation of provincial and municipal sports teams throughout the country. Non-Olympic sports teams were substantially reduced. By 1995, non-Olympic athletes comprised only 7.34 per cent of all elite athletes. In addition, team sports that demanded more investment than individual sports and that had no medal potential were terminated in most provinces and municipalities. Figure 10 shows the changes clearly.[10]

An outcome of this restructuring of elite sports teams was the decline in the number of elite athletes: from a total of 16,982 in 1990, for example, to 13,374 in 1994.[11] Obviously, this change was aimed at concentrating available resources on the elite Olympic stars. Olympic victory was considered symbolic of China's rising power – economic, political *and* athletic.

The arrangements for the Olympic and National Games not only guaranteed international victories, but also precipitated the expansion of elite (medal) sport across the country. The powerful municipalities and provinces, such as Shanghai, Guangdong, Shandong and Liaoning, possessed vast talent pools, with each employing over 1,000 elite athletes. Intense competition between them characterised the 1997 National Games.[12] Shanghai, for the first time, defeated its major rival Liaoning and topped the games. Guangdong, the defending champion, had to give way to them both. Clearly, by the 1990s, the centre of Chinese elite sport had gradually moved from the inland provinces to the economically developed coastal regions.[13]

FIGURE 10

NUMBER OF ELITE ATHLETES IN DIFFERENT SPORTS, 1979 AND 1992

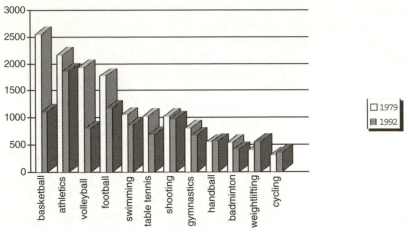

Nevertheless, the underdeveloped remote provinces and their newly established, enterprise-backed, sports associations did not abandon elite sport. Instead, they focused narrowly on their best sports. As a result, they achieved something of a breakthrough in the medal count at the 1997 Games. Thirty-one delegations shared the 327 gold medals. The era of a few powerful provinces and municipalities dominating the National Games had disappeared,[14] and elite sport success now characterised more of China than at any time in its modern history.

Market Economy and Institutional Reform

Although the sports community underwent some radical reform in the 1980s, as discussed in Chapter 4, by the early 1990s the operational mechanisms of sports management had not changed fundamentally.[15] The sports administration established in the 1950s had played an undeniable part in advancing Chinese sport. Victories in international competitions had proved its value. However, the structure of the administration, based as it was on a dominant authoritarian system, had serious weaknesses. Its main flaw lay in its juggernaut of centrally controlled organisations, with their tendency towards complacent inefficiency and lack of vigour.[16] The vastness and complexity of the country magnified these problems.

By 1993, to deepen sports reform, based on the experience of the last 15 years of reforms,[17] it was decided that sports reform should proceed in ten areas including the administrative system, the competition system, sports associations and sports training.[18] As in industry and agriculture, sporting reform took the approach of experimentation in selected units. Interestingly, men's sports – first football, later basketball and then tennis – were chosen as 'experimental' units. This was a pragmatic low-risk approach, embracing Chinese sportsmen whose performance was far from satisfactory. Their improvement could only add to the already successful state of Chinese sport. A breakthrough in male performance in these activities would be a pleasing bonus. Even if reform failed, it would not significantly affect the performance of Chinese sport in international competition.

In 1992 the Chinese Football Association took the lead in self-management after becoming independent from the First Competitive Sport Department (*di yi jinji yundong shi*)[19] of the NSC. Greater autonomy meant diminished government funding, for example, from three million yuan in 1991 to two million yuan in 1995. Yet by the mid-1990s the annual expenditure of the association had risen beyond ten million yuan.[20] Non-government funding provided the vast amount of the money required. This successful self-financing was copied by local football teams with some success. In 1996 the training budget for the provincial-level Qianwei Huangdao football team, for example, reached 26 million yuan. This was an incredible figure compared to the 1980s when the whole national table tennis squad had an annual budget of only about half a million yuan from the government.[21]

The only way these associations and clubs could achieve their new budgets was through market development. After 1992 a whole package of reforms was gradually introduced in football circles. To start with, the club system was widely adopted by football teams across the country. Although this system differed from the western market model, it was a significant step away from the socialist command economy model. It marked the departure from centrally planned sport to market-oriented sport. The club system prompted the establishment of the registration of athletes. By 1995, the number of registered players in the country had reached 6,700, significantly more than the 2,000 players prior to 1992.[22] Registration laid the foundation for the mobility of athletes, which will be discussed in Chapter 8. In addition, after 1994, western-style professional football competitions on a home-and-away basis came into being. Entrance fees, promotion and advertisement now became integral parts of sports competitions.[23] By the mid-1990s the commercialisation of sport had become quite phenomenal in China.

The Chinese Football Association's experiment paved the way for reform on a wider scale. After 1995 men's basketball, tennis and volleyball adopted the club system and professional league competitions. They were allowed to employ foreign players, to sell broadcasting rights and to sign lucrative sponsorship contracts. The experimentation with some men's sports resulted in progress in men's performances. At the 1996 Olympic Games, sportsmen won seven out of the 16 gold medals attained by the Chinese, and several swimmers, athletes and the men's basketball team qualified for quarter-final competitions. At the 2000 Olympic Games Chinese men won some 11.5 out of the 28 gold medals that the Chinese captured.[24] All this suggests that market-based reform provided some momentum for men's elite sport, although men's performances were still not as impressive as those of their female counterparts.

The constraints, confusions and contradictions generated by partial sports reform made comprehensive reform inevitable. By the mid-1990s 41 sports associations, affiliated to 14 sports management centres and covering 56 sports, had obtained freedom from the NSC to manage their sports. Two years later, the old department (*shi*) that was responsible for elite sport under the NSC ceased to exist. Now all sports were under the administration of 20 management centres that were public entities instead of government or Party agencies.

The decentralisation of sports institutions provided sports management centres with greater autonomy, but, of course, it also led to a decline in government investment.[25] Given the fact that the market economy was as yet far from mature in China, to obtain non-government sponsorship was not an easy job, especially for the less popular sports. Without sufficient financial support, performance would be under threat. In the face of the financial pressure, the directors of these associations and centres had to spend time as entrepreneurs in order to meet their financial needs. Most of these directors, however, were former officials of the NSC who had been substantially shaped by their previous experience in the central planning and administrative regime. They had little or no knowledge of marketing. Finding the right balance between market forces and the steady develop-ment of sport proved a complex matter for sports administrators. The transition to a market economy posed dilemmas and challenges for the sports community.

How to ensure international victory in the encouraging period of market-oriented reform was another challenge facing various associations. The Chinese Athletics Association (CAS) pioneered negotiations with local sports commissions on training budgets and performance quotas. Based on contracted quotas for the Olympic and Asian Games as well as World Championships medals,[26] the local sports commissions would receive training budgets and winning bonuses. However, if promised performance quotas were not achieved, the sports commissions would obtain no bonus and instead have to refund some of the budget received.[27] Liaoning, Shandong and Sichuan took the lead in signing agreements with the CAS.[28] This illustrates that although the provinces were heavily influenced by central policies, they were by no means merely passive respondents to central stimuli. They displayed discretionary behaviour and multiple compliance strategies. This process of bargaining served as a mutual constraint, itself part of China's unique response to economic reform. In short, the nation was moving neither towards capitalism nor away from socialism, but rather towards a mixed economy that combined state planning, government regulation and market forces and melded together private, collective, and state ownership.

Relationships between Elite and Mass Sport and between Coach and Athlete

Prior to economic reform, Chinese policy had been to combine mass and competitive sport, and to develop competitive sport based on mass sport. After China had resumed its place on the IOC, as already mentioned, the emphasis gradually shifted to elite sport. Some officials and academics argued furiously over the dialectic relations between mass and elite sport and questioned established sports guidelines.[29] As a consequence, in the mid-1980s the Olympic strategy was advocated. Despite being questioned in the late 1980s, when China performed poorly in the Seoul Olympic Games, the elite-oriented policy continued into the 1990s. However, by the mid-1990s it was coming under increasing challenge.

Now China had already fulfilled, some years in advance, the original target of quadrupling the 1980 GNP by the year 2000. People's living standards had improved dramatically, and at the same time their leisure time had increased following the adoption of the five-day working week in May 1995. Influenced by the international trend of 'sport for all', increasing numbers of people wanted to take part in sport as recreation. This demand, however, could not be fully met due to limited public access to sporting facilities, thus generating the criticism that international athletic success, so sought after during the previous two decades, was at the expense of mass sport.[30] Consequently, there was a growing demand for a greater emphasis on a national policy for, and investment in, mass sport. Against this background, in early 1995 the NSC established the 'national fitness programme'.[31] This programme represented a milestone in the history of mass sport in China.

To implement the programme many activities, including surveys of mass sport, fitness training, testing and monitoring were organised throughout the nation.[32] A number of publications on fitness and mass sport appeared. A new post of 'sports instructor for society', equivalent to coach and physical education teacher, was created. Sports stadiums and fields that had formerly been used for high-level training and competitions were gradually opened to the public.[33] Mass sport boomed.[34] In Beijing, the number of people using public sports facilities increased from 140,000 per month in 1995 to 530,000 in 1996.[35] Expenditure for mass sport in the capital was about six million yuan in 1996.[36] By the mid-1990s mass sport had joined elite sport as the second pillar of the sports edifice in China.

Given the increasing disparity in income between different occupations, and between city and rural dwellers, the popularity of sport was, to a great extent, confined to the urban areas and to affluent rural counties. Those with well-paid jobs or higher social status were more likely to engage in mass sport, especially in those activities that required facilities. The most visible example of this was the female ministers' tennis team[37] – women officials who regularly played tennis and took fitness classes. Despite the controversy over their privileged access to tennis, they set an example to women to be actively involved in sport.

The growing emphasis on mass sport, however, did not mean the downgrading of elite sport. Given that sport had been intricately intertwined with politics in the history of the PRC,[38] it was unlikely that China would change its priorities overnight from a medal-oriented strategy to a mass-oriented strategy. The Olympic strategy now went hand in hand with the national fitness programme. International sporting success was, and still is, a major instrument of political success and national inspiration.

This fact is reflected in the overwhelming proportion of the government budget that went into Olympic sports. To secure victory at the Atlanta Games in 1996, a special fund for Olympic-related sports facilities, nutrition and sports research reached 65 million yuan. Over 200 researchers were involved in 56 Olympic-related projects.[39] Moreover, between 1994 and 1996 China assembled 960 athletes across the country, more than twice the number of actual participants, to prepare for the universal sporting event.[40] This was undoubtedly an expensive approach. Although the details of the investment for the 1996 Olympic Games are not available, it has been alleged that the expenses were double of those for the games four years earlier. Indeed, these deliberate endeavours bore fruit at the 1996 Olympic Games – China retained its fourth place in the gold, and total, medal counts.

By the mid-1990s a growing diversification of interests had spawned a complex and at times confrontational process of change in the relationship between coach and athlete. The most prominent example comes from the experience of the much-talked-about 'Ma Family Army' of Chinese women's distance runners. The year following their victories at the 1993 Athletic World Championships, they received lucrative advertising fees, and payments for their successful presentation of an image as female athletes with ability, courage and determination.[41] These athletes played an active part in raising women's standing and in further changing traditional beliefs and attitudes about women, sport and professionalism. However, the economic rewards resulting from outstanding sporting achievements caused unexpected disputes and a resulting split between these sportswomen and their coach Ma Junren. In December 1993 the 10,000-metres world champion Liu Dong left coach Ma. The immediate reason was that she had not received the car awarded by the IAAF for a winning performance nor a pure one-kilogram gold medal given to her by the rich Hong Kong Chinese He Yindong. Ma had kept them both. In spite of her desire to continue athletic training, Liu was not allowed to continue in competition.[42]

The story of Liu Dong attracted prime media attention for over a year before a more astonishing event occurred: all but one of Ma's athletes abandoned Ma's training centre in Dalian.[43] The immediate reason was the same as in the case of Liu Dong: a dispute over money.[44] The deeper, long-term reasons for the split will be analysed in Chapter 7. The demise of such a high-profile sports community reflects the fact that after the inauguration of the market economy in the early 1990s social values underwent rapid and profound transformation. Sportswomen both were influenced by and promoted these social changes.

Disharmony between coach and athlete continued in the public domain with the rift between the 1995 world figure-skating champion Chen Lu and her coach in 1996. Once again, it was caused by a financial dispute. For three years before Chen's world fame began, Chen and her coach had received very favourable treatment from the state. About three-quarters of the annual budget (200 thousand yuan) for the entire national figure-skating team was used exclusively for Chen's training and competition abroad.[45] On top of this, Chen occasionally joined foreign skaters in commercial displays and obtained extra income from them. The fair sharing of these earnings became the source of conflict between Chen and her coach,[46] and as a result, she left the coach who had been with her for over a decade.

Financial concerns appeared to be the direct and most important cause of these confrontations. By the mid-1990s commercialisation had became pervasive, and splits had emerged in the sports community. With increased financial independence, athletes wanted to determine their own destinies – athletically, financially and socially. Inevitably, this posed a challenge to conventional ideas of conformity, loyalty and sacrifice of individual interest – the foundation of traditional sporting arrangements. Financial interests increasingly dominated relations between coaches and athletes. Undoubtedly, market-oriented reform and the associated social and cultural changes necessitated concomitant changes in sports management, and in the relationship between athlete and coach.

Coaches, who played a crucial part in bringing about the success of Chinese women in sport, were affected, of course, by the market economy. By the mid-1990s, China's surge towards becoming a consumer society was evident and it had become obvious to all that successful participation in it depended on one's income. When everybody tried to grab every opportunity to make money, coaches were no exception. Ma Junren, like his famous athletes, was involved in a number of commercial activities over and above various winning rewards. He received a house valued at 3.6 million yuan from the Zhejiang Shengda Company while his athletes obtained only 400,000 yuan in total in cash for advertising its products. In addition, Ma transferred the rights to produce his nutritious 'Life Nuclear Energy' (*shengmin helun*) drink to the Today's Group Company for ten million yuan. He also established his own Medical and Health-Care Product Company, of whose board he was chairman. These activities sparked controversy over Ma's role and coaching potential and involved him in two lawsuits as he attempted to transfer his patent to different companies.[47]

Like Ma, other local coaches ran their own businesses in tandem with their coaching. In the face of the pressures of commercialism, the complete commitment required of coaches was often compromised. Some even used their positions to accept bribes when recruiting and coaching athletes.[48] All this threatened to lower athletic standards, particularly in elite sports teams.

As the leader of the Shanghai gymnastic team remarked, 'In spite of working shorter hours, coaches in sports schools can earn more income [through charging for classes] than our coaches of the elite sports teams. This discrepancy adversely affects the commitment of elite team coaches to sports training.'[49] To create a contented group of dedicated coaches would be one of the challenges facing China in the process of market-driven reform.

Uncertainties over coaches' prospects intensified in the wake of economic reform. As noted in Chapter 4, coaches whose athletes did not win a place in national and international competitions found it hard to remain employed. To secure their coaching positions, some coaches pursued success during their four-year contracts in ways that ignored scientific training principles, at the possible expense of athletes and their future. Using drugs to enhance performance, it is alleged, was one of them. This issue will be discussed in the next chapter. Such short-sighted action endangered the whole of the future of Chinese, not to mention women's, sport. In summary, sports commercialism made relationships in elite sport more complex and more difficult.

Sportswomen and Women's Elite Sport in the 1990s

In the last decade of the twentieth century China consolidated its fourth position in the Olympic rankings. This achievement was largely attributable to Chinese women. In 1992 women not only outnumbered men in the Chinese delegation to the Olympic Games (132 to 118) but also won three-quarters (12) of the 16 gold medals. For the first time, women made their mark in establishing China as one of the major world powers in sport. Women athletes again outnumbered their male counterparts in the delegation to the 1996 Olympic Games: 200 to 110. Of the 16 gold medals won by Chinese, nine were won by women. They continued to be the backbone of Chinese elite sport.[50]

Olympic victories put women centre stage. They became the heroines of the nation,[51] and won enormous social esteem and prestige. For example, on their return from Barcelona, they were warmly received by people from all walks of life, including high-level officials. A reception was held by the Central Committee of the Chinese Communist Party and the State Council, in the People's Hall in Tiananmen Square on 16 August 1992, at which General Secretary Jiang Zemin and Premier Li Peng were present.[52]

In addition to social prestige, these Olympic winners obtained enviable material rewards. In 1992, gold, silver and bronze medallists obtained 80,000-, 50,000- and 30,000-yuan bonuses respectively from the central government (5.5 yuan was nearly equal to one US dollar at the time). This was topped up by various sponsorships from enterprises, businessmen and overseas Chinese. The 15-year-old Olympic gymnast Lu Li obtained sponsorship estimated to be at least a million yuan, a vast sum compared to the 1992 per-capita income of 1,020.9 yuan. Winning, however, could be a double-edged sword, stimulating athletes financially to fulfil their athletic ambitions, and at the same time undermining a long-term commitment to their career. Given the years of state investment, early retirement on the back of substantial earnings was undoubtedly a waste of resources. This was typified by Lu Li who, after her Olympic triumph, put an early end to her gymnastics career.[53] The successful athletes' enormous financial gains provoked debate over the desirability of rewards, as athletes were already given training equipment and free board, transportation and other benefits,[54] far beyond anything ordinary families could afford.[55] Market-driven reform did not always produce social harmony.

Reform not only challenged the old ways by introducing the new concepts of a market economy, but also brought about profound changes in the social structure and in social values in ways that were increasingly at odds with orthodox ideology.[56] Profit, competition and success became widely pursued aims. This is clearly reflected in the sports community. One very noticeable event concerned the well-known female diver Gao Min. In 1995 she auctioned one of her gold medals for 666,666 yuan (about US$80,000), six being a lucky number to the Chinese. This event, once again, generated an acrimonious debate over athletes' remuneration. Should athletes obtain huge bonuses and other income from activities such as advertising and auctions while the state provided them with free coaching, facilities, accommodation and food as well as salaries equal to those of ordinary factory workers? The deputy minister of the NSC, Liu Qi, offered strong support for the image of the new athlete: 'An athletic career differs from others. It is a career of youth. Athletes endure unimaginable hardship to achieve success.' Apparently, he persuaded Gao Min to set aside most of the money from the auction for her future life instead of donating it to a national disaster fund, as she had agreed to do under public pressure.[57] This pragmatism made individualism, inequality, and the treatment of talent and people as commodities gradually acceptable. Sport thus became a visible medium for communicating new national policies to the masses and helped validate the changing values in society.

Individuals may have benefited from the changes driven by the market economy approach, but in the short term, while some men's team sports experimented with market-oriented reform, most men's team sports and all women's team sports remained centrally planned and within the restricted confines of a limited and fixed government budget. This gave rise to problems: in the case of women basketball players below superstar status, for example, living within these financial constraints meant that the only affordable way to travel was by rail, which entailed long, stressful journeys before competitions. This contrasted sharply with the comfortable air travel available to their male counterparts. Furthermore, salaries for women professionals were well below those of their male colleagues. Such discrimination might well have affected women players' commitment. The Chinese women's basketball team dropped from Olympic and world silver medallists in 1992 and 1994 to ninth place in the 1996 Olympics and to twelfth place at the 1998 world championships.

Football provides a good example of an emerging and widening inequality between men and women in the same sport. Although the Chinese women's football team[58] won silver medals at the 1996 Olympics and the 1998 World Cup, it attracted few spectators and received insufficient sponsorship. In sharp contrast to the women's situation, the men's football team had never qualified for the Olympics or World Cup competitions, but enjoyed far more enviable financial rewards and the spotlight of the mass media. As already mentioned in the last chapter, in the 1980s women football players had far from comfortable training and living conditions. Although improvements were made in training facilities, living conditions and sponsorship following their rise to world prominence in the 1990s, women football players remained less well-rewarded than men in salaries, bonuses and transfer fees. Certainly, this state of affairs was not attractive to young promising players. Due to the shortage of young talent, most members of the Chinese women's football team at this time were aged between 28 and 30. Partly because of the lack of the promising young players, the team failed to get to the semi-finals at the 2000 Olympic Games. The world champion women's volleyball team of the 1980s was in the same predicament as the women's football team. It fell from being world champion in 1986 to seventh place at the 1992 Olympic Games.

There is some truth in the assertion that the deteriorating performance of women's team sport was associated with the shifting emphasis of sports policy from team sports to individual sports. This shift in emphasis is clear from the number of provincial women's football teams that ceased to exist and the number of players who were forced to end their training or go to other countries such as Japan to continue their football careers.[59] The number of women's volleyball teams in the national league was reduced from 35 in the 1980s to 20 in 1994.[60] Influenced by the cutting back of team athletes, basketball players in various sports schools decreased from 50,529 in 1980 to 30,640 in 1995 (a 40 per cent decline), and the number of coaches fell by 28 per cent from 2,794 in 1980 to 1,995 in 1998.[61] Women's team sports were under intense challenge in the context of market-oriented reform.

The inequality and uncertainty caused by reform had both a direct and an indirect impact on the morale of women's team sports. The training attitude of female athletes was a cause of concern. According to Wang Jian's mid-1990s survey, men's attitude to training was better than women's.[62] One reason lay in the disciplinary advantages available to the new club administrations. As volleyball coach Li Guizhi admitted:

> Managing a club team is relatively easier than managing state-owned provincial teams. Because violations of discipline, such as lateness for training, result in a fine, it is not worth being late. Under the new

system, financial interest governs people's behaviour. In contrast, our provincial team does not have the money to adopt this practice.[63]

Analysis: Illustrative Case Studies

As in the previous chapters, Beijing, Guangdong and Sichuan will be used as representative case studies to provide local illustrations of a general situation, covering the following issues:

- Sports developments in the 1990s;
- The market economy and sports reform;
- The influence of sporting reforms on both women's sport and sportswomen.

Beijing

As discussed in the previous chapter, from the mid-1980s Beijing became less influential in elite sport. This tendency continued into the 1990s. Beijing athletes won just 3.5 points at the Olympic Games in 1992,[64] coming 19th among the 30 municipalities and provinces in the country. Other areas did much better. Guangdong, for example, won 45 points at the 1992 games. This result might be associated with insufficient sports investment: in 1992, although Beijing ranked first in terms of per-capita sports budget – a result of having a smaller population than Shanghai, and indeed all the provinces – its sports expenditure was only 17,29 million yuan, 25th nationally among the municipalities and provinces.[65] Sports expenditure at this time arguably had a direct influence on the development of elite sport in Beijing.

Once Beijing declared its intention of hosting the 2000 Olympic Games, various sport-related activities were organised. For example, under the theme of 'Bid to host the 2000 Olympics', June 1992 was named 'sports month' in Beijing. Over 30,000 participants were attracted to 123 activities, including Olympic knowledge contests and marathon running.[66] To support the bid, Beijing's infrastructure was greatly improved.[67] The capital soon possessed 76 per cent of the stadiums and gymnasiums necessary for the Olympic Games. In addition, by the mid-1990s there were four training bases for elite sports teams. Half of the eight urban districts[68] in Beijing owned well-equipped sports centres, even though ten suburbs and counties remained under-equipped.[69] By the end of 1995, Beijing had 1.3 square metres of sports fields per head, a level well above the national average (0.65).[70] Despite all this effort and all the investment involved, Beijing lost the bid by two votes to Sydney (Australia).[71] The state media reacted as if the whole nation was plunged into depression.

Following the directive that the 1997 National Games would comprise only Olympic sports and martial arts, Beijing adjusted its elite sports policies and strategies. Its image had to be improved. Potential Olympic medal sports were increasingly emphasised. Incentive rewards were used to motivate both athletes and coaches: a winning bonus of 50,000 yuan for a gold medal was promised before the eighth National Games in 1997. Established coaches and athletes were further given monthly allowances of, for example, between 240 and 700 yuan for Olympic finalists placed first to eighth – see Table 10. Between 1995 and 1997 they also received nutrition subsidies (100 yuan per month) and had higher board standards.[72] In addition, a 'delivery bonus' was used to encourage sports schools to deliver athletes to elite sports teams. In 1996 the Beijing Municipal Sports Commission paid 1,700,000 yuan alone in bonuses of this type.[73] In short, a complicated system of wage and bonus structures evolved in the pursuit of good performance.

Such entrepreneurial incentives produced some positive results. Beijing athletes earned 100.5 points at the 1996 Olympic Games, ranking joint first with Hubei province in the national Olympic performance records.[74] Although Beijing women did not win any gold medals in the games, they were the key members of the silver-medal-winning football, baseball and handball teams: six members of the women's baseball team, three of the women's football team and three of the handball team were from Beijing. It should be noted that a number of the players were aged around 30.[75] They made a major contribution to Chinese success at the 1996 Olympic Games. In spite of this, the capital city failed to challenge the top three regions (Shanghai, Liaoning and Guangdong) at the 1997 National Games. Even worse, it dropped to fifth in the total score and sixth in the medal count. The effort to win back leadership in elite sport was left for the next century.

The truth of the matter was that Beijing's decline in elite sport is largely associated with ongoing market-oriented sports reform across the country. After a market economy was officially introduced in 1992, the marketing of sport became an irreversible trend. Sports clubs were created in 1993.[76] However, due to the need to make profits, not all clubs embraced profes-

TABLE 10

STANDARDS FOR ATHLETES' PERFORMANCE ALLOWANCES (YUAN/MONTH)

	1	2	3	4	5	6	7	8
OG	700	600	500	400	350	300	260	240
WC of OS	550	470	390	310	270	230	210	190
WC of non-OS	450	380	300	240	220	200	185	160
Asian Games	400	345	290	235	210	190	170	155
AG of OS	360	3320	280	220	200	180	160	145
NG, AC of non-OS	310	270	230	190	170	150	135	120
NC	280	240	200	175	155	140	125	110

Notes: WC=World championships; OG=Olympic Games; OS=Olympic sports; AG=National Games; NC=National Championships.

Source: Beijing shi tiwei (ed.), *1996 Beijing tiyu nianjian* [1996 Beijing Sports Year Book], Beijing: renmin tiyu chuban she, 1997, p.386.

sional sport. Sporting reforms such as the introduction of sports clubs were a process of learning and adjustment, and new problems and difficulties arose – two of them being inappropriate actions born of inexperience and insufficient sponsorship.[77] These affected Beijing's elite sport to some extent. Other places were shrewder, more dynamic and more successful.

Despite setbacks, failings and disappointments it was not all gloom – for women. The United Nations Fourth World Conference on Women in Beijing gave rise to an impetus to promote women's status in China, especially in Beijing. This was reflected in the increase in female sports officials and coaches in Beijing. In 1996, of 26 officials at the level of department director and above in the Beijing Municipal Sports Commission, six (22 per cent) were women.[78]

In the 1990s, corporate sponsorship and profits through business transactions rapidly increased and gradually became the main source of finance for sport in Beijing. In 1994, for example, of the 26.92-million-yuan sports budget in Beijing, 14.878 million yuan was earned through business activities, 4.907 million yuan was from government and 7.134 million yuan was from social sponsorship.[79] Thus government investment was only around 18 per cent, and social sponsorship was 26.5 per cent. Clearly, self-financing now became crucial to Beijing's elite sport, and compared to economically potent regions such as Shanghai (96.604 million yuan) and Guangdong (309.951 million yuan), Beijing's sports budget was now far inferior. It could not resist the intense challenge from these coastal regions in elite sport. Consequently, standards fell and Beijing's performance in international and national competitions became less and less impressive.

In summary, to raise the status of the nation's capital, the Beijing Sports Commission made every effort to restore its supremacy in elite sport. It achieved impressive results at the 1996 Olympic Games, in which Beijing women excelled at several team sports. However, various challenges and difficulties arising from market-oriented reforms made it hard, indeed impossible, for Beijing to reassert its dominance.

Guangdong

In the 1990s, Guangdong retained its leading position in economic development. Its average per-capita income was 2,356 yuan per year in 1992, higher than the national average of 1,990 yuan.[80] Thus it is no surprise that Guangdong had a much higher sports budget than Beijing or Sichuan. Of the total budget of 309.951 million yuan in 1994, some 258.282 million yuan was earned by sports communities through business activities, 26.391 million yuan was from government and 5.652 million yuan was from sponsorship.[81] Clearly, Guangdong was highly successful at self-financing its sport. In 1992, there were 24,921 enterprise-run sports teams in the province.[82]

As a measure of the province's entrepreneurial success, sporting organisations extended downwards from city level to town level. By the mid-1990s, some 803 out of the 1,672 towns (*zhen*) in Guangdong had established sports commissions.[83] This provided an organisational basis for the rapid development of sport. Multifarious financial schemes and multi-level sports organisations greatly bolstered Guangdong's elite sport.

Guangdong's economic power was reflected in the construction of a powerful facilities infrastructure. Between 1988 and 1992, 87 stadiums were built in the Pearl River delta,[84] the most rapidly developing area in the province. In Dong Guan, a newly expanded city in the delta, eight counties had already set up sports centres by the mid-1990s, and another eight were building them. In addition, a number of well-equipped, independent sports schools such as Guangdong Diving School and Foshan Lining Gymnastics School were built. This provision of sports facilities not only provided a resource base for increased sports participation, both mass and elite, but also raised the city's self-esteem.[85]

One interesting product of sporting reform was an improvement in athletes' educational standards. Of the 1,080 athletes in the province, 154 reached college level, 68 attended vocational schools and 333 finished senior high school. This was marked progress compared to the situation of a decade earlier, when few obtained a college education.[86] This change resulted to a considerable extent from more flexible academic courses and arrangements available for elite athletes. Now athletes could register as school or college students while they were pursuing athletic training. The relevant educational institutions sent teachers to sports centres to teach at agreed times. It was strongly believed that increased opportunities for higher education would ease parents' opposition to their children's participation in sport.

There was more. With the extension of 'opening up to the outside' in the 1990s, international sporting exchanges in Guangdong prospered. In 1995 alone, some 146 sports groups (646 people) travelled to 35 countries and regions including Hong Kong, Macao and Taiwan. Foreign sports visitors reached 1,200.[87] Thus, Guangdong itself was increasingly assimilated into the global sporting community. Numerous international and national sports competitions took place in the province, for example, the first Women's World Soccer Championships in 1991. These competitions enhanced the popularity of elite sport among women. For example, of the 18 members of the provincial judo team in the same year, ten were women.[88] Eleven Guangdong women competed at the 1992 Olympic Games. At the games Xing Fen won a gold medal in women's weightlifting. Four members of the Chinese women's football team that won a silver medal at the 1996 Olympic Games were from Guangdong.[89] Guangdong women had become an important segment of Chinese women's sport.

A strong economy, considerable investment in facilities and increased access to the outside world did not, however, guarantee outright success for Guangdong in competition with its provincial rivals. At the 1993 National Games, Guangdong was defeated by Liaoning, the north-eastern province, home of the famous Ma Family Army. Although Guangdong invested 120 million yuan to prepare for the 1997 National Games, and registered for 30 out of the 34 sports established at the games,[90] it failed to reclaim the Chinese crown of elite sport. Worse, it fell to third place in the total score, behind Shanghai and Liaoning, and fourth below Shanghai, Liaoning and Shandong in the gold medal count. Market forces could not achieve everything although they changed much.

How can lack of absolute success be explained? By the 1990s market forces had penetrated every corner of society in Guangdong. Entrepreneurship prevailed. But there was a snag in this: coaches and athletes were lured to make money in and out of sport. This undoubtedly undermined their commitment to sport. Although 60,000-, 40,000-, and 20,000-yuan bonuses from the Guangdong Provincial Sports Developmental Fund were awarded to the gold, silver and bronze medallists of the Barcelona Games,[91] these bonuses were not as attractive as those of other provinces. Due to higher living standards in Guangdong (2,356.33 yuan per year), winning bonuses in proportion to overall income were lower than in other provinces, for example, Sichuan (1,764 yuan). Then again, arguably, better living standards as well as entrepreneurship adversely affected the dedication of coaches and athletes. In short, the economic advantages mentioned earlier may well have been the cause of the Guangdong coaches' and athletes' reduced performance.

Guangdong demonstrates how market forces greatly influenced elite sport – positively and negatively. With its strong economy, Guangdong's sports expenditure soared and facilities improved. However, economic strength was not wholly synonymous with successful performance. Commercialised sport had a detrimental influence on elite sport through the distraction of coaches and athletes away from a commitment to athletic performance to a commitment to financial success. Guangdong's rating consequently fell at the two most recent National Games. Women were an integral part of Guangdong's elite sport, so women's elite sport was no exception to the situation outlined above. Nevertheless, in spite of the challenges arising from the market economy, Guangdong women were still influential in China's elite sport.

Sichuan

As the biggest province in China, Sichuan's gross 'national' product was 209.649 billion yuan in 1993, fourth among the provinces and municipalities in the country. However, Sichuan's per-capita income of 1,764 yuan in 1993 was below the national average of 2,706 yuan, and 25th among the country's municipalities and provinces.[92] This discrepancy was largely attributed to Sichuan's huge population of over 100 million. Due to its mountainous and isolated geographic location, Sichuan was less attractive to foreign investors than Beijing and Guangdong and, influenced by this economic situation, Sichuan's elite sport performance was only average. For example, Sichuan athletes earned 25 points from the 1992 Olympic Games. At these, the celebrated 'diving queen' Gao Min won the platform diving title and the shooter Zhang Shan defeated her male and female rivals to claim a gold medal, thereby helping to raise Sichuan's self-esteem.

Hosting sports events often facilitates the development of both elite and mass sport. However, due to its poor facilities, Sichuan found it too difficult and too expensive to host the National Games independently. To overcome this problem in 1993, for the first time, the National Games were co-hosted, by the two widely separate cities of Beijing and Chengdu. In preparation for the games, Sichuan's sports expenditure in 1992 reached 53.57 million yuan. Sports facilities in the province greatly improved. Benefiting from the advantageous position of being a host province, Sichuan achieved its best ever games results – fifth in the medal count and eighth in the points tally.[93] This encouraging performance stimulated the Sichuanese to continue their quest for athletic success.

In consequence, in the mid-1990s the Sichuan Provincial Sports Commission drafted a blueprint for the development of elite sport. It involved the continuity of provincial government investment in key sports such as athletics and swimming, and reliance on sponsorship for popular sports such as football, basketball and volleyball.[94] To rally significant support both from society at large and from individuals in the sporting community was a specific aim of this provincial sports policy.

As in other regions, sports sponsorship was diversified in Sichuan. In addition to 5.925 million yuan from the government, sponsorship reached 0.481 million yuan and revenue through business activities totalled 16.653 million yuan.[95] Due to volleyball's popularity, both men's and women's volleyball teams easily obtained sponsorship and in the mid-1990s actually pioneered the professionalisation of volleyball on the western model in China. As elsewhere the management of sport was shifting from exclusive government control to enterprise or club management.

Performance at the National Games, of course, continued to be the major concern of provincial sports officials. To produce good results at the eighth National Games in 1997, a specific strategy was formulated: to participate as widely as possible in events in order to compete strongly against other provinces in the total score rather than in the medal count. There were good reasons for this approach. First, a string of famous female athletes, including the 1992 Olympic gold medallist Gao Min, retired from the competitive arena after the 1993 National Games. Undoubtedly, their absence would affect Sichuan's potential for medals in 1997. This was clear from the 1996 Olympic Games, at which Sichuan athletes gained no medals. Second, there were changes in the scoring system of the National Games,[96] which meant that the number of entrants achieving top eight places had more weight than before in determining a province's placing. In addition, the exclusion of non-Olympic sports from the National Games meant the loss of sports in which Sichuan was much more successful, such as parachuting and sports acrobatics. Furthermore, the separation of Chongqing from Sichuan in 1997 reduced the province's competence since Chongqing athletes would now represent the new municipality. All these factors made it extremely difficult, if not impossible, for Sichuan to repeat its medal performances of 1993 at the National Games in 1997.

Its strategy, nevertheless, was reasonably successful – Sichuan achieved satisfactory results. Some 450 Sichuan athletes in 23 sports qualified for the final phase of the games in Shanghai. The province remained eighth in the total points in spite of the fall in the medal table from fifth to 11th.

These hard-earned results were largely attributed to the astounding achievements of Sichuan women. Women athletes captured first, second, fifth and sixth places in the 100-metre sprint; first, second and seventh places in the 100-metre hurdles; and first, third and seventh places in the long jump. The most astonishing result came from the sprinter Li Xuemei, who was timed at 10.9 seconds in the 100-metre sprint. This result outperformed that of the Olympic champion of the previous year, and cut 0.4 seconds off her own record at the World Athletics Championships a few months earlier. Unsurprisingly, these phenomenal results provoked suspicions of drug abuse. The suspicions were heightened when, a few months after the eighth National Games, woman's long-jump gold medallist Xiong Qiying was declared to be one of the 24 caught using drugs at the games.[97] In spite of the controversy over the reliability of Sichuan's performances, one thing is clear: women continued to be the backbone of its elite sport.

In the context of market-oriented economic reform, inland provinces such as Sichuan could hardly compete with the leading coastal provinces and municipalities in wealth and elite sport that was so directly influenced by economic progress. Nevertheless, Sichuan demonstrated that wealth was not everything and that motivation was not without its success. As a result of the National Games, elite sport continued to be the top priority of the Sichuan sports programme, and women remained essential to the programme.

These three case studies, then, demonstrate clearly that elite sport in China was influenced by the market economy developing in the 1990s. Commercialisation became pervasive. The practices of incentive rewards, sports clubs and professional sports teams became widespread. Public and private organisations sponsored sport. Interestingly, the three provinces responded in different ways to the new economic situation according to their specific circumstances. Economic reform was common in the whole of China to various degrees, but the response was varied in elite sport as in other things. Ironically, the rankings of the three sampled regions at the National Games all fell in 1997. An intense interprovincial rivalry now characterised China as a whole.

Conclusion

After Deng Xiaoping advocated a market economy in 1992, Chinese sport began a process of market-oriented reform. The club system, professional sports teams and athletes' transfer fees appeared and spread across the country. All this led to radical changes. By the end of 1997 sport administrative departments had been transformed from governmental sports agencies into independent management centres and associations. With the decentralisation of sports management local sports bodies continued to play an important part in directing sport.

In the transition to a market economy, the administration of sport became a mixture of state planning, government regulation and free-market forces. Conflicts and clashes surfaced between state planners and the market, between the state and individuals, and between coaches and athletes. Female sports stars were in the front line of these confrontations. An increased emphasis on individualism led not infrequently to overt questioning of the coaches' authority. Another outcome of reform was widening inequality in incomes and welfare benefits between different sports and athletes. As a consequence, while market forces provided opportunities for individual female sports stars, they also posed challenges to women's sport in general.

The promulgation of the national fitness programme demonstrated an increasing emphasis on mass sport. Nevertheless, as an important symbol of rising Chinese power in the world, elite sport was still the centre of Chinese sport as it approached the millennium. This was clearly manifested in the continued fierce rivalry between the provinces at the eighth National Games in October 1997.

Olympic Success, Drug Violations and Elite Women's Sport in the New China

In January 1998 Chinese swimmers became the target of accusations over drug abuse. Growth hormone was found in a flask in the Chinese swimmer Yuan Yuan's luggage at Sydney Airport on 8 January,[1] and one week later four other swimmers failed the pre-competition drug tests[2] at the World Swimming Championships in Perth. These events reinforced the long-standing suspicion that the Chinese were involved in a systematic national drug programme and forced Shen Guofan, a spokesman for the Chinese Foreign Ministry, to respond to questions at a press conference in Beijing on 15 January 1998. Drug abuse thus became a political issue. In the words of State Council Commissioner Li Tieying, 'This scandal brings disgrace to China's elite sport and damages the nation, its people and eventually the athletes themselves.'[3] Thus, at the very moment when China was making its most dramatic impact on world sport, it suffered a serious loss of face.

It appears that performance-enhancing drugs have been used widely in China. As such it is an unavoidable topic in any study of contemporary Chinese women's sport. However, the Chinese were, and still are, reluctant to speak about it. Drug-relevant publications have been simply descriptions of the international history of drug abuse or the negative medical and physiological consequences of drug taking. The only example of facing up to the issue within China has been Zhao Yu's *Qiangguo meng – Dangdai zhongguo tiyu de wuqu* [The Dream of Being a Superpower – The Traps of Contemporary Chinese Sport].[4] This literary work bravely exposed the widespread drug abuse in Chinese sport in the 1980s. However, there is still no specific study of the rise of drug abuse and its social and cultural roots in Chinese sport. There have been numerous articles on Chinese drug abuse in the western media, but they have been based for the most part on speculation or have been merely reports of positive tests as 'hot news', without adequate analysis. Thus, so although it is necessary, it is difficult to discuss drug-related issues in Chinese sport given the difficulty of obtaining information on drug-taking from published documents or even interviews.

To date many matters involving drug issues remain unclear. How were drugs introduced to China? What were the motives for Chinese athletes to take drugs? Were they coerced, or did they voluntarily take drugs? Was there a government-planned programme for administering performance-enhancing drugs? Will China crack down on drug abuse, and, if so, what impact will it have on its sport, women's sport in particular? All these questions require serious consideration.

Given the limited information available on drug use in China, this chapter will combine various sources including journals, newspapers (both western and Chinese), internet and official documents as well as interviews, to undertake a preliminary exploration of the issue. Swimmers will be the focus of this analysis for the simple reason that they have attracted the most attention.

Drug Culture versus Anti-Drug Campaigns

Employing substances to promote performance has a long history in world sport.[5] However, it was in the mid-1950s, when cyclists were tested drug-positive, that the issue of drug abuse first attracted international attention.[6] Alarmed by the increasing numbers of athletes using drugs to enhance performance, the International Olympic Committee (IOC) passed a resolution against doping in 1962 and introduced drug testing at both the Winter and Summer Olympic Games in 1968. Since 1972 full-scale testing has been carried out. Nevertheless, drug-taking was not stopped but became increasingly pervasive in western sport. By 1988, when the Canadian sprinter Ben Johnson was caught, 31 athletes had already been disqualified for drug use.[7]

Performance-enhancing drugs did not appear in China until the early 1980s, probably due to its exclusion from the IOC between the late 1950s and the late 1970s. After the 'open door' policy was embraced in 1979, China's cultural and technological exchanges with foreign countries expanded rapidly. Aided by modern telecommunications technology, the Chinese gained access to the latest information on advanced training methods, including drug technology.[8] Drug abuse in Chinese sport was essentially a by-product of the 'open door' policy.

In the 1980s, however, coverage of drug-related issues in the Chinese media was very limited. Most Chinese, including athletes and coaches, were ignorant of drugs. This ignorance, arguably, made early experimentation with drugs possible in the sports community. This state of affairs was clearly reflected in the remarks of one female swimmer from Shang Xi Province:

> I had no knowledge of drugs until the summer of 1986 when we joined the Beijing training camp. The doctors of the Beijing swimming team prescribed their swimmers Chinese medicine to increase strength. In the winter of 1987–88, our coaches gave us some pills. At first we thought that they were vitamin tablets. Later on, when we found out the truth, we stopped taking them.[9]

Ignorance at the time, to some extent, precipitated the dispersion of drugs to a wide range of sports and athletes.[10] As one famous speed skater in the early 1990s remarked:

> We knew nothing about drugs until the mid-1987 when a coach of the national swimming squad was invited to lecture to our coaches and team leaders. In February 1988, we were found drug-positive in a pre-Olympic international competition. We were banned for one year. We felt very embarrassed and distressed because we did not want voluntarily to take drugs. This incident was not reported in the domestic media.[11]

In 1989 the spread of drugs prompted China to announce a three-pronged anti-drug policy of 'strict prohibition, strict examination and strict punishment' (*yanlin jinzhi, yange jiancha, yanli chufa*). Subsequently, drug tests were introduced in major domestic competitions.[12] In 1990 some 165 athletes were screened, and three were positive (1.82 per cent).[13] However, these drug violators were neither punished nor named publicly. Instead, the excuse of 'misusing Chinese medicine' (*wufu zhongyao*) was offered to explain away drug-positive tests. This practice simply conveyed the Janus-faced attitude of officialdom to drug abuse. On the one hand, it confirmed the existence of the use of some kind of material by Chinese athletes. On the other hand, it denied an intentional violation of Olympic regulations because 'Chinese medicine' (*zhongyao*) was often both acceptable and accessible to ordinary people. Consequently, the term 'Chinese medicine' was being employed as a smokescreen for hiding drug offenders. Drug abuse increased, and between 1988 and 1991 nine Chinese athletes tested positive. After the female athlete Xiao Yanlin was found positive in an out-of-competition drug test carried out by the examiners of the International Amateur Athletics Federation (IAAF) in 1992,[14] drug-positive test results multiplied dramatically. In 1992 alone 24 Chinese athletes were caught red-handed with anabolic steroids.[15]

Embarrassed by the mounting drug incidents involving Chinese athletes in international competitions, China set up a special Anti-Doping Commission in 1992. Tough measures to punish drug abusers and those behind them – officials, coaches and doctors – were promised.[16] A deliberate effort was apparently made to combat the drug problem but, regrettably, these policies did not effectively contain drug abuse. In 1993 31 Chinese athletes tested positive.[17] In the same year the Chinese conducted 1,347 tests themselves, in which 1.56 per cent (21 athletes) read positive,[18] well above the 1.3 per cent in a worldwide IOC programme involving 80,000 athletes.[19] Drug abuse was spreading, becoming particularly acute in Chinese swimming. Between 1990 and 1998 there were 28 Chinese swimmers who tested positive (all but one for anabolic steroids), almost half the world total (59) of drug offenders in sport.[20]

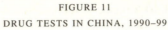

FIGURE 11

DRUG TESTS IN CHINA, 1990–99

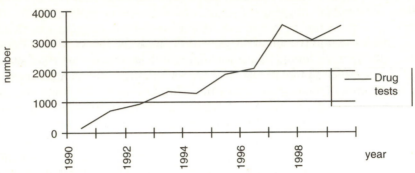

Concerned with the rising tide of drug incidence, from 1993 onwards China strengthened its anti-drug programme. Drug tests were given to a wider range of athletes (see Figure 11). As a result of this effort, of the 25 drug-test laboratories in the world in 1998, China was eighth in terms of the number of drug tests conducted – a marked progress compared to 17th place in 1994.[21] China invested considerable amounts of money in doping control programmes. Given the cost of drug testing, it cannot be denied that China now took the problem very seriously.

On 24 January 1994, for the first time, China named 24 drug-positive athletes[22] in *Zhongguo tiyu bao* [The China Sports Daily], and three months later an anti-drug education campaign was launched. 'Apart from facing mandatory sentences imposed by the international sports federations,[23] domestic penalties would now range from "moral criticism" to disciplinary and even legal action against offenders.'[24] Still, this new severity did not curb the use of performance-enhancing drugs. At the Hiroshima Asian Games in October 1994, 11 Chinese athletes (five of them women), including seven swimmers, tested positive for anabolic steroids.[25] This generated widespread speculation that Chinese women's achievement in sport was largely attributable to drugs.[26] In consequence, in 1995 the whole Chinese swimming team was barred from the Pan-Pacific Swimming Championships. The International Swimming Federation (FINA) also introduced random tests and an on-site investigation in China.[27] Drug scandals dealt China's image a heavy blow.

Further embarrassed by the international criticism and under escalating international pressure, in early 1995 China suspended for one year the nine coaches who were involved in the 31 cases of drug offences in 1994. Five of the coaches were from the national swimming squad.[28] Given the pervasiveness of drug misuse in the swimming world, the Chinese Swimming Association issued 'Regulations Against the Use of Forbidden Drugs' (*guanyu jinzhi shiyong weijing yaoping de guiding*), setting out tough penalties. If a swimmer tested drug-positive, the swimmer, the coach and the affiliated association would be disciplined. They would be banned from competitions for a minimum period of six months or for life depending on the seriousness of the offence. In addition, if a team had one drug-positive test, it would be subject to five out-of-competition drug tests. If two positive results occurred, the team would be ineligible for all the following year's domestic and international competitions. If six drug offences were found within a four-year period, the team would be disqualified from the National Games.[29] To fight against drug abuse was a requirement also written into the Sports Law (*tiyu fa*) that was enacted in 1995.[30] The law provides a legal basis for tackling drug abuse in sport. Consensus over the condemnation of drugs abuse was reached, at least ostensibly, within the sporting community. Nevertheless, as the director of the State Anti-Drug Committee, Yuan Weimin, sharply pointed out later: 'There is apparently ambiguity in some minds in the sports community as to whether or not they should deter athletes from using drugs.'[31] Some people were hesitating and waiting. This ambiguity made the implementation of various anti-drug policies doubtful. The dreadful predicament in Australia, described at the beginning of this chapter, became unavoidable.

Regarding drug offences in Chinese sport, one phenomenon should not be overlooked: in the 1990s drug-taking was spreading to young, inexperienced athletes. At the preliminary phase of the 1999 National City Games there were five drug-positive cases out of the 510 tests. Given that all the participants were junior and young athletes, this signalled a clear warning that drug abuse was spreading from adult to young athletes.[32] According to the doping laboratory of the National Sports Commission, most drugs that the young athletes took were cheap, accessible, strong and harmful steroids.[33] This state of affairs was worsened to some extent by easy access to drugs in society. 'There is no strict regulation or medical control; you can buy almost anything in a store.'[34] This casual management of medicine in the market certainly made it easy for drugs to spread among young athletes, and this spread could shake the foundations of China's sport. Aware of the horrifying consequences, the National Sports Bureau decided to introduce blood tests in the final phase of the City Games. If sample bottle 'A' tested positive for drugs, the athlete could be disqualified.[35] As a result of blood tests, four athletes were banned.[36]

In short, after the mid-1980s drug-taking and anti-drug campaigns coexisted in China. They were a recurrent element in elite sport, women's sport in particular, in the 1990s. For example, in 1997, some 18 out of the 24 drug-positive results involved women, mainly from athletics and weightlifting,[37] which suggests that 'the drug pestilence' was particularly rampant among women athletes. This attracted Chinese concern for the simple reason that women's performances in sport were China's glory. As the director of the National Athletic Centre, Duan Shijie, warned in March 1998: 'If drug abuses occur again in athletics, especially in the Ma Family Army, China's sport would collapse. This is not an exaggeration.'[38] China now went to the track in the battle against doping.

Behind the Drugs

How drug abuse originated in Chinese sport has been a question fascinating the sports world. It is speculated that East German coaches brought sophisticated doping techniques to China after being recruited in the mid-1980s.[39] Years later Chinese women swimmers achieved outstanding international successes,[40] similar to those of the former East Germany in the 1970s and 1980s.[41] It is undeniable that China employed East German as well as American, Russian and Australian coaches to raise athletic standards.[42] However, the Chinese seemed to value highly the German training regime especially. Reviewing the coach Klaus Nudalf's training, Qian Hong, one of his swimmers at the time and a 1992 Olympic champion, commented:

> He demanded similar high standards from our Chinese swimmers as he did of his European swimmers. He took us to Kunming, the capital city of Yunnan province in the south-west of China, for altitude training three times within the year. His methods, alternating between aerobic and anaerobic training, made us dizzy, caused us to have difficulty breathing and gave us sore muscles. Following a period of high-intensity training, we became stronger and our annual training load was greatly increased. We did in six months what we had previously done in one year. In short, before he came to China, our Chinese coaches did not have a full repertoire of training methods. By the time he left China, our Chinese coaches, combining his methods with China-specific situations and physical features, created a unique, individualised package of training methods.[43]

Based on a comparison of training methodologies between East Germany and the United States, Chen Yunpeng, the former head coach of the Chinese swimming team, claimed:

> The former East German training structure is superior to the American one. But the Americans held that the former east European countries, including East Germany, achieved good results by using drugs, and therefore did not study their training methods. This is their loss.[44]

Of course, it is most unlikely that coaches would admit to the use of drugs. As to the introduction of drugs by East German coaches, the matter is so sensitive that information on this point is very difficult to obtain. However, it has become dreadfully clear in the last few years that East German coaches used drugs to improve the performances of their athletes in many sports as a matter of course, and it is only reasonable to assume that they took these practices with them to China. What is reprehensible is the deceit involved. Athletes were informed that the pills supplied to them were health pills without any damaging effects.

It is still unclear who first introduced drugs to China. Anecdotal evidence suggests that sports researchers played an essential part. In other words, drugs in sport were a home-grown manifestation, at least to some extent. As mentioned in the earlier chapters, in the early 1980s China shifted its sports policy from an emphasis on friendship through sport to Olympic success. Sports research was utilised to optimise athletic performance, and to this end, drug research suddenly became a key project in almost all the research institutes across the country.[45] In 1993 there were 34 such institutes, at least one in each province.[46] These institutes recruited a number of medical or biochemical graduates and spent considerable amounts of money on advanced equipment for drug research. Sports researchers worked closely with coaches and athletes, supervising athletes' training, diet and possibly the use of drugs. Therefore, in the 1980s local sports researchers were the major agents in initiating the use of drugs in China. This fact has been largely overlooked by the West.

By the 1990s athletes had increased access to drug-related information through television, newspapers, the internet and foreign trips. They had more knowledge about drugs and their possible side-effects on their health. Thus it was difficult, if not impossible, for coaches to trick or pressurise athletes into taking performance-enhancing drugs. However, the number of athletes tested drug-positive climbed over time.[47] Why then did athletes want to use drugs? The 1990 national high-jump champion Zhang Tong has provided an answer: 'Nowadays some athletes themselves want to use drugs because of the lure of rewards and self-esteem. They want to be rich and they do not like to be despised by their friends for their poor performances.'[48]

Unsurprisingly, it seems that personal aspirations, pressure to achieve and the concomitant political and financial rewards are the prime reasons for drug abuse. As mentioned before, the economic reform unleashed in the late 1970s has resulted in radical changes in virtually every area of Chinese society. One of the marked changes is the replacement of Mao's egalitarianism by Deng's elitism. Since the early 1980s medal-winners in international competitions and the National Games have received attractive material and political rewards, such as good jobs, political promotion, enviable bonuses, decent houses and cars – the symbols of the good life in China.[49] Motivated by the chance of social prestige and material gains resulting from winning, some athletes have regarded drugs as a secret weapon ensuring sporting success. The swimmer Qian Hong has admitted: 'I would sacrifice everything for an Olympic gold medal, even if that would shorten my life by ten years.'[50] The high-jumper Zhang Tong has also confessed: 'If I could reach the top eight in the world with the aid of drugs, I would use them.'[51] These assertions reflect, to some extent, the prevalent attitude of Chinese athletes to drugs. It goes without saying that rich rewards could seduce a number of athletes and those behind them to seek quick success through the use of drugs. For them, these massive benefits could offset the risk of drug-taking.

Winning is perhaps, and understandably, especially attractive to athletes from lower-income backgrounds.[52] Indeed, a number of Chinese Olympic swimmers came from poor working-class families.[53] For them, the great wealth, power and fame achieved through sporting success could compensate for initial social handicaps and provide them with comfortable futures. Thus, some athletes risked damaging their lives to take drugs.

Perhaps the surge of drug abuse in China has deeper social and historic roots. As mentioned repeatedly, the century of humiliation by foreign invasion and 'semi-colonisation' after 1840 made the Chinese under communism obsessed with the desire to put behind them the image of the 'sick man of East Asia'. Sport was an effective instrument. With the resumption of its place on the IOC in 1979, China finally was able to take on its foreign rivals in international sporting contests. Winning Olympic medals now became a symbol of the rise of China in the world. By the mid-1980s China had reached the world level in table tennis, volleyball, diving and many other sports, but it still lagged behind the top nations in swimming and athletics. To change this unacceptable situation within a short time became the top priority in Chinese sport. As a result, various means, such as the establishment of the gold and silver awards, mentioned in Chapter 4, were used to promote these sports. Drug use might have been one of the means, although it was never acknowledged overtly. However, for some, what cannot be detected cannot be considered as against the rules of the IOC. This belief guided some coaches and athletes, who were often aided by researchers, to gamble on the use of drugs to maximise athletic performance. In short, the century of struggle for the improvement of China's image in the world made international success extremely important. Along with the desire for personal success, respect and acclaim, this national history to a considerable extent sowed the seeds of drug-taking in the Chinese sports community.

Drug violations occurred not only in international contests, but also in domestic competitions. This situation was largely caused by intensifying interprovincial competition. As mentioned earlier, the National Games have been the yardstick of every province's elite sports development. Local sports officials, coaches and athletes were, and are, often assigned medal quotas for the National Games. Performance was and is an exclusive prerequisite and criterion for budget and bonus allocation. Consequently, provinces have concentrated overwhelmingly on their rankings at the National Games.

It is not surprising then that best performances occur not infrequently at the National, rather than the Olympic, Games. For example, at the 1997 National Games[54] women's performances in the 100-metre and 1,500-metre[55] races, the 10-kilometre walk and the discus[56] equalled those of the first places in the 1997 World Championships, in which China did not win any gold medals.[57] Swimming is even more illustrative of this state of affairs. Chinese women swimmers in the annual list of the world top 25 across all 13 individual Olympic events jumped in number from 27 in 1992 to 96 in 1993 and from 22 in 1996 to 98 in 1997. Noticeably, 1993 and 1997 – the years of the National Games – saw a remarkable rise in world-level athletes. Although men swimmers' results were not so impressive as women swimmers' at the National Games, the same pattern was apparent: the number of Chinese swimmers in the world top 25 increased from three in 1992 to eight in 1993 and from six in 1996 to 20 in 1997.[58] Such phenomenal performances at the National Games attracted attention from the International Swimming Federation. In the last two months of 1997, it sent 20 groups of examiners to China to test its 23 swimmers. There were 104 drug tests.[59] The fluctuation in performances provides the clearest evidence that fierce inter-provincial competition could well be an incentive for some athletes to take drugs to ensure success at the National Games. Arguably, at least, to some extent, drug abuse was deeply enmeshed in state policy.

The pursuit of, and pressure to obtain, medals involved not just athletes but coaches and officials at various levels. For them the medal count was a performance indicator of employability, a manifestation of their achievement and a standard by which bonuses and promotions were to be secured. Take the case of Li Menghua, the director of the National Sports Commission (NSC) in the 1980s. As the head of sport's national governing body, he had to take responsibility for the poor showing of Chinese athletes at the Seoul Olympic Games in 1988 and as a result he resigned from his position on the NSC. Li alarmed other sports administrators: their official careers could be jeopardised by the unsuccessful performances of their athletes. In this case, most sports officials put a premium on athletic achievement. However, they could not openly oppose drug control or keep silent over drug abuse. They were thus put in a dilemma. This predicament tempted not a few to keep 'one eye open and one shut', and at most pay lip-service to the anti-drug campaign.

Probably, most officials did not overtly or directly involve themselves in discreditable drug activity, but it is quite likely they ignored or tolerated the violation of anti-drug policies. In view of this situation, NSC director Wu Shaozu commented bitterly later in 1998: 'Some people did not seriously join in the fight against drug-taking, but tried to exploit the regulations. After the outbreak of the drug scandals, they did not tell the truth.'[60] The result was, for example, that the International Swimming Federation criticised the Chinese Swimming Association for its lack of control over coaches and local swimmers. In the final analysis, it seems most unlikely that many national and provincial sports commission officials were unaware of the existence of widespread drug misuse among athletes. It was the hypocrisy, deceit and dishonesty of some sports officials that provided a climate in which drug-taking could survive.

In summary, no single reason can explain the growth of drug abuse in China's sport over the past 15 years. Explanation involves several factors:

> Whatever the political ideology, the stakes in international competition are high. Victory brings increased status for the individual and his/her family, it results in financial and career rewards, and it boosts the image of the nation. Defeat can result in personal humiliation, loss of career and it does nothing for the image of the athlete's nation.[61]

Of course, drug abuse affected women as well as men athletes. Whether more women than men resorted to, and were affected by, drugs is impossible to determine. Some women believe this to be the case in view of the superior performances of women in international levels.

Decentralisation and Drug Offences

As discussed in the last two chapters, decentralisation has been taking place throughout the country since the introduction of economic reform in 1978. In tune with this broad general trend, since the early 1980s sports management has been progressively decentralised. The NSC has moved gradually from direct management of sport to macro supervision of sport.

While the decentralisation granted individual sports associations and local sports administrations more freedom for their activities, it also led to diversified responses by local provinces to central sports policies. The leaders of regional sports commissions, state-run sports schools and sports teams progressively shifted their allegiance away from the central government to their members. Increasingly, they represented the constituents below them rather than the authorities above them.[62] 'You have policies, we have countermeasures' went a saying about local authorities that sabotaged central mandates. This strategy was exemplified in the anti-drug campaign. Some local officials tried to prevent their athletes from being caught in drug tests, or found an excuse for their drug offenders. A typical example concerns the drug scandal surrounding the Shanghai swimmers Xiong Guobing and Wang Wei in mid-1999. No sooner had the International Swimming Federation announced these two men's positive tests than the Shanghai Swimming Association claimed that the results were caused by some contaminated food that contained the banned elements.[63] The International Swimming Federation, however, rejected this explanation and banned both swimmers for three years.[64] Obviously, reduced central control and increased local autonomy have resulted in added difficulties and complications for the anti-drug campaign in this huge country.

There were other difficulties and complications in the relationship between local and central elements. Various national sports teams, of course, had played an indispensable part in guaranteeing Chinese success in international competitions. However, tensions and conflicts exist, and have existed, between provincial and national teams. Before the mid-1980s the coaches of national teams were virtually permanently employed and local coaches were unable to get even a foot in the door for their athletes in the national teams. This state of affairs hardly encouraged local coaches to deliver promising athletes. However, local coaches were in a cleft stick: if they did not put their athletes forward for national teams, their athletes would not obtain access to major international competitions and bring reflected glory on their coaches. This dilemma victimised athletes as much as coaches. The story of Li Xiaohui, the Asian discus champion in the mid-1980s, reflects this clearly:

> After I broke the national discus-throwing record in 1975, the national team wanted to recruit me. Our province did not agree and nor did I because the standard of coaching in my province was not below that of the national team. I remained in the provincial team and only joined the national team prior to international competitions. In 1980 we assembled in Beijing to prepare for the Olympic Games that summer. Then we went to West Germany to train. After we came back from West Germany, I wanted to test the training effect in a national competition. My coach and I wrote a letter to the Office of Olympic Games Preparation for permission. The national competition approached, but there was no word from the office. We were so anxious that we begged the team leader of our West Germany tour to talk directly to the director of the National Sports Commission, Li Menhua. With his intervention, I was allowed to leave Beijing for the competition. However, this action made some junior officials lose face. As a result, my coach and I were bitterly criticised for violation of discipline. Furthermore, I was even deprived of opportunities for international competition for a few years.[65]

In order to reduce the tension between national and provincial sports teams, in the early 1980s trials were introduced to select candidates for major international competitions. Immediately, competition intensified considerably between provincial and national teams, between different provincial teams and between coaches and athletes themselves. Coaches worked extremely hard to produce national athletes. To gain an edge in this fierce competition new training methods, including improved drug techniques, were a real temptation. This state of affairs was responsible for an expansion of drug-taking. Despite this fact, it is highly unlikely that China had a nationwide state-sponsored drug programme to enhance athletes' performances. China is a huge country with over 30 provinces, municipalities and autonomous regions, and with a population of over 1.2 billion. If a state drug programme had existed, it would have been extremely difficult to implement. Given the intense rivalry between national and provincial teams, and among provincial teams, 'even if there were a systematic use of drugs in professional teams, it is highly unlikely that the program would be centrally administered as it was in East Germany'.[66] Indeed, based on an investigation[67] in China in February 1998,[68] the International Swimming Federation rejected the assumption that China had a national drug-taking programme.[69]

From the mid-1980s onwards local coaches could accompany their athletes, if selected, to national teams. This change made it possible for a coach to work with an athlete for a long period of time. The 'swimming flowers' Qian Hong and Lin Li, for example, both spent over ten years with their coaches, learning new techniques, developing their abilities and rehearsing complex manoeuvres. To a considerable extent, these swimmers' success was a reflection of their coaches' abilities. Swimmers and coaches were 'locked together' by mutual interests. Coaches monitored virtually all of the variables that were considered relevant to training, from food to injuries, to even personal matters, such as make-up and clothes. As Qian Hong has revealed, 'My coach once destroyed my cosmetic box by stamping on it and tore up my Qiong Yiao novel about love affairs. I got very irritated at the time.'[70] Clearly, coaches exercised a great deal of personal control over their swimmers simply through the promise of ensuring sporting success. This close relationship between coaches and swimmers made it highly improbable that coaches did not know if their swimmers were taking drugs. It was very likely, therefore, that coaches were part of the drug deception in which their swimmers were involved.

One outcome of the decentralisation of national teams was an increased enthusiasm for producing world-level athletes in the provinces, which consequently produced a number of world and Olympic champions. For example, of the 30 track and field athletes selected for the 1996 Olympics, only nine were directly from the national athletics team.[71] The increasing representation of local athletes mounted a considerable challenge to the privileges and even the existence of the national teams, which were assembled a year at a time. The result was that in 1997 the centralised National Swimming Team was dissolved. National swimmers now remained in their home provinces and only met together for a short period before major international competitions.[72] The selection of national swimmers was now based on performances in national and international competitions. This innovation was expected to ensure fair competition and more equal opportunities, alleviate the arbitrary power of head coaches or officials of national teams, and stimulate the initiatives of local athletes and coaches. However, in practice, this change had at least one detrimental effect: it endangered the tight control of the National Swimming Association over drug abuse among elite swimmers. The surge of drug offences in 1997 was the eventual result.

As in industry and other fields, reforms in sport have been a complex process involving interaction between government, enterprises, sports officials, coaches and athletes. Moreover, reform has been bottom-up as well as top-down, propelling reforms far beyond the Communist Party's initial intentions.[73] The outcome has been that government at all levels has become a recipient as well as a leader of reform, and this is true of the anti-drug campaign. In view of the significance of sporting achievements for employment, promotion and welfare benefits, it is not surprising that success at the National Games often took precedence over doping control for local sports commissions. Even though state policy-makers wanted to curb the spread of drug abuse among Chinese athletes, they were frequently stymied by the common practices in various provinces across the country. Without local effort, China's international success would be far less extensive, and so national sports bodies had to compromise over their policies. Perhaps the most revealing illustration of the flexible relationship between central and local sports organisations is the half-year delay in announcing the names of the 24 athletes caught using drugs at the 1997 National Games. Arguably, this postponement allowed sufficient time for local provinces and municipalities to celebrate their achievements and reward their successful coaches and athletes. The plain fact is that the immediate exposure of drug offenders would have spoiled the atmosphere of celebration and detracted from the enthusiasm of the provinces for elite sport. This in turn could have undermined the development of elite sport in China. In short, the new relationship between the central and local governments in the context of market-driven reform, and also devolved power, made national doping control more difficult to implement.

Implementation was also made difficult by the attention given by the mass media to winners rather than to drug choosers – no doubt, to a large extent, as a result of government pressure. Winning provided the right headlines. Thus, overwhelming coverage by the press was frequently given to gold-medallists; in *Ba yunhui tebie baodao* [The Special Report on the Eighth National Games], for example, there was no space given to drug-related issues. When the Chinese drug scandals at the Perth world championships in early 1998 became world headlines, they were not reported immediately in the major domestic newspapers. A week later the news was given only minor attention in *Zhongguo tiyu bao* [The China Sports Daily] – in sharp contrast to the photographs and descriptions of winning swimmers on the front page.[74] Playing down the thorny issue of drug-taking, however, did not mean that it went away: it actually encouraged more athletes to take drugs. Consequently, the national anti-drug programme was also hindered by media coverage.

In summary, then, drug abuse in sports in China is intricately intertwined with administrative decentralisation and the devolution of decision-making power to lower levels. While decentralisation granted local provinces more autonomy, it also generated an important dysfunctional consequence – reduced central control over sporting matters involving drug-related issues. This consequence was exacerbated by the media. In other words, doping control was not a straightforward matter in China, but one replete with problems.

Drugs, Disgrace and Women's Sport in China

By the turn of the millennium, the politics of sport had 'become the politics of drugs in sport.'[75] By then drug abuse existed not just in China, but also in America[76] and many other countries. Australia's former Commonwealth discus champion Verner Reitererm claimed recently that 'all the leading countries in the Olympic Games have systems in place to help their athletes dodge the drug-testing process'.[77] However, Chinese drug problems have received an exceptionally high profile in the western media. This fact has brought enormous embarrassment to China and generated immense distrust of China throughout the world. In the words of Yuan Weimin, deputy director of the National Sports Bureau: 'The negative impact of the drug scandals on China and Chinese sport cannot be counteracted by any number of gold medals. It will need a long time and enormous energy to clear our name'.[78]

In the process of clearing China's name, the 'drug incident in Australia' in 1998 became a turning point. In the immediate aftermath of the 1998 World Swimming Championships, the Chinese Olympic Committee held an anti-drug meeting in Beijing. A committee was appointed to investigate the incident[79] and at the same time the Chinese Swimming Association announced 11 anti-drug measures. They imposed much severer penalties on drug offenders than the international organisations had.[80] Severe doping control measures had been put in place.

To root out the 'cancer' of drug abuse at the Asian Games in 1998, Chinese athletes were strictly screened. Priority was given to power-oriented sports such as athletics, swimming, weightlifting, cycling, boat-racing, canoe, wrestling and judo. For example, the national weightlifting squad carried out drug tests every month.[81] In the same year blood tests were introduced in China – earlier than the IOC, which did not adopt blood tests until the 2000 Olympic Games.[82] In 1998 the number of blood tests in China totalled 317.[83] In 1999 Chinese swimmers underwent not just blood tests but all kinds of test – 699 in total, the highest figure to date. The deputy director of the Chinese Swimming Association, Zhang Qiuping, claimed with justification that 'China's swimming follows the most demanding drug test standards in the world'.[84] For the first time, to be 'drug free' was given higher priority than medal quotas.

The tightening-up of domestic and international anti-drug policies has had an immediate impact on Chinese women's sport, especially in swimming and athletics. Women's swimming performances have declined dramatically. For example, at the end of 1998 the Chinese were outperformed, after a decade of dominance, by their Japanese counterparts at the Asian Games.[85] At the 1999 World Athletics Championships, China won just one gold medal and one silver medal, in the women's 20-kilometre walk.[86] At the 2000 Olympic Games, the Chinese won no medals in swimming and only one gold medal in athletics. The results speak for themselves.

Impressively perhaps, given China's lust for medals, these poor results did not weaken the country's determination to step up the war on drug abuse. On 5 January 1999, the National Sports Bureau announced its decree 'Rigorously Restraining the Practice of Drug-taking in Sport' (*Guanyu yange jinzhi zai tiyu yundong zhong shiyong xinfen ji xinwei de guiding*). This decree stipulated the disciplinary and appeal procedures associated with drug offences,[87] and provided a legislative basis for the uprooting of drug abuse from Chinese sport. In the new millennium doping control had become the priority of Chinese sports governing bodies.

To ensure tighter control over swimmers, the dismantled centralised national swimming team was re-established in 1999. Now swimmers were required to undergo drug tests at any time and anywhere without any conditions. To save China from drug disgrace at the Sydney Olympic Games, the Chinese conducted numerous domestic drug tests. For example, within the first six months of 2000 some 271 tests were carried out in swimming, of which 102 were on national swimmers.[88] Just two weeks before the Sydney Olympics, 27 athletes, including six from the controversial Ma Family Army,[89] and 13 coaches were unceremoniously kicked out of the Chinese delegation due to 'suspicious' drug test results.[90] Despite their absence, Chinese sport did not collapse as speculated. Instead, China achieved its best ever result – third in the medal count – in Olympic history. This accomplishment clawed back credit for Chinese sport, and women's sport in particular, since women did exceptionally well.[91]

In spite of stringent anti-drug policies, it is far from easy, of course, to extinguish the entrenched practice of drug abuse in the era of the market economy. In May 1999 the world 200-metre medley swimming record holder Wu Yanyan tested drug-positive in the National Swimming Championships. She was immediately banned for four years and expelled from the national swimming squad, and thus disqualified from the forthcoming Olympic Games.[92] However, this was not the end of the story. Claiming innocence, Wu Yanyan announced that she would launch a lawsuit against the Chinese Swimming Association.[93] Wu's case sparked controversy in the domestic and foreign media over the association's decision to expel not only Wu and her coach but also two other promising and drug-free swimmers.[94] This was thought by some to have an ulterior motive: China wanted to use this case to show the world its ruthlessness in combating drug abuse – crucial for winning the opportunity to host the 2008 Olympic Games. For the Chinese leadership, national interest and image take precedence over everything else; in fact, Wu lent her support to concern for China's image and temporarily shelved her lawsuit.[95] Despite cultural changes, traditional forces are still strong in Chinese society. Individualism does not invariably triumph over collectivism.

China's fight to control drug abuse will now be assisted by recent international developments. Internationally, the 'traditional ideological spectrum of left and right has been replaced by largely unacknowledged tensions between pro- and anti-doping factions within the ranks of athletes, sports officials, sports physicians and trainers'.[96] War between the two has been defused. The IOC and other international sports organisations have begun to clamp down tightly on drug offences. For example, in 1999 the International Swimming Federation issued new regulations on the punishment of drug abuses. According to the regulations, if a national association has had four drug-positive tests within a year, the association will be banned for a year.[97] In the 2000 Olympic Games, a blood test was introduced to detect EPO, one of the peptide hormones that increases the number of red blood cells in order to improve oxygen transport.[98] The Olympic oath, the pledge made by athletes to uphold free and fair games, was altered for the first time in 80 years to reflect the scourge of drugs in sport.[99] This tougher approach by international sports organisations will, to some extent, thwart dependence on drugs to enhance performance. With the enlarged list of banned drugs[100] and the introduction of new and complicated drug-test techniques it is now becoming extremely difficult to rely on drugs to enhance performance. Consequently, it will be hard, if not impossible, for Chinese women to repeat their previous accomplishments in athletics and swimming, at least in the foreseeable future.

There is no doubt that in recent years some coaches, researchers and even administrators have been involved in drug abuses in China. However, there is a danger of exaggerating the importance of drugs in the achievements of Chinese women's sport. 'Drugs such as steroids are not magic pills that guarantee success regardless of the qualities of the users. Athletes using steroids must practise just as hard as others to attain what may be only marginal benefit from use.'[101] Drugs may have helped improve some sports performances, but the overall success of Chinese women has certainly not been the exclusive result of drugs. This was confirmed most convincingly in the 2000 Olympic Games, in which, as we have noted, China came third.

A closer examination of results in the Sydney Olympics shows that the Chinese excelled mainly in diving, table tennis, badminton, gymnastics, shooting and weightlifting – see Table 11. These sports, with the exception of weightlifting, demand a combination of physical and psychological qualities involving coordination, accuracy and artistry as well as strength, speed and endurance. They can rarely benefit from drugs. Taking drugs might enhance power, but may at the same time undermine delicate balance and coordination skills. Surely the world dominance of Chinese women in these aesthetic and agile sports is not the result of drug abuse. It is largely attributable to the centrally controlled sports administration and training regimes. The 'one dragon' training system,[102] talent identification and screening practice,[103] early specialisation and professional coaches[104] as well as Olympic-oriented sports policies have proved their value. They have ensured Chinese success in world sport throughout the past decades, especially before drugs were introduced to China in the 1980s. This earlier success and the funda-

TABLE 11

DISTRIBUTION OF CHINA'S MEDALS AMONG SPORTS IN THE SYDNEY OLYMPICS

	DV	WL	TT	BD	GA	SH	JU	AT	TK	FE	CT	WR
gold	5	5	4	4	3	3	2	1	1			
Silver	5	1	3	1	2	2	1			1	1	
bronze		1	1	3	3	3	1			1		1
Total	10	7	8	8	8	8	4	1	1	2	1	1

Note: DV=diving; WL=weightlifting; TT=table-tennis; BD=badminton; GA=gymnastics; SH= shooting; JU=judo; AT=athletics; TK=taekwondo; FE=fencing; CT=cycling (track); WR=wrestling.

Source: http://www.Olympics.com/eng/countries/CHI/medal.html)

mental sources of later success should not be overlooked when drug-related issues are addressed.

Chinese women's rise to prominence is mostly the product of hard work and discipline. The justification for this assertion lies in the fact that most of the sports in which Chinese women have succeeded either demand skills based on time-consuming hard work or are formerly 'male' but newly introduced and hitherto unpopular as activities for women, such as weightlifting. Although hard work and dedication themselves do not ensure an absence of drug-taking, they certainly contribute to the success of Chinese female athletes. The female swimmer Qian Hong has argued:

> We always followed the instructions of coaches, for example, going to bed before ten o'clock, but the boys did not. They sometimes played cards until late at night. How could they work hard without a good rest the night before? Disobedience happened also in training. Boys were not as committed to training as girls.[105]

However, women's discipline was, and is, often synonymous with traditional obedience in China. As mentioned earlier, more often than not female athletes have been submissive to coaches' instructions and arrangements. In the past, if coaches or officials told them directly or even hinted to them that there was a need to take drugs to enhance their performance, they would very possibly do their bidding. Obedience, together with ambition, might therefore be the underlying causes for women's adoption of drugs, especially in the mid-1980s when athletes had little knowledge of drugs.

Conclusion

In the late 1970s China opened its door to the outside world and at the same time resumed its place on the IOC. With increased cultural and sporting exchanges between China and other countries, foreign ideas and advanced technology, including performance-enhancing drugs, were introduced to China. Driven by the desire to escape from the humiliating image of the 'sick man of East Asia', and ensnared by the seductive social and material rewards resulting from sporting success, not a few coaches, athletes and officials pursued a policy of winning at all costs. The result was that some athletes, with direct or indirect approval from coaches and officials, risked taking drugs to achieve outstanding performances. In consequence, after the mid-1980s positive tests multiplied and drug abuse became endemic in Chinese sport.

The emergence of drug abuse in China has its internal social and historical causes. With the introduction and acceleration of the decentralisation of sports management in the mid-1980s, local sports commissions and provincial sports teams acquired increased autonomy in the management of their own activities. Consequently, the central sports bodies found it more difficult to exercise tight control over sport in the country. They were often frustrated in their anti-drug campaigns and had to compromise on their doping-control policies. Nevertheless, under escalating international pressure, by the turn of the millennium China had started to crack down heavily on drug abuse in the sports community. The tightening domestic and international doping controls have already had their effect on, and will have a further effect on, women's elite sport in China. The worst may be over.

While the existence of drug abuse should not be denied, the role of drugs should not be exaggerated. In examining drug-related issues, it is unwise to overlook the positive practices of China's sports administrative system and training schemes, such as the 'one dragon' system, early athlete identification and screening processes, state sponsorship, the employment of full-time coaches, the preparation and training systems and more importantly, attitudes such as athletes' inspiration, determination and dedication. Nevertheless, the consequences of drug control are real. While it is likely that Chinese women will continue to dominate some sports, such as table tennis, diving and badminton, it will be extremely difficult, if not impossible, for them to maintain their supremacy in swimming and athletics in the foreseeable future.

New Women for a New Age: Conquest and Confrontation – Successful Sportswomen

The sports achievements of a country are determined by various and multiple macro and micro factors, involving historical traditions, social, economic and political systems, sports policy, strategy, administration and investment, the personal motivation and commitment of athletes and coaches, and, not least, family support. Thus, to fully explore the reasons for the rapid advance of Chinese women to world supremacy, these last factors (motivation, commitment and family support), self-evidently, should be taken into account. Earlier chapters have mainly considered the social and historical contexts that have framed women's sport in China. This chapter will turn to the sportswomen themselves in order to probe further the complex relationship between society, sport and gender in modern China.

In general, celebrated athletes have in recent decades received positive profiles in the Chinese media, and have been frequently and uncritically applauded by the media as national heroes and heroines.[1] Lu Guang's book *Zhongguo guliang* (Chinese Girls),[2] which was adapted for a television documentary, is a typical example. However, in the last decade there have appeared negative profiles of sportsmen and women, for example, Zhao Yu's book *Majiajun diaocha* (Investigations into the Ma Family Army).[3] As it boldly exposed hidden problems in the sporting community, and the 'Ma Family Army' in particular, it evoked intense debate over sport throughout China in the late 1990s. Yet, there is still a paucity of serious and thoughtful academic inquiry into female athletes' lives. What are the personal reasons for the success of Chinese women in international competitions? What characteristics do successful female athletes have? What effects has sport had on their personal and family lives? How do they assess their athletic careers? These questions have been touched upon earlier, but this chapter will discuss the role of sport in women's lives in rather more detail than hitherto through descriptions of three representative samples of female athletes: the women's world champion volleyball team, the world record holders of the Ma Family Army, and the Olympic medallist speed-skater Ye Qiaobo.

In order to present contemporary images – warts and all – of Chinese women in sport, this chapter will take advantage of both critical and complimentary comment by academics and journalists to supplement interviews carried out by the author. These sportswomen will be considered under the following headings: sacrifices and rewards; athletes and coaches; clash of gender ideals; and ambition in sport.

The Chinese Women's Volleyball Team: Sacrifices and Rewards

The Chinese women's volleyball team (CWVT) that won five world titles in the 1980s was established in 1976. Its first 12 players, selected from hundreds of elite players across the country, were physically powerful, with an average age of 20 and average height of 1.766 metres. They had different personalities and technical skills,[4] but importantly, they had already received two to five years of specialised training in their provincial elite sports teams. In other words, these young women started playing volleyball in the early 1970s (see Appendix 5). This fact underlies the point made in Chapter 3, that elite sport did not stand still throughout the decade of the Cultural Revolution (1966–76). The international sporting success of the early 1980s was, to a large extent, an extension of the solid development of elite sport in the 1970s. As Dong Tianshu, a former member of the women's volleyball team of the 1960s and now a volleyball researcher at the National Institute of Sports Research, explained:

> When sports teams resumed training in the early 1970s, the desire to enter the world rankings reared up again after being buried for many years. The best players of the 1960s, who did not realise their dream of being world champions, were now coaches of provincial teams across the country. They passed on their frustrated ambition to the younger generation and identified, selected and cultivated players with high standards. This momentous work provided a solid foundation for the breakthrough of Chinese women's volleyball in the 1980s.[5]

Clearly, local coaches made a great contribution to the CWVT's world success. The network linking local and national teams was largely shaped by the 'one dragon' training system,[6] mentioned earlier, by which athletes moved along a continuum – through a sports school, to a provincial sports team and then to the national team. This process consisted of a multi-layered identification, cultivation and monitoring of sports talents. The 'one dragon' system, underpinned by central planning and financing, provided talented athletes with opportunities for systematic long-term training – essential for sporting success.

To acknowledge the contribution of local volleyball advisers and performers is not to overlook the efforts and sacrifices made by CWVT coaches and players. Li Guizhi, a member of the team in the early 1980s,[7] has pithily described these:

> In the early 1980s, we virtually undertook whole-day training every

day except on Sundays, when we had only a half-day session. On average, we practised seven hours a day. Evenings were used for team meetings, political studies and watching volleyball videos.[8]

Training was clearly extremely demanding – indeed, excessively demanding. But it was successful. The head coach set performance criteria for every skill and tactic: if a player did not perform a skill properly the first time, she would be required to do it again and again without protest. Thus, a session could sometimes last over ten hours. The training load was unbelievably intensive. Lang Ping, the most famous outside attacker in the world, for example, had to attack the ball 200 or 300 times each session and roll on the floor 400 or 500 times. She frequently undertook squat exercises with 100kg weights 200 times in one session. This training often left her unable to stand up at its completion.[9] Its value was questionable: unfortunately and predictably, such heavy training resulted in chronic fatigue, injuries and illnesses, which affected almost all the players. Sun Jinfang, for example, had asthma and a lower back injury; Chao Huiying had a knee injury and tuberculosis; Lang Ping had gastritis and back pain. However, such injuries and ill-health did not stop players from training.

> As long as you could move you had to join training sessions. This was one of the hallmarks of the CWVT. During a training session at a camp in Chengdu, one of my team-mates had knee injuries. The only exercise she could do was half-squat holding. One day she remained in this static position several hours without a break. The result was that her sweat could fill half a wash basin.[10]

Nothing was left to chance. To get accustomed to anticipated future circumstances, the players of the CWVT were required to give up the habit of a noon nap – the conventional practice of Chinese sports teams – and to eat 'disgusting' western food. Travelling around the city in a coach for about an hour before training was specially incorporated into the schedule to overcome the problem of carsickness. Plane-sickness was another problem confronting the CWVT. In 1980, the team went to America for an international competition; after a flight of over 20 hours most girls felt discomfort and vomited when they arrived in the high-altitude host city. But they left the airport directly for their training venue without even going to their hotel for a rest. They practised, vomited and practised again. Fortunately, every girl brought a bucket with her, which was now used for this waste. In this way, the team quickly adapted to the high altitude and defeated the Americans the following day.[11] Whatever the human cost, success arose from such incredibly hard work and careful preparation.

One final illustration proves this point. The 'setter' of a volleyball team should possess qualities of patience, compromise, self-denial and even self-sacrifice because she passes the ball, sets strategies and organises the play.

In this role, she has to be ready to accept any complaint and forgive others in order to maintain the morale of the team. Sun Jinfang, however, playing as setter in the CWVT, was by nature a girl with a strong personality, pride and competitiveness. To cultivate the required qualities, she was specially trained to become tolerant of the requests of her team-mates, and even the wrong decisions of referees. She had to learn not to get upset when asked to do more exercises for no apparent reason.[12] After literally years of conditioning, Sun gradually internalised the desirable psychological qualities for a setter. As a result, she successfully captained the team to world victories in the early 1980s. What made these women bear this incredible training load was a genuine mixture of fierce patriotism, group loyalty, cultural values and, not least, success.

Sportswomen have the dual identity of athletes and women. Marriage is an important issue for Chinese women. However, sports success is often *more* important for most athletes. To prevent any possible conflict between marriage and career, the players of the CWVT were officially required not to have love affairs (which often led to marriage) before 25 years of age. Consequently, virtually all the volleyball players married later than women in general.[13]

Once the players were old enough for love affairs, they were immediately put under pressure by parents and friends to consider marriage. Ironically, being confined to a 'semi-sealed' sports team, these girls had little time and few opportunities to meet and date boys. Thus the question was how, when and where they could spot a future husband. Confronting the conflict between sport and marriage, these women adopted narrowly pragmatic strategies: relying on friends or relatives to locate and introduce them to future potential husbands or dating their male volleyball colleagues with whom they shared training venues. By way of illustration, on this point and the earlier point that sports success was more important than marriage, Cao Huiying, one of the first 12 players of the CWVT, was introduced through her sister to a factory worker in the autumn of 1978. Although everything – house and furniture – was ready for their wedding the following year, Cao insisted that the wedding should wait until she won a world title. When this goal was realised two years later, however, she once again postponed her wedding for the Asian Games and the World Championships in 1982, despite the fact that before these competitions she had been hospitalised for several months with knee injuries and pneumonia. In fact, it was not until 1983 that she stopped training and got married.[14] Cao is merely 'the tip of an iceberg' of Chinese sportswomen who pursued athletic success at the expense of personal pleasure. Victory in sport created an enormous sense of fulfilment and a hugely meaningful existence. Marriage offered no competition.

The sacrifices that the CWVT had endured were not in vain. As a pioneer of 'three big balls'[15] success, the team actually realised the dream of reaching world level – the dream of the first director of the National Sports

Commission (NSC), Marshal He Long.[16] Success brought these women considerable fame and popularity. As a result, they were awarded all kinds of honorary titles, including the Honourable Badge of Sport[17] and the Best Ten Athletes,[18] and even became political representatives to the National People's Congress.[19] Their celebrity status was unimaginable to normal people. Wherever they went, they stayed in five-star hotels, ate luxurious dinners and were provided with first-class guards for their security.[20] In some cities streets were even cordoned off to allow these star players to travel to the stadium.[21] Sporting success elevated these female players to the status of national heroines. Fame was unquestionably their spur. The high visibility of the CWVT made the players ideal icons of commercial products: domestic factories and international enterprises offered them various items such as domestic goods, clothes, bicycles and electric appliances. In addition, there were various winning bonuses from the state and local governments and rich overseas supporters. The state bonuses increased from 500 yuan in 1981 to 1,000 yuan in 1982, then to 7,000–15,000 yuan in 1984. Athletic achievements thus brought huge financial benefits to female sports stars. Intensive, almost unendurable, training had its compensation – material and social rewards.

Nevertheless, reward was a double-edged sword. Mounting political honours and financial prizes, while elevating the status of the players and bringing them considerable wealth, also corrupted them. The players became arrogant, undisciplined and lazy; they did not follow the instructions of their coaches and even openly contradicted them. The team became increasingly difficult to manage.[22] In addition, the endless social activities drained so much energy from the players that they could barely achieve designated training targets. However, such was their pre-eminence that, backed by top-level NSC officials, they could not be dismissed or even criticised. To compound matters, they often complained about their coaches' misconduct or inability to these NSC officials and even to the central government, to which they now had access. The consequence was that relations between coaches and players deteriorated badly, and coaches could hardly control the team.

This chaos made the collapse of the CWVT inevitable. The 1988 Olympic Games were the turning point. The team fell from first to third place and declined continuously thereafter. By the 1992 Barcelona Games, it had dropped to seventh place, and in 1994 the team even lost its dominance in Asia.[23] Bizarrely, each defeat resulted in the resignation of the head coach of the team: five head coaches resigned in succession between 1986 and 1994.[24] However, the defeats had little impact on the players. They continued to enjoy various privileges inherited from their past accomplishments. Clearly more cherished than their coaches, they were iconic heroines whose astounding successes lived long in the memories of many Chinese. Earlier success brought a substantial degree of immunity to criticism. Fortunately, the CWVT regained some momentum after the former attacker

Lang Ping took over as coach in 1995. The silver-medal performance at the 1996 Olympic Games regenerated Chinese confidence in the prestigious team. To this day, the team still has a higher profile and status than most other teams throughout the country.

The rise and fall of the CWVT reveal the complex and changing lives of modern women athletes. They had the strongest motivation for success, honour and glory, but initially it was often hidden beneath the mask of modesty, obedience and self-denial. The huge fame and financial rewards from winning raised their standing to iconic levels but at the same time undermined their commitment to hard disciplined training and competition, and resulted in an arrogance and petulance. that destroyed their relationship with their coaches. But such was their prestige that most Chinese forgave them. This generosity was ironic given the fact that successful male leaders (coaches) were normally powerful, valued and respected. Some women had come a long way in a short time.

The Ma Family Army: Coach, Athletes and Confrontation

The dominance of male coaches is no better exemplified than in the case of Ma Junren. The 'Ma Family Army' was actually the Liaoning Women's Long and Middle Distance Running Team coached by Ma Junren. It burst onto the world scene by winning three gold medals at the August 1993 World Athletics Championships in Stuttgart. The following month, in Beijing, the selfsame athletes systematically smashed a number of world records.[25] These achievements put these athletes and their coach in the international spotlight. How could these Chinese women, unknown before the 1993 World Championships, suddenly leap to prominence in several world events? How could a man without any personal athletic experience or higher education create world champions? Along with these questions went the suspicion of drug-taking,[26] which led to visits by IAAF random drug-testing squads to the Ma Family Army (on 15 December 1993 and 8 March 1994). However, all tests were negative. Due to the lack of detailed documentation and any deep comprehensive analysis of the Ma Family Army, suspicions have lingered on in the world sports community. The sudden withdrawal of a new generation of the Ma Family Army from the Chinese team for the Sydney Olympics – a consequence of 'suspiciousblood test results' – partially confirmed the lingered suspicion about their drug abuse. However, it is widely accepted that sport is influenced by, and meshes with, social, economic and cultural forces. Any single factor, even drug abuse, cannot explain the ascent of the Ma Family Army. The following pages will trace the journey of Coach Ma and his athletes to world success, and uncover some relevant social and economic facts that shaped this success.

When in 1980 the Chinese re-emerged in the world athletic arena after exclusion from the IOC and other sports organisations for over two decades, little was known about Chinese athletes and their training regimes. They were anonymous. Thus, when the Ma Family Army captured several world medals in 1993, they seemed aliens from another planet. How the Chinese turned into world champions almost overnight became a puzzle to the world.

The bewilderment of the world is simply a demonstration of its ignorance about Chinese sport. In China, it was, and still is, a common practice to 'test athletes domestically' before sending them abroad. An athlete who wants to become a representative at international competitions has to pass through extensive trials from city through provincial to national levels. This process normally takes a number of years. Given the size and population of the country, domestic competition is rarely less fierce than any Asian, not to mention any world, contest. The Ma Family Army is not exempt from this demanding process. Wang Junxia, who broke both 3,000-metre and 10,000-metre world records at the 1993 World Championships and received the Jesse Owens Award that same year, began her running at a young age and always won at schools athletic meetings. In 1988 she won a place at the Dalian Sports Boarding School due to her outstanding performance in a city-level athletic trial, extraordinary running ability, cardiovascular capacities and physical fitness. Over the next two years, her 1,500-metres time improved from four minutes 51 seconds to four minutes 13 seconds. In 1991 she participated in the National City Games, but produced an unsatisfactory result due to ill health. The following year she won the 10,000-metres title at the World Youth Athletics Championships.[27] This laid the foundation for her victory at the World Championships in 1993.

Qu Yunxia, the 3000-metres world champion in 1993, provides another revealing glimpse of the systematic training system. As she was always first in 800-metres and 1,500-metres events at school sports meetings, she was drafted into the district spare-time sports school to specialise in distance running in 1986. The next year she gained access to the provincial elite team and began her professional athletic training. Subsequently, she took part in a number of domestic and international competitions, including the National City Games in 1988, and between 1989 and 1992 the Second National Youth Games, the World Junior Championships, the World University Games and the Barcelona Olympics. This record illustrates that Qu's international success was a consequence of many years of specialised training. There was no short cut on the Chinese road to athletic success.

In the mid-1980s, of course, rapid changes were taking place in Chinese society. These, as stated earlier, included sport. To take one example of special relevance to sporting success, at the 1987 National Games the policy of tallying the total score of a province – not just the count of medals – was introduced. It brought about an immediate adjustment to sports teams throughout the country: it became sensible to invest in 'cold' (new and relatively low-level) activities in which it was considered easy to win medals. As a result, around the mid-1980s many provinces established teams for these activities. One of them was women's long- and middle-distance running. It suddenly turned into a 'hot' sport and became intensely competitive. For example, before 1984, the Japanese had dominated women's middle- and long-distance running in Asia. By 1988 Chinese women dominated all the events at 1,500-metres and above. Unquestionably, the 1987 shift in state policy and consequent provincial strategy directly and sensationally shaped the progress of women's long- and middle-distance running in China.

Now back to Liaoning, one of the leading sports provinces in China,[28] where considerable change took place in 1988. The newly established Provincial Sports Technical Institute introduced an employment system based on contracts. Against all kinds of opposition and pressure, the director of the institute, Chui Dalin, made a decision to dismiss 66 out of the 195 coaches. He declared that 'only those who can help make Liaoning's number of gold medals the highest in the country will be employed'.[29] Apart from those retained, a few were newly recruited from grass-roots schools. One of them was Ma Junren. Based on the principle of 'the strong survive and the weak die', provincial sports teams in Liaoning were reconstructed. Teams without able coaches or good performances were disbanded. Priority was given to some 20 events in which there was the potential to win national titles. This medal-oriented policy yielded remarkable results: Liaoning won far more medals than any other province and became the 'superpower' at the National Games of 1993.[30]

Ma Junren, a peasant's son[31] with only primary school education, temporarily taught physical education in a primary school for two years before he served in the People's Liberation Army for several years. In 1968 he enrolled at a normal school for an eight-month course for sports trainers. Thereafter, he became a physical education teacher at a rural middle school. After four years of hard work,[32] his athletic team was ranked first, and his basketball and table tennis teams were also among the top three in his town. These performances won Ma local fame and provided a springboard for his employment in a variety of different schools. Strikingly, whatever school he worked at, it always led the region in sport. A number of his students were admitted into either city sports schools or provincial sports teams. His early experiences in the army and in schools not only enhanced Ma's confidence and advanced his ability, but also demonstrated his personality and determination. These experiences strongly influenced his later coaching style and laid down stepping stones for his future success.

In 1980 Ma began to focus on women's long- and middle-distance running. He made every effort to learn the most advanced techniques and training methods from books, colleagues and competitions.[33] His diligence bore fruit. Two of his student athletes broke the Liaoning provincial 3,000-metres record. He was soon employed temporarily to coach the provincial marathon team for the coming National Games in 1983.[34] Unfortunately, his athletes did not achieve satisfactory results due to injuries arising from overwork.[35] This defeat dealt a heavy blow to Ma, and he was not retained as marathon team coach. However, the defeat taught him a lesson: that post-training recovery was crucial in ensuring athletic success.

Five years later, he was re-employed by the provincial athletic team. To seek a solution for the difficult issue of post-athletic recovery, he turned to Chinese medicine. Virtually every night he made nutritious chicken and ginseng, caterpillar (winter insect, summer grass)[36] and soft-shell turtle soups for his athletes. These substances, according to Chinese medicine, are effective in strengthening the body's immune system and keeping it healthy. In Ma's regime intensive training was now supplemented by special, expensive and nutritious foods.

This traditional performance-enhancing diet appeared to help take Ma's athletes to world supremacy. In 1988 Qu Yunxia and another Ma athlete, for the first time in Chinese history, came third and fifth respectively in the 1,500-metres at the Olympic Games. The following year, Ma's athletes captured four gold, two silver and two bronze medals at the second National Youth Games. In 1990 his athletes won the 800-metres and 1,500-metres titles at the third World Junior Championships in Bulgaria. The next year Qu Yunxia came third at the World University Games. Wang Junxia, Liu Dong and two others won gold medals for various distances at the 1992 World Junior Championships in Seoul. The year 1993 witnessed the overwhelming victories of the Ma Family Army at the World Athletic Championships and the National Games.

Due to its emerging potential for outstanding performance, from the late 1980s onwards the Ma Family Army received extremely favourable financial support from the Provincial Sports Commission. Any expenses incurred outside the budget could be reimbursed simply on handing in receipts. Consequently, its training expenses surpassed those of other teams two or three times over.[37] This preferential treatment provided the crucial support for the advancement of Ma's athletes to world sports celebrities. However, government funding did not cover the expensive nutritious foods. To secure the entrance of Qu Yunxia and Liu Li into the 1992 Olympic team, Ma and his other 14 athletes donated their half-year wages (from November 1991 to May 1992) to buy nutritious foods for these two potential stars. Ma even sold an 'expensive' dog to finance training.[38] Without question he made sacrifices: among other things, he slept only four hours a night in the years before his team succeeded globally.

Ma's women athletes appreciated his dedication and sacrifice, but at the same time detested his cruelty in training. Quite often Ma acted as pacemaker by driving ahead of his athletes on an old motorcycle with a sidecar, shouting and scolding without restraint. He admitted himself: 'I would scold and even beat them when they were lazy or disobedient, but I did this for their own good. If we were not prepared to suffer pain how could we win world championships?'[39] Partly due to his methods, Ma rarely arranged for his athletes to train with other teams. To some extent it was the combination of cruelty and concern that made up his unique training regime and created his 'special' women athletes – puritan, courageous and single-minded.

The Ma Family Army went to high altitudes five or six times a year, where they ran little short of a marathon almost every day. The exceptional training programme of 8,000km a year made their toenails black with bruising. Fortitude became the hallmark of the Ma Family Army. It was exemplified by Wang Junxia at the 1996 Olympic Games,[40] where she competed three times on three consecutive days in the 5,000-metres and 10,000-metres heats and the 5,000-metres final. To most athletes to do this was inconceivable, and virtually all her foreign rivals withdrew from one of the events in order to keep their energy for the other. But Wang Junxia wanted to win in *both* events. After winning the 5,000-metres title, she began vomiting and was struck with diarrhoea. Despite this distressing physical reaction, she competed in the 10,000 metres and reaped the harvest of her exceptional tolerance of hardship: a silver medal.

Hand in hand with the fortitude of his women athletes went the 'patriarchal' management of coach Ma. Due to exceptional autonomy in financial management, personnel arrangements and team administration, rarely seen in other sports teams across the country, Ma could manipulate his athletes at will. For example, his athletes were required to lead an almost militarised life, acting together as a group and wearing tracksuits all the time. Cosmetics boxes and fashionable clothes were taboo. These women were virtually isolated from society and their families, and did not visit their parents for three years. Without Ma's permission, they could not give interviews. They were further restricted by Ma's two strict rules: no love affairs and always short hair. To ensure the observance of the first rule, he demanded that the women's parents sign an agreement that if a team member had a love affair she would be sent back home. In other ways, he exerted total and extraordinary control. To handle his team effectively, Ma even tried to pre-arrange competition results within his team. In this way, he could balance athletes' prizes. As a consequence of this tight control, one of his female athletes later complained: 'We had absolutely no freedom. We were all on the brink of madness. The pressure was too intense. We could not take it any longer.'[41]

How could women in the 1990s tolerate such exhausting and cruel coaching, even for a time? There are some clues. First of all, the dream of a better life helped them face up to their predicament. Most of Ma's athletes came from impoverished rural areas. They had known hardship from an early age. They were discontented at what they had and wanted to change their lives completely. To win world competitions and bring prestige to the nation, their families and themselves was the motive force for their engagement in Ma's harsh distance-running regime. They believed that, without achievements in sport, they had nothing and they were nothing. As Wang Junxia explained after winning a world title: 'If I failed to reach that goal, all my life and all my efforts would be a waste.'[42]

Close family ties, the cornerstone of traditional Chinese culture for thousands of years, added momentum to these women's drive for success. The story of Qu Yunxia demonstrates this. Between June 1987 and the end of 1988 Qu was on trial for the provincial athletic team. She had to pay 40 yuan for living expenses per month. This was a large sum of money for a poor peasant family at the time. Her father and brother worked hard to save every penny to support her. Even so, over the next year Qu had only one suit of clothes, one pair of shoes and one pair of socks.[43] This state of affairs brought home to her forcefully that sports success was important not only for herself but also for her family. She represented a gamble by the whole family to improve its living standards. Consequently, family ties and a sense of reciprocal obligation reinforced her commitment. On the single occasion when Qu wanted to quit training due to its unbearable nature, her father's opposition stiffened her resolve: 'To achieve good results, you must work hard and go on no matter how difficult it is.'[44] In short, family support, responsibilities and pressures played their part in ensuring that Ma's athletes saw their training through.

Nevertheless, Ma's rigid 'patriarchal' management planted the seeds for eventual revolt. Liu Dong, one of Ma's best athletes, took the lead in challenging Ma's autocracy. She boldly disregarded Ma's instruction to leave the 800-metres title to one of her team-mates at the 1993 National Games. Her rebellion exasperated Ma. Furthermore, Liu broke Ma's rules forbidding long hair and boyfriends, which further irritated him. He saw Liu's disobedience as a threat to his authority. Confrontation broke out between them and came to a head when Ma hurled Liu's baggage out of a fifth-floor hotel window in a fit of temper.[45] Liu left the team and returned home. When Liu's parents asked Ma to take her back, he told the 23-year-old girl to remain at home and write a letter of 'self-criticism' to him every fortnight. In this way he attempted to maintain his self-respect and humiliate Liu. To her credit Liu resigned from Ma's 'family'.

Deplorably, Liu's peasant parents failed to give her full support in this dispute. They remonstrated with her: 'You ran to win glory for your country. It wasn't easy for your coach to train you. How can you give up? Your family has been suffering for you all these years. If you give up, we can't afford to keep you.'[46] Liu's parents had dreamed of renovating their ramshackle home and paying off their 5,000-yuan debts with her winning prizes. Liu was squeezed between personal desire for individual freedom, parental pressures and social expectations. She was crushed. After weeks of enduring her mother's anguish, she gave in. She returned to Ma to ask for forgiveness. Ma refused to grant it, claiming that Liu had not sufficiently admitted her mistakes. In addition, he claimed that if he took her back into his record-breaking squad, he would lose face. The National and Liaoning Sports Commissions both backed him, saying that the clash between Liu and Ma jeo-pardised the discipline of the team. The result was that Liu was left with no salary, no bonus, no job and no access to university because her dossier[47] was in Ma's hands.

Liu's story has wider resonance beyond Liaoning; it reflects an awakening awareness on the part of women of their individuality, and their increasing readiness to fight for their own long-term interests and challenge patriarchal convention. It also reveals that in a society with a deep-rooted respect for authority, it is still extremely difficult for a female athlete to challenge the superior male coach, the sports culture and the established order. She faces not just one man, but the whole system behind him and the traditional Confucian culture behind the system.

However, even the impossible can happen. The 'Liu Dong incident' was the prelude to the dissolution of the Ma Family Army. In December 1994 explosive news broke: all but one of the female athletes of the Ma Family Army had abandoned their coach Ma Junren. The immediate reason for this rupture was a dispute over the distribution of winning bonuses and prizes. The girls and their families complained that Ma hoarded their cash bonuses and prizes, including three Mercedes cars.[48] However, Ma protested that, in fact, he deposited each athlete's cash bonuses in a bank for them. Regarding the cars, he argued that he should have half of them according to the government policy of allocating prizes between coaches and athletes.[49] Money and prizes were the crux of the quarrel.

As mentioned in the last chapter, sporting success brought immense financial benefits to the Ma Family Army. Apart from a one-million-yuan bonus from the State Council, they received various endorsements, media work and sponsorships from a number of enterprises, companies and rich individuals.[50] For example, He Yingdong, a Hong Kong tycoon, presented Ma and his three world-champion athletes with pure one-kilogram gold medals and the rest of the team with 160,000 yuan. These bonuses comprised a huge amount of money for these athletes and, in particular, their families. They lifted these families out of poverty. Ma completely underestimated the impact of these rewards on these athletes and their families. As a result, ironically, family ties, which had underpinned the sportswomen's commitment in the beginning, precipitated the break-up of the world-famous team in the end.

Sharing out rewards unfairly was the immediate cause of the split-up of the Ma Family, but there were other deeper social and psychological reasons. With the advent of the era of reform in the late 1970s and China's gradual opening-up to western countries, international sporting exchanges brought frequent contact with the West. Together with modern technology and science came western ideas and values of equality and individuality. They had a direct impact on athletes, including the Ma Family Army, which became more independent and individualistic. Furthermore, the astounding achievements of the Ma Family turned once-poor young women, the protégés of coach Ma, into famous celebrities and national heroines. The leap in status had huge psychological reverberations. The athletes became confident and self-assertive. They were also eager to taste the fruits of years of sacrifice and suffering. The outcome was a direct challenge to the traditional strict authoritarian relationship between coach and athlete.

In the face of changes in circumstances and personalities, neither Ma nor his athletes had enough sense to compromise. They were simply not willing to meet each other halfway. After his 'army' deserted him, Ma Junren admitted: 'I take some responsibility for the break-up. My fault is that I did not find a way to manage these world champion athletes.'[51] In reality, it was impossible for him to find a way given his personal arrogance and 'patriarchal' mentality. It should not be overlooked that the international success of Ma's athletes not only changed the lives of these rural women, but also raised Ma to a status usually reserved for the senior officials of the Communist Party.[52] He too became a celebrity. He appeared on television to advertise his turtle extract and was heavily involved in other commercial activities.[53] With this heightened social and economic standing Ma became disdainful and intransigent. With growing arrogance on his side and increasing assertiveness on the athletes' side, the Ma Family Army was doomed to dissolve. The collision between the liberated female athletes and the unliberated coach to some extent symbolised a clash between the new individualism and the old corporatism.

In summary, the story of the Ma Family Army displays a series of contradictions – concern and cruelty, hardship and enjoyment, conformity and individuality, obedience and defiance – typical of the evolution of the elite sports team in China. To pursue a better life through sporting success was the initial motive force for enduring hardship, but the realisation of a better life then became the cause of rebellion against the source of hardship. The relationship between coach and athlete, once simple, became complicated – too complicated, on occasion, to endure even in the most successful cases.

Speed Skater Ye Qiaobo: Clash of Gender Ideals

Before the 1990s China had won little world recognition in winter sports. However, in the early 1990s, the female speed skater Ye Qiaobo won 11 world titles. Ye was not just excellent in sport; she had all-round capability. All this put her in the full glare of publicity. Jiang Zemin, the chairman of the National Military Commission at the time, and now the president of the country, acclaimed her as the finest role-model for Chinese athletes. Yuan Weimin, the deputy director of the National Sports Commission in the early 1990s, outlined Ye's uniqueness in the following words:

> She has a strong will. At the age of 28 she still has given no consideration to marriage – a 'personal issue' (*geren wenti*).[54] Some people say that 'she is mad about skating'. I appreciate this commitment. In addition, she feels no frustration and fears no defeat. She has determination

and courage to rise above failure. In 1988 she was banned from competition for one and a half years for a drug violation – a result of misusing a nutritious medicine.[55] Her morale did not collapse. Instead, she used the ban to motivate her to pursue skating success. This indomitable spirit is invaluable. Finally, she kept writing training diaries every day. Her handwriting and her English are very good. In short, she is excellent in several aspects.[56]

How could Ye achieve such remarkable accomplishments in both the sport and non-sport fields? Her life story may provide an explanation.

Like her father, an amateur decathlon athlete, Ye had been a talented athlete since childhood. She won all the children's group events in the championships in Changchun, the capital city of Jilin province in the north-east of China. However, none of the athletic coaches at sports schools recruited her due to her poor running posture. At the age of ten, she changed to skating. Her impressive competitiveness finally won her one of the four places in the city skating school. Two years later, she obtained a place in the People's Liberation Army Team and so began her professional skating career – receiving wages and having her service years taken into calculation (the basis for a welfare package).

However, the road towards success was filled with problems. One was a major injury. At 14, Ye suffered a dangerous half-dislocation of her cervical vertebra. As she faced the risk of paralysis in the event of another incident, her parents strongly objected to her continuing skating. They wanted her to return to school to receive a normal education. Obsessed with skating, Ye did not give in. With the close cooperation of her doctor, she made a full recovery.

Nevertheless, the pain and frustration of injuries never left Ye. She constantly suffered stretched tendons, torn soft bones and knee problems. To cope with her injuries, she received four hours of massage almost every day. As a result, year in and year out she had no leisure, no Christmas holiday and no Chinese New Year. When she travelled abroad without a doctor, she performed acupuncture on her own knee (she had learnt acupuncture at an institute of physical education). After years of acupuncture, the knee looked terrible. In spite of all her efforts, the injured knee continued to deteriorate. Six months prior to the 1994 Winter Olympic Games, five small bones (ossicles) were removed from her knee. Predictably, this operation affected her performance at the games.

Nonetheless, she was still shocked by her 13th place in the 500 metres. In this event she had earlier won 11 world titles. In despair, she debated whether or not to enter the next race, the 3,000 metres. Ye's father, who travelled with her, persuaded her to withdraw. He said: 'If you continue to compete, the result could be worse, which would provoke more criticism and do no good to your future.' Locking herself in a hotel room for two days, Ye recalled both the afflictions she had endured and the accomplishments she had achieved over the years. She told herself: 'You have already sacrificed so much. Why do you want to care about what others say? All you can do is to try your best. If you do not compete in the 3,000 metres, you will regret it for the rest of your life.' She made up her mind to compete, and at that moment, in her own words, 'It seemed that I was going into battle, wanting to "kill enemies", as many as I could.' Summoning up all her energy, she won an unexpected bronze medal. A measure of success was achieved through extraordinary single-minded determination.

This determination was the product of years of effort, sacrifice and suffering. One particular event left its mark. In the 1970s, training conditions were crude. Ye and her team-mates had to undertake special conditioning training on public roads. This training resulted in a traffic accident that took the life of a friend – and had both short- and long-term reverberations. In the immediate aftermath of the tragedy, Ye was both frightened of road training and scared of remaining in the room that she had shared with her deceased friend. To this day she remembers her on the 21st of every month, the day she died, burning paper money for her (an old custom to commemorate the dead). The consequence of this experience was that, no matter how hard her life was, Ye viewed it as acceptable because nothing was more precious than life. The death of a friend became one source of the commitment and perseverance that underpinned her skating successes.

The determination displayed in sport was extended to academic study. For years Ye taught herself Chinese literature, mathematics and other high-school curriculum subjects. Given the long exhausting training every day, this was extremely demanding. Self-discipline was crucial. In 1980 she began to learn English, first listening to the radio, and then listening to and watching television. In the face of opposition from coaches and the difficulties of fitting in her lessons between training sessions, she persevered. The result was that she mastered English: she corresponded with foreign coaches and friends in English, and had no need of an interpreter at press conferences and on foreign journeys. She represented the new image of Chinese female athletes – knowledgeable, modern, successful and confident – and won respect and admiration at home and abroad.[57]

Dedication to sport is not necessarily synonymous with a dull personality and a dull life. Ye had a special liking for fashion. Whenever she travelled abroad with her coach, she put all her training and competition items in her bags and asked her coach to carry an impressive range of fashionable clothes for her. She always dressed to present a favourable image of Chinese women. Furthermore, if her skating performance was unsatisfactory, she would put on her most beautiful clothes at the post-competition reception. In this way, she would feel better psychologically and at the same time would confuse her rivals, who would wonder how she could enjoy a party after suffering defeat in competition. These tactics, of course, were an illustration of the Chinese technique of 'saving face'.

Ye also designed a unique hairstyle for herself: her hair was cut short with a fringe that matched her face nicely. This style was supposed to show off an assertive and confident modern personality. At first people did not accept it – on one occasion she was mistaken for a boy when she went to a toilet – but later on the style became popular in the north of China. Interestingly, however, not long after she gave up competition, she changed her hairstyle back to a more conventional 'feminine' pattern. Her main reason for the change in hairstyle was marriage. She wanted to look gentle and slim – the prevailing ideal of women and crucial for the prospect of marriage. Indeed, Ye lost some weight after quitting skating and came close to the favoured image of the ideal Chinese woman. This 'U turn' reflects both contradictory contemporary demands on sportswomen (and women in general), and the necessary pragmatism of sportswomen in reconciling sports participation with the dominant gender demands in society. 'Being a sportswoman' is only part of life, but 'being a woman' continues through the whole of life.

Ye's story represents the complicated, demanding and multifaceted aspects of life for a modern Chinese sportswoman: the quest for attainment, the tolerance of hardship and the necessary psychological ability to balance success and defeat, commitment to sport and commitment to lifelong goals, and the different roles of daughter, athlete, future wife and eventual mother.

Steps to Success

Sport is taken up by people, biological organisms, in a special cultural context. For this reason, in sport biological and cultural factors interact. Physical and psychological qualities are the initial reasons that lead young people into involvement in sport. About 36 per cent of sampled athletes in Zhong Bingshu's 1996 survey[58] considered 'self' an important factor for engagement in sport. This is further confirmed by interviews conducted for this study. 'I was tall' and 'I always wanted to be the first' were often given as reasons by interviewees. This early motivation is reinforced by sports training regimes in China. It is normal for professional coaches to go to local schools or kindergartens to select potential athletes. Those identified will undergo extracurricular training in sports schools.[59] The Olympic swimming champion Zhuang Yong[60] is a typical product of this regime. When Zhuang was at kindergarten, a female coach, Xu Renhui from the Lu Wan District Sports School, identified her as having swimming talent. She had long arms and legs, big feet and hands, a large but light build with good buoyancy. In consequence, she joined the sports school. The coach Xu acted like – and was even more affectionate than – her mother; Zhuang often ate and slept in Xu's home.[61] In modern China, physical and psychological qualities often determine initial steps towards sporting success, but cultural contexts can, and do, tease out talent.

Sports school – the first step in an athletic career – is the bedrock of elite sport in China. The majority of successful athletes come from sports schools.[62] According to the IAAF council member Lou Dapeng, there were 3,575 sports schools in the country in the early 1990s, with more than 100,000 athletes aged between eight and 14. The most talented athletes moved to one of the 160 technical sports high schools.[63] As the primary task of the sports schools was, and still is, to identify and propel forwards future sports stars, all their students aimed to win a place in a provincial sports team. This is in sharp contrast to North America, where most high-school students take part in sport mainly for pleasure, for enhanced feelings of importance and improved social status.[64] Thus, the sports schools lay the foundation for the international success of Chinese athletes.

Admission to a provincial team represents the defining moment of an athletic career. As discussed in Chapter 1, once athletes have obtained a place in a provincial team, they begin specialised training and lead monotonous and militarised lives in a semi-sealed sports community. Through constant contact with sport, discipline, hard work, competition and teamwork, they are transformed into top athletes and professionalised by their coaches and team-mates. Thus, participation in elite sport has its own processes of socialisation, formalisation and role differentiation.[65] The provincial sports team provides a crucial site for the socialisation of sportswomen. Even more interestingly perhaps, the perception of their modern gender role is to an extent shaped by and passed on to the wider society by their sports subculture.

The national team is, of course, the pinnacle of elite sport in China – the head of the 'dragon' training system mentioned in earlier chapters. Virtually all the country's talented athletes are brought together in the national teams of various sports. Due to priorities in capital investment, resource allocation and opportunities for international competition, to join a national team is the target of, and a great honour for, elite athletes. To remain in a team, however, is tremendously hard. There is a highly competitive atmosphere in every national team. As the Olympic swimmer Qian Hong explained:

> There was no training atmosphere in my province. We competed to be lazy. But once you reached the national team, you felt energetic. Everyone competed to swim faster. You dared not relax. The national team played a crucial part in ensuring our success.[66]

In modern Chinese athletes' rise to national prominence, the family should not be overlooked. Family support provides the emotional stability that allows athletes to devote themselves to sport. Parents provide a strong source of encouragement and constant reinforcement ensuring sports participation during childhood, adolescence and adulthood.[67] Zhong Bingshu's survey shows that some 37.6 per cent of respondents considered family background the most influential factor behind their involvement in sport.[68] Interviews with famous sportswomen conducted for this study also confirm this (see the case studies in the Appendices).

Finally, achievements in sport are inseparable from the inner drive of athletes themselves. Goal-setting, as the psychologist Eswin Locke argues, affects performance by focusing attention, mobilising effort in relation to the demands of the task, enhancing persistence and encouraging individuals to develop strategies for achieving their goals.[69] Most of the sportswomen interviewed for this study stressed the significance of achievement-oriented goal-setting.[70] The need for achievement impels them to strive to realise their potential, to cope with hard training, and to withstand various difficulties and frustrations. Years of sports participation, in turn, further reinforce the inner drive to goal achievement.

Inner drive is essential for coping with the phenomenally heavier training regimes for women in modern China. Intensive training is widely adopted by sports teams in China: 'We often practised 1.5 hours in the early morning, four in the morning, 3.5 in the afternoon, and three in the evening (12 hours a day). Boys had a much shorter training time,'[71] stated a former gymnast from the He Lonqian provincial team. Another gymnast from Hebei province added: 'Sometimes our training session lasted from 2.00 p.m. to 10.00 p.m. without a break.'[72] In the mid-1980s Chinese female race-walkers underwent an average training of 5,000 to 6,000 kilometres per year, much more than their foreign rivals (about 3,000km). In contrast, Chinese male race-walkers were below their foreign counterparts in training intensity.[73] Hard work has certainly prepared Chinese women to succeed in sport. However, the intensive training invariably leads to sports injuries and illness – one of the prices that athletes pay in order to achieve success. In addition to the physical demands, female athletes in China are subject to tight emotional control by their coaches. As mentioned earlier, they are required to delay love affairs and marriages. Fortunately, these disadvantages can be offset by advantages – high social prestige, political positions and financial rewards – once athletes win international competitions. These, of course, are the rewards that initially stimulate athletes to attempt to fulfil their athletic promise, but acquiring these rewards poses a threat to the continual commitment of athletes. This is clearly seen in the cases of the Chinese women's volleyball team and the Ma Family Army. The sudden success and consequent massive rewards can result in a short-term performance peak and the premature retirement of athletes who have been under the tight control of the state, province and coach for years.

To make the point yet again, because it explains so much of contemporary, and certainly future, sport in China: sportswomen in China are normally submissive to their coaches before they achieve success in sport. However, once they become world celebrities, increasingly they are likely to openly contradict and oppose their coaches. Obviously, success is the agent of this change. After their international victories, these women are exposed to the media and other seductions. They are no longer confined to the militarised sports community, their awareness of their individuality is awakened and their appetite for luxury living is stimulated. They want nothing more than a comfortable life after years of hard training. Perhaps above all, they are eager for previously unknown freedoms after experiencing 'patriarchal' domination for so long. As a result, they mount challenges to the well-entrenched authoritarian relationship between coach and athlete. However, the long-established 'patriarchal' mentality does not give away without resistance. Coaches often remain potent and resilient. As a consequence, more and more confrontation becomes inevitable between the modern female athlete and the conservative male coach. To smooth the relationship between coach and athlete is now a priority, but extremely difficult given the irreconcilable demands of modern western ideas of individualism and equality and the traditional rigid hierarchical relations between the superior and the inferior, the old and the young, and men and women. The successful Chinese coach is immensely powerful. Changes are taking place, but they are not without troubles. They will not happen without further confrontation.

The main reason is that sports victories are often choreographed and directed by capable coaches. They are often very able individuals: dedication, knowledge, capability, intelligence and management are the essential qualities of a successful coach in China. Achievements in sport can provide a springboard for coaches to reach the highest levels of sports officialdom. The volleyball coach Yuan Weimin and the athletic coach Ma Junren are obvious examples in this regard. Yuan became the deputy director of the National Sports Commission in 1986 after leading his team to world supremacy. Ma Junren was promoted to deputy director of the Liaoning Provincial Sports Commission in 1998. These political appointments reflect to some extent the continuity of the Confucian scholar-official mentality in modern Chinese sport. To win fame for China in international sport is glorious, and to be an official with responsibility is glorious in modern China. That the two roles should merge today is hardly surprising. This state of affairs makes the advance of sportswomen towards greater emancipation difficult but not impossible. This issue will be further discussed in the next chapter.

In summary, Chinese women's achievements in sport are variously influenced by the determination and sacrifices of athletes, family support and dedicated full-time coaches, the authoritarian and systematic management of sports teams, ruthless winning-oriented sports policies, and the changing social and economic milieu.

Conclusion

The life-stories of selected modern successful female athletes reveal the essential importance of intensive training, the 'one dragon' training system, the value of the institutions of sports school and provincial and national elite sports teams, and the work of dedicated full-time coaches in ensuring the success of Chinese women in international sport. In addition, family ties and the physical and psychological qualities of athletes play their respective parts in ensuring sporting success. Achievement-oriented goal-setting stimulates women to pursue success in sport. It offers the chance of immense political and material rewards, and creates rare opportunities for upward social mobility. However, growing confrontations and conflicts between coaches and athletes often follow hard on sporting triumph. The way ahead has its problems. Nevertheless, the Chinese are facing up to one basic challenge of the new millennium created by successful sportswomen: how to transform the conventional authoritarian mode of sports management into a more democratic one.

Mobility, Stratification and Sportswomen in the New China

Social Mobility

Social mobility is the movement from one status to another within a strati-fied society.[1] In functionalist theory,[2] it is the device by which societies ensure that the most important positions are conscientiously filled by the best qualified and not suitable people.[3] There is some truth, if not the whole truth, in this assertion. In China, as discussed in the earlier chapters, sport certainly functions as a catalyst or mechanism for upward social mobility for a number of successful sportswomen who are considered suitable for eleva-tion because of their athletic performances. This differential sports perfor-mance leads to differential status both in the sporting community and in society in general. This differential ranking and rewarding of athletes, of course, is the embodiment of social stratification[4] – the ranking of positions in a society in terms of unequal power, prestige, or privilege.[5] The irony of this arrangement in a communist society pledged in theory to the equality of all is lost neither on the Chinese nor on global society. Theory is one thing, however, while life is another.

Social mobility and stratification are now central topics in sports sociology. Western sociologists began investigating sports-related social mobility and stratification in the 1960s. Gunther Luschen pioneered studies of the relationship between socio-economic status and sports involvement in West Germany in the late 1960s.[6] Roland Renson, utilising Belgian evi-dence, has categorised sport into four categories[7] associated with the social class structure: higher-class sport, upper-middle-class sport, lower-middle-class sport and lower-class sport.[8] J.W. Loy has suggested that participation in sport might help upward social mobility in four ways: sporting skills might be a springboard for an athlete to enter professional sport; sport might enhance his/her educational aspirations and attainment; success in college or professional sport might result in a former athlete being sought after and sponsored in business; finally, sport might help the individual achieve social mobility by inculcating attitudes and behaviours that have value 'off the field'.[9] These western studies provide a useful framework for the analysis of the social mobility and stratification of sportswomen in China.

Few surveys have been devoted to social mobility and stratification in Chinese sport. Due to a lack of survey data in general, and national representative data in particular, most of the literature concerning these issues is conjectural, anecdotal or at best descriptive. The result has been that little information on patterns of athlete mobility and stratification is available. However, in 1997 there appeared a well-received survey report by Zhong Bingshu on research undertaken in 1996. In his *Chengji ziben he diwei huode: woguo youxiu yundongyuan qunti shehui liudong de yanjiu* [Performance Capital and Status Attainment: Sport and Social Mobility among Chinese Elite Athletes], Zhong investigated the mechanisms of social mobility for athletes in China.[10] However, he did not analyse the gender dimension. Thus, in his inquiry a number of questions relevant to the social mobility of *sportswomen* – the subject of this study – are left unanswered because he did not take gender into account. Does participation in elite sport lead to upward social mobility for women? What social mobility characteristics exist in elite women's sport? What is the relationship between different sports and social mobility, and between sporting experience and post-sporting careers? This chapter, based on interview analysis and a national survey of elite athletes in 1996,[11] attempts to seek answers to the above questions. (For convenience, it is referred to as the '1996 survey' in this chapter; in 1997 it became the report by Zhong Bingshu mentioned above.)

In order to examine an athlete's mobility, self-evidently the socio-economic background of the family has to be considered. Before the early 1990s the Chinese were divided into three major classes[12] – worker, peasant and cadre. The worker and peasant constituted the manual class and the cadre was equivalent to the non-manual class in western terms. As most of the athletes surveyed started training before 1990, the analysis of their social origins uses these categories. In China, as in other countries, the social standing of the family is normally defined in terms of the father's occupation and the mother's is usually disregarded. This conventional male-derived model[13] of social mobility is problematic given that the majority of Chinese women have entered the labour force and have been important contributors to the family economy since the early 1950s. The influence of the mother's economic status and education on her offspring's involvement in elite sport should be considered – indeed, cannot be overlooked. Fortunately, the 1996 survey included details of mothers' occupations and education, although Zhong's 1997 report did not analyse these elements. They will be analysed here.

Occupational Prestige, Social Mobility and Sportswomen

In China, as we have noted, the 'career' of elite athlete has been viewed as an occupation since the establishment in the early 1950s of 'specialised' provincial sports teams throughout the country. It means that once a person joins a provincial, municipal or army sports team, she/he immediately obtains a formal occupational status equivalent to 'state worker' (see below) in terms of wages, city residence and welfare benefits.[14] After retiring from sport, she/he is given a job in either sporting or non-sporting fields. Thus, elite athletes constitute a special and favoured occupational group.[15] Occupational prestige, based on surveys of attitudes of a national cross-section,[16] is one of the most commonly used indicators in evaluating occupational position,[17] but before the late 1980s there were no such surveys in China. However, not a few people admired elite athletes at the time. It should be borne in mind that urban economic enterprises were owned exclusively by the state or collective, and private enterprises did not exist until 1980. However, there was a sharp difference between state and collective enterprises. The former tended to offer higher pay, more fringe benefits and greater job security, while the latter, involving neighbourhood factories and service shops, were characterised by lower pay, fewer benefits and less certain career prospects. In these circumstances, the position of 'state worker' with a secure post-sport job had an obvious appeal to numerous young people. As the female swimmer Yang Shengmei from Shanxi province has remarked: 'The motive for me to enter the specialised sports team was to have a job and have service years calculated. Whatever the job, permanent employment [the 'iron rice-bowl' – in Chinese, *tie fan wan*] would provide me with a secure future.'[18]

In short, the specialised sports team was the source of a paid and 'professional' sporting career – *and* a post-sporting career. To join a provincial sports team was to scale a peak in sport – an indication of considerable ability. The result was that successful athletes had a high profile and received attractive social and political rewards in the Maoist era (1949–76). The mountain climber Pan Duo, a daughter of a peasant slave in Tibet, is a typical example:

> Being the first woman to reach the highest summit [8,834 metres] in the world brought me glory that money could not match, and completely changed my life. Now I am the deputy director of the Wuxi City Sports Commission, responsible for athletes' training and foreign contacts.[19]

As noted earlier, achievement in sport not only brought visibility, prestige and pride to athletes themselves and to the coaches who trained them but also to their families. This is vividly illustrated in the story of the Olympic swimming champion Qian Hong:

> After I joined our provincial swimming team, especially after I achieved good results in national competitions, people's attitudes to my family underwent a U turn. In the past, my family was very poor and despised by relatives and neighbours. Now they admired my achievements and became more friendly towards my family.[20]

After economic reform was unleashed in 1978 and private enterprises and joint-venture companies emerged and expanded, state enterprises were no longer as seductive as before. Neither was the elite sports team. Fortunately, the absorption of China into the world sports family in 1979 added momentum to its elite sport and brought abundant opportunities for the best athletes to win glory for the nation, *and* fame and fortune for themselves. Outstanding athletes were given huge material incentives and political rewards. Deng Yaping, the double Olympic table tennis gold medallist in 1992, is a good example. She received a 1.16-million-yuan bonus plus a flat worth 0.4 million yuan, becoming the most highly rewarded athlete in 1992.[21] Other gold medallists also secured about 700,00–800,000 yuan, equal to a 400-year income for an ordinary Chinese.[22] The huge winning bonus for successful athletes was in sharp contrast to the tiny bonus of 400 yuan for a successful executive designer on the space shuttle project,[23] and consequently the supply of ambitious athletes did not dry up. This discrepancy, as already stated, generated intense controversy among the public, who questioned whether sporting victories should be emphasised at the expense of scientific research. However, this dispute itself simply reflects the fact that in the last two decades successful athletes in China have enjoyed exceptionally high social prestige and financial benefits, and have raised their social standings in society dramatically. The general career of elite athlete was placed about 25th out of 80 occupations in Guangzhou in 1990, 25th out of 100 occupations in Beijing in 1997[24] and 19th out of 100 occupations in Shenzhen in 1998.[25] Strikingly, the elite athlete was even ahead of company director, film star, fashion model and pop singer in occupational prestige. This high occupational prestige underlies the considerable contemporary possibilities for individuals to realise upward social mobility through involvement in elite sport.

Family Background, Social Mobility and Involvement in Sport

Origin and destination are two basic elements in the study of social mobility. In this analysis, the elite sports team is viewed as the destination, and the occupational classes of parents the origin, of the vertical intergenerational mobility of athletes. The 1996 survey shows that 57.7 per cent of the mothers and 31.1 per cent of the fathers of female athletes were from worker/peasant (manual) classes. In contrast, the figures for male athletes were 51.67 per cent and 23.31 per cent respectively.[26] These data have two implications. First, female athletes seemed to have lower class origins than their male counterparts in terms of the economic status of both fathers and mothers. This contrasts with G.R. Pavia's study of Australian athletes in the 1970s, in which he concluded that more female athletes (42 per cent) were from higher-class families than their male counterparts (33 per cent).[27] A similar result was reached in Hasbrook's study of the mid-1980s.[28] Second, more than half the athletes from both sexes were from non-manual classes in terms of the father's family. Given that the socio-economic origin of a family is conventionally measured in terms of the father's occupation, this implies that most athletes in China were from non-manual families. This contradicts the commonly held assumption that sport is essentially an activity engaged in by the children of the manual class in China.[29]

The above facts have their underlying explanations. First, women's sport is, to a large extent, associated with the communist ideology of equality between men and women and the practice of socialist public ownership in China. As mentioned in earlier chapters, the principle of equality has been preached in the country since the Communist Party took power in 1949. In spite of the persistence of gender stratification in society in general, in elite sport women have been provided de facto with equal access to facilities, coaching and competitions as well as to bonuses and other benefits. In addition, based on the public ownership principle of the socialist system, elite sport has been a centralised government-sponsored activity. Free coaching, access to facilities and expert medical care, free board and subsistence and clothing subsidies create a material basis for talented boys and girls from various family backgrounds, especially from lower social classes, to develop their athletic potential. It should be emphasised that athletic gifts and capacity have been the essential precondition to gain access to elite sport. Athletic talent, irrespective of class background, has ensured the above benefits. Elite sport in China is wholly meritocratic.

Nevertheless, the family, as an important source of socialisation in sport, has made its mark on athletes' sporting choices. The 1996 survey shows (see Figure 12 and Appendix 4b) that female athletes from the manual class (workers/peasants) were more likely to engage in 'strength' and combat sports, and swimming. Those from non-manual (cadre) families tended to take up ball games and demonstration sports. These tendencies have their cultural roots. Those sports – such as weightlifting, wrestling and judo – that were introduced to women in the early 1980s are characterised by 'sheer strength' or strenuous physical effort. To a certain extent they resemble manual labour. In traditional China, mental labour was considered superior to manual labour;[30] this cultural heritage is deeply embedded in the Chinese psyche and influences attitudes to sport. The result is that cadre parents are more likely to discourage their children from engaging in sheer strength and combat sports.

In summary, the 1996 survey displays clear gendered differences in the relationship between type of sport and family background (see Figure 13). The differences are statistically significant, particularly in combat sports and swimming (see Appendix 6, Table 2A). More female athletes involved in combat sports were from manual families in terms of father's occupation. One possible explanation is that combat sports emphasise strength and aggression, and are generally considered 'unfeminine'; they are therefore more likely to arouse opposition from some, if not all non-manual families (see below). The gendered selection of specific sports is clearly influenced by the phenomenon of class.

However, matters are rather more complex still. The education of parents affects the participation of their children in sport. When athletes within a social class – the cadre class – are examined, the 1996 survey shows that female strength sports athletes had a higher percentage of fathers with college education than male athletes, and the male athletes of small ball games had a higher percentage of fathers with college education than female athletes – see Figure 14. There were no marked gendered differences in other sports. These results are largely rooted in recent historic and cultural factors. First, most of the 'strength sports' were introduced to women after the mid-1980s, and presented them with fresh chances and challenges. Women could

FIGURE 12

PERCENTAGE OF PARENTS OF FEMALE ATHLETES FROM MANUAL CLASSES

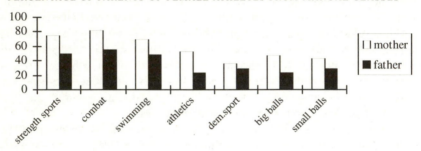

Note: Sport is categorised into these seven types in Zhong Bingshu, *Chengji ziben he diwei huode: woguo youxiu yundongyuan qunti shehui liudong de yanjiu* [Performance Capital and Status Attainment: Sport and Social Mobility among Chinese Elite Athletes]. *Strength sports* include weightlifting, cycling, sculling and yachting; *demonstration sports* include gymnastics, diving, figure-skating; shooting and archery; *big ball games* consist of volleyball, basketball, football, handball and water polo; *small ball games* consist of table tennis, badminton and tennis; and *combat sports* cover fencing, wrestling, boxing and judo.

FIGURE 13

PERCENTAGE OF ATHLETES' FATHERS FROM MANUAL CLASSES

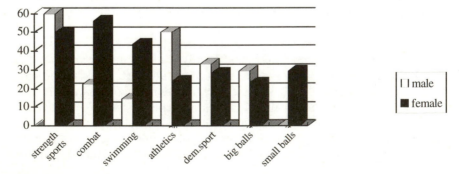

achieve success much more easily in these sports and at the same time advance their freedom. Arguably, parents with a better education were more sensitive to these newly available opportunities and encouraged their daughters to take up these sports. Second, games such as table tennis, tennis and badminton do not have direct physical contact and are less violent than football and basketball. For men they are more compatible with traditional Chinese sports, such as martial arts, and less opposed by parents with a higher educational background. In addition, the 'ping-pong diplomacy' of the early 1970s (see Chapter 3) enormously popularised table tennis across China, among both old and the young, men and women, intellectuals and workers. Against this backdrop, a number of table tennis stars became high-level sports officials. They included the former minister and deputy minister of the National Sports Commission, Zhuang Zhedong (1966–76) and Xu Yinsheng (1980–98), and the current deputy director of the National Sports Bureau, Li Furong. These promotions embodied the prospect of upward social mobility through achievement in table tennis, which increased the popularity of the sport, further attracting male middle-class athletes.

Interestingly, the mothers of both male and female athletes, as the 1996 survey shows, were more likely to be from worker and peasant classes than their fathers. This is probably associated with women's standing in society. It demonstrates that although women in China have taken up a wide range of occupations in society and their status has dramatically improved in the last half-century, the wife's original socio-economic status in a family often remains inferior to the husband's.[31] Women do not yet have full equality of career opportunity.[32] This state of affairs is to a considerable extent shaped by an amalgam of the legacy of traditional lack of respect for, and the corresponding low position of, women and the consequent division of labour.[33] Some Chinese women have achieved economic independence through taking up various newly available careers, but, as the Chinese scholar Wang Xiaopo has pointed out, their consciousness of equality of opportunity and individuality has not been fully awakened.[34] Furthermore, for a woman nothing is more important than looking after her husband and children and managing house-

FIGURE 14

PERCENTAGE OF ATHLETES' FATHERS WITH COLLEGE EDUCATION

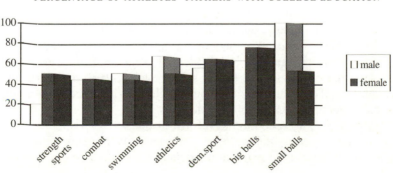

hold chores. This attitude is still entrenched in most Chinese minds.[35] In these circumstances, women shoulder the dual responsibilities of paid job and unpaid household chores. This double burden is likely to weaken further the opportunities for upward mobility. Indeed, a study by Tao Chunfang and her colleagues in 1992 reveals that the upward mobility rate for Chinese men was higher than for their women counterparts.[36] It should be noted, incidentally, that partly because of the existing disparity in upward mobility between men and women in society at large, mothers envisage sport as a possible vehicle for upward social mobility, especially for their girls. In sport, as already discussed, there is greater equality between men and women.

Geographical and Social Mobility of Sportswomen

In China an elite athlete often experiences three steps: student athlete, elite athlete and retired athlete. Each step is accompanied by geographical mobility. The first step in often involves a move away from home to sports school. Virtually all athletes live with their families initially, and go to sports schools for extracurricular training. The exceptionally talented are then selected for provincial elite sports teams, which are normally located in provinces' capital cities. These teams have an extraordinary magnetism for young people from rural areas. Before the early 1980s geographic mobility was extremely restricted due to the rigid national system of household registration, set up in 1955 and vigorously implemented between the late 1950s and the 1970s, which was called the *hukou* system. Each household possessed a registration book, the first page of which categorised the household and its members as 'agricultural' or 'non-agricultural':

> To move from a rural area to a city, one must hold an employment certificate from an urban employment department, or be enrolled in a university or have been granted permission by the authorities of urban household registration in the place of destination, and must then apply to migrate by going through the out-migration formalities in the place of origin.[37]

The *hukou* system[38] underpinned a rigid system of social stratification and allowed labour market segmentation.[39] However, movement from the countryside to the city existed in the world of sport because provincial sports teams could recruit extraordinarily talented athletes from rural areas. Nevertheless, the rigidity of the *hukou* system set limits to the recruitment of rural athletes. The result was that rural athletes comprised only a small proportion of the total number of elite athletes.

After China embraced economic reform in the late 1970s, control over population mobility was gradually and substantially relaxed.[40] Increasing numbers of people left their original residences for richer and more modern places. This movement set in motion a tidal wave of 'floating population' by the end of the 1980s, and, in tune with the times, sports teams were given much more room to recruit rural sporting talent. The Ma Family Army was a beneficiary of this policy. To escape arduous fieldwork in impoverished rural areas and to enjoy modern urban lives in cities are the major motives for rural athletes: 'They work hard at the beginning since they wish to obtain a place in the provincial team. Their parents will be most happy if they can obtain residence permission and have a job in the city,'[41] Ma Junren, the coach of the Ma Family Army, once commented. According to the 1996 survey, about a quarter of female elite athletes came from the countryside and none of them returned there after quitting training. Clearly, in the era of economic reform, as in the era of the Cultural Revolution, elite sports teams provide a channel to cities.

Figure 15 indicates that urban female athletes were overwhelmingly represented in ball games and demonstration sports. The life-stories of famous successful female athletes support these tendencies. All but one of the members of the 1980s Chinese women's volleyball team originated from cities. So did the 'five swimming flowers'[42] in the early 1990s. The author's interviews with elite athletes have provided reasons. 'The high jump is a sport with complicated techniques. The vast majority of jumpers are from cities,'[43] Zhang Tong, 1990 women's national high-jump champion, has claimed. 'Javelin throwers are normally from cities,'[44] Tan Guoli, the Asian record holder in the early 1980s, has observed. Urban athletes dominate those sports demanding elaborate skills and, perhaps more to the point, elaborate and expensive equipment and facilities and skilled coaches only available in cities and available to athletes at an early age.

As already mentioned, the 1996 survey shows that more than half the female athletes engaged in strength and combat sports were originally from the countryside (see Figure 15). These sports, such as weightlifting, judo, race-walking, and middle- and long-distance running, are less attractive to urbanites due to the 'repetitions of the same simple movement' and the arduous monotonous training, but, as already noted, they have features in

FIGURE 15

PERCENTAGE OF ATHLETES ORIGINATING FROM CITIES – 1996 SURVEY

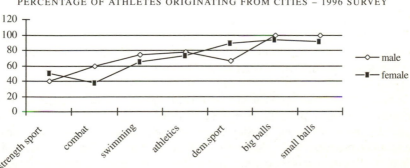

common with daily rural activities and require no expensive or sophisticated equipment. Thus, they are more acceptable and accessible to rural youth. Cheng Yuening, Olympic champion in the women's 20km walking event at the 1992 Barcelona Olympics, is a celebrated rural athlete:

> I was born in 1969 in a rural area in Liaoning province. My family, with eight children, was very poor. I had to walk or run to and from school about 20 miles twice a day. I began practising long-distance running and walking at the age of 15 when I was at secondary school.[45]

Participation in sport, then, creates a rare chance for rural girls and boys to flee the countryside, to win prestige, and to earn money for their families and themselves. As a consequence, to produce a sports star is a dream of many parents and to become a sports star is a dream of many children. Clearly, however, the type of sport and associated sports performance are inextricably woven into regional socio-economic environments and experiences. In China there is a considerable gap in living standards between the countryside and cities. In 1996, the average per-capita income of urban residents reached 4,377 yuan, but for rural residents it was only 1,926 yuan,[46] a differential of 2.27 compared to 2.7 in 1978.[47] As far as lifestyles and opportunities are concerned, the distinction between the rural and urban masses makes China a country of two nations.[48] Living in cities means better educational opportunities, a more stable income as a wage-earner, easier access to the mass media and above all, from the perspective of an athlete, better access to modern facilities and coaching. The famous swimmer Lin Li, merely one among many, provides the clearest evidence for this. Lin lived in Nan Tong city, Jiansu province. About 200 metres away from her home was a swimming pool attached to a spare-time sports school. She began swimming in this pool at the age of six. An opportunity such as this is not available to most rural children. Obviously, underdevelopment in the countryside blocks the way to a number of sports for rural athletes.

Migration occurs not only from the countryside to cities but also from small towns to large cities. As Zhang Tong, a national high-jump champion in 1990, stated:

> My motivation to enter the provincial sports school was to evade strict family discipline and to see the outside world – the cosmopolitan cities. Knowing nothing about sport, I left my home in a small town and went to Nanchan, the capital city of Jiangxi province.[49]

Like rural-urban population mobility, before 1980 interprovincial mobility was very limited. However, following the establishment of the 'special economic zones' in the same year, the economies of the coastal areas were boosted and moved well ahead of the interior provinces. The urban income disparities between the eastern (the coastal areas), central and western regions reached 1.41 to 0.95 to 1.0 respectively in 1994.[50] The prosperity and resultant various job opportunities in the coastal provinces made them attractive destinations for migrants, including athletes, and the deepening of economic reform necessitated a relaxation of control over population mobility. A 'temporary residence permit' was first given to those residents whose *hukou* belonged to other places. Later, some big cities experimented with selling urban *hukou*, with charges varying from 10,000 to 100,000 yuan.[51] Under these circumstances various individuals with special talents, including sporting ones, moved from the interior provinces to the coastal areas. Take Guangdong as an example. In 1982 only 0.52 per cent of its residents were migrants, ranking 22nd among the 29 provinces nationally. Eight years later, over five per cent of its population comprised temporary residents, far higher than in other provinces and municipalities. Shenzhen, the most attractive city in Guangdong, had one million temporary residents out of a population of 1.5 million.[52] Interregional migration increased with unprecedented speed and developed an irresistible momentum.

The winds of change were apparent in the sports community by the late 1980s, but the decision to grant athletes the freedom to choose where they would perform was still several years away. As the registration of athletes was still based on the system of *hukou*, most athletes continued to be tightly bound to their home provinces to which their *hukou* belonged. Without the transfer of their *hukou*, athletes could not move to other provinces. Thus, the conventional registration of athletes severely constrained the mobility of athletes between these provinces.

The year 1994 witnessed a significant shift in policy on athletes' mobility. To encourage more athletes to participate in the National City Games in October 1995, the National Sports Commission decreed that athletes could be exchanged between provinces without the transfer of *hukou*. As a result, the number of 'exchanged' athletes reached 185 across the country.[53] This innovation put down a marker for their eventual 'market freedom'.

In 1995 the first National Fair for the Exchange of Sports Information and Talent[54] was held in Shenyang, the capital city of Liaoning province. Although it came ten years later than the creation of a general free labour market, the fair represented a watershed in athletes' mobility. It legalised the transfer of athletes between different cities and provinces. During the fair, 80 people reached a deal and 292 drafted letters of transfer intention.[55] Two yachtswomen from the Dalian Navigation School became the first transferred athletes (to Shanghai) under the law. Not long after, the interprovincial migration of athletes escalated and transfers numbered 836 in 1996.[56] Athletes began to enter the national labour market to sell their skills and talent. Albeit not without local opposition, they were no longer tied to their home provinces.

Nevertheless, athletes' mobility was still in its infancy and far from mature. Illegalities were occasionally witnessed in transactions involving athletes, and a number of lawsuits were reported.[57] Threatened with a massive outflow of talented athletes, a number of provinces devised counter-measures to prevent athletes migrating.[58] Thus individuals wishing to move to other provinces often had to fight prolonged legal battles to secure a release from their original sports commissions. Change was under way, but not without hindrance.

To remove obstructions to the mobility of athletes, the National Sports Commission ordered that an 'exporting' unit could share the winning points earned by its former athletes with the 'buying' unit at the National Games – the most important sports event, of course, in China.[59] This policy precipi-tated an increase in athlete mobility across the country. At 1997's eighth National Games alone there were about 150 transferred athletes.[60] Shanghai, the host city of the games, was a major buyer of athletes. For its wrestling team alone, Shanghai secured three Liaoning wrestlers, including the retired former Olympic medallist Gao Dawei, and a coach from Beijing. To lure Gao to Shanghai, she was promised a flat with three bedrooms and 400,000 yuan in cash. Liaoning was unable to match such an offer.[61] Shanghai's endeavour paid off. Gao defeated her rival, the then current Olympic cham-pion Sun Fuming, winning a gold medal. Another Liaoning woman, Wang Xin, won a bronze medal for Shanghai at the 1997 National Games. Liaoning, the defending champions, became the major 'exporting' province: about half of the total of transferred athletes in the country came from there. Next was Guangdong, which released about 40 athletes to Hainan, Chongqing and Hunan.[62] Obviously, Shanghai, Liaoning and Guangdong, with the top three teams in the medal table for the 1997 National Games, played a leading part in the market for athletes one way and another.

The migration of athletes has also been closely linked to the global sports market since the early 1980s. Along with greater freedom of opportunity and movement, and a weakening of restrictions on travelling abroad, a great number of Chinese went to western countries to study, work or live. Given the gap in modern technologies and living standards between China and the west, going abroad was so attractive that it had become an unstoppable tor-rent by the end of the 1980s. Successful female athletes took advantage of various opportunities including scholarships, club employment, marital offers and even political asylum. In 1982 the female tennis player Hu Na from Sichuan[63] became a political refugee in the United States. This event provoked an immediate diplomatic crisis. In protest against American's entry offer, China temporarily terminated its sporting exchanges with the United States. Sport and politics were again twisted together. Hu Na, who was accused of being a traitor, found herself caught up in the first major crisis associated with athlete mobility.

Tension with the United States did not last long. China resumed its normal sports exchanges and sent a big delegation to the Los Angeles Olympic Games in 1984. At the games Chinese athletes for the first time won Olympic gold medals and became internationally celebrated. This vis-ibility created a number of opportunities for them to gain access to western countries, and as a result 'overseas' Chinese athletes snowballed in number and developed into 'overseas troops' (*haiwai bingtuan*). Table tennis alone had about 300 national players and coaches abroad in 1990.[64] Among them were the world champion He Zhili and the Olympic champion Chen Jing.[65] In the last decade, every year about 20 to 30 volleyball players have gone abroad to play.[66] According to Zhong's 1997 study, more than 15 per cent of Chinese Olympic athletes had taken up sport-related jobs in foreign countries.[67]

Faced with a massive exodus of outstanding athletes, in the late 1980s China issued a variety of directives to scale down the emigration. Now only elite athletes who were aged over 28 (for men) and 26 (for women), and who obtained consent from the National Sports Commission or individual national sports associations, could sign a contract with foreign clubs or agencies. These regulations certainly restricted the international outflow of athletes. However, along with the erosion of state manipulation in the era of market-oriented economic reform, by the 1990s individual athletes had obtained more freedom than ever to travel to foreign countries. The world shot-put champion Huang Zhihong[68] studied and trained in European countries for several years while she continued to represent China in international competitions. Ye Qiaobo,[69] world champion speed skater from 1989 to 1994, and Cheng Lu,[70] the first-ever Chinese world figure skating champion in 1995, both regularly visited foreign countries for training every year. They benefited professionally but also economically and psychologically from these foreign experiences. Their views of the world, women and sport were expanded. With consequently, greater self-assertion and individualism, they demanded more respect from coaches and wanted a more democratic relationship between coach and athlete. These demands, with others considered in earlier chapters, influenced the transformation of both sporting management and sporting culture in China.

Unsurprisingly, most of the 'overseas' Chinese female athletes specialised in gymnastics, diving, table tennis, volleyball and football – activities in which Chinese women had excelled internationally. With their departure went Chinese technical skills and training regimes. Consequently, the Chinese encountered more and more rivals in the sports that they had dominated, and even faced fierce challenge from overseas Chinese, now foreign nationals, who earlier had received years of professional training in mainland China.[71] This problem became acute in 1994 when He Zhili,[72] the former Chinese world table-tennis champion, represented Japan and won a gold medal at the Asian Games. Her victory over her former team-mates and world champions Deng Yaping[73] and Qiao Hong[74] greatly dented self-esteem in Chinese sporting circles. Her post-competition remark, 'It is the happiest moment in my life to defeat the Chinese', added salt to the wounds of defeat,[75] and aroused an intense nationwide debate on the issues of patriotism, performance and sporting management in China. He Zhili illustrates the fact that sporting globalisation makes the relationship between sport and the state increasingly complicated.

He Zhili was merely the tip of the iceberg. She, and others, signalled that the flight of outstanding athletes could endanger China's ambition to be a world sporting superpower. How to take advantage of the globalisation of sport to serve China's interests, while at the same time minimising its disadvantages, was clearly a major challenge. In the face of irresistible sporting globalisation, China began to learn the rules of the game. Now athletes were allowed to sign contracts with foreign clubs as long as they followed designated procedures, including limited periods abroad.[76] Sports associations, in addition to individuals, established various official links with international organisations and foreign clubs, and sent coaches and athletes abroad – but only for limited periods of time. These innovations were intended to secure the long-term retention of prominent coaches and athletes in China in order to ensure its success in world sport.

International movement was not all one-way traffic. By the late 1990s, with political, cultural and economic conditions improving in China, emigrant elite athletes began to return to China to develop their careers. Lang Ping, the former volleyball star, came back from America to coach the Chinese women's volleyball team between 1995 and 1998. The shot-putter Huang Zhihong, the swimmer Qian Hong and the skater Ye Qiaobo, mentioned above, all returned to China to study or run businesses. Several factors account for this counter-current. First, China's economic environment and living standards had improved considerably by the end of the twentieth century. With the commercialisation of sport, moreover, athletes could obtain lucrative wages and bonuses in addition to free clothing, food, accommodation and travel. The result was that the income gap between Chinese and western athletes had narrowed substantially. Second, with the transition to a market economy, there were, and are, plenty of business opportunities in China. The visibility of popular athletes can easily result in other job opportunities. Finally, cultural differences and language inability were, and are, major barriers facing Chinese athletes and coaches in foreign countries. Culture shock is real and lasting. For all the above reasons, at the turn of the century the tide of foreign migration in the sporting community gradually ebbed and some overseas Chinese came home.

Stratification, Post-Athletic Careers and Educational Opportunities

To some extent sport mirrors society. While it can encapsulate the contested and shifting dynamics of stratified societies, and challenge or reshape those dynamics, it remains essentially a stark embodiment of the realities of inequality and manifest forms of social division,[77] even in the most 'socialist' of nations.

Stratification, of course, exists between the successful and the less successful athletes in China. It is reflected strikingly in the following story. During the preparations for the 1996 Olympic Games, the Olympic and world gymnastic champions Li Xiaoshuan and Huang Liping could order dishes specially cooked for them in the public canteen and have massages at their preferred times. In contrast, other non-champion athletes had to eat the designated food and wait in a queue for a massage at a given time. This differential treatment was based on the rationale that 'the talented few are only produced if differential rewards are attached to such positions'.[78] For this reason, salary and bonus scales (see Table 12), food and medical standards, performance subsidies[79] and retirement allowances[80] are all based on achievement. Performance, resulting from talent, ability, ambition and hard work, determines the standings of athletes in the sporting community and society at large. In other words, achieved status is rewarded and ascribed characteristics such as class of origin, gender, race or kinship have less influence on the social status of athletes. Achieved status has become an essential part of the occupational subculture of elite sport. Once it is accepted by athletes, it influences their avocational and occupational lifestyles.[81] Elite sport acts as a source and a manifestation of a stratified society.

Along with this stratification, unsurprisingly, there is not infrequent jealousy and tension between athletes. The story of Huang Xiaomin, a female swimmer from Helongqiang province in the north-east of China, provides the clearest illustration of this:

> When Huang happily returned to the provincial swimming team with three gold medals from the National Junior Competition in 1982, she was insulted to her face by her team-mates. They shouted 'How terrific you think you are' and threw her belongings everywhere in their dormitory. Stubborn, proud and, more importantly, the youngest and fastest swimmer in the team, Huang was unable to stand this humiliation arising from jealousy. She escaped to her home hundreds of miles away. At the request of her coach, she came back to the provincial team, but was harassed again. Again she left and swore she would never return. She kept her promise, and joined the National Swimming Team.[82]

TABLE 12

SCALE OF WINNING BONUSES IN BEIJING

	1	2	3	4	5	6	7	8
National competition	2,400-4,000	1,200-2,000	720-1,200	600-1,000	540-900	480-800	420-700	360-600
National youth competition	600-1,000	420-700	360-600	300-500	240-400	180-300	120-200	120-200

Sources: Beijing shi tiyu yundong weiyuan hui [Beijing Sports Commission], *1996 Beijing tiyu nianjian* [Beijing Sports Yearbook], Beijing: Renmin tiyu chuban she, 1997, p.389.

Sponsored mobility is yet another phenomenon of sporting mobility in modern China. In one respect, athletes represent a unique group of individuals in the labour force. As a group, they are required to change their careers in mid-life. Thus, post-sport occupations, in particular the inevitable characteristic of intragenerational mobility for athletes, directly affect people's attitudes to elite sport. Zhong Bingshu stated in 1997 that 'the longer athletes remain in a sports team, the fewer chances they have of obtaining ideal non-sports jobs'.[83] Years of 'professional' training interfere with academic study and block the opportunities for other careers, as will be further discussed below. This has not been overlooked by the authorities. In the 1980s most athletes wanted to become coaches after retiring from training. 'Since I have played badminton for so many years, to be a coach is more suitable for me than any other career,'[84] Li Linwei, a female badminton player who won 43 gold medals and 13 world titles in her six years of international competition, once confessed. In the late 1980s, to ease anxiety about post-sport career prospects, the National Sports Commission endorsed a policy that Olympic and world medallists should be given job assignment priority. To be a provincial or national team coach was one of the jobs available. In China, a coach has a status equivalent to a teacher: in 1997 coaches ranked 20th out of a hundred occupations in occupational prestige in Beijing.[85] It is clearly an attractive occupation.

Political mobility is a further feature of elite sport. The spectrum of post-sport careers became diversified after the late 1980s. Many young people have long regarded a leadership position as one of the 'indispensable routes' – an attitude that has its cultural and historic origins. In Confucian society, personal dignity was determined by one's ability not only to establish oneself but also to take care of others. Thus, a person's level of independence and autonomy was measurable 'in terms of the degree to which one fulfils obligations and discharges responsibilities to family, community, state, and the world and heaven'.[86] To be an official and have power were the manifestations of success. This tradition was largely carried over into communist China.[87] As a consequence, a position in state or Party leadership has been frequently used to reward prominent people in various spheres, including sport. A number of successful sportswomen, such as Sun Jinfang, Zhang Rongfang and other volleyball players, were appointed to leadership positions in national or provincial sports establishments. These promotions highlight political opportunities for upward mobility through sport.

However, as noted earlier, to go abroad was another available route to upward social mobility for the Chinese in the late 1980s. The volleyball players Lang Ping and Yang Xilan went to the United States and Switzerland respectively after ending their playing careers. Due to their international sporting successes, such famous athletes had easier access to the West and survived better than most ordinary overseas Chinese. Li Xiaohiu's[88] story provides ample evidence of this:

I studied in Japan for five years. On arrival, I had no job and no scholarship. I could not speak Japanese either. Fortunately, with the support
of the Chinese Embassy in Japan, I obtained a scholarship from a
Japanese company. Thus, I did not need to wash dishes in restaurants
as many overseas Chinese students did. I understood fully that if I had
not been a famous athlete, the embassy would not have bothered to
contact relevant companies and colleges for me, and the company
would not have sponsored me either. Due to my sporting experience,
many professors wanted to have me as a student.[89]

There was yet another upward mobility route after the late 1980s. After
the policy of encouraging some people to 'get rich first' was advocated in
the mid-1980s, Chinese society became more materialistic. Many new
millionaires emerged and the income gap between citizens widened. In this
situation, to run a business became increasingly tempting in the 1990s.[90] Not
a few female sports stars started to run their own businesses, such as Qiu
Zhonghui Sports Equipment and Facility Company, Liang Yan Advertising
Company, Li Yuiming[91] Sports Entertainment Company and Guo Jung[92]
Food City Limited. Undoubtedly, their prominence in sport helped open various routes to entrepreneurship. The widely known stories of these successful athlete-businesswomen encourage many Chinese to dream of
upward mobility through sports involvement.

Nevertheless, not every professional athlete, of course, can realise post-
sport upward social mobility in sport. As sports-related careers are limited,
coaching posts are normally given only to successful athletes. Most ordinary
athletes have to move to other fields after they stop training. An investigation of the job assignments of retired athletes in the decade 1981–91 reveals
that only about 30 to 40 per cent of retired athletes gained sport-related jobs.
Others had their second careers in non-sport fields.[93] In addition, some athletes cannot acquire any job at all in the immediate aftermath of their retirement from sport. For example, of the 3,173 retired athletes in 1985, only
2,381 were quickly re-employed.[94] In other words, about a third of retired
athletes did not have an immediate job after quitting training. This situation
continued into the 1990s.[95] The post-sport career prospects of successful and
less successful athletes are symbolic of the stratified society. The fame
acquired during an athletic career is the most important predictor of immediate occupational attainment.[96]

Economic status and educational background, of course, are often interconnected. Education can provide a ladder to high-status and high-paying
occupations.[97] In China, sport can create educational opportunities for successful athletes, thus making upward mobility available indirectly if not
directly. The National Sports Commission issued a regulation in the mid-
1980s: 'Athletes who have won world top-three places can enrol at universities without an entrance examination and complete degree courses within
five to nine years.'[98] This policy created a channel between elite sport and

higher education, and more importantly, helped further alleviate public opposition to participation in elite sport. Due to the high visibility of famous athletes, universities competed to recruit them by providing them with favourable conditions, including studentships and priority in subject selection. Thus, a 'marriage' between the most famous athletes and the most prestigious universities resulted. At the renowned Qinhua University alone, there were over 40 well-known athletes in 1999.[99] For example, the skater Ye Qiaobo, went to the university for a master's degree course in industrial and business management after the 1994 Winter Olympic Games. She enjoyed various privileges, such as a one-bedroom flat instead of place in a dormitory with five or six other students, and one-to-one lectures by a specially appointed professor.[100] Such preferential treatment for star performers eventually became commonplace in higher educational institutions.

Such privileges are only open to a minority of established athletes. For the majority of less successful athletes, sport interferes with the attainment of their basic educational goals.[101] As athletes begin professional training at a relatively early age, their normal academic study is affected to some extent. The 1996 survey shows that 59 per cent of sampled sportswomen and 58 per cent of sportsmen went to elite sports teams before the age of 13 (see Appendix 6, Table 4d). More than half the women athletes in most sports received only primary-school education (Appendix 6, Table 4e). Due to their low educational achievements, some athletes found it difficult to obtain and retain ideal post-sport jobs. Their poor academic performance limited their confidence and their capacity in their new posts, and adversely affected future promotion. In elite sport there is, in fact, downward as well as upward mobility in post-sport careers.

Conclusion

The career of elite athlete, as we have seen, now has relatively high occupational prestige in China. This makes it highly likely that people from all classes can realise upward social mobility through engagement in elite sport. As talent plays a decisive part in access to elite sport, which is still sponsored mainly by the state, female athletes in China come from diversified family backgrounds. This sponsorship has specific advantages. The talented from all social backgrounds take advantage of this fact – a state of affairs that contradicts the widely held assumption that athletes are mainly from worker and peasant families. Elite sport is meritocratic.

However, there are some links between family background and the *type* of sport. According to the 1996 survey, the majority of athletes engaged in strength and combat sports and swimming were from manual classes, but fewer than half the participants in ball games and demonstration sports were from similar family backgrounds. Athletes from rural areas were more likely to engage in strength and combat sports. In addition, there were further interrelationships between sports involvement, socio-economic class and gender culture. In general, women athletes had slightly lower class origins than their male counterparts. Sportswomen from manual families were more likely to engage in combat sports and athletics; more middle-class (cadre) sportswomen than men engaged in combat sports and athletics. These facts are largely associated with the distinctive socio-economic development respectively of the countryside and cities, the characteristics of specific sports, the legacy of traditional culture, and the differential political and economic rewards arising from achievements in sport.

After the 'open door' policy was embraced in the late 1970s, geographical mobility between county and town, between small towns and cities, between provinces and between China and foreign countries became increasingly possible. Sporting success provides some athletes, women in particular, with a channel from the countryside to the cities, from small and undeveloped towns to large and cosmopolitan cities, and from China to advanced western countries. The overseas exodus of prominent athletes triggered a crisis due to the fear of a loss of Chinese dominance in key sports. Consequently, while the state sports governing bodies have encouraged the domestic exchange of athletes, they have tried to control the foreign emigration of athletes. For their part, local sports commissions have issued their own regulations to retain their outstanding athletes. In spite of this, international and inter-provincial mobility has accelerated since the 1990s as a by-product of the market economy.

Finally, whatever the official political ideology, stratification is rampant in Chinese elite sport, and in the last decade the associated social mobility has become more flexible and diverse. The huge visibility of successful sportswomen earns them a passport to modern cities and developed countries, access to commercial and educational benefits, and opportunities for a variety of high-status careers. However, less successful sportswomen face the disadvantages of poor academic performance, limited sports-related jobs and intense competition in non-sports careers. In the case of sportswomen, modern China has witnessed the phenomena of ever-increasing stratification, geographical mobility and social mobility – both upward and downward.

Gender Relations and
Sport in the New China:
Continuity, Change and Gender Culture

As has been noted in the Prologue, gender relations have been a focus of feminist studies since the 1970s.[1] It is widely accepted that gender inequality is a common feature of international contemporary social and cultural life. As also mentioned in the Prologue, some western scholars assume, based on analysis of western societies, that sport is a predominantly male preserve[2] and that male domination of sports institutions at all levels, from participation to coaching to administration, is widespread. Thus, for them, 'the female/male distinction will always be an irreducible organising principle in any symbolic system'.[3]

Although women's inequality is pervasive throughout the world, to generalise too freely about similarities is inadvisable, especially where Chinese sport is concerned. Given the significant differences between China and the West in terms of traditional culture, social systems, economic development and national priorities, simply to graft the western version of gender relations onto the Chinese world is unwise. In China, more women than men have succeeded in international competitions in the last two decades.[4] This has resulted in a startling phenomenon: the 'blossoming of the female and the withering of the male'.[5]

In Maoist China (1949–76) attention was heavily and at times exclusively focused on women's public roles in the workplace. Then, after economic reform was unleashed in the late 1970s, gender relations attracted the concerted attention of feminist writers[6] and academics.[7] However, they focused mostly on gender-related issues in the fields of employment, mass media and health care.[8] Sport has been virtually neglected in mainstream feminist studies, although arguably it has played a considerable part in strengthening and transforming social values and norms, and in promoting China's image in the world. In the sporting community itself there have been few surveys on gender relations in sport. As a result, as noted earlier, a number of questions have been, left for mostly unexplored. What is the nature of gender relations in the sports community in China? How do they affect Chinese women's performance in sport? What is the relationship between sportswomen and women in general? By exploring these questions, based on analysis rather than conjecture, a picture can be presented of gender relations in modern Chinese sport and their relationship to underlying cultural, historical and socio-economic changes in contemporary China. These matters have come up time and time again in the previous chapters. Here they are considered in more depth and more systematically, and earlier threads are thus pulled together.

Partnership in the Sports Community

Gender equality has been one of the Chinese Communist Party's primary principles. Based on the orthodox Marxist approach[9] to women's liberation, which argues that material structures determine relations between men and women, the Communist Party of China holds that gender equality can only be achieved through women's participation in 'social production' (*shehui shengchang*). Thus, as has already been made clear, after the CCP came to power in 1949 women were mobilised to step out of the home to take up paid jobs. This social innovation provided a basis for women, along with men, to engage in elite sport – which had become an occupation by the early 1950s, when a number of national and provincial 'specialised' sports teams were set up throughout the country. There was little sexual discrimination in the establishment of sports teams, the allocation of sports budgets, or the availability of sports facilities and equipment. As Lan Yalan, a former gymnast of the national team, has recalled: 'When I came to the national team in November, 1953, there were altogether 20 gymnasts (ten from each gender).'[10] De facto in sport – and from the start – socialism practised as well as preached the equality of women and men. By the late 1950s virtually every province in the country had set up elite teams for most sports and for both men and women, and Chinese women had started systematic and professionalised athletic training on a large scale – earlier, in fact, than in a number of western countries. Comparing America with China in terms of gender equality in sport, Susan Brownell has stated:

> If one takes the passage of Title IX[11] as the point when American sportswomen began to achieve legal parity with men, then 1972 was the year when the American situation approached the Chinese. That means American women lagged seventeen years behind Chinese women.[12]

This earlier entry of Chinese women into organised high-level sport provided a solid base for them to excel internationally in the following decades.

After the mid-1960s, as already discussed, elite women's sport expanded steadily in China. Between 1962 and 1978 the absolute number of female athletes increased from 3,552 to 6,348 and their percentage overall rose from 33.3 per cent to 38.3 per cent.[13] By 1994 the percentage of women athletes had climbed to 44 per cent. With the introduction of the 'Olympic Strategy' in the mid-1980s, as mentioned in previous chapters, successful sportswomen, due to their potential for international victory, have received prefer ential treatment. This was clearly manifested in the practice of 'training with a male sparring partner' (*nanpei nuilian*) adopted by a number of women's sports teams.[14] To ensure and maximise women's success in sport, these male partners have been widely employed to train with women. The famous Chinese women's volleyball team in the 1980s had full-time male training partners. The top eight female table tennis players in China were provided with 30 male training partners in preparation for the 1996 Olympic Games.[15] Xie Jun, the first Chinese world chess champion in 1995, was assisted by a number of male players. Judo was a relatively new sport for women, but the Chinese judoist Sun Fuming won a gold medal at the 1996 Olympic Games. She was convinced of the usefulness of male sparring partners:

> After masculinised training was advocated in women's judo in 1995, we always had over ten male team-mates as our rivals in training. One was a 17-year-old boy. I often threw him so vigorously that it brought tears to his eyes. He never complained about it. Once I hit him in the crotch by accident. His face turned pale and he rolled on the floor in unbearable distress. No sooner did he return from hospital than he started to train with me. I later hurt his legs and ribs several times. He even insisted on fighting me in bandages.[16]

From this description the boy was much more than a 'punch bag'. He was a willing patriot. Nevertheless, what is clear from the quotation is that the pursuit of international glory has created more than an equal environment for sportswomen in China.

How can men, who have been regarded as heads of their families and superior to women in Confucian society, sacrifice their own career aspirations to support women? There are several explanations. First of all, nationalism, as mentioned time and time again in the earlier chapters, has been a strong driving force in Chinese aspirations. In the nineteenth century, and indeed well into the twentieth century, China was continuously humiliated by the western powers. Although the socialist revolution initiated in 1949 has brought about fundamental social, political and cultural changes in the country, it has failed to raise Chinese living standards to western levels. In these circumstances, sporting victory, no matter whether by men or women, has been desperately needed to demonstrate socialist superiority and to create a strong image of communist China in the world. To be a world sporting power, symbolic of a strong nation, has been the ambition of generations of Chinese. This ambition was more furiously pursued after China rejoined the International Olympic Committee in 1979. To win prestige for the country, female athletes and those supporting them, including male sparring partners, made huge efforts to raise their standards. Given that women are more likely to win world championships, training with them is a national necessity. As a result, the 'national interest' takes precedence over any lingering male chauvinism. To be a woman's sparring partner, as in the case of Xie Jun's partner, is to be part of, and shaped by, patriotism.

Furthermore, in the light of Confucian tradition, the fact that men should sacrifice their own career prospects to be women's sparring partners is not wholly surprising. It is, in fact, part of the traditional Chinese *yin-yang* (female-male) philosophical inheritance. The ancient character *yin* signifies 'the sun hidden by clouds' and *yang* 'the sun shining over the land'. Lao Zi, the most influential yin-yang philosopher and the founder of Taoism – the indigenous religion of China – in the Late Spring and Autumn Period (770–475 BCE), held that 'Everything in the universe contains opposite yin and yang forces, which clash with each other. The normal relationship between, and the perfect standards for, yin and yang is "harmony".'[17] During the period of the Warring States (475–221 BCE), the yin-yang concept was used to explain the relationship between Heaven, Earth and man. It was later conceptualised as the basic concept of Chinese philosophy. The male is identified with Heaven and the female with Earth: Heaven is considered lofty and honourable, and Earth low and humble. Thus, the male is regarded as superior – strong and active – while the female is considered inferior – weak and passive. However, in spite of this hierarchical arrangement of man and woman, the yin-yang theory emphasises the integration of male and female qualities in order to reach balance and harmony. In the immediate context of this part of traditional philosophy, male assistance is proper to women's endeavours to succeed in sport. Thus, to some extent traditional yin-yang values provide a justification for cooperation between men and women within the sports community,[18] and help stimulate success in modern competitive sport.

There is another aspect of traditional culture and its influence on men and women that is relevant to the practice of 'male sparring partners'. James and Ann Tyson wrote in 1995:

> Chinese thinking is still ingrained with a tradition of absolute state dominance thousands of years old. Most Chinese still feel the pull of Confucian ideas that compel them to subordinate themselves to their families, communities and the state. They still have a weak sense of individual rights and no experience with self-rule.[19]

There is also the influence of the modern as well as the ancient to be considered. Undoubtedly, as a sparring partner, a man is in a subordinate position. This is emphatically at odds with a belief in traditional male superiority. However, in the 'New China' men and women have been bombarded with the idea of gender equality. Thus, it is not now so disgraceful to train with women despite an inevitable tension between the ideal of self-sacrifice and that of self-advancement. Also, on a practical note, being a woman's training partner has had certain advantages: enviable subsidies food and clothes, opportunities to go abroad, and political and material rewards for contributing to the woman's success.[20] No pragmatic Chinese would ignore these benefits. Clearly, the state authorities, with their capacity to offer practical inducements to adopt new attitudes have had enormous power in shaping gender relations in the sporting community. In fact, they have utilised both practical and psychological means. To win men's support, Chinese authorities have loudly asserted that without men's assistance Chinese women would not have made such remarkable achievements in sport. This praise of men and its associated maintenance of a sense of male superiority is therefore, to some extent, actually part of a strategy – to promote a belief in male and female partnership – that in turn is in pursuit of national success in sport. To this extent, the male-female partnership has been to the advantage of the state.

Training with male sparring partners, as the world wrestling champion Pan Yanping has pointed out, has not only advanced women's sport but also challenged traditional attitudes towards women.[21] This situation is in accordance with the observation that Jennifer Hargreaves has made of the West:

> To some extent, the traditional gender divisions that are imposed in most sports with separate male and female categories are broken down in judo. In many situations men and women train together without embarrassment and without any privileging according to sex.[22]

Male-female partnership in sport sets a good example for the transformation of gender relations in society at large, from male domination to partnership.

As a result of their success, as stated time and time again in earlier chapters, Chinese sportswomen enjoy an enviable status in the sporting community and the wider world. The following story is (up to a point) a good illustration. When the renowned Chinese women's volleyball team fell from grace[23] – a great blow to Chinese pride and identity – the female former volleyball player Lang Ping was invited back from America to coach the team in early 1995. Lang's appointment became 'hot' media news and a live television interview was screened throughout the country. Ismael Grasa, a Spanish visitor to China, commented: 'In Spain, a woman would never have been granted such visibility as Lang Ping.'[24] Paradoxically, this event highlights both the still extant significance *and* the insignificance of gender in serving the national interest in China. It is illustrated, perhaps with even greater clarity, in the remarks of Jing Dongxian, a world archery champion in the mid-1970s: 'From shooter to official I have not felt discrimination against women because I am not treated as a woman in my post.'[25] In other words, her success ensured her triumph over her femininity.

Reform: Male Coach and Female Athlete

A further close examination of the male-coach-female-athlete relationship can throw additional light on modern gender relations in sport. Influenced by multiple factors, including the organisational structure of sport, traditional culture, the personalities and educational and family backgrounds of both athletes and coaches, and, more importantly, the athletic capacities and performances of athletes, the male-coach-female-athlete relationship is undoubtedly complicated, diverse and dynamic, as has already been made clear. However, there is more to it than the real and growing confrontation mentioned earlier. Li Xiaohui, Asian shot-put champion in the early 1980s, has pointed out that 'A coach in China physically and mentally takes care of his athlete's health and skills, just as a father takes care of his daughter.'[26] The appropriateness of the father-daughter metaphor is underlined by the story of Olympic race-walking champion Chen Yueling. In the months leading to the 1992 Olympic Games, she rode pillion to save her energy for training. Her 60-year-old coach cycled between their residence and the training venue (a distance of 8km). As she observed him sweating and struggling, an ambivalent feeling arose within her. His harsh, even brutal attitude in training was forgotten and his imperious scolding was forgiven. She made up her mind that 'even if it were a sea of bitterness in front of me, I would jump into it. If I did not achieve a good result at the Olympic Games, it would be unfair to him.'[27]

This father-daughter relationship is pervasive in sporting communities in China. It locks the male coach and female athlete into a superior-inferior hierarchical framework but also locks them into a parent-child relationship. This is not surprising. In China an authoritarian state of affairs still characterises social relationships between superior and subordinate, teacher and student, coach and athlete, parent and child – a Maoist variation on the old Confucian theme of the 'three obediences'. It has remained intact, if adapted. Traditional forces have proved to be resilient: as in the past, to be quiescent, obedient, nurturing, hard-working, passive, supportive, self-sacrificing, and to please and be pleasing to others, particularly men – these have been the desired and desirable qualities of Chinese women as children and as adults. *Tinhua* (submissiveness) – children's conformity to adults – has often been praised and favoured by parents. However, this expectation of *tinhua* goes beyond the family circle.[28] To do what coaches demand is expected, encouraged and then normalised. Consequently, this quality of *tinhua* is gradually internalised by sportswomen through family, school, sports team and society. The male-coach-female-athlete relationship is, therefore, deeply embedded in past patriarchal norms, which have determined and still determine the authoritarian management style of Chinese sport.

In addition to the legacy of traditional culture, unique aspects of sport itself play a part in the formation of the coach-athlete relationship. As Harry Edwards put it:

> The coach is fully responsible for the team's victories and defeats, yet he has limited control in determining the outcome. Under these

circumstances, then, the coach insists on 'running a tight ship' and, consequently, a democratic leadership style would not enable the coach to maintain compliance under the tense conditions of a match where unquestioning obedience is required.[29]

Such features of sport suggest that the practice of obedience among athletes is far from being exclusively Chinese. Alan Tomlinson and Ilkay Yorganci's study of British coaches and athletes provides evidence of this beyond China. They claim that the female-athlete-male-coach relationship 'is typically based on a patriarchal autocratic mode of authority'.[30] However, as we have seen in the case studies in Chapter 7, for whatever reason, Chinese sportswomen seem to be more submissive to coaches than others. Both history and modernity play their part: it is through daily routines, complimentary remarks, punitive discipline and not least a sense of *esprit de corps* that obedience is reinforced and reproduced in sports teams. The volleyball player He Dai has revealed:

> Violating a coach's instruction always resulted in penalties not only for oneself but for the whole group. It was not worth getting others into trouble for one's own sake. Whenever I differed with the coach, I muttered to myself or kept my anger to myself.[31]

This self-restraint certainly contradicts the modern feminist requirement of self-assertion associated with female emancipation – with which, however, success in elite sport is not necessarily synonymous. Practical reality is certainly more complex than ideological requirements.

Athletes' compliance with coaches, of course, must not be interpreted naively as 'unconditional obedience'. Such an interpretation ignores the subtleties associated with modern gender relations in Chinese sport. Furthermore, quite often behind the overt submissiveness there is a covert defiance, which takes different forms, passive and active. The story of Li Guizhi, the former member of the Chinese women's volleyball team, offers a glimpse of this:

> When I left the national team in 1983 I was blamed for not 'eating bitterness' (*chiku*). In fact it was my poor health that had considerably affected the quality of my training. I felt frustrated. However, I believed that I was inferior to nobody. I was determined to prove my coaching critics wrong. I continued playing in my home province. My physical condition and skills improved dramatically. In 1988 I was ranked first nationally in terms of attacking performance. Yet I was not given opportunities to play in major international competitions until a year later, when a petition that requested the national team to employ me anew reached the Chinese Volleyball Association. This petition was signed by virtually all the head coaches of provincial teams throughout

the country. In response to this public pressure, in 1989 I was summoned back to the national team to play in the Asian Championships
and the World Cup tournament.[32]

Evidently, some Chinese women prove to be rather more than modest
and submissive; on appropriate occasions, they can be strong and assertive.
In spite of a general authoritarianism, it is hardly necessary to remark that
the relationship between coaches and athletes varies from sport to sport.
Interviewees have disclosed that a more equal relationship exists in some
high-level individual sports. As the national high-jump champion Zhang
Tong has stated:

> My male coach in the provincial sports team acted like my brother. We
> talked about training and life in general. Whenever he drafted a
> training plan, I was always consulted. I believe that to achieve good
> results in sport, an athlete must have questions in her mind and
> exchange ideas with her coach.[33]

However, as has been made clear earlier, there is another, more modern,
side to the authoritarianism coin. Following the adoption of a market
economy in China, western commercialism and individualism have accompanied modern technology into China and collided with Chinese indigenous
culture. In consequence, social values and norms have undergone profound
changes. According to an investigation of residents in five cities, including
Beijing, Shanghai and Guangzhou, in 1995, some Chinese now value independence and knowledge more and responsibility, honesty, belief, obedience
and imagination less than in some European and American countries.[34]
These developments have had their reverberations throughout the sports
community. Chinese athletes have become increasingly aware of their individual voices and rights. Many ideals and practices that were once regarded
as prestigious and valuable, such as collectivism and selflessness, have suddenly become dated and have been thrown out the window.[35] Accordingly,
the conventional authoritarianism typical of sports coaches, noted here and
in earlier chapters, has been questioned. Distinguished sportswomen, represented by the table tennis player He Zhili, the athlete Liu Dong and the
skater Chen Lu, have vehemently voiced their opposition to the manipula-
tive control and patriarchal domination of their coaches. Their actions have
tested the limits of coaches' tolerance and rocked the foundations of relationships between coaches and athletes. These protests reflect the growing
courage of women in expressing their individual needs and their desire to
control their own fates. Undeniably, such actions demonstrate progress
towards women's emancipation. Sport has served as one vehicle for the rein-
terpretation of the relationship between senior and junior and between men
and women, and as a model of interaction for people in the wider society.

In the era of economic reform, athletic performance has more than ever shaped the relationship between male coaches and female athletes. Performance brings women power. As Li Guizhi (quoted above) has remarked: 'Sometimes it is now the coach who appeals to athletes and compromises. Understandably athletes with good performances are more likely to be in this situation.'[36] Autocratic coaching has been eroding gradually, but new problems have surfaced: how to balance the increasing demands of athletes and the irreducible requirements of coaches, and how to resolve the contradiction between strict discipline and personal freedom. Reconciling these competing values is unlikely to be easy, but it is necessary to ensure the future of elite women's sport in China. In short, the relationship between coaches and athletes has seen change while continuity too has been apparent. The relationship is not simple and static, and it is replete with complexities and contradictions.

Family, Marriage and Careers in Sport

In China the family, still a fundamental component of society and still a significant source of gender relationships, has always been the centre of women's lives. Despite massive social change since 1949, a survey by Chinese Central Television in the mid-1990s showed that 97.4 per cent of women viewed the family as most important, followed by career (87.7 per cent), friends (79.3 per cent), politics (53.3 per cent), entertainment (25.4 per cent) and religion (12.2 per cent).[37] Things change yet things remain the same.

Nevertheless, to be economically independent has been considered fundamental to the full emancipation of women in China. As noted earlier, from the late 1950s onwards women began to enter various occupational fields on a large scale. Within a decade the category of 'housewife' had almost vanished in the country. In 1990 about 85 per cent of women aged between 16 and 54 had paid jobs. Women accounted for 44.96 per cent of the total labour force, above the world average of 34.5 percentage.[38] Since the 1950s Chinese women have indeed held up 'half the sky' of the Chinese economy.[39] Through their pursuit of careers, they have developed their potential outside the home and from this have derived, to an extent, a sense of the reality of women's liberation.

However, matters are still far from perfect. Due to the legacy of the powerful Confucian precepts described above, a married woman is still expected to become a good wife and mother: to look after, her extended family, to support her husband's career and to help educate her children. A national survey of 765 couples in 1994 indicated that only just over 21 per cent of husbands and wives shared the domestic chores, and that about 67 per cent of wives but only 14 per cent of husbands were exclusively responsible for housework.[40] Similar results have been found in other surveys.[41] The myriad domestic roles of cooking, cleaning and nurturing children make great demands still on most women's energy and time,[42] with the result that women are faced with the conflicting demands of paid job and unpaid housework.[43] This double burden is more than likely to generate considerable stress[44] and affect occupational performance. In view of this situation, in 1995 Margery Wolf noted caustically that 'the acceptance of the double burden as woman's lot by both Party and populace is the virtual acceptance of women's second-class status.'[45]

This situation rebounds on female athletes. They want to have happy and contented families, but family responsibilities can undermine their commitment to sport. To avoid the difficult double burden of family and career and prolong their athletic careers, in most teams young female athletes, as already observed, have been and still are discouraged from getting married. Until recently, having love affairs and getting married were taboo: love and marriage were considered somewhat unlooked-for distractions. In these circumstances, women in sport have often been forced to make a difficult choice: whether to end their athletic career at a relatively early age or delay marriage and family life.

The former decision means a waste of female talent. According to the available statistical data from the National Sports Commission (see Figure 16), in 1994 women athletes fell in number with the increase of age, and they were outnumbered by their male counterparts after 16.[46] This state of affairs suggests that sport is virtually an activity for girls who have not become women. The concentration of female athletes in the younger age groups is clearly rooted in an entrenched traditional culture that has defined women's proper place as the home and their proper roles as wife and mother. Thus, traditional culture has been, and to a certain extent still is, emphatically an impediment to an athletic career.

With ever-increasing opportunities for fame and financial rewards, the option to delay marriage and childbearing has been adopted by growing numbers of outstanding female athletes in recent years. The Olympic

FIGURE 16

OVERALL PERCENTAGE OF FEMALE ATHLETES IN VARIOUS AGE GROUPS, 1994

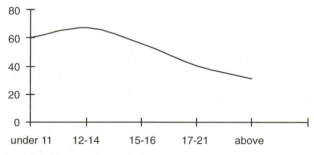

Source: Guojia tiwei jihua caiwu shi [Planning and Financial Department of the NSC], *Tiyu shiye tongji aianjian* [Statistical Yearbook of Sport], 1994.

swimmer Lin Li, the shot-putter Huang Zhihong, the table tennis player Qiao Hong, the basketball player Zheng Haixia and most of the Olympic silver-medal-winning football team[47] were all some 30 years of age when they participated in the 1996 Olympic Games. In their twenties and beyond they subordinated marriage and family obligations to their athletic commitments. Undoubtedly, this is a departure from, and represents a challenge to, the traditional idea of women and their purpose in life. In fact, by such actions sportswomen have initiated dramatic changes in the conceptualisation of femininity. Now such changes are increasingly common in society as a whole. In large cities such as Shanghai, Beijing and Guangzhou, women tend to have a family later rather than earlier in order to pursue individual development and personal careers.

Apart from their late marriages, a number of married sportswomen, exemplified most visibly, for example, by the famous 'diving queen' Gao Min,[48] have resumed competitive careers after having children. Impressively, these mother athletes have not been just ordinary participants, but medal contestants: for example, at the 1997 National Games, the high-jump gold medallist Jin Ling,[49] merely one of many, was the mother of a two-year-old son. The shot-putter Li Meishu provides an even more striking example. At 30, three years after her marriage, she won a bronze medal at the Seoul Olympic Games. She became a mother at 32 and at the age of 39 was still competing. At the 1997 National Games she was the oldest female athlete. These mother athletes, through their actions, have dealt a terminal blow to the myth that marriage and reproduction are the death of a woman's athletic career. The combination of athletic career with motherhood has proved that a woman can be successfully radical in sport, and successfully conservative in society. She can be a wife, mother and athlete simultaneously. Elite sport provides a means for the reconceptualisation of womanhood in China.

A major reason for the changing conceptualisation of women, of course, has been urban social transformation. The economic reform unleashed in 1978 has resulted in substantial improvements in living standards. Electric appliances, such as refrigerators and washing machines, are to be found in virtually every urban household. Convenience foods are now available in shops and have greatly saved cooking time. More importantly, the 'one child' policy adopted in 1980 has helped reduce the expense of raising children and shortened the maternity leaves that disrupt a woman's career and weaken her opportunities for promotion. Sportswomen are advantaged by such change. They can now dedicate themselves to a career after having a child almost as fully as any man. This is a critical precondition, among other things, for the resumption of fully professional training schedules and the retention of athletic careers for as long as success merits it.[50]

Be that as it may, to succeed in an athletic career still demands exceptional determination, particularly in coaching and administration. One female skating coach returned to training one and a half months after she had an operation for cancer, in which one breast and two ribs were removed.[51]

Perhaps this determination is sometimes misplaced. Feng Mengya, the former coach of three world table tennis champions and now deputy director of the Hubei Provincial Sports Commission, was concerned with nothing but coaching. She failed to give her sick son the attention he needed, and he became disabled.[52] Both cases illustrate the fact that too often female coaches have to sacrifice a great deal in their personal lives to ensure successful professional lives. This is especially true of the female coaches of national teams: the volleyball coach Lang Ping, the badminton coach Li Linwei, the figure-skating coach Li Minzhu and indeed many others have all endured long-term separation from their children and their husbands. The female national gymnastic coach Zhao Yaozhen is far from untypical:

> I work from early morning to late evening in the gym every day except on Sunday when I have a half day off. My husband is a football coach. He and my daughter remain in our hometown in Shanxi province. Sometimes I ask myself: 'Why should I lead so hard a life [a shared dormitory without television, telephone or bathroom in the national training centre]? Is it worth it?' Well, I have been in the gymnastic community since childhood. I hope, through my gymnasts, to realise my coaching potential. Fortunately, my husband gives me full support and encouragement. For this reason I will persist until I succeed.[53]

Certainly, some women now value their careers much more than before. However, this does not mean that the family has declined in importance. Women simply do not want to end their careers after having children. Nevertheless, due to the conflict between traditional female responsibilities and the modern pursuit of individual achievement, sacrifices have to be made. The sportswomen mentioned earlier, and many other sportswomen, seem sometimes to have drunk from a poisoned chalice. While they are elated by their career accomplishments, they often feel guilty about their families. Whenever their children are mentioned, their eyes fill with tears. They are coaches, but they are also wives and mothers, and not infrequently they are bruised by the conflicting demands of career and family.

Fortunately, these successful women have often won their men's support and understanding. In spite of the fact that the occupational success of the husband remains more acceptable in society, a capable wife is often encouraged to develop her career potential. One national survey in 1994 indicated that it was widely acknowledged by both men and women that the husband's support was essential for his wife's career success.[54] Indeed, the report made it clear that without a man's support, a career might well be impossible. Qiu Zhonghui has offered a vivid picture of this support:

> I stopped coaching in 1973 and began my job at the National Sports Research Institute. With the help of my engineer husband, I began to study and to invent a 'table tennis set machine', which mainly aimed at

imitating the European playing style. After ten years of experiments, I succeeded in 1982. Now I am busy running my own company and have no time to cook. I always buy a big box of fast-cooking noodles for my husband. He understands and backs my career.[55]

Qiu is merely the tip of an iceberg. In the mid-1990s in Beijing, about 80 per cent of wives and husbands shared household chores. In this respect, although women are still the main workers in the home, the trend towards egalitarianism in the family has received 'a social boost in contemporary China'.[56] By 2000 there was no longer a clear-cut division of labour between spouses in many families, especially in large cities. If required, men would stay at home and look after the children. Chinese women now spend only 0.7 to 1.9 hours longer than European and American women on household chores, while Chinese men now contribute 2.5 to 2.8 hours more than their foreign counterparts.[57] Shared domestic work effectively relieves women, to some extent, from the double burden of career and family responsibilities, and makes it possible for women, again to some extent, to realise their career ambitions. Without exaggeration, it can be claimed that gender relations in the family, which directly affect women's commitment to elite and other sport, have been gradually changing from male dominance to male and female partnership.

It should be pointed out that pragmatism has played an undeniable part in precipitating the changes in gender relations. Jing Dongxian, the deputy director of the Liaoning Provincial Sports Commission, has stated: 'Although certain feudal chauvinistic ideas persist deep in the mind of my husband, he treats me as a colleague not a working wife. This is to his advantage. Because I am more capable than him, he benefits.'[58] Thus, women justify their career aspirations on the grounds of both individual fulfilment and their contribution to the family economy. The transformation in family relations reflects the adaptation of cultural norms to changing political and economic circumstances, and to the practical benefits accruing to family members, including the husband.

In the past, Chinese husbands and wives rarely talked or even thought about mutual divorce. In traditional China, the husband had the indisputable right to divorce his wife for seven reasons: inability to bear a male heir, disobedience to parents-in-law, adultery, jealousy, incurable illness, gossiping and stealing.[59] After the People's Republic of China was established in 1949, and especially after economic reform was initiated in 1978, sweeping changes took place both in the family and in society. Although most Chinese still value long-lasting marriages, today people seem to have become increasingly aware of the tragic nature of unhappy marriages. The divorce rate in China rose from 0.07 to 0.15 per cent between 1980 and 1992,[60] higher than in Japan (0.13 per cent), but lower than in western countries.[61] Over decades of shouldering multiple responsibilities in society, Chinese women have always been capable; now, in the wake of political, legal and economic reforms, they are more independent and confident. They are no longer prepared completely to sacrifice their individualism to the family. Thus, in recent years, about 70 per cent of those filing for divorce have been women,[62] including some sportswomen.[63] Women are more determined than ever today to bury 'dead' marriages,[64] and to control their own lives. They are striving for a better and happier existence.

Opportunities and Challenges

Since the late 1970s competition has become extremely fierce in Chinese society. The female writer Zhang Xinxin[65] has used the metaphor of the jungle to describe the modern aggressive and competitive ethos of Chinese society. This new ethos is captured by Rudolf G. Wagner:

> The political and social environment becomes a jungle, populated by fierce and powerful crocodiles and elephants against whom the Bengal tiger has to struggle for existence ... both the man and the woman have set their minds on surviving in this jungle, and on surviving well.[66]

This free-for-all 'jungle' society has provided talented, skilful and capable women with opportunities to demonstrate their abilities.[67] Sport offers the pre-eminent example of Lang Ping, the world famous volleyball attacker in the 1980s. After taking over the Chinese women's volleyball team (CWVT) in 1995, she left her daughter with her husband in the United States and gave herself over totally to training the team. Under her demanding regime, the lost fighting spirit – the hallmark of the earlier world-champion CWVT – gradually returned. The team progressed from eighth place at the 1994 World Championships to the silver-medal position at the 1996 Olympic Games. Lang revealed to China and the world not only her coaching competence and her career commitment, but also her self-confidence and the courage to face challenges. She demonstrated that women could be as capable as men – perhaps even more capable – in coaching high-level sports teams. The result was that she won considerable and enhanced respect for women coaches through her efforts.

Nevertheless, conventional convictions die hard, and for women respect in sport can still be hard to come by. Although women have taken up sport successfully, with increasing social acceptance and individual self-esteem, sportswomen are sometimes regarded as 'lacking femininity'. Pan Yanping, the female world wrestling champion in 1992, has criticised those in society who are still prejudiced against female wrestlers: 'They think women wrestlers lack femininity. But in reality we are gentle and sensitive.'[68] Here lies the crux of the problem. Women athletes are expected to win medals for the nation by aggressive, competitive effort and at the same time maintain the pleasing 'female' characteristics of gentleness, delicacy and submissiveness. Sportswomen have rejected the equation of women with inferiority, but as Pan Yanping has clearly demonstrated, they have also accepted the traditional premise of 'natural' gender distinctions. To accommodate themselves to the still widely prevailing image of women, not a few female athletes wear colourful, modern fashions and cosmetics to 'prove' their femininity. Nevertheless, some have found conflicting professional and cultural demands difficult to reconcile. One possible by-product of this is that sports participation can, and does, adversely affect women's relations with men.[69] In their relations with men, some women athletes have found it difficult to 'change colour'. The role of chameleon has not been easy because of a rejection of hypocrisy and prejudice, a commitment to modern individualism or simply to the ingrained conditioning of years of athletic training, or indeed to a combination of all these things.

In seeking to assess the credits and debits of change in women's lives there is yet another point to consider. Socio-economic reform in China has certainly raised living standards for women along with men, but it has also led to the return of aspects of China's previous male-dominated society, reinforced by prevailing sexist features of western societies.[70] In the early 1990s, women in general received lower incomes than men: the mean income was 1,956 yuan for men and 1,633 for women.[71] Since the elimination in the mid-1980s of life tenure for cadres and the end of the 'iron rice bowl' employment policy, more female workers have been laid off (receiving 50–70 per cent of their normal wage while awaiting work at home).[72] Many protective measures and many of the benefits for women in industry have disappeared one after another.[73] Many rural women have returned to their homes to concentrate on household work and women college students have had difficulties finding placements.[74] In addition, about 80 per cent of children who have dropped out of school in impoverished rural areas have been girls.[75] Concubinism and prostitution, which disappeared after 1949, have re-emerged.[76] It is occasionally reported that women from urban centres are abducted, then transported to and 'sold' in remote isolated areas.[77] In short, in the era of economic reform the problems facing Chinese women have not been wholly alleviated but have in some ways intensified.[78]

With regard to gender issues in China, there is another alarming phenomenon – the shortage of female children. Although the preference for sons has diminished significantly in modern China, it continues to cast a long shadow, especially in rural areas where physical labour is still essential. Demographic data reveal that the sex ratio at birth – a measure of the number of boys born for every 100 girls – has been highly skewed since 1980. Whereas this ratio is normally about 105, in China it has increased over time, from 107 in the years prior to 1980 to 110 in 1986, and then 112 in 1989.[79] The ratio reached 113.8 by the mid-1990s and was even as high as 117 in some provinces.[80] This abnormal sex ratio suggests the loss of hundreds of thousands of girls,[81] a result of the strong desire for sons, aided by the use of modern technology such as amniocentesis and abortion, and even the cruel practice of infanticide.[82] The preference for sons reflects the deeply rooted cultural belief in female inferiority, which is far from being set aside.

The fourth Women's Conference of the United Nations, held in Beijing in 1995, provided an impetus for challenges to the deeply entrenched bias against women. In preparation for the conference, unprecedented volumes of previously unavailable information on women were distributed across China. A number of nongovernmental organisations for women and centres for women's studies were established. To show the world its commitment to female emancipation, the Chinese government made strenuous efforts to increase the numbers of female cadres in the Party and government bodies at various levels.[83] In the country as a whole, in the mid-1990s some 16 ministers, 18 provincial governors and more than 300 mayors (including deputies) were women.[84] Arguably, the Women's Conference has had, a positive impact on the improvement of women's status in China, but gender-related issues cannot be resolved overnight. In decision-making positions women's representation is still low. For example, in 1994 women occupied only six per cent of ministerial positions and 21 per cent of seats in the National People's Congress – the normal pinnacle of state power.[85] Women's inequality has not been wholly eradicated. An appropriate and desirable number of women's voices in decision-making has yet to be achieved.

Whatever gender dissatisfaction remains, sportswomen in China have been much better treated than women in general. Due to their sporting achievements, the best have acquired enviable social prestige and political favours,[86] and have received huge financial rewards, as discussed in previous chapters. Despite their improved situation, sportswomen have been underrepresented in decision-making positions on the governing bodies of sports. By the mid-1990s women accounted for only 8.9 percent of department directors and above in the National Sports Commission.[87] Approximately the same proportion is seen in coaching. Although Chinese women started to take up coaching careers on a large scale in the late 1950s, and women coaches have increased in number over time from 282 in 1962 to 878 in

FIGURE 17

MALE AND FEMALE COACHES AT DIFFERENT LEVELS, 1994

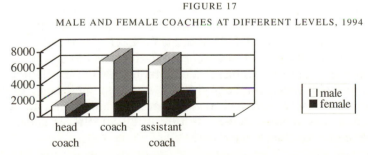

Source: Guojia tiwei jihua caiwu shi [Planning and Financial Department of the NSC], *Tiyu shiye tongji aianjian* [Statistical Yearbook of Sport], 1994.

1994,[88] they remained under-represented in coaching positions of elite sports teams in the mid-1990s.[89] Take the three sample regions of this study – Beijing, Guangdong and Sichuan – for example: in 1994, women coaches in elite sports teams accounted for just 14.77 per cent in Beijing, about 18.4 per cent in Guangdong and 20 per cent in Sichuan.[90] Clearly, there is an obvious gap between men and women in coaching positions in elite sport. Moreover, the percentage of women coaches is lower in head coaching positions than in assistant coaching posts (see Figure 17). It is clear that women are more likely to be employed in lower coaching positions. For example, by the mid-1990s female coaches in sports schools in Beijing reached 30 per cent, significantly higher than in elite sports teams.[91] Beyond question there appears to be a gender-based double standard with respect to promotion to the limited number of positions with high prestige and power. Self-evidently there is a marked difference between the proportion of women athletes and the proportion of women coaches.[92] The latter are still in short supply. In 1992 female coaches were only about 13 per cent of the total, but female athletes reached over 40 per cent of the total in elite sports teams over the whole country.[93] At the 1996 Olympic Games, while there were only ten women coaches out of a total of 73 coaches, 200 of the 310 athletes in the Chinese delegation were female.[94] This contrast reveals the uneven development of women's sporting representation. In the area of athletic performance they are well-represented; in coaching and management, they are poorly represented. To a very large extent women have freed themselves in one very important sphere – athletic performance. At the same time they are still imprisoned by past attitudes and assumptions.[95] There is little indication to date that this liberty, won with difficulty, has carried over from athletic performance to coaching and administration.

The above state of affairs, it must be stated yet again, is embedded to a considerable extent in Confucian ideas about women. Despite being continuously attacked throughout the century,[96] Confucian tenets remain extant in the psyches of many Chinese. An investigation into women's social status in 1991 shows that more than half the respondents (both men and women) believed that men were superior to women.[97] This is the modern equivalent of the old Chinese saying that 'women with their long hair are short-sighted'. In other words, they are preoccupied with the immediate present and not the future. They have narrow not broad vision. By extension, men have been assumed to be 'far-sighted', better coaches and administrators. As a result, gender stratification has persisted in important decision-making positions. Women's under-representation in high-level sports coaching and administrative positions[98] 'speaks to the strength of the continuing connection between sport and gender'.[99] Gender relations in sport remain, at least to some degree, 'a historically constructed pattern of power relations between men and women'.[100]

Conclusion

Gender relations in China, self-evidently, have evolved over time. They have not been static. They have certainly influenced, and been affected by, the recent development of elite women's sport. At an ideological level, gender equality was accepted, at least in theory, after the Communist Party took power in China. 'Women can do what men do' has been a widely cited slogan that has inspired numerous women to achieve their potential in various fields, not merely sport, since 1949.

Despite this fact, at a practical level the Confucian notion of women's inferiority has remained influential. Women's participation in modern sport is a testimony to their partially successful challenge to this belief in women's inferiority, yet women are still more obedient to coaches and administrators than their male counterparts. Ironically, perhaps the obedience of female athletes has contributed to their international successes. However, over-submissiveness often sows the seed of outright defiance. Distinguished female athletes have acquired confidence, assertiveness and autonomy through sport and now openly question the conventional patriarchal control of coaches. Women's defiance is an embodiment of their rising awareness and appreciation of individualism. Sportswomen have enjoyed more than equal rights and opportunities in athletics, yet they have been 'punished' in subtle and unsubtle ways for their gender with regard to leadership positions. The contrast between the high representation of female athletes and the low representation of women coaches in Olympic delegations is the clearest illustration of this state of affairs.

In the face of the double burden of paid job and household work that most married women in society have to shoulder, successful women athletes and coaches devote themselves to full athletic careers only by delaying marriage, delaying childbirth and sacrificing family responsibilities. To strike a positive note, fortunately, they often obtain encouragement from their families, especially their husbands. The relationship between men and women in society, in the sporting community in particular, has been moving towards partnership. To strike a negative note, this process, however, is by no means straightforward nor is it without problems. Women still have some way to go to reach parity with men in modern sport.

Elite Women's Sport in China: Bridging the Past and the Future

Past Action

In the last 50 or so years, since the People's Republic of China was established in 1949, elite women's sport in has evolved from embryo to maturity, and from relative invisibility to full international visibility. This process has been replete with challenges, complexities and complications and has also been deeply enmeshed with communist practices, state policy, economic trends, traditional forces and international politics.

From the outset, the new communist regime possessed enormous power to shape the course of both women's liberation and the associated development of women's sport. Central to both were the Marriage Law and the Land Law of 1950, which attacked the 'customs and habits of the feudal patriarchal system that had stretched back hundreds and thousands of years',[1] and granted women equal rights with men at home and in society in the 'New China'. These rights were fundamental to the change from women with crippled, shrunken feet to women with long strides who won Olympic championships. With the law at last on their side, and intoxicated by the belief that economic independence was the permanent basis of women's liberation – physical, sexual, social and economic – women threw themselves enthusiastically into various jobs. They became factory workers, schoolteachers, army officers and much else. Political and legal reform also paved the way for women to accept elite sport as an occupation. Specialised sports teams at the provincial level came into being one after another after 1952, while mass sport took off even earlier as the Chinese, preoccupied with rehabilitating their war-torn, inflation-damaged economy, used sport to improve people's health and physiques. Women, female students in particular, took up various physical activities. Some quickly demonstrated exceptional athletic talent and became the first generation of elite athletes.

As early as the mid-1950s, China had installed a centralised sports administrative system, modelled on the Soviet system, comprising the National Sports Commission (NSC), local sports commissions, national and provincial specialised sports teams, and spare-time sports schools as well as sports institutes. A coordinated network for athlete identification, testing and nurturing had also been put in place. These innovations provided the organisational platform for the take-off of elite women's sport.

Then, inspired by enthusiasm for the rapid construction of socialism, the Great Leap Forward (1958–60) was launched by Mao. Both elite and mass sport flourished: intensive training and technical innovation were promoted in order to accelerate China's advance to supremacy in world sport. However, as will-power took precedence over sports science, intensive training produced extensive injuries. As a result, a number of talented athletes had to end their competitive careers prematurely. Nevertheless, in spite of the waste of manpower and squandering of resources, the Great Leap Forward 'encouraged innovations and even more important the spirit of innovation'.[2] Looked at in retrospect, it left a positive mark on China's sport, reflected in the philosophy of intensive training and emphasis on personal initiative. Be that as it may, due to the combination of political arrogance, the lack of effective central planning and a three-year period of natural disasters (1959–61), the Great Leap Forward turned into a terrible economic catastrophe. Resources were in short supply, and consequently, the high tide of elite sport ebbed away.

Before China had fully recovered from the legacy of disaster, another even more traumatic movement – the Cultural Revolution (1966–76) – was next launched by Mao throughout the country. Made pitiless by Mao's theory of class struggle, the Red Guards, made up mostly of young students, immersed themselves in heartless and ferocious attacks on the 'four old things' and the 'five types of black elements' between 1966 and 1969. Unprecedented personal humiliation, physical assault, harsh imprisonment and numerous deaths resulted. All this set China on a course of political and social anarchy. Bombarded by the eight 'model operas', in which women were represented as sexually neutralised revolutionary militants, and fired by Mao's strident assertion that 'men and women are equal', many women embraced the Cultural Revolution. They gained new opportunities to express their wishes directly, to demand power in their own right and to demonstrate their abilities through their own actions, in pursuit of still unfulfilled emancipatory goals. To prove their equally ruthless capability for revolution, women now often dressed and acted like men. Ironically, this 'sameness', resulting from the keenness of women to meet male standards of performance, simply reflected an entrenched belief in men's superiority. Furthermore, women's rejection of traditional roles was as much a result of political manipulation as of women's awakened consciousness of liberation. Mao had cynically used women before to achieve his political ends and he was now doing so again.

One by-product of the attitudes and actions that typified the Cultural Revolution was that in the years between 1966 and 1971 elite sport suffered badly from the political chaos. A number of leading sporting figures were denounced, persecuted or even tortured and killed, the training of sports teams was disrupted, sports schools were closed down, and international sports contacts were sharply reduced. Fortunately, the destructive and violent confrontations between sectors of the Red Guards pursuing their various interpretations of ideological purity, which came to characterise the Cultural Revolution, subsided in 1969, and the party and state administration systems slowly began to reconstruct themselves. In 1970 provincial sports teams gradually resumed normal training. Nevertheless, 'politics in command' was still pervasive in society. Intellectuals were still denounced and academic studies were still discouraged. Apart from the endless political meetings, there were few other activities available to the young. In these circumstances, children from various backgrounds became enthusiastic about sport, which offered escape from political boredom and painful circumstances. This positive attitude to sport was reinforced by the 'Rustication Campaign' (1968–80), in which hundreds of thousands of urban youths were sent to the impoverished countryside to 're-educate' themselves through hard labour. There were limited channels for these 'educated youths' to return to the cities, and provincial sports teams provided one sure route. Thus, it is not surprising that elite sport picked up steadily in the first half of the 1970s. Female athletes once again made impressive progress and exhibited huge potential in a number of sports.[3] The early 1970s proved to be the prelude to a period of international victories from the late 1970s onwards.

After national entrance examinations for universities and colleges were reintroduced in 1978, higher education became a major ambition both for school students and higher education for the 'educated youths' who had been sent to the countryside. Education was viewed again as a path to a brighter personal future. In contrast, sport was no longer considered an important medium of social mobility. The number of students in ordinary spare-time sports schools decreased from 1977 onwards – see Table 13. This fall in sporting participation might well have been associated also with the national birth-control project. Initiated in the early 1970s, and tightened up after 1980 through the enforcement of the 'one child' policy, this project successfully reduced the birth rate, particularly in cities. The number of children below 14 decreased from 337,251,000 in 1982[4] to 308,067,000 in 1987.[5] This demographic change meant a reduced pool of talent available for elite athletes. In addition, the one child policy had an alarming and unforeseen social consequence: spoiled children unwilling to face up to harsh training regimes. Furthermore, due to high expectations for their only children, parents themselves now turned their backs on hard, demanding and short-lived careers in elite sport, and made sure their offspring did also.

TABLE 13

STUDENTS IN SPARE-TIME SPORTS SCHOOLS, 1976–82

	1976	1977	1978	1979	1980	1981	1982
number	280,866	278,183	225,977	188,148	157,426	158,357	158,812

Source: statistics of Department of Sports History of the State Sports Committee, 1992.

In consequence, these objectives – reducing the opposition of parents to their children's participation in sport, and improving academic opportunities and performance of elite athletes – were put at the top of the political agenda by the late 1980s. Now universities were allowed to possess, or co-sponsor with sports commissions, their own elite sports teams. Athletes would become students. This dual identity of athlete and student was expected to resolve the inherent conflict between academic study and athletic training. The outcome of this policy, as expected, was a small and steady number of elite athletes enrolling in prestigious universities. This access to higher education, to some extent, helped offset declining sports school enrolments across the country.

The pivotal third plenum of the Eleventh Central Committee of the Communist Party of China on 22 December 1978 marked a shift in the Party's priorities from class struggle to modernisation. Economic reform was inaugurated and radical change resulted in virtually every area of society, including sport. Mao's egalitarianism was abandoned, and material incentives and bonuses were introduced to motivate athletes and attract young people into sport. Next, both public and private sectors were encouraged to sponsor sport, and market forces began to play an increasingly important part in elite sport. When the market economy was embraced in the early 1990s, sports clubs, transfers and professional teams were created; commercialisation reared its profit-driven head in sport. However, it was not until the mid-1990s that fundamental changes were witnessed in sporting institutions. The five long-established elite-oriented departments under the NSC were gradually transformed into 20 sports management centres. These centres were gradually given financial and managerial autonomy, and consequently received ever-decreasing funding from government. This innovation led to changes in sporting policy, personnel allocation and financial budgeting. In turn, this has reshaped the contours of elite sport for both men and women in China.

Elite women's sport in China has frequently meshed with international political developments. The Sino-American confrontation from the 1950s to the early 1970s, and Sino-Soviet differences from the late 1950s to the early 1980s, had reverberations for China's relations with international sporting bodies. When China and Taiwan clashed over representation on the International Olympic Committee in the 1950s, America and its allies supported Taiwan. Insistent on a 'One China' policy, in 1958 China declared its withdrawal from the IOC and other international bodies. This action delayed Chinese women's worldwide visibility for at least two decades.

However, China did not abandon elite sport. It fell back on the principle of self-reliance, and deliberately created a variety of domestic competitions to stimulate enthusiasm for elite sport. The National Games were created in 1959 and became the most important sporting event in the country – the Chinese version of the Olympic Games. By 1997 eight National Games had taken place. Through the Games and other domestic competitions Chinese elite sport actually grew in size, advanced in quality and became firmly established.

To find a way out of its international isolation, China opted for normalising its relations with the United States in the early 1970s. Following the 'ping-pong diplomacy' period, described in Chapter 3, sports exchanges increased steadily between China and the West. In 1974 China regained its membership of the fencing, volleyball, swimming and ice hockey international federations.[6] In the same year Chinese athletes participated in the seventh Asian Games and won second place in the medal count, behind Japan. These international contacts laid the foundation for China's reconciliation with the IOC at the end of the 1970s. China at once began an all-out effort to win global respectability and esteem. The slogan 'friendship first, competition second', once sanctioned by Mao Zedong, was replaced by 'set out from Asia and join the ranks of the advanced world'. Chinese women led the way, quickly excelling internationally in diving, gymnastics, fencing and shooting as well as table tennis. In the 1980s the most impressive group of Chinese women was the Chinese women's volleyball team. Its six world titles in succession were greeted as 'the triumphs of the nation' (*minzu de shengli*).[7] They aroused the most intense patriotism right across the country, and served the image of women well. In the 20 years between 1978 and 1998, women made up 61.6 per cent of the Best Ten Athletes of the Year in China. Furthermore, only one of the Best Ten Athletes in 1998 was a man.[8] Clearly women have progressively overshadowed men in sport, sparking off a lasting nationwide controversy about male identity that still rages.[9]

Sporting success has brought female athletes enormous fame, prestige and benefits. Successful female athletes have become national celebrities and heroines. They enjoy enviable political, social and financial status; they have proved that success in sport can lead to upward social mobility, and that performance can determine standing both in the sporting community and in society at large.

Due to the contemporary global significance of sport, to become a world sporting power has been the persistent and ultimate dream of China – a nation that was terribly humiliated by western incursions (both military and economic) between the mid-nineteenth century and the mid-twentieth century. To realise this dream, considerable resources have been poured into elite sport. Fifteen gold medals at the 1984 Olympic Games were seen as vindicating the elite-oriented sports policy, and resulted in the creation of an 'Olympic Strategy' aimed at dominating the Olympic Games. However, the 1988 Olympics dealt a heavy blow to this ambition: the unforeseen fiasco of winning only five gold medals there simply reinforced Chinese determination to realise the strategy fully. The timing and activities of the National Games were adjusted to minimise the differences between National and Olympic Games. In addition, the performances of athletes in the Olympics were added to the records of their home provinces (previously only National Games performances were recorded) in order to stimulate local enthusiasm for the Olympics. In tune with these innovations, provincial sports teams throughout the country were reconstructed; consequently, by the mid-1990s, elite athletes concentrated overwhelmingly on *Olympic* sports. For example, athletics, shooting, wrestling, football and basketball had over 1,000 elite athletes each; gymnastics, weightlifting, judo, yachting, volleyball, table tennis and kayaking had from 500 to 1,000 elite athletes each. By contrast, elite athletes in non-Olympic sports numbered fewer than 50 each.[10] Clearly, Olympic victory, the public embodiment of national strength, has become the focus of national sporting policy.

Chinese women have been the prime beneficiaries of this winning-oriented policy due to their having greater potential than men for international success.[11] They have been provided with the best coaching, more than adequate financing and preferential arrangements, culminating in the use of male 'sparring partners' – a partnership in sport that set a good example for the transformation of gender relations in society at large. These special efforts paid off: Chinese women harvested a crop of gold medals in gymnastics, diving, badminton, table tennis, shooting, volleyball, weightlifting, wrestling, long-distance running, race-walking and swimming.[12]

Women in sport, when successful, may reap a bountiful harvest, but women in general have been faced with unforeseen difficulties and problems arising from market-oriented reform. Inequality in enrolment, employment and job promotion has accelerated since the mid-1980s. Ironically, women's dominance in elite sport, as mentioned earlier, may to some extent be attributed to their low status in other spheres in society – whatever their social class. When women are left with little or no possibility for upward social mobility in general economic circumstances, they may well be more committed to meritocratic elite sport that is based on competence, hard work and performance rather than on gender. The 1996 survey of Chinese elite athletes provides some evidence in support of this contention: female athletes had lower socio-economic backgrounds than male athletes. Arguably, the improvement of women's status in society at large historically might well have contributed to the greater participation of women in sport, but women's achievement in sport is not automatically synonymous with women's liberation. The combination of women's low status in sports decision-making positions with their high status in performance situations provides the clearest evidence of this. Thus, there is a pointed paradox for sportswomen in China. While they are superior on the athletics track and the like, they are inferior in sports management positions. Furthermore, while as performers they enjoy favourable conditions in sports communities, they live in a society that is increasingly driven by the rebirth of traditional Confucian doctrines and the birth of modern market forces. In these circumstances, Chinese sportswomen have to learn quickly how to negotiate both the legacy of past images *and* current practices to find a place in society without compromising their independence and at the same time realising their competencies.[13]

Women's success in sport is inseparable from their own endeavours and family support, and also from their capacity to build on the past. In China, not a few coaches and administrators have claimed that women are easier to manage because they are more obedient and work harder than men. To a large extent these assumed qualities of women are the combined products of Confucian influence and communist principle. Although Confucianism has been attacked continually over the last century, it is still apparent in Chinese society after more than 2,000 years. The roots of the prevalent pliancy of female athletes are buried deep in the Confucian 'three obediences' and cultivated, reinforced and internalised through family, school and sports team. Given the fact that most head coaches of sports teams are men, women's obedience to coaches and administrators symbolises, to some extent, their historical obedience to men. Women's submission has been attacked for decades and viewed as an unacceptable aspect of their lives in the past – far more so in the present. Yet achievement in modern sport might well be attributable, in part, to this obedience. Nevertheless, in the context of westernisation, individualism has been gradually awakened within female athletes. They have begun to question, and even attack, the 'common practices' and regulations that have been based on their absolute obedience. The table tennis player He Zhili and the athletes of the 'Ma Family Army' are typical examples of this defiance. The image of Chinese sportswomen is changing. They seem increasingly to be more independent, individualistic and assertive.

Regarding the Confucian legacy, there is another point to be made. According to Confucian ideas, after marriage a woman's main tasks are to help her husband and children to succeed in their lives, and to be responsible for domestic matters. This cultural tradition, still widely extant in society, does not favour women's commitment to sport. The result is that, until recently, female athletes were often required to avoid relationships with men and not get married. However, culture is in constant change. By the 1990s, not a few female athletes continued their competitive careers after marriage and even after starting families. Their action helped precipitate changes in gender relations both in the family and society; sportswomen are active agents in initiating social change.

The family has always been crucial in Chinese society. It is no different for sportswomen: the family is often the source of encouragement and dedication for participation in sport. In the interests of the family, father supports daughter, brother helps sister and husband backs wife to ensure their sporting success. Gender considerations come second to the family – a fact that itself mounts a challenge to the traditional gender order. However, following the incorporation of western individualism, family unity in general is diminishing. This is reflected in the increasing divorce rate in the last decade. Through decades of successful involvement in social, political and economic activities, Chinese women have become more self-assertive, ambitious and determined. More importantly, their self-awareness has been awakening in the light of economic reform and its opportunities for economic self-reliance. The burying of 'dead' marriages is one indication of this.

After two decades of opening up to outsiders, Chinese women's sport has become intertwined with global sport. From the 1980s onwards, a large number of Chinese athletes and coaches migrated abroad, and some foreign coaches and athletes came to China. As a result, China was assimilated more and more fully into the world sports scene. In conjunction with these exchanges, performance-enhancing drugs were brought to China in the early 1980s and gradually became endemic in the 1990s. Arguably, behind drug abuse was a significant socio-economic impulse. In the mid-1980s a con-tracted responsibility system was introduced, ranging from agricultural and industrial production to the sports community. Athletes' performance quotas became the sole criteria for the employment of, and bonus allocations to, coaches, administrators and athletes. In addition, winning a major event could result in enormous corporate sponsorship, advertising contracts and university studentships. In these circumstances, the win-at-all-costs men-tality ensnared not only a number of athletes, but also coaches, researchers and officials. The outcome was that some athletes, often assisted by coaches and researchers, took drugs to enhance their performance. The consequent upsurge of drug offences put China under intense international pressure to crack down on drug abuse. Indeed, various anti-drug policies and regula-tions were promulgated over the years. However, due to the ongoing decen-tralisation of management to provinces and cities, central sports bodies' control over drug offences was now weakened. Threatened by failure to meet contracted performance quotas unless they used drugs, some officials, especially local ones, often paid mere lip-service to the anti-drug campaign. Consequently, by the mid-1990s it became more and more difficult to imple-ment anti-doping policies.

Frank acknowledgement of the existence of drug abuse, however, should not be allowed to overshadow the positive aspects of Chinese sport, especially women's sport. First, before performance-enhancing drugs emerged in the country, Chinese women had already achieved success in a variety of sports. Second, drugs do not assist performance greatly in a number of sports such as gymnastics, diving and table tennis, which have witnessed Chinese dominance. Finally, the sports administration and training regimes established from the early 1950s – including early special-isation of training, the identification, screening and cultivation of athletes, and the 'one dragon' system from sports school to the national team and coaches' education – have been and still are the backbone of China's elite sport, and to a considerable extent, they have ensured Chinese progress to world prominence. The existence of drug abuse should not be denied, nor should it be exaggerated.

Although there have been twists and turns in the development of elite women's sport in China, the ambition to become a world sports power has never changed. Sport is a crucial part of Chinese attempts to be a world superpower. Chinese women's success in international sport is a product of the interaction of many factors, including communist ideology and the practice of equality, state planning of and control over elite sport, traditional gender culture, contemporary competitive conditions in the era of economic reform, China's integration into the global sports community and other nations' well-established male dominance in international sport. Contradiction, complexity and change all characterise elite women's sport in China.

Future Prospects

With regard to elite women's sport in China, the following questions about its future cannot, and should not, be avoided. Will China become a sports superpower early in this millennium? To this end, will state policy that has so favoured women's sport continue? In short, what is the future for elite women's sport and sportswomen in China? It is difficult, even impossible, to forecast this future with precision given the complex interplay of many macro and micro factors. However, several scenarios are possible in the first decade of the twenty-first century.

One is that Chinese women will surpass the sporting powers of America and Russia, and lead the world in most sports. Another is that Chinese women will regress in most sports. The former optimistic view is based on the assumption that the combination of China's huge population, its state-financed sports system, new economic stimulants, women's hard work and obedience, plus the disintegration of the Soviet Union, could well create, favourable conditions for Chinese women to rule the roost in world sport. By contrast, the latter view holds that two major factors could well collectively thwart China's ambitions in the new century: the decentralisation of sports management, which could well lead to total rejection of the 'one dragon' administration and training system, the cornerstone of past Chinese success; and the 'lust for money' mentality in the era of market-oriented reform and the consequent immediate gratification syndrome, which could well jeopardise systematic long-term training and lower athletic standards.

Neither of these two extreme scenarios is, however, likely. First, it is unlikely that Chinese women will have further remarkable achievements in the near future. In the light of the changes made so far and the unavoidable difficulties that lie ahead, the future of Chinese women's sport is far from ideal. Sustaining past success will be difficult, if not impossible, given that Chinese victories in such sports as athletics and swimming resulted in large measure, in the recent past, from the simultaneous occurrence of several sets of one-off circumstances: performance-enhancing drugs, the unstable political and social environment of the former Soviet bloc, and the huge incentives to win after long isolation from the international sports community. These factors, scarcely exist today and will in all probability have even less salience tomorrow.

First of all, under huge international and domestic pressure over drug scandals, the governing sports bodies in China have had to crack down vigorously on drug abuse. Some changes in strategies and sanctions are already under way. Tougher penalties[14] and more sophisticated testing technology will make drug-taking both more risky and more costly. Without reliance on drugs, there is little doubt that the Chinese will forfeit some successes in sports such as swimming in major world competitions.

Next, global sport is a dynamic process. If the countries of the former Soviet bloc gradually stabilise their economic and political situations, their sporting heritage and talent could again challenge Chinese women. America, the world's leading sporting power, will not easily surrender its dominance. With the backing of its strong economy, its advanced science and technology, and its attraction for sporting immigrants, America will continue to lead the world in elite sport. Thus, it is somewhat fanciful to believe that the Chinese will surpass the Americans in the Olympics in the first decade of the twenty-first century.

In addition, women's sport across the world has expanded quickly in the last two decades. The number of women athletes in the world has increased by two to three per cent at each Olympic Games. In 1996 women athletes numbered 3,779 (1,074 more than in the previous games), and women reached 35 per cent of the total number of participating athletes.[15] With the rapid expansion of women's sport globally, Chinese women will have more rivals and it will become even more difficult for them to retain their dominance in a number of sports, never mind achieving domination in new sports.

Moreover, the processes of 'marketisation', privatisation and globalisation under way in China since the mid-1980s will substantially reduce coaches' and administrators' ability to exercise autocracy over athletes. This will also bring uncertainty and challenge to women's sport. How to balance the irreducible discipline of sports training and the increasing demands of athletes will be a difficult task. It will certainly affect the future of Chinese women's sport.

Furthermore, the 'one child' policy might also impinge on elite women's sport. The preference for sons, though eroded significantly in the cities, persists in Chinese society, particularly in rural areas. A shortage of girls could result in a shortage of sportswomen. In addition, the 'little emperor' syndrome – where the only child in a family is spoiled and overindulged, and cannot endure hard work – will have an impact on sport. Athletes' commitment to the severe discipline required for women's competitive sport is likely to fall off. This will undoubtedly jeopardise women's sport in the coming years.

Finally, the deepening of market-oriented reform will create both fluidity and uncertainty in the political-economic system.[16] As state planning is gradually replaced by commercial marketing, many of the certainties in the planned system, such as free coaching and secure post-athletic jobs, will be under threat. Not only this, but China is a culturally decentralised country with a vast territory. While it might bring some advantages, a regime of only minimal regulation or control might cause even more problems than the existing system. As a result of the transition from old to new regimes, and the new coexistence of planning and market, Chinese sport can be expected to gain advantages but also to experience disadvantages. To identify the requirements and conditions for the effective combination of central planning with a market system is an urgent and difficult task. No matter what the outcome, one thing seems quite certain: there will be no return to the former planned system. The survival and development of women's sport will depend increasingly on its ability to create marketing activities that stimulate revenue.

In the final resort, whatever the difficulties and challenges, there are enough positive elements to make any marked deterioration of elite women's sport in China highly unlikely. First, China is still a developing country. Sport will continue to be needed to improve China's image in the world. Although the NSC, established in 1952, was downgraded to the level of National Sports Bureau in 1998 – a result of a restructuring of the institutional edifice[17] – it remains an independent institution under the State Council and its officials continue to enjoy the same social status and welfare benefits as before. This independent status reflects, to some extent, the continued importance of sport in the politics and culture of modern China. Without question, the state will continue its elite-oriented sports policy to ensure international success, and concentrate its limited resources on priority activities and athletes, including women athletes. The ongoing preparations for the 2008 Olympic Games in Beijing will fortify this policy at least in the first decade of the twenty-first century.

Second, ongoing market-oriented economic reform will bolster sporting investment. With the anticipated increased economic strength (China's GNP reached 959.33 billion yuan in 2001), the state will be able to support sport even more strongly than in the past. Simultaneously, with the advance of sports commercialisation, lucrative rewards, including corporate sponsorship, transfer fees and winning bonuses, will proliferate. They will entice greater numbers of young people into sport. As an effective medium to promote products internationally, Olympic sport is likely to gain more and more investment from public organisations, commercial enterprises and private individuals.

Third, a half-century of institutionalised administration of sport will not disappear overnight. Centralised talent identification and selection screening, systematic training from grass roots to international pinnacle, early specialisation, sports boarding schools, 'semi-professional' and professional elite teams, multi-level and well-structured systems of competition, coaches' preparation and evaluation are all hallmarks of Chinese sport. They will continue to underpin it.

Fourth, China's greatest assets are its population and increasing urbanisation. By the end of 1999, the Chinese population had reached about 1.259

billion.[18] This population provides a vast talent pool for all kinds of sports. More importantly, urbanisation is taking place in China at an accelerating pace. By 1996 about 43 per cent of the population were urban residents.[19] Due to better equipment and access to domestic and international competitions in cities, it is increasingly possible for more people to get involved in sport. Along with urbanisation, there is rising unemployment: the official unemployment rate rose from 2.6 per cent in 1993 to 3.1 per cent in 1997.[20] If the stood-down workers of state factories and enterprises were included, the real unemployment rate could well have been as high as 15–17 per cent in 1997.[21] This has resulted in unemployment anxiety among a number of workers, women in particular. According to a survey of 1,000 households in Beijing in 1996, the majority of respondents felt it had become an increasing struggle to survive in the previous two years, and 43.8 per cent considered the growing income gap to be the most serious social problem.[22] Under such employment pressure, it is possible that a number of young urbanites may once again regard elite sport, as they did in the early 1970s, as a means of gaining employment and a springboard to wealth. The widening income gap also could make sport as an occupation more and more acceptable.

It should be noted, incidentally, that in spite of urbanisation, the absolute number of rural dwellers continues to rise. They still outnumber the urbanites. In China, rural peasant incomes have always lagged well behind those of city residents. The ratio between rural and urban income widened from 1:1.7 in 1984 to 1:2.5 in 1993.[23] Arguably, the huge rural population, attracted by better living standards in cities, could be a major source of elite athletes in the coming decades.

In summary, China has both advantages and disadvantages in its attempts at ensuring continuous success in elite women's sport. The more plausible scenarios are less than dramatic. The most realistic is that China will move steadily from fourth to third place in the Olympics in terms of the medal count.[24] The most optimistic variant would be that it will become second in the world in sport. Any scenario raises problems. In the transition to a market economy, how to solve the contradiction of market values and centralised demands, how to reconcile national, sectional and individual interests, how to make athletes concentrate on sports training and not be distracted by seductive 'outside' lifestyles, and how to solve the conflict between the coach's authority and the athlete's individualism – answers to all these questions will determine the future of elite women's sport in China. In short, choices and dilemmas coexist in the new millennium. Given the large population and growing disparities between rich and poor, inland and coastal areas, and cities and countryside, athlete recruitment will not be too difficult. With the commercialisation of sport, a number of young people will consider sport a potentially lucrative career. Thus it is virtually impossible for Chinese women's sport to deteriorate. However, due to increasingly intense global rivalry, modern lifestyles, the 'one child' policy, the ongoing decentralisation of management and the concomitant decline in government funding, it is also highly unlikely that China could become the greatest sports power in the world in the near future. In the long term perhaps things might well be different. Is the twenty-first century to be 'China's century'? China will strive hard to see that it is.

Finally, elite women's sport is inseparable from sportswomen themselves. In the twenty-first century they will be faced with both challenges and opportunities. The challenges arise from, first, the 'patriarchal' tradition that remains embedded in many Chinese minds despite the half-century of advance to socialist equality. Women are still considered by not a few to be inferior to men. The existing inequality in promotion to leadership positions is the fruit of this cultural legacy. The double burden of a paid job and household chores could exhaust women and undermine their job prospects. In addition, as the former deputy minister of the NSC Zhang Caizhen commented: 'Society makes excessive demands on women. If they make any mistakes, it is very difficult for them to survive. China does not particularly favour women.'[25]

Second, unfolding market economic reform brings both opportunities and uncertainties for sportswomen. The market economy, based on contract and law, individuality and competition,[26] is a double-edged sword. While it requires fairness before the law, it is likely to develop the profit-before-everything mentality and the tendency to benefit oneself at the expense of others.[27] Driven by profit, more sponsorship is likely to go to men's sport – soccer for example – considering the overwhelming number of male spectators and the persisting stereotypes of women. Market forces could, at least in the short term, handicap women's sport, particularly the less popular and 'unfeminine' sports such as wrestling and weightlifting, without which world dominance would not be feasible.

Nevertheless, opportunities may be reasonably juxtaposed with challenges. Five decades of communist education and practice have instilled the belief in equality into most women's minds. Women have the courage and the capability to confront modern problems and dilemmas and overcome them. Sportswomen for their part today are aware of their possibilities and confident in their aspirations as never before. Women in general are conscious of their rights and ready to fight against social bias and injustice. 'They are striving for greater wealth, more meaningful lives, and freedom from harsh state controls in a grassroots movement that is shaping China's future and moving the world.'[28] The political, economic, cultural and social transformations under way in China and beyond will have reverberations for Chinese women *and* for Chinese sportswomen and their sport. If and when women's equality with men is fully achieved, women could well hold up more than half the sky – in Chinese sport and society.

Notes

Series Editor's Foreword

1. See page 228 of this book.
2. Ibid., p.1.

Prologue

1. Between 1950 and 1994 over 60 per cent of the 854 world-champion Chinese athletes, and 66 per cent of the 797 world-record Chinese athletes, were women. Reference from *Chinese Women Athletes: Marching Into the World Sports Arena*, pamphlet prepared for the UN Fourth World Conference on Women in Beijing.
2. China's rank in the Olympics progressed from eighth in 1988 to fourth in 1992 and 1996, and then to third in 2000.
3. Fu Yannong et al., 'Factors Determining the Recent Success of Chinese Women in International Sport', *International Journal of the History of Sport*, 14, 1 (April 1997), pp.172–7: Jim Riordan and Jinxia Dong, 'Chinese Women and Sports Success, Sexuality and Suspicion', *The China Quarterly*, 145 (March 1996), pp.130–52.
4. *Journal of Women and Sport: International Initiatives*, 31, 4 (1995), pp.13–15.
5. See Li Xiaojiang et al., *Huaxia nvxing zhi mi: zhongguo funv yangjiu lunji* [Mysteries of Chinese Women: Collection of Chinese Women's Studies], Shenghua, dushu, xinzhi shanlian shudian, 1990; Sha Jicai et al., *Dangdai zhongguo funv diwei* [Contemporary Chinese Women's Status], Beijing daxue chuban she, 1995.
6. Alison Dewar, 'Would All the Generic Women In Sport Please Stand Up? Challenges Facing Feminist Sport Sociology', *Quest*, 45 (1993), pp.221–9.
7. Susan Brownell makes a brave attempt but too frequently reveals her essential lack of understanding of Chinese cultural tradition and norms as in, for example, her comments on the situation of Chinese sport during the Cultural Revolution and the motive of elite athletes for sports participation (see Susan Brownell, *Training the Body for China: Sports in the Moral Order of the People's Republic*, Chicago, IL and London: University of Chicago Press, 1995). These issues will be discussed in relevant chapters of this book.
8. See Hao Qing, 'Dangdai zhongguo zhuanye jingji tizhi de tezheng yu pingjia' [The Characteristics and Evaluation of the Specialised Competitive Sports System in Contemporary China], *Tiyu kexue* [Sports and Science], 2 (1992).
9. Edward B. Tylor, *Primitive Culture: Researches into the Development of Mythology, Philosophy, Religion, Art and Custom*, Vol.1: *Origins of Culture*, Gloucester, MA: Smith, (1871) 1958, p.1.
10. Milton Singer, 'Culture: The Concept of Culture', in David L. Sills (ed.), *International Encyclopaedia of the Social Sciences*, Vol.3, New York: The Macmillan Company and The Free Press, 1979, p.539.

11. Clyde Kluckhohn, 'What Is Culture?', in Hu Wenzhong (eds), *Selected Readings in Intercultural Communication*, Changsha: Hunan Education Press, 1990, pp.37–45.
12. David D. Gilmore, *Manhood in the Making: Cultural Concepts of Masculinity*, New Haven, CT, and London: Yale University Press, 1990, p.224.
13. Ibid.
14. Helen Tierney (ed.), *Women's Studies Encyclopaedia*, New York: Peter Bedrick Books, 1991, p.153.
15. Suzanne Ogden, *China's Unsolved Issues: Politics, Development, and Culture*, Englewood Cliffs, NJ: Prentice Hall, 1989, p.18.
16. Confucius, a philosopher and teacher, lived between 551 and 479 BCE, when China was divided into warring feudal principalities. He saw it as the prime need of mankind to resolve the problem of human conflict and create conditions of peaceful coexistence and harmony with the universe. He found resolution of the problem in the concept of *Xiao* (filial piety). He defined this as serving parents during their lives and honouring them after their deaths. The central teaching of Confucianism is that nothing is more important to man than man, so Confucianism is essentially a humanistic philosophy.
17. He saw it as the prime need of mankind to resolve the problem of human conflict and create conditions of peaceful coexistence and harmony with the universe.
18. The Four Books: The Analects of Confucius; The Book of Mencius; Doctrine of the Mean; The Great Learning.
19. The Book of Odes; The Book of Documents; The Book of Changes; The Book of Rites; The Spring and Autumn Annals. These were first named the 'Five Classics' under the Han Dynasty in 136 BCE.
20. The Five Relationships: between father and son; ruler and ruled; husband and wife; elder brother and younger brother; and between friend and friend. Except for the last, all of these relationships were based on difference of status and expressed differences of power in society.
21. See Zhong Bingshu, *Chenji zhiben he diwei huode: woguo youxiu yundongyuan qunti shehui liudong de yangjiu* [Performance Capital and Status Attainment: Sport and Social Mobility among Chinese Elite Athletes], Beijing tiyu daxue chuban she, 1998, pp.182–3.
22. In China there are four grades for athletes: third, second, first and master grades, in ascending order. Most elite athletes are at first-grade level or above.
23. The respondents comprise 140 sports masters, including 27 international sports stars, and 134 first-grade athletes.
24. Chongqing became the fourth municipality in 1997; Hainan became a province in 1992; Hong Kong special administrative area was established when it was handed over from Britain to China in 1997.
25. http://www.bta.net.cn/travel.cn/cbeijing.htm.
26. Diving, swimming, table tennis, volleyball, basketball and gymnastics were imported to this southern province in the early years of the twentieth century (in reference to the evolution of modern sports in Guangdong, see *Guangdong shiliao* [Guangdong History Information], 1992 (1).
27. While the national annual growth rates of GNP and industrial output averaged 8.7 per cent and 10.1 per cent respectively from 1979 to 1991, in Guangdong the averages stood at 11.5 per cent and 20 per cent respectively. Data from Zhongguo tongji ju [Chinese Statistical Bureau], *1992 zhongguo tongji nianjian* [China Statistical Yearbook 1992], Beijing: Zhongguo tongji chuban she, 1992, p.3.
28. 'Guangdong yundong yuan' [Guangdong Athletes], *Guangdong tiyu shiliao* [Guangdong Sports History Information], 1 (1997), p.57.
29. Chongqing, which became an independent municipality in 1997, is included.
30. http://www.bta.net.cn/travel.cn/csichuan.htm.

31. The women's liberation movement of the 1960s fostered changes in gender divisions and sexual hierarchies in the direction of gender equality and developed a body of ideas about the systems of patriarchy. See Susan J. Birrell, 'Discourse on the Gender/Sport Relations: From Women in Sport to Gender Relations', *Exercise and Sport Science Review*, 16 (1988), pp.459–502.

32. Ibid. See also Martin Polley, *Moving the Goalposts: A History of Sport and Society since 1945*, London and New York: Routledge, 1998, pp.93–104.

33. Jennifer Hargreaves, 'Gender on the Sports Agenda', *International Review for Sociology of Sport*, 25 (1990), p.287.

34. Ann Hall, 'A "Feminine Woman" and an "Athletic Woman" as Viewed by Female Participants and Non-participants in Sport', *British Journal of Physical Education*, 3 (1972), pp.43–6; *Sport and Gender: A Feminist Perspective on the Sociology of Sport*, Ottawa, ON: Canadian Association for Health, Physical Education, and Recreation, 1978.

35. Susan Greendorfer, 'Role of Socializing Agents in Female Sport Involvement', *Research Quarterly for Exercise and Sport*, 48, 2 (1977), pp.304–10.

36. Birrell, 'Discourse on the Gender/Sport Relationship'.

37. M. Shoebridge, *Women in Sport: A Selected Bibliography*, London: Mansell, 1987; K. Dyer, *Catching Up the Men: Women in Sport*, London, Junction Books, 1982; B. Birkett and B. Peascod, *Women Climbing: 200 Years of Achievement*, London: A. & C. Black, 1989; Polley, *Moving the Goalposts*.

38. Nancy Theberge, 'Sport and Women's Empowerment', *Women's Studies International Forum*, 10 (1987), pp.387–93.

39. Birrell, 'Discourse on the Gender/Sport Relationship'.

40. B. Rogers, *The Domestication of Women*, New York: St. Martin's Press, 1980.

41. R.W. Connell, *Masculinities*, Cambridge: Polity Press, 1995.

42. George H. Sage, *Power and Ideology in American Sport: A Critical Perspective*, Champaign, IL: Human Kinetics, 1990, p.43.

43. B. Rogers, *The Domestication of Women*.

44. Christina K. Gilmartin et al., 'Introduction', in Christina K. Gilmartin et al. (eds), *Engendering China – Women, Culture, and the State*, Boston, MA: Harvard University Press, 1994, p.5.

45. Zhou Yanlin, 'Nan juan zhi de gainian he lilun zhi pipan yu chubu tansuo' [Criticism and Preliminary Exploration on the Concept and Theory of Patriarchy], in Jin Yihong and Liu Bohong (eds) *Shiji zhi jiao de zhongguo funv yu fazhang – lilun, jinji, wenhua, jiankan* [Chinese Women and Their Development at the Turn of the Century – Theory, Economy, Culture and Health] Nanjin: Nanjin daxue chuban she, 1998, pp.68–82.

46. For a definition of hegemony theory, see Alan G. Ingham and Stephen Hardy, 'Introduction: Sport Studies Through the Lens of Raymond Williams', in Alan G. Ingham and John W. Loy (eds), *Sport in Social Development: Traditions, Transitions, and Transformations*, Champaign, IL: Human Kinetics, 1993, pp.1–15.

47. Jennifer Hargreaves, 'Gender on the Sports Agenda', in Ingham and Loy, *Sport in Social Development*, p.179.

48. For example, it is not rare that women enjoy certain power in the family. In reference to the debate over power issues, see J.A. Mangan, 'Epilogue – Prospects for the New Millennium: Emancipation, Women and the Body', in J.A. Mangan and Fan Hong (eds), *Freeing the Female Body: Inspirational Icons*, London and Portland, OR: Frank Cass, 2001.

49. S. Wigmore, 'Gender and Sport – The Last 5 Years', *Sport Science Review*, 5, 2 (1996), pp.53–71.

50. Ann Hall, *Feminism and Sporting Bodies*, Champaign, IL.: Human Kinetics, 1996.

51. Birrell, 'Discourse on the Gender/Sport Relationship', p.492.

52. *The Past before Us: Twenty Years of Feminism: Feminist Review* (Special Issue), 31 (Spring 1989), p.1.

53. Michael A. Messner and Donald F. Sabo, 'Toward a Critical Feminist Reappraisal of Sport, Men, and the Gender Order', Michael A. Messner (ed.), *Sport, Men and the Gender Order*, Champaign, IL: Human Kinetics, 1990, p.7.
54. Ibid.
55. Alison Dewar, 'Would All the Generic Women in Sport Please Stand Up?', pp.221–9.
56. Michael Messner, 'Sports and Male Domination: The Female Athlete as Contested Ideological Terrain', *Sociology of Sport Journal*, 5 (1988), pp.197–211.
57. Tao Chunfang et al., *Zhongguo funv shehui diwei gaiguan* [Overview of Chinese Women's Social Status], Zhongguo funv chuban she, 1993.
58. About 5,000 people participated in the NGO Forum of the UN Fourth World Conference on Women. The Chinese hosted 47 specialised workshops. In addition, 8,000 training courses for the conference were held across the country, in which 1.91 million women were trained. Reference from Tan Shen, '1995 nian zhongguo funv jibeng qingkuang' [Chinese Women in 1995], in Jiang Liu (ed.), *Shehui lanpi shu – 1995–1996 nian zhongguo shehui xingshi fenxi yu yuce* [China in 1995–1996: Analysis and Forecast of the Social Situation], Beijing: Zhongguo shehui kexue chuban she, 1996, p.299.
59. He Zhenliang was chairman of the Chinese Olympic Committee and vice-chairman of the IOC. Zhang Caizhen was a female deputy minister of the National Sports Commission until 1995.
60. He Zhenliang, 'The Role of Chinese Women in the Olympic Movement', *China Sports* (September 1995), p.7; Zhang Caizhen, 'Zhongguo funiu tiyu fazhang huimou yu zhangwang' [Past Developments and Future Prospects for Women in Sport] *Tiyu wenshi* [Sport History], 1995 (4), p.6.
61. Lu Yuanzhen (interviewed by the author in Beijing in 1995) is professor of sports sociology at Beijing University of Physical Education.
62. Susan Brownell, *Training the Body for China*, p.209.
63. Lu Shiting et al., 'Rexian zhong de leng sikao – guanyu nvzi jinji tiyu yu qunzhong tiyu fancha de shehui xue qushi [Cool Thinking About a Hot Topic –Sociological Analysis of the Contrast between Woman's Competitive and Mass Sport], *Tiyu wenshi* [Sports Literature and History], 1995 (4), pp.18–19.
64. Statement by J.A. Mangan in his general introduction to the series *International Studies in the History of Sport*, published by Manchester University Press. See General Introduction to Stephen G. Jones, *Sports, Politics and the Working Class*, Manchester: Manchester University Press, 1985, p.1.
65. From the early 1820s actions against the opium trade were taken in China. Britain's desire to continue its illegal opium trade with China collided with imperial edicts prohibiting the addictive drug, and the First Opium War erupted in 1840. China lost the war; subsequently, Britain and other western powers, including the United States, forcibly occupied 'concessions' and gained special commercial privileges. Hong Kong was ceded to Britain in 1842 under the Treaty of Nanking, and in 1898, when the Opium Wars finally ended, Britain executed a 99-year lease of the New Territories, significantly expanding the size of the Hong Kong colony.
66. Kumari Jayawardena, 'Feminism and Revolutionary Struggles in China', in Kumari Jayawardena (ed.), *Feminism and Nationalism in the Third World*, London and New Delhi: Zed Books, 1986, p.187.
67. Footbinding seems to date back to the beginning of the tenth century, between the end of the Tang dynasty (618–906) and the beginning of the Song Dynasty. At first it was a practice of the aristocracy, and then it spread throughout the whole popula-tion. Footbinding took place between the ages of five and seven by bending back the foot and breaking the bone of the instep completely. A fashionable-sized foot was only three inches long at that time. Footbinding not only damaged women's bodies and limited their physical activities, but also restricted their emotional and mental

freedom, and made them more dependent on men.

68. Gymnastics was introduced to China in the 1860s, and mainly adopted in schools and the army from the end of the nineteenth century. Basketball was introduced to China in 1896. Athletics was introduced to China in the late nineteenth century. Football and volleyball appeared in Mainland China in the early twentieth century. National athletic competitions took place after 1910. See *Tiyu shiliao* [Sports History Information], 1–4 (1980); Jonathan Kolatch, *Sport, Politics and Ideology in China*, New York: Jonathan David, 1972, pp.8–11.

69. Kang Youwei (1858–1927), with the support of emperor Guanxu, led the 'hundred days' reform' in 1898. His policies were mainly concerned with the modernisation of the traditional examination system, the elimination of sinecures, and the creation of a system of modern education. After the failure of these reforms, he escaped to Japan, where he organised a 'society to protect the Emperor' in 1899 and ran a newspaper to protest against democratic revolution. He was the director of the Confucianism Society after 1913. He wrote many books and articles.

70. Liang Qichao (1873–1929) was a student of Kang Youwei. In 1895, he and Kang launched the 'Gong che shang shu' – a memorandum submitted to the emperor suggesting that China refuse negotiations with Japan, relocate the capital and carry out reforms. This statement was signed by 1,300 examinees for the scholar-officials from all 18 provinces of China. Liang was the chief writer of *Current Affairs* in Shanghai. Through his articles such as 'General Debate on Reform', he publicised the reform campaign. After the failure of the 'hundred days' reform', he escaped to Japan.

71. On 11 June 1898, the young emperor Guangxu formally announced the beginning of reform. More than 40 reforming edicts were issued to deal with almost every conceivable subject: setting up modern schools and reconstructing the examination system; revising the laws; promoting agriculture, medicine, commerce, inventions and sending students abroad; modernising the army, navy, police and postal system, etc. However, dowager empress Cixi and her conservative supporters opposed all these reforms, and on 21 September 1898, they instigated a coup, putting emperor Guangxu under house arrest and killing six leading reformers. The reform, which lasted 103 days, and was called 'the hundred days' reform', failed. See Jack Gray, *Rebellions and Revolutions: China from the 1800s to the 1980s*, Oxford: Oxford University Press, 1990, pp.132.

72. Kang Youwei and Liang Qichao advocated and initiated the banning of footbinding, and established schools for girls and women. Since it was believed that strong mothers produced strong sons for national revival, their intention was to strengthen national power in order to match western nations. For information on the anti-footbinding campaign, see Fan Hong, *Footbinding, Feminism and Freedom: The Liberation of Women's Bodies in Modern China,* London: Frank Cass, 1997, pp.62–9.

73. Nancy Bailey, 'Women's Sport and The Feminist Movement: Building Bridge', in Greta L. Cohen (ed.), *Women in Sport: Issues and Controversies*, London: Sage, 1993.

74. The May 4th Movement began when some 3,000 Beijing University students marched to Tiananmen Square, demanding that China's warlord government refuse to hand over German concessions to Japan after the end of the First World War. Thus, it was a political watershed in the country, paving the way for generations of protests. The movement developed into a call for democracy, science and equality. Traditional Chinese family and marriage customs were fiercely attacked. A multitude of popular periodicals and newspapers – *New Youth, The New Women, Women's Bell, Girls' Daily of Canton* and *The Women's Monthly* – introduced new ideas concerning women in society and western concepts of science, democracy and equality. The emancipation of women became a part of the widespread intellectual revolt against the Confucian code and all associated restraints.

75. Jiao Yunming, 'Lun jindai zhongguo de funv jiefang sixiang' [About Women's Emancipation in Modern China], in *Beijing daxue funv wenti di san jie guoji yantao hui lunwen ji* [Collection of Papers of the Third International Women Seminar in Beijing University], Beijing daxue chuban she, 1994, p.192.

76. Huang Jianheng, 'Jindai shiqi guangdong tiyu dashi ji' [Record of Major Sports Events in Guangdong in Modern Times], *Guangdong Tiyu shiliao* [Guangdong Sports History Document], 2 (1992), p.45.

77. Fu Zhiyuan, 'Wo suo liaojie de Chengdu jidu jiaohui nv qingnian hui ji nv qingnian hui yin ti zhuan kaiban tiyu de qingkuang [My Personal Knowledge of the Sports Development in the YMCA and the Musical and Sport Special School of the YMCA in Chengdu], *Sichuan tiyu shiliao* [Sichuan Sports History Information], 1984 (1), p.21.

78. Gao Huimin, 'Sishi niandai qian Hanyuan tiyu fazhan gaikuang' [Review of Sports Development Before 1940], *Sichuan tiyu shiliao* [Sichuan Sports History], 1984 (4), pp.13–15.

79. Sun Zhongda, 'Wusi hou sichuan xinxing tiyu yundong fazhang gaikuang' [General Situation of the Development of New Sports in Sichuan after the May 4th Movement], *Sichuan tiyu shiliao* [Sichuan Sports History Information], 1983 (1), p.6.

80. For women's sport before 1949, see Fan Hong, *Footbinding, Feminism and Freedom*.

81. Shi Liao zhu [History Group], Jindai shiqi Guangdong tiyu dashi ji [Major Events of Guangdong Sport in the Modern Period], *Guangdong tiyu shiliao* [Guangdong Sports History Document], (1992 (2), p.145.

82. Guojia tiwei wenshi gongzuo weiyuanhui & Zhongguo tiyu shi xuehui [The Working Commission of Sports History of the NSC and China Sports History Society] (eds), *Zhongguo jindai tiyu shi* [China Modern Sports History], Beijing tiyu xue yuan chuban she, 1989, pp.419–62.

83. Fan Hong, 'Socio-Historical Framework: Women and Sport in China', *WSPAJ*, 3, 1 (Spring 1995), p.16.

84. In the Chinese delegation to the Eleventh Olympic Games in 1936, Li Shen was the only woman among the 22 athletes.

85. Women's events were 19 (16.4%) in 1948, 30 (25.4%) in 1952, 40 (37%), 57 (50.9%) in 1968, and 85 (56.7%) in 1988 (as percentages of men's events). For details see Appendix 1.

86. See Susan Brownell, 'Representing Gender in the Chinese Nation: Chinese Sportswomen and Beijing's Bid for the 2000 Olympics', *Identities: Global Studies in Culture and Power*, 2, 3 (1996), pp.223–47.

87. Fewer than 300,000 girls, compared to more than 3.5 million boys, participated in school sport in 1971 in the USA. For details, see Martha Wilkerson, 'Explaining the Presence of Men Coaches in Women's Sports: The Uncertainty Hypothesis', *Journal of Sport and Social Issues*, Nov. 1996, pp.411–12.

88. Jennifer Hargreaves, *Sporting Females – Critical Issues in the History and Sociology of Women's Sports*, London: Routledge, 1994, p. 219.

89. George H. Sage, *Power and Ideology in American Sport: A Critical Perspective*, Champaign, IL: Human Kinetics, 1990, pp.47–53.

90. G.L. Cohen (ed.), *Women in Sport: Issues and Controversies*, London: Sage Publications, 1993, p.307.

91. Only one Chinese athlete, Liu Changchun, attended the 1932 Olympic Games. Four years later, 69 people were sent to Berlin by the Nationalist Government. In 1948 some 33 athletes participated in the London Games. However, Chinese athletes could not be found in the performance chart of the Olympic Games.

92. Min Jiayin (ed.), *The Chalice and the Blade in Chinese Culture: Gender Relations and Social Models*, Beijing: China Social Science Publishing House, 1995, pp.553–620.

93. Suzanne Ogden, *China's Unsolved Issues*, p.19.
94. Mao Zedong, 'Lun tiyu zhi yanjiu' [On Physical Education], *Xin qingnian* [New Youth] (April 1917).
95. Lin Yutang, *My Country and My People*, London: Heinemann, 1935, pp.41–74.
96. Peter Hain, 'The Politics of Sport and Apartheid', in Jennifer Hargreaves (ed.), *Sport, Culture and Ideology*, London: Routledge & Kegan Paul, 1982, p.233.
97. Gunther Lushen, 'The Interdependence of Sport and Culture', *International Review of Sport Sociology*, 2 (1967), pp.127–39.
98. Alan Hunter and John Sexton, *Contemporary China*, New York: St. Martin's Press, 1999, p.142.
99. Wang Xiaobu, 'nvxing yishi yu funv jiefang' [Women's Self-Awareness and Their Emancipation], *Dongfang* [Orient], 35, 5 (2000), pp.49–53.
100. Information Office of the State Council of PRC, 'The Situation of Chinese Women', *Beijing Review*, 6–12 June 1994, p.11.
101. Rong Gaotang et al.(eds), *Dangdai zhongguo tiyu* [Contemporary Chinese Sport], Beijing, 1984, p.121.
102. Guojia tiwei wenshi si [The Literature and History Department of the NSC], *Tiwei xitong zhiliao tongji* [Statistical Information on the Sports Community], 1992, p.12, and Guojia tongji ju [State Staistical Bureau] (ed.), *Zhongguo tongji nianjian* [Chinese Statistical Yearbook], Beijing: Zhongguo tongji chuban she, 1985, p.20.
103. See Chapter 2.
104. See Guojia tiwei wenshi si [The Literature and History Department of the NSC], 1992.
105. Three reasons contribute to this judgment. First, many sports have been introduced to women recently. Second, women's inequality is pervasive in the world, which leads to less investment in women's sport by many other countries. Finally, Chinese women have the historical heritage of hard work and obedience.
106. See Chapter 4.
107. Zhang Caizhen, 'Zhongguo funv tiyu fazhan huimou yu zhangwang' [Past Developments and Future Prospects].
108. Factories, businesses and public organisations were encouraged to sponsor competitions and sports teams. A number of business-owned elite sports teams emerged in China after the mid-1980s.
109. Guojia tiwei yu difan tiwei gongjian xunlian jidi mianling de wenti ji jiejue de jianyi [The Issues and Suggestions that Face the NSC and Local Sports Commissions In Co-building Training Bases], *Tiyu gongzuo qingkuang*, 622, 14 (1996), p.17.
110. The campaign of 'criticising Lin Biao and Confucius' in the latter stage of the Cultural Revolution (1973–76) marked the beginning of another effort to change long-standing perceptions of women, although its political target was Premier Chou Enlai, who emphasised the ethics of the great sage. Because the Confucian tradition had long been perceived as responsible for attitudes, values and behaviour inimical to socialist development, this fresh critique of Confucianism naturally led to a criticism, once again, of one of its main principles: male supremacy. Women in all walks of life, once more, were organised to study and analyse the origins and development of an ideological system in which oppression of women was a fundamental necessary premise. This campaign to some extent brought new life to women's consciousness of equality. Confucian teaching, as discussed in the first part of this chapter, was a main obstacle to women's participation in sport. Women, after violently criticising Confucianism, among other things, continued to refuse to subscribe to the long-standing belief in women's 'proper' inactivity. They took up every men's sport, and even competed with men. In short, criticism of Confucianism had an active impact on women's sport.
111. Kumari Jayawardena, 'Feminism and Revolutionary Struggles in China', in Jayawardena, *Feminism and Nationalism in the Third World*, p.185.
112. Gale Summerfield, 'Economic Reform and the Employment of Chinese Women', *Journal of Economic Issues*, 28, 3 (Sept. 1994), pp.715–32.

113. Li Xiaojiang, *Huaxia nvxing zhi mi: zhongguo funv yangjiu lunji* [Mysteries of Chinese Women], pp.1–12; Wang Xiaobo, 'Nvxing yishi yu funv jiefang' [Women's Self-Awareness and Emancipation].

Chapter 1

1. James Riordan, *Sport, Politics and Communism*, Manchester: Manchester University Press, 1991, p.52.
2. Earlier in 1950 the American-led United Nation forces crossed the 38th Parallel, which divides Korea into North and South. In response, in mid-October 1950, Chinese volunteers began to cross the Yalu river into North Korea to aid its army.
3. 'At present our sport must serve the people, serve national defence and promote people's health. Students, workers, peasants, citizen, militants and civil servants all have to become involved in sport' Vice-Chairman Zhu De (1886–1976), who was one of the major founders of the Communist Party, pointed out.
4. The development of and physical education and sport nationwide, from factories, schools, the army to government offices, in order to improve people's physique was incorporated into the first Five-Year Plan of the PRC. For the details, see Zhongguo tiyu nianjian bianji weiyuan hui [The Editorial Commission of Sport Yearbooks in China], *Zhongguo tiyu nianjian bianji 1949–1962* [Sports Yearbooks in China 1949–1962], Beijing: Renmin tiy chuban she, 1964, p.45.
5. See Zhu Zhengwu, 'Dui xin zhongguo sishi nian lai tiyu re de fenxi he dui weilai tiyu re de yuce' [Analysis of the Sports Craze during the Four Decades of New China and Predictions about its Future], in Zhongguo tiyu shi xiehui [China Sports History Association] (ed.), *Tiyu shi lunwen ji* [Collection of Papers on Sports History], Vol.6, Beijing: Renmin tiyu chuban she, 1989, p.10.
6. Meaning all economic activities in society.
7. Gu Shiquan, *Zhongguo tiyu shi* [Chinese Sports History], Beijing: Tiyu daxue chuban she, 1997, pp.340–8.
8. Jean-Marie Brohm (translated by Ian Fraser), *Sport – A Prison of Measured Time*, London: Ink Links, 1978, p.48.
9. The Party's administration from top to bottom includes: Central Committee; Regional Committee; Provincial, Municipal or Autonomous Region's Commission; City, District or Autonomous Prefecture's Commission; Factory, Commune Branch of Party Commission. The state administration from top to bottom includes: the State Council; Provinces, Autonomous Regions or Municipalities; Counties, Cities, Autonomous Prefectures, Districts and Communes (*Xian*).
10. Regarding the initial organisation of the NSC, see Jonathan Kolatch, *Sports, Politics and Ideology in China*, New York: Jonathan David, 1972, pp.100–9; regarding the duties of the commission, see Cao Xiangjun and Susan E. Brownell, 'The People's Republic of China', in Laurence Chalip, Arthur Johnson and Lisa Stachura (eds), *National Sports Policies: An International Handbook*, Westport, CT: Greenwood Press, 1996, p.78.
11. Elite athletes lived away from home and spent five to eight hours on athletic training each day. In addition to free food, training, clothes and coaching, athletes had wages equivalent to those of workers in factories. Furthermore, the period of an athlete's service was taken into account in the welfare package of his or her post-athletic career.
12. Interviewed in Beijing, September 1995.
13. Godwin C. Chu and Yanan Ju, *The Great Wall in Ruins: Communication and Cultural Change in China,* Albany, NY: State University of New York Press, 1993, p.80.

14. Li Xiaojiang (ed.), *Xingbie yu zhongguo* [Gender and China], Beijing: Shenghuo, dushu, xinzhi sanlian shudian, 1994, p.6.
15. When the PRC was created, the 'women's issue' was debated within the materialist framework set out in Engels's *Family, Private Property and the State*, which states that the roots of women's oppression lay in the denial of property and, through that, access to the public sphere as independent actors. Thus, women could not be liberated completely without economic independence. Those depending on husbands and disliking labour were criticised. All this was reflected in the speeches of the leading figures of the Women's Association of China, such as Song Qinglin's 'San Ba' jiliang yu jiating funv shengchang jianshe ['March Eighth' Anniversary and Housewives' Involvement in Production Construction]. For the details, see the journal *Xin zhongguo funv* [The New Chinese Women], issues between 1950 and 1951.
16. *The Constitution of the PRC*, 1954.
17. Song Qingling married Sun Yixian, the President of the Republic of China founded in 1911. After her husband died in 1925, she committed herself to the national revolution and patriotic war against the Japanese. After 1949 she was elected as a vice-chairwoman of the People's Central Government and vice-chairwoman of the PRC (twice). She was also an honorary chairwoman of the All China Women's Federation.
18. Shi Liang (1900–85) graduated from the Shanghai University of Law in 1927. Two years later, she was responsible for preparations for the establishment of the Jiangsu Provincial Association of Women. As a lawyer, she defended a number of Communist Party members and other progressive personages, for which she was jailed by the Nationalist government. During the Anti-Japanese War, she was actively involved in a variety of patriotic activities and campaigns. In the New China, she was appointed minister in the Justice Ministry and vice-president of the All China Women's Federation.
19. Altogether there were ten women in the National Commission of the Chinese People's Political and Consultative Conference in 1949.
20. Professor Wang's speech to the anniversary meeting of March Eighth Women's Day in Beijing University of Physical Education in 1995. She was a famous authority in the field of sports physiology.
21. The Marriage Law, banning compulsory betrothal, the marriage of children, infanticide, bigamy and concubinage, consists of eight sections and 27 articles. To publicise and implement the Marriage Law a mass campaign was staged throughout the country. Women activists were sent to factories and the countryside to publicise and prompt the implementation of the Marriage law. Books, pamphlets, drama and arts were used to popularise the law. For example, the women's magazine *Xin zhongguo funv* [The New Chinese Women], first published in July 1949, devoted a column to the topic of the Marriage Law in each issue throughout 1950–1.
22. Information Office of State Council of the PRC, 'The Situation of Chinese Women', *Beijing Review*, 6–12 June 1994, p.10.
23. Zhang Yun, 'Qinjian jianguo, qinjian chijia, wei jianshe shehui zhuyi er fendou'[Being Hardworking and Thrifty in order to Build the State and Home and Striving for the Construction of Socialism], in Zhongguo funv ganbu guanli xueyuan [The Cadre Management Institute of China] (ed.), *Zhongguo funv yundong wenxian zhiliao huibian* [The Collection of Documents of the Chinese Women's Movement], Vol. 2: 1949–83, Zhongguo funv chuban she, 1988, pp.315–17.
24. She was interviewed in Beijing in September 1995.
25. Hao Guiqiao, 'Zhigong Tiyu' [Workers' Sport], in Zhongguo tiyu wenshi xinxi bianji weiyuan hui [The Editorial Commission of China Sports Literature and History Information] (ed.), *Tiyu shiliao* [Sports History Information], Vol.11, Beijing: Renmin tiyu chuban she, 1984, pp.47–9.

26. All kinds of spare-time schools, evening schools and literacy classes were created to promote men's and women's education in both rural and urban areas immediately after the CCP took control of the country.

27. Zhongguo jiaoyu nianjian bianji shi [Chinese Education Yearbook Editorial Office], *Zhongguo jiaoyu nianjian 1949–1981* [Education Yearbook In China 1949–81], Beijing: Zhongguo baike quanshu chuban she, 1982, p.1037.

28. Information Office of State Council, 'The Situation of Chinese Women', p.11.

29. Zhongguo jiaoyu nianjian bianji shi [Chinese Education Yearbook Editorial Office], p.1037.

30. Physical education classes were normally co-educational and included team games and individual activities, including volleyball, basketball, athletics, gymnastics, soccer, badminton and martial arts.

31. Of the 3,160 students of Beijing University, 10 per cent of them had lung diseases. In North-East Normal University, about 8.1 per cent of junior students ceased their studies due to illness. For the details, see: Guojia tiwei zhengce yanjiu shi [The Policy Research Department of the NSC], 'Guojia tiwei dangzhu guanyu jiaqiang renmin tiyu yundong de baogao' [A Report on Strengthening People's Physical Culture and Sport by the Party Group of the NSC], in Guojia tiwei zhengce yanjiu shi [The Policy Research Department of the NSC] (ed.), *Tiyu yundong wenjian xuanbian 1949–1981* [Selected Collection of Document of Sport 1949–81], Beijing: Renmin tiyu chuban she, 1982, p.48.

32. In 1954 the NSC promulgated a nationwide physical fitness programme, *Lao Wei Zhi* [The Labour and Defence Programme], for students at secondary school level and above. This programme was first introduced in Beijing, Shanghai and Tianjin and then introduced to other parts of the country between 1951 and 1953 (see *Tiyu yundong wenjian xuanbian 1949–1981* [Selected Collection of Document of Sport 1949–81], pp.20–6).

33. Athletes of the national teams were often chosen from local provincial teams throughout the country according to their performance, potential and behaviour. The welfare package covering wages and bonuses and the like still had to be provided by the provinces.

34. They accorded with the six administrative regions, including North China, East China, Central-South China, South-West, North-West and North-East.

35. Yuan Weiming et al., *Zhongguo paiqiu shi* [Volleyball in China], Wuhan chuban she, 1994, p.73.

36. She was interviewed in Beijing in April 1995.

37. Several department directors under the commission, such as Han Fudong, the director of Ball Games Department, Zhang Zikui, the director of the Competition Department, and Zhong Shitong, the principal of the BIPE, all had military backgrounds.

38. For example, gymnasts Lan Yalan and Cheng Guide in the 1950s, Ma Yanhong and Wen Jia and the speed skater Ye Qiaobo, the volleyball players Cao Huiying, Chen Zhaodi and Yang Xi and many others in the 1970s and 1980s.

39. Rong Gaotang et al., *Dangdai zhongguo tiyu* [Contemporary Chinese Sport], Beijing: Zhongguo shehui kexue chuban she, 1984, p.111.

40. Students went to normal school in the morning and trained in sports centres in the afternoon. They lived in dormitories in the sports centres.

41. Nan Mu, 'Quanguo yeyu tiyu xunlian gongzuo yantao hui zongshu' [An Overview of the Seminar of Amateur Sports Training in China], *Tiyu gongzuo qingkuang* [The Situation of Sports Affairs], 655, 23 (1997), pp.8–11.

42. China adopted a Soviet model of social welfare centred on the workplace (*danwei*). The national or provincial sports commission functioned as a self-sufficient 'welfare society' (*danwei*), where coaches received employment and income protection and enjoyed benefits and services such as housing allocation, food and clothes subsidies

and medical care. Coaches were granted status equal to state cadres. All this favourable treatment stemmed from the demand that coaches should be completely dedicated to coaching.

43. Zhonghua renmin gongheguo tiyu yundong weiyuan hui [The NSC of the PRC], *Quanguo tiyu shiye tongji ziliao huibian 1949–1978* [Collection of Statistical Information on Sport in China, 1949–78], Beijing: Renmin tiyu chuban she, 1979, p.4.

44. Guojia tiwei wenshi si [The Literature and History Department of the NSC], *Tiwei xitong ziliao tongji* [Statistical Information on the Sports Community], 1992, p.10.

45. Beijing tiyu xueyuan yuanshi bianji zhu [The Editorial Group of the History of BIPE], Beijing: Tiyu xueyuan chuban she, 1993, p.2.

46. By1954 there were six institutes of physical education: Beijing, Shanghai, Xian, Wuhan, Tianjin and Chengdu.

47. Gu Shiquan, *Zhongguo tiyu shi* [Chinese Sports History], p.343.

48. The number of four-year course students was 79 in 1952, 733 in 1954, 1,675 in 1956, and 2,836 in 1957. The number in two-year courses was 246, 1,771, 1,024 and 416 respectively for these years. Date from the Sport History Department of The NSC, 1992.

49. 'Wuoguo 18 ge yundong xiangmu jishu fazhan ziliao'[Material on the Technical Development of 18 Sports In China], BIPE (ed.), *61 nian tiyu gongzuo huiyi cankao wenxian* [Reference Document of the 1961 Sports Conference], Beijing: Tiyu xueyuan (BIPE), 1964, p.73.

50. There were four grades for referees: from the highest to lowest level, national, first, second and third referee.

51. There were five grades for athletes: from highest to lowest level, sports master, first, second, third athlete and junior athlete (under 17). The criteria were revised in 1958 and 1963 before the system was suspended in 1966.

52. For further details, see Kolatch, *Sports, Politics and Ideology*, pp.171–4.

53. This will be further discussed in Chapter 9.

54. Women appeared in most sports, except football and weightlifting, in which Chinese men participated.

55. Guojia tiwei xuanchuang bu [Propaganda Department of the NSC], *Di yi jie quanguo yundong hui xuanchuan ziliao* [Propaganda Material of the First National Games] Vol.1, Beijing: Renmin tiyu chuban she, 1958, p.16.

56. Nationalists in Taiwan proclaimed their right to rule the mainland and occupied China's seat at the United Nations. Taiwan became Beijing's most irritating foreign policy problem.

57. Quanguo tiyu xueyuan jiaocai bianji weiyuan hui [Textbook Writing Commission of Institutes of Physical Education In China], *Tiyu shi* [Sports History], Beijing: Renmin tiyu chuban she, 1989, p.213.

58. She was interviewed in Beijing in August 1995.

59. *Quanguo tiyu shiye tongji ziliao huibian 1949–1978* [Collection of Statistical Information on Sport in China, 1949–78], pp.204–5.

60. Ibid., p.34.

61. Rong Gaotang, *Dangdai zhongguo tiyu* [Contemporary Chinese Sport], pp.218, 269.

62. Premier Zhou Enlai stated in his report to the Eighth Party Congress representatives in 1956: 'We must further develop physical culture and sport among the masses in order to improve people's physique, and advance our level of sport.'

63. China insisted, and still insists, that Taiwan is part of China, but the International Olympic Committee (IOC) invited both Taiwan and China, as two nations, to participate in the 16th Olympic Games. In protest against this decision, the All China Sport Federation declared that China would not send athletes to the Olympics. Later in 1958, China formally withdrew from the IOC and eight other international sporting organisations including those for gymnastics, swimming and athletics.

64. China sent its first sporting delegation to the Soviet Union for the period August to October 1950. In 1954, another group headed by the director of the NSC, Marshal He Long, visited the Soviet Union for two months.

65. Zhong Guangwen, 'Qingshaonian ertong yeyu tiyu xunlian qingkuang' [Sports Training in Spare-time Sports Schools for Young People], in *Tiyu shiliao* [Sports History Information], 11 (1984), p.98.

66. Dong Shouyi, who studied in America from 1923 to 1925, was elected member of the IOC in 1947. In the New China he was the deputy chairman of the All China Sports Federation [ACSF], and the chairman of the Sports Technique Committee of NSC in the 1950s. John Ma went to America twice from 1919 to 1920, and from 1925 to 1926. He was a professor at Qinghua University from 1914 to 1966. He was the deputy chairman (1949–55) and chairman (1956–66) of the ACSF. Xia Yian (in the United States from 1941 to 1945) was the deputy director of the Beijing Sports Commission, and the deputy president of the National Olympic Committee in the New China. Yuan Dongniu (deputy principal of Gansu Normal University), Wu Yunru (principal of the Shanghai Institute of Physical Education) and Xu Yinchao (deputy principal of the Beijing Institute of Physical Education) also studied in America in the 1920s and 1930s.

67. Yi Bei, 'Ji Beijing shi renmin tiyu dahui'[On Beijing Municipal People's Sports Meeting], *Beijing tiyu wenshi* [Beijing Sports Literature and History], 2 (Dec. 1986), pp.1–8.

68. Sun Xiaolin, 'Ji Beijing shi di er jie renmin tiyu dahui' [On the Second Beijing Municipal People's Sports Meeting], *Beijing tiyu wenshi* [Beijing Sports Literature and History], 2 (Dec. 1986), pp.14-18.

69. *Beijing tiyu wenshi* [Beijing Sports Literature and History], 1988 (3), pp.4–5.

70. After the PRC was established in 1949, the country consisted of six administrative regions. Each region sent a team to the national competitions. The People's Liberation Army (PLA) and the Railway Association participated in competitions independently.

71. Yi Bei, 'Beijing shi xuanba nanpai qiudui canjia huabei bisai' [Beijing City Selected Basketball and Volleyball Teams to Take Part in the North China Competitions], *Beijing tiyu wenshi* [Beijing Sports Literature and History], 1988 (3), pp.19–20.

72. Rong Gaotang, *Dangdai zhongguo tiyu* [Contemporary Chinese Sport], pp.190, 218.

73. Rong Gaotang, '61 nian xunlian gongzuo huiyi baogao' [A Report of the 1961 Sports Conference], in BIPE (ed.), *61 nian tiyu gongzuo huiyi cankao ziliao* [The Reference Document of the 1961 Sports Conference], 1961, p.2.

74. *Beijing tiyu wenshi* [Beijing Sports Literature and History], 3 (1988), pp.31–40.

75. In the early 1950s national teams such as those for basketball and football were affiliated to the Beijing Municipal Sports Commission. In addition, a number of student athletes from Beijing Institute of Physical Education also represented Beijing in national competitions.

76. *Quanguo tiyu shiye tongji ziliao huibian 1949–1978* [Collection of Statistical Information on Sport in China, 1949–78], p.4.

77. Beijing shi tiyu yundong weiyuan hui [The Beijing Municipal Sports Commission], 'Beijing shi zhongdian qingshaonian yeyu tixiao guoqu jinian jiaoxue xunlian de yixie xiangfa' [Some Ideas on Teaching and Coaching of Beijing Municipal Key Spare-Time Sports Schools For Young People in the Past Few Years], in Beijing tiyu xueyuan [BIPE] (ed.), *61 nian tiyu gongzuo huiyi cankao wenxian* [Reference Document of the 1961 Sports Conference], Beijing tiyu xueyuan (BIPE), 1964, pp.25–32.

78. Bai Shaoyi, 'Shi lun qingshaonian yeyu xunlian gongzuo lishi shang de jingyan he jiaoxun' [Experience and Lessons from the History of Spare-Time Sports Training for Young People], in Zhongguo tiyu shi xiehui [China Sports History Association], *Tiyu shi lunwen ji* [Collection of Papers on Sports History], pp.94–5.

79. *Quanguo tiyu shiye tongji ziliao huibian 1949–1978* [Collection of Statistical Information on Sport in China, 1949–78], pp.141–5.
80. According to Chen Dexin, who was interviewed at Beijing University of Physical Education (BUPE) in 1995. BUPE's antecedent was Beijing Institute of Physical Education. It was upgraded to university status in 1995.
81. Chen was an associate professor of gymnastics at BUPE.
82. Beijing tiyu xueyuan yuanshi bianji zhu [The Editorial Group of the History of BIPE], *Beijing tiyu xueyuan shi* [The History of Beijing Institute of Physical Education], pp.10–13.
83. March Eighth Day is International Women's Day. Various activities are organised to demonstrate women's capacities and in pursuit of the improvement of their status.
84. On 4 May 1919, some 3,000 students from Beijing University and other universities held a protest march against the Treaty of Versailles, in which the First World War Allies agreed that Japan should inherit the German privileges in Shangdong province. Their example touched off nationwide demonstrations, strikes and a boycott of Japanese goods. The government tried to repress these actions, but gave in under the pressure of the merchant communities in the country. China did not sign the peace treaty. In memory of this event, May Fourth Day is dedicated to Chinese youth.
85. Huang Zhouhui, 'Tiyu duanlian bangzhu tamen chengwei zhongguo de nv feixingyuan' [Physical Exercises Helped Them Become the Female Pilots of China], *Xin tiyu* [New Sport], May 1952, pp.30–1.
86. The interviewee was a principal of the spare-time sports school under BUPE.
87. The Guangdong Branch of the All China Sports Federation comprised an executive committee, a standing committee and a secretariat composed of a general affairs office, a financial office, an organisation office and an office of control. There were also competition, propaganda and education, help and guidance, research and welfare departments.
88. Wei Zhenlan et al., *Guangdong tiyu sishi nian* [Forty Years of Guangdong Sport], Guangzhou: Xin shiji chuban she, 1989, p.3.
89. *Quanguo tiyu shiye tongji ziliao huibian 1949–1978* [Collection of Statistical Information on Sport in China, 1949–78], pp.141–5.
90. Ibid., p.4.
91. Zhou Zhang, 'Jiefang hou gang ao huilai de tiyu jiaoshi, jiaolianyuan,yundongyuan' [The Athletes, Coaches and Physical Education Teachers from Hong Kong and Macao After Liberation], *Guangdong tiyu shiliao* [Guangdong Sports History Information], 1986 (2), p.59.
92. Li Sheng and Lin Shenhao, 'Guangdong sheng tiaoshui yundong' [Diving in Guangdong], *Guangdong tiyu shiliao* [Guangdong Sports History Information], 37, 1 (1992), pp.39–41.
93. At the games 627 young participants competed in athletics, swimming and gymnastics.
94. Lou Yangping, 'Guangdong shengzi: tiyu zhi gaishu' [An Overview of Guangdong Provincial Record: Sports Record], *Guangdong tiyu shiliao* [Guangdong Sports History Information], 1992 (3), p.41.
95. 'Guangdong sheng yundong hui' [Guangdong Provincial Games], *Guangdong tiyu shiliao* [Guangdong Sports History Information], 1987 (2), p.37.
96. Wei Zhenlan et al., *Guangdong tiyu sishi nian* [Forty Years of Guangdong Sport], p.130.
97. In 1912 a woman's sports school emerged in Guangzhou. Volleyball became an official sport for women at the Eighth Provincial Games of the Old China in 1921, four years later than for men. Women debuted at the National Games in 1922, in which Guangdong women won first place.
98. Cadre, in broad terms, means those who hold any post with leadership and authority

in the Party and non-Party bureaucratic hierarchies in the country. In most areas it is also applied to non-administrative teaching, medical and technical personnel. There are state and local cadres. A state cadre is paid on the basis of a nationwide ranking system that comprises 24 salary grades in urban areas and 26 in rural areas. Until the late 1980s there was an obvious distinction between cadres (*kanbu*) and the masses (*qunzhong*) in terms of power and privilege but little difference in income.

99. She was interviewed at BUPE in 1995.

100. Interviewee Huang Xinhe was a female professor and international gymnastics judge.

101. Guangdong women kept the 100m breaststroke swimming title for over 20 years, until 1984. They ranked first in gymnastics, second in the 200m sprint and third in two other athletic events at the First National Games.

102. Tang Minghui, 'Gengyun paitan san shi nian – ji sichuan nupai zhu jiaolian Wang Defen' [Three Decades of Work in the Volleyball Community – on Wang Defen, the Head Coach of Sichuan Women's Volleyball Team], *Sichuan tiyu wenshi* [Sichuan Sports History Documents], 6, 2 (1984), pp.30–4.

103. When the State Council was set up in 1954, the system of six administrative regions ceased to exist. Provinces and municipalities became the basic participating units in national competitions.

104. *Quanguo tiyu shiye tongji ziliao huibian 1949–1978* [Collection of Statistical Information on Sport in China, 1949–78], p.4.

105. Ibid., pp.141–5.

106. *Sichuan sheng zhi – tiyu zhi* [Sichuan Provincial Record: Sports Record] (draft). Kexue jishu chuban shi [Science and Technology Press, 1998].

107. In 1953, a group of Soviet gymnastics experts, including 22 of the world's best gymnasts, toured China and displayed their skills in different cities.

108. The top two teams of league B could be promoted to league A, of which the last two teams could be relegated to league B. This system was cancelled in the early 1960s when the nation experienced a difficult economic period.

109. *Sichuan sheng zhi – tiyu zhi* [The Record of Sichuan Province – the Record of Sport].

110. Lijian Hong, 'Sichuan: Disadvantage and mismanagement in the Heavenly Kingdom', in David S.G. Goodman (ed.), *China's Provinces in Reform: Class, Community and Political Culture*, London and New York: Routledge, 1997, p.210.

111. Zhu Chuandao et al., 'Yi shenhua gaige wei dongli, ba wosheng tiyu shiye tuixiang yige xin de fazhan jieduan – sichuan tiyu shiye fazhan de jiben zhuangkuang he 1988 nian – 1992 nian fazhan mubiao yu cuoshi' [Add Momentum to Reform and Raise Sichuan Provincial Sport to a New Stage of Development– The Basic Situation of Sports Development in Sichuan and the Goals and Measures for the 1988–92 Period], *Sichuan tiyu kexue* [Sichuan Sports Science], 1988 (4), p.6.

112. *Sichuan sheng zhi – tiyu zhi* [The Record of Sichuan Province – Record of Sport].

113. Towards the end of 1952 people's living standards improved remarkably and national industrial and agricultural production reached record levels.

114. In 1951 a nationwide campaign of 'Broadcast Gymnastics' – a set of callisthenics exercises accompanied by music – was advocated jointly by nine ministries including the All China Sport Federation, the Chinese Education Ministry, the All China Democratic Women's Federation and others. Broadcast Gymnastics immediately appeared everywhere. In the early 1950s, training courses for Broadcast Gymnastics were organised and the booklets and music tapes of the exercises sold out quickly. Broadcast Gymnastics became popular in schools, factories, government offices and even barracks.

115. The All China Sports Federation (ACSF) is a mass organisation involved with sport. Before the National Sports Commission was established at the end of 1952, the ACSF was in charge of sporting development throughout the country. Thereafter, it has been subordinate to the NSC.

116. For instance, a director of one village women's union in He Longqian province won two silver medals in the 60m and 100m sprints in the Provincial People's Sport Meeting in 1950. Reference from Pinglun yuan [Editorial], 'Fazhan funv tiyu yundong' [To Develop Women's Physical Education and Sport], *Xin tiyu* [New Sport], 1951 (8), p.10.

117. Sports activities in schools were very popular in the 1950s. Virtually all the interviewees who became athletes then were active school sports participants before being recruited into colleges of physical education or PLA sports teams.

118. At the 1956 World Volleyball Championships the Chinese women's team came sixth. After the Chinese weightlifter Cheng Jingkai broke a world record in 1956, the first ever, sport was utilised to build Chinese national identity in the world.

Chapter 2

1. The First Five-Year Plan started in 1953. Per-capita income increased from 119 yuan in 1952 to 168 yuan in 1957 reportedly. Based on Soviet experience, a centrally planned economy was created. Priority in investment was given to heavy industry, followed by light industries and agriculture.

2. Mao Zedong believed that industrial, agricultural, educational and scientific development should accelerate faster than was forecast. As a result, investment in capital construction surpassed the means of production, and salary increases outweighed the means of production. Credit loan was out of control, financial deficits appeared, and the market could not meet the demand.

3. Following the 'Hundred Flowers' campaign in 1956, in which intellectuals voiced their complaints and criticisms about the Party and state, between mid-1957 and mid-1958 an anti-rightist campaign was launched throughout the country. These criticisms and complaints were considered an attack by bourgeois 'rightists' on the Party. Some 552,877 people were denounced as rightists, among whom about 540,000 were unjustifiably labelled. Hence, some scholars have claimed that the GLF originated the collapse of the Hundred Flowers Campaign and the subsequent Anti-Rightist Campaign (Lu Tingyu and Hang Yinhong, *Zhonghua renmin gongheguo lishi ji shi: jiannan tangsuo* [Historical Record of the PRC: A Difficult Search] (1956–58), Beijing: Hongqi chuban she, 1994, p.17).

4. The first people's commune, 'the Sputnik Commune', was founded in Henan province in 1958. Peasants organised themselves into communes containing an average of 20,000 people. Within the communes were production brigades that were subdivided into several production teams. Each team usually consisted of one village, or 20 to 30 households. A system of work points was adopted. The people's commune combined industrial, agricultural, commercial, school and military organisations into one body. This institution was introduced into the cities on a large scale in 1960, but only existed for half a year. The commune was not officially abandoned in the countryside until the end of 1984.

5. In China the output of steel production was regarded as a yardstick of national strength. To surpass Britain in terms of steel production in two years, instead of the 15 years planned in 1956, became a target. Thus, the campaign of 'greatly smelting iron and steel' was launched across the country. Hundreds of millions of people including women, the old and the young joined the massive campaign, cutting down trees, digging coal and smelting steel. People brought every possible item from their home, even productive tools, to make iron and steel in the 'backyard factories'.

6. It was claimed that socialist construction would be basically completed in 1959 and then the transformation to communism would be finished in 1963. Xushui county in Hebei province even started to experiment with 'communism' in 1958. Members of communes were provided with free meals and other services. Unfortunately, some

people competed to see who could eat the most. This gave rise to abuse of the system. This experiment, unsurprisingly, came to an end six months later.

7. Evaluation of the GLF changed from praise during the campaign, partial rejection in the early 1960s, to renewed praise during the Cultural Revolution and complete rejection after the Cultural Revolution. For the details, see Xie Chuntao, *Dayuejin kuanlang* [The Raging Waves of the Great Leap Forward], Zhenzhou: Henan renmin chuban she, 1994, pp.1–4.

8. See Gu Shiquan, *Zhongguo tiyu shi* [Chinese Sports History], Beijing tiyu daxue chuban she, 1997; Chen Zhenghua et al., *Zhongguo ticao yundong shi* [Gymnastics in China], Wuhan chuban she, 1990; Yuan Weiming et al., *Zhongguo paiqou shi* [Volleyball in China], Wuhan chuban she, 1994 and various historical studies of other individual sports.

9. In the second session of the Eighth National Congress of the Party in 1958, they were set down as goals of future socialist reconstruction.

10. In agriculture, a production target for 12 years under normal circumstances was now shortened to one or two years. In industry, steel production increased tenfold within half a year (Lu Tingyu, *Zhonghua renmin gongheguo lishi ji shi: quzhe fazhang* [Historical Record of the PRC: Zig-Zag Developments] (1958–65), Beijing: Hongqi chuban she, 1994, p.75).

11. About 90 per cent of women were involved in field labour. Although women were only 18.6 per cent of state workers, they comprised over 80 per cent of the workforce in productive sections and welfare services run by urban communes.

12. She was interviewed in Beijing in 1997.

13. 'Mass line' (*qunzhong luxian*) is one of the Party's basic principles. It states the Party's dependence on the masses and the need for the Party to keep in constant contact with the masses. The major concept of the 'mass line' is 'from the masses, to the masses'.

14. Party and governmental officials, such as vice-premiers Chen Yi and He Long, stressed the importance of sport in keeping fit and serving the construction of economy and national defence (see *Tiyu bao* [Sports Daily] and *Xin tiyu* [New Sports] between 1958 and 1959).

15. Boastfulness was pervasive at the time. In sport, it was often stated that 100 per cent of people in schools or factories reached the standard of the Physical Fitness Programme. This was obviously impossible. In addition, it was reported that there were 16,000 spare-time sports schools, but in reality some existed only in name without a location or students.

16. In one district of Shanghai 18 housewives organised training groups among themselves and did exercises twice a day (see Chang Hsiangchao, 'Shanghai Is Leaping Forward', *China's Sports*, 1958 (3), p.13).

17. Zhuang Ping, 'Xin zhongguo tiyu zhanxian shang de funu' [Women in the Sports Field of New China], *Xin tiyu* [New Sport], 5 (1959), pp.7–10.

18. All over the country, college and middle-school students were encouraged to reach the appropriate standards in the 'Labour and Defence Programme' (*Lao wei zhi*). Training groups were organised according to age and sex. In 1958, about 10 million people were involved in the programme, greatly exceeding the figure of 890,000 in 1957.

19. Xinhua she [Xinhua News Agency], 'Shi nian jiaoyu da geming da fengshou' [Great Revolution and Great Harvest in Education in the Last Decade], *Renmin ribao* [People's Daily], 19 Sep. 1959.

20. Zhongguo jiaoyu nianjian bianji shi [The Editorial Office of Education Yearbook In China], *Zhongguo jiaoyu nianjian 1949–81* [Education Yearbooks in China: 1949–81], Beijing: Zhongguo baike quanshu chuban she, 1982, p.1037.

21. The NSC issued a 'Notice on Sports Work in 1958' in January 1958. It pointed out that counties, schools and factories and other entities should run their own sports schools.

22. Li Tan, 'Shaonian ertong yeyu tiyu xuexiao' [Spare-time Sports Schools for Juniors], Guojia tiyu wenshi xinxi bianji weiyuan hui [Editorial Commission of State Sports Literature and History Information] (ed.), *Tiyu shiliao* [Sports History Information], 11, Beijing: Renmin tiyu chuban she, 1984, pp.88–9.

23. Rong Gaotang et al., *Dangdai zhongguo tiyu* [Contemporary Chinese Sport], Beijing: Zhongguo Shehui kexue chuban she, 1984, p.445.

24. Zhonghua renmin gonghe guo tiyu yundong weiyuan hui [The NSC of the PRC], *Quanguo tiyu shiye tongji ziliao huibian 1949–1978* [Collection of Statistical Information on Sport in China, 1949–78], Beijing: Renmin tiyu chuban she, 1979, pp.34–9.

25. The Editorial, 'Looking Backwards – and Forwards', *China Sports*, 1958 (1), p.1.

26. Women ranked third in volleyball, fifth in basketball, seventh in gymnastics, and second in speed-skating, broke a number of world records in shooting and surpassed the former Soviet Union in some events (Rong Gaotang, *Dangdai zhongguo tiyu* [Contemporary Chinese Sport]).

27. The interviewee was a 1960s volleyball player and has been a volleyball researcher since 1970. The interview took place in Beijing in September 1997.

28. The number of parachutists increased from 38 in 1957 to 1,860 in 1960 (nearly a 50-fold rise). The number of people engaging in gliding increased from 544 in 1957 to 8,633 in 1960 (See Woguo 18 ge yundong xiangmu jishu fazhan Ziliao [Material on the Technical Development of 18 sports in China], Beijing tiyu xueyuan [BIPE] (ed.), *61 nian tiyu gongzuo huiyi cankao wenxian* [Reference Document of the 1961 Sports Conference], pp.80–105).

29. Zhang Canzhen, 'Gaige kaifang ge zhongguo dailai le shengmo' [What Has the Reform Brought to Chinese Sport?], *Xin tiyu* [New Sport], 1992 (4), p.5.

30. *Quanguo tiyu shiye tongji ziliao huibian 1949–1978* [Collection of Statistical Information on Sport in China, 1949–78], pp.204–5.

31. Ibid., p.105.

32. Xu Changyun et al., 'Tiaogao' [High Jump], in Xian Yalong (ed.), *Zhongguo youshi jingji xiangmu zhisheng guilv* [The Laws of Winning in China's Dominant Sports], Beijing: Renmin tiyu chuban she, 1992, p.436.

33. Cheng Zhenghua, *Zhongguo ticao yundong shi* [Gymnastics in China], p.300.

34. Guojia tiwei shangbing diaocha zhu [The Survey Group of the NSC on Injury and Illness], Guanyu zhishu yundongdui shanbing wenti de diaocao baogao [The Investigation Report on Injury and Illness of Sports Teams], *Tiyu kexue jishu zhiliao* [Sport Science and Technology Information], 81 (1961), p.37.

35. Cheng Zhenghua, *Zhongguo ticao yundong shi* [Gymnastics in China], p.304.

36. Interview took place in Beijing in September 1997.

37. In 1959, the Soviets started to restrict the flow of scientific and technological information to China.

38. In May 1957, the Americans installed on Taiwan Matador missiles capable of carrying tactical nuclear weapons against Mainland China. In August 1958, forces of the PLA bombarded the Nationalist base on Jinmen Island, near Xiamen (see Yongjin Zhang, *China in International Society since 1949: Alienation and Beyond*, London: Macmillan Press, 1998, p.23).

39. Taiwan under the governance of the Nationalist Party pressed for participation, but was not qualified under the IOC's own political criteria for membership: a national Olympic committee could only represent the territory and people controlled by its sponsoring regime. Since the Kuomintang no longer controlled most of China, it could no longer represent 'China' in Olympic competitions. In spite of the antagonism between Taiwan and the PRC, they were agreed upon one thing: there was only one China and Taiwan was part of it (see David B. Kanin, 'Ideology and Diplomacy: The Dimension of Chinese Political Sport', in Benjamin Lowe (ed.), *Sports and International Relations*, Champaign, IL: Stipes Publishing Company, 1978, p.268).

40. Woguo 18 ge yundong xiangmu jishu fazhan ziliao [Material on the Technical Development of 18 Sports in China], p.15.
41. Interviewee Qiu became a world table tennis champion in 1961.
42. Ibid.
43. *Tiyu bao* [Sports Daily], 21 Oct. 1963.
44. Gu Shiquan, *Zhongguo tiyu shi* [Chinese Sports History], Beijing tiyu xueyuan chuban she, 1989, p.320.
45. Rong Gaotang, '61 nian xunlian gongzuo huiyi baogao' [Report of the 1961 Sports Conference], Beijing tiyu xueyuan [BIPE] (ed.), *Tiyu gongzuo huiyi ziliao* [Material of Sports Working Conferences], Beijing tiyu xueyuan, 1964, p.1.
46. Zhong Guangwen, 'Qingshaonian ertong yeyu tiyu xunlian qingkuang [Situation of Sports Training of Spare-time Sports Schools for Young People], *Tiyu shiliao* [Sports History Information], 11 (1984), p.96.
47. Woguo 18 ge yundong xiangmu jishu fazhan: Tianjing [Material on the Technical Development of 18 Sports in China: Athletics], p.1.
48. Pinglun yuan [Editorial], Feiyue qianjin de woguo tiyu shiye [Greatly Leaping Forward Chinese Sport], *Renmin ribao* [People's Daily], 25 Oct. 1959.
49. Muztag Mountain is one of the peaks in the Himalayas.
50. According to statistics based on 14 provinces and municipalities, by April 1960 some 88.9 per cent of households and 88.6 per cent of residents in the countryside ate in public canteens. The figure even reached 99 per cent in Henan province (Lu Tingyu, p.9).
51. Between 1957 and 1958, in the countryside, the number of children in nurseries increased about seven times, while those in kindergarten increased 26-fold. By May 1960, in cities some 32,836 state nurseries and kindergartens accepted 1.746 million children, and 95,685 neighbourhood nurseries and kindergartens took care of 3.49 million children. For the details, see Zhongguo funv gangbu guangli xueyuan [The Cadre Management Institute of China] (ed.), *Zhongguo funv yundong wengxian ziliao huibian* [Collection of Documents of the Chinese Women's Movement], Vol.2, Beijing: Zhongguo funu chuban she, 1988, p.386.
52. Work units provided female staff with washing rooms, pregnant women with resting rooms and mothers and children with canteens and even dormitories (Zhongguo funv gangbu guangli xueyuan [The Cadre Management Institute of China], p.405).
53. Many local women were organised to run various neighbourhood factories, such as tailoring, shoemaking, food processing and chemical fertiliser manufacturing.
54. Gao Xioxian, 'China's Modernisation and Changes in the Social Status of Rural Women', in Christina K. Gilmartin et al., (eds), *Engendering China: Women, Culture, and the State*, Cambridge, MA: Harvard University Press, 1994, p.83.
55. Phyllis Andors, *The Unfinished Liberation of Chinese Women: 1949–1980*, Bloomington, IN: Indiana University Press, 1983, p.74.
56. The interviewee was a director of the political department in the Society of Sports History in China. Interviewed in August 1997.
57. Zhonghua renmin gonghe guo tiyu yundong weiyuan hui [The NSC of the PRC], Quemguo tiyu shiye tongji ziliao huibian, 1949–1978 [Collection of Statistical Information on Sport in China, 1949–1978], Beijing: Renmin tiyuchuban, she, 1979, p.105.
58. Yuan Weiming et al., *Zhongguo paiqiu yundong sh*i [The History of Volleyball in China], Wuhan chuban she, 1994, p.92.
59. In 1960 alone droughts and floods lasted over six months and virtually half of the crop fields suffered.
60. On the reasons for the breach in Sino-soviet relations, see Richard Lowenthal, 'Diplomacy and Revolution: The Dialectics of A Dispute', in Roderick Macfarquhar (ed.), *China Under Mao: Politics Take Command*, Massachusetts: The MIT Press, 1966, pp.425–48.

61. Whereas real average wages reportedly grew at 6.0% per annum between 1952 and 1957 and the rate fell to minus 0.8% between 1957 and 1963 (Christopher Howe, 'Labour Organisation and Incentives in Industry, before and after the Cultural Revolution', in Stuart R. Schram (ed.), *Authority, Participation and Cultural Change in China*, Cambridge: Cambridge University Press, 1973, p.237).

62. Edwin E. Moise, *Modern China: A History*, London and New York: Longman, 1986, p.155.

63. Zhonghua renmin gonghe guotiyu yundong weiyuan hui [The NSC of the PRC], 1979, op. cit., p.105.

64. 'The Crime of the Anti-Party, Anti-Military, Anti-Revolutionary, Revisionist Ho Lung', *Sports Battlefront*, 8–9 (9 Feb. 1967).

65. Ezra F. Vogel, *Canton Under Communism: Programs and Politics in a Provincial Capital 1949–1968*, Cambridge, MA: Harvard University Press, 1969, pp.269–70.

66. The Minister of Defence Marshal Peng Dehuai was dismissed due to his criticism of the policy of the GLF at the eighth plenum of the Central Committee held at Lushan in August 1959. He was denounced as a leader of an 'anti-Party' group at the Politburo. An unprecedented long list of appointments and removals followed. With reference to power struggles within the Party around the GLF, see David A. Charles, 'The Dismissal of Marshal Peng Dehuai', in Roderick MacFarquhar (ed.), *China Under Mao: Politics Takes Command*, Cambridge, MA: MIT Press, 1966, pp.20–33.

67. By 1966, the GNP in industry and agriculture had apparently reached 232.7 billion yuan, increasing by 80.9 per cent compared to 1956 (see Lu Tingyu, *Zhonghua renming gongheguo lishi ji shi* [Historical Record of the PRC] 1958–65, p.185).

68. China exploded its first atomic bomb in November 1964 and became one of the world's advanced nations in this field.

69. Sports boarding school was also named 'three concentration' sports school – boarding, study and training took place in the same place. The system was initiated in Shanghai in 1959. At a national seminar about sports schools in 1963, it was introduced to the whole country.

70. 'Shaonian ertong yeyu tiyu xuexiao' [Spare-time Sports Schools for Juniors], p.86.

71. Resembling China socially, economically and politically, Indonesia regarded the PRC as a powerful friend. When the Fourth Asian Games were convened in Jakarta in 1962, the Indonesian government refused to issue visas to nationals from Taiwan. As a result, the IOC disciplined Indonesia by suspending its membership indefinitely. To challenge the IOC, whose president was the American Avery Brundage, China and Indonesia initiated the New Emerging Forces Games for Asia, Africa and Latin America. It posed a real threat to the Olympic movement. For the details, see Swanpo Sie, 'Sport and Politics: The Case of the Asian Games and The Ganefo', in Lowe, *Sport and International Relations*, pp.283–94.

72. Zhong Guangwen, 'Qingshaonian ertong yeyu tiyu xunlian qingkuang [Training of Spare-time Sports Schools for Young People], p.96.

73. 'Guojia tiwei jueding shishi jiaolianyuan dengji zhi' [The National Sports Commission Decides to Implement Coaches' Ranking across the Country], *Tiyu bao* [Sports Daily], 13 May 1963.

74. In 1958 a ten-year sports development plan was formulated. This plan set goals of catching up with the world's advanced sports nations within the decade and a further 200 million people passing the Labour and Defence Programme (*Lao wei zhi*).

75. World records were created in weightlifting (four), rifle shooting (five), archery (six), aeroplane parachuting (nine) and model aeroplane flying (five). Of the new national records, 16 were events first introduced in China in 1965 (See Gu Shiquan, *Zhongguo tiyu shi* [Chinese Sports History], p.324).

76. The Labour and Defence Programme (*Lao wei zhi*) established the physical activities to be tested, the points for performances and overall standards to be met in order to receive an award. The standards were regarded as an important means of assessing

the overall success of physical policies. The focus was on the masses.

77. *Beijing tiyu wenshi* [Beijing Sports Literature and History], 1986 (3), p.113.
78. The Beijing women's volleyball team defeated the visiting Japanese national women's volleyball team in three straight sets in 1957, and the Czechoslovakian team in 1958. Its basketball team defeated the North Korean team in the same year.
79. They ran various classes for coaches, referees and others and helped produce more than 10,000 athletes. In 1960 the BIPE further sent about 300 teachers and students to over 500 local units across the country to popularise sport (Zhong Shitong, 'Luli jianshe xinxing de tiyu xueyuan, peiyang gongchan zhuyi xinren' [To Strive to Build Up the New Type of Institute of Physical Education and Cultivate the Communist New Man], *Beijing tiyu xueyuan* [Beijing Institute of Physical Education], 96 (1959), pp.1–4).
80. This department has been an important base for high-level sports coaches and administrators. It has produced about 4,000 sports talents over time. At present, some 600 students study in this department.
81. There were different courses, from four-year and two-year to three-month short-term courses and correspondence courses. Most coaches were ex-athletes. When they retired from competition, some of them were employed immediately as coaches for lower-level training. They could take part-time or correspondence courses. Some of them underwent academic study for two or four years and then became coaches. This system continues today.
82. She was interviewed in Beijing in 1995.
83. The interviewee was Huang Xinhe. Interview took place in 1995.
84. Ibid.
85. *Beijing tiyu wenshi* [Beijing Sports Literature and History], 1986 (2), pp.59–60.
86. Beijing shi tiyu yundong weiyuan hui [The Beijing Municipal Sports Commission], 'Cong Beijing shi zhongdian qingshao nian yeyu tixiao guoqu jinian jiaoxue xunlian zhong delai de yixie xiangfa' [Some Ideas from the Past Few Years' Teaching and Coaching of Beijing Municipal Key Spare-Time Sports Schools for Young People], Beijing tiyu xueyuan [BIPE] (ed.), *61 nian tiyu gongzuo huiyi cankao zhiliao* [The Reference Document of the 1961 Sports Working Conference], 10 (1964), pp.25–32.
87. *Quanguo tiyu shiye tongji ziliao huibian 1949–1978* [Collection of Statistical Information on Sport in China, 1949–78], pp.16–65.
88. Rao Yurong, 'Beijing nannv pai xia shangdong' [Beijing Men's and Women's Volleyball Teams Went to Shangdong], *Beijing tiyu wenshi* [Beijing Sports Literature and History], 1986 (2), pp.285–6.
89. Interviewee Cheng arrived at the Beijing Institute of Physical Education in 1953 as a student, achieved the grade of sports master in gymnastics in 1958, and was an associate professor at the institute when the interview took place in 1995.
90. He was interviewed in Shanghai in 1994.
91. Luo Yingqing, 'Xuexiao tiyu' [School Sport], *Tiyu shiliao* [Sports History Information], 11 (1984), p.75.
92. *Quanguo tiyu shiye tongji ziliao huibian 1949–1978* [Collection of Statistical Information on Sport in China, 1949–78], 1979.
93. *Beijing tiyu wenshi* [Beijing Sports Literature and History], 1986 (3), p.113.
94. Guijia tiwei xuanchuang bu [Propaganda Department of the NSC], *Di yi jie quanguo yundong hui xuanchuan ziliao* [Propaganda Materials of the First National Games], Vol.1, Renmin tiyu chuban she, 1958, p.13.
95. Li Tan, 'Shaonian ertong yeyu tiyu xuexiao' [Spare-time Sports Schools for Juniors], p.86.
96. Guangdong peiyang tiyu houbei rencai de zhuangkuang [Cultivating Sports Potentials In Guangdong], in Beijing tiyu xueyuan [BIPE] (ed.), *Tiyu gongzuo huiyi cankao zhiliao* [Reference Document of Sports Conference], 1962, p.1.
97. *Quanguo tiyu shiye tongji ziliao huibian 1949–1978* [Collection of Statistical

Information on Sport in China, 1949–78], pp.140–1.

98. Guangdong tiyu shi xuehui, huanan shifang daxue tiyu xi [Guangdong Sports History Society and Physical Education Department of South China Normal University], 'Guangdong youxiu yundong dui sixiang fazhanshi chutan' [Preliminary Studies of the History of the Administration of Elite Sports Teams in Guangdong], *Guangdong tiyu shiliao* [Guangdong Sports History Information], 1992 (3), p.1.

99. Wuoguo 18 ge yundong xiangmu jishu fazhan zhiliao [Material on the Technical Development of 18 Sports in China], p.5.

100. See 'Guangdong ticao yundong' [Gymnastics in Guangdong], 'Guangdong tianjing yundong' [Athletics in Guangdong], *Guangdong tiyu shiliao* [Guangdong Sports History Information], 1987 (2).

101. *Quanguo tiyu shiye tongji ziliao huibian 1949–1978* [Collection of Statistical Information on Sport in China, 1949–78], pp.16–65.

102. Guojia tiwei jihua caiwu shi [Planning and Finance Dept. of the NSC], *Tiyu shiye tongji nianjian (neibu ziliao)* [Statistics Yearbook of Sport, internal materials], 1994, p.16.

103. *Quanguo tiyu shiye tongji ziliao huibian 1949–1978* [Collection of Statistical Information on Sport in China, 1949–78], pp.144–5.

104. *Di yi jie quanguo yundong hui xuanchuan ziliao* [Propaganda Materials of the First National Games], 3, p112.

105. *Beijing tiyu wenshi* [Beijing Sports Literature and History], 1986 (3), p.113.

106. Jun Chang, *Wild Swans: Three Daughters of China*, London: HarperCollins, 1991, p.319.

107. Chris Bramall, *In Praise of Maoist Economic Planning: Living Standards and Economic Development in Sichuan since 1931*, Oxford: Clarendon Press, 1993, p.339.

108. Zhonghua renmin gonghe guo tiyu yundong weiyuan hui [The NSC of the PRC], 1979, pp.144–5.

109. 'Woguo 18 ge yundong xiangmu jishu fazhan Ziliao' [Material on the Technical Development of 18 Sports in China], p.5.

110. *Di yi jie quanguo yundong hui xuanchuan ziliao* [Propaganda Materials of the First National Games], pp.16–65.

111. Tang Minghui, 'Gengyun paitan sanshi zai – ji sichuan nvpai zhu jiaolian Wang Defen'[Thirty Years on the Volleyball Field – Documentary on the Head Coach of Sichuan Women's Volleyball Team Wang Defen], *Sichuan tiyu shiliao* [Sichuan Sports History Information], 6, 2 (1984), pp.30–4.

112. Cities and the countryside were instructed to develop sport to the same standard without any consideration of different lifestyles, facilities and equipment. For example, it was stated that every county should have a sporting stadium, gymnasium and swimming pool and two sports fields within five years. To meet these requirements, some places had to stop industrial and agricultural production to develop sporting facilities, invest considerable money in sport or falsify the figures on the development of such facilities.

Chapter 3

1. Power struggles continued in the Party both at central and local levels after the 1950s. In the aftermath of the utopian Great Leap Forward, President Liu Shaoqi and Party General Secretary Deng Xiaoping adopted pragmatic economic policies at odds with Mao's revolutionary vision. Dissatisfied with China's new direction and his own reduced authority, Chairman Mao Zedong launched a massive political attack on Liu, Deng and other pragmatists in the spring of 1966, charging them with

dragging China back toward capitalism. This launched the new movement – the 'Great Proletarian Cultural Revolution'. For further detail, see Ezra F. Vogel, *Canton under Communism: Programs and Politics in A Provincial Capital, 1949–1968*, Cambridge, MA: Harvard University Press, 1969, pp.317–20.

2. The 'socialist education movement' was also called the 'four clean ups' movement, namely to clean up politics, economics, organisation and ideas. It was launched in the country between 1963 and 1965 to correct 'unhealthy tendencies' that had appeared after the Great Leap Forward. Special working teams were organised to undertake the campaign.

3. A series of plays, novels, and essays written before the mid-1960s that had implicitly criticised Mao's policy were now subjected to attack, their authors were condemned and their supporters in the Party leadership were purged.

4. On 15 November 1965, Yao Wenyuan published his article 'Criticism of the Revised Historical Play *Hai Rui's Dismissal from Office*' (*Hai Rui ba guan*) in the Shanghai newspaper *Wenhui ribao* [Weihui daily]. Yao accused Wu Han, the author of the play and the deputy mayor of Beijing at the time, of being a dangerous class enemy who deliberately misinterpreted history. This aroused a nationwide debate over the nature of the play and the political stance of its author. Not long after, in early 1966, other popular pre-Cultural Revolution works were also assailed.

5. GNP reportedly decreased 9.4 per cent in 1967 and 4.5 per cent in 1968. National per-capita income in 1968 decreased 12.6 per cent compared to 1966. For details, see Guojia tongji ju (ed.), *Zhongguo tongji nianjian* [Chinese Statistical Yearbook], Zhongguo tongji chuban she, 1985, p.20.

6. The 'Resolution on Certain Questions in the Sixth Plenary Session of the Eleventh CCP Central Committee' in 1981 comprehensively evaluated the Cultural Revolution. Now it is widely accepted that the following factors were responsible for the Cultural Revolution. First, the power struggle within the party leadership led to the eruption of the political movement. Second, guided by the theory of class struggle that exaggerated the factionalism and antagonism in society, political movements were stressed in the New China. The anti-rightist campaign in 1957 and the socialist education movement in 1964 fed the leftist social climate. Third, Chinese social-psychological characteristics deeply rooted in an age-old agrarian society contradicted the demands of China's modernisation. The historic obedience to authority and Mao's cult drove Chinese, young people in particular, into the chaotic political movement.

7. Xinhua she guonei xinxi zhu [Domestic Information Group of Xinhua News Agency] (ed.), *Zhonghua renmin gongheguo dashi ji* [Documents on the Major Events of the PRC], Vol.3, Beijing: Xinhua chuban she, 1982, pp.85, 89; Xu Jin (ed.), *Zhonghua renmin gongheguo dashi ji* [Documents on the Major Events of the PRC], *1989–94*, Beijing: Kexue jishu wenxian chuban she, 1994; Lu Tingyu, *Zhonghua renmin gongheguo lishi jishi* [Historical Record of the PRC], Beijing: Hongqi chuban she, 1995.

8. Xiao Di (ed.), *Wenge zhimi* [The Mystery of the Cultural Revolution], Vol.5, Beijing: Zhaohua chuban she, 1993.

9. Xiao Jie (ed.), *Zhongguo zhiqing miweng lu* [The Secret Records of Chinese Educated Youths], Zuojia chuban she, 1993.

10. Zhongguo tiyu shi xuehui [Society of Chinese Sports History] (ed.), *Tiyu shi lunwen ji* [Collection of Papers of Sports History], Beijing: Renmin tiyu chuban she, 1989, pp.106–10.

11. Ibid., pp.119–24.

12. See Roderick L. MacFarquhar and John King Fairbank (eds.), *The Cambridge History of China*, Vol. xv: *Revolutions within the Chinese Revolution*, London: Cambridge University Press, 1991; Yue Daiyun and Carolyn Wakeman, *To the Storm: the Odyssey of a Revolutionary Chinese Woman*, Berkeley, CA: University of

California Press, 1985; Anne F. Thurston, *Enemies of the People: the Ordeal of the Intellectuals in China's Great Cultural Revolution*, New York: Knopf, 1987.

13. Donald. W. Calhoun, *Sport, Culture, and Personality*, 2nd edn, Champaign, IL: Human Kinetics Publishers, 1987, pp.141–56.

14. Zhong Qingyi, *The Effects of the 'Great Cultural Revolution' on Sport in China, 1966–1976*, Ph.D. dissertation, 1995, USA.

15. The circular announced the dissolution of the initial five-person Cultural Revolution Group and its replacement by another Cultural Revolution Group under the standing committee of the Politburo. Thereafter, a set of leftist theories, lines, policies and strategies were formulated, and people were called on to attack 'those taking the capitalist road' in the Party, the state and the Army as well as other fields.

16. Nie Yuanzi (born 1921) was a female Party secretary at Beijing University's philosophy department. She criticised the conservatism of the Party committee of the university and called on the students to overthrow it. As a result, the Party committee was dismantled and reorganised on 3 June 1966. After her wall-poster, Nie Yuanzi was promoted to director of the Cultural Revolution Committee of Beijing University, deputy director of the Beijing Municipal Cultural Revolution Committee and reserve candidate of the ninth Central Party Committee. She was arrested in 1978 for an 'anti-revolutionary crime' committed during the Cultural Revolution (Wen Lequn, Hao Ruiting (eds.), *Wenhua da geming zhong de mingren zhisheng* [The Rise of Famous People during the Cultural Revolution], Beijing: Zhongyang minzu xueyuan chuban she, 1993, pp.1–16).

17. One week later, Ye's poster message was broadcast throughout the whole country and a specific review article entitled 'To Cheer the Wall-poster from Beida [Beijing University]' was published in *Renmin ribao* [People's Daily], the official paper of the CCP.

18. Chairman Mao's 'My First Wall-poster: To Bombard Headquarters' was publicised on 5 August in 1966. It implied that there was a problem at the top-level leadership of the Party. Mao's wall-poster added fuel to the campaign and influenced the literary style of a whole generation.

19. Huang Kuangron was interviewed in July 1985 in Beijing.

20. The 'Resolution on the Proletarian Great Cultural Revolution' (16 articles) was passed at the 11th plenary session of the eighth national congress of the Party in August 1966.

21. The first Red Guards were students at a secondary school attached to Qinghua University in Beijing. They secretly set up the Red Guard organisation on 26 May 1966.

22. Mao wore the armband of the Red Guard at the mass rally in August to give personal approval to the organisation.

23. Within the three months after 18 August, Mao received delegations of teachers and students totalling more than 11 million. This gave a strong impetus to the massive Cultural Revolution.

24. Gordon A. Bennett and Ronald N. Montaperto, *Red Guard: the Political Biography of Dai Hsiao-Ai*, London: George Allen & Unwin, 1971, p.115.

25. In 1935, after breaking through the five encirclements launched by the Nationalists, the Red Army began the 25,000-*li* Long March (a *li* is equal to half a kilometre) through Hunan, Guzhou, Sichuan and finally to Yanan in December 1936. Of the 90,000 men who broke out of Jiangxi, only one in ten reached the new base in the north.

26. The interviewee is the director of the physical education department at the Normal University of Southern China in Guangdong.

27. All the names of streets, hospitals, shops and even bus stations that were considered outdated were replaced by 'revolutionary' and 'rebellious' names.

28. They are old ideas, old culture, old customs and old habits.

29. The Five Types of Black Elements comprised landlords, rich peasants, counter-revolutionaries, evildoers and rightists. Some 16,623 people were regarded as the 'Five Types of Black Elements' by October 1966 (Ma Yuping, *Zhongguo de zuotian he mingtian 1840–1987: Guoqing Shouche* [China's Yesterday and Today 1840–1987: Handbook of the National Situation], Beijing: Jiefangjun chuban she, 1989, p.754).

30. Lowell Dittmer, 'The Origins of China's Post-Mao Reforms', in Victor C. Falkenbeim (ed.), *Chinese Politics from Mao to Deng*, New York: Paragon House, 1989, p.57.

31. Fu Qifang came back from Hong Kong to Mainland China in 1952. He competed at the 24th world table tennis championships. After 1958, he coached the world champion men's table tennis team. From 1964 to 1966 he was the vice-chairman of China's Table Tennis Association. He committed suicide in 1967 after suffering humiliation, criticism and torture.

32. Rong Guotuan, born in Hong Kong, arrived in Mainland China in 1957. He joined the Guangdong provincial table tennis team and won the men's singles title at the world table tennis championships in 1959, becoming the first ever Chinese world champion. Due to his early days in Hong Kong he was accused of being a spy and enemy after the outset of the Cultural Revolution. He committed suicide in 1968, aged 30 (see Li Run (ed.), *Wenhua dageming zhong de mingren zhi shi* [The Deaths of Famous People during the Cultural Revolution], Zhongyang minzu xueyuan chuban she, 1993, pp.113–17).

33. Marshal He Long, a former Politburo member and one of the founders of the CCP, was subjected to two and a half years of slow torture before he died of diabetes in 1969. See Jung Chang, *Wild Swans: Three Daughters of China*, London: HarperCollins Publishers, 1991, p.391.

34. Yuan Weiming et al., *Zhongguo paiqou shi* [Volleyball in China], Wuhan chuban she, 1994, p.151.

35. Godwin C. Chu & Yanan Ju, *The Great Wall in Ruins – Communication and Cultural Change in China*, Albany, NY: State University of New York Press, 1993, p.79.

36. Interviewee Qou Zhonghui was a world table tennis champion in 1961 and a coach of the national table tennis team between 1963 and 1973. After 1973 she worked at the State Sports Research Institute as a researcher and administrator.

37. The National Sports Commission, chaired by vice-premier Marshal He Long, had placed emphasis on sports development, elite sport in particular. The NSC was relatively peripheral to political movements, compared to other ministries such as the Culturel Ministry. Between 1968 and 1971 the NSC was put under the control of the General Political Department of People's Liberation Army.

38. Interview, Beijing, 1997.

39. Yuan Weiming, *Zhongguo paiqou shi* [Volleyball in China], p.151.

40. Chen Zhenghua (ed.), *Zhongguo ticao yundong shu* [Gymnastics in China], Wuhan chuban she, 1990, p.376.

41. Weapons such as guns, tanks and cannons were used in some areas. The most serious incident happened in Wuhan city, the capital of Hubei province in central China. On 20 July 1967, about 100,000 people from the organisation 'Millions of Bold Warriors' (*baiwang yongshi*) and some soldiers demonstrated on the streets to protest against the speeches made by Xie Fuzhi and Wang Li – the agents of the Lin Biao and Jiang Qing coup in Hubei province. This event was soon declared to be anti-revolutionary by the Group of the Central Cultural Revolution. As a result, more than 184,000 people suffered beatings and several hundred died.

42. Guojia tongji ju [State Statistical Bureau](ed.), Zhongguo tongji nianjian [Chinese Statistical Yearbook], Beijing: Zhongguo tongji chuban she, 1985, p.20.

43. Guojia tiwei wenshi si [Literature and History Department of the NSC], *Tiwei xitong ziliao tongji* [Statistic Information of the Sports Community], 1992, p.12.

44. Zhonghua renmin gonghe guo tiyu yundong weiyuan hui [The NSC of the PRC], *Quanguo tiyu shiye tongji ziliao huibian 1949–1978* [Collection of Statistical Information on Sport in China, 1949–78)], Beijing: Renmin tiyu chuban she, 1979, pp.16–18.
45. As interviewee Yang Yizhuan remarked, 'most of these radical female rebels during the Cultural Revolution were students either in high school or in university, very few middle-aged or old women'.
46. Within the month of August, more than 114,000 families were searched and forced to hand over their houses; some 1,700 people were beaten to death; and over 85,000 were categorised into the 'five types of black elements' and forced to leave the capital (Deng Liqun (ed.), *Dangdai zhongguo Beijing* [Contemporary China in Beijing], Beijing: Zhongguo shehui kexue chuban she, 1989, p.168).
47. Interviewee Pan Yongzhi came to the Beijing Institute of Physical Education (now BUPE) to study in 1975 and became a teacher at the institute after graduation in 1978. Now she is a deputy director of the department of physical education at the university.
48. Jung Chang, *Wild Swans*, p.309.
49. Andrew F. Watson, 'A Revolution to Touch Men's Souls: The Family, Interpersonal Relations and Daily Life', in Stuart R. Schram (ed.), *Authority, Participation and Cultural Change in China*, Cambridge: Cambridge University Press, 1973, p.309.
50. Lucian W Pye, *The Mandarin and the Cadre: China's Political Cultures*, Ann Arbor, MI: Centre for Chinese Study, The University of Michigan, 1988, p.121.
51. Julia Kristeva, *About Chinese Women*, London: Marion Boyars, 1977, p.155.
52. Jing Lin, *The Red Guards' Path to Violence: Political, Educational, and Psychological Factors*. New York: Praeger, p.131.
53. The journal ceased publication between 1967 and 1972.
54. Rung Kao-tang, 'Sports Should Serve the People', *China's Sports*, 1 (1966), pp.1–5.
55. Jonathan Kolatch, *Sports, Politics, and Ideology in China*, New York: Jonathan David, 1972, p.162.
56. Two days after swimming across the Yangtze river, Mao returned to Beijing after an absence of eight months and took command of the Cultural Revolution.
57. Yan Jian, *Wenghua da geming zhong de dixia wengxue* [Unpublished Literature of the Cultural Revolution], Qinan: Zhaohua chuban she, 1993, p.17.
58. At six o'clock in the morning people stood in front of Chairman Mao's picture, wished him long life and then read a piece from Mao's works. Before sunset they again faced Mao's picture, summed up their daily work and lives and then sang the song 'Sailing on the Sea Relies on the Helmsman' (*Dahai hangxing kao duoshou*), which symbolised the role of Chairman Mao.
59. Guang Hong et al., 'Zhuang Zedong de sheng Luo' [The Rise and Fall of Zhuang Zedong], in Shi Reng (ed.), *Wenhua da geming zhong de minren zhi sheng jiang* [The Rise and Fall of Famous People during the Cultural Revolution], Beijing: Zhongyang minzu xueyuan chuban she, 1993, p.302.
60. Two years before the Revolution, Jiang Qing, the wife of Chairman Mao, made a speech, 'A Statement on the Revolutionary Beijing Opera', at the 'watch and emulation meeting' of Beijing Opera and Modern Operas. Her followers praised her as a leader and standard bearer for the revolution in art and literature.
61. Yan Jian, *Wenghua da geming zhong de dixia wengxue* [Unpublished Literature of the Cultural Revolution],
62. Zhong Qingyi, *The Effects of the 'Great Cultural Revolution'*.
63. Regarding the model opera, see Ellen R. Judd, 'Dramas of Passion: Heroism in the Cultural Revolution's Model Operas', in William A. Joseph (ed.), *New Perspectives on the Cultural Revolution*, Cambridge, MA: Harvard University Press, 1989, pp.265–82.
64. Robert L. Simon, *Sport and Social Values*, London and Englewood Cliffs, NJ: Prentice-Hall, 1985, p.104.
65. Mao's inscription on a photograph of a women's militia on 20 Sep. 1966 read:

These well-groomed heroines carry five-foot rifles,
On this parade ground in the first rays of the sun.
Daughters of China have uncommon aspirations,
Preferring battle tunics to red dresses.

66. Elisabeth Croll, *Changing Identities of Chinese Women*, Hong Kong University Press, 1995, pp.69–85.

67. Daqing's self-reliance, the management of its work force, and its high political consciousness channelled into solving production problems made it a model for industrial development.

68. The team consisted of 23 girls aged below 20. They worked alongside men, digging canals, building reservoirs and terraced mountainsides and gullies. This counteracted the effects of the most adverse weather.

69. The 19-year-old Guo Fengnian was a branch secretary of the Communist League of Dazhai commune in Xinyan county in 1966. She was later promoted to vice-secretary of Dazhai Commune Party Committee and vice-director of the Standing Committee of Provincial Revolutionary Commission in 1971. Three years later she became a member of Shanxi Provincial Committee in 1974 and an alternative member of the Central Committee of CCP in 1977. She was assigned to the Fruit Tree Research Institute in 1980. Now she is the general manager of the Dazhai Economic Development Company, and concentrates on profit-making instead of politics.

70. *Xinhua ribao* [Xinhua Daily], 6 July 1976.

71. Interviewed in 1995 in Beijing.

72. Women in all walks of life, once more, were organised to study and analyse the origins and evolution of an ideology of women's oppression. This campaign to some extent brought new life to women's consciousness of equality. A new set of principles came into being and directly challenged traditional values and attitudes held by and towards women.

73. It should be pointed out that this campaign was purposely manipulated by the Gang of Four. Through the allusive saga of conservative Confucian, it targeted Premier Zhou Enlai who emphasised the ethics of the great sage and protected a number of veteran party officials from torture.

74. In the 1969 ninth Party Congress, Jiang Qing (Mao's wife) and Ye Qun (Lin Biao's wife) were elected to the powerful Politburo. A campaign to recruit women into the party followed.

75. Guojia tiwei jihua caiwu si [Planning and Financial Department of the NSC], *Tiyu shiye tongji nianjian (neibu ziliao)*[Statistical Yearbook of Sport, internal materials],1994, pp.34–9.

76. Barbara Ehrenreich, 'Democracy In China', *Monthly Review*, Sep. 1974, pp.17–32.

77. Nancy E.Riley, 'Gender Equality in China: Two Steps Forward, One Step Back', in William A .Joseph (ed.), *China Briefing: the Contradiction of Change*, New York: M.E. Sharpe, 1997, p.85.

78. On 22 December 1968, *Renmin ribao* [People's Daily] published Chairman Mao's instruction: 'It is necessary that the educated young go to the countryside to be re-educated by peasants.' Immediately, about 17 million high-school students went voluntarily, or were forced to go, to the countryside and military construction camps in remote border areas, such as Helongjian, Inner Mongolia, Yunnan and Shanxi provinces.

79. Shou Xiaoyu was interviewed in 1994 in Beijing.

80. The author was in the same group as her in a preparatory workshop for the UN Fourth World Conference on Women in January 1995. Xiong undertook her postgraduate study at China's Academy of Social Sciences between 1978 and 1981, and went to the United States as a visiting scholar in 1988. Since 1981 she has been working at the Xinhua News Agency.

81. Delia Davin, *Internal Migration in Contemporary China*, Basingstoke: Macmillan Press, 1999, p.156.
82. Mao's works were read and the eight 'model operas' were heard and viewed, but no other books and songs were available.
83. Interviewee Pan Yongzhi, Beijing, 1996.
84. Interviewee Tang Guoli, who broke the Asian javelin record in 1980, was a coach in the sports boarding school affiliated to the BUPE when the interview took place in 1996.
85. Interviewee Jing Dongxian was shooting world record holder in the late 1970s.
86. Franz Michael et al., *China and the Crisis of Marxism-Leninism*, Boulder, CO and Oxford: Westview Press, 1990, p.160.
87. Interviewee Pan Yongzhi.
88. *Liaoning ribao* [Liaoning Daily], 19 July 1973. 'Two lines and thoughts' meant the proletarian revolutionary line and thought, and the bourgeois anti-revolutionary line and thought.
89. On 12 December 1973, *Beijing ribao* [Beijing Daily] published Huang's diary and a letter, in which criticism of teachers was voiced. On 28 December *Renmin ribao* [People's Daily] re-published the letter. Thereafter, students in primary and middle schools were encouraged to denounce their teachers for taking a revisionist educational line. After the end of the Cultural Revolution it was found out that the letter and diary were faked by others for political ends.
90. The interviewee was Huang Yaoling. Interview took place in 1996.
91. Guojia tiwei wenshi si [Literature and History Department of the NSC], p.11.
92. At the ninth congress of the CCP, Jiang Qing, Zhang Chunqiao and Yao Wenyuan were given no opportunity to address the Congress. Forty per cent of the new Central Committee were soldiers. No Red Guard leader became a full member of the Central Committee, and several purged former ministers reappeared. The message of the Congress was one of unity, stability and reconciliation.
93. Chief among these was Deng Xiaoping, who re-emerged in 1973 and was confirmed in 1975 in the concurrent posts of Politburo Standing Committee member, PLA chief of staff, and vice premier.
94. Guojia tiwei wenshi si [Literature and History Department of the NSC], p.12.
95. Ibid.,p.11.
96. Not only 'imperialist' countries such as the United Kingdom but also several 'friendly' countries such as India and Indonesia were under fierce assault. As a result, China became isolated and unpopular. By the end of 1969, the PRC had established diplomatic relations with only 50 countries, most of which were communist and newly independent states. Sino-Soviet relations reached a particularly tense stage, culminating in the armed clashes on Chenpao (Damansky) Island in the Ussuri River in 1969. Due to the withdrawal of diplomats, China had only one ambassador abroad, Huang Hua in Cairo, in 1969 (Yongjin Zhang, *China in International Society since 1949: Alienation and Beyond*, London: Macmillan Press, 1998, p.18).
97. Elizabeth Wright, 'China's Foreign Policy: Foreign Relations Since 1949', in Christopher Howe (ed.), *Studying China: A Source Book for Teachers in Schools and Colleges*, London: School of Oriental and African Studies, 1979, p.163.
98. On 4 April 1970 the Chinese player Zhuang Zedong sat beside an American player in a coach during the Tokyo World Championships. When they shook hands, they caught the attention of journalists. Three days later, the American team was invited to visit China. This tour was the prelude to the normalisation of Sino-American relations.
99. China had kept up sporting exchanges with Cuba, North Korea, Romania and other third-world countries.
100. Guojia tiwei [The NSC] (ed.), *Zhongguo tiyu nianjian, 49–91 jinghua ben* (xia ce) [Sports Yearbooks in China, 1949–91, Vol. 2], Beijing: Renmin tiyu chuban she, 1993.

101. Terry Monnington, 'Politicians and Sport: Uses and Abuses', in Lincoln Allison (ed.), *The Changing Politics of Sport*, Manchester: Manchester University Press, 1993, p.128.

102. The Gang of Four consisted of Mao's wife Jiang Qing, Zhang Chunqiao, Yao Wenyuan and Wang Hongwen. After criticising Wu Han's play *Hai Rui's Dismissal from Office*, Yao became one of the leaders of the CR. In the Shanghai January Revolution of 1967 Wang rose from a Shanghai factory security chief to a workers' leader. In the early 1970s he was head of the leftist stronghold of Shanghai. In 1973 he joined the Politburo at Mao's direction and a year later was promoted to vice-chairman and member of the Politburo Standing Committee. The Gang of Four allied themselves to advocates of radical leftist revolution in order to win their support. On 25 January 1981, after a lengthy trial, Jiang Qing and Zhang Chunqiao were sentenced to death, with two years' reprieve; Yao Wenyuan received a sentence of 20 years; and Wang Hongwen was given a life sentence.

103. It means that friendship took precedence over competition when Chinese played against Chinese or foreign players from the 'friendly' communist countries. Basically, this motto acted as an internal unifying force and presented a picture in which others could see communism's fraternal concepts in practice.

104. John M. Hoberman, *Sport and Political Ideology*, London: Heinemann, 1984, p.232.

105. Between 1973 and 1976 women created 22 out of the 40, 32 out of the 75, 36 out of the 87 and 36 out of the 76 national records respectively.

106. Pye, *The Mandarin and the Cadre*, p.60.

107. In order to guarantee Zhuang's success in winning the singles title three times in a row, Li was required to concede victory to his team-mate Zhuang Zedong in the World Championships.

108. Susan Brownell, *Training the Body for China: Sports in the Moral Order of the People's Republic*, Chicago, IL, and London: The University of Chicago Press, 1995, p.302.

109. Hoberman, *Sport and Political Ideology*, p.222.

110. Beijing tiyu xueyuan yuanshi bianji zhu [Editorial Group of the History of BIPE], *Beijing tiyu xuaxuan yuanshi* [The History of Beijing Institute of Physical Education], Beijing tiyu xuexuan chuban she, 1993, p.59.

111. Most of them had no sports background. Under the policy of 'running schools by opening up to society', students spent about a third of their time on physical labour and other political activities. Thus their academic performance was hardly satisfactory. Nevertheless, most of them became physical education teachers. Some became sports administrators and coaches.

112. Guojia tiwei ticao chu [Gymnastic Department of the National Sports Committee], *1973 ninan quanguo ticao xunlian gongzuo huiyi wenjian* [Document of the National Gymnastic Training Conference in 1973], Beijing tiyu xueyuan, 1973, p.26.

113. They won 33 gold, 64 silver and 27 bronze medals. They also broke one world record, 18 Asian records and 22 national records at the games (Gu Shiquan, *Zhongguo tiyu shi* [Chinese Sports History], Beijing tiyu daxue chuban she, 1997, p.363).

114. Rong Gaotang (ed.), *Dangdai zhongguo tiyu* [Contemporary Chinese Sport], Beijing: zhongguo shehui kexue chuban she, 1984, p.249.

115. Ibid., pp.192–194.

116. Zhong Qingyi, *The Effects of the 'Great Cultural Revolution' on Sport in China*.

117. Some even more absurd practices were seen during the period. For example, when the international compulsory routines for the 1976 Olympic Games were first adopted in gymnastic competitions, some skills in floor exercise and balance beam were considered manifestations of 'bourgeois' ideology. Gymnasts were required to do them in a 'revolutionary manner'. Otherwise, they would have up to 0.5 deducted from their score.

118. Athletes and coaches often went to villages, factories and the Army to undertake 'open door' training. Two months before the 1975 National Games Preliminary, the women's volleyball team of the PLA went to an army complex in Beijing for half a month. They joined the soldiers for study, even undertaking military duties.

119. In January 1976, Premier Zhou Enlai, a popular political figure, died of cancer. On 5 April, Beijing citizens staged a spontaneous demonstration in Tiananmen Square in Zhou's memory, with strong political overtones in support of Deng. The authorities forcibly suppressed the demonstration. Deng Xiaoping was blamed for the disorder and stripped of all official positions, although he retained his party membership.

120. Despite these changes in rhetoric, no fundamental difference existed between the 'show' and regular competitions except that the former did not publicise scores after a gymnast performed her/his routine.

121. Liang Heng and Judith Shapiro, *Return to China: A Survivor of the Cultural Revolution Reports on China Today*, London: Chatto & Windus, 1987, p.240.

122. Falkenheim, *Chinese Politics from Mao to Deng*, p.153.

123. H.W. James and Ann Tyson, *Chinese Awakenings: Life Stories from the Unofficial China,* Boulder, CO, and Oxford: Westview Press, 1995, p.1.

124. Hu Shen, 'Yige minchu zai chensi' [A Nation is Contemplating], *Renmin ribao* [People's Daily], 7 April 1988.

125. Zhong Guangwen, 'Qingshaonian ertong yeyu tiyu xunlian qingkuang'[Sports Training in Spare-time Sports Schools for Young People], *Tiyu shiliao* [Sports History Information], 1984 (11), p.98.

126. During the Cultural Revolution those who took the lead in attacking party organisations and administrators at all levels constituted a revolutionary rebel group and those who stood against them were labelled 'loyalists'.

127. Interviewee Yang Yizhuang, Beijing, 1996.

128. They were accused of being 'current anti-revolutionary elements'. For the details, see *Beijing tiyu wenshi* [Beijing Literature and History], 1982 (3), p.129.

129. Guojia tiwei jihua caiwu si [Planning and Financial Department of the NSC], p.16.

130. There were 106 schools of this kind across the country, which were run by the state council. In November 1969 about 500 teachers, officials and their family members from the Beijing Institute of Physical Education were sent to Wuqi gangxiao in Shanxi province. They laboured in arduous conditions.

131. *Beijing tiyu wenshi* [Beijing Sports Literature and History], 3 (1987), pp.132–3.

132. Ibid.

133. Ibid., pp.152–3.

134. See Bennett and Montaperto, *Red Guard: the Political Biography of Dai Hsiao-Ai.*

135. Ezra F. Vogel, *Canton under Communism*, pp.324–5.

136. Ye Chulin, 'Guangdong tiyu xingzheng jigou yange' [The Evolution of Sports Administration in Guangdong], *Guangdong tiyu shiliao* [Guangdong Sports History Information], 1996 (2), p.8.

137. Wei Zhenlan (ed.), *Guangdong tiyu sishi nian* [Forty Years of Guangdong Sport], Xin shiji chuban she, 1989, p.9.

138. Guojia tiwei jihua caiwu si [Planning and Finance Department of the NSC], p.16.

139. Guangdong tiyu shi xuehui, Huanan shifang daxue tiyu xi [Guangdong Sports History Society and Physical Education Department of South China Normal University], Guangdong youxiu yundongdui shixiang fazhan shi chutan [Preliminary Studies of the History of Administration of Elite Sports Teams in Guangdong], *Guangdong tiyu shiliao* [Guangdong Sports History Information], 1992 (3), p.3.

140. Wei Zhenlan, *Guangdong tiyu sishi nian* [Forty Years of Guangdong Sport], p.16.

141. Guijia tiwei xuanchuang bu [Propaganda Department of the NSC], *Tuanjie yu shengli de dahui – di sang jie quanguo yundonghui tongxin ji* [A United and Victorious Sports Meeting – Correspondence of the Third National Games], Beijing: Renmin tiyu chuban she, 1976, p.20.

142. Interview, Beijing, 1996.
143. A massacre was initiated by the 'Industrial Army' of Chengdu in Sichuan. In one clash, some 50 people were killed (see Liu Guokai, Anita Chan (ed.), *A Brief Analysis of the Cultural Revolution*, New York: M.E. Sharpe, Inc., 1987, p.135).
144. Class origin was the first qualification for the recruitment of the Party's new members and military servicemen, and for promotions in all organisations. 'Red Five Categories' (*hong wu lei*) were preferable: they comprised poor peasants, lower-middle peasants, workers, People's Liberation Army, and revolutionary cadres.
145. In Sichuan, the gross value of agriculture and industrial production apparently fell by 9.6 per cent and 23.8 per cent respectively, compared to the corresponding national figures of 9.6 per cent and 4.2 per cent. Data from Lijian Hong, 'Sichuan: Disadvantage and mismanagement in the Heavenly Kingdom', David S.G. Goodman (ed.), *China's Provinces in Reform: Class, Community and Political Culture*, London and New York: Routledge, 1997, p.208.
146. *Quanguo tiyu shiye tongji zhiliao huibian 1949–1978* [Collection of Statistical Information on Sport in China, 1949–78)], pp.107; 16.
147. The 'third front' of 1964–71 was a crash programme to build heavy industry in the south-west provinces, of which Sichuan was the core, away from the militarily vulnerable coastal and north-eastern areas. It was a response to perceived external dangers from the United States and the USSR.
148. *Quanguo tiyu shiye tongji zhiliao huibian 1949–1978* [Collection of Statistical Information on Sport in China, 1949–78], p.16.

Chapter 4

1. After Mao's death, the Gang of Four were put into jail. Factories began to return to normal production. Cadres and intellectuals who had been unjustly, falsely or wrongly accused or punished during and before the Cultural Revolution were rehabilitated gradually. In August, 1977, the Party's veteran leader Deng Xiaoping was reinstated to all of his previous posts at the 11th Party Congress. National entrance examinations for universities were resumed in the autumn of 1977.
2. Facing economic decline, administrative paralysis, severe unemployment and under-employment, which were the direct results of the Cultural Revolution, the third plenum decisively declared the goal of building socialism through the 'four modernisations' drive.
3. The primary tasks facing China were to expand rural incomes and incentives, to encourage experiments in enterprise autonomy, to reduce central planning, to establish direct foreign investment and to accelerate the pace of legal reform.
4. On 25 October 1979 the executive committee of the IOC drafted a resolution that the Chinese Olympic Committee was China's legal representative in the organisation. The Taiwan Olympic Committee was regarded as one of its local institutions and remained in the IOC. This resolution was passed by 62 votes to 17 votes one month later.
5. Between 1979 and 1994 Chinese athletes won 775 world titles, accounting for 96 per cent of the total won since the founding of the PRC in 1949.
6. Nian Naihua, 'Jingguo bu ran xumei – xi zhongguo nuzhi yundong xiangmu zhouxian shijie de yuanyin' [Women Are not Inferior to Men – An Analysis of the Reasons for the Rise of Chinese Women's Sport to World Level], *Tiyu bao* [Sports Daily], 9 March 1988; p.2; Liang Yan, 'Cong shuzhi kan xin zhongguo nvzi tiyu' [Data Reveal Women's Sport in New China], *Gongren bao* [Workers' Daily], 9 March 1988, p.4; Xin Jin, 'Zhongguo tiantan "yinsheng yangshuai" de san da qushi' [Three Major Inspirations Concerning the 'Female Wax and Male Wane' in China's Athletics], *Xin tiyu* [New Sport], 1988 (4), pp.32–3.

7. The system of household responsibility – the first step in decollectivisation – was gradually diffused from a few experimental counties to the whole country and greatly stimulated peasant entrepreneurial initiatives. Peasants were allowed to transfer contracted land to other skilled farms. They now had freedom to organise their time, and to engage in processing specific products or in non-farming activities.

8. Private and corporate enterprises increased from 1 million in 1981 to almost 3.4 million in 1984. For the details, see Craig Dietrich, *People's China: A Brief History* (2nd edn), Oxford: Oxford University Press, 1994, p.245.

9. Guojia tongji ju [State Statistical Bureau], '1984 nian quanguo shehui jingji fazhang gongbao' [Communiqué on National Economic and Social Development in 1984], *Renmin ribao* [The People's Daily], 9 March 1985.

10. The 'four big items' of watch, radio, sewing machine and bicycle in the 1970s were gradually replaced by colour television set, refrigerator, washing machine and video recorder.

11. Guojia tiwei wenshi si [Literature And History Department of the NSC], *Tiwei xitong zhiliao tongji* [Statistical Information of the Sports Community] (unpublished document), 1992, p.12.

12. Zhang Sunquan et al., 'Wuoguo tiyu sheshi jianshe de lilun yanjiu' [Theoretical Studies on the Building of Sports Facilities in China], *Tiyu kexue* [Sports Science], 1991 (1), pp.1–5.

13. A. Doak Barnett and Ralph N. Clough (eds), *Modernizing China: Post-Mao Reform and Development*, Boulder, CO: Westview Press, 1986, p.1.

14. Harry Harding, *China's Second Revolution: Reform after Mao,* Washington, DC: Brookings, 1987, pp.199–200.

15. Zhongguo tiyu nianjian bianji weiyuan hui [The Editorial Committee of Sports Yearbooks in China], *Zhongguo tiyu nianjian 1979* [Sports Yearbook in China, 1979], Beijing: Renmin tiyu chuban she, 1981, p.906.

16. Zhang Caizhen, 'Gaige ge zhongguo tiyu dailai le shenme [What Has the Reform Brought to Chinese Sport?], *Xin tiyu* [New Sport], 1992 (4), pp.4–6.

17. The third plenum decided to decentralise decision-making and control to promote enterprise autonomy. Meanwhile, the state endeavoured to smash the 'iron rice bowl' (*tie fanwan*) of expensive welfare benefits and guaranteed lifetime employment. As a result, market forces played a more and more important part and worker's wages were much more closely tied to efficiency of production.

18. Due to the emergence of panic buying and high inflation in early 1987 China had to temporarily suspend efforts to free prices. Not until June 1988 did China again free urban food and commodity prices. The government had to take strong measures to cool the overheated economy.

19. Lan Yan, 'Nvpai bingbai, shichu youyin' [The Defeat of Women's Volleyball Has Reasons], in Shi Hangbo (ed.), *Zhongguo tiyu de fengfeng yuyu* [Issues in Chinese Sport], Beijing nongye daxue chuban she, 1990, p.130.

20. Connie Squires Meaney, 'Market Reform and Disintegrative Corruption in Urban China', in Richard Baum (ed.), *Reform and Reaction in Post-Mao China,* London: Routledge, 1991, pp.137–8.

21. 'Shehui zhuyi tiyu de hualei – qiye he gaoxiao ban gao shuiping yundong dui' [Buds of Socialised Sports – Industrial Enterprises and Institutions of Higher Learning Run High-Level Sports Teams], Guojia tiwei [The NSC] (ed.), *Zhongguo tiyu nianjian 1986* [Sports Yearbook in China, 1986], Beijing: Renmin tiyu chuban she, 1987, p.10.

22. Tan Hua, 'Shi lun tiyu tizhi gaige de qianjing ji duice' [Prospects for Strategy of Sports System Reform], *Tiyu yu kexue* [Sports and Science], 1988 (1), p.21.

23. Guojia tiwei lianhe diaocha zhu [United Survey Group of the NSC], 'Guanyu 12 ge quanguo xing dangxiang yundong xiehui shiti hua gaige shidian qingkuang de diaocha' [Surveys of the Situation of 'Experimented' Reform of Turning the 12 Individual Sports Associations into Entities], Guojia tiwei zhengce fagui shi [The

Policy and Law Dept. of the NSC] (ed.), *Tiyu dangxiang xiehui shiti hua gaige yangtao wenji* [Collection of Papers on the Reform of Turning Individual Sports Associations into Entities], Beijing tiyu daxue chuban she, 1994, p.9.

24. The head coach had to be responsible for the comprehensive activities of training, competition and the management of political and educational affairs.

25. Zhang Caizhen, 'Gaige ge zhongguo tiyu dailai le shenme [What Has the Reform Brought to Chinese Sport?]

26. Guojia tiwei [The NSC], 'Ji wu qijian tiyu bixu jianchi gaige, kuochong daolu, zhixin fenlei zhidao yi qude gengda de chengjiu – quanguo tiwei zhuren gongzuo huiyi baogao'[During the Seventh Five-Year Period Sport Must Insist on Reform, Further Development and Conduct Management According to the Characteristics of Sports in order to Make Greater Progress – Reports of the National Meeting of Sports Commissions Directors], *Tiyu gongzuo qingkuang fanying* [Reflections on the Situation of Sports Affairs], 9 (April 1986), p.7.

27. Inflation at that time reached the highest level since 1949: in June 1988 the official rate was 19 per cent, but unofficially and more realistically, it was close to 40 per cent.

28. To ease the pain of the price reform, a two-track price system was introduced for a number of key commodities, namely fixed state-set prices for planned deliveries and flexible prices for above-plan production. This policy provided opportunities for official corruption.

29. In 1986 procuratorial organs handled 82,591 economic cases, a 54 per cent increase over the previous year. For the details, see Zuigao renming jiancha yuan gongzuo baogao [Work Report of the Supreme People's Procuratorate], *Zhongguo fazhi bao* [The China Legal Daily], 6 April 1987.

30. University students and other citizens in Beijing camped out in Tiananmen Square to mourn the death of Hu Yaoban, a leading advocate of reform, who had been blamed for the students' protests at the end of 1986 and forced to resign as the CCP General Secretary in January 1987. At the same time students protested against those who would slow down reform, and called for an end to official corruption and for the protection of freedoms guaranteed by the Chinese Constitution. Demonstrations also took place in many other cities including Shanghai, Chengdu and Guangzhou. Martial law was declared on 20 May 1989. Late on 3 June and early on 4 June, military units were brought into Beijing. They used armed force to clear demonstrators from the streets. There are no official estimates of deaths in Beijing, but most observers believe that casualties can be numbered in the hundreds.

31. International sports exchanges, especially those with the West, were cut short in the first two years after the suppression of the student movement.

32. John Gittings, *Real China: from Cannibalism to Karaoke*, Simon & Schuster, 1996, p.290.

33. For the details, see Guojia tongji ju [State Statistic Bureau] (ed.), *Zhongguo tongji nianjian* [Chinese Statistical Yearbook], zhongguo tongji chuban she, 1999, p.55.

34. The four zones are Shenzhen, Zhuhai, Shantou and Xiamen. They are situated in coastal areas near Hong Kong and Taiwan, where joint venture companies and even foreign-owned enterprises exist. They have opened up new opportunities for many Chinese.

35. The 14 coastal cities are Dalian, Qinhuangdao, Tianjin, Yantai, Qingdao, Lianyungang, Nantong, Shanghai, Ningbo, Wenzhou, Fuzhou, Guangzhou, Zhanjiang and Beihai.

36. Between 1978 and 1986 China's trade with foreign countries increased two and half times. It imported foreign technology valued at nearly $10 billion, attracted more than $8 billion in foreign investment and borrowed more than $20 billion from international financial markets and institutions (see Harding, *China's Second Revolution*, p.170).

37. Keun Lee, 'Making Another East Asian Success In China', in Chung H.Lee and

Helmut Recsen (eds), *From Reform to Growth: China and Other Countries in Transition in Asia and Central and Eastern Europe*, Paris: Organisation for Economic Cooperation and Development, 1994, p.186.

38. Luan Jujie ranked second at the youth world fencing championships in 1978 and the world fencing championships in 1981. She became an Olympic champion in 1984. Chen Xiaoxia won the women's platform diving title in 1979. Gao Fenglian won the world judo championships successively between 1986 and 1989. Wu Lanying broke shooting world records many times between 1981 and 1989.

39. She was interviewed in Beijing in June 1997.

40. They include the 1981 and 1985 World Cup, the 1984 Olympics, and the 1982 and 1986 world championships.

41. Zhao Yu, *Bingbai hancheng – Zhaoyu Tie Wenti baogao wenxue ji* [Defeat in Seoul –The Reports of Zhao Yu Tie Wenti], Beijing: Zhongguo shehui kexue chuban she, 1988, p.10.

42. The final game was between China and Japan. China would be champions provided they won two sets, no matter whether they defeated Japan or not. The Chinese women won the first two sets of the game, becoming too excited to concentrate on the remaining part of the game. As a result, they lost two sets in a row, which put them in a crucial position.

43. Rong Gaotang (ed.), *Dangdai zhongguo tiyu* [Contemporary Chinese Sport], Beijing: zhongguo shehui kexue chuban she, 1984, p.198.

44. Ibid.; Susan Brownell, *Training the Body for China: Sports in the Moral Order of the People's Republic*, Chicago,IL, and London: University of Chicago Press, 1995.

45. John Bale and Joe Sang, *Kenyan Running: Movement Culture, Geography and Global Change*, London: Frank Cass, 1996, p.39.

46. Tiyu zhangyue fazhang hui [Society of Sports Development and Strategic Research] (ed.), *Zhongguo tiyu nianjian 1985* [Sports Yearbook in China 1985], Renmin tiyu chuban she, 1986, p.16.

47. There were five competitive sport departments and a comprehensive department. Each competitive sport department took charge of one major sport or several similar small sports. For example, the first *shi* was responsible for ball games; the second *shi* was in charge of athletics, the third *shi* was for swimming and winter sports, and the fourth *shi* covered gymnastics, chess, weightlifting and so on.

48. Howard G. Knuttgen (ed.), *Sport in China*, Champaign, IL: Human Kinetics Books, 1990, p.111.

49. Guojia tiwei jihua caiwu si [Planning and Finance Department of the NSC], *Tiyu shiye tongji nianjian (neibu ziliao)* [Statistical Yearbook of Sport (internal information)], 1994, p.44.

50. Ibid., p.3.

51. Lin Shuying, '1987 Nian tiyu gaige de yi dabu' [A Big Stride in Sports Reform in 1987], Tiyu zhangyue fazhang hui [Society of Sports Development and Strategic Research] (ed.), *Zhongguo tiyu nianjian 1987* [Sports Yearbook in China,1987], Renmin tiyu chuban she, 1988, pp.133–4.

52. Shang Qiu et al., 'Gefu gezhong kunnan, zai huo jinpai zhongshu diyi – di shijie yayunhui zhongguo tiyu daibiao tuan de biaogao' [Overcoming Various Difficulties and Regaining First Place in the Gold Medal Count – Report of Chinese Sports Delegation at the 10th Asian Games], *Tiyu gongzuo qingkuang fanying* [Reflections on the Sports Situation], 24 (November 1986), p.13.

53. Editorial, 'Tiyu jie de yici duihua' [A Dialogue in the Sports Community], *Tiyu luntan* [Sports Forum], 1988 (1), p.9.

54. According to a poll on how many gold medals the Chinese would win, co-sponsored by China's *Sports Daily* and the American Kouda Company, only 1,536 out of 200,000 respondents predicted five or fewer gold medals going into Chinese pockets (Zhao Yu, *Bingbai hancheng* [Defeat in Seoul], p.9.

55. Guojia tiwei [The NSC], *Zhongguo tiyu nianjian 1986* [Sports Yearbook, 1986], p.3.
56. It is the title of a literary work by Zhao Yu – see note 41.
57. Li Hepu, '88 nian aoyunhui hou renmin riyi quexing de tiyu quanli yishi: tiyu gaige de nandian' [The Increasingly Awakening Consciousness of Sport after the 1988 Olympic Games: The Difficult Issues of Sports Reform], *Tiyu* [Sport], 1989 (7), p.11.
58. Zhao Yu, 'Qiangguo meng – dangdai zhongguo tie de wuqu' [Superpower Dream– Traps of Contemporary Chinese Sport], *Dangdai* [Contemporary], 1988 (2). It was republished as a monograph, and examples were published in more than 30 newspapers and magazines across the country.
59. Su Xuewen, Liu Ping et al., *Zhongguo ren 'dabai' zhongguo ren* [Chinese 'Defeat' Chinese], Beijing: Huayi chuban she, 1993, pp.306–7.
60. Dong Xinguang et al., 'Dui aoyun zhanlue xiangmu touru jiegou de fenxi yu duice jianyi' [An Analysis of the Investment Structure of the Olympic Strategy: Opinions about Relevant Measures], *Tiyu kexue* [Sports Science], 13, 4 (1993), p.8.
61. 'Zhongguo jianshe tiyu qiangguo yao zhuanghao "liangge zhanlue" – benbao zhaokai de lilun taolun hui fayang zhaiyao' [China Must Insist on the 'Two Strategies' to Become a Sports Power – Extracts of Speeches in the Theoretic Seminar Held by Sports Daily], *Tiyu bao* [Sports Daily], 2 May 1988, p.2.
62. '1989 nian quanguo tiwei zhuren huiyi dui tiyu jianguo, jingpai yishi, qunzhong tiyu yu jingji tiyu xietiao fazhang de yixie yilun [Discussions on Becoming a Sports Power, Gold-Medal Awareness, the Harmonious Development of Mass Sport and Elite Sport in the Conference of the National Sports Commissions' Directors], *Tiyu luntan* [Sports Forum], 1989 (3), pp.2–3.
63. Zhang Caizhen, 'Gaige ge zhongguo tiyu dailai le shenme [What Has the Reform Brought to Chinese Sport?], pp.4–6.
64. They won 16.5 gold meals in table tennis between 1979 and 1987 (men won only one) and 25 and 14 world titles respectively in badminton and diving. They also created world records in walking, shooting and weightlifting as well as judo, fencing, basketball and football. In 1987 the nation's 'Best Ten Athletes' in athletics were all women.
65. Guojia tiwei jihua caiwu si [Planning and Finance Department of the NSC], *Tiyu shiye tongji nianjian* [Statistical Yearbook], pp.18–21.
66. Interviewee Luo Ping is a professor of sociology in Wuhan University in Hubei province.
67. The interview took place in Beijing in June 1995.
68. The practice of conceding to team-mates can be traced back to the 26th world championships in 1961. At the time team leaders decided who should win or lose, even when the semi-final players were all Chinese in the men's competition. By the late 1980s this practice continued when Chinese competed against foreign rivals (see Liang Zuoxun, 'Cong "ran qiou" tanqi' [About 'Conceding to Rivals'], *Tiyu luntan* [Sports Forum], 1989 (6), pp.23–4).
69. Jennifer Hargreaves, *Sporting Females – Critical Issues in the History and Sociology of Women's Sports*, London: Routledge, 1994, p.289.
70. A. Doak Barnett and R.N. Clough, *Modernising China: Post-Mao Reform and Development*, Boulder, CO, and Oxford: Westview Press, 1986, p.20.
71. *Zhongguo tiyu bao* [China Sports Daily] first published an article in early August 1988 in which the head coach of the national table tennis team explained the reasons for He Zhili's removal from the team. Later it published another article written by a consultant for the team. Based on evidence, she questioned the decision to remove He from the team. Immediately, X*inhua she* [Xinhua News Agency], *Jiefan ribao* [Liberation daily] and *Guangming ribao* [Gguangzhou Daily] all joined the debate on the issues of fair competition, an athlete's individuality and the national interest.
72. 'About the bikini', *China Sports*, 1987 (3), p.13.
73. Ibid.

74. Sun Qinmei, 'Chenggong laizi dui shiye de zhizhu zuqiu' [Success Comes from Unrelenting Pursuit], in Guojia tiwei xuanchuan bu [Propaganda Department of the NSC] (ed.), *96 aoyun pinbo zhi ge* [Battle and Fighting Songs at the 1996 Olympic Games], Renmin tiyu chuban she, 1997, pp.171–2.

75. 'Nvzu xuyao guanai' [Women's Football Needs Attention], *Titan zhoubao* [Sports Weekly], 23 March 1999, p.3.

76. Chou Ming enrolled in the Beijing Institute of Physical Education in 1977 and passed the entrance examination for postgraduates in 1979. After he graduated in 1982 he started to coach the national swimming team and trained a number of world champions including Zhuang Yong and Le Jingyi.

77. Guojia tiwei wenshi si [Literature And History Department of the NSC], *Tiwei xitong zhiliao tongji* [Statistical Information], p.10.

78. 'Guojia tiwei tiyu tizhi gaige de queding (caoan)' [The NSC's Decision to Reform Sports System (draft)], Guojia tiwei [The NSC] (ed.), *1986 zhongguo tiyu nianjian* [Sports Yearbook in China], Beijing: Renmin tiyu chuban she, 1987, pp.75–87.

79. Godwin C. Chu and Yanan Ju, *The Great Wall in Ruins – Communication and Cultural Change in China*, Albany, NY: State University of New York Press, 1993, p.80.

80. Historically, and especially during the 800 years between the Song and Qing dynasties, Chinese intellectuals admired book knowledge and disparaged sports, and generally had rather weak physiques. They aimed at reaching high official positions through lengthy education and success in the imperial examinations. The sports ground was replaced by the examination hall.

81. Brownell, *Training the Body for China*, p.203.

82. Damlen McElroy, 'China's Little Emperors Fight Battle of the Bulge', *The Scotsman*, 23 Sep. 2000.

83. In 1978, China started to pursue agricultural reforms. The household responsibility system, which allowed peasants greater decision-making in agricultural activities, was introduced to help increase productivity and expand rural income and incentives. As a result, the commune system created during the Great Leap Forward in the late 1950s was dismantled in the early 1980s and rural per-capita real income apparently doubled.

84. Jan S. Prybyla, *Reform in China and Other Socialist Economies,* Washington, DC: The AEI Press, 1990.

85. Guojia tiwei wenshi si [Literature and History Department of the NSC], *Tiwei xitong zhiliao tongji* [Statistical Information], p.11.

86. Ibid.

87. Chu and Ju, *The Great Wall in Ruins*, p.112.

88. In Liaoning and many other places, some parents sent their children to sports schools to receive training on the basis of self-financing training events and coaching fees.

89. About 15,189 participants competed in 34 sports at the games. As a result, 11 world and 102 national records were broken. Meanwhile, a number of young sports stars emerged, including the volleyball player Lan Ping and gymnast Liu Yajun (see Tiyu Zidian bianji weiyuan hui [The Sports Dictionary Editorial Committee], *Tiyu zidian* [Sports Dictionary], Shanghai zidian chuban she, 1984, p.641).

90. Mou Junqing, 'Nuli fenjin, zaizhan hongtu – Beijing shi dangwei he zhengfu juxing tiyu gongzuo huiyi' [Strive to Advance and Recreate Great Prospects – Beijing Municipal Party Commission and Government Holds a Meeting on Sport], *Tiyu gongzuo qingkuang fanying* [Reflections on the Sports Situation], 4 (February 1986), pp.3–4.

91. Lu Yuanzhen and Lai Tiande, 'Dui Beijing shi quefa gao shuiping yundongyuan de shehui xue fenxi' [Sociological Analysis of the Lack of High Level Athletes in Beijing], in Beijing tiyu daxue keyan chu [Beijing University of Physical Education] (ed.), *Beijing tiyu daxue 45 nian xiaoqin kexue lunwen xuan* [Selection of Scientific

Papers for the 45th Anniversary of Beijing University of Physical Education], Beijing tiyu daxue chuban she, 1998, pp.168–73.

92. It was required that three half-days and three evenings were given to academic studies, but teaching periods were flexible in accordance with sports training and competition arrangements. Each subject had a certificate. Coaches were also encouraged to undertake academic studies. Reviews of coaches were organised once a year (Lin Yishan, 'Guanyu Beijing shi yiuxiu yundongdui wenhua jiaoyu naru jiaoyu jiegou gaige de diaocha' [A Survey of the Integration of the Academic Education of Elite Sports Teams into the Mainstream Educational Structure in Beijing], *Tiyu gongzuo qingkuang* [The Situation of Sports Affairs], 14–15 (July 1992), p.29).

93. The system of wages changed to structural scholarships consisting of studentships, study and training rewards, performance reward and retirement funds.

94. Ma Guitian, 'Jiefang sixiang, shenhua gaige, jiaqiang guanli, cujin Beijing shi tiyu yundong xietiao fazhan' [Liberating Thought, Expanding Reform, Strengthening Management and Promoting the Harmonious Development of Sport in Beijing], in Beijing shi tiwei [Beijing Sports Commission] (ed.), *Beijing tiyu nianjian 1992–93* [Beijing Sports Yearbooks 1992–3], Beijing: renmin tiyu chuban she, 1993, pp.5–6.

95. Liang Shiyin et al., 'Dui Beijing shi tiwei tigong dui bang zhuren fuzhe zhi xia de zhu jiaolian zheren zhi de diaocha' [A Survey of the Head Coach Responsibility System Under the Leadership of the Class Director in Beijing Municipal Sports Teams], *Tiyu gongzuo qingkuang* [The Situation of Sports Affairs], 13 (July 1992), pp.12–13.

96. Lin Shuying et al., 'Beijing tiyu gaige de shijian he kangfa' [Ideas and Practice of Sports Reforms in Beijing], *Tiyu gongzuo qingkuang fanying* [Reflections on the Sports Situation], 64 (March 1988), p.3.

97. Those who had once trained world, Asian or national champion athletes could get bonuses equivalent to 70 per cent of the pay of current coaches.

98. Guojia tiwei jihua caiwu si [Planning and Finance Department of the NSC], *Tiyu shiye tongji nianjian* [Statistical Yearbook], p.44.

99. Ibid., p.19.

100. Beijing spent five years preparing for the 1990 Asian Games, which greatly changed its appearance. In addition to the Asian Games Village with news centre, athletes' complex, entertainment palace and big hotels, 31 sports fields and stadiums and 46 training areas were built and refurbished. With the construction of new roads and flyovers in different parts of the city, a traffic network centring around the Asian Games Village and radiating out to all competition venues was formed. Computer communication and correspondence systems were all installed within five years (Yayunhui zhuwei hui [The Organising Committee of the Asian Games] (ed.), *1990 nian Beijing di yi jian yazhou yundonghui gongzuo baogao* [Working Report of the 1990 Asian Games in Beijing], Zhongguo aolinpike chuban she, 1992, p.120).

101. The Chinese government allotted 1.047 billion yuan and credited 0.23 billion yuan to the organising committee of the Asian Games in Beijing. The Beijing Municipal Government provided 0.58 billion yuan, and various counties and districts of Beijing donated about 0.7 billion yuan (Yayunhui zhuwei hui [The Organising Committee of the Asian Games], p.122).

102. Huang Zhenzhong, 'Funds Collection: the Concern of the Whole Nation', *China Sports*, 1990 (5), pp.2–3.

103. Beijing shi tiwei [Beijing Sports Commission], *Beijing tiyu nianjian 1992–93*, p.147.

104. Chen Wuan, 'Guangdong tiwei yi zhangyue yianguang guanzhu yeyu xunlian' [Guangdong Sports Commission Strategically Pays Attention To Amateur Training], *Tiyu gongzuo qingkuang fanying* [Reflections on the Sports Situation], 5 (March 1986), p.12.

105. Ye C., Guangdong tiyu xingzheng jigou yuan ge [The Evolution of Sports Administration in Guangdong], *Guangdong tiyu shiliao* [Guangdong Sports History Information], 1996 (2), p.8.

106. Of the top ten cities, assessed in 1990 in terms of social development in China, four were situated in the Pearl River delta. For the details, see Stewart Macpherson and Joseph Y.S. Cheng (eds.), *Economic and Social Development in South China*, Cheltenham: Edward Elgar, 1996, p.9.

107. Y.M. Yeung, 'Introduction', in Y.M. Yeung and David K.Y. Chu (eds), *Guangdong: Survey of a Province Undergoing Rapid Change*, Hong Kong: Chinese University Press, 1996, pp.7–11.

108. Zhongguo Tongjiju [Chinese Statistics Bureau], *Zhongguo tongji nianjian 1992* [Statistics Yearbook in China, 1992], Beijing: Zhongguo tongji chuban she, 1993, p.3.

109. Guojia tiwei jihua caiwu si [Planning and Finance Department of the NSC], *Tiyu shiye tongji nianjian* [Statistical Yearbook], p.45.

110. Wei Zhenlan, 'Gaige kaifan zhong de guangdong tiyu'[Guangdong Sport in the Period of Reform and 'Opening Up' to the Outside], *Tiyu wenshi* [Sport History], 59, 1 (1993), pp.56–8.

111. Ibid.

112. Guojia tiwei jihua caiwu si [Planning and Finance Department of the NSC], *Tiyu shiye tongji nianjian* [Statistical Yearbook], p.19.

113. Li Guoshun, Guangdong zhuqou yundong shi [Football History in Guangdong], *Guangdong tiyu shiliao* [Guangdong Sports History Information], 1992 (3), pp.53–4.

114. Wei Zhenlan (ed.), *Guangdong tiyu sishi nian* [Forty Years of Guangdong Sport], Guangzhou: Xin shiji chuban she, 1989.

115. Li Guoshun, Guangdong zhuqou yundong shi [Football History in Guangdong].

116. Ye Chulin, 'Guangdong tiyu xingzheng jigou yuange' [The Evolution of Sports Administration in Guangdong], *Guangdong tiyu shiliao* [Guangdong Sports History Information], 1996 (2), p.12.

117. Li lanfang, 'Quan shehui canru peiyan tiyu rencai' [All Sectors of Society are Involved in Producing Sports Talents], in Wei Zhenlan, *Guangdong tiyu sishi nian* [Forty Years of Guangdong Sport], p.33.

118. Zhou Feijing, 'Shengzhen shi dui zhangzhu tiyu danwei he geren geiyu shihui' [Shengzhen Rewards the Enterprises and Private Organisations that Sponsor Sport], *Tiyu gongzuo qingkuang* [The Situation of Sports Affairs], 13 (July 1992), p.7.

119. Shiliao zhu [Historical Information Group], 'Shanzhong quanhui qianhou wuosheng tiyu fazhan bianhua zhuangkuang' [Sports Changes and Development in Guangdong after the Third Plenum], *Guangdong tiyu shiliao* [Guangdong Sports History Information], 1992 (3), p.15.

120. Wang Pingshan, 'Guanyu wuosheng yundong gongzuo qingkuang huibao' [Report on Sports Development in Guangong], *Guangdong tiyu shiliao* [Guangdong Sports History Information], 1987 (3), pp.1–4.

121. 'Di er zhang: Jinji tiyu' [Chapter 2: competitive sport], *Sichuan shezhi: tiyu zhi* [Sichuan Provincial Record: Sports Record].

122. Guojia tiwei jihua caiwu si [Planning and Finance Department of the NSC], *Tiyu shiye tongji nianjian* [Statistical Yearbook], p.19.

123. Zhu Chuandao et al., 'Yi shenhua gaige wei dongli, ba wuosheng tiyu shiye tuixiang yige xin de fazhan jieduan – Sichuan tiyu shiye fazhan de jiben zhuangkuang he 1988–1992 nian fazhan mubiao yu cuoshi'[Add Momentum to Reform and Raise Sichuan Sport to a New Level – the Basic Situation of Sichuan Sports Development and the Goals and Measures for the 1988–92 Period], *Sichuan tiyu kexue* [Sichuan Sports Science], 1988 (4), p.8.

124. Guojia tiwei jihua caiwu si [Planning and Finance Department of the NSC], 1994, op. cit.

125. Zhu Chuandao, 'Yi shenhua gaige wei dongli, ba wuosheng tiyu shiye tuixiang yige xin de fazhan jieduan' [Add Momentum to Reform and Raise Sichuan Sport to a New Level], p.7.

126. Ibid.
127. Sichuan tiwei qunti chu [Mass Sport Department of Sichuan Sports Commission], Fazhang zhigong tiyu de yizhong hao xingshi – shi da qiye jian tiyu hezuo de qingkuang [A Good Means of Developing Workers' Sports – Sports Cooperation between the Ten Big Enterprises], *Tiyu gongzuo qingkuang fanying* [Reflections on the Sports Working Situation], 6 (March 1986), pp.2–6.
128. Lijian Hong, 'Sichuan: Disadvantage and Mismanagement in the Heavenly Kingdom', in David S.G. Goodman (ed.), *China's Provinces in Reform: Class, Community and Political Culture*, London: Routledge, 1997, p.200.
129. Zhu Chuandao, 'Yi shenhua gaige wei dongli, ba wuosheng tiyu shiye tuixiang yige xin de fazhan jieduan' [Add Momentum to Reform and Raise Sichuan Sport to a New Level], p.8.

Chapter 5

1. Paramount leader Deng Xiaoping visited the south of China in early 1992. He praised the development of Shengzhen, the most important of the four specialised economic zones initiated in 1980. Because of his personal view that the market system was not incompatible with the idea of socialism, he called for the establishment of a socialist market economy, which was an important ideological breakthrough.
2. In 1993 the gross domestic product (GDP) reportedly reached 3,138 billion yuan, an increase of 18.2 per cent over 1992, in spite of the rise in the cost-of-living average by 10.2 per cent and 3.2 per cent respectively for urban and rural inhabitants.
3. Guojia tiwei zhengce fagui si [Policy and Law Bureau of the NSC] (ed.), *Zouxiang 21 shiji de sikao—quanguo tiwei xitong lingdao ganbu lunwen ji* [Reflections on Approaching the 21st Century – Collection of Papers Written by Leading Cadres in the Sports Community Across the Country], Beijing tiyu daxue chuban she, 1996.
4. The most illustrative is the 'ping-pong diplomacy' discussed in Chapter 3.
5. Nicholos D. Kristof and Sheryl WuDunn, *China Wakes – the Struggle for the Soul of a Rising Power*, London: Nicholas Brealey, 1994, p.54; Zheng Fa, 'Deep Effects of the Beijing Asian Games', *China Sports*, 1992 (5), p.35.
6. At the Games Chinese athletes won 183 out of the 310 gold medals (60 per cent) in 29 sports, and broke several world records and over 100 Asian records.
7. Xu Qi, 'A New Height in Beijing', *China Sports*, 1992 (10), pp.36–7.
8. Chen Jinhua, '1993 nian quanguo jingji shehui fazhan jihua wancheng qingkuang de baogao ji 1994 nian quanguo jingji shehui fazhan jihua de caoan' [A Report on the Implementation of the 1993 National Economic and Social Developmental Plan (NESDP) and a Draft of the 1994 NESDP], *Renmin ribao* [People's Daily], 25 March 1994.
9. Guojia tiwei [NSC] (ed.), *Zhongguo tiyu nianjian, 49-91 jinghua ben* (xia ce)[China's Sports Yearbooks, 49–91 (vol.2)], Beijing: Renmin tiyu chuban she, 1993, p.202.
10. Guojia tiwei jihua caiwu si [Planning and Finance Department of the NSC], *Tiyu shiye tongji nianjian (neibu ziliao)* [Statistical Yearbook of Sport] (internal information), 1994, pp.20–3.
11. Zhang Yao, '1995 nian wuoguo shengqushi suoshu youxiu yundongdui qingkung fenxi' [Analysis of Provincial, Autonomous and Municipal Elite Sports Teams in 1995], *Tiyu gongzuo qingkuang* [The Situation of Sports Affairs], 610, 2 (1996), pp.6–8.
12. Before the end of the games, it was virtually impossible to predict results. When Ma Junren's athletes dominated the 1,500-metre and 3,000-metre races and gave Liaoning a number of medals, Shanghai's promising prospects were severely challenged.
13. The first eight provinces at the eighth National Games in the points tally were Shanghai, Liaoning, Guangdong, Shangdong, Beijing (The Army), Jinagshu, Sichuan and Henan.

14. Jin Zhan, 'Xuannian dengshen de quanyun zuoci zhizheng' [Unpredictable Rankings at the National Games], *Tiyu wenzai zhoubao* [Sports Digest Weekly], 482 (1997), p.1.
15. 'Wu Shaozu zhuren zai quanguo tiwei zhuren zuotan hui kaimushi shang de jianhua' [Speech By Wu Shaozu, director of the State Sports Commission, at the Opening Ceremony of the National Forum of Sports Commission Directors] (13 Nov. 1993), Guojia tiwei zhengce fagui si [Policy and Law Bureau of the NSC] (ed.), *Tiyu gaige wenjian xuanbian* [Collection of Documents on Sports Reform] (1992–95) (internal information), 1996, p.22.
16. Tan Hua, 'Shi lun tiyu tizhi gaige de qianjing ji duice'[Prospects for Strategy of Sports System Reform], *Tiyu yu kexue* [Sports and Science], 1988 (1), p.21.
17. Guojia tiwei [The NSC], 'Guojia tiwei guanyu shenhua tiyu gaige de yijian (1993)' [Opinions of the NSC on the Expansion of Sports Reform], Guojia tiwei [the NSC] (ed.), *Zhonghua renmin gongheguo tiyu fagui huibian* (1993–6) [Collection of Sports Laws and Regulations of the PRC], Xinhua chuban she, 1997, pp.11-45.
18. For the details, see Appendix 8.
19. There were five such departments under the NSC. The first *shi*, also called 'ball games *shi*', was responsible for the affairs of volleyball, football, basketball, handball and so on.
20. 'Wu Shaozu zhuren zai 1995 nian quanguo tiwei zhuren huiyi shang de zhongjie jianhua [Speech by Director Wu Shaozu at the 1995 National Forum of Sports Commission Directors)', Guojia tiwei zhengce fagui si [Policy and Law Bureau of the NSC] (ed.), 1996, p.57.
21. Wu Shouzang, 'Bayun jinchui gaige fen' [The Eighth National Games Promote Reforms], *Xin tiyu* [New Sport], 1997 (5), p.20.
22. 'Wu Shaozu zhuren zai 1995 nian quanguo tiwei zhuren huiyi shang de zhongjie jianhua' [Speech of Director Wu Shaozu in the 1995 Forum of Directors of Sports Commissions throughout the Country].
23. For example, in 1994 the head coach of Liaoning Far-East Football Club had a monthly salary of 3,000 yuan (about 350 US dollars), and players earned between 1,200 and 2,800 yuan. The playing bonus for each match was 300 yuan and the winning bonus was 2,000 yuan per person. With food subsidies of 900 yuan, a major player could earn 100,000 yuan a year (Xiao Mingweng, 'Liaoning yuandong zhuqiu julebu qiuyuan shoury zhi duoshao?' [Revelations about the Earnings of Players of Liaoning Far East Football Club], *Wuhuang shidai zhoukan* [Five Circles Times], 1994 (1), pp.21–23.
24. Men obtained 11.5 of the 28 gold medals that the Chinese attained in Sydney. The percentage of 41.1 is lower than the 46 per cent in 1996, but higher than the 35 per cent in the 1992 Olympics.
25. The state, in a break with past practices, agreed to allocate each association or centre the same fixed budget package as in previous years without reference to inflation. Five years later, the association had to finance itself.
26. Those sports commissions that promised first to third places at the Olympic Games would be awarded respectively 100,000, 60,000, and 30,000 yuan bonuses; those sports commissions who promised gold medals at the World Championships would receive 20,000 yuan each, and 10,000 yuan for silver and bronze. Those sports commissions that promised a gold medal at the Asian Games would receive 50,000 yuan.
27. Yang Ming, 'Zhongguo tianjin dachu "chengbao" zuhe quan' [China's Athletics Adopts the 'Contract' Agreement], *Tiyu wenzhai zhoubao* [Sports Digest Weekly], 502 (1998), p.2.
28. Liaoning promised six gold medals at the 1998 Asian Games, one gold medal and two to three medals at the 1999 World Championships and the 2000 Olympic Games respectively. Shangdong and Sichuan expected to win five and four gold medals at the Asian Games respectively, one medal at the World Championships and one medal at the Olympics respectively.
29. Wu Shaozhu, 'Shixin aoyun zhangye yao zhuodao shuoduan zhanxian, tuchu zhong-

dian' [To Implement the Olympic Strategy, Shorten the Battle Line and Concentrate on the Priorities], *Zhongguo tiyu bao* [China Sports Daily], 14 March 1989.

30. Apart from Zhao Yu's *Bingbai hancheng* [Defeat in Seoul], which criticised the Olympic-oriented sports policy, sports officials and academics began to question this policy after the 1988 Olympic Games (see Li Hepu, '88 nian aoyunhui hou renmin riyi juexing de tiyu quanli yishi: tiyu gaige de nandian' [The Increasingly Awakening Consciousness of Sports After the 1988 Olympic Games: The Difficult Issues of Sports Reform], *Tiyu* [Sport], 1989 (7), pp.11–12).

31. Ibid.

32. 'Zhongguo shehui tiyu xiangzhuang diaocha jieguo gongbu' [Promulgation of the Survey Results on Social Sport in China], *Zhongguo tiyu bao* [The China Sports Daily], 8 August 1998, p.1.

33. Public sports stadiums, which used to be privileged places for elite athletes or which were rented out for furniture exhibitions or ballroom dancing in the 1980s and the early 1990s, were now available to the public.

34. 'Sports months', broadcast exercises, aerobic dances, tai ji and other activities have been organised by local and national sports commissions, trade unions and education commissions. A number of families have established fitness facilities at home.

35. Li Hepu and Wang Runzhi, 'Beijing shi tiyu changguang zujian dui gongzhong kaifang' [Beijing Sports Stadium and Fields Gradually Open to Public], *Beijing wanbao* [Beijing Evening News], 13 Sep. 1996, p.7.

36. Beijing shi tiwei [Beijing Sports Commission] (ed.), *1996 Beijing tiyu nianjian* [Beijing Sports Yearbook], Beijing: renmin tiyu chuban she, 1997, p.266.

37. They consisted of the ministers and vice ministers of different ministries in Beijing.

38. Lv Shuting and Wang Yuan, 'Rexian zhong de leng shikao – guanyu nuizhi jinji tiyu yu qunzhong tiyu fancha de shehui xue qushi' [Cool Thinking about a Hot Topic –Sociological Analysis of the Contrast between Women's Competitive and Mass Sport], *Tiyu wenshi* [Sports Literature and History], 1995 (4), p.18.

39. Zhang Tianbai, 'Di 26 Jie aoyunhui ji zhongguo tiyu daibiaotua cansai qingkuang' [The Situation of the Chinese Delegation at the 26th Olympic Games],*Tiyu gongzuo qingkuang* [Situation of Sports Affairs], 624–5, 16–17 (1996), p.14.

40. Yuan Hongheng, 'Zhengqian jinzhen, zhujin gaige – Wu Shouzhang zai aoyun xuanba sai shang de jianhua' [Increase Competition, Promote Reform – Wu Shouzhang's Remarks on the Trials for the Olympic Games], *Beijing wanbao* [Beijing Evening News], 2 June 1996, p.8.

41. Chu Yue, 'Ma jia jun: Zaisheng huo xiaoshi?' [The Ma Family Army: Reborn or Disappeared?] *Dandai tiyu* [Contemporary Sport], March 1995, pp.4–6.

42. For the details, see Chapter 7.

43. On 11 Dec. 1994 Wang Junxia and two other girls went to Ma Junren's office to discuss the issue of bonus distribution. Insulted by Ma, they left without a resolution of the issue after a few hours' intense talk. That evening Wang Junxia and two other athletes left the training centre (Dalian) for home, and others (more than ten athletes) stayed in a hotel close to the training centre for a night. The next day a deputy director of the Liaoning Provincial Sports Commission went to mediate between Ma and his athletes, but no agreement was reached. The deputy director then took all these athletes back to the provincial capital, Shengyan.

44. Nao Qiang, 'Tiyu yu jingqian – cong Ma Jia Jun duiyuan lidui shuokai qi' [Sport and Money – Reflections on the Split in the Ma Family Army], *Beijing guangbo dianshi bao* [Beijing Broadcast and Television Newspaper], 10 Jan. 1995.

45. Shuan Ren, 'Chen Lu he yi zhegang luosan' [Why did Chen Lu Fail in Lausanne?], *Beijing wanbao* [Beijing Evening News], 19 April 1997, p.8.

46. In accordance with state policy on the distribution of winning bonuses, half of the amount goes to the state, and the another half is divided between coaches and athletes. But there is no specific rule for the distribution of other incomes.

47. Chu Yue, 'Ma jia jun: Zaisheng huo xiaoshi?'[The Ma Family Army: Reborn or Disappeared?].

48. Ni Zhiqing, the world high jump recorder in 1972, was sentenced to eight years in jail for accepting 57,000 yuan in bribes. For the details, see Li Jie, 'Qian tiaogao yun-dongyuang Ni Zhingqing shouhui bei panxing' [The Former High Jumper Ni Zhiqing was Sentenced to Jail for Eight Years for Accepting Bribes], *Renmin ribao* [People's Daily], 26 April 1995.

49. Interview, Beijing, 1997.

50. In 1993 Chinese women earned 77 out of the 103 world titles won by Chinese. In 1994 the Chinese broke 41 world records, of which 38 were won by women. Most impressive were women swimmers. In this year they won 12 championships and created five world records at the seventh World Swimming Championships. In 1995 Chinese women broke 11 world records, while their male counterparts broke only two.

51. Xinhua she guonei xinxi bu [The Domestic Information Department of the Xinhua News Agency] (ed.), *Zhonghua Renmin Gongheguo dashi ji* [Documents on the Major Events of the PRC] (1985–88), Xinhua chuban she, 1989, p.361.

52. Yu Jian, *Zhonghua renmin gongheguo lishi jishi: dachao yongdong* [Historic Record of the PRC: Moving Wave] (1990–92), Beijing: Hongqi chuban she, 1994, p.145.

53. Lu Li retired from training and competition immediately after the 1992 Olympic Games. Her parents were afraid that she would develop health problems if she continued training since she had had hepatitis before she participated in the Olympic Games. Of course, this is just one side of the story. Her victory at the Olympic Games won her and her family a fortune. Eventually she enrolled at the Beijing University of Foreign Language Studies to pursue a degree.

54. To prepare for the Olympic Games in 1992, each athlete was given 25 yuan for meals each day and 10 yuan for nutrition expenses.

55. Yu Jian, *Zhonghua renmin gongheguo lishi jishi: dachao yongdong* [Historic Record of the PRC: Moving Wave], pp.160–6.

56. Gordon White, 'The Decline of Ideocracy', in Robert Benewick and Paul Wingrove (eds), *China in the 1990s*, Basingstoke: Macmillan Press, 1995, p.65.

57. Liu's speech at the Beijing University of Physical Education, December 1995.

58. The team won the Asian Championships in 1988, reached the semi-finals in the first World Women's Soccer Championships in 1991and then picked up the Olympic silver medal in 1996.

59. 'Nuvzu xuyao guanan' [Women's Football Needs Attention], *Titan zhoubao* [Sports weekly], 23 March 1999, p.3.

60. Shu Shuicher, 'Zhongguo tiyu jie mianlin shichang jinji de tiaozhang' [Chinese Sport Community Faces the Challenge of the Market Economy], *Cankao xiaoxi* [Reference News], 12 Aug. 1994, p.4.

61. Wang Jiali, 'Nunan shangxin dao heshi' [When Will Women's Basketball Stop Grieving?], *Xin tiyu* [New Sport], 1998 (7), pp.8–11.

62. Wang Jian, 'Tiyu houbei rencai xunlian taidu de fazhang yu bianhua – dui jin 5 nian lai tiyu houbei rencai xunlian taidu de zhuizhong kaocha' [The Development and Changes in Training Attitudes of Young Sporting Talents – a Longitudinal Study of Training Attitudes in Young Sporting Talents in the Past Five Years], Zhongguo tiyu kexue xuehui [Chinese Sports Science Society] (ed.), *Di wu jian quanguo tiyu kexue dahui lunwen zaiyao* [Proceedings of the Fifth National Sports Science Congress], 1997, Beijing, p.33.

63. The interviewee is a coach of the Hebei Provincial Female Volleyball Team. She was interviewed in Beijing, 1995.

64. The NSC decided to integrate the results of the Olympic Games into those of the National Games. An Olympic gold medallist could get points for his/her province in the coming National Games.

65. 'Beijing shi quxian tixiao yeyu xunlian qingkuang diaocha baogao' [Report on

Amateur Training at District and County Level in Beijing], Beijing shi tiwei [Beijing Sports Commission] (ed.), *1995 Beijing tiyu nianjian* [1995 Beijing Sports Yearbook], Beijing: renmin tiyu chuban she, 1996, pp.101–13.

66. In addition, a special television programme documented Olympic history and the measures that Beijing had taken to ensure the success of its bid for the 27th Olympic Games. An exhibition entitled 'A More Open China Looks Forward to the 2000 Olympics' was held at the China Sports Museum. Moreover, a Chinese-language edition of the Olympic Charter was published in Beijing.

67. An overall scheme for the 2000 Beijing Olympics was designed, which included four sports centres, an Olympic village occupying an area of 60 hectares, a press centre covering an area of 100,000 square metres and many other projects. An expressway from the airport to the city and a large railway station were also newly established (Zhang Luya (ed.), *Shiji qing – zhongguo yu aolinpike yundong* [A Century of Contact – China and the Olympics], Renmin tiyu chuban she, 1993, p.204).

68. Dongcheng (east of the city), Xicheng (west of the city), Chongwen, Xuanwu, Chaoyang, Fengtai, Haidian, Shijingshan.

69. Beijing shi tiyu yundong weiyuan hui [Beijing Sports Commission], 'Beijing shi tiyu jiuwu jihua' [The Ninth Five-year Plan of Beijing Sport], Beijing shi tiwei [Beijing Sports Commission] (ed.), *1996 Beijing tiyu nianjian* [1996 Beijing Sports Yearbook], Beijing: renmin tiyu chuban she, 1997, p.73.

70. Ibid., pp.463, 466.

71. After it was revealed in 1999 that Australia had bribed some members of the IOC before the final vote, the Chinese were furious and questioned the reliability of the bid.

72. In the canteen of the Beijing Sports Brigade, three sections were arranged for athletes with different performances. The most expensive food, such as turtle, was for those expected to win gold medals in the coming National Games. The less expensive, but relatively dear food, such as king prawns, was for those with the potential of achieving top three positions in the games. Normal dishes were provided for the others.

73. '1996 nian Beijing shi tiyu gongzuo zhongjie (Annual Summary of Sports Work in Beijing in 1996)', Beijing shi tiwei [The Beijing Sports Commission] (ed.), *1996 Beijing tiyu ninjian* [Beijing Sports Yearbook], Beijing: renmin tiyu chuban she,1997, p.34.

74. Thirty-five Beijing athletes qualified in ten sports and won one gold, 7.5 silver and 0.5 bronze medals – one silver and one bronze were shared with competitors from other provinces (see *1996 Beijing tiyu ninjian* [Beijing Sports Yearbook], p.33).

75. Huo Ju and Li Gan, 'Qingchun yijiu, yingxiong rugu – Beijing nuchu sang laojian suxian' [The Same Youth, the Same Appearance– Sketches of Three Old Female Footballers from Beijing], *Qingnian Bao* [Youth Daily], 22 Oct. 1997.

76. Of the 35 sports clubs in Beijing in 1995, 23 (65 per cent) were established after 1993. They included football (13), basketball and table tennis (four each), tennis and golf (seven each), cycling, horse-riding, motor-racing, long-distance running, and winter swimming (one each). In 1996, registered football clubs numbered 20 in Beijing ('Guanyu Beijing shi tiyu julebu qingkuang de diaocha baogao' [Report on Sports Clubs in Beijing], *1996 Beijing tiyu nianjian* [1996 Beijing Sports Yearbook], pp.63–74).

77. Li Peiyun et al., 'Beijing shi tiyu julebu qingkuang diaocha' [Inquiry into the Situation of Beijing Municipal Sports Clubs], *Tiyu gongzuo qingkuang* [Situation of Sports Affairs], 615, 7 (1996), pp.2–6.

78. *1996 Beijing tiyu nianjian* [1996 Beijing Sports Yearbook], pp.483–5.

79. *Tiyu shiye tongji nianjian (neibu ziliao)* [Statistical Yearbook of Sport], 1994, p.694.

80. *Guangdong nianjian* [Guangdong Yearbook], 1993, p.646.

81. *Tiyu shiye tongji nianjian (neibu ziliao)* [Statistical Yearbook of Sport], 1994, p.694.

82. Shiliao zhu [Historic Document Group], 'Sanzhong quanhui hou woshen tiyu bianhua fazhan qingkuang' [Change and Development in Guangdong's Sport After the Third

Plenary], *Guangdong tiyu wenshi* [Guangdong Sports History Document], 1992 (3), p.2.

83. Wei Zhenlan, 'Gaige kaifang zhong de Guangdong tiyu' [Guangdong Sport in the Period of Reform and Opening up to the Outside], *Tiyu wenshi* [Sport History], 59, 1 (1993), pp.56–8.

84. Zhan Tianxiang and Zhang Junying, 'Zhujiang Sanjiaozhou qishi shehui fazhan pinggu' [An Assessment of the Social Development of Seven Cities in the Pearl River Delta], *Guangdong shehui kexue* [Social Sciences in Guangdong], additional volume, 1992, p.179.

85. Dong Liangtian, 'Shenhua gaige, nuli shixian Guangdong tiyu fazhan mubiao' [Expending Reforms, Striving to Realise Guangdong's Targets of Sports Development], Guojia tiwei zhengce fagui si [Policy and Law Bureau of the NSC] (ed.), 1996, pp. 234–5.

86. *Tiyu shiye tongji nianjian (neibu ziliao)* [Statistical Yearbook of Sport], 1994, pp.152–3.

87. *1996 Beijing tiyu nianjian* [1996 Beijing Sports Yearbook], p.37.

88. *Guangdong tiyu shiliao* [Guangdong Sports Historic Document], 1991 (1).

89. Chen Hanlin and Lin Shiyue, 'Guangdong nuzhi zhuqiou yundong' [Women's Football In Guangdong], *Guangdong tiyu shiliao* [Guangdong Sports Historic Document], 1997 (1), p.21.

90. Wang Xiaotian, 'Ba yun jun tuan [Troops at the National Games], *Tiyu wenhua yuekan* [Sports Cultural Monthly], Oct. 1997, pp.6–8.

91. Guangdong tiyu fanzhang jijin hui, 'Guanyu geiyu cangjia 25 jie aoyunhui qude youyi chengji de yundongyuan jiaolianyuan jianjin jianli de jueding' [A Decision to Reward the Successful Athletes and Coaches at the 25th Olympic Games], *Guangdong tiyu shiliao* [Guangdong Sports History Information], 1992 (3), p.9.

92. Lijian Hong, 'Sichuan: Disadvantage and Mismanagement in the Heavenly Kingdom', in David S.G. Goodman (ed.), *China's Provinces in Reform: Class, Community and Political Culture*, London and New York: Routledge, 1997, pp.199–203.

93. Huang Chenhui, 'Chuan jun didiao dongjin' [Sichuan Army Marches Eastwards With Low Quotas], *Tiyu wenzhai zhoubao* [Sports Weekly], 72 (1997), p.5.

94. Chen Baoming, 'Xin shiqi sichuan tiyu shiye fazhan zhi sikao' [Deliberation on the Development of Sichuan Sport in the New Era], Guojia tiwei zhengce fagui si [Policy and Law Bureau of the NSC] (ed.), 1996, pp.254–5.

95. Guojia tiwei jihua caiwu si [Planning and Finance Department of the NSC], 1994, p.694.

96. At the seventh games, the first place was awarded nine points and the eighth one point. By the eighth games, the first place got 13 points and the eighth five points.

97. Li Hepu, 'Lanyong weijin yaowu, 24 ming yundongyuan shou chufa' [Male Swimmers Were Caught Drug Positive and 24 Athletes Were Published], *Beijing wanbao* [Beijing Evening News], 7 April 1998, p.8.

Chapter 6

1. According to medical sources, there was enough of the drug Somatotropin to serve the entire Chinese team of 23 in Perth for the duration of their stay. Yuan Yuan was banned for four years and her coach for 15 years (Craig Lord, 'Caught Red-Handed – Amid Global Cries of "I Told You So", China Awaits its Fate in the Great Doping Scandal', *Sunday Times*, 11 Jan. 1998).

2. The urine samples of female swimmers Wang Luna, Wang Wei and Cai Huiyu and a male swimmer, Zhang Yi, contained traces of Triamterene, a diuretic that can be used as a masking agent to cover any traces of banned substances. Its use is interpreted as trying to manipulate a test and is therefore read as a positive result.

3. 'Li Tieying zai quanguo tiwei zhuren huiyi shang jianhua sishuo: zhongguo zhengfu

jianjue fandui shiyong xingfenji' [Reflections on Li Tianying's Remarks at the National Conference of Sports Commission Directors], *Zhongguo tiyu bao* [China Sports Daily], 17 Jan. 1998.

4. This work was first published in the magazine *Dangdai* [Contemporary], 1988 (2). The exposure of the dark aspects of Chinese sport, such as false age registration, corruption and drugs, provoked an intense nationwide controversy and debate in the late 1980s.

5. Doping was first reported in modern sport in 1865. After 1879 cyclists favoured ether and caffeine to delay the onset of fatigue sensations. In the 1930s some cyclists used strychnine and other stimulants, which were later adopted by body builders, footballers and track athletes. For the details, see Ellis Cashmore, *Making Sense of Sports* (2nd edn), London and New York: Routledge, 1996, p.150.

6. The Sports Council, 'History of Doping in Modern Sport', in Craig Donnellan (ed.), *Drugs and Violence in Sport: Issues for the Nineties*, no. 26, Cambridge: Independence Educational Publishers, 1995, p.27.

7. Ellis Cashmore, *Making Sense of Sports*, p.149.

8. China decided to establish a drug-testing laboratory in 1985. After four years of preparation and experiment, it successfully passed the IOC's standards and became the 20th qualified lab in the world (see Wang Chongli, *Wuhuang renshi xiang* [The Picture of the 'Five Ring' Community], Beijing: Zhongguo wenliang chuban she, 1995, pp.43–6).

9. The interviewee studied at the Beijing University of Physical Education between 1992 and 1996. She was interviewed in March 1996.

10. The female shooter Li Duihong was tested drug-positive in September 1987 and banned from competition for two years. The speed skater Ye Qiaopo was also found to be drug-positive in 1988 and was banned for one and a half years. These events were not publicised domestically at the time.

11. Interview took place in Beijing in 1995.

12. In 1989 the National Sports Commission issued 'Provisional Regulations on Testing for Banned Drugs in National Sports Competitions' (quangguo xing tiyu jingsai jiecha jingyong yaowu de zanxin guiding).

13. Guojia tiyu zhongju zhongguo qoweihui [The National Sports Bureau and the Chinese Olympic Committee], Zhongguo fan xingfenji shinian [A Decade of the Fight against Drug Abuse in China], http://www.sports.gov.cn.

14. Li Ping, 'Zhongguo xingfenji shoujian mianmian guan' [An Overview of Chinese Performance-enhancing Drug Tests], *Tiyu wenzhai zhoubao* [Sports Digest Weekly], 78 (14 April 1994).

15. Li Ke, 'Yanzheng de lichang – zhongguo fan xingfenji dahui xianchang suxie' [Stringent Attitude – Literary Sketches of the Anti-drug Meeting in China], *Beijing wanbao* [Beijing Evening News], 3 March 1995.

16. Xinhua She [Xinhua News Agency], 'Zhongguo ao wei hui fabiao shengming' [The Chinese Olympic Committee Makes a Pronouncement], *Beijing wanbao* [Beijing Evening News], 4 Dec. 1994.

17. Li Ke, 'Yanzheng de lichang' [Stringent Attitude].

18. Guojia tiyu zhongju zhongguo qoweihui [National Sports Bureau and Chinese Olympic Committee], Zhongguo fan xinfenji shinian [The Decade of the Fight against Drug Abuse].

19. Li Ping, 'Zhongguo xingfenji shoujian mianmian guan' [An Overview of Chinese Performance-enhancing Drug Tests].

20. 'Zhongguo xianru jinyao chouweng' [China Is Plunged into a Drug Scandal], http://www.zabao.com.sg/zaobao/games/pages/cjinyao200198.html.

21. Guojia tiyu zhongju zhongguo qoweihui [National Sports Bureau and Chinese Olympic Committee], Zhongguo fan xingfenji shinian [The Decade of the Fight against Drug Abuse].

22. Including Xin Feng, the first gold medallist at the 1990 Beijing Asian Games, who took drugs at the National Games in 1993 (see Wang Chongli, *Wuhuang renshi xiang* [The Picture of the 'Five Ring' Community], pp.25–7).

23. The IOC passed a resolution in January 1994 to ban athletes for two years for the first offence and to impose a life ban for the second offence.

24. 'Chinese Begin Crackdown', *Independent*, 6 April 1994.

25. Yang Aihua, the women's 400-metre freestyle world champion in the Rome World Championships, tested positive for testosterone in a random out-of-competition test on the eve of the Asian Games. Then two other female swimmers, Lu Bing and Zhou Gongbing, the athlete Han Qing and the cyclist Wang Yan were found to be in violation of drug regulations at the same games.

26. Brent S. Rushall and Brian Browne, 'China's Swimming: They've Done It Again!' *Swimnews Online*, http://www.swimnews.com/Mag/1996/JunMag96/chinaswim.shtml.

27. Karen Allen, 'Chinese Drug Test Confirms Suspicions', *USA Today*, 1 Dec. 1994.

28. They were Zhou Ming, Wang Lin, Chen Qin, Yao Ying and Mo Zhengjie (see 'China Bans Nine Coaches Over Drugs', *The Independent*, 1 March 1995).

29. Zhang Jun, 'Chunjie yongtian, changchu duliu'[To Clear the Swimming Community and Eradicate Drug Taking], *Beijing wanbao* [Beijing Evening News], 8 April 1995.

30. Articles 34 and 50 point to drug issues. For the details, see 'Zhonggua renmin gongheguo tiyu fa' [Sports Law of the People's Republic of China], *Zhongguo tiyu bao* [China Sports Daily], 1 Oct. 1995.

31. Xu Jiren et al., 'Zhongguo aoweihui zhaokai fang xingfenji dahui' [The Chinese Olympic Committee Holds an Anti-Drug Meeting], *Zhongguo tiyu bao* [China Sports Daily], 17 Jan. 1998.

32. Xiao Ming, 'Shi Tianshu: fei yao quanti xiaogan bu ke?' [Shi Tianshu: Would All Swimmers Be Dismissed?], *Tiyu zhoubao* [Sports Weekly], 13 Aug. 1999.

33. Ibid.

34. Craig Lord, 'The Medal Factory', *Sunday Times*, 9 May 1999.

35. Ibid.

36. Guojia tiyu zhongju zhongguo qoweihui [National Sports Bureau and Chinese Olympic Committee], Zhongguo fan xingfenji shinian [The Decade of the Fight against Drug Abuse].

37. Li Hemu, 'Lanyong weijin yaowu, er shi si ming yundongyuan shou chufa' [Male Swimmers Were Caught Drug Positive and 24 Athletes Were Punished], *Beijing wanbao* [Beijing Evening News], 7 April 1998.

38. Yang Ming, 'Zhongguo tianjing dachu "chengbao" zhuhe quan' [China's Athletes Adopt the 'Contract' Agreement], *Tiyu wenzhai zhoubao* [Sports Digest Weekly], 502 (1998).

39. In early 1986 an East German coach named Klaus Nudalf signed a contract with China to coach the national team for a year.

40. Although Chinese swimmers won three gold medals at the 1982 Asian Games, China still lagged behind the world's top nations until 1988, when the female swimmer Yang Wenyi broke the world 50-metre freestyle record. At the 1992 Olympic Games, six Chinese female swimmers won four gold and five silver medals. More astonishingly, at the seventh World Swimming Championships held in 1994, they won 12 of the 16 gold medals and set five new world records.

41. East German women won 44 gold, 32 silver and 15 bronze medals in 72 world championships between 1973 and 1986, a phenomenal record but one now discredited by evidence of a state-run drug programme (Craig Lord, 'China's Women Shake the World', *Sunday Times*, 11 Sep. 1994).

42. Initially, China sent coaches and swimmers to the United States and Australia to observe and train. Later experts and coaches from these two countries were invited to China to give lectures in the early 1980s. For example, Jianshu province, the home

of the Olympic Champion Lin Li, invited a female Australian coach to supervise its swimming team. In addition, some former Soviet Olympic champions and two East German coaches, including Klaus Nudalf, coached the national squad.

43. Interviewed in Beijing, 1997.
44. Zhou Zhongqiu, 'Chen Yunpeng de kangfa' [Views of Chen Yunpeng], *Youyong* [Swimming], 1994 (1), p.11.
45. 'Gaige kaifang shiwu nian zhongguo tiyu chengjiu huihuang' [The Remarkable Achievements of Chinese Sport during the One and Half Decades of Reform and Opening-up to the Outside], *Zhongguo tiyu bao* [China Sports Daily], 9 Feb. 1994.
46. Guojia tiwei jihua caiwu si [Planning and Finance Department of the NSC], *Tiyu shiye tongji nianjian (neibu ziliao)* [Statistical Yearbook of Sport] (internal materials), 1994, p.151.
47. After the start of drug testing in 1989, the number of offenders increased, for example, from 24 in 1993 to 31 in 1994.
48. Ibid.
49. In the transition to a market economy, the pursuit of materialism became pervasive. To be in a powerful position, to consume branded goods, and to have a house and money were the most envied achievements in Chinese society in the 1990s. For athletes and coaches these achievements were based on sports performances, without which they could not be acquired.
50. Interviewed on 12 August 1997.
51. Interviewee Chang Tong won the national championships and fourth place at the Asian Games in 1990. She studied at the Beijing University of Physical Education between 1992 and 1996. She was interviewed in Beijing in 1995.
52. This will be analysed in Chapters 7 and 8.
53. Zhuang Yong and Lin Li were both from factory worker's families with two children. Lin's mother was a housewife. Qian Hong and Yang Wenyi were from junior cadre families.
54. Forty-one world records were broken by 179 athletes, of whom 165 were women. For the details, see *Quan yunhui ziliao* [Information on the National Games], Guojia tiwei xingxi wang [Information Net of the National Sports Commission], http://www. sports.gov.cn.net.
55. A new generation of the Ma Family Army, represented by Jian Bo and Dong Yanmei, broke the 5,000-metre world record at the games.
56. Xu Shaolian, 'Zhongguo tianjin xian dasai yao chengji' [China's Athletics Should Target the World Competitions], *Dandai tiyu bao* [Contemporary Sports], 18–24 Nov. 1997.
57. Sun Baosheng, 'Zhongguo tianjin yundong huapo'[The Decline of China's Athletics], *Beijing wanbao* [Beijing Evening News], 8 Aug. 1997.
58. Lord, 'The Medal Factory'.
59. Wang Hui, 'Shi Tianshu tan xingfenji shijian' [Shi Tianshu Talks about the Drug Incidents], Lianghe zhaobao [United Morning News], 5 March 1998.
60. Xu Jiren, 'Zhongguo aoweihui zhaokai fan xingfenji dahui' [The Chinese Olympic Committee Holds an Anti-Drug Meeting].
61. James Riordan and Dong Jinxia, 'Chinese Women and Sport: Success, Sexuality and Suspicion', *The China Quarterly*, 145 (March 1996), p.132.
62. James Tyson and Ann Tyson, *Chinese Awakenings: Life Stories from the Unofficial China*, Boulder, CO: Westview Press, 1995, p.2.
63. 'Shiping beiwu wu yongjian'[Contaminated Food Led to Swimmers Being Misunderstood], *Yancen wanbao she qioumi shijie* [The Fans' World of the Ball Games of the Yancen Evening Daily Press], 19 Aug. 1999.
64. 'Qingbai zhongyu jinpai' [Honesty Is More Important Than Gold Medals], http://www.chinasports.com (jiuwen huicui [Collection of Old News]).

65. Interviewee Li Xiaohui (see case studies in Appendix), interviewed in Beijing, June 1997.
66. Susan Brownell, *Training the Body for China: Sports in the Moral Order of the People's Republic*, Chicago, IL, and London: University of Chicago Press, 1995, p.319.
67. Before sending a delegation to China, FINA expressed its confidence in China's own investigation of its drug scandals, and accepted the Chinese explanation that the four drug-positive swimmers had acted alone.
68. Anita Lonsbrough, 'FINA Send a Doping Taskforce to China', *Daily Telegraph*, 26 Jan. 1998.
69. Chao Jianjie and Li Hepu, 'Guoji yongliang daibiao tuan juxin fabuhui' [The FINA Delegation Holds News Conference], *Zhongguo tiyu bao* [China Sports Daily], 20 Feb. 1998.
70. Interviewed in August 1997.
71. Yuan Honghen, 'Zengqiang jingzheng, tuijin gaige –wu shouzhang tan aoyun xuanba sai' [Increase Competition, Promote Reform – Remarks by Wu Shouzhang on the Olympic Games Trials], *Beijing wanbao* [Beijing Evening News], 2 June 1996.
72. There are now three categories of national teams: the permanent one for most Olympic sports, the temporary one for major international competitions and the one represented by the national team championships of the year.
73. Tyson and Tyson, *Chinese Awakenings*, preface.
74. See *Zhongguo tiyu bao* [China Sports Daily], 8–15 Jan. 1998.
75. Mihir Bose, 'Desperate Americans Relax Border Controls', *Daily Telegraph*, 30 Sept. 2000.
76. Six days after C.J. Hunter, Marion Jones's husband, had failed a drug test (four positive tests in the last four months), the Americans had not named him and refused to name ten others who had tested positive (Bose, 'Desperate Americans relax border controls'). 'They do not declare after the A or the B, or even after the full process is over if the athlete is exonerated. So we never come to know about it. How are we supposed to monitor the situation and ensure that cases are treated in the same and fair way?' said Arne Ljungqvist, the senior vice-president of the IAAF. Subsequently anti-American sentiment was generated in the sports world. The United States were threatened with suspension from international athletics because of their rules over drug testing. The US Olympic authorities had prided themselves on their clean image, but the finger was now being pointed at them. (Owen Slot, 'US Athletes Facing Ban over Drug Testing', *Sunday Telegraph*, 1 Oct. 2000).
77. Owen Slot, 'Top Nations Accused of Masterminding Drug-Test Dodges', *Sunday Telegraph*, 17 Sep. 2000.
78. Xu Jiren, 'Zhongguo aoweihui zhaokai fan xingfenji dahui' [The Chinese Olympic Committee Holds an Anti-Drug Meeting].
79. Anita Lonsbrough, 'China Left to Carry Out Drugs Inquiry', *Daily Telegraph*, 19 Jan. 1998.
80. For example, those taking the first category of drugs would be sentenced to a life-time ban; local associations or clubs would be prohibited from competition for a year if two incidents of drug-positive tests happened in a year; the association would be withdrawn from the National Games and the National City Games in the event of four drug cases within four years (*Zhongguo tiyu bao* [China Sports Daily], 20 Feb. 1998).
81. Jian Pin, 'Zhongguo juzhong mianmian guan' [The Situation of Weightlifting in China], *Beijing wanbao* [Beijing Evening News], 1 Sep. 1999.
82. Zhang Jun, 'Zhongguo youyong: shengsi chunwang – zhongguo yongxie tan fandui xinfeng ji' [China's Swimming: Survive or Die – the Swimming Association Speaks about Combating Drug Abuses], *Beijing wanbao* [Beijing Evening News], 28 Aug. 1999.
83. Guojia tiyu zhongju zhongguo qoweihui [National Sports Bureau and Chinese

Olympic Committee], Zhongguo fan xinfenji shinian [A Decade of the Fight against Drug Abuse].

84. 'Zhongguo youyong fan xinfenji biaozhun zhuiyan' [Chinese Standards Against Banned Drugs Are the Strictest in the World], 23 Aug. 2000, http://www.eastday.com. cn/.

85. The Japanese swimmers won 15 gold medals, two more than the Chinese at the Asian Games (see Nick Thierry, 'Asian Games: Japan Reclaims Supremacy', http://swim-news.com/Mag1999/JanMag99/asiangames.shtml).

86. Jun Ming and Ha Kang, 'Liu Hongyu Wang Yan fen huo jinzhou jin yin pai' [Liu Hongyu and Wang Yan Won Gold and Silver Medals in Walking], *Beijing wanbao* [Beijing Evening News], 28 Aug. 1999.

87. 'Guojia tiyu zhongju lin (di yi hao): Guanyu yange jinzhi zai tiyu yundong zhong shiyong xinfen ji xinwei de guiding (zhangxin)' [The Decree of the National Sports Bureau (No.1): Regulations Strictly Forbidding the Use of Drugs in Sport], *Zhongguo tiyu bao* [China Sports Daily], 5 Jan. 1999.

88. 'Zhongguo youyong fan xinfenji biaozhun zhuiyan' [Chinese Standards Against Banned Drugs Are Strictest in the World].

89. Six of Ma's seven Olympic hopes exceeded the IOC standards in their blood test results and two of them were even positive in urine samples (Hui Wencui, 'Ma Jia Jun aoyun jixun shengmi shizhong you le xiaweng' [Reasons for the Mysterious Disappearance of the Ma Family Army], *Lianhe zhaobao* [United Morning News], 22 Oct. 2000.

90. 'China Drops 40 Members from Sydney Olympic Team', 8 Sep. 2000, *Yahoo! Singapore Sports,* http://sg.sports.yahoo.com/000908/1/5ka.html.

91. As mentioned in the Prologue, women won 16.5 out of the 28 Chinese gold medals at the 2000 Olympic Games.

92. 'Zhongguo yongxie dui Wu Yanyan jinsai 4 nian' [The Chinese Swimming Association Bans Wu Yanyan for Four Years], *Jinan ribao* [Jinan Daily], 18 July 2000.

93. 'Wu Yanyan: wo yan gao zhongguo yongxie' [I Want to Sue the Chinese Swimming Association], *Yangzhou dushi bao* [Yangzhou City News], 19 July 2000.

94. 'Wu Yanyan: wo bei ziji ren dadao le' [Wu Yanyan: I Was Defeated by Our Own People], http://www.eastday.com.cn, 17 July 2000.

95. 'Wu Yanyan "guanshi" chuxiang chongda zhuanji' [A Great Turn Around in Wu Yanyan's "Legal Case"], *Jinan ribao* [Jinan Times], 24 July 2000.

96. John Hoberman, 'Sport and Ideology in the Post-Communist Age', in Lincoln Allison (ed.), *The Changing Politics of Sport*, Manchester: Manchester University Press, 1993, p.29.

97. Zhang Jun, 'Zhongguo youyong: shengsi chunwang' [China's Swimming: Survive or Die].

98. 'Opinion Interview: Drug Buster', *New Scientist*, 16 Sep. 2000, p.45.

99. Peter Foster, 'Olympic Oath Against Drugs', *Daily Telegraph*, 16 Sep. 2000.

100. The IOC's banned list includes over 4,000 substances, which are grouped into six categories of drugs, including anabolic steroids, stimulants, narcotic analgesics, beta-blockers and diuretics.

101. Robert L. Simon, 'Good Competition and Drug-Enhanced Performance', in William J.Morgan (ed.), *Philosophic Inquiry In Sport*, Champaign, IL: Human Kinetics, 1988, p.213.

102. See next chapter.

103. Virtually all the Olympic and world champions were initially identified by profes-sional coaches in kindergarten or primary schools. For example, Zhuang Yong and Yang Wenyi, with their exceptional swimming talent and unique physical qualities, were picked out in kindergarten by coaches at the district sports schools in Shanghai.

104. There were about 1,000 professional swimming coaches throughout the country in the

mid-1980s. Most of the coaches of the national squad had university degrees, and knew at least one foreign language. Chou Ming, the deputy head coach of the team, may serve as a typical example. He began his coaching in 1982 after receiving a master's degree at the BIPE. He speaks two foreign languages. As early as the early 1980s he was using computers to serve his coaching. He introduced training methods to increase swimmers' strength and instructed swimmers on how to meditate. His intelligence and abilities made him one of the best coaches in the national team. At the same time he became the most controversial coach in the world due to the drug issue. He served a one-year ban when his swimmer tested positive for steroids in 1994. Two of the four drug offenders at the World Championships in 1998 were also his swimmers. Thus, he was once again banned from coaching after the championships.

105. She was interviewed in Beijing in 1997.

Chapter 7

1. This is reflected in the films *Nulan wuhao* [Number Five in the Female Basketball Team] and *Bingshang jiemei* [Sisters on Ice] in the 1950s, and literary works such as *Yangmei jian chuqiao* [Sword Comes out from the Flying Brows] in the early 1980s.
2. Lu Guang, *Zhongguo gulian* [Chinese Girls], Beijing: Renmin tiyu chuban she, 1981.
3. Zhao Yu, 'Majiajun diaocha' [Inquiries into the Ma Family Army], *Zhongguo zuojia* [Chinese Writer] 1998 (3), pp.1–213.
4. Gu Shiquan, *Jiannan de qidian yu luodian de huihuang – zhongguo titan beiwang lu* [The Difficult Take-off and the Marvellous Landing – Memorandum of Chinese Sport], Beijing: Jilin jiaoyu chuban she, 1994, p.155.
5. This interview took place in September 1997.
6. The national team symbolises the head of the dragon and the provincial elite teams and sports schools symbolise the body. The head leads the body, but all parts are interconnected and affect one another.
7. Li Guizhi was interviewed in Beijing in 1995.
8. Zhou Ping and Yi Ya, 'Zhongguo nvpai liu lian guan de xiwang zhi meng' [The Dream of Six Titles in Succession of the Chinese Women's Volleyball Team], *Tiyu chunjiu* [Sports Spring and Autumn], Feb. 1988, p.11.
9. Sun Weiyu et al., *Shijie 100 titan mingxing paihang bang* [The 100: A Ranking of the Most Famous Athletes in the World], Beijing: Zhongguo jinji chuban she, 1994, p.275.
10. Interviewee Li Guizhi.
11. Wang Han, 'Xianhua kaifang zhihou – cong zhongguo nvpai jingshen zhong xuexi shenme [After the Blooming of Fresh Flowers – What to Learn from the Spirit of the Chinese Women's Volleyball Team], *Wenhui bao* [Wenghui Daily], 28 Nov. 1981.
12. Wang Hongsheng (ed.), *Zhongwai tiyu mingxin qiwen qushi* [The Legends of Chinese and Foreign Sports Stars], Beijing: Huaxia chuban she, 1988, p.100.
13. The legal marriage age was, and still is, 20 for women and 22 for men, but the minimum age for the 'late marriage' advocated by the government is 23 for women and 25 for men.
14. Wang Hongsheng, *Zhongwai tiyu mingxing qiwen qushi* [Legends of Sports Stars], pp.81–3.
15. They are volleyball, basketball and football.
16. The vice-premier of the State Council and the first director of the NSC, Marshal He Long, stated that 'I will not close my eyes until the three big balls advance to world level'.
17. This honorary title, established by the National Sports Commission, is presented to eminent athletes and coaches.
18. Sun Jingfang was voted one of the best 10 athletes in China in 1981and 1982. Lan Ping was one of the best ten athletes in China five times in succession between 1980 and

1985, and was also voted the 'best player in Asia' twice, in 1984 and 1985. Yang Xilan was awarded the title 'model athlete' (*mofan yundongyuan*) and the first merit citation class of the General Political Ministry of the Army after she became famous at the 23rd Olympic Games in 1984 (see Chen Zhongguo, Wang Huaxin and Wang Guie, *Guan zhong guan: dangdai zhongguo titan chaoji mingxin diaoxiang* [Champions out of Champions: Sculptures of the Sports Superstars in Modern China], Shijiazhuang: Huashan wenyi chuban she, 1990, p.511).

19. Sun Jingfang was a representative at the 12th Party Congress; Zhang Rongfang was the commissioner of the sixth National Political and Consultative Committee in 1983.
20. Jin Shang, 'Hancheng fansi lu' [Reflections on the Seoul Games], in Shi Hangpo (ed.), *Zhongguo tiyu de fengfeng yuyu* [The Plight of China's Sport], Beijing: Beijing longye daxue chuban she, 1990, p.53.
21. Lan Yang, 'Nvpai bingbai shichu youyin' [The Defeat of Women's Volleyball Has its Reasons], in Shi Hangpo, *Zhongguo tiyu de fengfeng yuyu* [The Plight of China's Sport], p.141.
22. Jin Shang, 'Hancheng fansi lu' [Reflections on the Seoul Games], p.55.
23. At the 1994 Asian Games, the Chinese women's volleyball team was defeated by the Koreans and came second. At the following World Volleyball Championships China fell to eighth place.
24. After Yuan Weimin was promoted to deputy director of the NSC following victory in the 1984 Olympic Games, Deng Ruozeng, Zhang Rongfang, Li Yaoxian, Hu Jin and Li Xiaofeng coached the team successively.
25. In 1993 five members of the team successively broke three world records 13 times, winning five international gold medals. In particular, Wang Junxia knocked 42 seconds off the 10,000-metres record with 29 min 31.78 sec, and bettered the 3,000-metres record by 16.5 seconds, finishing in 8 min 06.11 sec.
26. How the Ma Family Army could run a marathon a day for six months of the year (300k 180m) without taking drugs was frequently questioned. In view of the fact that the performances of Ma's athletes were far better than any available drugs could ensure, some referred to these performances as the product of hard work and hunger for fame on the part of poor peasants. Some attributed them to a Chinese capacity for mental and physical endurance (see: 'Wang races to hat-trick', *The Independent,* 14 Sep. 1993; Jeff Hollobaugh, 'A Giant Awakens', *Track & Field News,* Dec. 1993, p.5).
27. Shu Zhishong, 'Wang Junxia chu shang' [Wang Junxia's Rise], *Xiangdai tiyu* [Modern Sports], Feb. 1994 (2), pp.23–26.
28. At the National Games Liaoning were third in 1983 and 1987, first in 1993 and second in 1997.
29. Zhao Yu, 'Majiajun diaocha' [Inquiries into the Ma Family Army], p.5.
30. Liaoning won 65 gold medals, followed by Guangdong (31) and Shanghai (28).
31. He was born in 1944. When he grew flowers, he was a well-known local grower. When he was a livestock farmer, he was again successful.
32. Besides physical education classes, he was responsible for the school's basketball, athletics and table tennis teams for both girls and boys. He had to leave home at 4:30 in the morning and rode a bicycle to school for the morning training session. He stayed there until 9:00 p.m. His students were unable to afford shoes and ran barefoot. Lacking school sports facilities and equipment, he built fields with students and used stones to practise discus-throwing.
33. When an international competition was taking place in Beijing in 1981, Ma was ill and hospitalised. He ignored his poor health and went to Beijing to watch the competition.
34. In an attempt to create a miracle at the games, he adopted intensive training for his athletes (960km a month, the highest load for female marathon athletes anywhere in the world and even more than that of Chinese male athletes).
35. Unfortunately his athletes all suffered pain in the anterior tibia muscles – a result of intensive training without effective rehabilitation methods. To tackle the problem, he

wanted his athletes to soak their feet in a herbal liquid. This indeed reduced their pain but softened the soles of their feet, which was not drawn to Ma's attention. He expected one of his best athletes to achieve a miraculous result at the games. However, her feet stopped her from reaching her potential. When she finally approached the finishing line, she fainted. Her feet astonished people: blood, skin tissue and shoes were so mixed together that her shoes could not be removed.

36. Caterpillar is a substance that, according to legend, was discovered over 1,500 years ago by herdsmen who said that their yaks became energised after eating it.
37. Guojia tiwei xuanchuan shi [Propaganda Department of the NSC] (ed.), *Ma jia jun* [The Ma Family Army], Beijing: Renmin tiy chuban she, 1994, p.109.
38. Ibid., p.20.
39. 'Ma's Secret Recipe is a Good Beating', *The Independent*, 23 March 1995.
40. After her split from Ma at the end of 1994, Wang's performance declined sharply due to unsystematic training and psychological distress. She was repeatedly defeated in domestic competitions in 1995. Doubts, disappointment and a lack of confidence in her performance were all expressed in the media, which further depressed her and destroyed her self-confidence. However, persuaded and encouraged by national and provincial government officials, she gave up the thought of ending her athletic career. Aided by her new coach Mao Dezheng and others, Wang restarted her arduous and dull training even harder than before. Overcoming sickness, injuries and mental anxiety, she gradually recovered her physical ability and psychological confidence.
41. 'Ma Army Set Up New Base Camp', *The Independent*, 1 June 1995.
42. Hollobaugh, 'A Giant Awakens', p.6.
43. Shu Zhishong, 'Majiajun de richu – Qu Yunxia' [The Ma Family Army's Sun Rising – on Qu Yunxia], *Dandai tiyu* [Modern Sports], Feb. 1994 (2), p.27.
44. Ibid.
45. 'Ma's Secret Recipe'.
46. Ibid.
47. In China, the dossier is the most important means of controlling people. It is the basis for virtually everything, including entrance for higher education, employment, promotion and mobility as well as service in the Army.
48. Chu Yue, 'Ma Jia Jun, zaisheng haishi xiaowan' [The Ma Family Army, Reborn or Disappeared?], *Dandai tiyu* [Contemporary Sport], March 1995, p.4.
49. According to a decree on the rating methods of international grand-prix competitions, issued in May 1988, athletes can keep any bonus below US$2,000. If the bonus is above this, they have to submit half of it to their units. This policy was relaxed in the 1990s. For the details, see: Zhonghua renmin gongheguo tiyu yundong weiyuan hui [NSC of the PRC], *Xianxin tiyu fagui huibian* [Collection of the Current Sports Laws and Regulations], Beijing: Renmin tiyu chuban she, 1990, pp.699–704.
50. Qing Tian, 'Ma Junren youhua shuo' [Ma Junren Has Something to Say], *Dangdai tiyu* [Modern Sport], April 1995, p.3.
51. Chu Yue, 'Ma Jia Jun' [The Ma Family Army], pp.4–6.
52. John Kohut and Nick Rufford, 'China's Golden Girl Runs Foul of Her Mean Ma', *Sunday Times*, 16 Jan. 1994.
53. See Chapter 5.
54. Personal issue (*geren wenti*) is a metaphor for marriage in China.
55. Before the drug issue became widely publicised, Chinese athletes who were caught using drugs were always reported to have misused Chinese medicine.
56. 'Yuan Weimin zai jiejian Ye Qiaobo shi de jianhua' [Yuan Weimin's Speech on Receiving Ye Qiaobo], *Tiyu gongzuo qingkuan* [The Situation of Sports Affairs] (internal publication), 519, 7 (1992), p.3.
57. She underwent her first knee operation in Norway, and was charged only ten per cent of the operation fee. After the 1994 Olympic Games she had a second operation in Germany free of charge.

58. Zhong Bingshu, *Chengji ziben he diwei huode: woguo youxiu yundongyuan qunti shehui liudong de yanjiu* [Performance Capital and Status Attainment: Sport and Social Mobility Among Chinese Elite Athletes], Beijing tiyu daxue chuban she, 1998, p.56.
59. Qi Ming, 'Zhuang Yong de yihan' [Zhuang Yong's Regret], in Chen Zhongguo and Deng Bian (eds), *Guan zhong guan* [Champions out of Champions], pp.297–313.
60. She won a 100-metres freestyle swimming silver medal at the 1988 Seoul Olympic Games. This was the first ever Olympic swimming medal won by a Chinese. Four years later she won a gold medal and created new Olympic records twice.
61. Qi Ming, 'Zhuang Yong de yihan' [Zhuang Yong's Regret], pp.297–313.
62. Between 1992 and 1996 China produced 361 world champions, of which 90 per cent once received training in various sports schools. All the gold medallists at the Atlanta games experienced sports school training (see Nan Mu, 'Quanguo yeyu tiyu xunlian gongzuo yantao hui zongshu' [Review of the National Coaching Seminar on Amateur Sport], *Tiyu gongzuo qingkuang* [The Situation of Sports Affairs], 655, 23 (1997), pp.8–11.
63. Jeff Hollobaugh, 'The Man Behind it all', *Track & Field News*, Dec. 1993, p.4.
64. Jin Wang and Diane M. Wiese-Biornstal, 'The Relationship of School Type and Gender to Motives for Sport Participation among Youth in the People's Republic of China', *International Journal of Sport Psychology*, 28, 1 (Jan.–March 1997), p.23.
65. John W. Loy et al., 1978, *Sport and Social Systems: A Guide to the Analysis, Problems and Literature*, Reading, MA: Addison-Wesley Publishing Company, 1978, p.181.
66. Interviewee Qian Hong, Beijing, 12 Aug. 1997.
67. Jay J. Coakley, 'Sport and Socialisation', *Exercise and Sport Sciences Reviews*, 21 (1993), pp.169–200.
68. Zhong Bingshu, *Chengji ziben he diwei huode* [Performance Capital and Status Attainment], p.56.
69. Paul Beashel and John Taylor (eds), *Advanced Studies in Physical Education and Sport*, Walton-on-Thames: Nelson, 1996, p.281.
70. See appendix 4.
71. Interviewed at the Beijing University of Physical Education, 1995.
72. Ibid.
73. Xin Jin, 'Zhongguo tianjin "yinsheng yangshuan" de san da qushi' [Three Major Inspirations Concerning the 'Female Wax and Male Wane' in China's Athletics], *Xin tiyu* [New Sport], 1988 (4), p.32.

Chapter 8

1. Caroline Hodges Persell (ed.), *Understanding Society: An Introduction to Sociology* (2nd edn), New York: Harper & Row, 1996, p.228.
2. Functionalists see stratification as inevitable and necessary for the 'good' of society (see R. Keith Kelsall and Helen M. Kelsall, *Stratification: An Essay on Class and Inequality*, London: Longman, 1974, p.22).
3. Grant Jarvie and Joseph Maguire, *Sport and Leisure in Social Thought*, London: Routledge, 1994, p.20.
4. Barry D. Mcpherson et al., *The Social Significance of Sport: An Introduction to the Sociology of Sport*, Champaign, IL: Human Kinetics, 1989, p.171.
5. Persell, *Understanding Society*, p.183.
6. G. Luschen, 'Social Stratification and Social Mobility among Young Sportsmen', in J.W. Loy and G.S. Kenyon (eds), *Sport, Culture, and Society: A Reader on the Sociology of Sport*, London: Macmillan, 1969, pp.258–76.
7. Roland Renson, 'Social Status Symbolism of Sport Stratification', in Fernand Landry (ed.), *Sociology of Sport: A Collection of the Formal Papers Presented at the*

International Congress of Physical Activity Sciences, Miami, FL: Symposia Specialists Inc., 1978, pp.191–200.

8. Higher-class sport: skiing, golf, field hockey, tennis, and fencing (individual sports that require a large outlay of money). Upper-middle-class sport: rowing, canoeing, horse riding, climbing and caving, skating, hunting and scuba diving (sports that adopt special equipment and complex apparatus). Lower-middle-class sports make use of balls, nets and targets, require teamwork or precise goal setting (basketball, korfball, volleyball, table-tennis, badminton, swimming, cycling and walking). Lower-class sports are either of an individual nature or they involve close bodily contacts as in martial sports or in rough team games: gymnastics, callisthenics and athletics events all adhere to the principle of surpassing and struggling with one's own bodily limitations. The above categories, of course, are only approximate generalisations – there is overlap.

9. Loy and Kenyon *Sport, Culture, and Society*, p.275.

10. Zhong Bingshu, *Chengji ziben he diwei huode: woguo youxiu yundongyuan qunti shehui liudong de yanjiu* [Performance Capital and Status Attainment: Sport and Social Mobility among Chinese Elite Athletes], Beijing tiyu daxue chuban she, 1998.

11. The sampled athletes numbered 274 and included 157 females. For the details, see Appendix 6, Table 4a.

12. The distinction between *kanpu* [cadres] and *qunzhong* [the masses] (workers and peasants) is obvious in China. In its broadest usage, 'cadre' includes all those who hold any post as a functionary in the bureaucratic hierarchies in China, from top to bottom. Generally, non-administrative teaching, medical and technical personnel are also included in this category.

13. Geoff Payne and Pamela Abbott (eds), *The Social Mobility of Women: Beyond Male Mobility Models*, London: Falmer Press, 1990, p.2.

14. Athletes have been officially categorised as state workers since 1964, when an 'Announcement about the Calculation of Service Term of Professional Athletes' was issued jointly by the Ministry of Domestic Affairs, the Ministry of Labour and the State Sports Commission (See *Guojia tiyu yundong weiyuanhui wenjian: Ming Fa* [Documents of the National Sports Commission: Ming Fa], 26; (80)Nao Zhong Ji Zi; 81, (80)Ti Zheng Zi, 253, 1980).

15. Eighty per cent of surveyed athletes held this viewpoint in 1996 (see Zhong Bingshu, *Chengji ziben he diwei huode*, p.44).

16. Reinhard Bendix and Seymour Martin Lipset (eds), *Class, Status, and Power: Social Stratification in Comparative Perspective* (2nd edn), London: Routledge & Kegan Paul, 1967, p.574.

17. A.B. Hollingshead, *Two-Factor Index of Social Position*, New Haven, CT: privately printed, 1957; W.L. Warner et al., *Social Class in America*, Chicago. IL: Social Research Association, 1949; P.M. Blau and O.D. Ducan, *The American Occupational Structure*, New York: John Wiley &Sons, 1967.

18. Interviewee Yang Shengmei was a swimmer in the Shangxi provincial team. The interview took place at the Beijing University of Physical Education in 1995.

19. The interview was carried out during the UN Fourth World Conference on Women in Beijing in Sep. 1995.

20. The interviewee was Qian Hong. Interview took place in 1997 in Beijing.

21. One US dollar was worth about 6.45 yuan in 1992.

22. Wang Chongli, *Wuhuang renshi xiang* [Picture of the 'Five Ring' Community], Beijing: Zhongguo wenliang chuban she, 1995, pp.70–1.

23. Ibid.

24. Ma Yihua, 'Jiaolianyuan yundongyuan shehui shenwang jiaogao' [Coaches and Athletes have Relatively High Social Status], *Zhongguo tiyu bao* [China Sports Daily], 27 Dec. 1997.

25. Dong Yu, 'Shenzhen ren ping kang ban zhong zhiye' [Shenzhenese Opinions about the Prestige of 100 Occupations], *Zhongguo funu bao* [China Women's Daily], 24 July 1998.

26. For information on survey respondents, such as type of sport and family background, see Appendix 5: Tables 1–5.

27. G.R. Pavia and T.D. Jaques, 'The Socio-economic Origin, Academic Attainment, Occupational Mobility and Parental Background of Selected Australian Athletes', in Landry, *Sociology of Sport*, p.90.

28. C.A. Hasbrook, 'The Sport Participation – Social Class Relationship: Some Recent Youth Sport Participation Data', *Sociology of Sport Journal*, 1986 (3), pp.37–47.

29. Susan Brownell, *Training the Body for China: Sports in the Moral Order of the People's Republic*, Chicago, IL, and London: University of Chicago Press, 1995, p.224.

30. People who laboured with their minds felt that they were born to dominate those who laboured with their hands (see Edwin E. Moise, *Modern China: A History*, London & New York: Longman, 1986, p.25).

31. For example, domestic violence existed in certain families. On this issue, see Zhu Dongwu, 'Zhizhi jiating baoli keburonghuan [To Stop Domestic Violence is an Urgent Task], *Gongren ribao* [Workers' Daily], 2 Sep. 1994.

32. This includes employment and promotion. For further details, see Zhang Liming, 'Zhaogong zhong xingbie jishi xiexiang youwai gaibian [The Phenomenon of Gender Discrimination in Employment Will Be Overcome], *Jiangfang ribao* [Liberation Daily], 25 Oct. 1994; Liu Delian, 'Nu gangpu chengzhang de zhangai ji duice' [The Obstacle to the Promotion of Female Cadres and the Measures to Solve the Problem], *Gongre ribao* [Workers' Daily], 1 Nov. 1994.

33. See section on Confucianism in Prologue.

34. Wang Xiaopo, 'Nvxing yishi yu funv jiefang' [Women's Self-awareness and Their Emancipation], *Dongfang* [Orient], 35, 5 (2000), pp.49–53.

35. See Chapter 9.

36. Tao Chunfang (ed.), *Zhongguo funv shehui diwei geiguan* [An Overview of Chinese Women's Social Status] Vol.1, Beijing: Zhongguo funu chuban she, 1993, p.122.

37. Ma Xia, 'Changes in the Pattern of Migration in Urban China', in Lincoln H. Day and Ma Xia (eds), *Migration and Urbanization in China*, Armonk, NY: M.E. Sharpe, 1994, p.4.

38. The enforcement of the *hukou* system depended on the rationing system. Between the 1950s and the early 1980s grain, oil, cloth, fuel and many other products were rationed.

39. Delia Davin, *Internal Migration in Contemporary China*, London: Macmillan Press, 1999, p.39.

40. In 1985 the State Council formulated a new economic policy that allowed peasants to enter cities to run shops and do other service work.

41. 'Gan xiang, gan gang, gan dong – Ma Junren zai Liaoning tiwei ganbu jiaolianyuan dahui shang de baogao' [Dare to Think, Dare to Act – Ma Junren's Report at the Meeting of Cadres and Coaches of Liaoning Provincial Sports Commission], Guojia tiwei xuanchuan si [Propaganda Department of the NSC] (ed.), *Ma jia jun* [The Ma Family Army], Beijing: renmin tiyu chuban she, 1994, p.38.

42. Female swimmers Zhuan Yong (who won the 100-metres freestyle Olympic title and created two new Olympic records in 1992), Yang Wenyi (who smashed the 50-metres freestyle world record in 1988 and became an Olympic champion in 1992), Lin Li (who won an Olympic gold medal in 1992 and a bronze in 1996 in the 200-metres medley), Qian Hong (who became the Olympic 100-metres butterfly champion in 1992) and the Asian champion Huang Xiaomin.

43. Zhang Tong, a national high-jump champion in 1990, was interviewed at the Beijing University of Physical Education in 1996.

44. Interviewee Tang Guili, Beijing, 1996.

45. Cheng Yuening was interviewed in Lausanne, Switzerland, in 1996.

46. 'China's 1992–1996 Socio-economic Development' [http://www.chinese embassy. org.uk/Economy/Press.pl.449.html].

47. Weng Jieming (ed.), *Zhongguo fazhan baogao shu (1998): Zhongguo fazhan zhuangkuang yu qushi* [Report on China's Development (1998): Situations and Trends in China's Development], Beijing: Zhonggong zhongyang danxiao chuban she, 1999, p.336.
48. Linda Wong, 'China's Urban Migrants – The Public Policy Challenge', *Pacific Affairs*, 67, 3 (Fall 1994), p.351.
49. Interviewee Zhang Tong.
50. Zhu Qingfan, '1995–1996 nian renmin shenghuo zhuankuan' [People's Living Standards in the Year 1995/96], in Jiang Liu (ed.), *Shehui lanpi shu – 1995–1996 nian zhongguo shehui xinshi fenxi yu yuce* [Social Blueprint: an Analysis and Forecast of China's Social Situation in the Year 1995/96], Beijing: Zhongguo shehui kexue chuban she, 1996, p.151.
51. For the details, see Kaming Chan & Li Zhang, 'The Hukou System and Rural-Urban Migration in China: Processes and Changes', *The China Quarterly*, 160 (Dec. 1999), pp.818–55.
52. Joseph Cheng Yu-shek and Maurice Brosseau (eds), *China Review 1993*, Hong Kong: The Chinese University Press, 1993, p.1912
53. Sun Baosheng, 'Tiyu rencai de jiaoliu shizai bixin' [The Exchange of Sports Talents is a Trend], *Beijing wanbao* [Beijing Evening Daily], 31 Oct. 1995.
54. At the first fair for sporting talents, about 130 representatives from provincial sports commissions, enterprise sports associations, sports colleges and the army across the country were present.
55. Liaoning tiyu yundong weihuan hui [Liaoning Sports Commission] (ed.), *Liaoning tiyu nianjian* [Liaoning Sports Yearbook], Shengyan: Liaoning gushu chuban she, 1996, p.7.
56. Wu Shouzang, 'Bayun jinchui gaige feng' [The Eighth National Games Promote Reforms], *Xin tiyu* [New Sport], 1997 (5), p.21.
57. Zhao Yongsheng, the former world 50km walking champion from Liaoning, signed a contract with Chongqing Jinhui Wankui Walking Club that assembled 69 former national, Asian or world champions in 1997. Before the National Athletics Centre approved his registration, he signed another contract with Hebei Provincial walking team. Thus, a dispute surfaced between Chongqing and Hebei. As a punishment for this illegal action, the NAC decided to expel Zhao from the National Squad, cancelled his place for the coming Asian Games and temporarily terminated his registration (He Bing, 'Zhao Yongsheng shijian fanshi lu' [Reflections on the Zhao Yongsheng Incident], *Beijing wanbao* [Beijing Evening News], 11 April 1998).
58. For example, the Inner Mongolian Sports Commission, educational bureau, and labour and personnel bureau co-issued regulations to tightly control the outflow of athletes in 1986; Zejian Provincial Sports Commission and the provincial security bureau co-issued a notice on strengthening control over the mobility of sporting talents and strictly handling the outflow of from the province in 1992 – see Guojia tiwei zhengce fagui shi (ed.), *Difang tiyu fagui zhidu huibian (xiace)* [Collection of Local Sports Laws and Regulations] (second volume), 1995, pp.64–5; pp.173–4).
59. Guojia tiwei [The NSC], 'Guojia tiwei guanyu shenghua tiyu gaige de yijian' [The View of the NSC on Expanding the Sports Reform], in Guojia tiwei fagui si [The Law and Regulation Department of the NSC] (ed.), *Tiyu gaige wenjian xuanbian* [Selection of Document on Sports Reform] (1992–95), Beijing: Xinhua chuban she, 1997, p.31.
60. Tong Xin, 'Liudong dajun nengfuo chengwei zhongguo tiyu junheng fazhang de chouma' [Whether the 'Mobile Army' Can Promote the Balanced Development of Sport in China], *Tiyu bao* [Sports Daily], 30 Oct. 1997.
61. Duan Lianyue, 'Aoyun guanjun bingbai quanyun' [The Olympic Champions Were Defeated at the National Games], *Tiyu zhoubao* [Sports Weekly], 9 Sep. 1997.
62. Tong Xin, 'Liudong dajun nengfuo chengwei zhongguo tiyu junheng fazhang de chouma' [Whether the 'Mobile Army'...].

63. Hu Na, born in 1974, won the international tennis White House Cup in Mexico in January 1982. As the first Chinese tennis champion, she became popular, was given the honorary title of 'New Long-March Fighting Worker' and became a leading member of the Young Communist League. Her picture appeared on the cover of the magazine *New Sport*. Three months later she sought political asylum in America.

64. Zhang Minxian, 'Zai riben de waiguo yundongyuan' [Foreign Athletes in Japan], *Guowai tiyu dongtai* [Sports Development Abroad], 1991 (8), pp.58–59.

65. He Zhili went to Japan in 1990 and Chen Jing went to Taiwan after the 1992 Olympic Games.

66. Xu Shaolian, 'Paiqiou waiyuan denglu jinmen' [Foreign Volleyball Players Arrive in Tianjin], *Titan zhoubao* [Sports Weekly], 9 Feb. 1999, p.5.

67. Zhong Bingshu, *Chengji ziben he diwei huode*, p.112.

68. Huang Zhihong won the world shot-put championships in 1991 and 1993. She went to England to study and train for a year, and then transferred to the Netherlands for a period of time. To pay her coaching fees, she sold the car awarded to her by the FIFA for her victories. She participated in the 1996 Olympic Games and returned to China in 1996. In 1997 she undertook a master's degree course at Qinghua University, and also hosted a television programme.

69. See Chapter 7.

70. See Chapter 6.

71. Apart from He Zhili, the national table tennis players Chen Jing and Ji Baoxian went to Taiwan and Hong Kong respectively, and competed against mainland Chinese players at the Asian Games and World Championships.

72. He Zhili married a Japanese and went to Japan in 1989. She became a Japanese citizen in 1992.

73. Deng Yaping began playing table tennis at the age of five. By 1997 she had already won 18 world titles. As the world first seed, she won 1992 and 1996 Olympic titles in both female single and double events. She defended her title at the 1997 National Games. Thereafter, she entered Qinghua University to study, and specialised in economic management. In early 1998 she was sent to Cambridge University to study English.

74. Qiao Hong was the playing partner of Deng Yaping. They won the women's doubles titles at the 1992 and 1996 Olympic Games and at various world championships.

75. Long Xiong, 'Dangdai zhongguo titan da jiaodian renwu'[Focused Sports Figures in Contemporary China], *Haishang wentan* [Haishang Literary Circle], 1996 (4), pp.4–11.

76. Athletes apply, through their affiliated provincial or municipal sports commissions, to the relevant national sports associations, which will assess them in terms of age and duration of retirement from training. If they meet the official requirements, they are allowed to sign a contract with foreign employers. The association, the local provincial sports commission and athletes themselves all share the income from the foreign clubs.

77. John Horne, Alan Tomlinson and Garry Whannel (eds), *Understanding Sport: An Introduction to the Sociological and Cultural Analysis of Sport*, London and New York: E. & F.N. Spon/Routledge, 1999, p.123.

78. Jarvie and Maguire, *Sport and Leisure in Social Thought*, p.21.

79. In Beijing, an Olympic gold medallist receives extra bonuses of 700 yuan a month, and those ranking from second to eight places between 240 and 600 yuan. In short, the winning bonus varies according to the nature and grade of competitions and the type of sport (Olympic or non-Olympic). The highest monthly subsidy for a national champion is 280 yuan.

80. There is a complicated scale for this allowance: 400 yuan for those with less than two playing years, 600 yuan for three playing years, 800 yuan for over three years, and every extra playing year equivalent to a month's allowance up to a maximum of ten months. The champions in National or Asian Games and the world top three in

Olympic sports can get the retirement allowance according to their actual playing years, without any number of years (see Beijing shi tiyu yundong weiyuan hui [Beijing Sports Commission], *1996 Beijing tiyu nianjian* [Beijing Sports Yearbook], Beijing: Renming tiyu chuban she, 1997, p.389)

81. John W. Loy et al., *Sport and Social Systems*, Reading, MA: Addison-Wesley Publishing Company, 1978, p.181.

82. Liu Wenbiao, 'Huang Xiaomin xuexing yu gexing' [The Personality and Characteristics of Huang Xiaomin], Chen Zhengguo (ed.), *Guan zhong guan: dangdai zhongguo titan chaoji mingxin diaoxiang* [Champions out of the Champions: Sculpture of Sports Superstars in Modern China), Shijiazhuang: Huashan wenyi chuban she, 1990, pp.276–84.

83. Zhong Bingshu, *Chengji ziben he diwei huode*, p.125.

84. 'Chongsuo zixin, zaichuan huihuang' [Rebuild Self-confidence and Recreate Brilliance], Zhongyan dianshi tai tiyu bu [Sports Dept. of China Central Television] (ed.), *Tiyu shalon wenji* [The Collection of the Sports Salon], Beijing: Guoji wenhua chuban gongshi, 1995, p.224.

85. Ma Yihua, 'Jiaolianyuan yundongyuan shehui shenwang jiaogao' [Coaches and Athletes have Relatively High Social Status].

86. Tu Wei-ming (ed.), *Confucian Traditions in East Asian Modernity: Moral Education and Economic Culture in Japan and the Four Mini-Dragons*, Cambridge, MA: Harvard University Press, 1996, p.8.

87. Feng Zusheng and Lin Yingnan, *Kaifang yu fengbi: zhongguo chuantong shehui jiazhi quxiang jiqi dangqian liubian* [Opening Up Versus Closing Down: The Chinese Traditional Value Orientation and its Current Changes], Shijiazhuang: Hebei renmin chuban she, 1987, p.253.

88. She was the Asian shot-put champion at the 1978 and 1982 Asian Games, and retained the Asian record for ten years between the mid-1970s and the 1980s. After ending training, she went to Japan in 1987. She undertook her Ph.D. studies between 1994 and 1997 at the Beijing University of Physical Education.

89. Interview took place in Beijing in June, 1997.

90. Jin Shang, 'Han Cheng Fan Si Lu' [Reflections on the Seoul Games], in Shi Hangpo (ed.), *Zhongguo tiyu de fenfen yuyu* [The Plight of China's Sport], Beijing nongye daxue chuban she, 1990, p.53.

91. An attacker in the CWVT in the early 1990s.

92. A member of the CWVT in the late 1980s.

93. Wang Guangyu et al., 'Woguo youxiu yundongyuan tuiyu anzhi xianzhuang ji duice yanjiu' [Job Assignments of Retired Athletes and the Improvement of Policy in China]; also Tian Maijiu et al., 'Woguo youxiu yundongyuan tuiyu anzhi qingkuan ji gaijin duice' [The Situation of Job Assignments of Retired Athletes and the Improvement of its Policy], both in Guojia tiwei zhengce fagui shi (ed.), *Tiyu xitong ruan kexue yanjiu lunwen ji* [The Collection of Research Papers on Soft Science in the Sports Community], Beijing: Renmin tiyu chuban she, 1994, pp.20–2 and pp.101–13.

94. Guojia tiwei jihua caiwu si [Planning and Finance Department of the NSC], *Tiyu shiye tongji nianjian* [Statistical Yearbook of Sport], Beijing: Renmin tiyu chuban she, 1994, pp.42–3.

95. There were 4,530 retired athletes in 1990, but only 3,404 were assigned jobs after they stopped training. The corresponding figures in 1992 were 3,859 and 2,260.

96. Zhong Bingshu, *Chengji ziben he diwei huode*, pp.124–5.

97. Christopher Jencks et al., *Who Gets Ahead? The Determinants of Economic Success in America*, New York: Basic Books, 1979.

98. Li Zhenhui and Dai Jinshong, 'Tiyu mingxin "jinjun" daxue ketan' [Sports Stars 'March' to University Classroom], *Beijing Wanbao* [Beijing Evening News], 12 Sep. 1998.

99. Ibid.

100. The interviewee was Ye Qiaobo. Interview took place in 1995 in Beijing.
101. Loy, *Sport and Social Systems*, p.227.

Chapter 9

1. Jennifer Hargreaves, 'Gender on the Sports Agenda', *International Review for Sociology of Sport*, 25 (1990), p.287.
2. See K.Fasting, 'Gender Inequality in Leisure and Sport', in A. Tomlinson (ed.), *Sport in Society: Policy, Politics and Culture*, 43, Eastbourne, UK: Leisure Studies Association, 1990, pp.94–104; Anita White, 'Women Coaches: Problems and Issues', *Coaching Focus*, 6 (1987), pp.2–3.
3. Susan Brownell, *Training the Body for China: Sports in the Moral Order of the People's Republic*, Chicago, IL, and London: University of Chicago Press, 1995, p.220.
4. See Prologue.
5. This phenomenon arose when women had many more remarkable achievements in international competitions than men in the early 1980s. It was also reflected, incidentally, in show business. More actresses than actors won international recognition.
6. For example, the woman writer Zhang Jie published *The Ark* (1982) and *Love Should Not Be Forgotten* (1984). The former tells the story of three single women with meaningful jobs who have to fight against male chauvinism, gossip and humiliations because of their sex. The latter is about an elderly woman and her lifelong passion for a man to whom she has hardly spoken. Both have a message that is extremely radical in the context of Chinese society: it is better not to marry at all than to marry someone you do not love. They provoked a fierce debate on modern love and marriage.
7. In the seminar on Women and Development in China in 1993, the concept of gender was introduced. Four years later it became the focus of the same seminar.
8. Jin Yihong, 'Qianyian' [Foreword], in Jin Yihong and Liu Buohong (eds), *Shiji zhi jiao de zhongguo funv yu fazhang – lilun, jinji, wenhua, jiankan* [Chinese Women and Their Development at the Turn of the Century – Theory, Economy, Culture and Health], Nanjin daxue chuban she, 1998, pp.1–7.
9. According to Engels's *The Origin of the Family, Private Property and the State*, the roots of women's oppression lie in the denial of property and, through that, access to the public sphere as independent actors.
10. She was a national gymnastics champion in the 1950s and a coach of the national team from 1963 to 1994. She was interviewed in Beijing in 1994.
11. Title IX of the Education Amendment Act was enacted in 1972. It is widely regarded as the most influential piece of US legislation affecting women's athletics. It ushered in an era of participation without parallel in women's sports history. Between 1972 and 1981, the number of female high-school athletes jumped from 294,000 to almost 2 million. The number of college women athletes increased from 16,000 in 1972 to 158,000 in 1991, an almost 900 per cent increase. By 1988, 35 per cent of high school participants were girls and the number of sports open to them had more than doubled (see George H. Sage, *Power and Ideology in American Sport: A Critical Perspective*, Champaign, IL: Human Kinetics, 1990, pp.47–53).
12. Brownell, *Training the Body for China*, p.226.
13. Zhonghua renmin gongheguo guojia tiyu yundong wei yuan hui [National Sports Committee of the PRC], *Quanguo tiyu shiye tongji zhiliao huibian* [Collection of Statistical Information on Sport in China] (1949–78)], Beijing: Renmin tiyu chuban she, 1979, p.101.
14. The term 'sparring partner' is borrowed, of course, from boxing, where the partner's task is to help the main boxer improve his skill and competence. In China the task of

the male sparring partners is to promote women's, rather than their own, performances in sport.

15. Deng Yaping, 'Liang ge hao xiang' [Try to Make a Good Showing], in Guojia tiwei xuanchuan bu [Propaganda Department of the NSC] (ed.), *'96 Aoyun pingbo zhi ge* [Battle and Fighting Songs at the 1996 Olympic Games], Beijing: Renmin tiyu chuban she, 1997, p.100.

16. Sun fuming, 'Yinxiong zai wuo beihou [Heroes behind Me], in *'96 Aoyun pingbo zhi ge* [Battle and Fighting Songs], pp.27–8.

17. Min Jiayin (ed.), *The Chalice and the Blade in Chinese Culture: Gender Relations and Social Models*, Beijing: China Social Science Publishing House, 1995, p.23.

18. Ibid., p.619; Brownell, *Training the Body for China*.

19. James and Ann Tyson, *Chinese Awakenings: Life Stories from the Unofficial China*, Boulder, CO, and Oxford: Westview Press, 1995, p.3.

20. Until recently coaches, especially those working in provincial teams, had limited access to foreign countries. Salaries in the West were higher than in China. However, sparring partners could obtain opportunities to coach abroad and, more importantly, could be promoted to administrative and coaching positions. For example, Wang Biao, the team manager of the national table-tennis team, went to Kuwait to coach after being a sparring partner in the team; Yao Zhengxu, the deputy director of the National Table Tennis Management Centre, was also a sparring partner for a time. Interestingly, the sparring partners of the Chinese female tennis stars Li Fen and Yi Jingrong, who entered the world top 50 rankings, ended up as their coaches and husbands.

21. She was interviewed at the Beijing University of Physical Education in 1995.

22. Jennifer Hargreaves, *Sporting Females – Critical Issues in the History and Sociology of Women's Sports* (London: Routledge, 1994), p.281.

23. At the 1988 Olympic Games the Chinese women's volleyball team came fourth. Expected to recover their prominence at the 1992 Olympic Games, they dropped out of the top eight teams.

24. Grasa was interviewed in Beijing in 1995.

25. Jing Dongxian was interviewed in Beijing in 1995.

26. She was undertaking Ph.D. studies at the Beijing University of Physical Education when the interview took place in June 1997.

27. Lei Guangming, 'Leishui qingwu le tiantan – ji nvzi 10 gongli jinzhou ao yun guanjun Chen Yueling' [Tear Stains in Paradise – On Chen Yueling, the Women's Olympic 10Km Walking Champion], in Wu Shaozu (ed.), *Tong xiang aoyun guanjun zhi lu* [The Road towards Olympic Champions], Shanghai: Huadong shifan daxue chuban she, 1993, p.203.

28. Jing Lin, *The Red Guards' Path to Violence: Political, Educational, and Psychological Factors*, New York: Praeger, 1991, p.127.

29. Donald W. Ball and John W. Loy, *Sport and Social Order: Contributions to the Sociology of Sport*, Addison-Wesley Publishing Company, 1975, p.25.

30. Alan Tomlinson and Ilkay Yorganci, 'Male Coach/Female Athlete Relations: Gender and Power Relations in Competitive Sport', *Journal of Sport & Social Issues*, 21, 2 (1997), p.152.

31. She was interviewed in Beijing in June 1995.

32. Li Guizhi was interviewed in 1995 in Beijing.

33. Zhang Tong was interviewed in 1996 in Beijing.

34. Yuan Yue, '1995–1996 nian zhongguo chengshi shehui wending yu gongzhong xintai' [Urban Stability and Public Opinion in 1995–96], in Jiang Liu (ed.), *1995–1996 nian zhongguo shehui xingshi fenxi yu yuce* [China in 1995–96: Analysis and Forecast of the Social Situation], Beijing: Zhongguo shehui kexue chuban she, 1996, p.119.

35. Qi Ming and Tian Yubao, 'Zhongguo titan neimu de shenceng baoguang' [The Exposure of the Chinese Sports Community], in Shi Hangpo (ed.), *Zhongguo tiyu de fenfen yuyu* [The Plight of China's Sport], Beijing nongye daxue chuban she, 1990, p.3.

36. Li Guizhi was interviewed in Beijing in 1995.
37. *Beijing qingnian bao* [Beijing Youth Daily], 13 Sep. 1995.
38. Zhonghua renmin gongheguo guowuyuan xinwen bangongshi [The News Office of the State Council of the PRC], 'Zhongguo funv zhuangkuang' [The Situation of Chinese Women], *Renmin ribao* [People's Daily], 3 June 1994.
39. *Zhonghua renmin gonghe guo zhixing 'tigao funv diwei de neiluobi qianzhang xin zhanlue' de guojia baogao* [National Report on the Implementation of the Nairobi Strategy of Promoting Women's Status by the PRC], *Renmin ribao* [People's Daily], 11 Oct. 1994.
40. Zhou Weiweng, 'Chenshi zhiye funv de jiating juese' [Urban Career Women's Family Role], in Shao Jiechai (ed.), *Dangdai zhongguo funv diwei* [Contemporary Chinese Women's Status], Beijing daxue chubang she, 1995, p.118.
41. Based on 2,200 questionnaires in 1994, Luo Shi found that about 39.1 per cent of female respondents and 8.59 per cent of males were exclusively responsible for household chores, while 32.72 per cent of couples shared them. (Luo Xin, 'Zhongguo zhiye nuxin jiaoshe chongtu de tedian jiji biaoxiang – jian wenjuang shuju fenxi' [Characteristics and Manifestations of Role Conflict of Career Women in China – Data Analysis of Questionnaires], in Sa Lianxiang (ed.), *Zhongguo nvxing jiaoshe fazhang yu jiaoshe chongtu* [Women's Role Development and Role Conflict in China], Beijing: Zhongguo renmin daxue nuxin yanjiu zhongxin, Minzhu chuban she, 1995, p.69.
42. According to a survey of towns in Hebei province, women spent 4.38 hours per day on housework, while men spent only 2.17 hours. Data from Huang Dezhi and Feng Chunfeng, 'Chapter 11: Relationships between the Sexes in the New Age of Reform and Open Policy', in Min Jiayin, *The Chalice and the Blade in Chinese Culture*, p.550.
43. With reference to this issue, see Tong Shaoshu, 'Shuangcong jiaoshe chongtu zhong de zhongguo funv fazhang wenti' [Issues on the Development of Chinese Women with the Conflict of Double Roles], *Zhejian xuekang* [Zhejian Academic Journal], 1994 (1), pp.67–70; Yang Zhi, 'Dangdai zhongguo nvxing jiaoshe chongtu de xianzhuang, yuanyin yi gaishan tian' [Female Role Conflict in Modern China: Present State, Causes and Suggestions for Improvement], in Sa Lianxiang, *Zhongguo nuxin jiaoshe fazhang yu jiaoshe chongtu* [Women's Role Development and Role Conflict in China], p.32.
44. Lai G., 'Work and Family Roles and Psychological Well-being in Urban China', *Journal of Health and Social Behaviour*, 36, 1 (1995), pp.11–37.
45. Margery Wolf, *Revolution Postponed: Women in Contemporary China*, Stanford, CA: Stanford University Press, 1985, p.73.
46. Data from Guojia tiwei jihua caiwu si [Planning and Financial Department of the NSC], *Tiyu shiye tongji nianjian (neibu ziliao)* [Statistical Yearbook of Sport] (Internal Information), 1994.
47. Huo Ju and Li Gan, 'Qingchun yijiu, yingxiong rugu – Beijing nuchu sang laojian suxian' [The Same Youth, the Same Appearance - Sketches of Three Old Female Footballers from Beijing], *Qingnian Bao* [Youth Daily], 22 Oct. 1997.
48. After the 1992 Olympic Games, she retired and got married. Not long after, she emigrated to Canada and gave birth to a son.
49. Jin Ling, Asian female high-jump record holder in the late 1980s, re-emerged in national competitions the year after she gave birth to her son. She won the 1997 National Games.
50. Deford, F., 'An Old Dragon Limbers Up: Sports in China, a Special Report', *Sports Illustrated*, 15 Aug. 1988, pp.36–43.
51. According to interviewee Ye Qiaobo, a famous speed-skater in the 1980s and the early 1990s.
52. According to interviewee Qiu Zhonghui, a former table-tennis champion.
53. She was interviewed in Beijing in March 1996.
54. About 95 per cent of sampled women and 93.1 per cent of sampled men praised the

importance of husband's support for women's successful careers. For the details, see Luo Xin, 'Zhongguo zhiye nuxin jiaoshe chongtu de tedian jiji biaoxiang' [Characteristics and Manifestations of Role Conflict of Career Women in China], p.83.

55. The interviewee was Qiu Zhonghui.
56. Chong-chor Lau, 'The Chinese Family and Gender Roles in Transition', in Joseph Cheng (ed.), *China Review 1993*, Hong Kong: Chinese University Press, 1994, pp.13, 20.
57. Lu Yuanzheng, *Zhongguo tiyu shehui xue* [Sports Sociology of China], Beijing tiyu daxue chuban she, 1996, p.94.
58. The interviewee was Jin Dongxian. Interview took place in 1995 in Beijing.
59. Du Fangqin, 'Zhenyin daode zhonghe tan' [An Overview of Chastity and Morality], in Li Xiaojiang (ed.), *Huaxia nvxing zhi mi* [The Mystery of Chinese Women], Beijing: Shenghua, dushu, xinzhi sanliang shudian, 1990, p.99.
60. Zhongguo Tongji ju [China's Statistical Bureau], *Zhongguo 1993 nian tongji nianjian* [1993 Statistical Yearbook of China], Beijing: Zhongguo tongji chuban she, 1994, p.93.
61. Meng Xianfan, G*aige dachao zhong de zhongguo nvxing* [Chinese Women in the Tide of Reform], Beijing: Zhongguo shehui kexue chuban she, 1995, p.174.
62. Xue Ninglan, 'S*hi jiasuo haishi shengjing: zhongguo nvxing yu fa zongheng tan'* [Shackle or Bible: Horizontal and Vertical Remarks on Chinese Women and Law], Beijing: zhongguo renmin daxue chuban she, 1992, p.89.
63. Two members of the world champion CWVT are divorced.
64. Li Ruiying, 'Lianai hunying jiating guannian de bianhua jiqi duice' [Changes in the Values of Love and Marriage and Measures to Deal with Them], *Guangming ribao* [Guangming Daily], 9 Feb. 1994.
65. Zhang Xinxin is a female writer who ripped away the facade of sexual equality in the early 1980s. Her works include 'How Did I Miss You' (*Wo dumo shinian ni*), 'On the Same Horizon' (*Zai tongyi qipao xiang shang*), 'The Dream of Our Generation' (*Womeng zhe yi dai ren de meng*) and 'The Last Haven' (*zui hou de bifen gang*). She bluntly points out that men and women do not have the same starting-line in modern competition. She emphasises the conflicts between family, love and career that beset women.
66. Rudolf G. Wagner, 'The PRC Intelligentsia: A View from Literature', in Joyce K. Kallgren (ed.), *Building a Nation-State: China after Forty Years*, Berkeley, CA: Institute of East Asian Studies, University of California, 1990, p.175.
67. For the details, see Zhonghua renmin gonghe guo guowu yuan xinwen banggong shi [News Office of the State Council of China], *Zhongguo funv wengti baipi shu* [White Paper on the Situation of Women in China], Beijing, 1994.
68. From 1991 to 1995 she studied at the Beijing University of Physical Education. She was interviewed in Beijing in June 1995.
69. Female athletes in such sports as wrestling, shot-put and weightlifting have more difficulties finding boyfriends or husbands. Because of this, they are allowed to get married while they are in training.
70. Nicholas D. Kristof and Sheryl Wudunn, *China Wakes - The Struggle for the Soul of a Rising Power*, London: Nicholas Brealey Publishing, 1994, p.214.
71. John Knight and Song Lina, 'Why Urban Wages Differ in China', in Keith Griffin and Zhao Renwei (eds), *The Distribution of Income in China*, New York: St Martin's Press, 1993, p.248.
72. According to a survey of 11 provinces, by the end of 1987 about 64 per cent of the laid-off workers were women. For the details, see Meng Xianfan, G*aige dachao zhong de zhongguo nvxing* [Chinese Women on the Wave of Economic Reform], p.49.
73. As enterprises gradually become self-financing and self-managing in the new period of economic reform, maternity and childcare welfare is burdensome. Thus, most of them tried to cut the benefits that women had enjoyed in the pre-reform period.

74. Not until the early 1990s were students assigned to employers by the universities in which they had enrolled. After 1987 most graduates returned by employers to universities and colleges were female. In 1987, the prestigious Beijing University had over 100 female graduates rejected by employers (see *Zhongguo funv bao* [Chinese Women's Newspaper], 31 July 1987).

75. Xue Ninglan, S*hi jiasuo haishi shengjing* [Shackle or Bible], p.143.

76. Fu Yu, 'Qingchu "jingshe yapian" keburonghuan: quanguo fulian fu zhuxi Huang Jicha tan "shaohuang" "dao fei"' [The Urgent Task of Clearing up 'Spiritual Opium': On 'Anti-Pornography' and 'Anti-Illegality' – Remarks by Huang Jichao, Deputy Chairwoman of the National Women's Association], *Renmin ribao* [People's Daily], 18 Nov. 1994.

77. For example, between 1995 and mid-1996 cases of abduction reached 7,221 and 7,547 women and children in Sichuan. For the details, see Weng Jieming (ed.), *Zhongguo fazhang baogao shu 1998 nian: zhongguo fazhang zhuangkuang yu qushi* [Report on Chinese Development, 1998: Trends in China's Development], Beijing: Zhonggong zhongyang dangxiao chuban she, 1998, p.332.

78. Li Xiaojiang, 'Gaige dachao zhong de zhongguo nvxing' [Chinese Women in the Reform Era], in Li Xiaojiang (ed.), *Zhongguo nvxing de kunhuo* [The Puzzles Facing Chinese Women], Beijing: Shenghuo, dushu, xinzhi shanglian shudian, 1990, p.391.

79. Zheng Xiaoying (ed.), *Zhongguo nvxing renkou wengti yu fazhang* [The Female Population and Its Development in China], Beijing daxue chuban she, 1995, p.265.

80. Nancy E. Riley, 'Gender Equality in China: Two Steps Forward, One Step Back', in William A. Joseph (ed.), *China Briefing: The Contradictions of Change*, New York: M.E, Sharpe, 1997, p.95.

81. Bill Brugger and Stephen Reglar, *Politics, Economy and Society in Contemporary China*, London: Macmillan, 1994, p.294.

82. Ibid.

83. The Central Committee of the CCP and the China Women's Association required in 1990 that by the end of the twentieth century every city/county-level Party and government organisation should have at least one female cadre. For the details, see *Renmin ribao* [People's Daily], 11 Oct. 1994.

84. Lu Meiyi and Zheng Yongfu, 'The Women's Movement and Women's Liberation in China', in Min Jiayin, *The Chalice and the Blade in Chinese Culture*, p.531.

85. United Nations, *The World's Women, 1995: Trends and Statistics*, New York: United Nations, 1995, p.174.

86. Brownell, *Training the Body for China*, p.96.

87. Zhang Caizhen, 'Zhongguo funv tiyu fazhang huimou yu zhanwang' [Review and Projection of Chinese Women's Sports Development], *Tiyu wenshi* [Sport History], 1995 (4), p.8.

88. Guojia tiwei jihua caiwu si [Planning and Finance Department of the NSC], *Tiyu shiye tongji nianjian (neibu ziliao)* [Statistical Yearbook of Sport] (internal information), 1994, p.39.

89. Guojia tiwei wenshi si [Literature and History Department of the NSC], *Tiwei xitong zhiliao tongji* [Statistical Information on the Sports Community], 1992, pp.2, 6.

90. *Tiyu shiye tongji nianjian* [Statistical Yearbook of Sport], 1994, pp.152–3.

91. Ibid.

92. In 1994, in Guangdong the percentage of female coaches was 18.4 per cent, but that of athletes was 38.7 per cent. In Sichuan the figures were 20 per cent and 43.5 per cent respectively.

93. *Tiwei xitong zhiliao tongji* [Statistical Information on the Sports Community], 1992.

94. 'Zhongguo aoyun daibiao tuan jiaolianyuan yundongyuan mingdan' [List of Coaches and Athletes in the Chinese Delegation to the Olympic Games], *Beijing wanbao* [Beijing Evening News], 17 June 1996.

95. Ellis Cashmore, *Making Sense of Sports* (2nd edn), London and New York: Routledge, 1996, p.145.

96. Confucianism has been challenged violently and frequently in the twentieth century, especially during the period of the May Fourth Movement (1919) and the Cultural Revolution (1966–76). Confucianism was once again attacked in the anti-Lin and Confucius campaign in the Cultural Revolution (see Chapter 3).

97. Wang, Jia, '40,000 diaocabiao xiansi zhongguo funv de shehui diwei' [Data Reveal the Social Status of Chinese Women: Investigation of 40,000 Questionnaires], *Zhongguo funv* [Chinese Women], 1992 (1), pp.24–5.

98. After Zhang Caizhen stepped down from the position of deputy minister of the National Sports Commission, there was no woman in the minister-level leadership of the NSC. There is only one female principal in the ten sports university/institutes affiliated to the NSC.

99. Ellen J. Staurowsky, 'Women Coaching Male Athletes', in Michael A. Messner and Don F. Sabo (eds), *Sport, Men, and the Gender Order: Critical Feminist Perspectives*, Champaign, IL: Human Kinetics, 1990, p.163.

100. R. Connell, *Gender and Power*, Cambridge: Polity Press, 1987, pp.98–9.

Epilogue

1. Chen Yiyun (translated by S. Katherine Cambell), 'Out of the Traditional Halls of Academe: Exploring New Avenues for Research on Women', in Christina K. Gilmartin (ed.), *Engendering China: Women, Culture, and the State*, Cambridge, MA: Harvard University Press, 1994, p.76.

2. Ezra F. Vogel, *Canton Under Communism: Programs and Politics in a Provincial Capital, 1949–1968*, Cambridge, MA: Harvard University Press, 1969, p.269.

3. Within the two years 1974 and 1975, they broke seven world records in archery and shooting. Female alpinist Pan Duo became the first woman in the world to climb Mount Everest from its northern slope in 1975.

4. Jersey Liang et al., 'Zhonghua renmin gongheguo renkou nianning' [The Age of Population in the People's Republic of China], *Hehui kexue yu yixue* [Social Science and Medicine], 23 (1986), p.1354.

5. State Statistical Bureau, 'China's Population Structure', *Beijing Review*, 5–11 Dec. 1988, p.31.

6. David B. Kanin, 'Ideology and Diplomacy: The Dimension of Chinese Political Sport', in Benjamin Lowe et al., (eds.), *Sports and International Relations*, Champaign, IL: Stipes Publishing Company, 1978, p.273.

7. According to a survey of 1,500 youths in Guangzhou, 81 per cent of respondents held this view (see Stanley Rosen, 'Students and the State in China: The Crisis in Ideology and Organization', in Arthur Lewis Rosenbaum (ed.), *State and Society in China: The Consequences of Reform*, Boulder, CO: Westview Press, 1992, p.171).

8. Yuan Honghen, 'Benjie 'shijia' pingxuan, huojianzhe nannu bili wei 1:9: zhongguo tiyu yinsheng yanshuai toushi' [The Ratio of the 'Best Ten' Athletes Selected This Year was 1:9: An Exploration of the Female Blossoming and the Male Withering in Chinese Sport], *Beijing wanbao* [Beijing Evening News], 9 April 1999.

9. Since the mid-1980s the phenomenon *yinsheng yanshuai* [blossoming of the female and withering of the male] has been questioned and debated throughout the country.

10. Zhang Yao, '1995 nain woguo sheng qu shi suoshu youxiu yundong dui qingkun fenxi' [Analysis of Provincial, Autonomous Regions and Municipal Elite Sports Teams in 1995], *Tiyu gongzuo qingkuang* [The Situation of Sports Affairs], 610, 2 (1996), pp.6–8.

11. Three contributions contribute to this judgement. First, many sports were newly introduced to women. Second, women's inequality is pervasive in the world, leading to less investment in women's sport in many other countries. Finally, Chinese women have the historical heritage of hard work and obedience.

12. See Jim Riordan and Jinxia Dong, 'Chinese Women and Sports Success, Sexuality and Suspicion', *The China Quarterly*, 145 (March 1996), pp.130–52.
13. Nancy E. Riley, 'Gender Equality in China: Two Steps Forward, One Step Back', in William A. Joseph (ed.), *China Briefing: The Contradictions of Change*, Armonk, NY: M.E. Sharpe, 1997, p.107.
14. See Chapter 6.
15. Zhang Tianbai, 'Di 26 jie aoyunhui ji zhongguo tiyu daibiaotua cansai qingkuang' [Situation of the Chinese Delegation at the 26th Olympic Games], *Tiyu gongzuo qingkuang* [The Situation of Sports Affairs], 624–5, 16–17 (1996), p.9.
16. Suhan Breslin, 'Centre and Province in China', in Robert Benewick and Paul Wingrove (eds), *China in the 1990s*, London: Macmillan, 1995, p.65.
17. The number of ministries and commissions was reduced from 40 to 29 in 1998. For details, see 'Reports on Ninth NPC (National People's Congress) and CPPCC', *China Daily*, 6 March 1998, p.1.
18. http://www.chinatoday.com/general/a.htm£popu.
19. 'Quarterly Chronicle and Documentation', *The China Quarterly*, 153 (March 1998), p.199.
20. 'Quarterly Chronicle and Documentation', *The China Quarterly*, 154 (June 1998), p.461.
21. John Gittings, *Real China: From Cannibalism to Karaoke*, London: Simon & Schuster, 1996, p.272.
22. Zhen Xing et al., 'Beijing shehui fazhan xingshi zonghe pingjia yu yuce' [Synthetic Evaluation and Forecast of Beijing Social Development], in Hou Yulan (ed.), *1996–1997 Nian Beijing shehui xingshi fenxi yu yuce* [Analysis and Forecast of the Social Situation: Beijing 1996–97], Beijing: Tongxin chuban she, 1997, pp.19–36.
23. John Gittings, *Real China*, p.270.
24. This was written before the 2000 Olympics.
25. Interviewed in Beijing, 1996.
26. Zhou Dongtao and Tan Z. (eds), *Zhuangui de zhongguo* [China in Transition], Beijing: Gaige chuban she, 1996, pp.217–18.
27. Ibid., p.220.
28. James Tyson and Ann Tyson, *Chinese Awakenings: Life Stories from the Unofficial China*, Boulder, CO: Westview Press, 1995, p.2.

Bibliography

In Chinese

Unpublished sources

Guojia tiwei [National Sports Commission], *1961–63 tiyu gongzuo huiyi zhiliao* [Material of Sports Work Conferences], Beijing tiyu xueyuan (Beijing Institute of Physical Education), 1964.

Guojia tiyu yundong weiyuanhui wenjian: Ming Fa [Documents of the National Sports Commission: Ming Fa] 26, (80)Nao Zhong Ji Zi; 81, (80)Ti Zheng Zi, 253 (1980).

Guojia tiwei ticao chu [Gymnastic Department of the National Sports Commission], *1973 nian quanguo ticao xunlain gongzuo huiyi wenjian* [Documents of the 1973 National Training Gymnastics Conference] (Beijing tiyu xueyuan, 1973).

Guojia tiwei wenshi si [Literature and History Department of the NSC], *Tiwei xitong ziliao tongji* [Statistical Information on the Sports Community], 1992.

Guojia tiwei zhengce fagui si (ed.), *Difang tiyu fagui zhidu huibian (xiace)* [The Collection of Local Sports Laws and Regulations (second volume)], 1995.

Guojia tiwei zhengce fagui si [Policy and Law Department of the NSC] (ed.), *Tiyu gaige wenjian xuebian 1992–1995 (neibu zhiliao)* [Collection of Document on Sports Reform 1992–95 (Internal Information)] (Beijing tiyu daxue chuban she, 1996).

Guojia tiwei zhengce fagui si [Policy and Law Department of the NSC] (ed.), *Zouxiang 21 shiji de sikao – quanguo tiwei xitong lingdao ganbu lunwen ji* [Reflections on Approaching the 21st Century – Collection of Papers Written by Leading Cadres of the Sports Community Across the Country] (Beijing tiyu daxue chuban she, 1996).

Sichuan sheng zhi: tiyu zhi [Sichuan Provincial Record: Sports Record] (draft).

'Woguo 18 ge yundong xiangmu jishu fazhan ziliao' [Material on the Technical Development of 18 Sports in China], in Beijing tiyu xueyuan [BIPE] (ed.), *61 nian tiyu gongzuo huiyi cankao wenxian* [Reference Document of the 1961 Sports Conference] (Beijing tiyu xueyuan [BIPE], 1964), pp.1–160.

Zhong, B., *Chengji ziben he diwei huode: woguo youxiu yundongyuan qunti shehui liudong de yanjiu* [Performance Capital and Status Attainment: Sport and Social Mobility among Chinese Elite Athletes], Ph.D. dissertation, Beijing University of Physical Education, 1997.

Published articles

'1989 nian quanguo tiwei zhuren huiyi dui tiyu jianguo, jingpai yishi, qunzhong tiyu yu jingji tiyu xietiao fazhang de yixie yilun' [Discussions on Becoming a Sports Power, Gold-Medal Awareness, the Harmonious Development of Mass Sport and Elite Sport in the Conference of the National Sports Commission's Directors], *Tiyu luntan* [Sports Forum], 1989 (3), pp.2–3.

A, Di, 'Jujian Zhengtang – Aoyun jianli xiezheng' [Huge Bonus Causes Shake-up – Analysis of Olympic Rewards], *Tiyu zhi chun* [Spring of Sport], 125 (Jan. 1993), pp.3–5.

Bianji [Editorial], 'Tiyu jie de yici duihua' [A Dialogue in the Sports Community], *Tiyu luntan* [Sports Forum], 1988 (1), pp.9–10.

Bianji [Editorial], 'Feiyue qianjin de woguo tiyu shiye' [The Advance of Chinese Sport], *Renmin ribao* [People's Daily], 25 Oct. 1959.

Chao, F. and Huang, Y., 'Chendu shi bufen jiazhang dui jingji tiyu taidu de chouyang diaocha [Survey of Some Parents' Attitudes to Elite Sport], *Sichuan tiyu kexue* [Sichuan Sports Science], 1989 (2), pp.25–7.

Chao, J. and Li, H., 'Guoji yongliang daibiao tuan juxin fabuhui [The FINA Delegation Holds News Conference], *Zhongguo tiyu bao* [China Sports Daily], 20 Feb. 1998.

Chen, B. and Lin, P., 'Guangyu tiyu yundong rencai jiaoliu de yanjiu' [A Study of Sports Talents' Mobility], *Sichuan tiyu kexue* [Sichuan Sports Science], 1988 (1), pp.6–10.

Chen, H. and Lin S., Guangdong nvzi zuqiu yundong [Women's Football in Guangdong], *Guangdong tiyu shiliao* [Guangdong Sports History Document], 1997 (1), pp.21–2.

Chen, J., '1993 nian quanguo jingji shehui fazhan jihua wancheng qingkuang de baogao ji 1994 nian quangji shehui fazhan jihua de caoan' [Report on the Implementation of the 1993 National Economic and Social Development Plan (NESDP) and the Draft of the 1994 NESDP], *Renmin ribao* [People's Daily], 25 March 1994.

Chen, W., 'Guangdong tiwei yi zhanlue yianguang guanzhu yeyu xunlian' [Guangdong Sports Commission Pays Attention to Amateur Training with a Strategic Vision], *Tiyu gongzuo qingkuang fanying* [Reflections on the Sports Situation], 5 (10 March 1986, pp.12–13.

Chu, Y.,'Ma jia jun: zaisheng haishi xiaowan?' [The Ma Family Army: Reborn or Disappeared?] *Dandai tiyu* [Contemporary Sport], March 1995, pp.4–6.

Dong, X. et al., 'Dui aoyun zhanlue xiangmu touru jiegou de fenxi yu duiche jianyi' [An Analysis of the Investment Structure of the Olympic Strategy Events and Opinions about Relevant Measures], *Tiyu kexue* [Sports Science], 13, 4 (1993), pp.8–10.

Dong, Y., 'Shenzhen ren ping kang ban zhong zhiye' [Shenzhenese Opinions about the Prestige of One Hundred Occupations], *Zhongguo funv bao* [Women's Daily of China], 24 July 1998.

Duan, L., 'Aoyun guanjun bingbai quanyun' [Olympic Champions Were Defeated at the National Games], *Tiyu zhoubao* [Sports Weekly], 9 Sep. 1997.

Fu, Y., 'Qingchu "jingshe yapian" keburonghuan: quanguo fulian fu zhuxi Huang Jicha tan "shaohuang" "dao fei"' [The Urgent Task of Clearing up 'Spiritual Opium', 'Anti-Pornography' and 'Anti-Illegality' – Remarks by Huang Jichao, Deputy Chairwoman of the National Women's Association], *Renmin ribao* [People's Daily], 18 Nov. 1994.

Fu, Z., 'Wuo shuo liaojian de Chengdu jidu jiaohui nu qingnian hui ji nu qingnian hui yin ti zhuang kaiban tiyu de qingkuang [My Personal Knowledge of Sports Development in the YMCA and the Musical and Sport Special School of the YMCA in Chengdu], *Sichuan tiyu shiliao* [Sichuan Sports History Information], 1984 (1).

'Gaige kaifang shiwu nian zhongguo tiyu chengjiu huihuang' [The Remarkable Achievements of Chinese Sport during the One and Half Decades of Reform and Opening-up to the Outside], *Zhongguo tiyu bao* [China Sports Daily], 9 Feb. 1994.

Gao Huimin, 'Sishi niandai qian Hanyuan tiyu fazhang gaikuang' [Review of Sports Development Before 1940], *Sichuan tiyu shiliao* [Sichuan Sports History], 1984 (4), pp.13–15.

Guangdong tiyu fanzhang jijin hui, 'Guanyu geiyu cangjia 25 jie aoyunhui qude youyi chengji de yundongyuan jiaolianyuan jianjin jianli de jueding'[A Decision to Reward Successful Athletes and Their Coaches at the 25th Olympic Games], *Guangdong tiyu shiliao* [Guangdong Sports History Information], 1992 (3), p.37.

Guangdong tiyu shi xuehui, Huanan shifan daxue tiyu xi [Sports History Society, Physical Education Department of the South China Normal University], Guangdong youxui yundongdui shixiang fazhan shi chutan [A Preliminary Study of the History of the Administration of Guangdong Elite Sports Teams], Guangdong tiyu shiliao [Guangdong Sports History Information], 1992 (3), pp.1–3.

'Guojia tiwei jueding shishi jiaolianyuan dengji zhi' [National Sports Commission Decides to Implement Coach's Ranking across the Country], *Tiyu bao* [Sports Daily], 13 May 1963.

Guojia tiwei shangbing diaocha zhu [The Survey Group of the NSC on Injury and Illness], Guanyu zhishu yundongdui shanbing wenti de diaocao baogao [Report on Injury and Illness of Sports Teams], *Tiyu kexue jishu ziliao* [Sport Science and Technology Information], 81 (1961), pp.3–7.

Guojia tiwei [The NSC], 'Ji wu qijian tiyu bixu jianchi gaige, kuochong daolu, zhixin fenlei zhidao yi qude geda de chengjiu – quanguo tiwei zhuren gongzuo huiyi baogao' [During the Seventh Five-year Period Sport Must Insist on Reform, Further Development and Efficient Management According to the Characteristics of Each Sport in order to Make Greater Progress – Reports of the National Conference of the Sports Commission Directors], *Tiyu gongzuo qingkuang fanying* [Reflections on the Sports Situation], 9 (April 1986), pp.7–8.

Guojia tiwei yu difan tiwei gongjian xunlian jidi mianling de wenti ji jiejue de jianyi [The Issues and Suggestions that Face the NSC and Local Sports Commissions In Co-building Training Bases], *Tiyu gongzuo qingkuang*, 622, 14 (1996), pp.16–18.

'Guojia tiyu zhongju lin (di yi hao): Guanyu yange jinzhi zai tiyu yundong zhong shiyong xinfen ji xinwei de guiding (zhangxin)' [The Decree of the National Sports Bureau (No.1): Regulations Strictly Forbidding the Use of Drugs in Sport], *Zhongguo tiyu bao* [China Sports Daily], 5 Jan. 1999.

Guojia tongji ju [State Statistical Bureau], '1984 nian quanguo shehui jingji fazhan gongbao [Communiqué on National Social and Economic Development in 1984], *Renmin ribao* [People's Daily], 9 March 1985.

Hao Q., 'Dandai zhongguo zhuangye jinji tizhi de tezheng yu pingjia' [The Characteristics and Evaluation of the Specialised Competitive Sports System in Contemporary China], *Tiyu kexue* [Sports and Science], 2 (1992).

He, B., 'Zhao Rongsheng shijian fanshi lu' [Reflections on the Zhao Rongsheng Event], *Beijing wanbao* [Beijing Evening News], 11 April 1998.

Hu, S., 'Yige minchu zai chensi' [A Nation is Contemplating], *Renmin ribao* [People's Daily], 7 April 1988.

Huang, C., 'Chuan jun Didiao Dongjin' [Sichuanese March Eastwards with Low Quotas], *Tiyu wenzhai zhoubao* [Sports Digest Weekly] 72 (1997), p.5.

Huang, J., 'Jindai shiqi guangdong tiyu dashi ji' [Record of Major Sports Events in Guangdong in Modern Times], *Guangdong tiyu shiliao* [Guangdong Sports History Document], 2 (1992).

Huang, Z., 'Tiyu duanlian bangzhu tamen chengwei zhongguo de nv feixingyuan' [Physical Exercises Helped Them Become the Female Pilots of China], *Xin tiyu* [New Sport], May 1952, pp.30–1.

Hui, W., 'Ma Jia Jun aoyun jixun shengmi shizhong you le xiaweng' [Reasons for the Mysterious Absences from the Ma Family Army], *Lianhe zhaobao* [United Morning News], 22 Oct. 2000.

Huo, J. and Li, G., 'Qingchun yijiu, yingxiong rugu – Beijing nvchu sang laojian suxian' [The Same Youth, the Same Appearance – Sketches of Three Old Female Footballers from Beijing], *Qingnian Bao* [Youth Daily], 22 Oct. 1997.

Jian, P., 'Zhongguo juchong mianmian guan' [The Situation of Weightlifting in China], *Beijing wanbao* [Beijing Evening News], 1 Sep. 1999.

Jin, Z., 'Xuannian dengshen de quanyun zuoci zhizheng' [Unpredictable Rankings at the National Games], *Tiyu wenzai zhoubao* [Sports Digest Weekly], 482 (1997), p.1.

Jun, M. and Ha, K., 'Liu Hongyu Wang Yan fen huo jinzhou jin yin pai' [Liu Hongyu and Wang Yan Won Gold and Silver Medals in Walking], *Beijing wanbao* [Beijing Evening News], 28 Aug. 1999.

Li, D. and Luo X., 'Huang Zhihong: yi ren san tai xi' [Huang Zhihong Plays Three Roles], *Xin tiyu* [New Sport], 1997 (5), p.22.

Li, G., 'Guangdong zuqiu yundong shi' [Football History in Guangdong], *Guangdong tiyu shiliao* [Guangdong Sports History Information], 1992 (3), pp.53–4.

Li, H. and Wang R., 'Beijing shi tiyu changguang zujian dui gongzhong kaifang' [Beijing Sports Stadiums and Fields Gradually Open to Public], *Beijing wanbao* [Beijing Evening News], 13 Sep. 1996.

Li, H., ' Lan young weijin yaowu, er shi si ming yundongyuan shou chufa' [Male Swimmers were Caught Drug Positive and 24 Athletes were Punished], *Beijing wanbao* [Beijing Evening News], 7 April 1998.

Li, H., '88 nian aoyunhui hou renmin riyi quexing de tiyu quanli yishi: tiyu gaige de nan-dian' [The Increasingly Awakening of a Consciousness of Sports after the 1988 Olympic Games: the Difficult Issues of Sports Reform], *Tiyu* [Sport], 7 (1989), pp.11–12.

Li, J., 'Qian tiaogao yundongyuang Ni Zhingqing shouhui bei panxing' [The Former High Jumper Ni Zhiqing was Sentenced to Jail for Eight Years for Accepting Bribes], *Renmin ribao* [People's Daily], 26 April 1995.

Li, K., 'Yanzheng de lichang – zhongguo fan xingfenji dahui xianchang suxie [Stringent Attitude – Literary Sketches of the Anti-drug Meeting in China], *Beijing wanbao* [Beijing Evening News], 3 March 1995.

Li, P., 'Zhongguo xingfengji shoujian mianmian guan' [An Overview of Chinese Performance-Enhancing Drug Tests], *Tiyu wenzhai zhoubao* [Sports Digest Weekly], 14 April 1994, p.3.

Li, P. et al., 'Beijing shi tiyu julebu qingkun diaocha' [Inquiry into the Situation of Beijing Municipal Sports Clubs], *Tiyu gongzuo qingkuang* [The Situation of Sports Affairs], 615, 7 (1996), pp.2–6.

Li, R., 'Lianai hunyin guannian de bianhua jiqi duice [Change in the Values of Love and Marriage and Measures to Deal with them], *Guangming ribao* [Guangming Daily], 9 Feb. 1994.

Li, S. and Lin, S., 'Guangdong sheng tiaoshui yundong' [Diving in Guangdong], *Guangdong tiyu shiliao* [Guangdong Sports History Information], 37, 1 (1992), pp.39–41.

Li, T., 'Shaonian ertong yeyu tiyu xuexiao' [Spare-time Sports Schools for Juniors], Guojia tiyu wenshi xinxi bianji weiyuan hui [Editorial Commission of State Sports Literature and History Information] (ed.), *Tiyu shiliao* [Sports History Information], 11, Beijing: Renmin tiyu chuban she, 1984, pp.88–9.

'Li Tieying zai quanguo tiwei zhuren huiyi shang jianhua sishuo: zhongguo zhengfu jianjue fandui shiyong xingfenji' [Reflections on Li Tianying's Remarks at the National Conference of Sports Commission Directors], *Zhongguo tiyu bao* [China Sports Daily], 17 Jan. 1998.

Li, Z. and Dai, J., 'Tiyu mingxin "jinjun" daxue ketan' [Sports Stars 'March' to University Classroom], *Beijing Wanbao* [Beijing Evening News], 12 Sep. 1998.

Liang, J., et al., 'Zhonghua renmin gongheguo renkou nianning' [The Age of Population in the People's Republic of China], *Hehui kexue yu yixue* [Social Science and Medicine], 23 (1986).

Liang, S. et al., 'Dui Beijing shi tiwei tigong dui bang zhuren fuzhe zhi xia de zhu jiaolian zheren zhi de diaocha' [A Survey of the Head Coach Responsibility System Under the Leadership of the Class Director in Beijing Municipal Sports Teams], *Tiyu gongzuo qingkuang* [The Situation of Sports Affairs], 13 (July 1992), pp.12–13.

Liang, Y., 'Cong shuzhi kan xin zhongguo nvzi tiyu' [Data Reveal Women's Sport in New China], *Gongren bao* [Workers' Daily], 9 March 1988.

Liang, Z., 'Cong "ran qiou" tanqi' [About 'Conceding to Rivals'] *Tiyu Luntan* [Sports Forum], 1989 (6), pp.23–4.

Lin, S. et al., 'Beijing tiyu gaige de shijian he kangfa' [The Ideas and Practices of Sports Reforms in Beijing], *Tiyu gongzuo qingkuang fanying* [Reflections on the Sports Situation], 64 (4 March 1988), pp.3–5.

Lin, Y., 'Guanyu Beijing shi yiuxiu yundongdui wenhua jiaoyu naru jiaoyu jiegou gaige de diaocha' [A Survey of the Integration of the Academic Education of Elite Sports Teams into the Mainstream Educational Structure in Beijing], *Tiyu gongzuo qingkuang* [The Situation of Sports Affairs], 526–7, 14–5 (1992), pp.29–32.

Liu, D., 'Nu gangpu chengzhang de zhangai ji duice [The Obstacle to the Promotion of Female Cadres and the Measures to Solve the Problem], *Gongre ribao* [Workers' Daily], 1 Nov. 1994.

Long, X., 'Dangdai zhongguo titan da jiaodian renwu' [Focused Sports Figures in Contemporary China], *Haishang wentan* [Haishang Literary Circles], 1996 (4), pp.4–11.

Lou, Y., 'Guangdong shenzhi: tiyu zhi gaishu' [An Overview of Guangdong Provincial Record: Sports Record], *Guangdong tiyu shiliao* [Guangdong Sports History Information], 1992 (3), p.41.

Lu, S. and Wang, Y., 'Rexian zhong de leng shikao – guanyu nvzhi jinji tiyu yu qunzhong tiyu fancha de shehui xue qushi' [Cool Thinking About a Hot Topic – A Sociological Analysis of the Contrast Between Women's Competitive and Mass Sport], *Tiyu wenshi* [Sports Literature and History], 1995 (4), pp.18–19.

Ma, Y., 'Jiaolianyuan yundongyuan shehui shenwang jiaogao [Coaches and Athletes Have Relatively High Social Status], *Zhongguo tiyu bao* [China Sports Daily], 27 Dec. 1997.

Mou, J., 'Nuli fenjin, zaizhang hongtu – beijing shi dangwei he zhengfu juxing tiyu gongzuo huiyi' [Strive to Advance and Re-create Great Prospects – the Beijing Municipal Party Commission and Government Holds a Meeting on Sport], *Tiyu gongzuo qingkuang fanying* [Reflections on the Sports Situation], 1986 (4), pp.3–4.

Nan, M., 'Quanguo yeyu tiyu xunlian gongzuo yantao hui zongshu' [Review of the National Coaching Seminar on Amateur Sport], *Tiyu gongzuo qingkuang* [The Situation of Sports Affairs], 655, 23 (1997), pp.8–11.

Nao, Q., 'Tiyu yu jingqian – cong Ma Jia Jun duiyuan lidui suokai qu' [Sport And Money – Reflections on the Split in the Ma Family Army], *Beijing guangbuo dianshi bao* [Beijing Broadcast and TV Newspaper], 10 Jan. 1995.

Nian, N., 'Jingguo bu ran xumei – xi zhongguo nvzhi yundong xiangmu zhouxian shijie de yuanyin [Women Are Not Inferior to Men – An Analysis of the Reasons for the Rise of Chinese Women's Sport to World Level], *Tiyu biao* [Sports Daily], 9 March 1988.

'Nvzhu xuyao guanan' [Women's Football Needs Attention], *Titan zhoubao* [Sports Weekly], 23 March 1999, p.3.

Pinglun yuan [Editorial], 'Fazhan funv tiyu yundong' [To Develop Women's Physical Education and Sport], *Xin tiyu* [New Sport], 1951 (8), p.10.

Pinglun yuan [Editorial], 'Feiyue qianjin de woguo tiyu shiye' [Chinese Sport Greatly Leaping Forward], *Renmin ribao* [People's Daily], 25 Oct. 1959.

Qing, T., 'Ma Junren youhua suo' [Ma Junren Has Something to Say], *Dandai tiyu* [Contemporary Sport], 4 (April 1995), p.3

Rao, Y., 'Beijing nannv pai xia shangdong' [Beijing Men's and Women's Volleyball Teams Went to Shangdong], *Beijing tiyu wenshi* [Beijing Sports Literature and History], 1986 (2), pp.285–6.

Shang, Q. et al., 'Gefu gezhong kunnan, zai huo jinpai zhongshu diyi – di shijie yayunhui zhongguo tiyu daibiao tuan de biaogao' [Overcoming Various Difficulties and Regaining First Place in the Gold Medal Count – Report of the Chinese Sports Delegation at the 10th Asian Games], *Tiyu gongzuo qingkuang fanying* [Reflections on the Sports Situation], 24 (Nov. 1986), pp.13–14.

Sichuan tiwei qunti chu [The Mass Sport Department of the Sichuan Sports Commission], Fazhan zhigong tiyu de yizhong hao xingshi – shi da qiye jian tiyu hezuo de qingkuang [A Good Means of Developing Workers' Sport – Sports Cooperation Between the Ten Big Enterprises], *Tiyu gongzuo qingkuang fanying* [Reflections on the Sports Situation], 6 (March 1986), pp.2–6.

'Shiping beiwu wu yongjian' [Contaminated Food Lead to Swimmers Being Misunderstood], *Yancen wanbao she qioumi shijie* [The Fans' World of the Ball Games of the Yancen Evening Press] 19 Aug. 1999.

Shiliao zhu [Historic Document Group], 'Sanzhong quanhui hou woshen tiyu bianhua fazhan qingkuang' [Change and Developments in Guangdong Sport after the Third Plenum], *Guangdong tiyu wenshi* [Guangdong Sports History Documents], 1992 (3), pp.2–15.

Shuan, R., 'Chen Lu he yi zhegang luosan' [Why Did Chen Lu Fail in Lausanne?], *Beijing wanbao* [Beijing Evening News] 19 April 1997.

Shu, S., 'Zhongguo tiyu jie mianlin shichang jinji de tiaozhang' [The Chinese Sports Community Faces the Challenge of the Market Economy], *Cankao xiaoxi* [Reference News], 12 Aug. 1994.

Shu Z., 'Wang Junxia chu shang' [Wang Junxia's Rise], *Xiangdai tiyu* [Modern Sports], 2 (Feb. 1994), pp.23–26.

Shu, Z., 'Majiajun de richu – Qu Yunxia' [The Sunrise of the Ma Family Army – on Qu Yunxia], *Dandai tiyu* [Contemporary Sport], 2 (Feb. 1994), pp.27–30.

Sun, B., 'Tiyu rencai de jiaoliu shi zai bixin' [The Exchange of Sports Talents Is Inevitable], *Beijing wanbao* [Beijing Evening News], 31 Oct. 1995.

Sun, B., 'Zhongguo tianjin yundong huapo' [The Decline of China's Athletics], *Beijing wanbao* [Beijing Evening News], 8 Aug. 1997.

Sun, X., 'Ji Beijing shi di er jie renmin tiyu dahui' [On the Second Beijing Municipal People's Sports Meeting], *Beijing tiyu wenshi* [Beijing Sports Literature and History], 2 (Dec. 1986), pp.14-18.

Sun, Z., 'Wusi hou sichuan xinxing tiyu yundong fazhan gaikuang' [The General Situation of the Development of New Sports in Sichuan After the May Fourth Movement], *Sichuan tiyu shiliao* [Sichuan Sports History Information], 1983 (1), pp.6–7.

Tan, H., 'Shi lun tiyu tizhi gaige de qianjing ji duiche' [Prospects for Strategy of Sports System Reform], *Tiyu yu kexue* [Sports and Science], 1988 (1), pp.21–23.

Tan, S., 'Dangdai zhongguo funv zhuangkuang de fenxi yu yuce' [Analysis and Prediction of the Situation of Contemporary Chinese Women], *Shehui xue yanjiu* [Sociological Studies], 1994 (3), pp.69–77.

Tang, M., 'Gengyun paitan sanshi zai – ji Sichuan nvpai zhong jiaolian Wang Defen' [Thirty Years on the Volleyball Court – Documentary on the Head Coach of Sichuan Women's Volleyball Team Wang Defen], *Sichuan tiyu shiliao* [Sichuan Sports History Information], 6, 2 (1984), pp.30–4.

Tong, S., 'Shuangcong jiaoshe chongtu zhong de zhongguo funv fazhan wenti' [Issues Regarding the Development of Chinese Women and the Conflict of Double Roles], *Zhejian xuekang* [Zhejian Academic Journal], 1994 (1), pp.67–70.

Tong, X, 'Liudong dajun nengfuo chengwei zhongguo tiyu junheng fazhan de chouma' [Whether the 'Mobile Army' Can Promote the Balanced Development of Sport in China], *Tiyu bao* [Sports Daily], 30 Oct. 1997.

Wang, H., 'Xianhua kaifang zhihou – cong zhongguo nupai jingshen zhong xuexi shenme' [After the Blooming of Fresh Flowers – What to Learn from the Spirit of the Chinese Women's Volleyball Team], *Wenghui bao* [Wenghui Daily], 28 Nov. 1981.

Wang, H., 'Shi Tianshu tan xinfenji shijian' [Shi Tianshu Talks about the Drug Incidents], *Lianghe zhaobao* [United Morning News], 5 March 1998.

Wang, Jia, '40,000 diaocabiao xiansi zhongguo funv de shehui diwei' [Data Reveal the Social Status of Chinese Women: Investigation of 40,000 Questionaires], *Zhongguo funv* [Chinese Women], 1992 (1), pp.24–5.

Wang, J., 'Nvnan shangxin dao heshi' [When Will the Women's Basketball Stop Grieving], *Xin tiyu* [New Sport], 1997 (7), pp.8–11.

Wang, P., 'Guanyu wuosheng yundong gongzuo qingkuang huibao' [Report on Sports Development in Guangong], *Guangdong tiyu shiliao* [Guangdong Sports History Information], 1987 (3), pp.1–4.

Wang, X., 'Ba yun jun tuan' [Troops at the National Games], *Tiyu wenhua yuekan* [Sports Cultural Monthly], Oct. 1997, pp.6–8.

Wang, X., 'Nuxing yishi yu funv jiefang' [Women's Self-Awareness and Their Emacipation], *Dongfang* [Orient], 35, 5 (2000), pp.49–53.

Wei, Z., 'Gaige kaifan zhong de guangdong tiyu' [Guangdong Sport in the Period of Reform and 'Opening Up' to the Outside], *Tiyu wenshi* [Sport History], 59, 1 (1993), pp.56–8.

Wu, S., 'Bayun jinchui gaige fen' [The Eighth National Games Promote Reforms], *Xin tiyu* [New Sport], 1997 (5), pp.20–1.

Wu, S., 'Wu Shouzhang tongzhi tang beizhang aoyunhui' [Comrade Wu Shouzhong's Remarks on Preparation for the Olympics], *Tiyu gongzhuo qingkuang* [The Situation of Sports Affairs], 14–15 (1995), pp.9–13.

Wu, S., 'Shixin aoyun zhangye yao zhuodao shuoduan zhanxian, tuchu zhongdian' [To Implement the Olympic Strategy, Shorten the Battle Line and Concentrate on the Priorities], *Zhongguo tiyu bao* [China Sports Daily], 14 March 1989.

'Wu Yanyan: wo yan gao zhongguo yongxie' [I Want to Sue the Chinese Swimming Association], *Yangzhou dushi bao* [Yangzhou City News], 19 July 2000.

'Wu Yanyan "guanshi" chuxiang chongda zhuanji' [A Great Turn Around in Wu Yanyan's 'Legal Case'], *Jinan ribao* [Jinan Times], 24 July 2000.

Xiao, M., 'Liaoning yuandong zhuqiu julebu qiuyuan shoury zhi duoshao' ['Revelations about the Earning of Players of Liaoning Far-East Football Club], *Wuhuang shidai zhoukan* [Five Circles Times], 1994 (1), pp.21–3.

Xiao, M., 'Shi Tianshu: fei yao quanti xiaogan bu ke?' [Shi Tianshu: Would All Swimmers Be Dismissed?], *Tiyu zhoubao* [Sports Weekly], 13 Aug. 1999.

Xinhua She [Xinhua News Agency], 'Zhongguo ao wei hui fabiao shengming' [The Chinese Olympic Committee Makes a Pronouncement], *Beijing wanbao* [Beijing Evening News], 4 Dec. 1994.

Xin, J., 'Zhongguo tiantan 'yinsheng yangshuai' de san da qushi' [Three Major Inspirations Concerning the 'Female Wax and Male Wane' in China's Athletics], *Xin tiyu* [New Sport], 1988 (4), pp.32–33.

Xu, J. et al., 'Zhongguo aoweihui zhaokai fang xingfengji dahui' [The Chinese Olympic Committee Holds an Anti-Drug Meeting], *Zhongguo tiyu bao* [China Sports Daily], 17 Jan. 1998.

Xu, S., 'Paiqiou waiyuan denglu jinmen' [Foreign Volleyball Players Arrive in Tianjin], *Titan zhoubao* [Sports Weekly], 9 Feb. 1999.

Xu, S., 'Zhongguo tianjin xian dasai yao chengji' [China's Athletics Should Target the World Competitions], *Dandai tiyu bao* [Contemporary Sports], 18–24 Nov. 1997.

Yang, M., 'Zhongguo tianjin dachu "chengbao" zhuhe chuan' [Chinese Athletes Adopt the 'Contract' Agreement], *Tiyu wenzhai zhoubao* [Sports Digest Weekly], 502 (1998), p.2.

Ye, C., 'Guangdong tiyu xingzheng jigou yange' [The Evolution of Sports Administration in Guangdong], *Guangdong tiyu shiliao* [Guangdong Sports History Information], 1996 (2), pp.8–12.

Yi, B., 'Ji Beijing shi renmin tiyu dahui' [On Beijing Municipal People's Sports Meeting], *Beijing tiyu wenshi* [Beijing Sports Literature and History], 2 (Dec. 1986), pp.1–8.

Yi, B., 'Beijing shi xuanba nanpai qiudui canjia huabei bisai' [Beijing City Selected Basketball and Volleyball Teams to Take Part in the North China Competitions], *Beijing tiyu wenshi* [Beijing Sports Literature and History], 1988 (3), pp.19–20.

Yuan, H., 'Zhengqian jinzhen, zhujin gaige – Wu Shouzhang zai aoyun xuanba sai shang de jianhua' [Increase Competition, Promote Reform – Wu Shouzhang's Remarks on the Olympic Games Trials], *Beijing wanbao* [Beijing Evening News], 2 June 1996.

Yuan, H., 'Benjie 'shijia' pingxuan, huojianzhe nannu bili wei 1:9: zhongguo tiyu yinsheng yanshuai toushi' [The ratio of the 'best ten' athletes selected this year was 1:9: The exploration of the female blossoming and the male withering in China's sport], *Beijing wanbao* [Beijing Evening News], 9 April 1999.

'Yuan Weimin tongzhi zai jiejian Ye Qiaobo shi de jianhua' [Yuan Weimin's Speech on Receiving Ye Qiaobo], *Tiyu gongzuo qingkuan* [The Situation of Sports Affairs]

(Internal Publication), 519, 7 (1992), p.3.

Zhang, C., 'Gaige ge zhongguo tiyu dailai le shengmo' [What Has Reform Brought to Chinese Sport?], *Xin tiyu* [New Sport], 1992 (4), pp.4–6.

Zhang, C., 'Zhongguo funiu tiyu fazhan huimou yu zhangwang' [Review and Projection of Chinese Women's Sport Development], *Tiyu wenshi* [Sport History], 1995 (4), pp.5–8.

Zhang J., 'Chunjie yongtian, changchu duliu' [Clear the Swimming Community and Eradicate Drug Taking], *Beijing wanbao* [Beijing Evening News], 8 April 1995.

Zhang, J., 'Zhongguo youyong: shengsi chunwang – zhongguo yongxie tan fandui xinfeng ji' [Chinese Swimming: Survive or Die – the Swimming Association Speaks about Combating Drug Abuses], *Beijing wanbao* [Beijing Evening News], 28 Aug.1999.

Zhang, L., 'Zhaogong zhong xingbie jishi xiexiang youwai gaibian [The Phenomenon of Gender Discrimination in Employment Will Be Overcome], *Jiangfang ribao* [Liberation Daily], 25 Oct. 1994.

Zhang, M., 'Zai riben de waiguo yundongyuan' [Foreign Athletes in Japan], *Guowai tiyu dongtai* [Developments in Sport Abroad], 1991 (8), pp.58–9.

Zhang, S. et al., 'Wuoguo tiyu sheshi jianshe de lilun yanjiu' [Theoretical Studies on the Building of Sports Facilities in China], *Tiyu kexue* [Sports Science], 1991 (1), pp.1–5.

Zhang, T., 'Di 26 jie aoyunhui ji zhongguo tiyu daibiaotua cansai qingkuang' [The Situation of the Chinese Delegation at the 26th Olympic Games], *Tiyu gongzuo qingkuang* [The Situation of Sports Affairs], 624–5, 16–17 (1996), pp.9–11.

Zhang, Y., '1995 nian woguo sheng qu shi suoshu youxiu yundong dui qingkung fenxi' [Analysis on Provincial, Autonomous Regions and Municipal Elite Sports Teams in 1995], *Tiyu gongzuo qingkuang* [The Situation of Sports Affairs], 610, 2 (1996), pp.6–8.

Zhan, T. and Zhang J., 'Zhujiang Sanjiaozhou qishi shehui fazhan pinggu' [An Assessment of the Social Development of Seven Cities in the Pearl River Delta], *Guangdong shehui kexue* [Social Sciences in Guangdong] (additional volume 1992), pp.179–82.

Zhao, Y., 'Qiangguo meng – dangdai zhongguo tie de wuqu' [The Dream of Being a Superpower – the Trap of Contemporary Chinese Sport], *Dangdai* [Contemporary], 1988 (2).

Zhao, Y., 'Majiajun diaocha' [Inquiries into the Ma Family Army], *Zhongguo zuojia* [Chinese Writer], 1998 (3), pp.1–213.

Zhong, G., 'Qingshaonian ertong yeyu tiyu xunlian qingkuang' [Sports Training in Spare-time Sports Schools for Young People], *Tiyu shiliao* [Sports History Information], 11 (1984), pp.98–102.

'Zhongguo aoyun daibiao tuan jiaolianyuan yundongyuan mingdan' [List of Coaches and Athletes in the Chinese Delegation to the Olympic Games], *Beijing wanbao* [Beijing Evening News], 17 June 1996.

'Zhongguo jianshe tiyu qiangguo yao zhuanghao "liangge zhangye" – benbao zhaokai de lilun taolun hui fayang zhaiyao' [China Must Insist on the 'Two Strategies' to Become a Sports Power – Extracts from Speeches at the Theoretical Seminar Held by the Sports Daily], *Tiyu bao* [Sports Daily], 2 May 1988.

'Zhongguo shehui tiyu xiangzhuang diaocha jieguo gongbu' [Promulgation of the Survey Results on Social Sport in China], *Zhongguo tiyu bao* [The China Sports Daily], 8 Aug. 1998, p.1.

'Zhongguo yongxie dui Wu Yanyan jinsai 4 nian' [The Chinese Swimming Association Bans Wu Yanyan for Four Years], *Jinan ribao* [Jinan Daily], 18 July 2000.

Zhonghua renmin gongheguo guowuyuan xinwen bangongshi' [The News Office of the State Council of the PRC], 'Zhongguo funv zhuangkuang' [The Situation of Chinese Women], *Renmin ribao* [People's Daily], 3 June 1994.

'Zhonghua renmin gongheguo nzhixin "tigao funv diwei de neiluobi qianzhang xin zhanlue" de guojia baogao' [National Report on the Implementation of the Nairobi Strategy on Promoting Women's Status by the PRC], *Renmin ribao* [People's Daily], 11 Oct. 1994.

'Zhonggua renmin gongheguo tiyu fa' [Sports Law of the People's Republic of China], *Zhongguo tiyu bao* [China Sports Daily], 1 Oct. 1995.

Zhong, S., 'Luli jianshe xinxing de tiyu xueyuan, peiyang gongchan zhuyi xinren' [To Strive to Build Up the New Type of Institute of Physical Education and Cultivate the Communist New Man], *Beijing tiyu xueyuan* [Beijing Institute of Physical Education], 96 (1959), pp.1–4.

Zhou, F., 'Shengzhen shi dui zhangzhu tiyu danwei he geren geiyu shihui' [Shengzhen Rewards the Enterprises and Private Organisations Who Have Sponsored Sport], *Tiyu gongzuo qingkuang* [The Situation of Sports Affairs], 52, 13 (1992), p.7.

Zhou, P. andYi, Y., 'Zhongguo nupai liu lian guan de xiwang zhi meng' [The Dream of Six Titles in Succession for the Chinese Women's Volleyball Team], *Tiyu chunjiu* [Sports Spring and Autumn], Feb. 1988, p.11.

Zhou, Z., 'Chen Yunpeng de kangfa' [Views of Chen Yunpeng], *Youyong* [Swimming], 1994 (1), p.11.

Zhou, Z., 'Jiefan hou gangao huilai de tiyu jiaoshi jiaoliangyuan yundongyuan' [Physical Education Teachers, Coaches and Athletes from Hong Kong and Macao After Liberation], *Guangdong tiyu shiliao* [Guangdong Sports History Information], 1986 (2), p.59.

Zhu, C. et al., 'Yi shenhua gaige wei dongli, ba wuosheng tiyu shiye tuixiang yige xin de fazhan jieduan – sichuan tiyu shiye fazhan de jiben zhuangkuang he 1988 – 1992 nian fazhan mubiao yu cuoshi' [Add Momentum to Reform and Raise Sichuan Provincial Sport to a New Level of Development – the Basic Situation of Sports Development in Sichuan and the Goals and Measures for the 1988–92 Period], *Sichuan tiyu kexue* [Sichuan Sports Science], 1988 (4), pp.7–12.

Zhu, D., 'Zhizhi jiating baoli keburonghuan [To Stop Domestic Violence is an Urgent Task], *Gongren ribao* [Worker's Daily], 2 Sep. 1994.

Zhuang, P., 'Xin zhongguo tiyu zhanxian shang de funv' [Women in the Sports Field of New China], *Xin tiyu* [New Sport], 1959 (5), pp.7–10.

'Zuigao renmin jiancha yuan gongzuo baogao' [Report of the Supreme People's Procuratorate], *Zhongguo fazhi bao* [China Legal Daily], 6 April 1987.

Published books and chapters in books

Beijing shi tiyu yundong weiyuan hui [Beijing Sports Commission], 'Beijing shi zhongdian qingshaonian yeyu tixiao guoqu jinian jiaoxue xunlian de yixie xiangfa' [Some Ideas on the Teaching and Coaching of Beijing Municipal Key Spare-Time Sports Schools for Young People in the Past Few Years], in Beijing tiyu xueyuan [BIPE] (ed.), *Tiyu gongzuo huiyi ziliao* [Material of Sports Conferences] 1964, pp.25–32.

Beijing shi tiyu yundong weiyuan hui [Beijing Sports Commission], 'Beijing shi tiyu jiuwu jihua' [The Ninth Five-year Plan of Beijing Sport], in Beijing shi tiwei [Beijing Sports Commission] (ed.) *1996 Beijing tiyu nianjian* [1996 Beijing Sports Yearbook] (Beijing: Renmin tiyu chuban she, 1997), pp.68–74.

Beijing tiyu xueyuan xuanshi bianji zhu [The Editorial Group of the History of the BIPE], *Beijing tiyu xuaxuan yuanshi* [History of the Beijing Institute of Physical Education] (Beijing tiyu xuexuan chuban she, 1993).

Beijing tiyu xueyuan [BIPE], *Beijing tiyu xueyuan zhi* [Annals of the Beijing Institute of Physical Education] (Beijing tiyu xueyuan chuban she, 1994).

'Beijing shi quxian tixiao yeyu xunlian qingkuang diaocha baogao' [Report on Amateur Training at District and County-level in Beijing], in Beijing shi tiwei [Beijing Sports Commission] (ed.) *1996 Beijing tiyu nianjian* [1996 Beijing Sports Yearbook] (Beijing: Renmin tiyu chuban she, 1997), pp.101–13.

'1996 nian Beijing shi tiyu gongzuo zhongjie (Annual Summary of Sports Work in Beijing in 1996)', in Beijing shi tiwei [Beijing Sports Commission] (ed.), *1996 Beijing Sports Yearbook* [Beijing Sports Yearbook] (Beijing: Renmin tiyu chuban she, 1997), pp.30–6.

Cai, F., *Huaxia shengxue-rujiao yu zhongguo wenhua* [Chinese Religion – Confucianism and Chinese Culture], Chengdu: Sichuan renmin chuban she 1995.

Chen, B., 'Xin shiqi sichuan tiyu shiye fazhan zhi sikao [Deliberation on the Development of Sichuan Sport in the New Era], in Guojia tiwei zhengce fagui shi [Policy and Law Department of the NSC], *Tiyu gaige wenjian xuebian 1992–1995* (neibu ziliao) [Collection of Document on Sports Reform 1992–5 (Internal Information)] (Beijing tiyu daxue chuban she, 1996), pp.248–57.

Chen, Z., Wang, H. and Wang, G. (eds), *Guan zhong guan: dangdai zhongguo titan chaoji mingxin diaoxiang* [Champions out of Champions: Sculptures of the Sports Superstars in Modern China] (Shijiazhuang: Huashan wenyi chuban she, 1990).

Chen, Z. (ed.), *Zhongguo ticao shi* [Gymnastics in China] (Wuhan chuban she, 1990).

'Chongsuo zixin, zaichuan huihuang' [Rebuild Self-confidence and Recreate Brilliance], in Zhongyan dianshi tai tiyu bu [Sports Department of China Central Television] (ed.), *Tiyu shalon wenji* [The Collection of the Sports Salon] (Beijing: Guoji wenhua chuban gongshi 1995), pp.222–33.

Deng, L. (ed.), *Dandai zhongguo Beijing* [Contemporary Beijing in China] (Beijing: Zhongguo shehui kexue chuban she, 1989).

Deng, Y., 'Liang ge hao xiang' [Try to Make a Good Showing], in Guojia tiwei xuanchuan bu [Propaganda Department of the NSC] (ed.), *'96 aoyun pingbo zhi ge* [Battle and Fighting Songs at the 1996 Olympic Games] (Beijing: Renmin tiyu chuban she 1997), p.100.

Dong, L., 'Shenhua gaige, nuli shixian Guangdong tiyu fazhan mubiao' [Expanding Reforms, Striving to Realise Guangdong's Targets of Sports Development], in Guojia tiwei zhengce fagui shi [Policy and Law Department of the NSC], *Tiyu gaige wenjian xuebian 1992–1995* (neibu zhiliao) [Collection of Document on Sports Reform 1992–5 (Internal Information)] (Beijing tiyu daxue chuban she, 1996), pp. 233–47.

Du, F., 'Zhenyin daode zhonghe tan' [An Overview of Chastity and Morality], in Li Xiaojiang (ed.), *Huaxia nvxing zhi mi* [The Mystery of Chinese Women] (Beijing: Shenghua, dushu, xinzhi sanliang shudian 1990), pp.87–123.

Feng, Z. and Lin, Y., *Kaifang yu fengbi: zhongguo chuantong shehui jiazhi quxiang jiqi dangqian liubian* ['Opening Up' Versus 'Closing Down': Chinese Traditional Value Orientation and Its Current Changes] (Shijiazhuang: Hebei renmin chuban she, 1987).

Gu, S., *Jiannan de qidian yu luodian de huihuang – zhongguo titan beiwang lu* [The Difficult Take-off and the Marvellous Landing – Memorandum Book of Chinese Sport] (Changchun: Jilin jiaoyu chuban she, 1994).

Gu, S., *Zhongguo tiyu shi* [Chinese Sports History] (Beijing: Beijing tiyu xueyuan chuban she, 1989).

Gu, S., *Zhongguo tiyu shi* [Chinese Sports History] (Beijing: Beijing tiyu daxue chuban she, 1997).

Guang, H. et al., 'Zhuang Zedong de sheng Luo' [The Rise and Fall of Zhuang Zedong], in Shi, R. (ed.), *Wenhua da geming zhong de mingren Zhi sheng jiang* [The Rise and Fall of Famous People during the Cultural Revolution] (Beijing: Zhongyang minzu xueyuan chuban she,1993), pp.292–302.

Guangdong she tongji ju [Guangdong Statistical Bureau], *Guangdong tongji nianjian 1994* [Guangdong Statistical Yearbook 1994] (Beijing: Zhongguo tongji, 1994).

Guangdong sheng tongji ju, *Qianjinzhong de guangdong: 1949–1988 nian guangdong shehui jingji fazhan qingkuang* [Guangdong Forging Ahead: The Character of Guangdong's Social and Economic Development, 1948–88] (Hong Kong: Dadao wenhua, 1989).

Guangdong tiyu yundong weiyuan hui [Guangdong Sports Commission], *Guangdong tiyu nianjian* [Guangdong Sports Yearbook] 1993.

'Guanyu Beijing shi tiyu julebu qingkuang de diaocha baogao' [Report on Sports Clubs in Beijing], in Beijing shi tiwei [Beijing Sports Commission] (ed.), *1996 Beijing tiyu nianjian* [1996 Beijing Sports Yearbook] (Beijing: Renmin tiyu chuban she, 1997), pp.63–74.

Guo, J. et al., *Len xian kang aoyun* [Coolly Looking at the Olympic Games] (Beijing: Zhongguo guanbo dianshi chuban she, 1998).

Guo, L. et al., '1995 nian Beijing shi renkou fazhan ji qi duiche' [Population Development in Beijing in 1995 and the Associated Strategy], in Hou Yulan (ed.), *1996–1997 nian Beijing shehui xingshi fenxi yu yuce* [Analysis and Forecast of the Social Situation: Beijing 1996–7] (Beijing: Tongxin chuban she, 1997), pp.37–42.

Guojia tiwei [The NSC], 'Guojia tiwei guanyu shenghua tiyu gaige de yijian' [The View of the NSC on Expending Sports Reform], Guojia tiwei fagui shi [The Law and Regulation Department of the NSC] (ed.), *Tiyu gaige wenjian xuanbian* [Selection of Documents on Sports Reform] (1992–5) (Beijing: Xinhua chuban she, 1997), pp.31–7.

Guojia tiwei [The NSC] (ed.), *Zhongguo tiyu nianjian, 49–91 jinghua ben* (xia ce) [Sports Yearbooks in China, 49–91 (two volumes)] (Beijing: Renmin tiyu chuban she, 1993).

Guojia tiwei [The NSC], 'Guojia tiwei guanyu shenhua tiyu gaige de yijian (1993)' [Opinions of the NSC on the Expansion of Sports Reform], in Guojia tiwei [the NSC] (ed.), *Zhonghua renmin gongheguo tiyu fagui huibian* (1993–1996) [The Collection of Sports Laws and Regulations of the PRC] (Xinhua chuban she, 1997), pp.11–45.

Guojia tiwei jihua caiwu shi [Planning and Financial Department of the NSC], *Tiyu shiye tongji nianjian (neibu ziliao)* [Statistical Yearbook of Sport] (Internal Information), 1994.

Guojia tiwei lianhe diaocha zhu [United Survey Group of the NSC], 'Guanyu 12 ge quanguo xing dangxiang yundong xiehui shiti hua gaige shidian qingkuang de diaocha' [Survey of the Situation of 'Experimental' Reform: Turning the 12 Individual Sports Associations into Autonomous Entities], in Guojia tiwei zhengce fagui shi [Policy and Law Department of the NSC] (ed.), *Tiyu dangxiang xiehui shiti hua gaige yangtao wenji* [Collection of Papers on Turning Individual Sports Associations into Autonomous Entities] (Beijing tiyu daxue chuban she, 1994), pp.9–15.

'Guojia tiwei tiyu tizhi gaige de queding (caoan)' [The NSC's Decision to Reform the Sports System (draft)], in Guojia tiwei [The NSC] (ed.), *1986 zhongguo tiyu nianjian* [Sports Yearbook in China] (Beijing: Renmin tiyu chuban she, 1987), pp.75–87.

Guojia tiwei wenshi gongzuo weiyuanhui & Zhongguo tiyu shi xuehui [The Working Commission of Sports History of the NSC and China Sports History Society] (eds), *Zhongguo jindai tiyu shi* [China Modern Sports History], Beijing tiyu xue yuan chuban she, 1989, pp.419–62.

Guojia tiwei wenshi si [Literature and History Department of the NSC], *Tiwei xitong ziliao tongji* [Statistical Information on the Sports Community], 1992.

Guojia tiwei xuanchuang bu [Propaganda Department of the NSC], *Di yi jie guanguo yundong hui xuanchuan zhiliao* [Propaganda Material of the First National Games] Vol.1 (Beijing: Renmin tiyu chuban she, 1958).

Guojia tiwei xuanchuang bu [Propaganda Department of the NSC], *Tuanjie yu shengli de dahui – di sang jie quanguo yundonghui tongxin ji* [A United and Victorious Sports Meeting – Correspondence of the Third National Games] (Beijing: Renmin tiyu chuban she, 1976), p.20.

Guojia tiwei xuanchuang si [Propaganda Department of the NSC] (ed.), *Ma jia jun* [The Ma Family Army] (Beijing: Renmin tiy chuban she, 1994).

Guojia tiwei xuanchuang si [Propaganda Department of the NSC] (ed.), *'96 Aoyun pingbo zhi ge* [Battle and Fighting Songs at the 1996 Olympic Games], (Beijing: Renmin tiyu chuban she, 1997).

Guojia tiyu yundong weiyuan hui [The NSC] (ed.), *Zhongguo tiyu nianjian* [Sports Yearbook in China] (1986, 1987) (Beijing: Renmin tiyu chuban she, 1987, 1988).

Guojia tiwei zhengce fagui si (ed.), *Tiyu xitong ruan kexue yanjiu lunwen ji* [Collection of Research Papers on Soft Science in the Sports Community] (Beijing: Renmin tiyu chuban she, 1994).

Guojia tiwei zhengce yanjiu si [The Policy Research Department of the NSC], 'Guojia tiwei dangzhu guanyu jiaqiang renmin tiyu yundong de baogao' [A Report on Strengthening People's Physical Culture and Sport by the Party Group of the NSC], in Guojia tiwei zhengce yanjiu si [The Policy Research Department of the NSC] (ed.), *Tiyu yundong wenjian xuanbian 1949–1981* [Selected Collection of Document of Sport 1949–81] (Beijing: Renmin tiyu chuban she, 1982).

Guojia tongji ju [State Statistical Bureau], *Zhongguo tongji nianjian* (1992, 1995, 1999) [Chinese Statistical Yearbook (1992, 1995, 1999)] (Beijing: Zhongguo tongji chuban she, 1992, 1995, 1999).

He, X. (ed.), *Zhongwai wenhua zidian* [Dictionary of Chinese and Foreign Culture] (Haerbing: Hei longjian renmin chuban she, 1989).

Hou, Y. (ed.), *1996–1997 nian beijing shehui xingshi fenxi yu yuce* [Analysis and Forecast of the Social Situation: Beijing 1996–97] (Beijing: tongxin chuban she, 1997).

Hu, S., *Weilai bushi meng* [The Future is not a Dream] (Beijing: Baishang chuban she, 1992).

Jia, P. and Sun, X. (eds), *Zhongguo zhishi fenzi da liebian* [Fission of Chinese Intelligensia] (Beijing: Minzhu yu jianshe chuban she, 1997).

Jiang, L. (ed.), *Shehui lanpi shu – 1995–1996 nian zhongguo shehui xingshi fenxi yu yuce* [China in 1995–96: Analysis and Forecast of the Social Situation] (Beijing: Zhongguo shehui kexue chuban she, 1996).

Jin, S., 'Hancheng fansi lu' [Reflections on the Seoul Games], in Shi Hangpo (ed.), *Zhongguo tiyu de fengfeng yuyu* [The Plight of China's Sport], Beijing: Beijing longye daxue chuban she, 1990, p.53.

Jin, Y. and Liu, B. (eds), *Shiji zhi jiao de zhongguo funv yu fazhan – lilun, jinji, wenhua, jiankan* [Chinese Women and Their Development at the Turn of the Century – Theory, Economy, Culture and Health] (Nanjin: Nanjin daxue chuban she, 1998).

Jiao, Y., 'Lun jingdai zhongguo de funv jiefang shixiang' [About Women's Emancipation in Modern China], in *Beijing daxue funv wenti di san jie guoji yantao hui lunwen ji* [Collection of Papers of the Third International Women's Seminar in Beijing University] (Beijing: Beijing daxue chuban she, 1994), pp.187–201.

Lan, Y., 'Nupai bingbai shichu youyin' [The Defeat of Women's Volleyball Has its Reasons], in Shi, H. (ed.), *Zhongguo tiyu de fenfen yuyu* [The Plight of China's Sport] (Beijing nongye daxue chuban she, 1990), pp.130–42.

Lei, G., 'Luishui qingwu le tiantan – ji nvzi 10 gongli jinzhou ao yun guanjun Chen Yueling' [Tear Stains in Paradise – on Chen Yueling, the Women's Olympic 10km Walking Champion], in Wu Shaozu (ed.), *Tong xiang aoyun guanjun zhi lu* [The Road towards Olympic Championship] (Shanghai: Huadong shifan daxue chuban she, 1993), pp.199–203.

Li, F. and Liu, J. (eds), *Zhaigui duokui: shijie guanjun dansheng ji* [To Win the World Titles – the Birth of the World Champions] (??? 1992), pp.1–35.

Li, J. (ed.), *Titan nv mingxin* [Female Stars in the Sports Community] (Beijing: Guoji wenhua chuban she, 1994.)

Li, L., 'Quan shehui canru peiyan tiyu rencai' [All Sectors of Society Are Involved in Producing Sports Talents], in Wei, Z. (ed.), *Guangdong tiyu sishi nian* [40 Years of Guangdong Sports] (Guangzhou: Xin shiji chuban she, 1989), pp.29–33.

Li, R. (ed.), *Wenhua dageming zhong de mingren zhi shi* [The Deaths of Famous People during the Cultural Revolution] (Beijing: Zhongyang minzu xueyuan chuban she,1993).

Li, Q., *Dangdai zhongguo shehui fenceng yu liudong* [Social Stratification and Mobility in Contemporary China] (Beijing: Zhongguo jinji chuban she, 1993).

Li, X., 'Gaige dachao zhong de zhongguo nvxin' [Chinese Women in the Reform Era], in Li, X. (ed.), *Zhongguo nvxin de kunhuo* [The Puzzles Facing Chinese Women] (Beijing: Shenghuo, dushu, xinzhi shanglian shudian, 1990).

Li, X. (ed.), *Huaxia nvxing zhi mi* [The Mystery of Chinese Women] (Beijing: Shenghua, dushu, xinzhi sanliang shudian 1990).

Li, X. (ed.), *Xinbie yu zhongguo* [Gender and China] (Beijing: Shenghuo, dushu. xinzhi sanliang shudian, 1994).

Liaoning tiyu yundong weiyuan hui [The Liaoning Sports Commission] (ed.), *Liaoning tiyu nianjian* [Liaoning Sports Yearbook] (Liaoning guji chuban she, 1996).

Lin, S., '1987 nian tiyu gaige de yi dabu' [A Big Stride in Sports Reform in 1987], in Tiyu zhangyue fazhan hui [Society of Sports Development and Strategic Research] (ed.), *1987 zhongguo tiyu nianjian* [1987 Sports Yearbook] (Beijing: Renmin tiyu chuban she, 1988), pp.133–4.

Liu, W., 'Huang Xiaomin's xiexin yu gexin' [The Personality and Character of Huang Xiaomin], in Z. Chen (ed.), *Zhongguo ticao shi* [Gymnastics in China] (Wuhan chuban she, 1990), pp.276–84.

Lu, T., *Zhonghua renmin gongheguo lishi jishi* [Historic Record of the PRC] (Beijing: Hongqi chuban she, 1995).

Lu, Y., *Zhongguo tiyu shehui xue* [Sports Sociology of China] (Beijing tiyu daxue chuban she, 1996), p.94.

Lu G., *Zhongguo gulian* [Chinese Girls] (Beijing: Renmin tiyu chuban she, 1981).

Lu, Y., *Tiyu de shehui wenhua shenshi*[Social and Cultural Reflections on Sport] (Beijing tiyu daxue chuban she, 1998).

Lu, Y., *Zhongguo tiyu shehui xue* [Sports Sociology of China] (Beijing: Beijing tiyu daxue chuban she, 1996).

Lu, Y., *Jinji, zhongguo: jinji wenhua yu zhongguo de guomin xin* [Competition and China: the Culture of Competition and Nationalism in China] (Beijing: Zhonghua gongshang lianghe chuban she, 1997).

Lu, Y. and Lai, T., 'Dui Beijing shi quefa gao shuiping yundongyuan de shehui xue fenxi' [Sociological Analysis of the Lack of High Level Athletes in Beijing], in Beijing tiyu daxue keyan chu [Beijing University of Physical Education] (ed.), *Beijing tiyu daxue 45 nian xiaoqin kexue lunwen xuan* [Selection of Scientific Papers for the 45th Anniversary of Beijing University of Physical Education] (Beijing tiyu daxue chuban she, 1998), pp.168–173.

Luo, X., 'Zhongguo zhiye nvxing jiaoshe chongtu de tedian jiji biaoxiang – jian wenjuang shuju fenxi' [The Characteristics and Manifestations of Role Conflict among Career Women in China – Data Analysis of Questionnaires], in Sa, L. (ed.), *Zhongguo nuxin jiaoshe fazhan yu jiaoshe chongtu* [Women's Role Development and Role Conflict in China] (Beijing: Zhongguo renmin daxue nvxin yanjiu zhongxin, Minzhu chuban she, 1995), pp.61–86.

Lv, T., and Hang, Y., *Zhonghua renming gongheguo lishi ji shi: jiannan tangsuo* [Historical Record of the PRC: A Difficult Search] (1956–8) (Beijing: Hongqi chuban she, 1994).

Lv, T., *Zhonghua renming gongheguo lishi ji shi: quzhe fazhang* [Historical Record of the PRC: Zig-Zag Developments] (1958–65) (Beijing: Hongqi chuban she, 1994).

Ma, G., 'Jiefang sixiang, shenhua gaige, jiaqiang guanli, cujin Beijing shi tiyu yundong xietiao fazhan' [Liberating Thought, Expanding Reform, Strengthening Management and Promoting the Harmonious Development of Sport in Beijing], in Beijing shi tiwei [The Beijing Sports Commission] (ed.), *Beijing tiyu nianjian 1992–93* [Beijing Sports Yearbooks 1992–3] (Beijing: Renmin tiyu chuban she, 1993), pp.5–6.

Ma, Y., *Zhongguo de zuotian he mingtian 1840–1987 guoqing shouce* [China's Yesterday and Today: Handbook of the National Situation between 1840 and 1987] (Beijing: Jiefangjun chuban she, 1989).

Mao Zedong, 'Lun tiyu zhi yanjiu' [On Physical Education], *Xin qingnian* [New Youth] (April 1917).

Meng, X., *Gaige dachao zhong de zhongguo nvxing* [Chinese Women in the Tide of Reform] (Beijing: Zhongguo shehui kexue chuban she, 1995).

Qi, M. and Tian, Y., 'Zhongguo titan neimu de shenceng baoguang' [The Exposure of the Chinese Sports Community], in Shi, H. (ed.), *Zhongguo tiyu de fenfen yuyu* [The Plight of China's Sport] (Beijing nongye daxue chuban she, 1990), pp.3–15.

Qi, M., 'Zhuang Yong de yihan' [Zhuang Yong's Regret], in Chen, Z., Wang, H. and Wang,

G. (eds), *Guan zhong guan: dangdai zhongguo titan chaoji mingxin diaoxiang* [Champions out of Champions: Sculptures of the Sports Superstars in Modern China] (Shijiazhuang: Huashan wenyi chuban she, 1990), pp.297–313.

Qiou, S. (ed.), *Gongheguo zhongda shijian he juece leimu* [The Inside Story of the Decision-Making on the Important Events in the PRC] (Changchun: Jinji ribao chuban she, 1997).

Qunti bu [Department of Mass Sport], 'Beijing shequ tiyu fazhan de xianzhuan ji duiche [The Present Situation and Strategy for Sports Development of the Beijing Communities], in Beijing shi tiwei [The Beijing Sports Commission] (ed.), [????] *1996 Beijing Sports Year-Book* (Beijing: Renmin tiyu chuban she,1997), pp.115–136.

Rong, G., '61 nian xunlian gongzuo huiyi baogao' [Report of the 1961 Sports Conference], in Beijing tiyu xueyuan [BIPE] (ed.), *Tiyu gongzuo huiyi ziliao* [Material of Sports Conferences] 1964, pp.1–3.

Rong, G. et al. (eds), *Dangdai zhongguo tiyu* [Sport in Contemporary China], (Beijing: Zhongguo shehui kexue chuban she, 1984).

Sha, J. (ed.), *Dangdai zhongguo funv diwei* [Contemporary Chinese Women's Status] (Beijing daxue chuban she, 1995).

Sha, L. (ed.), *Zhongguo minzhu xin* [The National Character of China], Vol.1 (Beijing: Zhongguo renmin daxue chuban she, 1989).

Sha, L. (ed.), *Zhongguo minzhu xin* [The National Character of China], Vol.2 (Beijing: Zhongguo renmin daxue chuban she, 1990).

'Shehui zhuyi tiyu de hualei – qiye he gaoxiao ban gao shuiping yundong dui' [Buds of Socialised Sports – Industrial Enterprises and Institutions of Higher Learning Run High–Level Sports Teams], in Guojia tiwei [The NSC] (ed.), *Zhongguo tiyu nianjian 1986* [Sports Yearbook in China,1986] (Beijing: Renmin tiyu chuban she, 1987), pp.10–12.

Su, X., Liu, P. et al., *Zhongguo ren 'dabai' zhongguo ren* [Chinese 'Defeat' Chinese] (Beijing: Huayi chuban she, 1993).

Sun, F., 'Yinxiong zai wuo beihou' [Heroes Behind Me], in Guojia tiwei xuanchuan bu [Propaganda Department of the NSC] (ed.), *96 aoyun pingbo zhi ge* [Battle and Fighting Songs at the 1996 Olympic Games] (Beijing: Renmin tiyu chuban she 1997), pp.27–8.

Sun, Q., 'Chenggong laizi dui shiye de zhizhu zhuiqou' [Success Comes from Unrelenting Pursuit], in Guojia tiwei xuanchuan bu [Propaganda Department of the NSC] (ed.), *96 aoyun pinbo zhi ge* [Battle and Fighting Songs at the 1996 Olympic Games] (Renmin tiyu chuban she, 1997) pp.171–2.

Sun, W. et al., *Shijie 100 titan mingxing paihang bang* [The 100: A Ranking of the Most Famous Athletes in the World] (Beijing: Zhongguo jinji chuban she, 1994).

Tao, C. (ed.), *Zhongguo funv shehui diwei geiguan* [An Overview of Chinese Women's Social Status] (Beijing: Zhongguo funv chuban she, 1993).

Tan, S., '1995 nian zhongguo funv jibeng qingkuang' [Chinese Women in 1995], in Jiang Liu (ed.), *Shehui lanpi shu – 1995–1996 nian zhongguo shehui xingshi fenxi yu yuce* [China in 1995–1996: Analysis and Forecast of the Social Situation] (Beijing: Zhongguo shehui kexue chuban she, 1996).

Tian, M. et al., 'Woguo youxiu yundongyuan tuiyu anzhi qingkuan ji gaijin duice' [Job Assignments of Retired Athletes and the Improvement of Policy], in Guojia tiwei zhengce fagui shi (ed.), *Tiyu xitong ruan kexue yanjiu lunwen ji* [Collection of Research Papers on Soft Science in the Sports Community] (Beijing: Renmin tiyu chuban she, 1994), pp.101–13.

Tiyu zhanlue fazhan hui [Society of Sports Development and Strategic Research] (ed.), *Zhongguo tiyu nianjian 1985* [Sports Yearbook in China 1985], Renmin tiyu chuban she, 1986.

Tiyu zidian bianji bu [Editorial Department of Sports Dictionary], *Tiyu zidian* [Sports Dictionary] (Shanghai zidian chuban she, 1984).

Tuanjie yu shengli de dahui – di sang jie quanguo yundonghui tongxin ji [A Sports Meeting with Union and Victory – Correspondence of the Third National Games] (Beijing: Renmin tiyu chuban she, 1976).

Wang, B. et al., *Zhongguo zai shikao – '92 da xieshi* [Rethinking China: the Picture of 1992] (Beijing: Zhuanli wenxian chuban she, 1993).

Wang, C., *Wuhuang renshi xiang* [A View of the 'Five Ring' Community] (Zhongguo wenliang chuban she, 1995).

Wang, G. et al., 'Woguo youxiu yundongyuan tuiyu anzhi xianzhuang ji duice yanjiu' [Job Assignments of Retired Athletes and the Improvement of Policy in China], in Guojia tiwei zhengce fagui shi (ed.), *Tiyu xitong ruan kexue yanjiu lunwen ji* [Collection of Research Papers on Soft Science in the Sports Community] (Beijing: Renmin tiyu chuban she, 1994), pp.20–2.

Wang, H. (ed.), *Zhongwai tiyu mingxin yiwen qushi* [The Legends of Chinese and Foreign Sports Stars] (Beijing: Huaxia chuban she, 1988).

Wang, J., 'Tiyu houbei rencai xunlian taidu de fazhan yu bianhua – dui jin 5 nian lai tiyu houbei rencai xunlian taidu de zhuizhong kaocha' [The Development and Changes in Training Attitudes of Young Sporting Talents – a Longitudinal Study of Training Attitudes in Young Sporting Talents in the Last Five Years], in Zhongguo tiyu kexue xuehui [Chinese Sports Science Society] (ed.), *Di wu jian quanguo tiyu kexue dahui lunwen zaiyao* [Proceeding of the Fifth National Sports Science Congress] (Beijing: 1997), pp.33–4.

Wang, J., 'Beijing shi tiyu gongzhou yao luli shixiang liangge gengben xing zhuangbian' [Beijing's Sport Has to Undergo Two Fundamental Changes], in Guojia tiwei zhengce fagui shi [Policy and Law Department of the NSC] (ed.), *Tiyu gaige wenjian xuebian 1992–1995* (neibu zhiliao) [Collection of Document on Sports Reform 1992–95 (Internal Information)] (Beijing tiyu daxue chuban she, 1996), pp.86–95.

Wen, L. and Hao, R. (eds), *Wenhua da geming zhong de mingren zhi sheng* [The Rise of Famous People during the Cultural Revolution] (Zhongyang minzhu xueyuan chuban she, 1993).

Wei, Z., (ed.), *Guangdong tiyu sishi nian* [Forty Years of Guangdong Sport] (Guangzhou: Xin shiji chuban she, 1989).

Weng, J. (ed.), *Zhongguo fazhan baogao shu (1998): zhongguo fazhan zhuangkuang yu qushi* [Report on China's Development, 1998: Trends in China's Development] (Beijing: Zhonggong zhongyang danxiao chuban she, 1998).

Wu, B., *Xiandai zhongguo ren – cong guoqu zhouxiang weilai* [Contemporary Chinese – from Past to Future] (Shengyan: Liaonin daxue chuban she, 1992).

'Wu Shaozu zhuren zai quanguo tiwei zhuren zuotan hui kaimushi shang de jianhua' [Speech of Wu Shaozu, director of the State Sports Commission, at the Opening Ceremony of the National Forum of Sports Commission Directors] (13 Nov. 1993), in Guojia tiwei zhengce fagui shi [Policy and Law Department of the NSC] (ed.), *Tiyu gaige wenjian xuebian 1992–1995* (neibu zhiliao) [Collection of Document on Sports Reform 1992–95 (Internal Information)] (Beijing tiyu daxue chuban she, 1996), pp.19–35.

'Wu Shaozu zhuren zai 1995 nian quanguo tiwei zhuren huiyi shang de zhongjie jianhua' [Speech of Director Wu Shaozu at the 1995 National Forum of Sports Commission Directors], in Guojia tiwei zhengce fagui shi [Policy and Law Department of the NSC] (ed.), *Tiyu gaige wenjian xuebian 1992–1995* (neibu zhiliao) [Collection of Document on Sports Reform 1992–95 (Internal Information)] (Beijing tiyu daxue chuban she, 1996), pp.57–60.

Xiao, D. (ed.), *Wenge zhimi* [The Mystery of the Cultural Revolution], Vol.5 (Zhaohua chuban she, 1993).

Xiao, J. (ed.), *Zhongguo zhiqing miweng lu* [The Secret Records of Chinese Educated Youth] (Beijing: Zuojia chuban she, 1993).

Xie, C., *Dayuejin kuanlang* [The Raging Waves of the Great Leap Forward], Zhenzhou: Henan renmin chuban she, 1994.

Xinhua she guonei xinxi zhu [Domestic Information Department of the Xin Hua News

Agency] (ed.), *Zhonghua renmin gongheguo dashi ji* [Documents of the Major Events of the PRC], Vol.3 (Beijing: Xinhua chuban she, 1982).

Xinhua she guonei xinxi zhu [Domestic Information Department of the Xin Hua News Agency] (ed.), *Zhonghua renmin gongheguo dashiji* [Documents of the Major Events of the PRC] (1985–8) (Beijing: Xinhua chuban she, 1989).

Xong, Y. (ed.), *Miang dui 21 shiji de xuanzhe – dangdai funv yanjiu zhui xin lilun gailang* [Choice in the Twenty-first Century – An Overview of the Latest Theories of Contemporary Feminist Studies] (Tianjin: Tianjin renmin chuban she, 1993).

Xu, C. et al., 'Tiaogao' [High Jump], in Xian Yalong (ed.), *Zhongguo youshi jinji xiangmu zhisheng guilu* [The Laws of Winning in China's Dominant Sports] (Beijing: Renmin tiyu chuban she, 1992).

Xu, J. (ed), *Zhonghua renmin gongheguo dashi ji* [Documents on the Major Events of the PRC] (1989–94) (Beijing: Kexue jishu wenxian chuban she, 1994).

Xue, N., *Shi jiasuo haishi shengjing: zhongguo nvxin yu fa zongheng tan* [Shackle or Bible: Horizontal and Vertical Remarks on Chinese Women and Law] (Beijing: zhongguo renmin daxue chuban she, 1992).

Yan, J., *Wenghua da geming zhong de dixia wengxue* [Unpublished Literature of the Cultural Revolution] (Qinan: Zhaohua chuban she, 1993).

Yang, Z., 'Dangdai zhongguo nvxing jiaoshe chongtu de xianzhuang, yuanyin yi gaishan tian' [Female Role Conflict in Modern China: Present State, Causes and Suggestions for Improvement], in Sha, L. (ed.), *Zhongguo minzhu xin* [The National Character of China], Vol.?? (Beijing: Zhongguo renmin daxue chuban she, 1995), pp.30–43.

Yayunhui zhuwei hui [Organising Committee of the Asian Games] (ed.), *1990 nian Beijing di yi jian yazhou yundonghui gongzuo baogao* [Working Report of the 1990 Asian Games in Beijing] (Zhongguo aolinpike chuban she, 1992).

Yi, J., *Tiyu wenhua xue gailun* [General Review of China's Sports Culture] (Taibei: Wenjin chuban she youxian gongshi, 1998).

Yuan, W. (ed.), *Zhongguo paiqou shi* [Volleyball in China] (Wuhan: Wuhan chuban she, 1994).

Yu, J., *Zhonghua renmin gongheguo lishi jishi: dachao yongdong* [Historical Record of the PRC: Moving Wave] (1990–2) (Beijing: Hong qi chuban she, 1994).

Yuan Y., '1995–1996 nian zhongguo chengshi shehui wending yu gongzhong xintai' [Urban Stability and Public Opinion in 1995–6], in Jiang, L. (eds), *1995–1996 nian zhongguo shehui xingshi fenxi yu yuce* [China in 1995–6: Analysis and Forecast of the Social Situation], Beijing: Zhongguo shehui kexue chuban she, 1996, pp.112–24.

Zhao, Y., *Bingbai Hancheng – Zhaoyu Tie Wenti Baogao Wenxue Ji* [Defeat in Seoul – the Report of Zhaoyu Tie Wenti] (Beijing: Zhongguo shehui kexue chuban she, 1988).

Zhang, L. (ed.), *Chuantong xue yinlun—zhongguo chuantong wenhua de duowei fangshi* [Tradition Study – Multi-dimensional Thinking about Chinese Traditional Culture] (Beijing: Zhongguo renmin daxue chuban she, 1989).

Zhang, L. (ed.), *Chuantong wenhua yu xiangdai hua* [China's Traditional Culture and Modernisation] (Beijing: zhongguo renmin daxue chuban she, 1987).

Zhang, L. (ed.), *Shiji qing – zhongguo yu aolinpike yundong* [A Century of Contact – China and the Olympics] (Beijing: Renmin tiyu chuban she, 1993).

Zhang, Z., *Aoyun chao yong zhonghua hun* [The Olympic Wave Stirs the Chinese Soul] (Beijing: Zhonggong zhongyang danxiao chuban she, 1996).

Zheng, X. (ed.), *Zhongguo nvxin renkou wengti yu fazhan* [The Female Population and Its Development in China], Beijing daxue chuban she, 1995.

Zhong, B., *Chengji ziben he diwei huode:woguo youxiu yundongyuan qunti shehui liudong de yanjiu* [Performance Capital and Status Attainment: Sport and Social Mobility Among Chinese Elite Athletes] (Beijing tiyu daxue chuban she, 1998).

Zhongguo funv gangbu guanli xueyuan [The Cadre Management Institute of China] (ed.), *Zhongguo funv yundong wengxian ziliao huibian* [Collection of Documents on the Chinese Women's Movement], Vol.2 (Beijing: Zhongguo funv chuban she, 1988).

Zhongguo jiaoyu nianjian bianji shi [Editorial Office of Education Yearbooks in China], *Zhongguo jiaoyu nianjian 1949–1981* [Education Yearbooks in China 1949–1981] (Beijing: Zhongguo baike quanshu chuban she, 1982).

Zhonghua renmin gongheguo guojia tiyu yundong wei yuan hui [National Sports Committee of the PRC], *Quanguo tiyu shiye tongji zhiliao huibian* [Collection of Statistical Information on Sport in China] (1949–78) (Beijing: Renmin tiyu chuban she, 1979).

Zhonghua renmin gongheguo tiyu yundong weiyuan hui [The NSC] (ed.), *Xianxin tiyu fagui huibian (1949–1988)* [Collection of Current Sports Laws and Regulations (1949–88)] (Beijing: Renmin tiyu chuban she, 1990).

Zhonghua renmin gongheguo tiyu yundong weiyuan hui [The NSC] (ed.), *Zhonghua renmin gongheguo tiyu fagui huibian* [Collection of Sports Laws and Regulations in China] (1993–6) (Beijing: Xinhua chuban she, 1997).

Zhonghua renmin gongheguo guowu yuan xinwen banggong shi [News Office of the State Council of China], *Zhongguo funv wengti baipi shu* [White Paper on the Situation of Women in China] (Beijing, 1994).

Zhongguo tiyu nianjian bianji wieyuan bu [Editorial Committee of Sports Yearbooks in China], *Zhongguo tiyu nianjian 1979* [Sports Yearbook in China, 1979] (Beijing: Renmin tiyu chuban she, 1981).

Zhongguo tiyu shi xuehui [Society of China Sports History] (ed.), *Tiyu shi lunwen ji* [Collection of Papers on Sports History], Vol.6, Beijing: Renmin tiyu chuban she, 1989.

Zhongguo tongji ju [Chinese Statistical Bureau], *Zhongguo 1993 nian tongji nianjian* [1993 Statistical Yearbook in China] (Beijing: Zhongguo tongji chuban she, 1994).

Zhongyang dianshi tai tiyu bu [Sports Department of China Central Television] (ed.), *Tiyu shalun wenji* [Collection of the Sports Salon], Beijing: Guoji wenhua chuban gongshi, 1995.

Zhou, D. and Tan, Z. (eds), *Zhuangui de zhongguo* [China in Transition] (Beijing: Gaige chuban she, 1996).

Zhou, W., 'Chenshi zhiye funv de jiating juese' [Urban Career Women's Family Role], in Shao Jiechai (ed.), *Dangdai zhongguo funv diwei* [Contemporary Chinese Women's Status], (Beijing daxue chubang she, 1995), pp.114–23.

Zhou, Y., 'Nan juan zhi de gainian he lilun zhi pipan yu chumu tansuo' [Criticism and Preliminary Exploration on the Concept and Theory of Patriarchy], in Jin, Y. and Liu, B. (eds), Shiji zhi jiao de zhongguo funv yu fazhang – lilun, jinji, wenhua, jiankan [Chinese Women and Their Development at the Turn of the Century – Theory, Economy, Culture and Health] (Nanjin: Nanjin daxue chuban she, 1998).

Zhu, Q., '1995–1996 nian renmin shenghuo zhuankuan' [People's Living Standards in the Year of 1995–96], in Jiang, L. (ed.), *Shehui lanpi shu – 1995–1996 nian zhongguo shehui xingshi fenxi yu yuce* [China in 1995–96: Analysis and Forecast of the Social Situation] (Beijing: Zhongguo shehui kexue chuban she, 1996), pp.143–56.

Zhu, Z., 'Dui xin zhongguo sishi nian lai tiyu re de fenxi he dui weilai tiyu re de yuce' [Analysis of the Sports Craze during the Four Decades of New China and Predictions about its Future], in Zhongguo tiyu shi xiehui [China Sports History Association] (ed.), *Tiyu shi lunwen ji* [Collection of Papers on Sports History] (Beijing: Renmin tiyu chuban she, 1989) Vol. 6, pp.9–14.

Periodicals and newspapers

PERIODICALS

Beijing tiyu wenshi [Beijing Literature and History]
Beijing tiyu xueyuan xuebao guangdong tiyu shiliao [Guangdong Sports History Information]
Dongfang [The Orient]
Guangdong tiyu shiliao [Guangdong Sports History Information]
Guowai tiyu dongtai [Sports Developments Abroad]
Xi tiyu [New Sport]

Haishang wentan [Haishang Literature Circles]
Shehui kexue yu yixue [Social Science and Medicine]
Sichuan tiyu kexue [Journal of Sport and Science in Sichuan]
Sichuan tiyu shiliao [Sichuan Sports History Information]
Tianjin tiyu xueyuan xuebao [Journal of the Tianjin Institute of Physical Education]
Tiyu gongzuo qingkuang fanying [Reflections on the Sports Situation]
Tiyu gongzuo qingkuang [The Situation of Sports Affairs]
Tiyu kexue [Sports Science]
Tiyu shiliao [Sports History Information]
Tiyu wenhua yuekan [Sports Culture Monthly]
Tiyu wenshi [Sport History]
Tiyu zhi chun [Spring of Sport]
Youong [Swimming]
Zhongguo Funv [Chinese Women]

NEWSPAPERS
Cankao Xiaoxi [Reference Information Daily]
Beijing wanbao [Beijing Evening News]
Beijing ribao [Beijing Daily]
Beijing qingnian bao [Beijing Youth News]
Liaoning ribao [Liaoning Daily]
Lianhe zhaobao [United Morning News]
Jinan ribao [Jinan Times]
Renmin ribao [People's Daily]
Shijie jinji daobao [World Economic Herald]
Tiyu zhoubao [Sports Weekly]
Tiyu wenzhai zhoubao [Sports Digest Weekly]
Xinhua ribao [Xinhua Daily]
Zhongguo tiyu bao [China Sports Daily]
Zhongguo funv bao [Women's Daily of China]

In English

Dissertations

Breslin, S.G., *Changing Centre-Province Relations in the People's Republic of China in the 1980s* (Ph.D. dissertation, University of Newcastle, 1993).
Chen, D., *The Contract Management Responsibility System in China: An Institutional interpretation*, (Ph.D. dissertation, Aston University, 1993).
Chen, J., *Chinese Television Broadcasting in Transition – Between the Party and the Market* (Ph.D. dissertation, University of Sussex, 1995).
Cherrington, R.L., *Why Bother to Study? The Reform Generation of Educated Youth in 1980s China* (Ph.D. dissertation, University of London, 1995)
Du, H., *The Process of Transition from Central Planning to a Market-oriented Economy – A Study of the Impact of Decentralisation on the Cotton Textile Enterprises in China* (Ph. D. dissertation, University of Sussex, 1993).
Han, X., *Interdependence and the Problems of Adaptation: The Case of China in the 1980s* (Ph.D. dissertation, London School of Economics, University of London, 1993).
Kerr, D., *Contrasting Russian and Chinese Perspectives on the Future of Asia* (Ph.D. dissertation, University of Glasgow, 1995).
Lei, C.L., *Shifting Central-Provincial Relations in China: The Politics of Fixed Asset Investment in Shanghai and Guangdong, 1978–93* (Ph.D. dissertation, School of Oriental and African Studies, University of London, 1995).

Li, F., *Theory of Productive and Unproductive Labour: An Analysis of Chinese Commercial Development* (M.Sc. dissertation, University of Cambridge, 1991).

Li, Y., *The Challenges to Deng Xiaoping's Policy of Indirect Leadership over the Arts in China, 1979–1989* (Ph.D. dissertation, City University, 1994).

Lin, C.Z., *Marxian Economic Categories and Problems of Centralised and Decentralised Planning in China* (D.Phil. dissertation, University of Oxford, 1990).

Liu, H., *Markets, Marketing, and Marketing Behaviour – An Empirical Examination in China and Britain* (Ph.D. dissertation, University of Warwick, 1991).

Mao, Y., *Modern Chinese Universities and Adult Education with Particular Reference to Shandong Teachers' University in China and the University of Nottingham in Britain* (Ph.D. dissertation, University of Nottingham, 1990).

Sheehan, J., *Conflict Between Workers and the Party-State in China and the Development of Autonomous Workers' Organizations 1949–1984* (Ph.D. dissertation, School of Oriental and African Studies, University of London, 1996).

Takahara, A., *The Politics of Wage Reform in Post-Revolutionary China* (Ph.D. dissertation, University of Sussex, 1988).

Zhang, L-F., *After Mao: Cinema and Chinese Society – a Sociological Analysis of the Chinese Cinema (1978–92)* (Ph.D. dissertation, University of Leicester, 1995).

Zhong, Q., *The Effects of the "Great Cultural Revolution" on Sport in China, 1966–1976* (Ph.D. dissertation, University of Idaho, USA, 1995).

Published articles

'About the Bikini', *China Sports*, 1987 (3), p.13.

Allen, K., 'Chinese Drug Test Confirm Suspicions', *USA Today*, 1 Dec. 1994, p.40.

Andors, P., 'The "Four Modernisations" and Chinese Policy on Women', *Bulletin – Concerned Asian Scholars*, 13 (1981), pp.44–56.

Bierling, J. and G. Murray, 'The Emerging Powers: China, Singapore, Hong Kong and Taiwan', *Current Sociology*, 43, 1 (1995), pp.65–96.

Birrell, S.J., 'Discourse on the Gender/Sport Relationship: from Women in Sport to Gender Relations', *Exercise and Sport Science Review*, 16 (1988), pp.459–502.

Bose, M., 'Desperate Americans Relax Border Controls', *Daily Telegraph*, 30 Sep. 2000.

Brownell, S., 'Representing Gender in the Chinese Nation: Chinese Sportswomen and Beijing's Bid for the 2000 Olympics', *Identities – Global Studies in Culture and Power*, 2, 3 (1996), pp.223–47.

Carlile, F., 'Why the Chinese Must Not Swim at Atlanta '96', *Inside Sport*, Nov. 1995, pp. 18–29.

Chan, A., 'Looking Back at the Chinese Cultural Revolution', *Problems of Communism*, March–April 1988, pp.68–75.

Chan, A. and R.A. Senser, 'China's Troubled Workers', *Foreign Affairs*, March–April 1997, pp.104–17.

Chan, K.. and Li Zhang, 'The Hukou System and Rural-Urban Migration in China: Processes and Changes', *China Quarterly*, 160 (Dec. 1999), pp.818–55.

Chang, H., 'Shanghai Is Leaping Forward', *China Sports*, 1958 (3), p.13.

Cheng, C., 'Mainland China's Transition from a Planned to a Market Economy: New Breakthroughs and Hurdles', *Issues and Studies: Journal of Chinese Studies*, 30, 8 (Oct. 1994), pp.74–93.

'China Bans Nine Coaches Over Drugs', *Independent*, 1 March 1995.

'Chinese Begin Crackdown', *Independent*, 6 April 1994.

Coakley, J.J. 'Sport and Socialisation', *Exercise and Sport Sciences Reviews*, 21 (1993), pp.169–200.

Craig, L., 'China's Women Shake the World', *Sunday Times*, 11 Sep. 1994.

Craig, L., 'Caught Red-handed', *Sunday Times*, 11 Jan. 1998.

Craig, L., 'The Medal Factory', *Sunday Times*, 9 May 1999.

Deford, F., 'An Old Dragon Limbers Up: Sports in China, A Special Report', *Sports Illustrated*, 15 August 1988, pp.36–43.

Dewar, A., 'Would All the Generic Women in Sport Please Stand Up? Challenges Facing Feminist Sport Sociology', *Quest*, 45 (1993), pp.221–9.

Dubois, P., 'Participation in Sports and Occupational Attainment: a Comparative Study', *Research Quarterly*, 49 (1978), pp.28–37.

Ehrenreich, B. 'Democracy in China', *Monthly Review*, Sep. 1974, pp.17–32.

Fan Hong, 'Socio-Historical Framework – Women and Sport in China', *WSPAJ*, 3,1 (Spring 1995), pp.15–17.

Foster, P., 'Olympic Oath Against Drugs', *Daily Telegraph*, 16 Sep. 2000.

Fu, Y. et al., 'Factors Determining the Recent Success of Chinese Women in International Sport', *International Journal of the History of Sport*, 14, 1 (1997), pp.172–7.

Greendorfer, S., 'Role of Socializing Agents in Female Sport Involvement', *Research Quarterly for Exercise and Sport*, 48, 2 (1977), pp.304–10.

Gray, W., 'China's Drugs "Cheats" Claim', *Daily Telegraph*, 20 Oct. 1997.

Hall, A, 'The Discourse on Gender and Sport: from Femininity to Feminism', *Sociology of Sport Journal*, 5, 4 (1988), pp.330–40.

Hall, A., 'A "Feminine Woman" and an "Athletic Woman" as Viewed by Female Participants and Non-Participants in Sport', *British Journal of Physical Education*, 3 (1972), pp.43–6.

Hall, A., 'Gender and Sport in the 1990s: Feminism, Culture, and Politics', *Sports Science Review*, 2, 1 (1993), pp.48–68.

Hargreaves, J., 'Where's the Virtue? Where's the Grace? A Discussion of the Social Reproduction of Gender through Sport', *Theory, Culture and Society*, 3 (1986), pp.109–21.

Hargreaves, J., 'Gender on the Sports Agenda', *International Review for Sociology of Sport*, 25 (1990), pp.287–305.

Hasbrook, C.A., 'The Sport Participation–Social Class Relationship: Some Recent Youth Sport Participation Data', *Sociology of Sport Journal*, 3 (1986), pp.37–47.

He, Z., 'The Role of Chinese Women in the Olympic Movement', *China Sports*, Sep. 1995, pp.7–8.

Hollobaugh, J., 'A Giant Awakens', *Track and Field News*, Dec. 1993, pp.5–6, 24.

Hollobaugh, J., 'The Man Behind It All', *Track and Field News*, Dec. 1993, p.4.

Huang, Y., 'Information, Bureaucracy, and Economic Reforms in China and the Soviet Union', *World Politics*, 47, 1 (1994), pp.102–34.

Huang, Z., 'Funds Collection: The Concern of the Whole Nation', *China Sports*, 1990 (5), pp.2–3.

Information Office of the State Council of the PRC, 'The Situation of Chinese Women', *Beijing Review*, 6–12 June 1994, pp.1–12.

Joseph, W., 'A Tragedy of Good Intention: Post-Mao Views of the Great Leap Forward', *Modern China*, 12 (Oct. 1986), pp.419–57.

Jung, K., 'Sports Should Serve the People', *China Sports*, 1966 (1), pp.1–5.

Karklins, R. and R. Peterson, 'Decision Calculus of Protesters and Regimes: Eastern Europe 1989', *Journal of Politics*, 55, 3 (1993), pp.588–614.

Kohut, J. and N. Rufford, 'China's Golden Girl Runs Foul of Her Mean Ma', *Sunday Times*, 16 Jan. 1994.

Krotee, M.L. and Wang Jin, 'A Sociocultural View of Physical Education and Sport in the People's Republic of China', *Journal of the International Council for Health, Physical Education and Recreation*, 26, 1 (1989), pp.9–14.

Lai, G., 'Work and Family Roles and Psychological Well-being in Urban China', *Journal of Health and Social Behaviour*, 36, 1 (1995), pp.11–37.

Lonsbrough, A., 'China Left to Carry Out Drugs Inquiry', *Daily Telegraph*, 19 Jan. 1998.

Lonsbrough, A., 'FINA Send a Doping Taskforce to China', *Daily Telegraph*, 26 Jan. 1998.

'Looking Backards and Forwards' (Editorial), *China Sports*, 1958 (1), p.1.

Loy, J.W., 'Social Origins and Occupation Mobility of a Selected Sample of American Athletes', *International Review for Sociology of Sport*, 7 (1972), pp.5–23.

Lushen, G.,'The Interdependence of Sport and Culture', *International Review of Sport Sociology*, 2 (1967), pp.127–39.

'Ma Army Set Up New Base Camp', *Independent*, 1 June 1995.

'Ma's Secret Recipe Is a Good Beating', *Independent*, 23 March 1995.

Manion, M., 'The Electoral Connection in the Chinese Countryside', *American Political Science Review*, 90, 4 (1996), pp.736–48.

McElroy, D., 'China's Little Emperors Fight Battle of the Bulge', *The Scotsman*, 23 Sep. 2000.

McElroy, D., 'China's Children to Fight Obesity at "Fat Camp"', *Sunday Telegraph*, 24 Sep. 2000.

Messner, M., 'Sports and Male Domination: The Female Athlete as Contested Ideological Terrain', *Sociology of Sport Journal*, 5 (1988), pp.197–211.

Montinola, G. et al., 'Federalism, Chinese Style: The Political Basis for Economic Success in China', *World Politics*, 48 (1995), pp.50–81.

Nathan, A., 'Is Chinese Culture Distinctive?' *Journal of Asian Studies*, 52, 4 (1993), pp. 923–36.

Nee, V., 'The Emergence of a Market Society: Changing Mechanisms of Stratification in China', *American Journal of Sociology*, 101, 4 (1996), pp.908–49.

Nee, V.and Peng, L., 'Sleeping with the Enemy: A Dynamic Model of Declining Political Commitment in State Socialism', *Theory and Society*, 23 (1994), pp.253–96.

O'Brien, K. and Li, L., 'The Politics of Lodging Complaints in Rural China', *China Quarterly,* 143 (1995), pp.756–83.

'Opinion Interview: Drug Buster', *New Scientist*, 16 Sep. 2000, pp.44–7.

'The Past Before Us: Twenty Years of Feminism', *Feminist Review*, 31 (Special Issue, Spring 1989).

Pavia, G.R, 'An Analysis of the Social Class of the 1972 Australia Olympic Team', *Australian Journal of Physical Education*, 61 (1973), pp.14–19.

Rawki, T.G., 'Implications of China's Reform Experience', *China Quarterly*, 144 (Dec. 1995), pp.1150–73.

Riordan, J. and Dong, J., 'Chinese Women and Sport: Success, Sexuality and Suspicion', *China Quarterly*, 145 (1996), pp.130–52.

Rung, K., 'Sports Should Serve the People', *China Sports*, 1966 (1), pp.1–5.

Slot, O., 'US Athletes Facing Ban over Drug Testing', *Sunday Telegraph*, 1 Oct. 2000.

Slot, O., 'Top Nations Accused of Masterminding Drug-Test Dodges', *Sunday Telegraph*, 17 Sep. 2000.

State Statistical Bureau, 'China's Population Structure', *Beijing Review*, 5–11 Dec. 1988, pp.30–32.

Summerfield, G., 'Effects of the Changing Employment Situation on Urban Chinese Women', *Review of Social Economy*, 52, 1 (1994), pp.40–59.

Summerfield, G., 'Economic Reform and the Employment of Chinese Women', *Journal of Economic Issues*, 28, 3 (1994), pp.715–33.

Theberge, N., 'Sport and Women's Empowerment', *Women's Studies International Forum*, 10 (1987), pp.387–93.

Tomlinson, A. and I. Yorganci, 'Male Coach/Female Athlete Relations: Gender and Power Relations in Competitive Sport', *Journal of Sport and Social Issues*, 21, 2 (1997), pp.134–55.

Walder, A., 'Local Governments As industrial Firms: An Organizational Analysis of China's Transitional Economy', *American Journal of Sociology*, 101, 2 (1995), pp.263–301.

'Wang Races to Hat-trick', *Independent*, 14 Sep. 1993.

Wang, J. and D.M. Wiese-Biornstal, 'The Relationship of School Type and Gender to Motives for Sport Participation Among Youth in the People's Republic of China',

International Journal of Sport Psychology, 28, 1 (1997), pp.13–24.

White, A., 'Women Coaches: Problems and Issues', *Coaching Focus*, 6 (1987), pp.2–3.

Wigmore, S., 'Gender and Sport – The Last 5 Years', *Sport Science Review*, 5.2 (1996), pp.53–71.

Wilkerson, M., 'Explaining the Presence of Men Coaches in Women's Sports: The Uncertainty Hypothesis', *Journal of Sport and Social Issues*, Nov. 1996, pp.411–12.

Wong, L., 'China's Urban Migrants – The Public Policy Challenge', *Pacific Affairs*, 67, 3 (Fall 1994), pp.335–55.

Xie, Y., 'Measuring Regional Variation in Sex Preference in China: A Cautionary Note', *Social Science Research*, 18 (1989), pp.291–305.

Xie, Y. and Hannum, E., 'Regional Variation in Earnings Equality in Reform-Era Urban China', *American Journal of Sociology*, 101, 4 (1996), pp.50–92.

Xu, Q., 'A New Height in Beijing', *China Sports*, 1992 (10), pp.36–7.

Zhang, W., 'Bodybuilding: A New Stage of Development', *China Sports*, 1987 (3), pp.7–8.

Zheng, F., 'Deep Effects of the Beijing Asian Games', *China Sports*, 1992 (5), pp.35–6.

Published books and chapters in books

All China Women's Federation, *The Second Report of the Implementation of the Nairobi Forward-Looking Strategies for the Advancement of Women's Status* (Beijing, 1994).

Allison, L. (ed.), *The Changing Politics of Sport* (Manchester: Manchester University Press, 1993).

Andors, P., *The Unfinished Liberation of Chinese Women 1949–1980* (Bloomington, IN: Indiana University Press, 1983).

Bachman, D., *Bureaucracy, Economy, and Leadership in China: The Institutional Origins of the Great Leap Forward* (Cambridge: Cambridge University Press, 1991).

Bale, J., and J. Sang, *Kenyan Running: Movement Culture, Geography and Global Change* (London and Portland, OR: Frank Cass, 1996).

Bale, J., and J. Maguire (eds), *The Global Sports Arena: Athletic Talent Migration in an Interdependent World* (London and Portland, OR: Frank Cass, 1994).

Ball, D.W. and J. W. Loy, *Sport and the Social Order: Contributions to the Sociology of Sport* (Reading, MA: Addison-Wesley Publishing, 1975).

Barlow, T.E. (ed.), *Gender Politics in Modern China* (Durham, NC, and London: Duke University Press, 1993).

Barnett, A.D. and R.N. Clough (eds), *Modernising China: Post-Mao Reform and Development* (Boulder, CO: Westview Press, 1986).

Baum, B.R., *Reform and Reaction in Post-Mao China: The Road to Tiananmen* (London and New York: Routledge, 1991).

Beashel, P. and J. Taylor (eds), *Advanced Studies in Physical Education and Sport* (Walton-on-Thames, Canada: Nelson, 1996).

Beauvoir, S. de, *The Second Sex*, translated and edited by H.M. Parshley (London: Pan Books, 1988).

Bell, M.W. et al., *China at the Threshold of A Market Economy* (Washington, DC: International Monetary Fund, 1993).

Bendix, R. and Seymour Martin Lipset (eds), *Class, Status, and Power: Social Stratification in Comparative Perspective*, 2nd edn (London: Routledge & Kegan Paul, 1967).

Benewick, R. and P. Wingrove (eds), *Reforming the Revolution: China in Transition* (London: Macmillan, 1988).

Benewick, R. and P. Wingrove (eds), *China in the 1990s* (London: Macmillan, 1995).

Bennett, G.A. and R.N. Montaperto, *Red Guard: The Political Biography of Dai Hsiao-Ai* (London: George Allen & Unwin, 1971).

Bilton, T. et al. (eds), *Introductory Sociology*, 3rd edn (London: Macmillan, 1996).

Birkett, B. and B. Peascod, *Women Climbing: 200 Years of Achievement* (London: A. & C. Black, 1989).

Blanchard, K. et al., *The Anthropology of Sport: An Introduction* (Westport, CT: Bergin & Garvey, 1985).

Blau, P.M. and O.D. Ducan, *The American Occupational Structure* (New York: John Wiley & Sons, 1967).

Bloodworth, D., *Chinese Looking Glass* (London: Secker & Warburg, 1967).

Bramall, C., *In Praise of Maoist Economic Planning: Living Standards and Economic Development in Sichuan since 1931* (Oxford: Clarendon Press, 1993).

Breiger, R.L. (ed.), *Social Mobility and Social Structure* (Cambridge: Cambridge University Press, 1990).

Brohm, J.M., translated by Ian Fraser, *Sport – A Prison of Measured Time* (London: Ink Links, 1978).

Brownell, S., *Training the Body for China: Sports in the Moral Order of the People's Republic* (Chicago, IL, and London: University of Chicago Press, 1995).

Brownmiller, S., *Against Our Will: Men, Women and Rape* (New York: Simon and Schuster, 1975).

Brugger, B. and S. Reglar, *Politics, Economy and Society in Contemporary China* (London: Macmillan, 1994).

Cahn, S.K., *Coming on Strong: Gender and Sexuality in Twentieth-Century Women's Sport* (New York: The Free Press, Toronto: Maxwell Macmillan, 1994).

Calhoun, D.W., *Sport, Culture, and Personality*, 2nd edn (Champaign, IL: Human Kinetics, 1987).

Cashmore, E., *Making Sense of Sports*, 2nd edn (London and New York: Routledge, 1996).

Centre for Social Development and Humanitarian Affairs, *Women in Politics and Decision-Making in the Late Twentieth Century: A United Nations Study* (Dordrecht, Netherlands: Martihus Nijihoff, 1992).

Chalip, L., A. Johnson and L. Stachura (eds), *National Sports Policies: An International Handbook* (Westport, CT: Greenwood Press, 1996).

Chan, A., *Children of Mao: Personality Development and Political Activism in the Red Guard Generation* (London: Macmillan, 1985).

Chang, J., *Wild Swans: Three Daughters of China* (London: Harper Collins, 1991).

Cheng, J.Y. and M. Brosseau (eds), *China Review 1993* (Hong Kong: Chinese University Press, 1993).

Chinese Women Athletes: Marching into the World Sports Arena (pamphlet for UN Fourth World Conference on Women, Beijing, 1995).

Chipp, S.A. and J.J. Green (eds), *Asian Women in Transition* (University Park, PA: Pennsylvania State University Press, 1980).

Chow, R., 'Violence in the Other Country: China as Crisis, Spectacle, and Women', in C.T. Mahanty (ed.), *Third World Women and the Politics of Feminism* (Bloomington, IN: Indiana University Press, 1991), pp.81–100.

Chow, R., *Woman and Chinese Modernity: The Politics of Reading Between West and East* (Minneapolis, MN: University of Minnesota Press, 1991).

Chu, G.C. and Y. Ju, *The Great Wall in Ruins – Communication and Cultural Change in China* (Albany, NY: State University of New York Press, 1993).

Cleverley, J., *The Schooling of China* (Sydney, London and Boston, MA: George Allen & Unwin, 1986).

Ci, J., *Dialectic of the Chinese Revolution: From Utopianism to Hedonism* (Stanford, CA: Stanford University Press, 1994).

Coakley, J.J., 'Children and Sport Socialisation Process', in D. Gould and M.R. Weiss (eds), *Advances in Paediatric Sport Sciences: Vol.2, Behavioural Issues* (Champaign, IL: Human Kinetics, 1995), pp.43–60.

Coakley, J., *Sport in Society: Issues and Controversies*, 5th edn (St Louis, MO: Mosby, 1994).

Cohen, G. L. (ed.), *Women in Sport: Issues and Controversies* (London: Sage, 1993).

Connell, R.W., *Masculinities* (Cambridge: Polity Press, 1995).

Connell, R.W., *Gender and Power* (Cambridge: Polity Press, 1987).

Coote, A. and P. Pattullo, *Power and Prejudice: Women and Politics* (London: Weidenfeld & Nicolson, 1990).

Costa, D.M. and S.R. Guthrie (eds), *Women and Sport: Interdisplinary Perspectives* (Champaign, IL: Human Kinetics, 1994).

Craig, C., *Neither Gods Nor Emperors* (Berkeley, CA: University of California Press, 1994).

Cray, J., *Rebellions and Revolutions: China from the 1800s to the 1980s* (Oxford: Oxford University Press, 1990).

Croll, E.J., *Feminism and Socialism in China* (London: Routledge & Kegan Paul, 1978).

Croll, E.J., *Chinese Women Since Mao* (London: Zed Books, 1983).

Croll, E.J., *Changing Identities of Chinese Women* (Hong Kong University Press, 1995).

Curtin, K., *Women in China* (New York: Pathfinder Press, 1979).

Davin, D., *Internal Migration in Contemporary China* (London: Macmillan, 1999).

Davis, D. and E.F. Vogel, *Chinese Society on the Eve of Tiananmen: The Impact of Reform* (Cambridge, MA: Harvard University Press, 1990).

Dernberger, R.F. (ed.), *China's Development Experience in Comparative Perspective* (Cambridge, MA: Harvard University Press, 1980).

Dietrich, C., *People's China: A Brief History*, 2nd edn (Oxford: Oxford University Press, 1994.

Dittmer, L., *Liu Shao-ch'i and the Chinese Cultural Revolution: The Politics of Mass Criticism* (Los Angeles, CA: University of California Press, 1974).

Donnellan, C. (ed.), *Drugs and Violence in Sport*, Vol.26 (Cambridge: Independence Educational Publishers, 1995).

Donnellan, C. (ed.), *Drug Abuse in Sport* (Cambridge: Independence Educational Publishers, 1998).

Dunning, E. (ed.), *The Sociology of Sport: A Selection of Readings* (London: Frank Cass, 1971).

Dunning, E.G., J.A. Maguire and R.E. Pearton (eds), *The Sports Process: A Comparative and Developmental Approach* (Champaign, IL: Human Kinetics, 1993).

Dyer, K., *Catching Up the Men: Women in Sport* (London: Junction Books, 1982).

Eckstein, A., *China's Economic Development: The Interplay of Scarcity and Ideology* (Ann Arbor, MI: University of Michigan Press, 1975).

Elias, N. and E. Dunning, *Quest for Excitement: Sport and Leisure in the Civilising Process* (Oxford: Blackwell, 1986).

Elizen, D.S. and G. Sage, *Sociology of American Sport* (Dubuque, IA: Wm.C.Brown, 1978).

Engels, F., *The Origin of Family, Private Property and the State*, translated by A. West (London: Lawrence and Wishart, 1972).

Evans, H., *Women and Sexuality in China: Female Sexuality and Gender Since 1949* (New York: Continuum, 1997).

Evans, P.M., *John Fairbank and the American Understanding of Modern China* (New York: Basil Blackwell, 1988).

Fairbank, J.K., *The United States and China*, 4th edn, enlarged (Cambridge, MA: Harvard University Press, 1983).

Falkenheim, V.C. (ed.), *Chinese Politics from Mao to Deng* (New York: Paragon House, 1989).

Fan Hong, *Footbinding, Feminism and Freedom – The Liberation of Women's Bodies in Modern China* (London: Frank Cass, 1997).

Fasting, K., 'Gender Inequality in Leisure and Sport', in A. Tomlinson (ed.), *Sport in Society: Policy, Politics and Culture*, 43 (Eastbourne: Leisure Studies Association, 1990, pp.94–104).

Featherstone, M. (ed.), *Global Culture: Nationalism, Globalization and Modernity* (London: Sage, 1990).

Fei, X., *From the Soil: The Foundations of Chinese Society*, translation and critique by Gary Hamilton and Wang Zheng (Berkeley, CA: University of California Press, 1992).

Gerth, H. and C.W. Mills (eds), *From Max Weber: Essays in Sociology* (New York: Oxford University Press, 1946).

Giddens, A., *Sociology: Introductory Readings* (Cambridge: Polity Press, 1997).

Gill, D.L. (ed.), *Psychological Dynamics of Sport* (Champaign, IL: Human Kinetics, 1986).

Gilmartin, C.K., G. Hershatter, L. Rofel and T. Whyte (eds), *Engendering China: Women, Culture, and the State* (Cambridge, MA: Harvard University Press, 1994).

Gilmore, D.D., *Manhood in the Making: Cultural Concepts of Masculinity* (New Haven, CT, and London: Yale University Press, 1990).

Gittings, J., *Real China: from Cannibalism to Karaoke* (London: Simon & Schuster, 1996).

Glaeser, B. (ed.), *Learn from China? Development and Environment in Third World Countries* (London: Allen & Unwin, 1987).

Goodman, D.S.G. (ed.), *China's Provinces in Reform: Class, Community and Political Culture* (London: Routledge, 1997).

Griffin, K., and Zhao, R. (eds), *The Distribution of Income in China* (New York: St Martin's Press, 1993).

Grummitt, K., *China Economic Handbook* (London: Euromonitor, 1986).

Gruneau, R.S., 'Sport, Social Differentiation and Social Inequality', in Donald Ball and John Loy (eds), *Sport and the Social Order* (Reading, MA: Addison-Wesley, 1975), pp.117–84.

Giele, J.Z., *Women and the Future: Changing Sex Roles in Modern America* (London: Collier Macmillan, 1978).

Guttmann, A., *Women's Sport: A History* (New York: Columbia University Press, 1991).

Guttmann, A., *Games and Empires: Modern Sports and Cultural Imperialism* (New York: Columbia University Press, 1994).

Graves, N. and V. Varma, *Working for a Doctorate: A Guide for the Humanities and Social Sciences* (London and New York: Routledge, 1997).

Hall, A., *Sport and Gender: A Feminist Perspective on the Sociology of Sport* (Ottawa: Canadian Association for Health, Physical Education, and Recreation, 1978).

Hall, A., *Feminism and Sporting Bodies* (Champaign, IL: Human Kinetics, 1996).

Hall, C., *Daughters of the Dragon: Women's Lives in Contemporary China* (London: Scarlet Press, 1997).

Hamrin, C.L., *China and the Challenge of the Future: Changing Political Patterns* (Boulder, CO: Westview Press, 1990).

Hamilton, G., 'Overseas Chinese Capitalism', in Tu, W. (ed.), *Confucian Traditions in East Asian Modernity* (Cambridge, MA: Harvard University Press, 1996), pp.328–42.

Hao, Y. and Huan, G., *The Chinese View of the World* (New York: Pantheon, 1949).

Harding, H., *China's Second Revolution: Reform After Mao* (Washington, DC: Brookings Institution, 1987).

Hargreaves, J. (ed.), *Sport, Culture and Ideology* (London: Routledge and Kegan Paul, 1982).

Hargreaves, J., *Sporting Females – Critical Issues in the History and Sociology of Women's Sports* (London and New York: Routledge, 1994).

Hoberman, J., *Sport and Political Ideology* (London: Heinemann, 1984).

Hoberman, J., 'Sport and Ideology in the Post-Communist Age', in Lincoln Allison (ed.), *The Changing Politics of Sport* (Manchester: Manchester University Press, 1993. pp.15–36).

Holland, J. (ed.), *Debates and Issues in Feminist Research and Pedagogy: A Reader* (Clevedon: Multilingual Matters/Open University, 1995).

Hollingshead, A.B., *Two-factor Index of Social Position* (New Haven, CT: privately printed, 1957).

Holt, R. and J.A. Mangan (eds), *European Heroes: Myth, Identity, Sport* (London and Portland, OR: Frank Cass, 1996).

Hong, L., 'Sichuan: Disadvantage and Mismanagement in the Heavenly Kingdom', in D.S.G. Goodman (ed.), *China's Provinces in Reform: Class, Community and Political*

Culture (London: Routledge, 1997).

Honig, E. and G. Hershatter, *Personal Voices: Chinese Women in the 1980s* (Stanford, CA: Stanford University Press, 1988).

Horne, J., A. Tomlinson and G. Whannel (eds), *Understanding Sport: An Introduction to the Sociological and Cultural Analysis of Sport* (London and New York: E. & F.N. Spon, 1999).

Hsu, I.C.Y., *The Rise of Modern China*, 4th edn (New York: Oxford University Press, 1990).

Huang, D. and Feng, C., 'Chapter 11: Relationships between the Sexes in the New Age of Reform and Open Policy', in Min, J. (ed.), *The Chalice and the Blade in Chinese Culture: Gender Relations and Social Models* (Beijing: China Social Science Publishing House, 1995), p.550ff.

Hunter, A. and J. Sexton, *Contemporary China* (New York: St. Martin's Press, 1999).

Ingham, A.G. and J.W. Loy (eds), *Sport in Social Development: Traditions, Transitions, and Transformations* (Champaign, IL: Human Kinetics, 1993).

Jackson, S. (ed.), *Women's Studies: A Reader* (New York: Harvester Wheatsheaf, 1993).

Jancar, B.W., *Women Under Communism* (Baltimore, MD: Johns Hopkins University Press, 1978).

Jarvie, G. and J. Maguire, *Sport and Leisure in Social Thought* (London: Routledge, 1994).

Jayawardena, K. (ed.), *Feminism and Nationalism in the Third World* (London: Zed Books, 1986)

Jencks, C. et al., *Who Gets Ahead? The Determinants of Economic Success in America* (New York: Basic Books, 1979).

Jing L., *The Red Guards' Path to Violence: Political, Educational, and Psychological Factors* (New York: Praeger, 1992).

Joint Economic Committee of the United States Congress (ed.), *China's Economic Dilemmas in the 1990s: The Problems of Reforms, Modernization, and Interdependence*, Vol.1 (Washington, DC: US Congress Joint Economic Committee, 1991).

Jones, S.G., *Sports, Politics and the Working Class* (Manchester: Manchester Univerisity Press, 1985).

Joseph, W., *The Critique of Ultra-leftism in China, 1958–1981* (Stanford, CA: Stanford University Press, 1984).

Joseph, W.A., C.P.W. Wong and D. Zweig (eds), *New Perspectives on the Cultural Revolution* (Cambridge, MA: Harvard University Press, 1989).

Judd, E., 'Dramas of Passion: Heroism in the Cultural Revolution's Model Operas', in Joseph, W.A., C.P.W. Wong and D. Zweig (eds), *New Perspectives on the Cultural Revolution* (Cambridge, MA: Harvard University Press, 1989), pp.265–282.

Kallgren, J.K. (ed.), *Building A Nation-State: China after Forty Years* (Berkeley, CA: Institute of East Asian Studies, University of California Centre for Chinese, 1990).

Kanin, D.B., 'Ideology and Diplomacy: The Dimension of Chinese Political Sport', in B. Lowe, D. Kanin and A. Strenk (eds), *Sports and International Relations* (Champaign, IL: Stipes Publishing Co., 1978), pp.268–74.

Kelliher, D., *Peasant Power in China: The Era of Rural Reform, 1979–1989* (New Haven, CT: Yale University Press, 1992).

Kelsall, R.K. and H.M. Kelsall (eds), *Stratification: An Essay on Class and Inequality* (London: Longman, 1974).

Kenyon, G.S. (ed.), *Sociology of Sport* (Chicago, IL: Athletic Institute, 1969).

Kluckhohn, C., 'What Is Culture?' in Hu Wenzhong (ed.), *Selected Readings in Intercultural Communication* (Hunan jiaoyu chuban she, 1990), pp37–45.

Knuttgen, H.G. (ed.), *Sport in China* (Champaign, IL: Human Kinetics, 1990).

Kolatch, J., *Sports, Politics, and Ideology in China* (New York: Jonathan David, 1972).

Kristof, N.D. and S. WuDunn, *China Wakes – The Struggle for the Soul of a Rising Power* (London: Nicholas Brealey, 1994).

Kristeva, J., *About Chinese Women* (London: M. Boyars, 1977).

Lam, W., *China after Deng Xiaoping* (Singapore: John Wiley & Sons, 1995).

Landry, F. et al. (eds), *Sociology of Sport: A Collection of the Formal Papers Presented at the International Congress of Physical Activity Sciences* (Miami, FL: Symposia Specialists, 1978).

Larson, W., *Women and Writing in Modern China* (Stanford, CA: Stanford University Press), 1998.

Lau, C., 'The Chinese Family and Gender Roles in Transition', in Cheng, J. (ed.), *China Review 1993* (Hong Kong: Chinese University Press, 1994), pp.13–20.

Lee, H.Y., *The Politics of Chinese Cultural Revolution* (Berkeley, CA: University of Ccalifornia Press, 1978).

Lee, C.H. and H. Recsen (eds), *From Reform to Growth: China and Other Countries in Transition in Asia and Central and Eastern Europe* (Paris: Organisation for Economic Co-operation and Development, 1994).

Lee, H.Y., *China's Party-State* (Berkeley and Los Angeles, CA: University of California Press, 1990).

Levenson, J.R., *Confucian China and Its Modern Fate*, Vol.2 (London: Routledge & Kegan Paul, 1964).

Lewis, S., 'Marketization and Government Credibility in Shanghai: Federalist and Local Corporatist Explanations', in D. Weimer (ed.), *The Political Economy of Property Rights* (Cambridge: Cambridge University Press, 1997), pp.259–87.

Liang, H. and H. Shapiro, *Return to China: A Survivor of the Cultural Revolution Reports on China Today* (London: Chatto & Windus, 1987).

Li, C., *China: The Consumer Revolution* (Singapore: John Wiley & Sons (Asia), 1997).

Lieberthal, K.G. and D. Lampton (eds), *Bureaucracy, Politics, and Decision-Making in Post-Mao China* (Berkeley, CA: University of California Press, 1992).

Lin, J., *The Red Guards' Path to Violence: Political, Educational, and Psychological Factors* (New York: Praeger, 1991).

Lin, Y., *My Country and My People* (London: Heinemann, 1935).

Liu, B., *People or Monsters? And Other Stories and Reportage from China after Mao* (Bloomington, IN: Indiana University Press, 1983).

Liu, G., *A Brief Analysis of the Cultural Revolution,* edited by A. Chan (Armonk, NY: M.E. Sharpe, 1987).

Loy, J.W, B.D. McPherson and G. Kenyon, *Sport and Social Systems: A Guide to the Analysis, Problems and Literature* (Reading, MA: Addison-Wesley, 1978).

Luschen, G., 'Social Stratification and Social Mobility Among Young Sportsmen', in J.W. Loy and G.S. Kenyon (eds), *Sport, Culture, and Society* (London: Macmillan, 1969), pp.258–76.

Luschen, G., 'On Sociology of Sport – General Orientation and Its Trends in the Literature', in O. Grupe, D. Kurz and J.M. Teipel (eds), *The Scientific View of Sport* (Heidelberg: Springer-Verlag Berlin, 1972), pp.119–54.

Luschen, G., and G.H. Sage (eds), *Handbook of Social Science of Sport* (Champaign, IL: Stipes Publishing Co., 1981).

Lu, H., *The True Story of Ah Q*, English edition (Boston, MA: Cheng & Tsui, 1921).

Lu, M. and Zheng, Y., 'The Women's Movement and Women's Liberation in China', in Min, J. (ed.), *The Chalice and the Blade in Chinese Culture* (Beijing: China Social Science Publishing House, 1995), pp.479–535.

MacFarquhar, R. (ed.), *China Under Mao: Politics Takes Command: A Selection of Articles from the* China Quarterly (London: MIT Press, 1966).

MacFarquhar, R., and J.K. Fairbank (eds), *The Cambridge History of China*, Vol.14: *The Peoples Republic* (Cambridge: Cambridge University Press, 1987).

MacFarquhar, R.L. and J.K. Fairbank (eds), *The Cambridge History of China*, Vol.15: *Revolutions within the Chinese Revolution* (Cambridge: Cambridge University Press, 1991).

Macpherson, S. and J.Y.S. Cheng (eds), *Economic and Social Development in South China* (Cheltenham: Edward Elgar, 1996).

Mahanty, C. T., A. Russo and L. Torres (eds), *Third World Women and the Politics of Feminism* (Bloomington, IN: Indiana University Press, 1991).

Mangan, J.A., *Physical Education and Sport: Sociological and Cultural Perspectives* (Oxford: Basil Blackwell, 1973).

Mangan, J.A. and R.J. Park (eds), *From 'Fair Sex' to Feminism: Sport and the Socialization of Women in the Industrial and Post-Industrial Eras* (London: Frank Cass, 1987).

Mangan, J.A., 'Epilogue – Prospects for the New Millennium: Emancipation, Women and the Body', in J.A. Mangan and Fan Hong (eds), *Freeing the Female Body: Inspirational Icons*, in series Sport in the Global Society (London and Portland, OR: Frank Cass, 2001).

Ma, X., 'Changes in the Pattern of Migration in Urban China', in L.H. Day and Ma Xia (eds), *Migration and Urbanization in China* (Armonk, NY: M.E. Sharpe, 1994).

McMillan, J. and B. Naughton (eds), *Reforming Asian Socialism: The Growth of Market Institutions* (Ann Arbor, MI: University of Michigan Press, 1996).

Mcpherson, B.D. et al., *The Social Significance of Sport: An Introduction to the Sociology of Sport* (Champaign, IL: Human Kinetics, 1989).

Messner, M. and D. Sabo (eds), *Sport, Men, and the Gender Order: Critical Feminist Perspectives* (Champaign, IL: Human Kinetics, 1990).

Michael, F. et al., *China and the Crisis of Marxism-Leninism* (Boulder, CO: Westview Press, 1990).

Min, J. (ed.), *The Chalice and the Blade in Chinese Culture: Gender Relations and Social Models* (Beijing: China Social Science Publishing House, 1995).

Moise, E.E., *Modern China: A History* (London and New York: Longman, 1986).

Monnington, T., 'Politicians and Sport: Uses and Abuses', in Lincoln Allison (ed.), *The Changing Politics of Sport* (Manchester: Manchester University Press, 1993), pp.125–50.

Morbeck, M.E. (ed.), *The Evolving Female – A Life-History Perspective* (Princeton, NJ: Princeton University Press, 1997).

Myers, R.H. (ed.), *Two Societies in Opposition: The Republic of China and the People's Republic of China after Forty Years* (Stanford, CA: Hoover Institution Press, 1991).

Nathan, A. (ed.), *China's Crisis* (New York: Columbia University Press, 1990).

Nathan, A. J., *China's Transition* (New York: Columbia University Press, 1997).

Naughton, B., *Growing Out of the Plan: Chinese Economic Reform 1978–1993* (Cambridge: Cambridge University Press, 1995).

Oakley, A., *Subject Women* (Oxford: Martin Robertson, 1981).

Ogden, S., *China's Unresolved Issues: Politics, Development, and Culture* (Englewood Cliffs, NJ: Prentice-Hall, 1989).

Pavia, G.R. and T.D. Jaques, 'The Socio-economic Origin, Academic Attainment, Occupational Mobility and Parental Background of Selected Australian Athletes', in F. Landry et al. (eds), *Sociology of Sport: A Collection of the Formal Papers Presented at the International Congress of Physical Activity Sciences* (Miami, FL: Symposia Specialists, 1978), pp.90–104.

Payne, G. and P. Abbott, *The Social Mobility of Women: Beyond Male Mobility Models* (London: Falmer Press, 1990).

Persell, C.H., *Understanding Society: An Introduction to Sociology*, 2nd edn (New York: Harper & Row, 1996).

Phillips, W.N., *Anabolic Reference Guide*, 6th edn (Golden, CO: Mile High Publishing, 1991).

Polley, M., *Moving the Goalposts: A History of Sport and Society Since 1945* (London: Routledge, 1998).

Price, F., *Education in Modern China*, 2nd edn (London: Routledge & Kegan Paul, 1979).

Prybyla, J.S., *China and the Crisis of Marxism-Leninism* (Washington, DC: American Enterprise Institute, 1990).

Prybyla, J.S., *Reform in China and Other Socialist Economies* (Washington, DC: AEI Press, 1990).

Przeworski, A. et al., *Sustainable Democracy* (Cambridge: Cambridge University Press, 1995).

Pye, L., *The Spirit of Chinese Politics: A Psychocultural Study of the Authority Crisis in Political Development* (Cambridge, MA: MIT Press, 1968).

Pye, L., *The Dynamics of Chinese Politics* (Cambridge, MA: Oelgeschlager, Gunn & Hain, 1981).

Pye, L., *The Mandarin and the Cadre: China's Political Cultures* (Ann Arbor, MI: Center for Chinese Studies, University of Michigan, 1988).

Pye, L., *The Spirit of Chinese Politics* (Cambridge, MA: Harvard University Press, 1992).

Reddings, S. G., 'Societal Transformation and the Contribution of Authority Relations and Cooperation Norms in Overseas Chinese Business', in Tu, W. (ed.), *Confucian Traditions in East Asian Modernity* (Cambridge, MA: Harvard University Press, 1996), pp.310–27.

Renson, R., 'Social Status Symbolism of Sport Stratification', in F. Landry et al. (eds), *Sociology of Sport: A Collection of the Formal Papers Presented at the International Congress of Physical Activity Sciences* (Miami, FL: Symposia Specialists, 1978), pp.191–200.

Riley, N.E., 'Gender Equality in China: Two Steps Forward, One Step Back', in W.A. Joseph (ed.), *China Briefing: The Contradictions of Change* (Armonk, NY: M.E. Sharpe, 1997), pp.79–108.

Riordan, J., *Soviet Sport: Background to the Olympics* (Oxford: Blackwell, 1980).

Riordan, J., *Sport, Politics and Communism* (Manchester: Manchester University Press, 1991).

Riordan, J. and R. Jones, *Sport and Physical Education in China* (London: E. & F.N. Spon, 1999).

Riskin, C., *China's Political Economy: The Quest for Development* (Oxford: Oxford University Press, 1987).

Rogers, B., *The Domestication of Women* (New York: St. Martin's Press, 1980).

Rosen, S., *Red Guard Factionalism and the Cultural Revolution in Guangzhou* (Boulder, CO: Westview Press, 1982).

Rosen, S., *The Role of Sent-Down Youth in the Chinese Cultural Revolution: The Case of Guangzhou* (Berkeley, CA: University of California, 1981).

Rosen, S., 'Students and the State in China: The Crisis in Ideology and Organisation', in A.L. Rosenbaum (ed.), *State and Society in China: The Consequences of Reform* (Boulder, CO: Westview Press, 1992), pp.167–91.

Rowbotham, S., *Women, Resistance and Revolution* (Harmondsworth: Penguin Books, 1972).

Sage, G.H., *Sport and American Society: Selected Readings* (Reading, MA: Addison-Wesley, 1980).

Sage, G.H., *Power and Ideology in American Sport: A Critical Perspective* (Champaign, IL: Human Kinetics, 1990).

Salisbury, H.E., *To Peking – and Beyond: A Report on the New Asia* (London: Hutchinson, 1973).

Sapsford, R. and V. Jupp (eds), *Data Collection and Analysis* (London: Sage/Open University, 1996).

Schell, O. and D. Shambaugh (eds), *The China Reader: The Reform Era* (New York: Vintage Books, 1999).

Schram, S.R, *Ideology and Policy in China Since the Third Plenum: 1978–1984* (London: University of London Press, 1984).

Schram, S.R. (ed.), *Authority, Participation and Cultural Change in China* (Cambridge: Cambridge University Press, 1973).

Schrecker, J.E., *The Chinese Revolution in Historical Perspective* (New York: Praeger, 1991).

Shaw, Y. (ed.), *Mainland China: Politics, Economics, and Reform* (Boulder, CO: Westview Press, 1986).

Shaw, Y. (ed.), *Changes and Continuities in Chinese Communism*, Vol.2: *The Economy, Society, and Technology* (Boulder, CO: Westview Press, 1988).

Shih, C., *State and Society in China's Political Economy: The Cultural Dynamics of Socialist Reform* (London: Lynne Rienner, 1995).

Shoebridge, M., *Women in Sport: A Selected Bibliography* (London: Mansell, 1987).

Short, P., *Mao: A Life* (Loondon: Hodder & Stoughton, 1999).

Sie, S., 'Sport and Politics: The Case of the Asian Games and the Ganefo', in B. Lowe, D. Kanin and A. Strenk (eds), *Sports and International Relations* (Champaign, IL: Stipes Publishing Co., 1978), pp.283–94.

Simon, R.L., *Sport and Social Values* (London and Englewood Cliffs, NJ: Prentice-Hall, 1985).

Simon, R.L., 'Good Competition and Drug-Enhanced Performance', in W.J. Morgan and K. Meier (eds), *Philosophic Inquiry in Sport* (Champaign, IL: Human Kinetics, 1988), pp.198–219.

Singer, M., 'Culture: The Concept of Culture', in D.L. Sills (ed.), *International Encyclopaedia of the Social Sciences* (New York: The Macmillan Company and The Free Press, 1979).

Smith, R.J., *China's Cultural Heritage*, 2nd edn (Boulder, CO: Westview Press, 1994).

Sparhawk, R. et al., *American Women in Sport, 1887–1987* (New York: Scarecrow Press, 1989).

Spence, J.D., *The Gate of Heavenly Peace: The Chinese and Their Revolution 1895–1980* (New York: Viking, 1981).

Sports Council, 'History of Doping in Modern Sport', in C. Donnellan (ed.), *Drugs and Violence in Sport*, Vol.26 (Cambridge: Independence Educational Publishers, 1995), p.27.

Stavis, B., *China's Political Reforms* (New York: Praeger, 1988).

Stone, G., 'Some Meanings of American Sport: An Extended View', in G.S. Kenyon (ed.), *Aspects of Contemporary Sport Sociology* (Chicago, IL: Athletic Institute, 1969), pp.5–16.

Tang, T., *The Cultural Revolution and Post-Mao Reforms: A Historical Perspective* (Chicago, IL: University of Chicago Press, 1986).

Thurston, A. F., *Enemies of the People: The Ordeal of the Intellectuals in China's Great Cultural Revolution* (New York: Knopf, 1987).

Tierney, H. (ed.), *Women's Studies Encyclopaedia* (New York: Peter Bedrick Books, 1991).

Tsou, T., *The Cultural Revolution and Post-Mao Reforms: A Historical Perspective* (Chicago, IL: University of Chicago Press, 1986).

Tu, W. (ed.), *China in Transformation* (Cambridge, MA: Harvard University Press, 1994).

Tu, W. (ed.), *Confucian Traditions in East Asian Modernity: Moral Education and Economic Culture in Japan and the Four Mini-Dragons* (Cambridge, MA: Harvard University Press, 1996).

Tylor, E.B., *Primitive Culture: Researches into the Development of Mythology, Philosophy, Religion, Art and Custom* (Gloucester, MA: Smith, 1871 [1958]).

Tyson, J. and A. Tyson, *Chinese Awakenings: Life Stories from the Unofficial China* (Boulder, CO: Westview Press, 1995).

United Nations, *The General Socio-Economic Situation in Asia and Pacific Area* (New York: United Nations, 1991).

United Nations, *The World's Women, 1995: Trends and Statistics* (New York: United Nations, 1995).

Vir, D., *Sport and Society* (New Delhi: Classical Publishing Co., 1989).

Vogel, E.F., *Canton Under Communism: Programs and Politics in A Provincial Capital 1949–1968* (Cambridge, MA: Harvard University Press, 1969).

Voy, R., *Drugs, Sport, and Politics* (Champaign, IL: Leisure Press, 1991).

Wang, J.C.F., *Contemporary Chinese Politics*, 5th edn (Englewood Cliffs, NJ: Prentice-Hall, 1995).

Warner, W.L. et al., *Social Class in America* (Chicago, IL: Social Research Association, 1949).

Watson, A., 'A Revolution to Touch Men's Souls: The Family, Interpersonal Relations and Daily Life', in S.R. Schram (ed.), *Authority, Participation and Cultural Change in China* (Cambridge: Cambridge University Press, 1973), pp.291–330.

Watson, J.L. (ed.), *Class and Social Stratification in Post-Revolution China* (Cambridge: Cambridge University Press, 1984).

Weber, M., *The Religion of China: Confucianism and Taoism*, translated and edited by Hans H. Gerth (Glencoe: The Free Press, 1951).

Wenzhong, H. (ed.), *Selected Readings in Intercultural Communication* (Changsa: Hunan Education Press, 1990).

White, G., 'The Decline of Ideocracy', in R. Benewick and P. Wingrove (eds), *China in the 1990s* (London: Macmillan, 1995).

White, L.T., *Policies of Chaos: The organizational Causes of Violence in China's Cultural Revolution* (Princeton, NJ: Princeton University Press, 1989).

Wolf, M., *Revolution Postponed: Women in Contemporary China* (Stanford, CA: Stanford University Press, 1985).

Wright, E., 'China's Foreign Policy: Foreign Relations Since 1949', in C. Howe (ed.), *Studying China: A Source Book for Teachers in Schools and Colleges* (London: School of Oriental and African Studies, 1979), pp.157–68.

Xia, D. and M. (eds), *Migration and Urbanization in China* (New York: M.E. Sharpe, 1994).

Yeung, Y.M. and D.K.Y. Chu (eds), *Guangdong: Survey of a Province Undergoing Rapid Change* (Hong Kong: Chinese University Press, 1996).

Young, M.B. (ed.), *Women in China: Studies in Social Change and Feminism* (Ann Arbor, MI: University of Michigan Press, 1973).

Yu, C., 'On the Reactions of Chinese Culture Against the Western Challenge: The Other Side of Modernisation', in B. Glaeser (ed.), *Learning from China? Development and Environment in Third World Countries* (London: Allen & Unwin, 1987), pp.13–31.

Yue, D. and C. Wakeman, *To the Storm: The Odyssey of A Revolutionary Chinese Woman* (Berkeley, CA: University of California Press, 1985).

Zhang, Y., *China in International Society since 1949: Alienation and Beyond* (London: Macmillan, 1998).

Zheng, W., *Women in the Chinese Enlightenment: Oral and Textual Histories* (Berkeley, CA: University of California Press, 1999).

Zheng, Y., *Discovering Chinese Nationalism in China: Modernisation, Identity, and International Relations* (Cambridge: Cambridge University Press, 1999).

Zito, A. and T.E. Barlow (eds), *Body, Subject and Power in China* (Chicago, IL: University of Chicago Press, 1994).

Periodicals and newspapers

PERIODICALS
American Journal of Sociology
Beijing Review
China Sports
China Quarterly
Journal of Economic Issues
European Sociological Review
Inside Sport
International Journal of the History of Sport
International Review for the Sociology of Sport

International Review of Sport Sociology
Journal of Economic Issues
Journal of Sport and Social Issues
Modern China
Monthly Review
Quest
Social Science Research
Sports Illustrated
Track & Field News
Journal of Sport and Social Issues
WSPAJ

NEWSPAPERS
China Daily
The Independent
The Sunday Times (UK)
The Times
The Daily Telegraph
The Sunday Telegraph
The Scotsman

Websites (Chinese and English)

http://sg.sports.yahoo.com/
http://www.bta.net.cn/
http://www.chinasports.com/
http://www.chinatoday.com/
http://www.chinese-embassy.org.uk/
http://www.eastday.com.cn/
http://www.olympics.com/
http://www.sports.gov.cn/
http://www.swimnews.com/
http://www.zabao.com.sg/

Appendices

Year	New Events	
1900	**Tennis** (unofficial)	
1904	**Archery** (unofficial)	
1908	**Figure skating**	
1912	**Equestrian**	
1920	**Swimming**:	300-metres freestyle, springboard diving
	Yachting:	mixed, finn class
1924	**Fencing**:	foil, individual
	Swimming:	200-metres breaststroke
1928	**Athletics**:	100-metres, 800-metres, 4 x 100-metres relay, high-jump, discus
	Gymnastics:	team competition
1932	**Athletics**:	80-metres hurdles, javelin
	Yachting:	mixed, star class
1948	**Athletics**:	200-metres, long jump, shot put
	Canoeing:	kayak singles, 500-metres
1952	**Gymnastics**:	individual all-around, apparatus finals
	Swimming:	100-metres butterfly
1956	**Canoeing**:	Kayak pairs, 500-metres
	Fencing:	foil
	Swimming:	4 x 100-metres medley relay
1960	**Yachting**:	mixed flying Dutchman class
	Athletics:	400-metres, pentathlon
1964	**Swimming**:	400-metres individual medley
1968	**Volleyball**	
	Shooting:	mixed skeet shooting
	Swimming:	200-metres freestyle, 800-metres freestyle, 200-metres backstroke, 100-metres breaststroke, 200-metres butterfly, 200-metres individual medley
1972	**Athletics**:	1,500-metres, 100-metres hurdles (replaced the 80-metres) 4 x 400-metres relay
	Archery:	individual single-round
	Canoeing:	kayak slalom singles
	Yachting:	mixed Soling class
1976	**Basketball**	
	Handball	

APPENDIX I (Cont'd)

Year	New Events	
1976	**Yachting**:	mixed tornado class
	Rowing:	single sculls, double sculls, quadruple scull, coxless pairs, coxed fours, eights
1980	**Field hockey**	
1984	**Athletics**:	3,000-metres, marathon, 400-metres hurdles, heptathlon (replaced the pentathlon);
	Canoeing:	Kayak fours, 500-metres
		Cycling: road race
	Rhythmic gymnastics:	all-around
	Shooting:	sport pistol; small-bore rifle, three positions; air rifle
1988	**Athletics**:	10,000-metres; 800-metres wheelchair
	Archery:	team competition
	Cycling:	1,000-metres sprint
	Table-tennis	
	Shooting:	air pistol
1992	**Judo**	
	Badminton	
	Biathlon	
1996	**Football**	
	Softball	
	Beach volleyball	

Note: Chinese women started to compete on a large scale at the Olympic Games in 1984.

Sources: Janet Woolum (ed.), *Outstanding Women Athletes*, Phoenix, AZ: Oryx Press, 1992; *Women in the Olympic Movement* (Document of the Women's Conference of the IOC), Department of International Cooperation, IOC, 1996.

APPENDIX II

LIST OF INTERVIEWEES

name	year of birth	place of birth	field	present position
Wang Yirun	1915	Beijing	sports physiology	professor
Liu Guangde	1928	Shanghai	sociology	professor
Xiu Huangzhi	1933	Hunan	sports official	deputy principal of BUPE
Lan Yialan	1934	Sichuan	national gymnastics champion	coach of national team
Zhang Caizhen	1934	Beijing	sports official	deputy minister of NSC
Zhou Dechi	1934	Shanghai	law	director of a department of Ministry of Justice
Qiu Zhonghui	1935	Yunan	world table tennis champion	deputy director of NSRI, manager of sports shop
Yang Yizuan	1935	Hunan	national javelin record holder	principal of BUPE spare-time school
Zheng Fenrong	1937	Shandong	world high jump record holder	ACSF deputy general secretary
Cheng Biyin	1937	Fujian	international gym judge	associate professor
Cheng Dexing	1937	Jiangsu	gymnastics master	associate professor
Weng Yijing	1938	Guangdong	diving	professor
Liang Chengyu	1938	Beijing	gymnastics coach (male)	head of Beijing municipal gymnastics team
Huang Xinhe	1938	Guangdong	national gymnastics champion	professor, international judge
Niu Shenrong	1938	Beijing	sports official	president of IBF, member of IOC
Pan Duo	1939	Tibet	world alpinism record holder	deputy director of city sports commission
Chang Shuying	1939	Beijing	interpreter	deputy director of foreign affairs office in NSC
Lu Yuanzhen	1939	Beijing	sports sociology (male)	professor
Guo Zhi	1939	Shanxi	parachuting world record holder	deputy director of NSC sports history department
Dong Tianshu	1940	Henan	national volleyball player	Sports Research Institute of NSC
Lo Ping	1941	Hunan	sociology	professor, Central China Normal University
Chao Qixiao	1942	Beijing	official	deputy director of trade union in Chemical Industry Ministry
Feng Meiyun	1943	Beijing	sports science	professor, director of sports science department, BUPE
Lou Buyue	1945	Zhejiang	gymnastics	head coach of Zhejiang gymnastic team
Shou Xiaoyu	1950	Beijing	swimming	administrator in CSA

APPENDIX II (Cont'd)

name	year of birth	place of birth	field	present position
Huang Kuanrong	1950	Jining	gymnastics	director of PE department, South Normal University
Wen Yichan	1952	Beijing	sports administrator (male)	deputy principal, Beijing youth sports school
Pan Yunzhi	1953	Liaoning	table tennis player	deputy director of PE department, BUPE
Jing Dongxian	1957	Liaoning	shooting world record holder	deputy director, Liaoning Sports Commission
Li Xiaohui	1957	Hebei	Asian shot-put champion	Ph.D. student in sports science
Huang Yialing	1961	Ningxia	athletics	teacher at BUPE
Tang Guoli	1961	Shandong	Asian javelin record holder	coach at BUPE
Qian Hong	1961	Hubei	sports reporter	Xinghua News Agency
Zhao Yaozhen	1960	Shanxi	gymnastics master	coach of national team
Li Guizhi	1962	Bebei	member of CWVT	coach of Hebei volleyball team
Ye Qiaobo	1964	Jining	world champion speed-skater	postgraduate, Qinhua University
Zhang Tong	1968	Jiangxi	national high-jump champion	student at BUPE
Chen Yueling	1969	Liaoning	Olympic walking champion	emigrated to United States
He Dai	1970	Shanxi	volleyball player	student at BUPE
Qie Hong	1971	Hebei	Olympic swimming champion	businesswoman in China
Yang Shenmei	1971	Shanxi	provincial swimmer	student at BUPE
Pang Yianping	1972	Guangdong	world wrestling champion	student at BUPE
Chai Xu	1972	Shanghai	Army volleyballer	student at BUPE
Zhu Ping	1973	Liaoning	provincial gymnast	student at BUPE
Yuan Fan	1975	Liaoning	Army volleyballer	student at BUPE
Chang Luna	1975	Liaoning	provincial swimmer	student at BUPE
Wang Zheng	1977	Hebei	provincial gymnast	student at BUPE
Wang Rong	1977	Hebei	provincial gymnast	student at BUPE

Abbreviations: BUPE: Beijing University of Physical Education; NSC: National Sports Commission; NSRI: National Sports Research Institute; CSA: Chinese Swimming Association; ACSF: All China Sports Federation

APPENDIX III
INTERVIEW QUESTIONS

1. The background of interviewee, including age, birthplace, family members, educational level and parents' employment.

2. When did you start and stop sports training?

3. Why did you take up sport? How many hours did you exercise each day?

4. What were the attitudes of people to sport and how was women's sport viewed in general at that time?

5. What were the salaries, bonuses and advantages for athletes and coaches at that time?

6. Did you have serious sports injuries? If so, why did you continue your sports career after severe injury or illness?

7. Do you wish to continue your sports career if you succeed or become famous in sport? Why?

8. What are the main factors in your success in sport?

9. What is the relationship between you and your coach(es)?

10. Do you regret being a sportswoman?

11. What do you think of athletes having love affairs? What are coaches' attitudes to them?

12. How do you solve the contradiction between a paid job and household work? Are you equal to your husband at home?

13. What do you think of the notion that 'man is responsible for outside affairs and woman for family affairs'? Is this still a common belief?

14. Do you consider a man cleverer and more capable than a woman?

15. Have you experienced unfair treatment by reason of your gender?

16. How many female decision-makers are there in your working unit?

17. Has sport been a means to increased status among friends, colleagues and in the community?

18. Has sport led to greater personal freedom?

19. Is sport an efficient avenue to female emancipation in China?

20. Does China respect women more because of the international achievement of its women athletes?

21. Has your own sporting success made you feel valued in society?

22. Has sport in the last decade become more and more valuable to women in terms of importance, respect and contentment?

23. Will sport be a means of steadily increasing women's opportunities for self-realisation, self-confidence, personal freedom and personal status in the next ten years?

24. If women become freer, have more leisure and obtain higher wages, will they be less determined to work hard to succeed in sport?

25. Looking back, has sport played a useful role in helping women to be freer, happier, more fulfilled?

26. If sport has done some or all of these things, is it for a few, many or most women?

APPENDIX IV
INTERVIEW EXCERPTS

Qiu Zhonghui

First Chinese female table tennis world champion in 1961

I was a sports enthusiast at secondary school. I joined the basketball, volleyball and athletics teams. In 1951 my school set up a table tennis team, which was selected from over 1,000 students. I was the captain of the team. We participated in the Yunnan provincial competition the same year. As a result, I qualified for the forthcoming South-West Administrative Area competition in Chengdu, the capital city of Sichuan province. At the time there was no railway linking Yunnan and Sichuan. We had to travel by bus for a week. Although I was the youngest (16) of the four players from our province and I had never previously been out of our town, I was responsible for the routine management of this group on the trip to Sichuan. Once we arrived in Chengdu, we immediately joined the competition. I won a silver medal. This qualified me for the following national competition. Although I was not among the top eight who formed the national team, I impressed people by my young age, small size and competitiveness. Consequently, I was asked to join the national team. My table tennis career then took off.

In 1994 I became a manager of a sports shop named after myself. Not a few thought that I was eager for money. In fact, I just wanted to realise my potential in various ways. Without ambition, I would vegetate. I will not leave a penny to my three children. They all have satisfactory jobs and successful careers. ... Being busy at my business, I have no time to do housework or cook for my family. My husband understands me and gives his full backing to my career.

Pan Duo

First woman to reach the highest summit in the world in 1975

As a daughter of a peasant slave in Tibet, I was very poor and even begged for a living with my mother and sister before the Chinese Communist Party took over Tibet in 1952. Later, I became a worker in a textile mill. When a climbing team was set up in Tibet in 1955, I joined it. I later became a member of the national mountaineering team and created women's world records in 1959 and 1961. Two years later, I married the deputy political commissar of the team, who is now the principal of a middle school. We had planned not to have children until I conquered the highest summit in the world. However, the eruption of the Cultural Revolution (1966–76) led to the dismantling of the mountaineering team. I had to return home and then raised three children in succession. In 1975 a national climbing camp was organised in Beijing in an attempt to conquer the Himalayas. My third child was only five months old. To join the camp I stopped breastfeeding, leaving him with a colleague in Beijing and the other two children with my husband's relatives in Jiangsu province. Driven by state pressure and personal aspiration, I overcame various difficulties and finally vanquished the Himalayas. In spite of the risky nature of mountain climbing – a state of affairs that worried my husband and his relatives all the time – they fully supported my sporting career. They helped bring up my three children.

Lan Yalan

National gymnastic champion in early 1950s; national coach for over three decades

I did not marry until I stopped training at 29. During my pregnancies at the ages of 33 and

44 I continued coaching until I went into labour. After 56 days of maternity leave, I returned to my gym, leaving my children with a babysitter during the daytime. My two children went to kindergarten at about 20 months. As I committed myself to gymnastics day and night, I did not take good care of my children, especially the older one. He received only junior school education and eventually qualified to become a taxi driver. I felt guilty about it. Instructor Wu [her husband] and I understand each other. After he stopped coaching, he spent a lot of time and energy taking care of the family.

Jing Dongxian

World shooting record holder in 1975

After the 1984 Olympic Games I was offered a chance to go to America. However, I did not take up the offer because my husband was reluctant and feared that I would abandon him if I went there. However, when my husband wanted to go abroad, I arranged for him to go to Japan to coach shooting. Although he was provided with a good salary and accommodation, he came back within a year. Eventually he wanted to go abroad again because he could not cope with China any more. With my support, he left for America. In short, he depends on me too much.

I stopped training at 31 (in 1988) to have a child. Not long after, I was asked to coach the national team. Due to my absence from shooting for two years, I was afraid that I was not conversant with the latest training trends. So I rejected the offer and remained in Liaoning province. In 1990 I was sent to Russia to study for half a year. After I returned home I was involved in the preparations for the Liaoning Provincial Games, in which yet again I demonstrated my ability and skill. This ensured my nomination to the post of deputy director of the Provincial Sports Commission. Now I enjoy many of the privileges of a provincial-level cadre, such as a car with a paid driver and a dinner party almost every night. Although I am not as rich as those in business, I am contented with my lifestyle. With the social status I enjoy in China I have no wish to emigrate.

Li Guizhi

Member of the Chinese women's volleyball team between 1981 and 1989 and head coach of the Hubei provincial volleyball team

I joined the Hubei provincial volleyball team in 1976. Within a year I grew so quickly (from 1.72 metres to over 1.80 metres) that a normal diet could not meet my growth requirements. However, medical supervision was very backward, if not non-existent, at the time. I always felt dizzy, nauseous and weak. This physical condition undoubtedly affected my training. At first coaches accused me of not working hard. After a period of time, I went to hospital to have a medical examination. The tests showed that I was anaemic with a haemoglobin count of six grams. Thereafter, the intensity of my training was reduced.

At the end of 1980 I was admitted to the newly established national youth volleyball team. Ten months later I moved up to the Chinese women's volleyball team, which had just won the World Cup. Due to my shorter playing history, I was not as skilful and experienced as other players. The result was that I was always a reserve in international competitions. In addition, I had not completely recovered from anaemia. It still affected my training. Unfortunately, this brought me a reputation for not 'eating bitterness' [working hard]. In these circumstances, I demanded to return to my home provincial team, promising to rejoin the national team once I became mature and more experienced. This request, however, gave me the further reputation of being difficult. At that time team discipline took precedence over the individuality of players. They were absolutely submissive to coaches and were not encouraged to voice their own opinions. It seemed that players had no rights. Eventually, I left the CWVT at the end of 1983, with a reputation for defiance. I was regarded as a bad example to the whole nation. This negative image lingered for a long time. ...

In order to qualify for a flat from my work unit, I married in 1987 (marriage was the precondition). My husband, four years older than me, used to serve in the Army, and played basketball as a pastime. Now he is a cameraman in our sports brigade. He gave me full support. In 1993, when I was 31, I was pregnant and intended to have an abortion in order to participate in the coming National Games. However, doctors persuaded me to keep the baby. It should be noted that the members of the Chinese women's volleyball team gave birth relatively later than women in general. They all received backing from their husbands. This happened also in our provincial team. Perhaps things have changed over time. Women do not want to be bound to family tasks at too early an age.

When I was an athlete, coaches arranged everything for us. Thus, I was very poor at self-management. I did not even know how to buy a train ticket for home. Now players have more freedom and autonomy than our generation. Due to my own experience, I pay attention to my players' opinions on coaching and their physical and psychological state before and after training.

Zhang Tong

National high-jump champion in 1990

Against my parents' wishes, I joined the provincial sports school in Nanchang, the capital city of Jiangxi province. Within the first week I wept over 20 times due to the arduous training and the rude and rough attitudes of my team-mates. I wanted to go back home, but my father's admonition at my departure – 'once you have chosen your way, you have to continue; otherwise, you are not accepted by the family' – put an end to my self-pity. I had to persevere. Indeed, I persevered. My father later gave me the fullest backing to my athletic career.

From sports school to provincial and then national sports teams, I was constantly at odds with my team-mates due to my insistence on employing my own ideas. I was considered a strong, and even self-willed, girl. For this reason, many coaches did not want me to be admitted to the provincial team. Fortunately, the coach who was in charge was different. However, I did not speak to him for three months. The reason was that I had grown up in a military compound where I had hardly talked to any male. As athletes, we were not allowed to have love affairs. I did not intend to have a boyfriend. In my view, those who fell in love with boys were often too emotional. I think that people should not have love affairs until they have a secure position in society.

In retrospect, my sports experience broadened my view of the world, and enhanced my endurance of hardship. Sport brought me glory and grief, fame and envy. I think women have their own advantages in society. Indeed, now they sometimes have higher status than men, especially in cities. The issue of women's liberation should be focused on women in the rural and poor areas.

Chen Yueling

1992 Olympic walking champion

I broke the world 10km walking record at the 1987 National Games and won the Asian Championships in 1989. I retained the national champion title for many years. However, these achievements were accompanied by numerous defeats. At the 1987 World University Games I was expelled from the race as a result of receiving three yellow cards. Four years later, with improved techniques and enriched experience, I confidently approached the World Cup. However, when I led other competitors in the competition, I became the target of the referees. As a consequence, a red card ended my efforts. Being frustrated at these results, I cried and shouted at my coach: 'I am the most unlucky person in the world. Once I attract the attention of the referees I am disqualified no matter how I walk. I will not compete any longer.'[1] For days I could not sleep. I either sang loudly or yelled hysterically. My 60 year-old coach fully understood my feeling. Although he himself was maybe more depressed – his team had no successful results after two of his four athletes were expelled from competition – he patiently analysed my situation with me. This moved me deeply. He had sacrificed so much within a decade. Faced with the repeated defeats of his athletes, he had not collapsed. 'I am his best athlete at the moment. If I did not compete at the Olympic Games, who could? Should younger athletes compete?'[2] To prepare for the 1992 Olympic Games, I was determined to change my style of walking to avoid penalties. I went to Qinghai plateau to undergo arduous training. To get used to the high-temperature environment of the Barcelona Olympics, I walked at midday through the streets in a temperature of over 35 degrees. ...

Notes

1. Lei Guangming, 'Luishui qingwu le tiantan – ji nuzi 10 gongli jingzhou aoyun guangjun Chen Yueling' [Tear Stains in Paradise – On Chen Yueling, the Women's 10km Olympic Walking Champion], in Wu Shaozu (ed.), *Tongxiang aoyun guanjun zhi lu* [The Road Towards Olympic Championship], Shanghai: Huadong shifan daxue chuban she, 1993, p.199.
2. Ibid., p.200.

BACKGROUNDS OF THE MAJOR PLAYERS IN THE CWVT IN THE 1980s

name	date of birth	year of marriage	year and place when started playing	year of entry back to elite team	year of entry to CWVT	year of retire-ment	present job/place
Cao Huiying	1954	1983	1970 BIPE (Hebei countryside)	1973 PLA	1976	1983	deputy general manager of CSTC
Chen Zhaodi	1955	1983	1970 BIPE (Hangzhou)	1973 PLA	1976	1983	senior colonel, director of art and sports department in GPMPLA
Sun Jinfang	1955	1983	1971 Suzhou SSS	1971 Jiangshu	1976	1983	deputy director of Jiangshu SC
Yang Xi	1956	1984	1970 BIPE (Hebei)	1973 PLA	1976	1983	businesswoman in US
Zhang Rongfang	1957	1985	1970 Chengdu	1971 Sichuan	1976	1985	deputy director of TB of NSC
Zhou Xiaolan	1957	1985	1971 Shanxi SSS	1973 Shanxi	1977	1985	1988–95 deputy director of NSC volleyball department; now in US
Lan Ping	1960	1987	1974 Beijing SSS	1976 Beijing	1978	1987	CWVT coach, 1995–98; now in US
Liang Yan	1961.	1988	1974 Chengdu SSS	1977 Sichuan	1979	1987	deputy director, Liang Yan Sports Advertising Company
Yang Xilan	1961	Dec. 1988	Tianjin	1976 PLA	1982	1989	Switzerland

Abbreviations: SSS = spare-time sports school; Vol. = volleyball; TB of NSC = Training Bureau of the National Sports Commission; SC = Sports Commission; CWVT = Chinese Women's Volleyball Team; CSTC = Chinese Sports Travel Company; GPMPLA = General Political Ministry of the People's Liberation Army.

APPENDIX VI

1996 SURVEY OF ELITE ATHLETES IN CHINA

TABLE A1

NUMBER OF SAMPLED ATHLETES IN DIFFERENT SPORTS

	athletics	swim-ming	big ball games	small ball games	strength	demon-stration	combat sports session	total sports
male	27	16	27	3	15	9	20	117
female	29	25	30	17	12	28	16	157
total	56	41	57	20	27	37	36	274

TABLE A2

PERCENTAGES OF ATHLETES FROM MANUAL CLASS FAMILIES IN VARIOUS SPORTS

type	mothers			fathers		
	male athletes	female athletes	Z test	male athletes	female athletes	Z test
strength sports	80	75	0.311	60	50	0.520
combat sports	60	81.3	1.379	22.2	56.2	2.031*
swimming	51.9	69	1.309	14.3	48.3	2.603**
athletics	33.3	52.9	0.626	50	24	1.713+
dem sports	62.5	36	1.660+	33.3	28.6	0.268
big ball games	40.7	46.7	0.456	29.6	23.3	0.503
small ball games	33.3	42.9	0.510	0	29.4	1.084

+ = $p<0.10$; * = $p<0.05$; ** = $p<0.01$. dem: demonstration.

TABLE A3

PERCENTAGES OF URBAN ATHLETES IN VARIOUS SPORTS

type	no	percentage	male	female	Z test for difference between sexes
strength sports	27	44.2	40	50	0.520
combat sports	36	50	60	37.5	1.342
swimming	41	69.6	74.1	64	0.699
athletics	56	75.4	77.8	72.4	0.394
dem sports	37	83.8	66.7	89.3	1.600
big ball games	57	95	100	93.3	0.432
small ball games	20	95	100	94.1	1.160

TABLE A4

ATHLETES' AGES ENTERING SPORTS TEAMS

type	no	percentage of athletes under 13	male %	female %	Z test for difference between sexes
strength sports	27	33.3	40	25	0.822
combat sports	36	36.1	45	25	1.240
swimming	41	36.8	18.5	53.3	2.720**
athletics	56	48.2	37	55.2	1.365
dem sports	37	75	100	70.6	1.084
big ball games	57	86.5	66.7	92.9	2.000*
small ball games	20	95.1	100	92	1.160

* =p<0.05; ** = p<0.01

TABLE A5

ATHLETES ABOVE PRIMARY EDUCATION LEVEL IN VARIOUS SPORTS

type	no	percentage of athletes	male %	female %	Z test for difference between sexes
strength sports	27	82.5	100	66.7	3.300**
combat sports	36	73.2	81.5	65.5	1.351
swimming	41	58.2	60	56.3	0.224
athletics	56	55.6	80	25	2.858**
dem sports	37	45	66.7	41.2	0.819
big ball games	57	34.1	37.5	32	0.362
small ball games	20	21.6	55.6	10.7	2.846**

APPENDIX VII

CHINESE FEMALE ATHLETES TESTED DRUG-POSITIVE

Name	Sport	Date and Competition
Li Duihong	shooting	1987 pre-Olympic competition
Wang Xiuli	speed-skating	1988 pre-Olympic competition
Ye Qiaobo	speed-skating	1988 pre-Olympic competition
Zhong Hua	modern pentathlon	1988 World Championships
Xiao Yanlin	athletics	1992
Wu Dan	volleyball	1992 Olympic Games
Wang Wenya	shot put	1993
Xin Fen	weightlifting	1993 National Games
Zhou Xin	swimming	January 1993
Yang Aihua	swimming	1994 Asian Games
Lu Bing	swimming	1994 Asian Games
Zhou Gongbing	swimming	1994 Asian Games
Han Qing	athletics	1994 Asian Games
Wang Yan	cycling	1994 Asian Games
Zhong Weiyue	swimming	1994 World Cup Series, Beijing leg
Zhang Xiaoli	weightlifting	1997 National Games
Xiang Fenlan	weightlifting	1997 National Games
Tan Yanying	weightlifting	1997 National Games
Han Wengpo	weightlifting	1997 National Games
Chen Xiaomin	weightlifting	1997 National Games
Jin Chunlan	weightlifting	1997 National Games
Du Linmei	weightlifting	1997 National Games
Li Zhongying	cycling	1997 National Games
Shi Yunli	athletics	1997 National Games
Ma Jinmei	athletics	1997 National Games
Wu Guihua	athletics	1997 National Games
Xiong Qiying	athletics	1997 National Games
Chen Xuehui	athletics	1997 National Games
Jiang Limei	athletics	1997 National Games
O Yanlan	athletics	1997 National Games
Peng Yinghua	athletics	1997 National Games
Wang Yanin	athletics	1997 National Games
Yuan Yuan	swimming	1998 World Championships
Wang Luna	swimming	1998 World Championships
Wang Wei	swimming	1998 World Championships
Cai Huiyu	swimming	1998 World Championships
Wu Yanyan	swimming	July 2000, Jinan, China

APPENDIX VIII

EXTRACTS FROM TWO IMPORTANT DOCUMENTS OF THE NATIONAL
SPORTS COMMISSION

1. *From Guojia tiwei guangyu tiyu tizhi gaige de jueding (chaoan) [Decisions of the National Sports Commission to Reform Sports Systems (draft)], April 1986*
   * Shen youxiu yundongdui ying yi geren xiangmu (tianjin, youyong deng) wei zhu, jiti xiangmu zhubu xiang chengshi, changkuang qiye he dazhuan yuanxiao guodu [Provincial elite sports teams should concentrate on individual sports such as athletics and swimming, and the management of team sports should be gradually extended to cities, factories and enterprises as well as universities].
   * Jizhong renli, wuli, chaili zhongdian baozheng aoyun xiangmu zhong tianjin, youyong deng yingxiang da, jiangpai duo de xiangmu, yiji woguo de youshi xiangmu he duan shijian keyi shangqu de xiangmu [To focus personnel, material and financial resources on Olympic sports with high visibility and medal events at which the Chinese have performed well or can advance within a short time].
   * Ge xiangmu yundongdui zhubu xiang zhu (zhong) jiaolian fuzhe zhi guodu [All sports teams should gradually change to the head coach responsibility system].
   * Quanyunhui, qingyunhui, shaoshu minchu yundonghui, chengyunhui mei sinian yici, lungliu zai sheng qu shi juxin, qingyunhui zhi jinxin aoyunhui xiangmu de bisai [The National Games, the Youth Games, the Minority Ethnic Games and the City Games should now take place every four years in different provinces, autonomous regions and cities. Only Olympic sports are to be contested at the Youth Games].

Source: Guojia tiyu yundong weiyuan hui [NSC] (ed.), *1987 zhongguo tiyu nianjian* [Yearbook of Chinese Sport, 1987), Beijing: Renmin tiyu chuban she, 1988, pp.75–87.

2. *From Guojia tiwei guangyu shenhua tiyu gaige de yijian [The Opinions of the National Sports Commission on Extending Sports Reform], 24 May 1993*
   * Jinyibu gaige tiyu xingzheng guanli tizhi, jiaqian hongguang tiaogong nengli [There should be a strengthening of macro supervision through continuing reform of the administrative system];
   * Jiakuai yundong xiangmu xiehui shitihua bufa, jianli juyou zhongguo tese de xiehui zhi [There should be an acceleration of the process of turning sports associations into autonomous entities and establishing sports associations with Chinese characteristics];
   * Jianli jizhong yu fenshan xiang jiehe, duoqiang duikang de xunliang tizhi [There should be a training system combining concentration with decentralisation, and promoting competition];
   * Gaige jingsai tizhi, shixing fenji fenlei guangli [There should be a transformation of the competition system to suit the characteristics of specific sports and various levels of performance];
   * Jianchi shehuihua fangxiang, jiakuai qunzhong tiyu de fazhang [There should be a utilisation of social resources to speed up the development of mass sport];
   * Yi changyehua wei fangxiang, zenqiang tiyu ziwo fazhang nengli [There should be an enhancement of the entrepreneurship-oriented reforms];
   * Zhuanhuan keji, jiaoyu yunxing jizhi, jiakuai tiyu kexuehua [There should be a change in approaches to sports research in order to speed up the 'scientification' of sport];
   * Shixing quan fangei duiwai kaifang, tuozhang guoji yu diqu jie de tiyu jiaowai [There should be a comprehensive opening up to the outside and a broadening of international and inter-regional sports exchanges];
   * Wanshan jili jizhi he yueshu jizhi, tuidong beitao gaige [There should be an improvement of the rewards and punishment systems to advance reform];
   * Cong shiji chufa, jiqi wentuo di tuijin tiyu gaige [There should be a vigorous and steady advance of sports reforms based on the specific situation of each region].

Source: Guojia tiwei [National Sports Commission] (ed.),Zhonghua renming gongheguo tiyu fagui huibian (1993–1996) [Collection of the Laws and Regulations on Sport in China], Beijing: Xinhua chuban she, 1997, pp.11–45.

APPENDIX IX

SIGNIFICANT EVENTS FOR WOMEN AND SPORT IN THE NEW CHINA

Year	Events
1949	Establishment of People's Republic of China.
1950	Establishment of All-China Sports Federation; China's involvement in Korean War begins (to 1953); promulgation of Marriage Law and Land Law.
1951	National volleyball and basketball competitions; establishment of national teams for these sports.
1952	The Army Games; establishment of National Sports Commission; delegation of 40 to Helsinki Olympic Games.
1953	Establishment of provincial sports commissions, and national and provincial sports 'specialised' teams; convening of international and national competitions.
1954	Participation in Summer World Collegiate Games.
1955	Emergence of spare-time sports schools.
1956	Boycott of Olympic Games due to issue of 'two Chinas'; 49 athletes awarded title of Sports Master.
1957	World record (1.77 metres) attained by female high jumper Zheng Fenrong.
1958	Promulgation of ten-year plan for sports development; advent of Great Leap Forward; China's withdrawal from IOC and eight other international sports organisations.
1959	First National Games; Chinese women set world shooting and mountain climbing records.
1960	Withdrawal of Soviet experts from China; beginning of three years of difficult economic conditions.
1961	Qiu Zhonghui wins women's single title at world table tennis championships held in Tianjin, China.
1962	Readjustment of sports teams.
1963	Victory at first New Emerging Force Games in Jakarta; convening of basketball Tournament of Friendly Countries in Beijing; endorsement of new ranking systems for athletes, referees and coaches.
1964	Japanese coach invited to coach Chinese women's volleyball team.
1965	Second National Games in Beijing, at which a number of world and national records are created.
1966	Start of decade-long Cultural Revolution, and deaths of some prominent sports figures.
1967	Interruption of normal training and competition.
1968	Start of Rustication Campaign.
1969	End of chaotic fighting between factions of Red Guards.
1970	Recovery of some sports teams and international competition; 'ping-pong' diplomacy.
1971	Taking up of China's seat at United Nations; national sports competitions restored.
1972	China-America United Communiqué; normalisation of China-Japan relationship.
1973	Taking up of China's seat on Asian Sports Committee.
1974	China's renewed participation in Asian Games – second in points tally.
1975	Three women's world shooting records at third National Games in Beijing.
1976	'Sports Revolution' attacking 'medals and trophyism'; Mao's death.
1977	Normalisation of national competitions; reintroduction of national university and college entrance examinations.
1978	Third Plenum of Eleventh Central Committee of Chinese Communist Party; eighth Asian Games in Bangkok.

APPENDIX IX (Cont'd)

Year	Events
1979	Recovery of China's seat on IOC; fourth National Games in Beijing; Ma Yanhong wins bars title at World Gymnastics Championships
1980	China's participation in Winter Olympic Games, and boycott of Moscow Summer Olympic Games.
1981	Chinese women's volleyball team wins World Cup.
1982	Chinese women's basketball team ranked third at World Championships.
1983	Fifth National Games in Shanghai.
1984	China participates in Los Angeles Olympic Games, winning 15 gold medals; emergence of sports lottery; corporations and individuals sponsor sports.
1985	Advocacy of Olympic Strategy.
1986	Emergence of elite sports teams in universities; introduction of head coach responsibility system.
1987	Start of sports commercialisation at sixth National Games in Guangzhou.
1988	China's defeat at Seoul Olympic Games; numerous world records in women's weightlifting and swimming.
1989	Student democratic movement; world shot-put title for Huang Zhihong at Athletics World Cup.
1990	Asian Games in Beijing, at which China dominates medal table.
1991	Policy of incorporating Olympic results into scoring of the National Games; Huang Zhihong wins world championships; Xie Jun becomes world chess champion.
1992	China wins 16 gold medals at Olympic Games (12 by women); introduction of club system, professional teams and athletes' registration in football.
1993	'Ma Family Army' wins three world titles at World Athletics Championships and creates 1,500-metre, 3,000-metre and 10,000-metre world records at seventh National Games held in Beijing and Chengdu; radical reform of sports institutions gets under way.
1994	11 Chinese athletes proved drug-positive at Asian Games; bronze medal in 1,000 metres speed skating won by Ye Qiaopo at Winter Olympics.
1995	World figure-skating champion Chen Lu; split-up of Ma Family Army; UN World Conference on Women held in Beijing; promulgation of 'National Fitness Programme' and Sports Law; first Sports Talent Fair.
1996	16 Chinese gold medals at Atlanta Olympic Games (nine won by women).
1997	Eighth National Games in Shanghai; reforms of sports institutions under NSC.
1998	Female swimmer Yuan Yuan caught with illegal drugs at Sydney Airport, and four other swimmers tested drug-positive in Australia; National Sports Commission reorganised into National Sports Bureau.
1999	Chinese women's football team runner-up at World Cup tournament.
2000	Chinese ranked third in count of gold medals (28) and total medals (59) at Olympic Games in Sydney.

APPENDIX X

CHINESE GOLD MEDALLISTS AT THE SYDNEY OLYMPIC GAMES

events		gender	name
1	Artistic gymnastics parallel bars	m	Li Xiaopeng
2	Artistic gymnastics team	m	
3	Badminton singles	m	Ji Xinpeng
4	Diving 3m springboard	m	Xiong Ni
5	Diving synchronized 3m springboard	m	
6	Diving 10m platform	m	Tian Liang
7	Shooting 10m running target	m	Yang Ling
8	Shooting 10m air pistol	m	Cai Yalin
9	Table tennis doubles	m	Wang Liqin/ Yan Sen
10	Table tennis singles	m	Kong Linghui
11	Weightlifting 77kg category	m	Zhan Xugang
12	Badminton singles	f	Gong Zhichao
13	Badminton doubles	f	Ge Fei/Gu Jun
14	Artistic gymnastics balance beam	f	Liu Xuan
15	Diving synchronized 10m platform	f	
16	Diving 3m springboard	f	Fu Mingxia
17	Athletics 20km walk	f	Wang Liping
18	Judo 78kg category	f	Tang Lin
19	Judo Heavyweight +78kg	f	Yuan Hua
20	Shooting 10m air pistol	f	Tao Luna
21	Table tennis single	f	Wang Nan
22	Table tennis double	f	Wang Nan/Li Ju
23	Taekwondo over 67kg	f	Chen Zhong
24	Weightlifting 63kg category	f	Cen Xiaomin
25	Weightlifting 53kg category	f	Yang Xia
26	Weightlifting 69kg category	f	Lin Weining
27	Weightlifting 75kg category	f	Ding Meiyuan
28	Badminton doubles	mixed	Zhang Jun/Gao Ling

APPENDIX XI

	China				United States				Russia			
	G	S	B	total	G	S	B	total	G	S	B	total
2000 total	28	16	15	59	39	25	33	97	32	28	28	88
f	16.5	7	11	33	19.5	6	15	40.5	11	14	8	33
%	*58.9*	44	73	56	*50*	24	45	42	*34*	50	29	37.5
1996 total	16	22	12	50	44	32	25	101	26	21	16	63
f	9	11	6	26	19	7	6	32	6	7	5	18
%	*56*	50	50	52	*43*	22	24	32	*23*	33	31	29

G: gold; S: silver; B: bronze

Index